ucap,ustx E 668.C085 1000
W9-BZJ-728

THOSE TERRIBLE CARPETBAGGERS

BOOKS BY RICHARD NELSON CURRENT

Those Terrible Carpetbaggers

Arguing with Historians: Essays on the Historical and the Unhistorical

Speaking of Abraham Lincoln: The Man and His Meaning for Our Times

Northernizing the South

Wisconsin: A Bicentennial History

The History of Wisconsin: The Civil War Era, 1848-1873

United States History (with Alexander DeConde and Harris Dante)

Three Carpetbag Governors

Lincoln and the First Shot

John C. Calhoun

American History: A Survey (with T. Harry Williams and Frank Freidel)

The Lincoln Nobody Knows

Lincoln the President: Last Full Measure (with J. G. Randall)

Daniel Webster and the Rise of National Conservatism

The Typewriter and the Men Who Made It

Secretary Stimson: A Study in Statecraft

Pine Logs and Politics: A Life of Philetus Sawyer, 1816-1900

Old Thad Stevens: A Story of Ambition

EDITED BY RICHARD NELSON CURRENT

Reconstruction in Retrospect: Views from the Turn of the Century

Sections and Politics: Selected Essays by William B. Hesseltine

The Political Thought of Abraham Lincoln

Reconstruction, 1865-1877

Words That Made American History (with John A. Garraty)

Advance and Retreat, by J. B. Hood

Mr. Lincoln, by J. G. Randall

THOSE TERRIBLE CARPETBAGGERS

Richard Nelson Current

New York Oxford
OXFORD UNIVERSITY PRESS
1988

Oxford University Press

Oxford New York Toronto
Delhi Bombay Calcutta Madras Karachi
Petaling Jaya Singapore Hong Kong Tokyo
Nairobi Dar es Salaam Cape Town
Melbourne Auckland

and associated companies in
Beirut Berlin Ibadan Nicosia

Published by Oxford University Press, Inc.,
200 Madison Avenue, New York, New York 10016

Library of Congress Cataloging-in-Publication Data
Current, Richard Nelson.
Those terrible carpetbaggers.
Includes index. 1. Reconstruction. 2. United States—Politics and government—1865-1877. I. Title. II. Title: Carpetbaggers.
E668.C985 1988 973.8 87-11061
ISBN 0-19-504872-5

9 8 7 6 5 4 3 2 1
Printed in the United States of America
on acid-free paper

To Kenneth M. Stampp
For More than Fifty Years a Friend

Contents

Cast of Characters *ix*

Foreword *xi*

1. The Omen of Peace & Reunion (1865-1866) *3*
2. Go South, Young Man! (1865-1866) *24*
3. We Poor Southern Devils (1865-1867) *46*
4. To Reconstruct This Godforsaken Country (1867-1868) *68*
5. I Believe in the People (1867-1868) *91*
6. The Spirit of the Rebellion (1868-1869) *112*
7. Turbulent and Lawless Men (1868-1869) *132*
8. Some Good and Some Bad (1868-1872) *153*
9. The War Still Exists (1869-1872) *172*
10. Juries Are All Ku Klux (1869-1872) *193*
11. The Best-Abused Man (1869-1872) *214*
12. The Leprous Hands Upraised (1869-1872) *236*
13. Guttersnipes from the North (1872) *261*
14. The Leopard Don't Change His Spots (1873-1875) *282*
15. Political Death of the Negro (1873-1876) *306*
16. This Pathway of Political Reform (1873-1876) *328*
17. The Abandonment of Southern Republicans (1876-1879) *349*
18. A Fool's Errand (1877-1881) *367*
19. Only a Carpetbagger (1877-1907) *383*
20. Lies, Unmitigated Lies (1877-1933) *401*

Afterword *422*

Acknowledgments *426*

Notes *427*

Index *459*

Illustrations follow page 256

Cast of Characters
in the order of their appearance

HENRY CLAY WARMOTH (1842-1931). Once an Illinois farm boy, he arrived in Louisiana as a Union army officer, became governor of the state at twenty-five, remained to prosper as a sugar planter, and lived on into the time of Huey Long, who viewed him as something of a model.

HARRISON REED (1813-1899). After a Wisconsin career as newspaperman and town promoter, this Massachusetts native went to Florida as a federal jobholder, won election as governor of the state, and afterward stayed on as an orange grower and state booster.

GEORGE E. SPENCER (1836-1893). Born in New York, educated in Canada, admitted to the bar in Iowa, he went to Alabama as a Union army officer, returned to the state afterward as a federal jobholder, was Alabama Republican boss and U.S. senator for nearly a dozen years, and later invested in mines and ranches in Nevada.

WILLARD WARNER (1826-1906). Ohio farm boy, Marietta College graduate, California Forty-niner, Ohio manufacturer, Union general, he bought an Alabama plantation after the war, won election as U.S. senator from Alabama but lost to Spencer in a power struggle, and finally succeeded as an iron manufacturer in Alabama and Tennessee.

ALBERT T. MORGAN (1842-1922). After a Wisconsin boyhood he was badly wounded in the war, then failed at cotton planting in Mississippi, became sheriff and Republican boss of Yazoo County, was driven out of Mississippi, and later tried to make a living from silver in Colorado while his mulatto wife and daughters went their own way as song-and-dance team.

ROBERT K. SCOTT (1826-1900). He moved from Pennsylvania to Ohio, got rich as a physician, merchant, and land speculator, rose to a generalship in the Union Army, acquired an opium habit, headed the Free-

Freedmen's Bureau in South Carolina after the war, served two terms as governor of South Carolina and, after returning to Ohio, killed his adolescent son's drinking companion.

ALBION W. TOURGEE (1838-1905). Born in Ohio, educated at the University of Rochester, he was badly wounded in the war, moved to North Carolina to get a fresh start, served as state judge and law codifier but left before his best-selling novel *A Fool's Errand* appeared, and spent the rest of his life as a writer, editor, and advocate of equal rights for blacks.

DANIEL H. CHAMBERLAIN (1835-1907). Massachusetts-born, Yale B.A., Harvard LL.B., he served briefly as an officer of black troops, tried cotton planting in South Carolina, became attorney general and then governor of the state, and afterwards was a successful New York lawyer and anti-black pamphleteer.

ADELBERT AMES (1835-1933). A Maine native and West Point graduate, he made a heroic record as a Union general, was named military governor of Mississippi under Reconstruction, became U.S. senator and then governor of Mississippi, and eventually made a fortune as a Massachusetts businessman.

POWELL CLAYTON (1833-1914). He studied engineering at a military college in Pennsylvania, his native state, moved to Kansas, helped to conquer Arkansas as a cavalry commander, remained to plant cotton, became Arkansas governor and U.S. senator, and later promoted railroads in the state and served as ambassador to Mexico.

Foreword

Anyone who claims to know anything about American history can tell you who the carpetbaggers were. They were, of course, Northerners who went south after the Civil War to take advantage of the Negro vote, gain election to office, and get rich by plundering the Southern people. Having waited for the real soldiers to subdue the South, these soldiers of fortune followed at a safe distance, like jackals in the track of a lion. They were as poor as they were greedy and unscrupulous, each of them managing to carry all he owned in a carpetbag, a popular kind of valise made of carpeting material. Hence the name and byword *carpetbagger*.

Men of this sort, meddling in places where they did not belong, governed and misgoverned along with their black and "scalawag" henchmen for a decade or so. During those years they spent so wildly as to run up astronomical state debts, even though they levied confiscatory taxes upon the unfortunate planters and other property owners. In a grotesque carnival of corruption, they diverted fabulous amounts of public funds to private use. All the while, they incited the blacks to such extremes of self-assertion as to destroy the harmonious relations that would otherwise have prevailed between the former masters and the former slaves.

Such, in brief, is the reputation that carpetbaggers have long had and, generally speaking, still have. But there may be human beings hidden behind the stereotype. This book undertakes to bring ten of these characters into the open, so as to see what kind of men—or what kinds of men—they really were and what role or roles they actually played in the postwar Reconstruction of the Southern states. These ten are among the most notorious of the hundreds of carpetbaggers who had a part in that story. At least nine of the ten would undoubtedly be included in any expert's list of the dozen most important.

What follows here is not a series of separate biographical sketches.

Instead, the history of Reconstruction is presented through interwoven accounts of the careers of the ten men. The story is told from the standpoint of these participants in it, not from the usual standpoint, which has been that of their enemies. While trying to see things as the carpetbaggers saw them, the book strives for objectivity in the sense of relying on the critical use of sources and revealing the pertinent facts whether favorable or unfavorable to the subjects.

THOSE TERRIBLE CARPETBAGGERS

CHAPTER 1

The Omen of Peace & Reunion (1865-1866)

By noon on March 4 the incessant chill rains of the past three days had finally let up, but the sky was still rather dark and the atmosphere gloomy. Thousands of people milled about with mud underfoot at the east of the Capitol, waiting for the inauguration to get underway. Though bedraggled and miserable, especially the women in their ruined finery, they mostly had an eager and expectant look. The war was approaching the end of its fourth long year, and peace seemed almost in sight. What word of hope and cheer would the President bring?

No one in the crowd showed greater interest than a tall, very slender young man, not yet twenty-three, who had a self-assured manner and, despite his youth, a way of getting close to important personages and events. This young man, who bore the name of Abraham Lincoln's hero Henry Clay, had met President Lincoln almost two years before. In the summer of 1863 Henry Clay Warmoth had come to Washington from the battlefield of Vicksburg to clear his name. Lieutenant-Colonel Warmoth he then was—or had been until General Ulysses S. Grant removed him from command. Grant accused him of having been a.w.o.l. and having aided the enemy by giving the press an exaggerated report of Union losses. Warmoth insisted he had been on sick leave and had actually underestimated the casualties, and he got statements from fellow officers and other pieces of evidence to verify his claim.

In Washington, on that previous occasion, Warmoth hurried to the White House and, after waiting for other callers to depart, managed to get a private interview with the President. Lincoln listened sympathetically to the youthful officer, then put his documents in a large envelope, endorsed it, and told him to take it to Joseph Holt, the judge advocate general of the army. As Lincoln and Warmoth walked, chatting, down the White House steps together, the tall Warmoth felt that Lincoln, in his stovepipe hat, towered over him.

During the next couple of weeks, while his case was under consideration, Warmoth wandered about "like a nervous boy" (as he confessed to himself), seeing the sights in the nation's capital, a city that struck him as "the most licentious and corrupt place in the U. S." He resolved to keep away from temptation and to think seriously about his future. "Hard study strict morality & determined honesty are the only sure means to prosperity and usefulness," he penciled neatly in the small leatherbound diary he carried with him. But, unable to resist temptation entirely, he soon met other young army officers, made instant friends of them, and joined them in what he referred to as "a heavy time." Another day, left to himself, he visited the Smithsonian Institution and, while there, weighed himself on scales that were on exhibit. They indicated only 115 pounds, though he stood more than six feet. "Soon we will see what I will weigh hereafter," he thought to himself, and he had more than mere physical weight in mind.

Hereafter he was indeed to make at least something of a mark on the scales of American history. He was to become one of the most famous—or most notorious—of all the so-called carpetbaggers in the postwar South. But that was yet a few years in the future. More immediately, during his 1863 mission to Washington, he exerted sufficient influence to get from the commander in chief an order restoring him to his rank in the army, with back pay. And now, in March 1865, he was in the capital on a different errand. This time he was there as a lawyer, up from Union-occupied New Orleans, and he was seeking to influence the government in the interest of a wealthy client. Again, as before, he was to spend more time in sightseeing than on business.

And the first big sight to see was Lincoln's second inauguration. When the President and the procession emerged from the Capitol, to take their places on the temporary wooden platform outside, Warmoth joined in the tremendous shout that arose from the crowd, and then in the roar of applause when Lincoln stepped forward to deliver his inaugural. Lincoln had just picked up his manuscript and started to read when suddenly, for the first time in days, the clouds parted and sunlight flooded the scene. Warmoth saw not only the sun but also the moon and a bright star. "Oh! the spectacle. Oh! the Omen!" he said to himself. "May God grant that it is the omen of peace & reunion."

Over the now silent multitude Lincoln's clear, high voice rang out, every word audible even at a considerable distance. "Both parties deprecated war," he was saying, "but one of them would *make* war rather than let the nation survive; and the other would *accept* war rather than let it perish." Here he was interrupted by prolonged cheering, which compelled him to pause, with dramatic effect, before adding: "And the war came." Soon he was through with the inaugural, the shortest any President had ever delivered. He stirred up tears as well as cheers when he concluded: "With malice toward none; with charity for all; with firmness in the right as God gives us to see the right, let us strive on to finish the work we are in; to bind up the nation's wounds; . . . to do all which may achieve and cherish a just and a lasting peace, among ourselves and with all nations."[1]

That evening Warmoth went to the President's reception at the White House. He "had a shake of Mr. Lincoln's hand, a low bow from Mrs. Lincoln & greetings from Major Hay," that is, John Hay, Lincoln's private secretary, whom Warmoth had got acquainted with during his 1863 visit to Washington. But what most impressed Warmoth about the affair this evening was the way Lincoln treated one of his guests, the former slave and abolitionist Frederick Douglass, whom policemen had just now tried to eject from the executive mansion on the assumption that no black person could have been invited. "Mr. Lincoln took Douglass' hand between his two," Warmoth observed, "& said, My Dear Sir I am glad to see you! What did you think of my address? The reception of Douglass was the most cordial of any I saw."

A month later Washington celebrated the tidings that General Robert E. Lee and his Army of Northern Virginia had abandoned the Confederate capital, Richmond. On the night of April 4 the city was aglow with fireworks and illuminations of all kinds, including candles and lamps in the windows of downtown stores, public buildings, and private houses. The next afternoon, with a pass from the War Department, Warmoth got aboard a government steamboat bound for General Grant's headquarters at City Point, downriver from Richmond. The only other passengers were a young army captain, a senator from New York, and the Vice President of the United States, Andrew Johnson.

On the voyage the four spent the afternoon and evening together, and Warmoth got well acquainted with the Vice President. A good man, Warmoth judged him. Johnson had about him an aura of dependability, with his solid physique, his heavy features, his grim expression, and his attitude of dogged dignity. Certainly, from Warmoth's point of view, Johnson held correct opinions. As a senator from Tennessee, remaining loyal when his state seceded, he had spoken on behalf of the common man of the South and had ridiculed the aristocratic pretensions of Jefferson Davis, who he said really belonged to nothing more than a "bastard, scrub aristocracy." As military governor of conquered Tennessee, Johnson had assured the slaves that he was the Moses who would lead them out of bondage. Now, as Vice President, he was still talking bitterly about the rebel leaders.

The next day Warmoth managed to get passage, as one of the Vice President's party, on a steamer to Richmond. As the vessel steered cautiously up the James River, the passengers could see signs of the recent warfare, among them "a good many torpedoes marked by the navy." At the landing a fine carriage, lately the personal vehicle of Jefferson Davis, picked up the travelers and took them to what had been the executive mansion of the Confederate president and what was now the headquarters of General Godfrey Weitzel, commanding the local Union forces.

From there, the distinguished visitor and his traveling companions made their way to the nearby Spotswood House, where the general had reserved rooms for them.

On the following three days Warmoth went about the enemy capital to see the sights, sometimes walking, sometimes riding a horse that General Weitzel provided. "All the business portion of the city is in ruins—about one third of the city," Warmoth discovered. According to the rumors he heard, the Confederate authorities had deliberately put the torch to the place (though in fact the fire had started accidentally at the time of the Confederate evacuation). "Libby Prison & Castle Thunder was saved although all the houses were burned around them." In these two tobacco warehouses thousands of Union soldiers had languished as prisoners, and Warmoth had once had a bad dream in which he was confined in an overcrowded and foul-smelling Libby. Of both places he remarked: "They are now full of rebels." Riding out, he found "a most beautiful country" surrounding Richmond. The havoc of war appeared, in contrast, all the more deplorable.

Where and when the war would cease was still a question. Somewhere to the west of Richmond was Lee's army, and somewhere in pursuit of it was Grant's. On Sunday night, April 9, Warmoth in his hotel room was hoping to get a few hours of good sleep before rising early for the return trip to Washington. Around midnight, much to his annoyance, he awoke to the roar of repeated cannon fire. Soon he learned that Lee had surrendered to Grant at Appomattox and that Union guns near Richmond were saluting the Union victory. "God bless the country & its people." So Warmoth phrased the feelings that now surged through him. "May peace & good will be speedily restored & swords be beaten into plough shares, & we learn to fight no more. The rebellion is over. God Almighty be praised."[2]

Back in Washington again, Warmoth was among the throng that, on the evening of April 11, gathered in front of the brightly lit White House to serenade the President. Once more the city was all lighted up. "A most magnificent illumination," it seemed to Warmoth. The night was misty, and the reflection of the Capitol's illuminated dome, in the moist air above it, could be seen for miles. On the other side of the Potomac, high on the bluff, rockets blazed and colored lights shone at Arlington, the old Lee home, and hundreds of former slaves gathered there to sing "The Year of Jubilee." Outside the White House, meanwhile, the crowd listened to band music, displayed patriotic banners, gave cheer after cheer, and called for the President. When he finally appeared, at an upstairs window, the outburst was deafening. After he had begun his response, however, the crowd remained remarkably quiet. His speech was not what most of the serenaders had expected; it was longer, more formal, more serious.

Lincoln was dealing with the difficult problem of Reconstruction—of what to do with the states of the defeated Confederacy—a matter on which Northerners were already expressing sharp disagreement. Some were saying the Southern states, having seceded from the union, had lost their equal membership in it and had become mere territories. Some maintained that, before being restored to their former place, these states should make voters as well as freedmen of their slaves. Lincoln now said the question whether the states were in or out of the Union was a "merely pernicious abstraction"; the important thing was to get them back into their "proper practical relation" with the Union as soon as possible. He urged the prompt readmittance of Louisiana, Warmoth's adopted state, which had been reorganized under Lincoln's plan. The new Louisiana constitution would provide freedom but not the franchise for blacks, though it would permit the legislature to give them the vote (if the legislature should ever choose to do so).

Good Friday, April 14, was a perfect spring day in Washington. Warmoth took advantage of the weather by going on a long walk. He reflected on his yesterday's encounter with General Grant, whom he had run across in the dining room of the Willard Hotel. Not in the least nonplused, he had shaken hands with the conquering hero and congratulated him on his great success. Grant seemed to remember Warmoth perfectly but, so far as Warmoth noticed, no longer felt any resentment over that Vicksburg affair of 1863, when Warmoth frustrated Grant's attempt to get rid of him. Today Grant was consulting with Lincoln and the cabinet in regard to Reconstruction. The Grants had been invited to attend the theater with the Lincolns tonight, but declined.

On Saturday morning flags flew at half mast, church bells tolled, and black drapery, covering the previous bunting, flapped in the rain and wind. "The elements seem to mourn the calamity, for today it rains, & the Heavens are thick with clouds," Warmoth commented in his journal. "Yesterday so beautiful & the air so dry & clear with a happy President & a happy people. Today a dead President murdered by a citizen of the United States, a mourning people, & the city, the country & the Heavens mourning & weeping at his loss." From a friend who had been in last night's audience at Ford's Theater, Warmoth received a vivid, first-hand account of the assassination and heard that the assassin was the well-known actor J. Wilkes Booth, whom he had seen and admired in the role of Richard III.

On Easter Sunday, Warmoth was thoroughly depressed. "Slept poorly," he noted. "I smoke too many cigars and the excitement of yesterday made me very nervous. When I would wake from my troubled sleep, the first thing that would enter my mind would be Sic Semper Tyrannis, the South is avenged, & the description I have of Booth's walking across the stage after the murder of the President."

Later in the day Warmoth and an army-officer friend called on the new President, Andrew Johnson, who had a temporary office in the Treasury Building while Mrs. Lincoln continued to occupy the White House and Lincoln's body lay in state in its East Room. President Johnson readily recognized his recent traveling companion and was "very polite & affable" toward his young visitors, who "had a good long talk with him." Johnson demonstrated patience and fortitude as well as politeness and affability, for he had already been beset by callers, not to mention the sudden responsibilities of the presidency. This morning he had held a cabinet meeting, then had received a delegation of Republican congressmen. To all he gave assurances that he would carry on Lincoln's Reconstruction program, but he also gave the impression that he would be more severe than Lincoln in dealing with rebel leaders. Treason is a crime, he was saying, and crime must be punished. He believed, as most Northerners did, that Lincoln's murder had resulted from a Confederate plot, and he was shortly to issue a proclamation calling for the arrest of Jefferson Davis as the chief of the conspirators. Warmoth came away convinced that, lamentable though Lincoln's death might be, the country was still in good hands.

Warmoth stayed in Washington long enough to finish the legal business that had brought him there, to attend Lincoln's funeral, and to accompany the funeral train as far as New York City on its roundabout route to Springfield, Illinois. Sad though the occasion was, he left Washington with a good deal of satisfaction. He had earned a very large fee, his first significant one as a practicing lawyer.[3]

After getting off the train in St. Louis, Warmoth called on his "little sisters" at their school and "had a sweet pleasant visit" with them. Then, with his father, he went aboard the *Henry Ames,* one of the floating palaces of the Mississippi River, bound for New Orleans. By the time the paddle wheels had begun to churn the muddy water, the great riverboat contained as many passengers as it could comfortably carry. Lots of Northerners were heading south, now that the war was over.

Warmoth's father was only going along for the ride, with no intention of remaining long. He was a saddle and harness-maker from McLeansboro, in southern Illinois. He had married a state senator's daughter, Eleanor Lane, who died after bearing him five children. Henry, the oldest of them, was only ten or eleven at the time. The boy got what education he could from attending the village school, setting type in the local print shop, and studying the law books his father had acquired as a justice of the peace. When not yet quite eighteen, Warmoth moved to Lebanon, Missouri. There, by answering a few simple questions to the satisfaction of a committee of lawyers, he gained admission to the bar. Then he put up a sign and started to practice. "The sign was a big one," he was to recall long afterward, "because I knew that I didn't know much law and I thought to accomplish the same purpose by as much advertising as possible." He had practiced only a year when the war came and he went off with a Missouri regiment he helped to raise for the Union army.

His father was not feeling well when he got on the *Henry Ames*, but he began to improve once the week-long voyage had begun. "There were two parties of ladies on board going to New Orleans," Warmoth recorded. "Dancing every night." He always had very little difficulty in striking up acquaintance with men, and still less with women. He quickly joined in the merriment. His father, by no means an old man yet, eventually recovered enough to take part, too.

At Vicksburg the boat stopped long enough for Warmoth and his father to go on a carriage ride with an army comrade still stationed there. Streets in the town, which stood on a high bluff, were cut through and along the hills in such a way as to leave high, cliff-like banks and huge loaf-like remnants of earth. Relics of the six-month siege and bombardment still remained, though the maimed tree branches were largely hidden by the greenery of spring, many of the bomb-shelter caves had been filled in, and most of the fortifications were crumbling away. From the heights, overlooking a rough wooded terrain with deep ravines, Warmoth could point out to his father approximately where he had been when he was wounded on the day the siege began. And, much farther off, they could almost see the place where Grant's army had landed when, earlier, Warmoth had helped it cross the river and get behind Vicksburg.

Between Baton Rouge and New Orleans, a distance of nearly one hundred miles, the boat moved along the top of a ridge, where the river ran above the surrounding country, the river having built up its own banks and these having been raised still higher by the construction of levees. From the upper decks the passengers could get a sweeping view of the low, flat land on either side. Great sugar plantations stretched away to the remote edge of a cypress forest. Manor houses, some pillared and porticoed, others with low roofs and wide verandas, appeared one after another, most of them in the shade of carefully planted trees. At a discreet distance, in the rear, stood the cabins built for the slaves. Many of the plantations were beginning to give evidence of neglect, the fields uncultivated, the fences sagging, the buildings in need of paint or repair.[4]

The scene had deeply moved Warmoth when he first beheld it, more than a year earlier, while he was on his way to the Department of the Gulf to resume his military service. He was then confirmed in the antislavery feelings he had acquired during the war, after seeing black troops in action. He blamed slavery for "the woes of this war." If, instead of depending on their slaves, the rebels had had to work for a living, "there would have been no time for treason." Still, Warmoth could not help envying the masters who had enjoyed a rich and splendid life in this once prosperous sugar country. "It is perfectly lordly to live down here, with such refinements," he thought. "But the war has rid these people of their property & labor, reduced prosperity & happiness to destruction & mourning." In time, recovery was to come and Warmoth was to get his wish. There would be a day when the saddler's son from Illinois would live the lordly life of a Louisiana sugar planter.

On May 6, seven days after setting out from St. Louis, the *Henry Ames* docked in New Orleans, now the capital of Louisiana, formerly one of the busiest ports in the United States, and once again becoming a very busy place. Here the river front followed an S-curve seven miles long, with wharves on one side of the broad, flat-topped levee and city streets on the other. Vessels of all kinds, large and small, steam and sail, ocean ships and riverboats, were constantly departing and arriving, loading and unloading. Wagons and carts were picking up or depositing crates, boxes, sacks, bales. Not only passengers but also merchants, crewmen, and stevedores, black and white, kept coming and going.

For all the din and dirt—not to mention the long stretches of humid heat and the frequent epidemics—New Orleans had a magnetic fascination for Warmoth, as it did for many others from the North. Here was a lush and almost tropical atmosphere, with banana plants, orange trees, magnolias, live oaks hung with Spanish moss that moved in the slightest breeze, and roses and oleanders that bloomed colorfully even in midwinter. Here was the exotic charm of old France and old Spain in architecture, festivals, and food. Here, too, were plays, concerts, balls, and other amusements for practically every taste. And here, for Warmoth, were the many friends, both male and female, that he had made in a year's residence.[5]

Within hours after his return to New Orleans, Warmoth went to a concert, with a lady on each arm, and sat in the special box of his best friends in the city, General Nathaniel P. Banks and his wife. It was most pleasant to be with the genial Bankses once again. The general, commanding the Department of the Gulf, was not yet fifty and was still trim, dapper, and really quite handsome with his black hair and mustache. His vivacious wife had a somewhat regal air and a well-known fondness for stylish clothes and lavish parties. Warmoth vividly remembered meeting her at a party about a year before. He had noted at that time: "Mrs. Banks complimented me by saying that when she saw me she was taken back to old times—that I looked talked & acted just like Genl Banks when he was young. I blushed. Thanked her and felt better. Danced with her." Less than a week after that, General Banks insisted on making Warmoth the judge of the local provost court.

Judge Warmoth tried thirty cases on his very first day. "Everybody said I did well." He continued to do a satisfactory job during the several months he held the military judgeship. But he had little success when he attempted to raise the level of soldier morality by eliminating brothels and limiting beer sales. He could not even keep his own conduct quite up to the standard he set. He continued to drink and smoke in spite of his twenty-second birthday resolution to "not drink liquor of any kind nor smoke cigars or use tobacco in any way." After a night out with several army companions he confessed to his diary: "All tight but me, and I not very sober, not tight though."

By the beginning of 1865 Warmoth was out of the army and in private practice as a lawyer. "Will . . . prosecute any claims against the Government before either of the Departments," he advertised. "Prize claims attended to." The federal government had confiscated large quantities of cotton on the assumption that it belonged to the Confederacy, but individuals claimed much of it as their property. These claimants had to sue in the federal courts, before which no attorney could appear without swearing he had never willingly borne arms against the United States. So Warmoth needed to expect little competition from ex-Confederates, and since cotton now fetched a very high price, he could anticipate correspondingly large fees. Of all the many charms of New Orleans, one of the most appealing to him was, no doubt, the money-making opportunities it seemed to offer.[6]

Soon after his return to New Orleans, Warmoth began to notice on the streets the Confederate veterans who, in rapidly growing numbers, were coming home from the war. These recent rebels seemed to think they were as good as anybody else. "I suppose," Warmoth observed, "they expect to go into business and take part in governmental offices as if they had always been loyal citizens." If such men should regain control of the state, Warmoth would find his own prospects dimmed. Not only that. He would also see in jeopardy the aims for which he and his comrades had fought so long and hard. The supremacy of the Union government, the complete eradication of slavery, both would be in considerable doubt.

Already the new governor, J. Madison Wells, was taking steps to restore the old ruling class to power. Though once the owner of four cotton plantations and many slaves, and in 1861 an ardent secessionist, Wells had played along with the Louisiana Unionists and emancipationists who undertook to reconstruct the state in accordance with Lincoln's plan. Yet no sooner was he governor than he began to turn his recent associates out of office and put ex-Confederates in. General Banks did what he could to resist. Exercising his military authority, he countermanded all of the removals and installed one of his army officers as New Orleans mayor in place of Wells's appointee.

On the evening of May 17 the Banks sympathizers, prominent among them Warmoth, staged a rally in Lafayette Square to back President Johnson and the policy they thought he was going to follow. Warmoth made the most important speech. From a torchlit platform he assured the crowd that, having talked with the President, he knew they could depend on him. In the reconstructed South, Warmoth continued, the former slave was going to "stand upright and free in the midst of Southern chivalry and assert his right to life, liberty, property, and political equality." Ex-slaves must be enfranchised and ex-Confederates, both the leaders and the rank and file, must be at least temporarily disfranchised. Louisiana plantations would have to be "divided up into small farms" and "cultivated by the industry of freemen," who thus would be given "an interest in the soil."[7]

Before long, Warmoth realized all too well that Johnson had no such black Utopia in mind for Louisiana or for any other Southern state. The President took the side of Governor Wells and removed General Banks from command. Then he announced his plan for the restoration of the seceded states, a plan that would require them to abolish slavery, disavow secession, and repudiate their war debts, but not to enfranchise the former slaves and certainly not to give them land. Nor did he propose to disfranchise the whites who had supported the Confederacy. Instead, he offered amnesty to all except those who had held high civil or military positions in it or who owned property worth more than $20,000 (that is, the comparatively wealthy planters). He made it clear that men excluded from the blanket pardon could apply to him for individual pardons, and soon he was granting these at a rapid rate.

Disillusioned with Johnson, as most Republicans throughout the country were, Warmoth decided to go into politics and oppose the President's party and program. He knew from his recent experience on the platform in Lafayette Square that he had both a taste and a talent for politics. At least, he could harangue a crowd. From a book he was reading, he derived a bit of additional inspiration, if not also a historical model. The book was a biography of Robespierre, the Jacobin leader of the French Revolution who presided over the Reign of Terror. "The history of that man is quite remarkable," Warmoth concluded after staying home an entire day to read. "He seemed by dint of determination and pertinacity to carry everything before him." But, of course, Robespierre ended up a victim of the guillotine.

The first step for Warmoth would be to organize a Republican party in Louisiana. Such a party could emerge from a combining of three main elements. One of these consisted of Free State men, native or long-resident whites who had helped to make the constitution of 1864, and some of whom were now willing to go beyond it in respect to Negro rights. A second source of Republican membership would be the growing number of Northerners, many if not most of them mustered-out Union soldiers and officers, arriving in the state. But, as a rule, these newcomers appeared to be more interested in profit than in principle. To gain the trade of Southern whites, many were all too ready to echo them in slurring "niggers" and "nigger-lovers." The third and numerically much the most important Republican group would have to be the Afro-American, a group that included not only recent field hands and house servants but also thousands who never had been slaves. But the

Afro-Americans, whether long free or lately freed, would have to get the vote if they were to count as Republicans.

During June and July, in cooperation with older and more experienced local activists, Warmoth took steps toward the forming of a new party. First, he called a meeting in his law office to organize what he referred to as a Union club. Then he presided over a gathering to set up a National Republican association. For the time being he avoided the term *party*, since some of the free men of color objected that the Republican party in the North was not yet committed to the suffrage cause. With Warmoth again presiding, his association appealed to the disaffected Negroes by adopting the platform of the Friends of Universal Suffrage, an organization to which both white and colored reformers belonged.

Despite his conciliatory efforts, Warmoth was already beginning to antagonize prominent members of the New Orleans colored community, which numbered more than 18,000. These people were quite distinct from the recently emancipated field hands. Many were light-skinned mulattoes, hard to tell from whites, and quite a few were well educated and well-to-do. They thought of themselves as the natural leaders of the Negro race. Though they once had welcomed the assistance of white radicals, native and Northern, they were now becoming suspicious of men like Warmoth. Two of the most influential were the brothers Charles Roudanez, a physician who had studied at a French medical school and at Dartmouth College, and Jean Baptiste Roudanez, an engineer and building contractor who published the *New Orleans Tribune*. In the *Tribune* the members of the community could read that, once they had the ballot, they would have a certain amount of political power. "And while we can wield that power in our own hands, and use it in the interest of equality, why should we look to others to do our work, and, perhaps, to politicians to make tools of us all?"[8]

In the midst of his effort to create a party, Warmoth made the mistake (as he was soon to view it) of going off to Houston, Texas, to serve as a federal agent in disposing of cotton the government had seized as Confederate property. In the August heat and dust of Houston he fell ill with what his doctor diagnosed as bilious fever. When, after an absence of forty-four days, he got back to New Orleans, he was still too weak for work or politics, and he was thoroughly disgusted at having lost so much time and money, his medical and other expenses having more than eaten up his government salary.

While convalescing, he had letters from erstwhile army comrades to cheer him a bit. On "the historic fields of Dixie" a Missouri friend had, as he now reminded, "often listened with unfeigned pleasure to jokes and narratives" from Warmoth. "The echo of your clarion voice even at this late date has not died away," this correspondent added. "Everybody says bully for Warmoth and more especially your many lady admirers whose names are Legion." Another friend, now living in Salt Lake City, had much to say about Mormon women and what he imagined to be their sexual appetite and their preference for "Gentile" men. "You would kill yourself here in about one year."[9]

Warmoth was not yet quite himself when, late in September, the Friends of Universal Suffrage held their convention at Economy Hall. Neverthless, he was very much on hand as the leader of the smaller of two factions. The delegates, more than a hundred of them from twelve parishes, almost evenly divided as to race, chose Thomas J. Durant as convention president by acclamation. The lean, sallow, cadaverous Durant, an eloquent lawyer, Philadelphia-born but a New Orleans resident for three decades, had been active in the wartime Free State movement. He now threw his powerful support to Warmoth's side when one of Warmoth's black followers proposed to drop the name Friends of Universal Suffrage and adopt, instead, the name Republican party of Louisiana. Over noisy opposition the motion finally carried, and thus the state's Republican party came into being.

The convention proceeded to adopt a platform based on the theory which some Republican leaders in Congress were already proclaiming: There was no longer a state of Louisiana. By seceding, it had ceased to exist (as had the other members of the late Confederacy). What was left was only a territory, like the territory of Utah or Montana or Idaho. Governor Wells was no more than a pretender, since Congress had never approved the 1864 constitution under which he claimed authority. A valid constitution must be the work of all the United States citizens in Louisiana, and by virtue of emancipation these now included blacks.

Warmoth gathered strength enough to get to his feet and offer an additional resolution, to the effect that this convention should go ahead and immediately draw up a new constitution with a provision for Negro suffrage. He managed to speak to the point at some length. "During the latter portion of his eloquent speech," the secretary recorded in the official proceedings, "Mr. Warmoth was interrupted every now and then by the most enthusiastic applause; and when he sat down, it was amidst stamping of feet, clapping of hands, and lusty cheers." But opponents argued that, if the 1864 convention had had no real constitution-making authority, this 1865 one had even less. Warmoth's proposal was voted down.

Finally the delegates got around to nominating the party's ticket—or, rather, its candidate, for there was to be only one. In keeping with their own logic, these Republicans could not very well run men for state offices or for congressional seats, since there was no state to be officered or represented. Still, the territory of Louisiana, like the territory of Utah or Montana or Idaho, would be entitled to send a territorial delegate to Congress. The convention offered this nomination to Durant and, when he declined, gave it to Warmoth. Conventioneers clamored for another speech, but Warmoth did not feel up to it. "The wildest excitement and confusion followed," he jotted down the next day, much pleased by his selection. "It was indeed very complimentary to me, a boy and really a stranger."[10]

Warmoth had only contempt for the Democratic convention that met a few days later. "The convention was full of unpardoned Confederates," he heard. "Several persons were put on the ticket who have not been pardoned." Wells now became the Democratic candidate for re-election as governor. There was, of course, no Democratic nominee for territorial delegate to Congress. Having no opponent, Warmoth could hardly lose, but he wanted to do more than win. For moral effect, he wanted to get as large a vote as possible.

So, during October, his health improving, he campaigned strenuously. At one rally, in the Custom House on a rainy night, he faced an audience that, according to a newspaper reporter, looked "dark as a thundercloud" because of dim lights and "Afric's tawny hue." He recounted a recent interview with the pretended governor of the state. "I told Governor Wells that the niggers were going to vote" (here the crowd interrupted with laughter); "that they were going to vote for me" (more laughter), "and I asked him to use his influence to make the vote heavier" (prolonged applause). After an election-eve rally, this one in the old Opera House, Warmoth could only smile as he read the account of the event in the unfriendly *Daily Crescent*. This paper said he had "exhibited most singular intellectual qualities, oscillating between the gravity of the owl and the levity of the monkey. He wound up his buffoon discourse by advising his hearers to commence early in the morning and vote all day for him for Congress."

Warmoth could smile again at the result of the voting on November 6. There were, in Louisiana that day, two separate elections and two sets of polling places, the official and the unofficial, the one open only to whites and the other to whites and blacks, the one offering Democratic candidates and the other a single Republican candidate. He received 19,105 unofficial ballots, according to the Republican tally, and a few thousand write-ins on official ballots, according to his own estimate. If these write-ins had been counted, as he believed, he would have outpolled Wells.

A week later the Republicans held a victory celebration at the Orleans Theatre. Warmoth informed the large audience, two-thirds of which was colored, that he would "regard his election as the proudest achievement of his life, if he should live to be a thousand years old." Addressing the blacks, he joked: "When I get back North I am going to get a Yankee to invent a machine which will pump out your black blood and pump in white blood." He had to wait for the laughter and applause to subside before continuing: "There will be no trouble then about your voting, for all you will have to do will be to wash your faces and go to the ballot box." More seriously, he assured them that they were kept from voting not because they were unqualified—"the negro population of this city is not the ignorant and degraded people they are represented to be"—but because Southern whites were prejudiced and Northern whites were, too.[11]

As Warmoth prepared to leave for Washington, he was aware of growing hostility against blacks and also against men like himself. According to a newspaper report, a local judge had charged a grand jury against "a class of adventurers who infest the city and parishes of the State without any occupation except to teach the negroes insubordination to the laws of the State by instructing them that they have a right to vote, etc." Such "treason" was not to be tolerated, and two men accused of it were being held in jail. Warmoth sent the clipping to Senator John Sherman, of Ohio, so the senator might know how Union men were faring in Louisiana under President Johnson's restoration plan.

For Warmoth, this new life had its risks but also its delights. On a drizzly November afternoon he dined with several cronies at a restaurant in the French Quarter. He had, for his expenses as territorial delegate, $1,000 that the party had raised from the contributions of the faithful, mostly black. After lingering too long over the excellent dinner, he barely made it to the dock on time. The next day, though the weather remained dreary, there was a pleasantly thrilling time on the *Lady Gay* as she got into a race with other boats steaming up the Mississippi. "We were making fifteen miles an hour," Warmoth boasted to his diary. "We passed the Magenta, Fashion & Magnolia. We cleared the string."[12]

Waiting for Warmoth at the Washington railroad station were Michael Hahn and Alfred Shaw. Hahn, a lawyer, born in Bavaria, educated at the University of Louisiana, had opposed the state's secession in 1861 and had become the first governor under the new constitution in 1864. He was now hoping to gain admission to Congress as one of the senators from the Free State. Shaw, a former schoolteacher, had also been active in the Free State movement.

The next day, December 1, Hahn and Shaw conducted Warmoth to the Capitol and introduced him to the Pennsylvania congressman Thaddeus Stevens and to the chief clerk of the House of Representatives, Edward McPherson, in McPherson's office. The seventy-three-year-old Stevens made an unforgettable impression, his face grimly taut, his hollow eyes burning, his reddish-brown wig sitting askew on his hairless head. Though hobbled by rheumatism as well as a clubfoot, he could still terrify his colleagues with the lash of his sarcasm. Indeed, he had a reputation as dictator of the House. Toward the much younger McPherson, however, he displayed the feeling of a kindly uncle. He had secured the job of chief clerk for McPherson, the son of a former business associate of his in Gettysburg, where he had settled years ago as a fledgling lawyer from Vermont.

The old man welcomed his visitors from Louisiana, and he readily shared with them his views and his plans. In his opinion the Southern states, having fought and lost a war, were now "conquered provinces" and, as such, merely territories. He was determined to keep them indefinitely in a territorial condition. The first step was to exclude from Con gress those men coming from the South and claiming seats as duly elected representatives of states that President Johnson pretended to have restored. Those claimants would not have a chance. One of the duties of the chief clerk was to call the roll when Congress met to organize, as it was to do in just three days. McPherson was simply going to omit the names of the men from the states of the late Confederacy. But Stevens gave Warmoth to understand that he did not mean to exclude *him,* at least not for long. "Old Thad says," as Warmoth understood him, "I am the only man who will be admitted from the Southern States."

Warmoth had a privileged place—a seat on the floor of the house—from which to view the political drama that was to be staged when Con gress met at noon on December 4. It was a sunny, spring-like day. Well-dressed ladies and gentlemen, eager to watch the show, thronged the corridors and galleries of the newly carpeted and furbished Hall of Representatives. When McPherson, calling the roll, passed over Horace Maynard's name, Maynard rose to protest. He, after all, had been a congressman from Tennessee in 1861 and, like his colleague Andrew Johnson, then a senator from Tennessee, had remained with the union when his state left it. But the clerk now refused to recognize him. While Maynard repeated his effort to gain the floor, Warmoth edged forward in his seat, ready to get up and reply if Maynard should succeed in making a speech. But Stevens managed to organize the House just as he had planned, without admitting Maynard or anyone else from a seceded state. That evening, Warmoth celebrated by dining at the Metropolitan Club, along with Congressman George S. Boutwell of Massachusetts and other important people. "Had a good time."

During the next few weeks, as the Joint Committee on Reconstruction began to consider the terms on which the Southern states might be readmitted, Warmoth continued to enjoy the privilege of a place on the House floor. Though not yet officially recognized as a delegate from the territory of Louisiana, he was getting more recognition than the men who came to Washington as congressmen from the state of Louisiana. They could only look on from the House galleries. Charles Sumner, the powerful senator from Massachusetts and foremost advocate of immediate suffrage for Southern blacks, assured Warmoth that he was "privileged on the floor of the Senate" as well as the House.

A kind of Radical pet, Warmoth went on hobnobbing with leading Radicals, the Republicans who demanded a stern program of Reconstruction. He was more than welcome when, with the young journalist Whitelaw Reid, he called at the residence of the Chief Justice of the United States, Salmon P. Chase. Long a widower, Chase lived with his two beautiful daughters—Kate, twenty-five, and Nettie, a few years younger—in a house that belonged to Kate's husband, the Rhode Island millionaire William Sprague IV. Kate Chase Sprague, already the belle of Washington, aspired to become the first lady of the land by putting her father in the White House. Warmoth had visited the family the previous March (when Kate was six months' pregnant with her first child), and he and Chase had "had a long talk about matters in the South," Chase confiding that he favored Negro suffrage. Since then, Chase had gone on a Southern tour, in the course of which he revealed his Radicalism, if not also his presidential ambition, in public remarks. Now Warmoth the ladies' man, on this second visit, again gave his attention to the father instead of the daughters. "Reid entertained the ladies & I & the Chief Justice had a long & interesting talk on politics. I received a cordial invitation to come again soon."

Warmoth also had a good visit with General Benjamin F. Butler, who happened to be in Washington and had been consulting with Stevens on the "political crisis." Warmoth had met Butler, too, when previously in Washington, and had breakfasted with him and his wife. Mrs. Butler was a cultured and charming person, formerly an actress. Ben Butler was not much to look at, what with his paunchy figure, his bald dome and long hair fringing it, his drooping eyelids and mustache, and his peculiar, mismatched eyes. Yet he was nobody's fool, and on some people he exerted an almost hypnotic influence. Of all the Union generals, he was much the worst hated in the South. He had preceded Banks in command of occupied New Orleans and had disciplined its rebellious citizens with such severity as to gain the name "Beast" Butler. His Louisiana experience made him especially fascinating to Warmoth, who noted: "Had an interesting time with him."

Still, friendly though the Radicals were, Congress came to its Christmas recess without having officially admitted Warmoth as a territorial delegate. "A very bad day," he wrote in his hotel room on Sunday, December 24. "Read the whole of St. Matthew in the New Testament today. Received letters from N. O. and answered them."[13]

Some of the news from New Orleans was amusing enough. "Judge Warmoth," the Democratic *New Orleans Times* editorialized, " . . . is an ambitious young gentleman of great volubility of tongue—one of that dangerous class who think it 'better to reign in hell than serve in heaven.' Having a strong dash of the demagogue in his composition, he coquetted for a while after his arrival here with the white element of our population, but finding that darkness to him was more promising than light, he joined himself to the ebony idol, and now claims to be the mouthpiece of the blackest sort of republicanism." When he left for Washington after his "farce of an election," the paper went on, "the true citizens of this State looked upon the whole thing as a harmless joke." But now it has to be taken seriously, for "the spurious representative of a deluded negro constituency is likely to be accepted by sectional fanaticism while the legal representatives of the white people of the South are thrust aside." That editorial was good enough to keep, and Warmoth put the clipping away for eventual inclusion in his scrapbook.

On the whole, the reports from the South in general and from Louisiana in particular were increasingly ominous. The legislature of Louisiana, like that of every other ex-Confederate state, was adopting a black code that made it legal to arrest blacks for vagrancy and compel them to work out their fines. Governor Wells was using the new militia, or "patrol," consisting of Confederate veterans, to harass recalcitrant blacks. The late rebels were in complete control of the state. "These miserable traitors proclaim in the public streets and in the social circle that as soon as the Union troops are withdrawn they will make short work of Union men," one correspondent wrote from New Orleans. Another warned: "If left to themselves there is not the shadow of a doubt that at present the people here would re-enslave the black man—or at least make him a mere serf." All this only strengthened the conviction Warmoth already held. Congress must do more than the President had done to reconstruct the Southern states. If these states should rejoin the Union under Johnson's plan, the rebels would soon dominate not merely the South but the entire country.[14]

While the Republicans in Congress were resuming consideration of the danger and of ways to meet it, Warmoth in January 1866 made a trip to New York City to attend a high-society reception honoring Schuyler Colfax, the speaker of the House of Representatives. At this affair Warmoth met and chatted with a large number of notables, among them the nation's most influential newspaperman (Horace Greeley), its most distinguished legal scholar (David Dudley Field), and its most famous historian (George Bancroft). He was not overawed. "Had a jolly time and came home tight," he congratulated himself. "Stopped at the New York Hotel, where all rebels stop. It was fun to see how soon I was found out by the guests. I was the 'observed of all observers' . . . . It is certainly a very sassy thing for a man of my political views" to stay at such a hotel. "But anything for fun." Before leaving the big city, he went to a clothier to order a new suit, visited a phrenologist to have his skull examined, and attended a theater to see Edwin Booth in *Hamlet.* He also had at least one sober and sobering thought: "Men are foolish things—afraid of God, but will not acknowledge his power."

After his return to Washington he spent the whole day, February 1, in the Hall of Representatives lobbying in his own behalf. He had another opportunity to mix pleasure with business when he received a note from Mary Harlan, the daughter of the Secretary of the Interior and a frequent date (and the future wife) of Lincoln's son Robert. Mary was asking Warmoth to escort her to a series of receptions that evening, and he gladly did so. Nineteen years old, the graduate of a finishing school, she was well trained in the feminine graces and was delightful company. The next day Warmoth presented to the chief clerk of the House a formal petition requsting admittance as the territorial delegate from Louisiana. Then Miss Harlan picked him up at the Capitol and took him to his hotel in the carriage she was sharing with General John M. Schofield.

The day after that, Warmoth went to one of Kate Chase Sprague's fabulous receptions, where he mingled with Generals William T. Sherman, George G. Meade, and George H. Thomas. Afterwards he was pleased to hear from Alfred Shaw that another guest had asked: "Shaw, who is this fellow Warmoth? I meet him everywhere I go. Chief Justice Chase introduced me to him last night at Mrs. Sprague's reception. He walks with such a lordly air! Who is he?"

Once he had formally applied for admission to Congress, Warmoth at first was confident he would soon get it. He was also confident that the Republicans in Congress soon would replace the President's Reconstruction policy with much stricter requirements of their own. Thaddeus Stevens wanted to confiscate Southern plantations and divide them among the freed people, forty acres to each family head, but he was willing to accept, as a stopgap, a measure that would bar ex-Confederate leaders from public office and would reduce the congressional representation of the Southern states. His committee was working on such a constitutional amendment. More immediately, the Republicans thought it urgent to prolong the life of the Freedmen's Bureau, which they had recently set up as a temporary army agency to look after the liberated slaves, and which was helping to protect the freedmen against virtual reenslavement under the black codes. On February 19, Johnson vetoed the new Freedmen's Bureau bill with a message that amounted to a declaration of war against the Radicals.

The outcome of the struggle between President and Congress was uncertain, but to Warmoth the fact was becoming more and more evident that, whatever Congress did, it would do it without accepting him as an official member. On February 21 he wrote to Thomas J. Durant, chairman of the Republican state central committee of Louisiana, to say he thought he could no longer serve the party or the state by remaining in Washington. By his presence he had already made the point that Louisiana was, or ought to be, nothing but a territory. "Bid all of my friends good bye at the Capitol," he recorded a week later. "Dined at the Secretary of the Interior's. Mrs. Harlan & Daughter took me to the R. R. Depot & remained with me until the train started—7 ½ P.M."[15]

"I cannot tell you anything about your dear little Miss Harlan," Warmoth read in a letter from his friend Alfred Shaw after returning to New Orleans. "I think that little affair of yours with the young creole lady on Canal St a more difficult problem to solve than the territory of Louisiana. It can't be solved satisfactorily both to Miss Harlan and her."

Whatever the feelings of the young creole lady, the feelings of most white Louisianans and especially of the women, it seemed to Warmoth, were growing more and more hostile toward men recently arrived from the North. "Our dear ladies are the most bitter of all our population," he thought. A year after the Confederate surrender the spirit of rebellion was stronger, or at any rate more openly expressed, than it had been at the time. This spirit received a stimulus both from the Radical frustration of Johnson's plan and from Johnson's obstruction of Radical measures. After vetoing the Freedmen's Bureau bill he had done the same to a civil rights bill. Congress was soon to override both vetoes.

In April 1866 a white Republican of St. James parish, upriver from New Orleans, informed Warmoth that the Democrats there were persecuting blacks and threatening to break up the new party. "Our only hope heretofore has been in Congress; but we can but begin to give way under the persevering intention of the President to veto all bills calculated to advance our cause, or to at least give us hope." In January, General Philip H. Sheridan, now the commander of the Military Division of the Gulf, had remarked optimistically that the South was fast becoming "Northernized." In June the general emphasized the restlessness of the people and the need for additional troops.[16]

Meanwhile Warmoth was giving more and more attention to politics and less and less to the practice of the law. In the state and municipal courts he was arguing few cases or none at all, since he was practically disqualified by the prejudice of juries against him. The immediate aim of Louisiana Republicans, he now believed, should be to redraft the state constitution so as to give the vote to blacks. As a member of the Republican executive committee, he moved that the party hold an election to choose delegates to a new constitutional convention. But Governor Wells—who had switched back from the Democrats to the Republicans—proposed, instead, that the party reconvene the old convention, the one that had adjourned in 1864. This way, the election of new delegates would be unnecessary; the previous ones could simply get together again and add such amendments as they desired. Either the Wells or the Warmoth procedure would be extralegal if not downright illegal. In any case, most of the party leaders preferred the Wells plan.

The date set for the reassembling of the constitutional convention was Monday, July 30, and the place was the Mechanics' Institute building, which was being used as a temporary state capitol. On the day before, Warmoth made the following notation: "The Republicans held a large meeting at the Mechanics' Institute on Friday night to endorse Congress & the call of the convention. The Governor has issued his proclamation . . . and everybody favorable to it are in good spirits. The press & the Democracy are mad against it. It is hoped that it will pass off without trouble whichever way it may terminate." This was to prove a fragile, unavailing hope.[17]

On July 30, shortly before noon, Warmoth strode along broad Canal Street on his way to the Mechanics' Institute, to observe the proceedings there. He was perspiring in the midsummer heat, which was already sticky and oppressive and was steadily getting worse. There was a tension as well as a heaviness in the air, and he felt it all the more strongly as he reached the corner of Dryades, the side street on which the Mechanics' Institute was located. On the corner stood dozens of young white men, their arms folded, their gaze fixed ominously on the crowd, mostly black, that had gathered in front of the convention building. Inside it Warmoth found the people apprehensive, half-expecting the police to appear and put them under arrest. Soon after twelve the convention was called to order, the prayer was said, and the roll was taken. Responses came from only twenty-six delegates, too few for a quorum, and so the convention adjourned, to meet again in just one hour.

As Warmoth left and made his way to Canal Street, he noticed that the knots of hostile, glaring young toughs had greatly increased. A block farther on he went into the house at 150 Canal and told a couple of his friends what was going on. In a few minutes he was interrupted by the sound of gunfire outside. Stepping out on the balcony, he and his friends looked up the street. The young men who had been waiting were now deploying like skirmishers and shooting continually as they advanced toward the Mechanics' Institute and disappeared around the corner. Policemen began to arrive on the double quick, two, three, perhaps four hundred of them. Suddenly two black men came running down the street, and after them hundreds of white men and boys throwing stones. Right in front of where Warmoth stood, the two blacks fell to the pavement. He watched them quiver and die when policemen walked up to them and shot them. A little later the policemen only looked on as the rabble knocked down a poor old Negro and kicked and stomped him. Then the two men at the side of Warmoth, fearing that the mob might recognize and turn upon him, pulled him back inside the house.

His host, one of his comrades of the Vicksburg compaign, slipped out to find General Absalom Baird, the commander of the local contingent of federal troops, and tell him what was happening. In about half an hour, as a white and a black regiment approached, Warmoth reemerged to watch. White civilians were still attacking black ones. And police were dragging along and beating an elderly white man, a member of the ill-fated convention, while fifty or sixty of the rabble, brandishing guns and knives, trailed behind with yells of "Shoot him!" "Hang him!" "Kill him, God damn him!" But the infantry, with bayonets pointed, soon cleared the streets and brought an end to the rioting.

Then Warmoth and his associates walked down Canal to St. Charles Street, ate at a French restaurant, and went on to the St. Charles Hotel. In this stately edifice, with white pillars and porticoes, they found their mutual friend Alfred Shaw, one of the convention delegates. From him they learned that the rioters had besieged the Mechanics' Institute, battered their way into the building, and shot and stabbed as many as they could, without mercy. The police had attempted to escort the white leaders to safety, and Shaw himself, while under police protection, had been shot, though not seriously wounded. Some of the others, among them ex-Governor Michael Hahn, were badly hurt but would recover. Still others were dead or dying. And now the proprietor of the St. Charles came up to Shaw and told him he would have to find quarters elsewhere. Shaw asked why, but the proprietor merely turned and walked away. Warmoth followed him and demanded a reason. The man replied that "the guests would not stay in the same house with a Black Republican." What a change had come over New Orleans! This hotel had once been the headquarters of General Butler.

Warmoth and Shaw obtained a carriage and rode around the city for several hours to see and hear what they could. "The impression amongst Union men," they discovered, "is that the attack was premeditated murder. That the city government planned it, as it is certain they executed it." Warmoth sought out General Baird and got from him the estimate that thirty-nine blacks had been killed and hundreds wounded. (A later estimate had 3 whites and 34 blacks dead and 17 whites and 119 blacks hurt—all of them Republicans.) One policeman had collapsed from the heat, ten had been injured, and one member of the mob had died from a shot in the back of the head, probably an accidental shot from the gun of another mob member or a policeman. As Warmoth summed it up in his journal entry for Monday, July 30, 1866: "A dark day for the city of New Orleans."[18]

CHAPTER 2

Go South, Young Man! (1865-1866)

On the ship approaching the Atlantic coast of Florida, just below the Georgia line, passengers could make out the low silhouette of the town of Fernandina. As the ship docked, near the little wooden building that served as a customhouse, they could see that Fernandina, with its rambling structures of weather-beaten wood, was not much of a place. The home of nearly 800 whites and 600 blacks, this was nevertheless one of the largest communities in the entire state, which as yet was hardly settled at all except along its northern edge. The town appeared to have the potential of a future metropolis. With its deep and well-protected natural harbor, it seemingly ought to grow into a great seaport once it had a sufficiently developed hinterland.

To one of the arrivals the sight brought memories both sweet and bitter, memories of a lovely friend and a vicious foe, of hope renewed and hope deferred. But this man showed no emotion. If the other passengers noticed him at all, they probably assumed, mistakenly, that Harrison Reed was a banker or perhaps a merchant intending to reestablish his business in Florida. Rather short and slight, Reed was unimpressive in appearance. He had a comparatively large head that was bald on top, long graying hair that hung down from the tonsure, and a long graying beard that descended from his cheeks and chin, but not from his upper lip, which was clean-shaven. His thick-rimmed eyeglasses gave him an owlish look, and his pious, calculating, unobtrusive manner added to the effect. He was no longer young—he was past fifty—but perhaps he was not too old to begin anew. Florida might yet prove to be the frontier of his dreams.[1]

Like millions of other Americans of his time, Harrison Reed had spent a good part of his life in pursuit of the horizon. Born near Boston, he moved with his parents and his four brothers and three sisters to a Massachusetts town a little farther away and then to Castleton in central Vermont. Here the father ran a hotel and traded in cattle, and here Harrison grew up, attended the local academy, and worked as a printer's apprentice. Then, setting out on his own, he went west to Troy, New York, where he clerked in a general store. At the age of twenty-two he made the westward jump to the newly settled town of Milwaukee, in what was about to be reorganized as the territory of Wisconsin. There he and the rest of the family joined two of his brothers who had gone on ahead and started a hardware business.

Wisconsin seemed a land of promise at the time Harrison Reed arrived, and during the next quarter-century it did develop wondrously, first as a territory and then as a state. Some enterprisers made fortunes there. Reed tried hard to do the same. He took up storekeeping, newspaper publishing, and land speculating. He moved from Milwaukee to Madison, then to Neenah and back to Madison again. He gained the support of influential men, such as Solomon Juneau, the founder of Milwaukee, and James Duane Doty, the strong-willed territorial governor. (He did not win the favor of Wisconsin's wealthiest citizen, the banker and railroad promoter Alexander Mitchell, though one of Reed's sisters married him.) Through his efforts he managed to support a wife, two sons, and a daughter, and he made a respectable record of accomplishment, most notably as a co-founder of the village of Neenah. Loyally he served the cause of first the Whig and then the Republican party. No Wisconsinite was more devoted than he to the old Whig principles of government aid to business—through protective tariffs, transportation improvements, and the establishment of a national bank—or the new Republican principle of resistance to the spread of slavery. Yet real success, both economic and political, kept eluding Reed.

At the outbreak of the Civil War he pulled up stakes once more and headed for Washington, D.C., where he resigned himself temporarily to the life of a petty bureaucrat. An employee of the Treasury Department, he devoted himself, as all such employees were expected to do, not only to the interests of the public but also to those of the department head, Salmon P. Chase, then as always a presidential hopeful. After a year Reed's daughter, Georgiana, died, and before long his wife, Anna Louise, followed her.

"The ghosts of my own buried hopes would throng me until I would give up in despair," Reed a little later reminisced about this period of his life. "We cannot recall our dearest ones who are gone, but it lightens many a burden of life & illumines many a cloud to reflect that they await us on the 'shining shore,' where we may yet join them & spend an eternity with them 'basking in the sunshine of God.'" Try as he would, Reed could not keep his mind off his sad memories. "I often indulge myself in communion with the loved & lost & feel sometimes anxious to close this rough pilgrimage & be with them. It will not be long & may the light that comes from those mansions where our loved ones dwell cheer & lighten our pathways & keep us from wandering after the things that 'perish with the using.'"

In the midst of his mourning an opportunity to wander after such things presented itself to Reed. According to a recent act of Congress, a federal tax was to be imposed on real estate in the South. To pay the tax and keep his property, an owner must demonstrate his loyalty to the United States. If the owner failed to do so, the property would be forfeited to the federal government, which could then sell it. Treasury officials were to follow the armies into the conquered areas of the Confederacy and administer the law. Reed received, from Treasury Secretary Chase, an appointment as one of three tax commissioners for Florida.

In January 1863 Reed and his two colleagues landed at Fernandina, on a narrow coastal strip that Union troops had occupied. He found Florida a promising frontier, "one of undeveloped resources and latent wealth" that "could render it one of the finest states in the Union," one needing only enterprise to attain "a degree of prosperity unknown to even the North." But, for the time being, he had to devote himself to his duties as a tax commissioner—assessing the local real estate, advertising to notify absent owners of taxes due, and holding auctions to dispose of forfeited property.[2]

At first the three officials got along reasonably well with one another and performed their task smoothly enough. Then Reed grew increasingly suspicious of one of his associates, Lyman D. Stickney. A Vermonter by birth, Stickney had gone to the South before the war and had been on good enough terms with the Florida secession legislature of 1860-61 to obtain a land grant from it, yet later claimed to be a Unionist refugee from the state. Now, as a tax commissioner, he seemed to spend less time in serving the purposes of the government than in serving the interests of himself and those of the Florida Railroad, a large landholder in the Fernandina area. Soon he departed for the North and left Reed and John S. Sammis, the latter elderly and unenergetic, to carry on by themselves.

Reed and Sammis proceeded to auction off houses and lots on which no one had paid the tax. Each of the two men bought for himself two square blocks of Fernandina real estate, and Reed bid in a lot for each of his two sons. Reed and Sammis also sold homes to many freed slaves at prices these poor people could afford. Stretching the law a bit, the commissioners allowed blacks to buy without competitive bidding the premises they were already occupying. Reed disposed of one house with a value of $3500 for a mere $25. This large and rather imposing residence, one of the best in town, belonged to Joseph Finegan, who was hardly in a position to redeem it since he was away on duty as a general in the Confederate army. The Finegan house was already in use as a Negro orphanage.

Reed could never forget the young woman who ran the orphanage and who bought the mansion. She was Chloe Merrick, daughter of the very respectable Susbanus Merrick of Syracuse, New York. An agent of the Freedmen's Aid Society of Syracuse, Chloe had come south in the wake of the Union armies, like dozens of other Yankee maidens, to help educate the children of the former slaves. With the support of Northern charity she set up schools in both Fernandina and St. Augustine. She could hardly keep from stirring the heart of the lonely widower Reed. Chloe had such a romantic name, and she was so diligent in good works. But she was so young, scarcely half his age, and his bereavement was so recent. Well, at least he could wait and hope.[3]

Before the summer's end Reed had to leave Fernandina and Chloe. Stickney was denouncing him and Sammis for having made the sales without Stickney's participation, and Stickney had the backing of his superiors in Washington, including Chase. Reed went to Washington to defend himself, but Chase would not even listen to him. So Reed appealed to his Wisconsin political friends. "A year ago I went out as an officer of the government, to find relief from an overburdened heart, in a new field, where I thought to be useful in assisting the great mission of freedom & civilization which has been forced upon the nation," he explained to Congressman John F. Potter. "I have embarked in schemes for the benefit of the freedmen & I want to live in Florida to assist in bringing it in as a free state & in regenerating the slavery cursed territory." But "this villainous man" Stickney had frustrated him. "He is the most unmitigated scoundrel I ever met & a wily, sharp, dangerous man in any position & particularly to one who is naturally confiding like myself."

A friend of Stickney's described Reed as a "fussy old granny," and Stickney himself called him a "damn fool." Stickney complained: "Reed hangs around like the itch. I can hardly meet him without spitting in his face." Stickney won out. Chase ordered a resale of the Fernandina properties and compelled Reed to resign his Treasury job. Desperate to get back to Florida, Reed begged Wisconsin Republicans to find another position for him there. The best they could do for him at the moment was a Washington assignment in the Post Office Department, where ex-Governor Alexander W. Randall of Wisconsin was Assistant Postmaster General. Reed finally got a chance to resume his Florida career when President Andrew Johnson appointed him as a special postal agent to supervise the mails of the state.[4]

When Reed reappeared in Fernandina in June 1865, Chloe was still there, and so was Stickney. She had managed to retain the Finegan house for her orphanage, which was flourishing, as were her schools. She was beginning to find new employment for children and youths in her care. Through the Freedmen's Bureau she obtained places for them in New York and New England where they could escape from peasantry and become house servants for the Yankee well-to-do.

Stickney was the local leader of the Chase-for-President cause. Chase, though now Chief Justice, continued to hold the loyalty of many Treasury employees. On his Southern tour his ship put in at Fernandina, and he invited Stickney aboard for consultation. Reed took alarm. Now decidedly (and understandably) anti-Chase and pro-Johnson, he feared the Chase men were using Treasury jobs and funds to put together a political machine in the South. They were said to be lining up the blacks and scheming to use their vote. As postal agent, Reed himself controlled a certain amount of federal patronage. But if the Treasury people should have their way, Stickney would again get the upper hand.

Reed hastened to send off, for the benefit of Johnson, a warning in regard to the nefarious designs of Chase. "He has advised his friends here to organize the colored men & prepare them to vote & that their action shall be sustained by the Supreme Court—holding that there is no legal authority or power to deny suffrage." So wrote Reed in his fastidiously neat and tiny penmanship. "Secret organizations of blacks & non-resident whites or outsiders imported here as agents of the Treasury &c. have been commenced." The Chase men intended to "override the resident white citizens" on the grounds that all of them were disloyal. But there *was* a "loyal element here," and the President should recognize it in making federal appointments. Certainly he should appoint an old Floridian as provisional governor to oversee the reorganization of the state under the Johnson plan. A good man for the position would be William Marvin, a jurist, a scholar, and for twenty-five years a Florida resident.[5]

Before receiving Reed's recommendation of Marvin, the President had already decided to make him provisional governor. Marvin had no sooner taken office than he discouraged the Chase faction of Treasury agents by suspending the sale of confiscated property. Touring the state, he told both whites and blacks what to expect from the Johnson plan. Blacks had heard the rumor that on New Year's Day 1866 the federal government was going to provide each of them with forty acres and a mule. Marvin assured them: "The President will not give you one foot of land, nor a mule, nor a hog, nor a cow, nor even a knife or fork or spoon." In an address to the constitutional convention he had called, he instructed the delegates not to consider Negro suffrage. "Neither the white people nor the colored people are prepared for so radical a change in their social relations," he explained. "Nor have I any reason to believe that any considerable number of the freedmen desire to possess this privilege."

Reed thoroughly approved the course that Florida was taking under the direction of President Johnson and Governor Marvin. Reed's opinions carried some weight, for he now was not only the federal postal agent but also the editor of the leading Republican newspaper in the state, the *Jacksonville Florida Times.* He had nothing to say against the ex-Confederates who dominated the constitutional convention. "Such 'rebels' will make faithful citizens," he editorialized. Nor did he object to the former slaveholders and Confederate veterans who filled the offices in the reorganized state government.

Jacksonville, Reed's second home in Florida, was only slightly more populous than Fernandina and was less than a day away. From Fernandina the boat steamed down the coast and up the broad and quiet St. John's River, rousing sleepy alligators and stirring pelicans to flight. Forests hid the banks except for an occasional clearing with a shack that passed for a mansion. Orange groves could be developed along the St. John's, as they already had been elsewhere in northern Florida. Near St. Augustine the former secretary to President Lincoln, John Hay, owned a productive and profitable grove that Treasury commissioners had sold for unpaid taxes. It cost Hay $500 and its previous year's crop was said to be worth $2500. At Jacksonville some wooden stores, a few brick warehouses, and a billiard saloon faced the river along the main street, which was deep in sand, as were all the other streets and roads in the vicinity. Black soldiers policed the town. With its lumber, tar, and turpentine trade increasing day by day, Jacksonville was beginning a rapid recovery from the war.[6]

The town had a future, and so did Harrison Reed. Squelching his onetime nemesis Lyman D. Stickney, he was to become the first Republican governor in the history of Florida. He was to win the heart and hand of Chloe Merrick. And he was to acquire, on the bank of the St. John's River, a farm and orange grove of his own. Yet he was never quite to achieve the kind of success he hungered for.

Railroads in northern Alabama, like many of those elsewhere in the fallen Confederacy, were not yet back to normal and would not be for months. Here and there the bridges were still out. Near Decatur, for example, nothing was left of the once imposing high-level bridge except the tall stone piers, and railroad passengers had to cross the Tennessee River in a barge, which black men operated. Rolling stock was generally the worse for wear, and occasionally a boxcar with benches had to serve as a coach. Nevertheless, the trains were crowded now that peace had come. Among the arrivals were many men from the North.

This part of Alabama, though different from more southerly areas of the state, had attractions of its own. Here were high and thickly wooded ridges, not much good for farming, but here also were cultivated slopes and valleys with a more or less fertile soil of red clay. Farms were small and Negroes few. The inhabitants, especially in the Tennessee Valley, had felt little enthusiasm for the Confederacy. They had welcomed the Union troops who occupied the valley in 1862, and on the whole they were well disposed toward the civilian invaders of 1865, most of whom till recently had worn the uniform of blue.

What drew the newcomers was, in a word, cotton. After four years of blockade and disruption, cotton was scarce and its price high, much higher than before the war. And the cost of land, whether to rent or to buy, was much lower than it had been. One reason was that the owners generally lacked the capital to improve and cultivate the land themselves. If the soil here was less productive than in central or southern Alabama, it was also less expensive. Here even a man of modest means could afford to purchase or to lease. Fortunes seemed to await enterprising cotton cultivators from the North.

To grow cotton, though, was not the quickest or easiest way to make money out of it. Hoarded away were thousands and thousands of bales that Alabamians claimed as their private property and Treasury agents claimed as confiscated assets of the Confederate government. A Northerner with ready cash and the right connections could get his hands immediately on quite a bit of cotton. If he had to pay a high price for it, he could hope to resell it for a still higher price.

The possibilities for profit were quite clear to Colonel George Eliphaz Spencer when he came back to Alabama's Tennessee Valley. Spencer knew the area well. Here, in 1863, he had recruited enough white Alabamians to form a Union cavalry regiment, which he thereafter commanded. In the spring of 1865 he was still in the army and, like a great many other officers, had just been awarded the brevet (honorary) rank of brigadier-general. But—again like many other volunteers—he would face an uncertain future if he should remain in the shrinking postwar army. Now twenty-eight years old, he had to look for another career, one that might be at least as gratifying as military command. "I am strongly of the opinion that I should settle somewhere South," he confided to General Grenville M. Dodge, his fellow Iowan, his erstwhile superior in the Army of the Tennessee, and still his obliging friend. "I think the chances of making a fortune there the best."

For the moment, Colonel Spencer was in Alabama primarily for the purpose of influencing state politics. He was working for the appointment of William H. Smith, a native wartime Unionist, as provisional governor of the state. He remembered Smith's coming to General Dodge—after the Union occupation of Corinth, Mississippi, in 1862—and agreeing to serve as a paid spy for him. Recently Spencer had called upon President Johnson three times to urge Smith's appointment, and now he was holding meetings and gathering petitions in Smith's behalf. If he should succeed in putting Smith in office, Spencer could expect to wield, at least temporarily, a certain amount of power in Alabama affairs. "If I succeed," he decided, "I shall settle in Ala. at once and claim it for my home."[7]

Resigning from the army (on Independence Day, appropriately enough) Spencer continued to travel back and forth between Philadelphia and northern Alabama. His wife, a twenty-five-year-old career woman, lived in Philadelphia. Born in England, she had grown up in the United States, bearing the exotic and un-English though mellifluous name of Bella Zilfa. Bella was the author of a recent novel, *Ora, the Lost Wife,* and she was writing another, *Tried and True: A Story of the Rebellion.* She also edited a newspaper, the *Philadelphia Post,* in which she was purchasing a one-third interest. Still, she had time to involve herself in her husband's activities and associates. When he congratulated General Dodge on receiving from the citizens of St. Louis a gift of silver plate, Spencer said he would much like to see the gift—"but having been one of Sherman's bummers it might not be safe to place so much temptation in my way"—and he added: "Mrs. Spencer first saw [a report of] it in one of the northern exchanges & was as pleased as though it had been given to herself."

Spencer failed to persuade President Johnson to appoint Smith, though Johnson reportedly had "ordered that all appointments must & shall be given to actual & bona fide residents of the different localities." Disgusted with Johnson, but still hopeful of a Southern career, Spencer wrote to General Dodge on August 1:

> When you get out of the army I wish you would come South & operate. We are bound to succeed ultimately and if we can't any other way we can by "Negro Suffrage." I have been figuring with the radicals & think I am in the ring. As I was in business with Gov Sprague I can get his & the Chase influence & expect, when Congress meets, to knock this provisional governor system higher than a kite. I am in favor of Negro Suffrage or reducing all these states to the position of territories & keeping them so for years to come or until the leaders are all dead or have left the country. This is the only safe course of procedure.[8]

During the summer and fall Spencer was busily buying cotton in Alabama. By mid-October he had accumulated a thousand bales, in which he held a quarter-interest (partners who had helped finance the deal held the rest). He estimated that he would have spent 28 cents a pound for the cotton, including transportation, by the time it reached New York, and that he could dispose of it there for 60 cents. With a profit of 32 cents per pound, or $160 per 500-pound bale, the thousand bales would bring a total of $160,000, of which his share would come to $40,000 (at a time when a day laborer in the North would do extremely well to make $400 in a year). "I think," he congratulated himself, "I shall make a good year's work out of it." But, at Tuscaloosa, he had to wait for the Black Warrior River to rise, so he could send his cargo down to Mobile and out to market.

After selling the cotton he would, "like Micawber, wait for something to turn up." The political prospect in Alabama, so far as the immediate future was concerned, was no longer encouraging at all. Spencer explained to Dodge:

> Politics has played out. The rebels control all the southern states and a Yankee stands no show. The test for every officer here must be, has he been in the Confederate Army? If he has not been loyal to the South he is immediately removed. No loyal Union man can hold a position in the South if the President's policy is carried out. I am in hopes that when Congress meets that something may be done.

Until Congress did something, there would be at best but limited scope for a man like Spencer in the South. Meanwhile, he might as well move on. His twenty-ninth birthday was approaching, and there was little time to lose. Already, before the war, he had gone west in search of opportunity. Born in northern New York, the son of a surgeon, he had studied at a college in Montreal and then had located in Iowa, where at the age of twenty he became secretary of the state senate and at twenty-one was admitted to the bar. He now decided to try his luck still farther west, in California. But in due time he was to return to Alabama, and much of Reconstruction politics in that state was to revolve around a personal rivalry between him and another ex-colonel of the Union army—Willard Warner.[9]

Alabama's most desirable lands were located in the Black Belt, a strip of rich black soil stretching across the south central part of the state. Before the war, this rolling prairie had been converted into some of the largest and wealthiest cotton plantations in the entire South. Though the Black Belt was accessible by rail, planters generally relied on the Alabama River to send out their crops and to bring in supplies. Passengers and goods from the North could go down the Mississippi or sail from an Atlantic port and, at Mobile, transfer to an Alabama riverboat (much smaller and cruder than a floating palace of the Mississippi).

As the boat steamed slowly up the meandering Alabama, experienced Southern planters and prospective Northern planters on board had a chance to exchange opinions. A few of the Alabamians were confident that their former slaves would work willingly as free laborers, but most thought compulsion would be necessary. "The nigger is going to be made a serf, sure as you live," one of them asserted, expressing the hope and expectation of many others. They agreed, however, that serfdom could be made effective only after the federal government had withdrawn the Freedmen's Bureau and the troops. For the time being, all was uncertainty for the Southerners, many of whom would therefore be glad enough to lease or sell their land. Quite different was the outlook for the Northerners. "The Yankees have faith in Sambo and propose to back their faith with abundant capital," the traveling newsman Whitelaw Reid reported. "If they succeed, their cotton fields are better than Nevada mines."

Three days and three hundred miles after leaving Mobile, the boat arrived at Selma, on the farther edge of the Black Belt. Here the Confederate arsenal, foundry, rolling mill, and munitions warehouses lay in ruins, and private houses and stores were only beginning to be rebuilt after the devastating raid by James H. Wilson's cavalry at the very end of the war. On the way from Selma to Montgomery, a hundred miles farther upriver, Wilson's route could be traced by the charred remnants of railroad depots, plantation gin-houses, and other buildings. Some foundries, machine shops, and cotton warehouses were destroyed in Montgomery itself, but otherwise there was little damage to the state's capital (and after Mobile its largest city, with a prewar population of 10,000). Attractively spread out on gentle hills, Montgomery continued to be graced by its colonnaded mansions and to be crowned by its domed capitol, which was painted to look like granite. Here, as at Mobile, the cotton business boomed during the postwar months.[10]

Several miles below Montgomery lay the plantation that, in the autumn of 1865, thirty-nine-year-old Willard Warner was operating and was about to buy. One corner of it touched upon the Alabama River and had a landing where steamboats could load and unload freight. The property, roughly two-and-a-half miles long and one-and-a-half wide, was divided into 80-acre to 150-acre fields, which were bounded by hedges. Here and there were groves of hickory and walnut. For the coming season, Warner intended to plant 700 acres in cotton and at least 200 in corn. This was good land; it ought to yield close to a bale of cotton per acre.

By December, Warner had thirty hands at work and was expecting soon to have forty. They were plowing, cutting corn stalks, cleaning out ditches, and doing all that was necessary to prepare for the planting. Women plowed and hoed like men, but were paid less—$8 a month plus rations as compared with $10 for men. Serving as his own overseer, Warner rode out to the fields along with his laborers early each morning. Altogether, there were 59 Negroes on the plantation, 23 of them small children. Only a few, young or old, could read. On Fridays Warner personally held classes on the third floor of the gin-house to teach the illiterate. On Sundays he taught Sabbath school in the same large room.

For him, the life of a Southern planter was agreeable enough. Indeed, he could be quite happy—if only his beloved Eliza were still alive. She was often on his mind, and so were his seven-year-old son, Willard, Jr., and five-year-old daughter, May, who were staying with their mother's parents in Ohio.

He took what time he could to write to young Willard and tell him about plantation life, particularly the aspects of it that might appeal to a boy. "It is warm and pleasant as summer here," though Christmas was not far away. "Cane poles grow, thousands of them, on the place. You can get plenty of fishing poles. There are squirrels, ducks, coons, possums, in abundance, and some wild turkeys." Warner had tried raccoon meat and had found it excellent, but he certainly did not have to depend on hunted game. He owned 17 milk cows, 58 beef cattle, and 200 hogs. "I just ate dinner alone & had nice sweet potatoes, ham, corn & wheat bread and turnips & milk & butter, all good & well cooked." "If I stay all winter . . . I want you to come and you shall have a pony and saddle & bridle to ride with me." "Be a good boy. God bless you and May. Your loving Papa."[11]

The thought of Eliza brought the past to mind. Warner's earliest memories were of an Ohio farm, first his father's and then, after his mother's death when he was five, his uncle's, where he was mostly raised, in the Licking Valley east of Columbus. After earning a B.A. and an M.A. degree from Marietta College he returned to the farm for a few years and then, with three companions, joined the earliest of the Forty-niners in the California gold rush. The trip to San Francisco—by way of the Mississippi River, the Gulf of Mexico, the Isthmus of Panama, and the Pacific Ocean—took more than five exhausting months. After nearly three years of hard work at placer mining, the lone survivor of his little group of Ohio gold seekers, Warner made his way back home without a fortune but with savings large enough to help him start a business. He founded and became the general manager of the Newark Machine Works, which manufactured steam engines, sawmill machinery, and threshing machines.

Ever since his return from California he had been courting Eliza Woods. The two lovers confided their innermost moods to one another. "I find a secret pleasure in wandering about the old farm," he wrote when they were apart. "I love to sit under the old trees by the stream and . . . to recall my thoughts and anticipations, to look at the picture of the future as painted by boyish fancy, and compare the bright rainbow coloring, its sunset tints, with the real picture which time has made, with its sunlight and shade, its tones and shadows." But he would not allow her to be sad. "Just in the dawn of beautiful womanhood, your life should be bright as sunset glow." She grew more and more impatient to be married: "When I am your wife, I will be kind, & loving, & when we go to our little home, humble tho' it be, I will make it glad & bright that you may love me more." But they delayed the wedding for four years, until he was well established in business, by which time he was twenty-nine and she was twenty-three.[12]

Already he was a rising politician as well as an up-and-coming businessman. One of the first Ohioans to join the Republican party, he took an active part in its first national campaign, in 1856. By 1860 he was important enough to be a delegate to the party's presidential nominating convention and to be the object of an urgent and confidential appeal from Salmon P. Chase, at that time Ohio's governor and favorite son. Chase wanted to be sure that Ohio Republicans would bring up no name except his own at the Chicago convention. If his state remained solidly behind him he thought he could win: "With New England, a considerable part of New York, & the Northwestern States added to my own strength, the nomination would be secure enough." At Chicago, after Chase's hopes proved illusory, Warner felt free to vote for Abraham Lincoln. When Lincoln's election led to the secession of the Southern states, Warner discovered a silver lining in the ominous cloud: "*The great result* . . . of this now impending crisis will be the destruction of the system of slavery, and . . . the *slaveholders* are to be the unwitting instrument in the hands of God to work out this great result."

Once the war had begun, Warner did his part to bring about the victory for Union and freedom. He served in the campaigns that culminated at Fort Donelson, Corinth, Vicksburg, Chattanooga, Atlanta, Fort Fisher, and Raleigh. Along the way he rose from major to colonel and (brevet) major-general. In the midst of the war, after less than eight years of married life, he received the shocking news of Eliza's death. At the war's end he mailed his son a few souvenirs: $500 in Confederate currency and a sliver of wood from the North Carolina farmhouse where General Joseph E. Johnston had surrendered to General William T. Sherman. "We have accomplished what we aimed at, despite traitors & Copperheads, and I shall ever be glad that I was in at the end of the war," he told the boy. "If your Mother was living, how happy we should all be in our home, with her with us. But we must submit to the will of God as cheerfully as we can."

By summer he was out of the army and back in Ohio politics. In October he won election to the state senate. Then he went south to the plantation in Alabama, a state to which his war service had never brought him. During a few months in early 1866 he was in Ohio to attend the legislative session, but by April he was in Alabama again. The plantation, which he had left in the care of a partner, was doing splendidly. Already the cotton plants were leafing out, and the corn was four to six inches high. To Warner, this first springtime there, the whole place looked like a great and beautiful garden.[13]

An occasional visitor at Warner's plantation was Eliza's brother William B. Woods, a (brevet) brigadier-general commanding the federal troops in Alabama, with headquarters at Mobile. Warner's example encouraged his brother-in-law to become an Alabama planter also. "I believe it is the policy of the President to appoint Southern citizens to fill offices in the South when suitable persons can be found," General Woods wrote from Mobile to Ohio Senator John Sherman. "I consider myself a citizen of Alabama, or that I will be as soon as my muster out takes effect. I have purchased a plantation in this State, have stocked it, and am preparing to plant, and as soon as discharged from the military service will bring my family here."

According to some reports, Woods and other Northerners aspiring to be planters had to contend against the hostility of native whites. For example, the *Chicago Tribune* (February 23, 1866) published the following letter from a Union officer who had been stationed in Alabama for four postwar months:

> The facts are that in Alabama there is a class of men, intelligent and usually wealthy, who take a correct view of the condition of things in that State, and who certainly desire Northern men to come in among them with their cap-

ital, to engage in planting, trading, manufacturing, &c. But the majority of the people are still very bitter and opposed to Northern men coming into the State. I am satisfied that were the federal troops withdrawn from the State, in some localities Northern men would be compelled to leave. It is estimated that five thousand men from the North have already settled in that State, bringing with them their capital, and have engaged principally in planting cotton. Already threats have been made that no "Yankee" shall be permitted to sell or ship his cotton next fall. As a consequence many of them are making arrangements to arm and drill their negro laborers, for the purpose of protecting themselves and property after the troops are withdrawn. Gen. Woods, commanding the Department, has signified his willingness to furnish them with arms and ammunition.[14]

But Warner did not believe such reports, and from his plantation he wrote to Senator Sherman in mid-April to refute them:

All very quiet here. I was met, on my return, with the greatest kindness by all with whom I had become acquainted last fall. My partner, who has been here on the plantation *alone* all winter, has met only the kindest treatment and the *heartiest encouragement* from all our neighbors. I have yet to hear (and I inquired of the [Freedmen's] Bureau in Montgomery) of the first instance, in this State, of injury to Northern men. A Northern man who is not a natural fool, or foolish fanatic, may live pleasantly anywhere in Alabama, without abating one jot of his self-respect or independence.

It followed, in Warner's opinion, that the Radical Republicans were wrong and President Johnson was right. Hate and fanaticism were delaying the reestablishment of national unity: "Fanaticism on the part of men, of whom Sumner is a type, in whose view the Negro stands as the embodiment of all the virtues and woes of humanity," and vengefulness as reflected in "Stevens' crazy, hateful schemes." There should be equal justice for all, without regard to color, and the franchise should be given only to the intelligent, whether black or white. "The Negro is safe enough, for two men want to hire, at good wages, each one, to say nothing of Civil Rights bills, Freedmen's Bureau, and Constitutional Amendment." Congress should promptly readmit the Southern states as restored under the Johnson plan. At the recent session of the Ohio senate Warner had introduced a resolution to this effect (it did not pass).

Warner found that, on the question of Reconstruction, he had the full endorsement of General Sherman, on whose staff he had served during the war and who remained a close friend. He heard from Sherman:

Young men, such as you, have gone south. I found Memphis and Arkansas full of them. You can work negroes with good profit to yourself and good results to the negro, and to the country. . . . We now have the power to transform that vast area, heretofore kept in a low state of civilization by causes for which this generation was not responsible, to the very highest, by education, by industry, by patience, by forbearance and the simple practice

> of that charity which is the foundation of religion and wisdom. Congress can't do it by all the test oaths and voluminous trammelings of statutes, but the young men of this country can and will.

After reading one of Warner's letters General Sherman forwarded it to his brother, Senator Sherman, with the notation: "I think this letter will repay a perusal. It is from Willard Warner, who was a *real* abolitionist before the war."

One of the government's unfortunate policies that, in Warner's view, were based on hatred of the South—the policy that affected him the most directly—was the federal tax of three cents a pound on cotton. By June 1866, when his cotton plants were blooming, their colors fluctuating from white to straw or pink, his plantation looked more than ever like a huge flower garden. But his prospects of profit were fading as the cotton price declined. The tax enabled foreign growers, who had sprung up during the wartime shortage, to undersell Americans in the markets of the world. Unless the law was quickly repealed, Warner would be lucky to break even with the present crop. "Many Northern men, & Southern too, will be glad to make expenses this year," he protested to Senator Sherman. "I beg of you, don't tax us for the benefit of India, China, Brazil & Africa." Yet, for the time being, the tax was neither repealed nor reduced.

The cotton bubble had burst. Now that Northerners in Alabama could no longer expect to get rich quick as planters, most of them were going home. Warner was one of the minority that stayed on.[15]

Cotton had been even more of an attraction in Mississippi than in Alabama. Ox carts loaded with cotton bales were creaking through the streets of Vicksburg, the state's river entrepôt, when Albert T. Morgan and his brother Charles arrived there in the fall of 1865. In the rush of Northerners to Mississippi the Morgans were rather late. They had taken time to explore the agricultural possibilities of the West before trying those of the South.

Aspiring pioneers themselves, the Morgans came from a pioneering family. Albert could remember his father's telling of the move from New Hampshire to northern New York, where the family cleared enough of the primeval forest to make a farm, and where Albert was born into what then became a brood of eight children (ultimately ten: seven boys and three girls). He could also remember—though, again, only from his parents' account—the long trek to Wisconsin, where his father rose to become the proprietor of a wheat warehouse and a general store, and where he himself grew up, in the village of Fox Lake.

Albert was eighteen years old and a student in Oberlin, Ohio, preparing to enter Oberlin College, when he heard the news that Southerners had fired on the American flag at Fort Sumter. Just one week later, back home in Fox Lake, he enlisted as a private in what became Company A of the 2d Wisconsin Regiment. Eventually he was to be promoted to captain and was to be brevetted lieutenant-colonel. At the second battle of Bull Run he was captured but was soon exchanged. At Gettysburg he fell when an ememy bullet struck him in the left thigh, passing inside the bone and out through the buttock. After several months in military hospitals the wound had healed and the bone swelling had gone down, but he was permanently lame. Nevertheless, he returnd to service and, when his three years of duty were up, reenlisted. Outside of Petersburg, during the siege, he suffered a relapse and was overcome by general fatigue and abdominal weakness and pain. Yet, after a brief sick leave and a visit home, he was at the Virginia front again. He was not finally mustered out until July 1865, and by that time he was seriously ill with malaria.

Four years earlier Albert had been a robust five-feet-ten 175-pounder with a clear, healthy, tan complexion. Now, at twenty-two, he was a sallow 145-pound weakling with a sagging belly that only Dr. Fitch's patented London Abdominal Supporter could comfortably hold up, and with a shriveled leg that quickly tired and began to drag when he walked.[16]

His brother Charles, ten years older, also a war veteran, proposed that the two of them look around, as soon as Albert was able to travel, for a place to get a new start in life. Early in September they took a train from Wisconsin to Kansas and spent three days investigating the prospects of farming on the plains. According to Northern newspapers, with their reports of fortunes to be made in cotton planting, the chances were considerably better in the late Confederacy. "Go west, young man," had been Horace Greeley's advice to the ambitious before the war. Now, the Morgans were beginning to think, the slogan ought to be changed to "Go south, young man!"

Acting on this revised principle were prospectors on almost every Mississippi steamboat heading downriver, and large numbers of them, like the Morgans, disembarked at Vicksburg. Hotels were full by the time Albert and Charles landed there, and they had to find accommodations in a private home. Land agents offered plantations of all sizes for sale or rent and were only too glad to show them to newcomers. For most of a month the Morgans looked at the places still available without finding anything that exactly suited them. Then, from another guest at the house where they were staying, they heard of a fine plantation near Yazoo City, about a hundred miles above Vicksburg. Charles made an inspection trip, arranged tentatively for a lease, returned to inform Albert, and immediately went north for supplies, equipment, and additional funds.

The next evening Albert took a steamer up the lazy Yazoo to see the land for himself and to confirm the deal. Arriving at Yazoo City the next morning, a glorious November day, he promptly registered at a hotel. But when he called on the owner of the property, Mrs. J. J. B. White, she and her husband, with true Southern hospitality, insisted that he stay with them.

That Sunday he climbed the high bluff on the east and got a view of the town, hemmed in between the bluff and the river. Two and a half miles to the north, on the other side of the river, he could glimpse through the woods the nearest edge of the plantation. It was called Tokeba—from "took a bar," the local people thought, since this had once been bear-hunting country (a spurious bit of etymology, but at least it suggests the pronunciation). As he looked around from the height, Albert had no thought of politics, local or national. He did not dream that someday he would be, if not monarch of all he surveyed, at least sheriff and Republican boss of Yazoo County.

Early the following day Albert and his host, Colonel White, a Confederate veteran, set out to explore Tokeba, Albert on a mouse-colored mule, the colonel on a little, old gray horse. On the way the colonel had much to say about the undependability of the "nigra," a word he pronounced with a snap that connoted a sense of mastery. He did not mention the fact that, by order of the local head of the Freedmen's Bureau, he was under bond to keep the peace after having threatened, on the street in front of his house, to kill a crippled black veteran of the Union army.[17]

Ferrying across the river at the upper end of the plantation, the two men inspected the gin-house and the quarters, consisting of cabins for 125 or more hands. Next they proceeded to the mansion, which stood amid chinaberry and magnolia trees on a low knoll, where they had good views of the curving river to the north, east, and south. Nearby was the colonel's study, a one-room building that would serve as an office. From here the men rode over the fields to a cypress swamp, which marked the plantation's southern boundary.

After having examined the property, Albert eagerly put his name to the contract that Charles had already signed. It appeared to be a real bargain. Here were 900 acres of open, arable land, and since the Morgans were agreeing to a three-year lease, the Whites were lowering the rental from $10 to $7 an acre, one-half of the annual total to be paid each year in advance. And the Whites were throwing in the stand of cypress, with permission to cut and use or sell the timber as the Morgans saw fit.

While awaiting Charles's return Albert took up residence at Tokeba and began to recruit a labor force. Standing on the street corners in town were knots of freedmen looking for work, but Albert soon found that the most promising among them had families remaining on their former master's plantation. To obtain the best workers, he had to provide accommodations also for their dependents. Many of the blacks, half expecting a division of the land at Christmas or New Year's, hesitated to hire out to anybody. Nevertheless, Albert soon succeeded in employing the hundred-odd hands he needed. For the first time he felt unfriendliness on the part of native planters, who resented his taking their labor away from them. Even the politeness of Colonel and Mrs. White was wearing thin.

Charles returned from the North with encouraging news. He had made two vital arrangements: one with a Wisconsin lumberman to bring down a sawmill and a crew of skilled workers, and the other with an Illinois capitalist to help finance both the planting and the sawmilling venture. By the spring of 1866 Tokeba was alive with sounds of productive activity. The singing of the plow people, men and women, could be heard from the mansion and the office, and the whine of the whirling saws could be heard as far away as Yazoo City. Much of the cypress lumber the Morgans sold locally and on credit.

They were too busy to pay much attention to what was going on in the wider world. According to Northern newspapers, conditions for Northerners were growing much worse in Mississippi than in Alabama. "Northern men are being driven out." Those who stayed on would suffer, in Mississippi as elsewhere, from the drop in the price of cotton. Before the summer's end the Morgans realized that they would have a very poor crop, partly because of their late start. Soon they were running short of cash.

Albert decided to ride into town and try to collect on overdue bills for lumber. Not yet fully recovered from a spell of malarial chills and fever, he could barely mount and sit his horse. In Yazoo City he called on one of the debtors, an ex-Confederate captain and the proprietor of a drug store. The captain said he would be able to pay up in a week or so, and the two parted pleasantly enough.

As Albert left the store and walked down the street, using his folded umbrella as a cane, he heard someone following him and turned around to see it was the captain. Red-faced, the big man addressed him (as Morgan recalled): "What in the hell do you mean, you Yankee son of a bitch? By God, sir, I'll have you bear in mind that I pay my debts. I'm a gentleman, by God, sir, and if you don't know it, I'll teach you how to conduct yourself toward one, damn you!" So saying, the captain knocked Albert down with a blow to the ear, jumped on him, and beat him about the head and face while other gentlemen gathered in a ring to watch and to cheer the captain on: "Kill the damn Yankee! Kill him, damn him!" [18]

Signs of desolation and ruin—deserted buildings, grass-grown streets, weed-filled gardens—were still to be seen in Charleston when General Robert Kingston Scott arrived there in January 1866. The city had been gradually recovering as men from the North repaired and occupied shell-damaged or burnt-out stores and brought in stocks of merchandise for sale. Charlestonians often resented the influx of Yankees and "Yankee notions" ("notions" in the sense of both ideas and goods). But the newcomers, many of them, viewed

Charleston as needing reformation even more than the rest of the South, since this had been the very hotbed of secession.[19]

The last time Scott was here, nearly two years earlier, he had come as a prisoner of war. Now, as the army officer in charge of the South Carolina Freedmen's Bureau, he could wield a certain degree of military authority over the city and the state. And less than two years later General Scott was to be Governor Scott, the state's first Republican chief executive.

At thirty-nine he was a fine figure of a man, six-feet-two (rather tall for that time), straight as an arrow, the kind who stood out in a crowd. He had the rugged features of his Scottish ancestors: a broad forehead beneath his abundant brown hair, a beetle brow overhanging his blue eyes, and sharp lines around his mouth and sculptured chin. Though commanding, his presence was by no means intimidating, for his expression and manner were frank and friendly. His splendid physique helped him to keep secret the fact that he was on the way to becoming an opium addict.

His drug problem had begun soon after his capture, outside of Atlanta. In a boxcar taking him and other prisoners to Macon, Georgia, he was sitting in the doorway with his feet dangling when the guard sitting beside him dozed off. Quickly Scott threw himself off the moving train. He landed on his back and bumped down a steep embankment. The injury to his spine was excruciating, yet he managed to subsist for several days and to make his way up the Ocmulgee River a considerable distance toward the Union lines, only to be recaptured and sent to Charleston. Released in a prisoner exchange after a few months there, he rejoined his regiment in time to take part in the march from Atlanta to the sea. His army doctors, like other physicians of the period, considered opium (in its diluted, liquid form of laudanum or in its concentrated, powdered form of morphine) as the most indispensable of remedies. The doctors prescribed it for his recurring pain.

In character and accomplishment Scott struck his acquaintances as a typically American self-made man, one who, relying on his native abilities, had taken advantage of the frontier's possibilities and had grown with the growing country. His career bore out this impression. He was born in the Allegheny Valley above Pittsburgh, Pennsylvania, the son of a War of 1812 veteran who had moved there from a farm near Harrisburg, and the grandson of a Revolutionary War veteran who had moved from a farm near Philadelphia. At sixteen he set out on his own for the Old Northwest, stopping in Columbus, Ohio, to attend Central College and then Sterling Medical College. At twenty-four, after practicing medicine for a few years in Ohio, he crossed the Great Plains and the Rocky Mountains to look for gold and to resume his practice in California. He found his fortune not on the Pacific Coast, which he left after a year, but back in Ohio, in Henry County, in the northwestern part of the state. Here he prospered as a physician and surgeon after his patients chanced to survive a cholera epidemic. He prospered even more when he invested his fees in real estate and in general merchandising. By the outbreak of the Civil War, though not yet thirty-five, he was already a highly successful doctor, land dealer, and merchant.

Now he became a highly successful soldier as well, rising from major in 1861 to brigadier-general and (brevet) major-general in 1865. Not one to shun the thick of battle, he had his horse shot under him at Shiloh. He won the respect of his subordinate officers, who presented him an engraved gold watch after the fighting was over. He felt only contempt for officers whose main concern seemed to be rank and pay, and early in the war he had considered resigning in protest against a superior he accused of such a concern. "I did not come into the service for the money I will receive," he declared, "as I can make more at home." Nor did he remain in the service to make money, and when he returned to the South in January 1866, he was following military orders and not pursuing some new economic opportunity.[20]

As assistant commissioner of the Freedmen's Bureau for South Carolina, Scott faced urgent and complex responsibilities, some of which are suggested by the Bureau's full name: Bureau of Freedmen, Refugees, and Abandoned Lands. Just before the close of the war Congress had set up this agency as a branch of the army to provide relief, employment, resettlement, education, and protection for blacks making the transition from slavery to freedom. Despite the best efforts of the head commissioner, General Oliver Otis Howard, the Bureau remained inadequately funded and staffed, and in the spring of 1866 it would have expired entirely if Congress had not repassed over President Johnson's veto the bill to enlarge its powers and prolong its life.

Scott inherited the assignment of adjusting the conflicting land claims of former masters and former slaves. On the Sea Islands—the low, flat country separated from the mainland only by narrow lagoons—the last of the masters had fled at the coming of Union troops in the spring of 1862, and the slaves then divided the plantations into farms under the supervision of the occupation authorities. In January 1865, General Sherman in his Special Field Order No. 15 set aside the entire coastal area below Charleston for the exclusive settlement of black refugees, including the thousands who had flocked to his army. Later in 1865, by pardoning the previous owners of the land, President Johnson enabled them to seek recovery of it, and he further assisted them through his directives to the Freedmen's Bureau. The assistant commissioner for South Carolina at that time, General Rufus Saxton, resisted the dispossession of the blacks, believing it violated the government's promises to them. Commissioner Howard had to remove Saxton, and he replaced him with Scott.[21]

When Scott took over the Charleston office, he found everything in confusion and no records to help him straighten matters out, since Saxton had taken the records with him. Nevertheless, Scott proceeded with what he readily recognized as a "delicate and arduous" task—that of determining the validity of property claims along the coast. He was beset by both blacks and whites. Some of the blacks held unassailable titles, having purchased at Treasury agents' tax sales. Others possessed only assurances and hopes. Scott had to explain, as patiently and carefully as he could, that Sherman's order had not converted the whole area into a "permanent inheritance" for blacks. A claimant under the order must have a certificate entitling him to a specified plot, which he must have cultivated and must be living on. After Scott and his agents had examined the claims, he reported that, of the approximately 40,000 blacks (men, women, and children) on the disputed lands, only 1,565 held valid titles. Whites who lost out accused him of favoritism to blacks.

Certainly Scott was more considerate of the freedmen than were some of the regular army officers, with whom he soon came into jurisdictional conflict. According to law, the Bureau had supervision over labor contracts as well as land disputes, but on the Sea Islands the commander of the Charleston army post interfered in both matters. The commander, (brevet) Brigadier-General James C. Beecher, was a brother of Harriet Beecher Stowe, the author of *Uncle Tom's Cabin*. General Beecher ordered all freedmen residing on a plantation to agree to work for the planter or leave the plantation in ten days. "In executing this order," Scott learned, "he exhibited more zeal than judgment or humanity; he sent small detachments of troops to different plantations with instructions to offer to the people the alternative of accepting such contracts as he himself should dictate, or such of those offered by the planters as he should approve, or of leaving the premises." And that was not the worst of it. "The officers of these detachments, in many instances, took from the freedmen their certificates [of land ownership], declared them worthless, and destroyed them in their presence." Scott protested to Beecher's superior, but Beecher and his officers continued to defy the Bureau on the Sea Islands.

In the state as a whole, Scott was more successful in supervising contracts, and by the summer of 1866 the Bureau agents under his direction had arranged 8,000 agreements involving 130,000 laborers. He warned planters that the Bureau would seize their land if they violated the agreements by firing workers without cause. He warned workers that the Bureau would eject them from the land if they failed to live up to the terms. Early in the season the reports he received from around the state encouraged him to believe that the system was operating well and that the cotton crop would be large and profitable. But before long the reports indicated that many planters, in their concentration on the money crop, were neglecting foodstuffs. In some areas famine threatened.

From the time he took charge of the Bureau, Scott had given much of his attention to providing relief for the destitute, white as well as black. Planters, he discovered, were turning away the aged and infirm among their former slaves, leaving them to shift for themselves and, if no help came, to starve along the roadsides. The Bureau set up camps and hospitals to care for these "wretched victims of slavery." Its agents also issued food and clothing to the desperately needy. "On issuing days," Scott observed, "might be seen the white lady of respectability, standing side by side with the African, both waiting their turn to receive their weekly supply of rations."[22]

As food became scarce, Scott thought the Bureau should enlarge its charity. The "appalling fact" was that many planters, for want of provisions, would have to abandon their plantations and turn away even the able-bodied blacks to starve. Scott proposed to feed all the hungry, including those who were strong enough to work. But he again ran into military opposition when he talked to General Daniel E. Sickles—who had shot and killed his wife's paramour in 1859, had lost a leg at Gettysburg, and was now in command of the military district that included South Carolina. Sickles said that to give rations to the able-bodied would only "encourage idleness," and he cited as his authority the governor of the state, James L. Orr. Scott asked Commissioner Howard whether he might not disregard the opinions of Orr and Sickles. "I am perhaps better qualified to judge of the necessity than either of them," he explained. "I have . . . in some instances given a small amount of provisions to persons other than those who are unble to work."

In handling disputes between landowners and laborers, Scott realized that there was something to be said for the former as well as the latter, and he tried to be fair to both. Disagreements often arose when the planter tried to collect, in cotton, what he claimed his workers owed him for supplies he had advanced. Scott advised one black: "Some of the people will try to evade the payment of fair and just accounts against them for provisions furnished while cultivating their crops. All such claims the people must be made to understand cannot be evaded. They should secure the creditor against loss; but he cannot take their cotton and fix the price. The people should . . . have the advantage of the highest price in the market." Scott found he had to intervene also to keep blacks from cheating one another, as in the case of the "colored man from New Jersey" who "made quite a fortune out of the people by buying their cotton at one quarter of its value." There were some "bad men" on each side. "I have been compelled at all times," Scott informed Howard, "to keep a check on the extravagant demands of both the white and black men."

But Scott could feel no sympathy with the whites in the race conflict that seemed to be intensifying. In Charleston, soon after his arrival, white policemen and black soldiers engaged in a bloody affray, a mob gathered in support of the police, and an infantry regiment had to fire on the mob to rescue the troops. From the upcountry came frequent reports of outrages upon both blacks and Unionist whites. Gangs of mounted outlaws, calling themselves Regulators, rode about terrorizing these people, whipping them, shooting them, tying them up by the thumbs. The state government had little power and still less inclination to put down the disturbances. The federal authorities could not do much, since they would need cavalry to catch the harrying horsemen but had only infantry in South Carolina.

After seven months in the state, Scott unburdened himself in a letter to an old physician friend in Henry County, Ohio. "You have doubtless heard a great deal of the Reconstructed South, of their acceptance of the results of the war, of their great claims . . . [to be] the only true friends the Negro had, etc., etc. Well, Doctor, this may all be true, but if a man in Henry County had the list of Negroes murdered in a single county in this most loyal and Christian state, he would think it a strange way of demonstrating his kindly feelings toward them." The (white) Southerners contended that they must care for the "darkies" because the darkies were like children. "As a general thing, however, those killed are the smart Negroes, who have the *insolence* to assert their *rights.*" Most Southerners were "barbarians"; some were decent enough at heart but lacked the moral courage to speak out against the atrocities. "I sometimes feel perfectly disgusted at the whole Southern people." The outlook for race relations in South Carolina was ominous. "The Negro predominates in this state about three to two whites and while he holds the balance of power numerically he will refuse to submit to the demands of his former master. And on the other hand this generation of white men will not overcome the education of two centuries, and therefore I regard a compromise as almost hopeless. Hence the two races can only live together by the presence of a sufficient military force to protect both."

White Southerners generally denounced the army and the Freedmen's Bureau as meddlers in local affairs and demanded that they both be withdrawn. But Scott found that, in private conversation, some of the leading whites admitted they considered the troops necessary for their own protection. Prominent whites publicly as well as privately endorsed his administration of the Bureau, and certainly he was efficient, conscientious, and just. Even the Democratic *Charleston Daily News* conceded "the integrity of purpose and the propriety of deportment of General Scott."[23]

CHAPTER 3

We Poor Southern Devils (1865-1867)

North Carolina must be the place. The state's provisional governor had responded most encouragingly. In his letter, dated at Raleigh, June 16, 1865, and written in his own hand, he said the price of farms was extremely low in North Carolina. "Capital would find ready and very advantageous investments in sections of this state where the productivity of the soil is very great." Skilled labor was in demand. "There is nothing in the feeling of the loyal people of this state which would make it unpleasant for northern labor to come into our midst." Those words of the governor's would be especially reassuring to an innocent reader who failed to notice exactly what the governor was saying—namely, that hospitality could be expected from the *loyal people* of the state but not from the population as a whole. Similarly reassuring was the invitation in the postscript: "Should any of the young gentlemen or yourself come to North Carolina I would be most happy to welcome you to our state, and to show you the fraternal feeling which the loyal people of the state entertain for their northern brothers." [1]

Albion W. Tourgee (he pronounced the name Toor-ZHAY) ran his one good eye over the letter again and again. He discussed it with his wife, Emma, who also read and reread it. Now twenty-seven, Tourgee was yet to find the way to a satisfactory career, though he had tried the legal, journalistic, and teaching professions. Certainly he did not wish to remain the principal of an academy for the rest of his life. Though he liked the outdoors he could not undertake anything requiring heavy labor, for he had a bad back, a painful reminder of the first battle of Bull Run. Once quite athletic, he now could neither remain standing nor sit still for very long at a time. His back seemed particularly troublesome during the long winter months here in Erie, Pennsylvania, when the chill damp wind swept in from Lake Erie. The doctors thought he would do better in a milder and sunnier climate. Taking everything into account, he had decided to form an association of young men, acquire land somewhere in the South, and cooperate in farm management and possibly in other enterprises. Hence his letter of inquiry to the North Carolina governor, whose response more than met all expectations.

Tourgee's life had prepared him somewhat better intellectually than physically for success. He was born on a farm in the northeastern corner of Ohio (not far from Erie, Pennsylvania), the descendant of Huguenot refugees from France, successive generations of whom had migrated from Rhode Island to the Massachusetts Berkshires, then to New York's Hudson Valley, and finally to Ohio's Western Reserve. One of the earliest—and saddest—things he could remember was his mother's dying on a bleak and wintry day when he was not yet five. At twelve, unable to get along with his stepmother, he went to Lee, Massachusetts, to live with his mother's relatives and to attend school. At fourteen he lost the sight of his right eye when he watched too close as a playmate exploded a percussion cap. Later he returned to Ohio to study at Kingsville Academy, near his father's farm. At the academy he fell in love with a fellow student, a neighboring farmer's daughter, the bright and blooming Emma Kilbourne. He was growing into a slender, dark-haired, strong-featured, and (despite his blind eye) quite handsome young man. Emma fully reciprocated his affection. The two kept up a warm correspondence after he left for the University of Rochester. There he stood out as a scholar, one more interested in literature than in politics.

At the war's outbreak Tourgee along with some of his fellow students promptly enlisted in a New York regiment. He was in time to take part, to his lasting sorrow, in the very first big battle. As the Army of the Potomac fled from Bull Run in a rout, the wheel of a speeding gun carriage struck him in the back. After a three-day coma he came to in a Washington hospital, to find himself paralyzed from the waist down. It was almost a year before he could walk without crutches. While recovering, he received his B.A. from Rochester (getting academic credit for his military service), studied law in Ashtabula, Ohio, and made recruiting speeches in the vicinity. Then, returning to the war as lieutenant of an Ohio company, he got a piece of shrapnel in his hip at Perryville and, after being captured at Murfreesboro, spent four months in Confederate prisons. As soon as he was released he met and married Emma in Columbus, Ohio. In a few weeks he was again in the army. He fought at Chickamauga, but at Chattanooga he reinjured his back in a fall. His disability kept him from promotion, and he protested by resigning from the army at the end of 1863.

The next spring, after admission to the Ohio bar, he joined a Painesville law firm. Soon he quit to take a job with an Erie newspaper, then left that to become a teacher in and the principal of Erie Academy. Quickly dissatisfied also with this, he was ready to try something new, something far away, when that fateful letter arrived from North Carolina.[2]

A month later he was in New York City, ready to board a southbound coastal steamer, *El Cid*. His mood kept fluctuating. After taking the train from Erie, he had struggled against a rising fear that, as he confided in a note to Emma, he would "find some insuperable obstacle in the way" of his "southern scheme." If only she could be here in the city with him! Sometime, perhaps, they could spend a few days here for the honeymoon they had never had a chance to take. Meanwhile he was further discouraged and depressed by what he heard from some "heavy capitalists," who did not think much of the enterprise he had in mind. Then, just before the ship sailed, his spirits rallied. "I have faith that God will open a way," he insisted to Emma. The prospects for his "highest success" were brighter than ever. "It will come, Darling, in some form or another."[3]

During three days and nights of a rough voyage he was miserably seasick, and after going ashore at New Bern, North Carolina, he got nauseous again as the earth seemed to rock and sway like the ship. New Bern, an old town of handsome residences, unscarred by the war, had been under Union military control since the spring of 1862. Northerners now dominated the place. Army officers or federal officials occupied many of the houses, and other Yankees, some of them former sutlers, ran the hotel and most of the stores. A couple of newcomers were digging up and making a profit out of rosin that local turpentine distillers had long since discarded as a worthless by-product. On the outskirts of town was a brand-new city of log cabins, which sheltered several thousand refugees from slavery.

The day after landing at New Bern, still rather queasy, Tourgee hurried on the hundred-odd miles to Raleigh, riding in reasonable comfort on the North Carolina Railroad, which Union army engineers had restored to fairly good shape. Raleigh had been the terminus of Sherman's march through Georgia and the Carolinas, and just three months before Tourgee's arrival Sherman had gone out from here to accept the surrender of the last important Confederate army still in the field, the army of Joseph E. Johnston. Now this city of about 8,000, half white, half black, was peaceful enough, with no visible sign of war damage. It remained a pleasant place to live, at least for most of its white inhabitants, with its big old trees, elegant houses, spacious yards, and broad, well-shaded streets.

From the railroad station Tourgee made his way to the center of town, where on a ten-acre lot the state capitol stood among wide-branching oaks. The capitol was quite impressive from the outside—a well-proportioned, copper-domed, classical-style building of light-gray native stone. On the inside the peeling paint, tarnished gilding, and general disrepair betrayed a lack of upkeep, as did the condition of most public structures in the South. Access to the provisional governor's office was easy. Here, greeting Tourgee like a father and a friend, stood a slight and rather frail-looking but nervously energetic man of forty-seven, with a neatly trimmed beard and a clean-shaven upper lip. His voice was soft and his dark blue eyes were kindly. This was Governor Holden, on whom the state's future as well as Tourgee's seemed for the moment to depend.

William W. Holden had what many North Carolinians considered a checkered past. Born one county away from Raleigh—in what some called bastardy and others politely referred to as obscurity—Holden had made his own way in the narrow world he knew. He worked as a printer in the capital, then edited the *Raleigh Star,* a Whig paper, and at twenty-five became editor of the *North Carolina Standard,* the foremost Democratic journal in the state. In editorial after editorial he demanded justice for the poor white. Remove all property requirements (but not the racial restriction) from the right to vote! Make the large planter pay his fair share of the cost of government by increasing the tax on slaves! When the sectional crisis of 1860-61 came, Holden (like most of his fellow North Carolinians) was at first a Unionist and then, after the firing on Fort Sumter and President Lincoln's call for troops, a secessionist. In the midst of the war he ran for governor, and lost, on a platform calling for peace.

A Whig, a Democrat, a Unionist, a secessionist, a war advocate, a pacifist—Holden appeared to be a politician of frequent twists and turns. Yet, in fact, a certain consistency underlay his career. He was always against the aristocrats, always on what he believed to be the common people's side. Toward the planter class he remained resentful, bitter, a bit pugnacious. In background and attitude he was much like Andrew Johnson, a Raleigh native, also born in poverty. No wonder President Johnson chose him to serve as provisional governor of the state.[4]

"Gov Holden is progressing with the great work before him," the Kentucky journalist Henry M. Watterson assured Johnson after a Raleigh visit at the end of June 1865. "He is a calm, clear, systematic, laborious gentleman." The governor was busy appointing temporary local officials: mayors, constables, county commissioners, justices of the peace. Hundreds of his appointees were former jobholders under the Confederacy, for whom he had to get pardons from the President before the men could take office again. This did not delay the work of reorganization so much as did the inadequacy of the mail service, which the Post Office Department was yet to restore throughout the western reaches of the state. In the circumstances Holden thought it best to put off for a while the calling of a constitutional convention. "He hopes, however," Watterson reported, "that by the beginning of next year he will have all the machinery of State government in complete operation."

Late in July, when Tourgee appeared in Raleigh, Holden was still desperately busy, but he readily found time for his visitor from the North. Indeed, his personal welcome was fully as cordial as his letter of invitation had been. In consequence of the "late disastrous rebellion," the people of North Carolina now suffered from terrible impoverishment, the governor was frank to say. That was why they were willing to rent or sell their land at such a bargain. That was why they were glad to see Northern capital and skill come in. "Nearly all the mechanical labor of this country has been swept away by the Conscript Acts," Holden explained, "and those [Northern workers] of a high order would only have to compete with the uncertain and unskilful negro—and would soon drive him to such other work as is more suited to his ability and knowledge." Tourgee was thoroughly satisfied with the interview as he left the statehouse.

After two days in Raleigh, a second conference with the governor, and conversations with land dealers, Tourgee possessed all the information he needed. Surely he would have no difficulty in obtaining suitable land. A single Raleigh real estate firm was advertising sixty-three separate tracts, all available on easy terms. It would not be necessary to go on to other Southern states, as Tourgee earlier had thought he might do. It would not even be necessary to travel further in North Carolina, since "all the state" with anything to sell appeared to be in Raleigh or to have an agent here.

So far, Tourgee had succeeded in his mission. He was feeling better in the stomach, thought himself well enough for the trip home, and was eager to get back to Erie and to Emma. Anyhow, he dared not stay much longer where he was, for these July days and nights were hot even for Raleigh, and he was "as near oil as a melted man could be and retain his identity as one of the genus." Yet he decided to remain a little longer when an Ohio lieutenant, facing a court-martial, asked him to serve as his attorney.

While waiting, Tourgee received a letter from Emma, who indicated that her own and their friends' enthusiasm continued high. One young couple, Seneca and Hattie Kuhn, were already members of the "association," and Seneca was now suggesting that another young couple, the Pettengills, be allowed to join. Hattie Kuhn expressed the anticipatory thrill of the whole group. "She hopes to hear from you soon that you are ready to transplant them to a grand cabin in North Carolina."[5]

Eighty-five miles west of Raleigh on the North Carolina Railroad lay the town of Greensboro. Fifty miles south of Danville, Virginia, the town was also accessible by the Piedmont Railroad, now that the tracks had been rebuilt where Stoneman's Union cavalry had destroyed them on the day of Lee's surrender. Except for Stoneman's raid and Johnston's demobilization, which took place in Greensboro, the war had not directly touched this part of the state. Physically, Greensboro remained much the same as it had been for years. Within its one woodsy square mile dwelt not quite 2,000 people, who found a livelihood here because this was a rail junction, a market town, and a county seat.

Guilford County, centering on Greensboro, could boast no great cotton plantations but had quite a few lesser plantations or farms growing a good deal of corn and smaller amounts of tobacco, sorghum, and fruit. Except for a clearing here and there, with a cultivated field or an abandoned and sedge-filled patch, the rolling hills of red clay were covered with a thick forest of oak, hickory, beech, and pine. The larger Guilford landowners generally had depended on the labor of slaves and, for months after Lee's and Johnston's surrenders, could hardly believe that slavery had been or ever would be abolished. In September 1865 the Freedmen's Bureau agent in Greensboro was receiving several appeals a day from blacks who came in from the countryside and complained of having been shot, beaten, or abused in other ways.

During the postwar months very few Northerners settled in this area. Most of those going to North Carolina were to be found in the coastal region, where they looked for opportunities in rice or cotton planting, lumbering, tar and turpentine production, general merchandising, and other enterprises. Still, if lacking in new arrivals from the North, Greensboro and Guilford County contained a large minority of old residents who, throughout the war, had remained inwardly loyal to the Union or, at any rate, had felt very little attachment to the Confederacy. Most numerous among these loyalists or Unionists were the Quakers, whose ancestors were some of the earliest settlers here, and whose religion inclined them to oppose both slavery and war. Prominent among the local Quakers was the Mendenhall family.[6]

Cyrus P. Mendenhall owned, among other real estate, a 750-acre tract lying four miles west of Greensboro on the Salem road. Besides dwellings, greenhouses, and other buildings, this property consisted of standing timber, farming land, and the West Green Nursery, with a stock of various shrubs and apple, peach, pear, apricot, nectarine, plum, cherry, and ornamental trees. Mendenhall, hoping to rent out the property, found an eager tenant when he met that young man from the North, Albion W. Tourgee.

After returning to Pennsylvania from his summer visit in North Carolina, Tourgee traveled to Greensboro with Emma in the fall. His business associates Seneca Kuhn and R. T. Pettengill and their wives soon joined the Tourgees. Emma's parents and a few other friends and relatives were to follow. Tourgee and his partners agreed to lease the Mendenhall property for fifteen years, beginning October 15, 1865, at $1,000 a year. The partners established the firm of A. W. Tourgee & Co. to operate the nursery and the farm, to practice law, and to engage in other, unspecified occupations. Money to finance the ventures came from the savings of Tourgee and his associates and from the contributions of his father-in-law.

At first Tourgee preoccupied himself with his promising new business, but before long he began to turn his attention more and more to politics. Events in North Carolina demanded that he do so. He had arrived in time to observe, though not to vote in, the state's first postwar general election. In it the old Confederates decisively triumphed over the old Unionists. Provisional Governor Holden, running for regular governor of the state as reorganized under the Johnson plan, went down in defeat.

Holden's victorious opponent, Jonathan Worth, was bitterly anti-Northern in a way that Holden had never been or had long since ceased to be. After taking the governor's office, Worth related to a newspaper reporter from the North that, during the Union occupation of Raleigh, Sherman's "bummers" had invaded Worth's nearby plantation, driven off his sheep and cows, and stolen his bacon after forcing his slaves to tell where it was hidden. "Of all the malignant wretches that ever cursed the earth, the hangers-on of Sherman's army were the worst," said Governor Worth. "It can't be expected that the people should love a government that has subjugated them in this way."

During that winter the state government did nothing to improve the condition, or even to assure the safety, of the blacks whom the North Carolina constitution as well as the United States Constitution now declared free. According to the assistant commissioner of the Freedmen's Bureau, in January 1866, there were so many cases of "robberies, frauds, assaults, and even murders, in which white persons were the agents and freed people the sufferers," that "no records of them could be kept, one officer reporting that he had heard and disposed of as many as a hundred and eighty complaints in one day."

Reports and rumors of the mistreatment of blacks distressed Tourgee. Before the war he had been no abolitionist, but, advancing into the South with the Union army, he was struck by the warm welcome he and his comrades received from the slaves. In 1862 he expressed his own emotion (though not necessarily his comrades') in the following verse:

> Then there came the kindly feeling,
> Swelling every patriot breast,
> That to lift these trodden children
> From the dust, was God's behest.

Now, at the West Green Nursery, Tourgee was doing what he could to lift the blacks by giving employment at good wages to as many as he could afford to hire.[7]

Tourgee was also concerned about the treatment of loyal whites. In the war days thousands of white North Carolinians, as civilians and as soldiers, had risked life and liberty to further the Union cause. From the strongly Unionist mountain counties enough men volunteered to fill more than four Federal regiments. From the coastal counties, after the Union occupation of them, two additional Federal regiments were raised. "But their present lot is one of local dishonor & infamy," the former lieutenant-colonel of the 2d North Carolina Union Volunteers lamented in February 1866. "The rebellion which they fought to overcome has succumbed, and the Union which they fought to maintain has reasserted its imperial authority. But what recognition or reward have they?" None at all. They were left out when the legislature provided artificial limbs for the state's maimed veterans of the Confederate army.

Most of the Union veterans were isolated, uninformed, illiterate, or for other reasons incapable of applying for disability pensions from the federal government. Even the able-bodied were at a terrible disadvantage. "Now these Unionists are being persecuted while former rebels hold all the government jobs in the state," the onetime surgeon of the 3d North Carolina Mounted Infantry (Federal) protested in May 1866. Tourgee, as a lawyer in the federal district court, was unsuccessfully pressing the claims of Unionists who had suffered losses at the hands of Sherman's foragers.

For redress of their many grievances the loyal people of North Carolina, black and white, could look only to Congress. The Reverend George William Welker, pastor of Greensboro's German Reformed church, stressed this point in a letter to Thaddeus Stevens. As a Pennsylvanian by birth, though a North Carolinian for nearly a quarter-century, Welker thought he could quite properly appeal to the Pennsylvania congressman. "There are enough loyal men in this state to fill all federal offices," he told Stevens, "but not enough loyal men to elect them." He begged him not to let the leaders of the rebellion back into Congress.

Though Stevens himself wanted to keep the rebels out indefinitely, he could not impose his will on the Joint Committee on Reconstruction, which finally presented its first Reconstruction plan in June 1866. This took the form of a proposed constitutional amendment, the fourteenth. If adopted, the Fourteenth Amendment would not give Negroes the vote, but it would pressure the Southern states to do so by threatening to reduce their congressional representation if they did not. It would also guarantee blacks their civil rights—or at least would forbid the states to deny or infringe those rights. And it would prohibit ex-Confederate leaders from holding any office, federal or state, until Congress should lift the ban. Once a Southern state had ratified the amendment, that state's senators and representatives presumably could take their seats in Congress. The Tennessee legislature promptly ratified, and Tennessee was immediately readmitted to its place in the union. But the rest of the states delayed.

As the congressional elections of 1866 approached, the proposed Fourteenth Amendment loomed as the big issue between the Radical Republicans and the President. The Radicals made it their platform as they campaigned on behalf of themselves and other Radical candidates. Johnson's adherents stood by his Reconstruction plan and insisted on the prompt readmittance, without further conditions, of all the former Confederate states. In mid-August the Johnsonites, among them prominent ex-Confederates, staged a "National Union" convention in Philadelphia to rally their forces and launch their campaign. To offset the

Johnsonites' show, the Radicals scheduled a convention of "Southern Loyalists" to meet in Philadelphia in September.

In response to the call for loyal delegates from the South, the Unionists of Guilford County gathered late in August in the Quakers' Deep River Meeting House, outside of Greensboro. Among those present were such notable members of the Society of Friends as Nereus Mendenhall, brother of Cyrus Mendenhall, from whom Tourgee and his associates were renting the West Green Nursery. Dominating the Deep River meeting were the youthful Tourgee and the older Welker, the Pennsylvania-born preacher. Under the lead of these two the Guilford Unionists not only endorsed the proposed Fourteenth Amendment but went considerably beyond the Radical platform. They adopted Tourgee's resolution for "impartial suffrage" regardless of race, that is, for allowing any man to vote "who knew the worth of a ballot and was loyal." Then they chose Tourgee as their delegate to the September convention in Philadelphia.[8]

The convention itself was not to start until Monday, September 3, but there were to be preliminary activities, and Tourgee got to Philadelphia good and early, on Friday, August 31, to find excellent accommodations where he had reserved them at the Union League headquarters and hotel. The Union League, with chapters in cities throughout the North, had originated during the war as a propaganda arm of the Republican party and was turning into a social as well as a political club. "Oh, it warms one's soul to be among loyal warm hearted Union men again," Tourgee promptly wrote to Emma. "You would never have dreamed that such enthusiasm could grow up over anything less holy than religion itself." He was sorry he had left Emma behind, suffering as she was from some mysterious and painful affliction of the foot. He hoped she would join him later, while he was still in the North.

On Saturday two more men from North Carolina arrived, and they elected Tourgee chairman of the state's delegation, which with additional arrivals was eventually to reach a total of nine, four of them Northern-born. On this day and the next, representatives from the various Southern states kept coming in, and Tourgee made the acquaintance of a number of them. One of the most conspicuous was the head of the Louisiana delegation, a man whose name everybody soon knew—Henry Clay Warmoth. This man was younger, taller, slimmer, and more handsome than Tourgee, but not a whit further advanced in Radicalism. On Sunday evening, before their final preparatory conference, the delegates bowed their heads in a prayer meeting. In their minds the cause they represented was, quite literally, no less holy than religion itself.

On Monday the proceedings were to start with a grand parade. In the morning the loyalists from the South gathered in Independence Square, where they joined a group of Republicans from the North who had come to welcome their brethren and thus to symbolize the reunification of the country under the party's auspices. One of the notable Northerners was Benjamin F. Butler, "Beast Butler" to Confederates, once the commander of occupied New Orleans, now a candidate for Congress from Massachusetts. Another was Frederick Douglass, once a slave in Maryland, then an abolitionist orator and the publisher of the *North Star* in Rochester, New York—and now the only black man among the Northern delegates in Philadelphia.

About eleven o'clock the Union League members, nearly a thousand of them, led off the procession. After them walked the Northern and Southern conventioneers, each wearing a ribbon with the name of his state on it. Then came a string of colorfully decorated carriages in which rode lame Union veterans in their blue uniforms. Behind them marched three or four hundred still vigorous comrades, also in blue. A long line of Republican citizens, dressed in their holiday best, followed on foot. Ably bringing up the rear were Philadelphia firemen with their gaudy trappings, brightly polished engines, and spirited brass bands. The midday sun was hot, much too hot for some of the marchers, but not hot enough to discourage spectators, who thronged the streets to applaud and wave flags. Warmoth, as he strode along, estimated that the crowd must total more than 100,000, perhaps as many as 300,000!

When the procession reached the Union League building, the delegates went inside for the ceremonies by which the Northerners were to welcome the Southerners. Frederick Douglass entered arm-in-arm with a young white friend, the Radical journalist Theodore Tilton. "This blending of colors is deemed inartistic as well as inexpedient at the present time," Tilton reported to the *New York Times*. "The country is not quite prepared to see the negro, no matter how talented, seated on terms of equality beside the white man in deliberative bodies. Singularly enough, Mr. Douglass is in better favor with the Southern delegates than with the Northern. These latter say that Douglass' being in this Convention will cost them 10,000 votes in the country." Certainly, among the Southern delegates, neither Warmoth nor Tourgee was in the least embarrassed by the presence of the great black orator.

After the ceremonies the Southern delegates, nearly three hundred of them, went off to National Hall to organize their convention, while their Northern hosts remained at the Union League rooms, waiting for an invitation to take part in the official proceedings—and waiting in vain. This was to be the loyalists' own show. The stage was well set for it. Behind the platform in the commodious hall could be seen a huge Lincoln portrait, draped in mourning, and above it a tremendous canvas scroll bearing the motto of the French Revolution: "Liberty, Equality, Fraternity." From the ceiling hung gigantic American flags. On the walls were more flags and also posters with quotations from both Lincoln and Johnson, including the latter's statement on taking over the presidency:

"Treason must be made odious, and traitors must be punished and impoverished." After the call to order, a fine brass band struck up, the delegates sang "The Star-Spangled Banner," a minister offered prayer, and the convention proceeded to elect a temporary chairman, appoint committees, and listen to speeches. At one point the audience chimed in with three cheers for the Union and freedom and three groans for the "dead dog in the White House."

In the evening some of the loyalists were to address the public from the balcony in front of the Union League house, though dark thunderclouds continued to threaten after a heavy shower at sundown. A crowd of several thousand had gathered in the square opposite the building, and one of the North Carolina delegates was speaking—saying the Unionists of the South were worse off under Andrew Johnson than under Jefferson Davis—when the Wide Awakes appeared and interrupted. These young men (members of a Republican youth organization that had campaigned for Lincoln throughout the North in 1860), each dressed in shining white and carrying a flaming torch, went through graceful maneuvers and saluted the Southern guests on the balcony while a band throbbed with patriotic sounds. Lightning flashed and rain poured down. The Wide Awakes, their torches sputtering out, ran for cover. So did the crowd.

On Tuesday morning Douglass argued eloquently for black suffrage in a speech at the Union League house. When, later, the Southern loyalists convened again in National Hall, the admitted delegates totaled more than four hundred. Of this number, only a little more than a third (144) came from the states yet to be readmitted to the Union. The great majority represented Tennessee, already readmitted, and the border states of Missouri, Kentucky, West Virginia, Maryland, and Delaware in addition to the District of Columbia. Tennessee alone had 81 delegates, and Maryland and the District together had 87, as compared with Louisiana's 18 and North Carolina's (at the moment) 7 delegates. Nevertheless, Louisiana's Warmoth and North Carolina's Tourgee were about to emerge as the two most influential men in the entire convention. The two were to exert their influence mainly through the committee to report on the condition of the "non-reconstructed" states, a committee of which Warmoth was chairman and Tourgee his most active colleague. Both men also served on the committee to prepare resolutions and an address to the nation.

On Wednesday, as committees and caucuses met, the convention divided along geographical lines. Though there were exceptions, the delegates from the border leaned less toward Radicalism than did those from the South, and those from the North were still less radical. The Northern and border-state men—excepting Douglass, among others—wanted the convention to endorse the proposed Fourteenth Amendment and nothing more. Warmoth, Tourgee, and most of the other loyalists from the South were determined to call, in addition, for the imposition of

Negro suffrage and the complete reorganization of the ex-Confederate states. These loyalists, while excluding the Northern representatives from the convention, could not avoid them in the lobbies of the convention hall, in the hotels, or on the streets. The more cautious and conservative men kept buttonholing the more radical ones and pleading with them to bear in mind the necessities of practical politics.[9]

That evening another mass meeting took place outside the Union League building. Watching from his room there, while writing to Emma again, Tourgee estimated that at least ten thousand people had gathered. "I never saw such a crowd before," he wrote. "Oh! This is a hearty city and you may be sure we poor Southern devils appreciate its hospitality and heartiness." After the day's activities, Warmoth noted: "Splendid lot of men from different Southern states." And surely one of the most splendid, from his point of view, was his enthusiastic fellow committeeman Tourgee.

On Thursday the two men struggled, along with other radicals, to win over to their own position the committee on resolutions. But border-state representatives dominated that committee, and when the chairman presented its report that evening, he made no mention of Negro suffrage or state reorganization, but merely endorsed the congressional plan—which would permit the present regimes to remain in power in the South if they would only ratify the Fourteenth Amendment. An angry debate ensued. Then the border-state men, having a large majority in the convention as well as on the committee, easily adopted their report. At once a Maryland delegate moved to adjourn *sine die,* and the motion carried. But the Southern loyalists still had business to attend to; they had yet to hear from Warmoth's committee on the "nonreconstructed" states. So the loyalists got together, resolved to let their border-state brethren go home, and prepared to meet again on the following day.

Since arriving in Philadelphia, Tourgee had not slept as much as four hours any night and had managed to keep going only on determination and nervous energy. His worst deprivation of sleep was about to occur. Shortly after midnight the cry of "Fire!" routed him and other guests out of their rooms at the Union League hotel. "It will be entirely destroyed," an overhasty reporter predicted in a dispatch to the *New York Times.* Actually the Philadelphia fire fighters, as impressive on duty as on parade, managed to confine the flames to the top floor, where the laundry and the servants' quarters were located.

On Friday morning the delegates remaining in Philadelphia assembled once more in National Hall. Only about half the previous day's number was present; most of the border-state men had left. From their point of view, what was now in session was a mere rump, but in the view of such men as Warmoth and Tourgee this was, at last, the true convention of Southern loyalists, and today was its climactic and decisive phase. Many excited delegates now wanted to be heard, and several got the floor, one after another, to introduce resolutions or make speeches. The only black among all the convention members, a Mr. Randolph from Louisiana, rose to thank the Union League for its hospitality and to intimate that last night's fire was the deed of an arsonist, who most likely had acted on Johnson's orders.

Finally Warmoth took the floor for the main business of the day, the presentation of the report on the "non-reconstructed" states, a report most of which he himself had written. As he read, he had to stop repeatedly for applause. Johnson, he said, was putting the rebels back into power instead of punishing them for their crimes. Warmoth proceeded to give a long account of the New Orleans massacre, so much of which he personally had witnessed. He went on:

> The state of affairs which led to the massacre is believed to be the legitimate result of the reconstruction policy of Andrew Johnson. There can be no safety for the country against the fell spirit of Slavery, now organized in the form of serfdom, unless the Government shall confer on every citizen in the States we represent the American birthright of impartial suffrage and equality before the law. It is a policy which will finally regenerate the South itself. It will be the crowning act of glory to our free Republic, and when done will be received, as was the act of Emancipation, with joy and praise throughout the world as the final realization of the promises of the American Declaration of Independence.

When Warmoth finished, the North Carolinian Daniel Goodloe rose to say that, while he himself favored Negro suffrage, he thought it ought to wait until white Southerners were ready for it and would adopt it of their own free will. Tourgee, his nerves on edge from sleeplessness and near-exhaustion, came to Warmoth's support with a speech he delivered partly from prepared notes and partly from the inspiration of the moment. He must insist on Negro suffrage, he said, for he had definite instructions from two thousand Unionists in his state to do so. He was here to claim justice, liberty, protection, and salvation for the loyal white men as well as the black men of the South.

> Rebels are confident, arrogant, and insulting. Union men are depressed and fearful. Without protection for the present and future, there is no hope but in exile. The depressing influence of these things upon the union men of the South is something sickening to contemplate. Bowed down and crushed by the foul weight of Rebellion for four years, they are still further humiliated by the stinging taunt—"See what your friends have done for you. They have given *us* all the power and left you more completely at our mercy than you were during the war."

While he was speaking, Tourgee too received applause from time to time, but nothing like the tumult of cheers and clapping that greeted Frederick Douglass when he entered the hall. After this interruption,

Goodloe broke in to ask whether blacks, once given the suffrage, would actually be allowed to go the polls and vote. Tourgee replied that they would. In his nervous exhilaration he also said other things he was not sure of, some of which he was later to have cause to regret.

Randolph added to the argument for Negro suffrage. As the only representative of four million blacks in the South, he urged the Republicans to do justice to his people. If the Republicans did not, they would regret it, he said, for when the time came that Negroes did vote, they would remember their friends and not forget their foes. But several other delegates spoke against the proposal as inexpedient. Then was heard a call for the previous question. Warmoth suggested that only the delegates from the "non-reconstructed" states be included in the balloting. It was agreed. On the question of adopting the report there were 66 yeas and 11 nays. Tourgee was the only delegate from North Carolina who voted yea.[10]

While the Southern loyalists were meeting in Philadelphia, their archfoe Andrew Johnson was traveling about on what the newspapers called a "swing around the circle." He was going out to Chicago to dedicate a monument to Stephen A. Douglas, Lincoln's great Democratic rival who had died just before the war but who until now had remained without an appropriate memorial. Johnson was taking a roundabout route. From Washington he went first to Philadelphia, where he appeared on August 28, only a few days before the opening of the loyalists' convention, to find a cheering crowd at the railroad station but no official welcome from the city council. Then he proceeded to Chicago by way of New York City, Buffalo, and Cleveland, and returned through Indianapolis and Pittsburgh, arriving back in Washington on September 15.

At each big city en route Johnson had stopped to make a speech. Repeatedly he insisted that *he,* not the Radicals, was following Lincoln's policy. Again and again he said *they,* not he, were the real traitors and disunionists, since they stood in the way of his efforts to reunite the country. His aim was to persuade voters to vote for candidates who would support him and his program. For the first time in American history, a President was out campaigning in a mid-term congressional election.

At their convention the loyalists had decided to counteract the Johnson tour by sending out selected speakers who, in both a political and a geographical sense, would cover much the same ground. There would be one significant difference in routing. Instead of swinging around through Chicago to honor the Democrat Douglas at his monument, the loyalists would swing around through Springfield, Illinois, to honor the Republican Lincoln at his tomb. They chose both Warmoth and Tourgee, among others, to make the trip, each on his own. "We are going on a great electioneering tour after the President's," Tourgee wrote to Emma, to explain the prolongation of his absence from home. He had been getting no letters from her, and he begged her to write to him.

From Philadelphia, Tourgee went to Erie, in the opposite corner of the state. After visiting friends and relatives and resting up, he crossed the state to its northeastern corner, to campaign in rural Susquehanna and neighboring counties for a week or more. Almost every day he made one or two or three speeches, and almost every day he dashed off a note to Emma. "I have ridden about thirty miles over rough county roads," he told her on September 19, "spoken two hours and been in the rain for three or four hours since, and have but a few minutes to write before the mail goes out . . . and only time to say 'I love you darling.'" Then he recrossed the state to Pittsburgh, to retake the stump there and in surrounding towns. "I speak so frequently that it completely exhausts my nervous energy and the constant excitement makes me a constantly worn out man," he wrote from Pittsburgh on October 3. Yet he would not have it otherwise, for he possessed a mission and a message, and he knew he was "doing good for the great cause." The message:

> Fellow Citizens and Comrades in Blue . . . . When the great heart crushing crisis of Rebellion came, with you I donned the blue and fought for the starry banner. The march, the battlefield, the defeat, the victory, the rebel dungeon and the glad release have all brought their burdens of joy or of sorrow to my heart. We are brothers bound to each other by the memory of the blood we have shed, the sufferings we have endured, and the comrades whom we mourn. We are bound together by the memory of the great glory which overspread our skies, when the sunlight of peace drove the war clouds from our horizon. . . . We rejoiced too soon. The battle of liberty was but half fought when we sung our paean. . . . When you came to your happy homes I went to my desolated one, and while you have been enjoying the well earned fruition of your victories I have been watching the rallying of our enemies and noting the precursors of the coming storm. I come here tonight as one of the pickets of the Grand Army of American Liberty to report to you what I have seen in my lonely beat upon the Southern front—the unmistakable signs of the mustering of Treason's hosts, to warn you to be at your posts and not to be found sleeping.

Tourgee stayed on in Pittsburgh to await the Pennsylvania election, which was set for October 9, about a month ahead of election day in most of the states. The outlook inspirited him. "If the 'Rebs' could see what I have seen they would . . . quietly back down and be still," he assured Emma. "They will have a harder row to hoe when Congress meets again than they have ever had before." As expected, the Republicans won a sweeping victory on October 9, sending to Congress an increased number of determinedly anti-Johnson men from Pennsylvania. Leaving for Philadelphia afterward. Tourgee planned to go on from there to New York and eventually to Illinois to join his fellows at Lincoln's tomb. He expected to find, awaiting him in Philadelphia, a stack of accumulated letters from Emma, from whom he had heard only once since leaving Greensboro in August. Sure enough, there was some mail for him in Philadelphia—and also a parcel containing a revolver for him. After reading the mail he knew there was nothing for him to do except to call off the rest of his trip and go back at once to North Carolina.[11]

Meanwhile Warmoth had gone from Philadelphia to New York City. On the night of September 12 he was one of the speakers at the Cooper Institute. In his talk he said he did not want to see the Southern states represented in Congress until those states had been reconstructed in such a way that all the loyal white and black people in them were completely safe. His hearers cried out in agreement, one of them yelling: "That's the talk!" They cheered again when he declared that the federal government had the power and the right to hang every rebel in the South. And the applause was even louder when he concluded by telling them to elect congressmen who would "undo everything that Mr. Johnson had done" and who would see that "none but men who have been true to the flag, without distinction of race or color," should share in governing the country.

From New York, Warmoth went on to Boston with a touring team of Republican campaigners. "The Mayor & City Council took us in carriages all around the City of Boston," he recorded, "& at one o'clock took us to Faneuil Hall where there was a big meeting, presided over by Genl Butler." Warmoth "spoke at Faneuil Hall & then went over & spoke at Tremont Temple. The Boston people wanted to stay up all night with us." On to Hartford, Connecticut, and to Albany and Troy, New York. In Albany, Warmoth dined with a United States senator, drove out to see the city with another distinguished citizen, and visited a soldiers' home and spoke to 250 broken-down veterans. "They wept and cheered us." Next, to Poughkeepsie, where there was a "splendid audience" and where the famous humorist and lecturer Josh Billings (Henry Wheeler Shaw) sat on the platform. After heading west with his fellow stump-speakers, Warmoth summarized the events of September 20:

> Met a large delegation in a special car at Erie, headed by the Mayor of Cleveland to receive us. Jolly bunch. Arrived at Cleveland after dark. Notwithstanding the rain, a large procession of torches met us and escorted us to the hotel. Here in front of the hotel were crowded together two thousand people, to welcome us. The rain ceased & several of us spoke from the balcony. I spoke. At 10 o'clock we had a splendid banquet at which the Mayor presided. I with others spoke in response to the toasts. The Mayor gave me my health. I spoke in reply on the subjects of the day, which was much appreciated. Had a splendid time with the boys of Cleveland.

On to Sandusky and another "Good time" there. Farther on, Warmoth "spoke at Wasson to a large crowd of radicals in the day time & to a splendid audience in White Hall, Toledo, at night." He lay over at

Toledo on Sunday, September 23, and dined with a group including another popular humorist, Petroleum V. Nasby (David Ross Locke), the editor of the *Toledo Blade*. On Monday he went alone to Napoleon, Ohio. "I spoke at 2 o'clock to a crowded house, for two hours, & they requested me to speak again at night, which I did, to a splended audience. They all say I made a great many votes & consolidated opinion on negro suffrage."

So it went for the rest of September, through October, and into November. On to Indianapolis and other Indiana cities; Chicago, Galesburg, Macomb, and Quincy in Illinois; and across the Mississippi to St. Louis, Missouri. Then back to Illinois and Springfield, where the group of campaigners paid their respects at Lincoln's tomb and disbanded. "Mrs. Oglesby gave me a party at the executive mansion," Warmoth exulted privately in Springfield. Finally he went back to New York State for twenty or thirty more performances before election day.

Warmoth, in New York City, read the returns from around the country with great satisfaction. The Republican triumph was even more decisive than he had expected it to be. In the new Congress the Republicans would hold considerably more than a two-thirds majority. Congress would be veto-proof. The Radicals could impose on the South a plan of their own—if they could agree among themselves on what to require in addition to the Fourteenth Amendment.[12]

"My Darling Husband: . . . I pray you may speedily be restored in health and safety to my arms," Emma Tourgee had written from the West Green Nursery near Greensboro.

> Your entire ignorance of the storm brewing here, which has increased from a cloud no bigger than a man's hand to a perfect hurricane of indignation and falsehood, seems strange enough. The Editor of the *[Greensboro] Patriot* cannot let you alone but every week his paper is filled with all the meanest low-lived falsehoods that can be thought of against your character. Your speech in the Convention at Phil. seems to be rather more than he can endure and that is his particular point of attack. Some one is kind enough to send us the papers—with such notes as these in pencil marks on the margin: "The nasty dog! He knows he lied when he said this. He had better look out! Beware! &c &c."

This was the news that had brought Tourgee abruptly back home from Pennsylvania.[13]

Tourgee did not realize the full extent to which Governor Worth was responsible for the vicious campaign of vilification and threat. In the *New York Herald* Worth had read an account that convinced him Tourgee's convention speech was "a tissue of lies from beginning to end." The *Herald* quoted Tourgee as saying (in Worth's paraphrase) "seven hundred loyal men had petitioned Prest. Johnson for redress from the rebel depredations, and this petition was referred back to the disloyal Govr. of that State and came back to the authorities of their own town." And that was not the worst of Tourgee's prevarications. "He says in a further statement that he had recently been informed, by a Quaker, that he (the Quaker) had seen fifteen murdered negroes dragged out of one pond." Worth determined to expose the "lying villain" who had been "purporting to represent 2000 North Carolinians."

Born and bred in Guilford County, the son of a Quaker mother, Worth was beside himself with indignation at what he considered the slurs of an outsider. Running for reelection as governor, he was also calculating the political value, to himself, of Tourgee's published remarks—which in confidence he recognized might be "most effectively used in the canvass." He was at least as disingenuous as Tourgee, however, when he denied having received from President Johnson and having rejected a petition from 700 North Carolina loyalists. He had indeed received and rejected the petition, though it came from a presidential intimate rather than directly from the President, and it contained fewer than 700 names. Furthermore, in making such an issue as he did of the story of fifteen black corpses in a single pond, Worth was evading the dreadful fact of the all-too-frequent murders of blacks in the county and the state.

The basic issue between Worth and Tourgee was one of race. "We who were born here will never get along with the free Negroes," Worth believed. "The fools and demagogues of the North insist they must be our equals. This will not be tolerated. As an inferior race they will degenerate and retard all prosperity." Tourgee was one of those "fools and demagogues of the North" who advocated racial equality. That, rather than his exaggerations, was the real reason Worth hated him.

After reading the *New York Herald* report of Tourgee's speech, Worth immediately composed a long letter to the editor of the Democratic *Greensboro Patriot* and another to Nereus Mendenhall, one of the Quakers who had attended the Deep River Meeting House caucus that sent Tourgee to the loyalist convention in Philadelphia. Worth urged the editor to denounce Tourgee and called upon Mendenhall to repudiate him. The editor readily responded with diatribes in his paper, but Mendenhall showed no willingness to cooperate. So Worth wrote him again:

> The public know that you participated in the meeting which delegated Tourgee to the Phila. Convention. They have read his speech there. While uncontradicted by the persons who sent him, he must be regarded, and he has a right to claim, that he was a true exponent of their views and opinions. From the *place* where the meeting was held and your participation in it, the inference is generally drawn that the Quakers, who are remarkable for their unity of action and among whom you are a prominent man, endorse the view that Union men are oppressed by the civil authorities of the State—that they are in favor of disfranchising the great body of the white men of the State and allowing universal suffrage to the recently emancipated

> negro—that you favor a constitutional amendment which would exclude from office [former] Gov. [William A.] Graham and every other prominent man in N. C., who have always stood up for the Quakers.

Still, the Quakers of Guilford County refrained from publicly disowning Tourgee or disavowing his views.[14]

Other local people, under the prodding of the *Greensboro Patriot,* not only disowned but denounced him. They addressed anonymous letters to him, for Emma to open and worry about in his absence. "The course you have taken in Guilford County and in the late Philadelphia convention has rendered you vile oily odious to nine tenths of the Southern people," she read in one unsigned missive postmarked Greensboro. "Your stay in North Carolina had better be short if you expect to breathe the vital air." Another one, somewhat less literary: "It is about time that your lying tong[ue] was stopped, and if you ever show your ugly face in Guilford County again I will take care with some of my friends that you find the bottom of that *niger pond* you have been talking so much about."

There also came, addressed to Mrs. Tourgee herself and signed only "The friend of all loyal people," a well-meant letter that was hardly less terrifying. The writer, obviously a woman, blushed to say she had been hearing even ladies talk of tar and feathers, and she advised Mrs. Tourgee to persuade her husband to stay away till things quieted down. "I was born in the South and know the character of the Southern people. There is a class of ignorant people which has always been under the influence of the more intelligent and designing and have always done their miserable work." With that, Emma could have agreed even more emphatically than she doubtless did—had she known of the correspondence of the intelligent and designing Governor Worth.

Instead of urging her husband to keep away for a while, Emma begged him to come home at once. When she realized from his letters that hers were not reaching him, she dispatched as a personal messenger, to deliver not only her pleas but also her husband's revolver, a youth from Erie who had been living with the Tourgees and working at the nursery. The boy never succeeded in catching up with the itinerant Tourgee, but finally left the letters and the parcel at Erie, for them to be forwarded to Philadelphia.

On his return to Guilford County, Tourgee found the situation fully as bad as Emma had described it—or even worse. Emma herself was in poor condition, both physically and emotionally. She was still recovering from her puzzling foot ailment. The doctor did not know what else to call it, so he diagnosed it as neuralgia, and he advised her to stay in bed and prop the foot up on a pillow, but she had too much to do to spend her days that way. She was already tense when the hate campaign began, and now the hostility all about her was seriously telling on her nerves.[15]

Tourgee's partners, Kuhn and Pettengill, were omitting his name from their correspondence and advertisements and were pretending, as

Emma put it, that "such an obnoxious individual" was "no longer connected with them in business." Apparently Kuhn and Pettengill were too late in disavowing Tourgee and his radicalism, for the business of the firm (never very successful) was already falling off. Only grudgingly would Pettengill provide the Tourgee household with potatoes from the common store, and both the Pettengills and the Kuhns seemed to resent the presence of Emma's parents, who would doubtless be *"turned out of doors* by my *Lord Kuhn* or *Lady P."* if those worthies should have their way.

The black employees of the nursery were overjoyed at Tourgee's return. They were behind in their pay and unable to get their due from Pettengill or Kuhn. "They have had but half rations for some time and not a cent of money," Emma said, "and [with] the cold weather coming on they need their winter clothing—and no money nor no promise of any." She had been distributing a little cash among them and occasionally inviting them to a meal, but she did not have the means to do right by them. They looked to Tourgee, not to Kuhn or Pettengill, as their protector and friend, though at the moment he did not have the necessary means, either. "There is not a colored man on the place," Emma told him, "who will stay another year if you sell out."

Either Tourgee or his partners must sell out, for he and they were at an impasse. Before the end of autumn Kuhn and Pettingill transferred their interests to Tourgee, and he assumed the partnership's debts, which were steadily mounting. Thus miserably ended, after scarcely more than a year's trial, the association of young men that Tourgee idealistically had counted on to start a happy, cooperative life in the South.

Tourgee now made an agreement with a new partner, who was to take charge of the nursery and receive, for his services, one-half of the gross receipts. He joined with another partner to set up a real estate agency. And he got together with a third, a former Union army surgeon from Michigan, to publish a newspaper.

The weekly *Union Register* of Greensboro began publication on December 1, 1866, with the frank avowal that it was to be a "thoroughly and unreservedly loyal" paper. Flattering the people of Greensboro, the editors announced that they had chosen this place not only because of "its central location and peculiar telegraph and railroad communications" but also because of the "well known enterprise of its inhabitants." Yet, gratuitously insulting many of the people, the editors said they aimed to raise the South from its "slough of ignorance and prejudice." Prejudice continued and increased. Posters advertising the *Union Register* were repeatedly torn down, and Tourgee blamed "the principal citizens of Greensboro" for condoning and even encouraging the vandalism. During the winter of 1866-67, for all his clever dialect poems and political satires, his venture into journalism did not do well financially.

Neither did his reorganized nursery business, his newly launched real estate operation, or his occasional resorts to the legal profession. When he did practice law he appeared only at the federal bar. He refused to enter the local or state courts, since to do so would be to recognize the Jonathan Worth regime, which he considered completely illegitimate. That fall and winter, depressed as he was by his economic prospects, he could find no compensatory cheer when he looked at developments in state politics.

In the North Carolina elections of 1866 the voters returned Worth to the governorship and sent an increased majority of pro-Worth Conservatives to the general assembly. Afterwards the governor advised them not to ratify the Fourteenth Amendment, and they were glad to comply. (Except for Tennessee, none of the former Confederate states ratified the amendment.) The governor also counseled the legislators to discontinue the public schools, and again they complied. He thought "the Common School system had better be discouraged, for a time, and thus avoid the question as to educating negroes." The consequence was that most white children in the state had no schools at all, while black children could attend those the Freedmen's Bureau provided in cooperation with the Freedmen's Aid Societies of the North.

If the Fourteenth Amendment went much too far to please Worth and his followers, it did not go nearly far enough, of course, to satisfy Tourgee and other radical loyalists in North Carolina. These radicals had parted from ex-Governor Holden when he limited his platform to the amendment alone, but after its defeat even the Holdenites came out for Negro suffrage, at least in a qualified form. Though the white Unionists combined their forces, they would not have a majority in the state until black Unionists got the vote. And blacks could get the vote only from Congress. In February 1867 the Unionists of Guilford and Randolph counties met and petitioned Congress to create loyal governments in the South by first making it a territory and then enfranchising former slaves and disfranchising former rebel leaders.[16]

To the prayers of Tourgee and others, Congress responded more or less adequately with the Reconstruction Act of March 2, 1867. According to this law, the ten excluded states were to be temporarily divided into five military districts, each of which was to be placed under the command of an army general. The generals were to see to the holding of new constitutional conventions and the formation of new state governments. Black men were to be eligible to vote and hold office, and so were the rank and file of Confederate veterans, but not (for the time being) the military officers or civil officials of the late Confederacy. The states, once properly reorganized, must ratify the Fourteenth Amendment. When they had met every requirement, they would be restored to the Union, and the military rule would terminate.

Just six months earlier, at the Philadelphia convention, only a minority of the Republicans present had agreed with Warmoth and Tourgee that the delegates ought to declare for a more thoroughgoing Reconstruction than the Fourteenth Amendment would mean. And now most of what Warmoth and Tourgee had been advocating was the law of the land, though neither man was entirely satisfied with the Reconstruction Act, for it failed to do one thing that both had advocated—namely, to reduce the South to the condition of a territory.

CHAPTER 4

To Reconstruct This Godforsaken Country (1867-1868)

When Congress passed the Reconstruction Act, on March 2, 1867, Willard Warner was in Columbus, Ohio, attending to his duties as a state senator—duties that kept him from his Alabama plantation during the winter months. He did not like the new law. Congress, he believed, should merely have made an explicit offer to readmit any state ratifying the Fourteenth Amendment by the end of the congressional session on March 4. If thus assured of readmittance, Alabama would have ratified promptly, and other states would have followed suit. So Warner thought, and he had urged the idea, in vain, upon his good friend John Sherman, the United States senator from Ohio.

Still, the law could have been worse from Warner's point of view, and it would have been worse if Thaddeus Stevens and Charles Sumner had had their way. The Stevens bill would have left the states indefinitely in a kind of limbo. The Sherman bill—the one that finally passed—would restore them to full membership in the Union once they had reorganized with Negro suffrage and had ratified the Fourteenth Amendment. Warner congratulated Sherman for having offered a "rebuke to the fierce fanaticism and unholy sectional ambition of Sumner in seeking to grind the South to powder and to not only enfranchise the Negroes but to disfranchise the whites and make Negro states." Warner told Sherman further: "I have long felt that you would sooner or later be compelled to do violence to your conceptions of right or part company with Sumner and Stevens *who don't want Union.*"

To Warner it seemed only fair that Ohio should give blacks the vote now that Alabama was being compelled to do so. The Ohio constitution still contained the qualifying word *white* in its suffrage clause. "What do you say to the question of *now* submitting the question of striking the word white from our Constitution?" Warner wrote to Sherman, this time asking instead of offering advice. "Its success is doubtful if submitted, though I think it may possibly be carried if the party *unites solidly* in it." Ohio Republicans failed to unite solidly on it, and Ohio voters defeated it in a referendum later in the year. Sherman's Ohio, like Stevens's Pennsylvania, refrained from joining the small group of Northern states (there were only seven of them) that allowed blacks to vote.[1]

Once the Ohio legislative session was over, Warner returned to his Alabama plantation to entertain some of his relatives there and to look after the growing crops. By June his cotton was coming up well and his melons were ripening, though his corn was suffering for want of rain. On June 4 about fifty whites and a hundred blacks met in nearby Montgomery to organize a state Republican party and make plans for electing delegates to the constitutional convention that the Reconstruction Act required.[2]

As yet, Warner took a less active part in Alabama politics than did George E. Spencer, that other quondam Union general who had looked for opportunities in the state at the close of the war. Spencer had found little to keep him in Alabama at that time, but the Reconstruction Act opened new possibilities for him, and in April, soon after its passage, he came back from California. Through the influence of his old army friend Grenville M. Dodge, now in Congress, he secured a job as federal register in bankruptcy for the fourth congressional district of Alabama. In June he was staying in Decatur with his wife, Bella, the aspiring journalist and novelist. He was watching political developments in the state and planning to take control of the new party.

If the party was to succeed in Alabama, Spencer believed, the largest possible number of ex-Confederates must be kept out of politics. The Reconstruction Act seemed to disfranchise only those who had held high military or civil positions in the Confederacy. To clarify the law on this and other points, Congress passed a supplementary act (March 23, 1867) which did not eliminate confusion but did give greater initiative to the commanding general in each military district of the South. Spencer looked to Congressman Dodge and Dodge's Radical colleagues to provide further clarification: "I sincerely hope that you will make the 'Reconstruction Act' so plain that a wayfaring man, though a fool, can understand it."

Spencer was delighted, meanwhile, to see that the commanding general of the district embracing Georgia, Florida, and Alabama was making the law plain enough. This officer was John Pope, the same man who had led the Army of the Potomac to disaster in the second battle of Bull Run. After giving general instructions to the registration boards in the three states under his command, Pope added some special instructions for the boards in Alabama. The Alabama registrars were to disqualify all who had engaged in the rebellion or had given aid and comfort to the enemies of the United States in any way. "The parents who gave a son, in armed hostility, food and clothing for his own use, might do so without hostile intent," Pope said. "If he gave him a horse, gun, or anything else to be used for hostile purposs, he thereby gave aid and comfort to the enemy." This order both pleased and surprised Spencer, disfranchising as it did much larger numbers than had been expected. "Under Pope's order," he was confident, "we can carry Alabama and secure it permanently to the Republican party. And without it we will have to give everything over to the Rebels."

During that summer and fall things continued to go well for Spencer in his political—though not in his personal—life. After settling in Tuscaloosa and taking up his duties as federal register in bankruptcy, he found business brisk and fees generous, so much so that he expected to make at least $5,000 a year and possibly as much as $10,000. He also did well in party affairs, though he ran into opposition from William H. Smith, the Alabamian who had defected to the Union in 1862 and had been Spencer's choice for provisional governor in 1865. Smith now disagreed with Spencer about the wisdom of excluding all former Confederates from politics. Republicans of the Smith faction were willing to accept any Southerner, regardless of his past, who would cooperate with them in the future. But Spencer's views and not Smith's prevailed among a majority of the delegates when the constitutional convention met in November.[3]

By that time, life had lost most of its meaning for Spencer. On August 1, after a brief illness, his beloved Bella suddenly died. He had not recovered from the blow when he, too, came down with the fever. In October, still weak and depressed, he opened his soul to his old comrade Dodge:

> I am completely broken down in spirits and care but little for the future. I feel that my duty is to remain here and help reconstruct this Godforsaken and miserable country. It is truly an awful place to live in, but since we have the colored men to help us we can outvote them [the ex-rebels] and I think if it becomes necessary we can outfight them. I have lost all my ambition and have but little heart to engage in political life. While I remain here I cannot help doing it.
>
> We will send an entire Republican delegation to join you from this State. I can go to Congress, if I wish, but at present I do not feel like it. Six months may change my views. I stand as well as any Union man in the State and do not believe that there is any man in the party who wields more influence than I do.[4]

While Spencer grieved in Tuscaloosa, Warner had other worries on his plantation near Montgomery. He, too, was a widower, but more than three years had gone by since Eliza's death, and so his grief was less fresh and sharp. Still, he had difficulties that Spencer was exempt from. Running a cotton plantation was, at the moment, much less remunerative than holding a good federal job. "The average cost of the cotton raised in the South this year has not been less than $75 per bale of 500 pounds," Warner complained to Senator Sherman. "The price now is in

Montgomery $65.00 per bale and out of this we must pay $12.50 tax." At that rate, growers would still lose $10 a bale even if the tax were repealed, as Warner again insisted it must be. "Two years cotton planting have ruined two thirds of the Northern men engaged in it, and nearly all the Southern planters are broken."

To make up for his losses in planting, Warner needed the income he could get from a political office. Before the end of 1867 he decided to run for Congress from Alabama, though he was still a member of the state senate in Ohio. He knew he would have difficulty in obtaining the nomination from the Republicans of the Montgomery district, for he would face the competition of a Union veteran who had a connection with the Freedmen's Bureau. So Warner appealed to Sherman to intercede with Wager Swayne, the Alabama Bureau head: "Can't you aid me through influence with Gen. Swayne who I think can control the nomination?" Warner also called on Swayne at his office in Montgomery.

But Swayne, while praising Warner as a "valued friend," professed to be steering clear of local politics. "I do not think that General Warner will seek the position," he replied to Sherman, "for the reason that one at least of the candidates has been for two years actively and conspicuously at work for equal rights, while the necessities of Gen. Warner's position have kept him from the Alabama public." His chances for the Montgomery nomination fading, Warner turned to Sherman again and proposed that Congress increase Alabama's representation by providing places for one or two congressmen-at-large. "If this is done I think I can get chosen to one of them." Once more, he was to be disappointed.[5]

Warner was not to be a candidate when the qualified Alabama voters went to the polls in February 1868 to accept or reject the new constitution and to elect congressmen and state officials. As the elections approached, Republicans were apprehensive at signs that the Democrats (or Conservatives, as many of them preferred to call themselves) were coming to life. Democrats in the state were encouraged by gains that their fellow partisans made in Pennsylvania, Ohio, and other Northern states in local elections in the fall of 1867. "Since the elections in Ohio & Penna.," Spencer observed, "the Rebels are very jubilant and talk of the time when they are again going to commence hanging." Spencer and other Alabama Republicans feared that, considering the backlash of those returns, Congress might hesitate to continue with Radical Reconstruction. "I hope that Congress will not back down one peg but go ahead," Spencer told Congressman Dodge, "and that the first thing they will do will be to pass a general impeachment law and then impeach the President."[6]

Spencer and his followers were further outraged when, a little more than a month before the Alabama elections, President Johnson suddenly removed two high-placed favorites of Alabama Radicals—the commander of the military district, General Pope; and the state head of the Freedmen's Bureau, General Wager Swayne. Among those who took particular offense at this was Charles W. Buckley, a Presbyterian preacher from Illinois who had come to Alabama as the chaplain of a black regiment, who had served two years with the Freedmen's Bureau in the state, and who now held the place on the Republican ticket that Warner had aspired to— as candidate for Congress from the Montgomery constituency. Buckley protested to Illinois Congressman Elihu B. Washburne:

> The removal of Genls Pope and Swayne has taken from the work of reconstruction two able and experienced leaders. Their loss to the Union men of this state is irreparable, and their removal is followed by such an outburst of rebel hostility, such defiant speeches and actions, that we are on the very eve of violence and bloodshed. No man today can enter the canvass and openly and publicly work for reconstruction without taking his life in his hands. Rebels, who call themselves Conservatives, are using all the force and violence necessary to defeat the new constitution. The rebels are organizing Conservative Clubs and War Clubs for the express purpose of keeping the colored people from the polls. We are in great danger now of being conquered by our old enemy and the fruits of our long struggle lost. If our new commanders are not heartily in favor of the present plan of reconstruction, so evenly are the scales balanced, we must go down, and Northern men must leave the South. Congress must not only be firm, but keep a faithless Executive from obstructing our work.[7]

President Johnson succeeded, temporarily, in obstructing the work of the Radicals in Alabama. His replacements for Pope and Swayne did not support the congressional plan as these two had done. When the elections were held, opponents of the plan were in charge of most of the polling places. Registered voters of Conservative sympathy stayed away from the polls and—through trickery, threats, force, and economic pressure—kept thousands of registered blacks away. After several days of balloting, the official count gave 70,812 votes for the new constitution and only 1,005 against it. But there were 170,812 registered voters, and the law required a majority of them for approval, so the constitution failed to pass. "Had he [Swayne] remained in command here our work would have been comparatively easy, and success certain," a Northern-born Republican reported from Montgomery. "Unfriendly military management has killed us."

While Radicals were downcast, Conservatives were overjoyed. The *Montgomery Mail,* speaking of "dead Radicalism in Alabama," said "she leaves a family of carpet-baggers and scalawags to mourn her loss." These terms were new to political discourse in the state—*carpetbaggers,* meaning Northern-born white Republicans who had arrived since the beginning of the Civil War; *scalawags,* meaning white Republicans who were either Southern-born or long resident in the South.

In the recent elections the Conservatives had put up no slate. A scalawag, William H. Smith, had won the governorship, and another had gained a place in Congress. The remaining four state offices and five congressional seats had gone to carpetbaggers. None of the victors could take office, however, until Alabama had been restored to complete statehood.

Foreseeing the tactics of the Conservatives, some of the Republicans had urged, before the elections, that Congress change the law so as to require only a majority of the voters actually balloting (and not a majority of all those registered) to ratify one of the new state constitutions. After the elections the Republicans revived and intensified the demand, and Congress responded with the supplementary law of March 11, 1868.[8]

By that time Warner had hopes of getting a government job at last. If Senator Sherman could not help him go to Congress, perhaps Sherman could at least obtain for him the secretaryship of the United States Senate. One of Warner's erstwhile fellow officers on General William T. Sherman's staff, Jacob D. Cox, recommended him as a gallant soldier, earnest Republican, and highly moral man. "He has now been some two years in Alabama, where he has fixed his home, & from many sources I learn that he has been recognized there as one of the leaders of the Republican party in that State."[9] This Senate job, too, fell through. As for Republican leaders in Alabama, time was yet to tell which of the three—the scalawag Smith and the carpetbaggers Spencer and Warner—would come out on top.

After winding up his autumn 1866 electioneering tour from New York to Illinois and back to New York, Henry Clay Warmoth had returned to New Orleans by way of St. Louis and the Mississippi River. He enjoyed the company of his father, who spent the winter months in New Orleans with him, gaining nine pounds and improving in health and looks. Warmoth himself remained slim and trim, while sporting a fashionable and becoming mustache, but he used up little of his youthful energy during the months following his return. "Since then I have read & studied, done no business," he noted as March 1867 approached, after a long lapse in his diary-keeping. "Attend to politics a little."

By the time March arrived, bringing warm and even hot and dusty days, Warmoth was beginning to attend to politics a great deal. He was busily enrolling Union veterans in the Grand Army of the Republic and expecting soon to have 5,000 to 6,000 men in the local department, of which he was provisional commander. The G.A.R., in the process of formation throughout the country, was to serve as an auxiliary of the Republican party. Promising though his future was in Louisiana politics, Warmoth for the moment faced an embarrassment that could impair his standing as a party leader. He was charged with having embezzled money from the federal government when, in July 1866, he was a treasury agent in Houston, Texas. Now he would have to take time from politics to make another trip to Houston, but knowing he was innocent he fully expected to be cleared—as indeed he was soon to be.

After his father's departure, Warmoth made new arrangements for bachelor living. His landlady at 139 Custom House Street ("a very unfortunate & unhappy woman, very nervous, poor, and as ugly as Satan") cursed him for leaving but could not keep him from moving to 130 Magazine Street. While rooming there, he was going to have his meals at a nearby boardinghouse. His social life continued in its usual course. On Sunday, March 3, he went to the theater with a lady friend to see the famous actor Joseph Jefferson in the perennially popular stage version of *Rip Van Winkle*. "We were delighted with it," Warmoth recorded. "It was the best thing I ever saw. The humor & the pathos was beautifully displayed." But the play was only a brief distraction. "The great event of the last few days is the passage over the veto of the President [of] the Military Bill which enfranchises 4,000,000 of blacks and disfranchises certain rebels."[10]

It was an exaggeration, of course, to say the Reconstruction Act enfranchised 4,000,000 blacks, since that was the approximate total of black men, women, and children in the South, and the act gave political rights only to the men. Still, the numbers were very large—in Louisiana, almost half of the adult males. The task for Warmoth and other aspiring Republican leaders was to organize them, bring them out to vote, and see that they voted right. Before long, it was clear that the job was not going to be easy. As an Ohioan operating a large plantation in northeast Louisiana observed:

> The South is making a great effort to control the negro vote. It will, for the present, be successful to some extent. In large cities and towns, on public thoroughfares, where the negro is more intelligent and is in constant communication with the outside world, he will generally vote right. So also will all who have been soldiers or indeed served in any capacity in the army. But in the interior & out-of-the-way places, they will vote very generally as their old masters direct. Indeed, the latter do not hesitate to boast of the reckless course they intend to pursue to control the negro vote in their respective communities.[11]

During the spring, Warmoth kept up a correspondence with both white and black politicians to advise and encourage them. They should form Republican clubs, hold frequent meetings, have someone at the polls to see that black voters knew which ballot was which. "I think they will go all right here but there will be a strong pressure against them as the white men intend to influence their vote," Warmoth heard from a Freedmen's Bureau agent in Thibodeaux, southwest of New Orleans. A member of the board of registrars in Vermilion Parish, in the Cajun country, complained to Warmoth that blacks were slow to register. "The reason why the colored men did not sooner come forward," the board member explained, "may be safely said to be false representations made by the whites." He added: "It will probably be a difficult matter to get Republican clubs organized in this parish with a small population so widely spread over a large country, and, worst of all, I have not yet found any educated men among them nor even a man who can read or write." As for white "Union men," they were extremely scarce and they, too, were illiterate.

To encourage blacks to register, Warmoth decided in August to "go into the parishes" along with Thomas W. Conway, recently head of the Louisiana Freedmen's Bureau. In the sugar region the planters were still suffering from a lack of capital, and stretches of once-rich cane fields had reverted to weeds and brush even along the Bayou Teche, an area that had been the "garden spot" of the state. "Sugar houses of the best construction, groups of cabins for the 'hands,' all neatly whitewashed, orange groves & live oak trees, made a sort of paradise to the eye—but with the Devil of Slavery in it," a sympathetic traveler from Massachusetts reported. "Now the devil has been exorcised, but in his going out has torn everything to pieces." Some of the planters, unable to hire or feed their hands between seed-time and harvest, had been hoping for federal government loans on their growing crop. Most of the whites, especially the women and the youths, were newly embittered when the government gave them Negro suffrage instead of financial aid. Warmoth and Conway, on their trip through the countryside, could sense the rising hostility. Still, they managed to attract and to harangue tremendous crowds of blacks.

Warmoth was helping to prepare the voters for the election to be held on September 27 and 28, when they were to decide whether or not a constitutional convention should meet and, if it did, who the delegates should be. He and other Republican campaigners had the support of the federal troops in trying to prevent intimidation of prospective black voters so long as General Philip H. Sheridan remained in command of the military district. Three weeks before the election President Johnson removed Sheridan because of the general's Radical proclivities. So Warmoth was greatly relieved when the returns finally came in. The proposition for holding a convention carried by 75,083 to 4,006, and of the 98 elected delegates a large majority were Republicans and nearly half (45) were blacks.[12]

Though not himself a delegate, Warmoth played a leading role in the convention when it met (from November 23, 1867, to March 9, 1868) in the Mechanics' Institute, recently the scene of riotous bloodshed and still the temporary capitol. On the third day the delegates decided to admit Warmoth and a few others to the privileges of the floor. That same day the convention received from him a copy of the New York constitutional manual and a letter in which he recommended it for the delegates' use. The manual contained the text of all the state constitutions, and the convention would do well, Warmoth suggested, to select or adapt the most up-to-date features of each. Throughout the nearly four-month session he labored to exert his persuasive powers upon the delegates. His mastery was shown when a majority agreed to lower, from thirty-five to twenty-five, the minimum age for governor. Warmoth was twenty- five.

The *New Orleans Tribune* demanded to know why the convention had seen fit to make this change. Of course, the *Tribune's* publisher, Dr. J. B. Roudanez, knew perfctly well that the purpose was to make Warmoth eligible for the governorship. A leader of the comparatively well-off "free persons of color," Roudanez presumed to speak for all the blacks, including the recent slaves. In his paper he had been saying: "We have more than the ballot: we compose a majority of the State, and with the help of our radical white friends, we . . . are the masters of the field. Everything depends on the colored race." Roudanez did not insist that the governorship belonged to a black, but he was determined that it should go to someone other than Warmoth.

As the time for nominations approached, the Louisiana Republicans divided into two quite distinct factions: the Pure Radicals and the White Republicans. "The active portion of the party in Louisiana is composed largely of white adventurers, who are striving to be elected to office by black votes," the *Tribune* commented. "Some of these intend, if elected, to give a share of offices to colored men. We admit that, but they will choose only docile tools, not citizens who have manhood." Warmoth suspected that the Pure Radical leaders were plotting to "Africanize" Louisiana and convert it into a Negro state comparable to Haiti or Liberia.

When the Republicans met to choose their candidates, on January 14, 1868, the *Tribune* faction backed the wealthy Negro Francis E. Dumas for governor. On the first ballot Dumas got 41 votes and Warmoth 37, but others received a scattering of votes, and Dumas lacked a majority. On the next ballot Warmoth led 45 to 43 and was nominated. Dumas refused to run for lieutenant-governor, but Oscar J. Dunn, a Negro house painter, accepted the second place on the Warmoth ticket. The Pure Radicals now chose a slate of their own, at the head of which they put James G. Taliaferro, a prewar planter and slaveowner and a wartime Unionist whom the Confederates had imprisoned.

The Republicans having thus split, the Democrats decided not to run a gubernatorial candidate but, instead, to let their followers increase the anti-Warmoth vote. Democratic newspapers concentrated their fire on Warmoth. The *New Orleans Times,* for one, said that ever since his arrival in Louisiana he had been "flitting from this State to the North and West every few months" and seldom appearing in the courts, though he professed to be a lawyer. "The future historian of the politics of this State will be puzzled, to a perplexing degree," the *Times* editorialized, "to know upon what basis, real or imaginary, this *modest* young gentleman stands for the highest executive of a State, to the great body of whose people he is an entire stranger, and in which he is a mere accidental and temporary sojourner."[13]

But Warmoth and his journalistic backers held their own in the campaign. The *New Orleans Republican* described a mass meeting in and around the Mechanics' Institute—"that building rendered sacred by the blood of the martyrs of the ever-memorable July thirtieth, 1866"—as a display of "magnificence seldom witnessed in New Orleans." In the main speech of the occasion Warmoth denounced the Democrats for abusing Congress on account of the Reconstruction Act. "What has Congress done that merits the condemnation of rebels?" he demanded. "They are prisoners, enemies captured in war, with no rights, no privileges, no anything but what the government in its magnanimity sees proper to give them." While using his rhetoric on the Democrats, Warmoth turned the patronage against the dissident Republicans. He and Conway persuaded Edward McPherson, the clerk of Congress, to take the federal printing away from the *New Orleans Tribune* and give it to the *St. Landry Progress,* a pro-Warmoth paper (and later to the *New Orleans Republican,* of which Warmoth became part owner).

Warmoth recognized a hindrance, and the Democrats a help, in Winfield Scott Hancock, the general whom President Johnson had appointed to replace Philip H. Sheridan as commander of the Louisiana-Texas military district. Himself a Democrat and a future presidential candidate of the Democratic party, Hancock had absolutely no use for the Reconstruction Act, and he tried as hard to sabotage it as Sheridan had tried to make it work. Hancock revoked an order of Sheridan's requiring that blacks be listed as prospective jurors, and he removed nine New Orleans council members whom he considered objectionable. Yet he asserted the supremacy of the state governments over the military authority, thus flouting the will of Congress, which had specified that state and local officeholders were to be subordinate to the district commanders in their efforts to enforce the Reconstruction Act.

One incident in particular showed the affinity between Hancock and the ex-rebels, or so it seemed to one Republican from the North, who witnessed the event. On March 4 the local firemen marched in a parade and then filed by the St. Charles Hotel—the wartime headquarters of Benjamin F. Butler—where Jefferson Davis now was staying. With heads uncovered, the firemen paid their respects to the "Ex-President" while Davis stood watching at a parlor window. Then the men sang the Confederate favorite *The Bonnie Blue Flag* and sent up repeated cheers in which they coupled the name of Hancock with that of Davis. According to the disgusted Republican observer, "It was a great triumph for *Davis & Hancock.*"

Soon after that, General-in-Chief Ulysses S. Grant having ordered him to reinstate the city councilmen he had removed, Hancock resigned as district commander. But Hancock had already done his worst, from the viewpoint of Republicans, to stack the cards against them. And his successor, General Robert C. Buchanan, was no better. While the ballots from the April 16–17 election were still being counted, a Republican from Ohio complained:

> The military were against us, the police were against us, and so were five hundred deputy sheriffs. Buchanan signed an order which justified arrests for very slight cause, and the sheriffs and policemen arrested for merely asking a man to vote the Republican ticket. Hundreds of arrests were made for no cause and parties lodged in jail and by the terms of the military orders could not be released until the election was over. The commissioners of election were against us. The commissioners changed ballots while putting them in the boxes—and ballots were changed before counted. Negroes were intimidated & coaxed and every means resorted to to prevent their voting or to induce them to vote the [Pure Radical] Republican ticket.
>
> Hancock played the devil. He appointed the registrars and he appointed the commissioners. Hancock picked out every scoundrel he could find and lent his aid to every scheme of the rebels.

Even so, the Warmoth Republicans had no real cause to worry. When the tally was complete, it showed that the people had ratified the new constitution by a vote of 66,152 to 48,739. And they had elected Warmoth governor by a bigger margin, though a smaller total: 64,951 to 38,046.[14]

On rainy and chilly nights toward the end of the Mississippi winter the fireplace blazed in the old mansion on Tokeba plantation. Albert T. Morgan, his brother Charles, their partner Mr. Ross, and occasionally a Yankee neighbor or a Negro employee warmed themselves in front of the fire and talked of their prospects and their problems. If they listened for it they could hear the murmur of the Yazoo River, already swollen and still rising, as it made its winding way through the darkness outside. Should it overflow its banks, it could kill the growing cotton.

The partners—Morgan, Ross & Company—desperately needed a good harvest this season of 1867. They had already spent more than $36,000 on their planting enterprise. All they had to show for the investment was the previous year's crop of only 68 bales, worth less than $14,000, besides their horses, mules, oxen, wagons, plows, harness, and other equipment. The partners also had invested $11,000 in their sawmill, which was yet to pay for itself. So they were "cramped for money," as Albert put it.

A more serious threat than the rising water was the mounting unfriendliness of the ex-Confederates. Rebecca White, from whom the Morgans rented Tokeba, did her best to stir up hostility. She shocked her friends with the report, for example, that Albert had declared a black wench to be every bit as good as a white lady. The passage of the Reconstruction Act further aroused resentment against the Morgans and other Union veterans, a total of nineteen of whom were residing in Yazoo County. Neither the Morgans nor anyone among their former comrades could appear on the streets of Yazoo City without being harassed or insulted in some way. At the approach of a Northerner the local ladies would gather up their skirts and turn their backs. The men would huddle in front of the delivery window at the post office and make it awkward for the Northerner to pick up his mail, or they would block the sidewalk and tell him to walk in the street along with the "niggers."[15]

There was no point in protesting to any of the local authorities—sheriff, mayor, constable, justice of the peace, or clerk or judge of the circuit court—since all of them were former Confederate army officers and were scornfully anti-Yankee and anti-black. Albert Morgan had tried appealing to the sheriff after a black man complained that nothing was being done to prosecute his son's killer, who was the son's one-time master and recent employer. The sheriff made no serious effort to press the case. The mayor required a permit, costing a dollar a year or more, for any black person to reside in Yazoo City. "The government of this city is particularly faulty and corrupt," the local Freedmen's Bureau agent thought; "a number of the places of business are kept open on the Sabbath, and the number and character of the houses of debauchery is almost incredible for a place of this size. The mayor shows no disposition to give justice to the freedmen."

In the eyes of the Yazoo establishment the Morgans were compounding their villainy by setting up schools for black children. On Tokeba the Morgans had their employees tear down the old slave jail and use its hewn logs to build a schoolhouse. The hands, many of them once chattels of Colonel J. J. B. White and his wife Rebecca, enjoyed the symbolism as well as the actuality of this transformation of the jail. Soon the "Morgan school" contained thirty-one pupils eagerly studying the first, second, third, or even fourth reader. When the Morgans' sister Mollie came down from the North with a friend to teach in the school, both of the young women were ostracized by Yazoo society. Meanwhile the Morgans provided lumber and the services of a carpenter to help add a schoolroom to a small wooden Negro church in town. Before long, white youths were gathering around this humble structure and, with their "nigger shooters" (slingshots), were breaking the windows and making life miserable for the teacher and her little charges.[16]

With the coming of spring the Yazoo and its tributaries rose still higher, and for several weeks most of the land remained under water. Attendance at the Tokeba school fell off, many of the pupils being unable to get there from the neighboring plantations where they lived. More serious, the cotton crop was now definitely going to suffer. About two-thirds of the plantation laborers in the area worked for a share of the crop, and the rest for wages. Expecting a harvest too poor to live on, sharecroppers began to leave their landlords—thus violating their contracts—and tried to hire themselves out to an employer. Some of the planters used threats and violence to hold their tenants and enforce the contracts. The Freedmen's Bureau agent, anticipating trouble, recommended to the military authorities that they station a few troops at Yazoo City. All along, planters had objected to the Bureau's intervening in their relations with tenants or hired hands, and the planters became doubly indignant when the Bureau agent made the rounds of the plantations to see that the blacks registered to vote. The whites acquired yet another grievance when, in response to the agent's request, a company of cavalry arrived.

Albert Morgan himself had occasion to resent the Bureau's interference in what he considered his own affairs. He got so angry with one of his laborers that he told him to leave Tokeba at once and without taking his wife with him. The man went to the Bureau official to complain, and the agent sent him back with a request that Morgan allow him to stay a little longer and that Morgan refrain from separating him and his wife. "The Col. [Morgan] soon called and stated that he was a Northern man, had fought for four years for the National banner, and that he was now trying to plant and needed discipline on his place. Thought I would be satisfied that he would do justice to the freedman." So the agent reported. "He remarked that he ran his own plantation and that the military authorities had no right to interfere. He left the office in a great passion and his expressions were not tempered at all with flattery to myself."[17]

Morgan was becoming more and more irascible because of his bad luck as a planter. Once the spring flood had subsided, the firm's six hundred acres of cotton surprisingly began to recover, and by July there was a quite promising stand. Then armyworms started across the fields in regiments. In little more than a week these voracious green-and-yellow-striped caterpillars consumed most of the tender plants, leaving the fields practically as bare as if a fire had swept through them. The Morgans could salvage a little of their cotton, and they could count on a few hundred acres of corn, but to keep going they would have to rely mainly on the sawmill. The high water had actually helped their lumber business by enabling them to float out some previously inaccessible cypress logs. They were confident that at least they would be well able to pay their semiannual rent of $3,150 when it fell due on December 1.

In August, three months before the due date, the sheriff appeared with a court order "attaching and levying on the following property To wit one saw mill & fixtures one hundred tier of logs more or less one hundred thousand feet of lumber more or less." Colonel White, as attorney for his wife, had told the local judge he had reason to suspect that the Morgans were going to remove their assets and then default on the rent. The Morgans now offered to give security for the payment of everything they prospectively owed Mrs. White, but neither she nor the judge nor the sheriff relented in the slightest. Instead, the sheriff ordered the Morgans not to operate the mill, and he put an armed guard over it to see that they did not. Of course, they needed to keep the mill running in order to meet their obligations. To them it was becoming perfectly obvious that the Whites and the local authorities were conspiring to ruin them.

"The case has assumed the form of a persecution on account of principles instead of a prosecution for just claims," the Bureau agent informed the military district headquarters. "Capt. Charles E. Morgan is an unassuming quiet Christian man" (whatever might be said of his hot-headed younger brother Albert). The agent received the reply that his duties were "required more particularly in cases relating to the colored people" and that "no action from here" was "deemed necessary" in the Morgan case. The Morgans themselves appealed to the district commander, and he did order two postponements of the sheriff's sale, but he finally concluded there were "no just grounds for military interposition." The sheriff proceeded to dispose of the Morgans' property for a fraction of its value to see that the rent was paid—one whole month before the rent was due.[18]

Having lost the mill and the accumulated logs and lumber, the partners in Morgan, Ross & Company could not afford to go on operating the plantation. They had no choice but to wind up their entire business. This they did, and Ross went back to Illinois, much the poorer for his Mississippi venture. The Morgans were left with very little except debts, which they owed not only to friends and relatives who had invested in the firm but also to laborers who had not received all the pay due them. For the Morgans, the dream of economic opportunity in the South, after less than two years of trying to make it a reality, had ended in utter disillusion. Yet they decided to stay on. Now that the Southern states were about to be radically reconstructed, perhaps a new day was dawning in Mississippi—a new day with new opportunities for young men from the North.

Until the Morgans faced the destruction of their lumbering and planting business, they had been too closely preoccupied with making it a success to give much attention to local politics. Other Yankees in the Yazoo country were busily organizing a Republican party and preparing for the fall elections, at which the voters were to indicate whether they wanted a constitutional convention and who their delegates should be. To make nominations, the Republicans scheduled a mass meeting for September 21 in Yazoo City. Blacks flocked into town from the surrounding countryside to take part.

Now the United States cavalrymen stationed in Yazoo City had a chance to show dramatically which side they were on. They were here presumably to protect the blacks as well as to preserve order and assure justice in disputes between blacks and their white landlords or employers. So, at first, the leading whites looked upon the soldiers as oppressors. Then the best families began to exercise their Southern hospitality and charm on the commanding officer of the cavalry company, Second Lieutenant Daniel Hitchcock. They invited him to their homes, wined and dined him, and let him know that they cherished only the kindliest feelings toward their former slaves and toward the Union—whatever their feelings might be toward Yankee adventurers who attempted to mislead the blacks. If Lieutenant Hitchcock had ever been inclined to sympathize with the local Republicans, black or white, he soon changed his mind about them.

On September 21, when the Republicans gathered in Yazoo City, the lieutenant demonstrated that he was in league with the local establishment. He dispatched a note to his friend the mayor: "Having heard that some of the freedmen who are in town attending a political meeting have been drinking and are going about armed, and fearing you may have some disturbance, I send you a party of men whom you can use in case of necessity." There was no necessity. Among the more than three thousand blacks present, a few had brought pistols, but the Freedmen's Bureau agent collected the weapons and deposited them in his office. No one in the crowd showed signs of drunkenness or rioting. No, the Republicans proved to be the victims rather than the perpetrators of violence. From behind a fence of upright boards a white man threw stones into the crowded field, striking one black in the forehead and seriously injuring him. Then, acting on the mayor's orders, a squad of cavalry rode in, broke up the meeting, and drove out of town every black who could not show a license from the mayor permitting him to remain as a paid-up resident.[19]

Later, without benefit of a formal nomination, three ex-officers of the Union army announced themselves as candidates for the three places allotted to the area in the constitutional convention. The November election was only a few days away when a group of blacks, including some of his recent employees, came to Albert Morgan and requested him to run. He preferred a native Southern white Unionist as one of his running mates, but after failing to find a suitable and willing one he agreed to combine with a fellow Union veteran and a Negro blacksmith. Hence the voters could choose between two Republican tickets, but they could not choose a Democratic one, since the ex-Confederates did not bother to put up candidates. The ex-Confederates concentrated on trying to defeat the proposition for holding a constitutional convention. During the election, which took five days (three of the fifteen polling places being open each day), anti-Republican whites gathered around the ballot boxes not to vote but to coax or coerce the blacks. Morgan and other candidates went from place to place to counteract the opposition by campaigning on the spot.

The Morgan ticket having carried the county, and the convention proposition having carried the state, Morgan at the age of twenty-seven could look forward to the overthrow of the old regime in Yazoo and in Mississippi. A veritable revolution was under way. From it Morgan was to emerge as, temporarily, a "dictator" in the eyes of local whites and a "savior" in the eyes of local blacks. For the time being, though, he could barely find the means to get to the convention or to survive until it met. Once it had begun, he could count on receiving travel expenses of forty cents a mile and compensation of $10 a day—income that would be a lifesaver. Fortunately, he had managed to hide a small quantity of lumber and save it from the sheriff's sale. With the proceeds he paid his share of his ticket's campaign expenses: one-third of $61, most of which had gone for printing ballots (each set of candidates provided its own), a small amount for hiring horses, and not a cent for "treating" the voters to the usual whiskey and cigars. He also bought a new suit to wear at the convention, and he had enough left over to pay his way to Jackson, where the convention was to meet on January 7, 1868, in the capitol.

On a cold January morning Morgan boarded a stagecoach in front of the Yazoo City post office. As the coach started out he could see men and boys on the street making faces at him and could hear them yelling: "Halloa, polecat!" "Where ye goin', polecat?" "G'wain ter de nigger convention?" His fellow passengers, even the Northern drummers among them, had only scowls for him. Twenty-six miles east of Yazoo City he caught the southbound train, on which he encountered further displays of scorn. In Jackson he soon stood out as a leader among the 97 delegates, of whom 79 were Republicans, 23 Northerners (19 of them Union veterans), and 18 blacks.[20]

Less than a week after the opening of the convention Morgan introduced and got passed a resolution for a committee to look into Governor (and former Confederate General) Benjamin G. Humphrey's recent proclamation (December 9, 1867) warning blacks against any attempt to rise up and seize the planters' lands. Certainly, with the advent of winter, there had been signs of increasing discontent and indeed desperation on the part of blacks. The cotton yield was so slim that many sharecroppers found themselves in debt to the landowner, and many laborers were without work or savings, their hard-pressed employers having long since discharged them. Rather than see their families starve, some of the blacks were slaughtering the planter's hogs and stealing his corn. Like former slaves elsewhere, those in Yazoo County had been disappointed in their hopes for a redistribution of property—"forty acres and a mule"—at Christmas or New Year's in 1865-66 and again in 1866-67. Now, in 1867-68, with Radical Reconstruction in progress, hopes were revived. "There is an idea existing among the freedmen that there are large portions of land in the state which is to be given them, and all the necessary implements furnished by Govt. to cultivate it," a new Freedmen's Bureau agent reported from Yazoo City on December 31, 1867, "and some of the freedmen have informed me they were told so by political speakers." But if any of the freedmen were plotting to kill the owners and take the land by force, Governor Humphreys would or could give no evidence of it when the investigating committee called on him.

Morgan left his mark on the incipient constitution as a member of the franchise committee, which he managed to dominate. He missed some of its early sessions because of illness, a recurrence of his malaria and other war-related ailments. When he returned to the committee, a majority of its members favored a plan to disfranchise only those whom the Fourteenth Amendment would bar from office (essentially the one-time military and civilian leaders of the Confederacy), and to disfranchise them only for a time. He now prepared to disfranchise them permanently and to do the same to all who refused to swear: "I admit the political and civil equality of all men, so help me God." The Fourteenth Amendment provision would disqualify only about 2500 men in Mississippi; the oath would likely prove an obstacle to a much larger number.

After the franchise committee had approved the Morgan proposal, the convention as a whole proceeded to debate it with some heat. Charles H. Townsend, a Northern delegate but a rather conservative one, offered a comparatively mild substitute and demanded a roll call, which the president of the convention refused. Townsend then called the president an autocrat and, after provoking a noisy argument, challenged another Northerner to a fight. This man declining, the feisty though still convalescent Morgan offered to take his place and followed Townsend outside to the capitol grounds. There, after the two had sparred a while, other delegates and then bystanders joined in, until constables arrived to stop the mêlée. Finally the convention adopted the Morgan article.

When, in the spring, the stage brought Morgan back to Yazoo City for a visit with his brother and their friends, the downtown loafers had a new epithet for him—one that sounded to him like "key-ah-pit-ba-ah-ger-r-r." But he and his associates could find encouragement in the progress the convention was making. Still, the Democrats were coming to life. Their newspapers throughout Mississippi were ridiculing the "Nigger Convention," the "Black and Tan Menagerie." The delegates, the *Jackson Clarion* was saying, "have no constituency outside of the ignorant black rabble whom they are seeking to convert into convenient tools for the promotion of their own selfish ends." As the convention dragged on, not concluding its sessions until the middle of May, the talk of conservative Southern whites grew more and more ugly. There was reason to doubt whether, in the forthcoming elections, the new constitution would carry, burdened as it was with Morgan's disfranchising clause.[21]

March in Jacksonville was certainly not the wintry month that Harrison Reed had known up North in Neenah, the Wisconsin town of which he was co-founder. Nor did Florida seem likely to chill his hopes in the way that Wisconsin repeatedly had done. Here, on this balmy and backward edge of the sunny South, was surely the arena where at last, after fifty-three years of life, he might successfully exercise his political and promotional talents. The long-range outlook for the state's development had been looking better and better to him ever since his return nearly two years before. To be sure, one thing essential for his happiness was now missing: the presence of the lovely Chloe Merrick, who, after founding and operating black orphanages in Florida, had gone off to do the same in the Carolinas.

Not that Reed himself was particularly concerned about the welfare of blacks. He was much more interested in the construction of railroads and the encouragement of trade. These things, he believed, required close cooperation between enterprising Northerners like him and enterprising Southerners like David Levy Yulee, a Jewish immigrant from the West Indies who had become Florida's leading railroad builder and one of its United States senators before the war. Reed wanted to join with Yulee and other prewar Floridians to form a party that could reconstruct the state in the way that would be best for business. He had no enthusiasm for the Reconstruction Act, with its directive for Negro suffrage. Good Johnson man that he was, he would have preferred to see the state continue under the President's restoration plan.

Reed occupied a strategic position from which to influence Florida politics. He was still Johnson's appointee as postal agent for the state and, as such, had a certain amount of federal patronage to dispense. More than most postal agents, he also had direct access to the resources of the Post Office Department, for he was an old friend of the postmaster general, the ex-governor of Wisconsin, Alexander W. Randall. Still, if Reed were to emerge as a leader of the Florida Republican party, he would have to control quite a few votes of newly enfranchised blacks. And he had much less appeal for them than did another federal officeholder in the state, Thomas W. Osborn.

A New Jersey native, Osborn had graduated from Madison (now Colgate) University, gained admittance to the New York bar, and then fought four years for the Union, rising to the rank of colonel. After the war he headed the Freedmen's Bureau in Florida for a time. While doing so, he managed to please the former masters without antagonizing the former slaves. He was accepted socially by conservative whites. Leaving the Bureau, he took a job as federal register in bankruptcy and formed a partnership with a leading secessionist of 1861 to practice law in Tallahassee. Once the blacks had become prospective voters, he began quietly organizing them as a secret society, the Lincoln Brotherhood.

Reed needed to get the support of Osborn, with Osborn's following among both blacks and Bureau agents, and at the same time to hold the support of property-owning, business-minded Floridians. It proved difficult to do. In March 1867 Reed and Ossian B. Hart, son of the founder of Jacksonville, brought together two hundred of the area's wealthiest men to form the Jacksonville Republican Club. Reed and Hart then arranged for the club to call a state Republican convention in July. By that time, Osborn was beginning to be suspect among the former Confederates, and so was Reed. Governor David S. Walker wrote to Yulee in regard to Osborn: "While he has been proposing to us the most conservative sentiments, he has been all the while deluding the negroes into joining secret leagues. . . . Reed is no better." In fact, Reed himself thought Osborn was going too far in catering to blacks. Reed said he was suspicious of anyone who was always "bowing and scraping to persons of that race."

Already Reed was facing a new threat to his position in the party, a threat which made it all the more urgent for him to patch up his alliance with Osborn on the one hand and with such men as Walker and Yulee on the other. The new danger arose from a combination of three Radical politicians, Liberty Billings, Daniel Richards, and William U. Saunders. Billings, a native of Maine and for a time a Unitarian minister in New Hampshire, had first appeared in Florida as the chaplain of a Negro regiment. Richards, a New Yorker by birth and an Illinoisian by residence, had come in 1866 as an agent of the Treasury Department. Saunders, a mulatto and an erstwhile Baltimore barber, had arrived with the Union army during the war. With the financial backing of both the national Union League and the Republican congressional campaign committee, Billings and Richards and Saunders went from plantation to plantation to enroll blacks in local chapters of the League. The three traveled in a wagon behind a team of mules, and so the men themselves came to be known as the Mule Team.

Reed had the satisfaction of seeing the Mule Team fail to dominate the July convention that he had helped to sponsor. But the three Radicals, along with like-minded Republicans, then held a separate meeting and nominated a competing slate of candidates for the constitutional convention. The Democrats refrained from putting up a ticket. They merely hoped, by dissuading blacks from going to the polls and by staying away themselves, to defeat the proposition for remaking the state's fundamental law. To do so would be a sizable task for the Democrats. According to a special state census of 1867, whites outnumbered blacks by approximately 82,000 to 72,000, but nearly a fifth of the white men were temporarily disfranchised under the Reconstruction Act. The registration from July to September produced a list of only 11,148 whites as compared with 15,434 blacks qualified to vote. Substantially all the blacks (if free to vote as they wished) could be expected to vote Republican, and so could at least 1,000 and perhaps as many as 2,000 of the whites.[22]

The November returns amounted to a setback for both the Democrats and the Reed Republicans. Though narrowly, the convention proposition carried, and the Radicals won a majority of the convention seats. All three members of the Mule Team were elected as delegates. One of the three, Billings, had beaten out Reed's Southern friend Ossian B. Hart. "God is good and the '*radical team*' has triumphed," Richards exulted.

"Three 'humble individuals'—Colonel Liberty Billings, Colonel Wm U. Saunders, and myself—have literally created the Republican party in Florida and *made* a convention with two thirds if not three fourths our friends."[23]

Reed was now very much on the defensive, but he had yet to marshal his full resources, and soon the odds appeared to change in his favor. Right after the November election the Republican congressional campaign committee ceased channeling funds for the Florida party through the Mule Team. Later the Radicals in Florida lost and Reed and his faction gained a powerful ally when Johnson replaced Pope with George Gordon Meade as commander of the district. Then, in January 1868, Reed returned from a Washington visit with promises of increased support from his friends in the administration and in Congress. Not only could he draw upon Postmaster General Randall for large amounts of cash but he would also distribute the congressional campaign committee's money that previously had been at the disposal of his factional foes. So he was well equipped to compete with them for mastery of the constitutional convention, which General Meade had scheduled to meet in Tallahassee on January 20.

The railroad trip frm Jacksonville to Tallahassee, 160 miles to the west, was slow and tedious, the train stopping a long time at every station and overnight at Lake City. Finally, at the journey's end, there was excitement enough. Tallahassee was not a very big town, having as it did a resident population, more black than white, of slightly less than two thousand (in comparison with Jacksonville's slightly more than two thousand). With the convention in the offing, though, the Tallahassee streets, bars, billiard parlors, inns, and boardinghouses overflowed with a growing crowd of restless strangers—delegates, lobbyists, soldiers, gamblers, whores, beggars, curiosity-seekers, and miscellaneous hangers-on. Reed, no delegate but the foremost of the lobbyists, occupied a suite in the leading hotel. From his headquarters there he could command his forces among the delegates in the nearby capitol, a gleaming white edifice a bit reminiscent of the Italian Renaissance and, in its setting of live oaks, really quite imposing for a place so remote and primitive as Tallahassee.[24]

Reed soon discovered that Billings, Richards, and Saunders were getting the jump on him. They had arrived early and had instructed other Radical delegates to do the same. With a hired team of mules and a carryall, the Mule Team saw that its followers, most of them black and poor, were picked up at the railroad station and taken to a rented house, to receive free room and board. "We find it necessary to do this," Richards explained privately, "as our delegates may be placed under obligations to other parties and under influences we shall deplore."

On opening day, January 20, only 30 delegates answered the roll call in the capitol. The number elected to the convention was 46, of whom 18 were black and the rest almost evenly divided between Northerners and

Southerners. A few of the Southerners were wartime Unionists who, still resenting their treatment at the hands of Confederates, were as Radical as any of the blacks or the Mule Team three themselves. The great majority of the delegates present on that first day were Radical in spirit, and before the day was over the team had succeeded in organizing the convention and electing Richards as its president.

For the next ten days Reed and his forces struggled to keep the Radicals from going ahead and drawing up a Radical constitution. As additional delegates arrived, he invited to his hotel headquarters and blandished those he thought susceptible. One of them was Philadelphia-born Jonathan C. Gibbs, a Presbyterian preacher with a "good intelligent yellow African face" and with an education from Dartmouth College and the Princeton Theological Seminary—all in all, perhaps the most cultured and certainly the most eloquent member of the convention. Gibbs used some of his eloquence to describe, on the convention floor, what had just transpired between him and Reed. "Who is this agent of Andrew Johnson who is manipulating members?" Gibbs demanded, after saying he had found colored delegates drunk on Reed's whiskey at the hotel. "It is the man who said to me on coming here, if you will come along with me we can harmonize all troubles and make a constitution to suit us. I simply replied, how dare you make such a proposition?"[25]

While Reed's ally Thomas W. Osborn rallied the anti-Radicals in the capitol, Reed made plans to expel the Radical leaders and seize control of the convention. He expected to win a majority to his side through an enticement that Gibbs (for the moment) might resist but others could not. Delegates were becoming more and more hard up, since they were being paid not in money but in scrip, the state's rather vague promises to pay. With the funds at his command, Reed could offer to cash the scrip—but only after the convention had been purged and reorganized.

It had been raining nearly every day, and the thunder was quite heavy at times. "Perhaps the stormy weather affects the minds and acts of the political thunderers now present in Tallahassee," the *New York Tribune*'s local correspondent wrote on January 29. "Certain it is there is a storm brewing." The reporter elaborated:

> The stormy element of the Convention and lobby, known as the "Reed Party," "Conservative Party" or "Opposition Party" (that is, opposition to the Billings party), comprises, its members believe, strength enough to oust Billings from his seat whenever they can bring the guns to bear which they have been mounting, under cover of darkness and caucus, every night since the Convention met.
>
> The bitterness existing between these factions is almost as bitter as between Radicals and Rebels. The "opposition" complaint is that "strangers have come into the State and have undertaken its reorganization without giving the 'Southern loyalists' a fair share of the responsibilities and honors of reconstruction." As an impartial observer, I do not see the point of this argument. It is true that Messrs. Billings, Richards, and Saunders, &c., are

> claimed to be non-residents, or ineligible to seats, and, for aught I know, may be "political adventurers" who have come into the State for the purpose of reconstructing it . . . but I cannot help noting among those opposed to "the mule team" there are also some "Yankee adventurers," including Messrs. Dennett, Osborn, Purman, Cessna, &c., in the Convention, and the great power behind the throne, Harrison Reed, United States Mail Agent and, as some persons fear, a secret agent of Andrew Johnson to prevent reconstruction at all hazards, even if it must be by breaking up the Convention.

Reed thought his men were ready to counterattack the next morning, Thursday, January 30. It dawned the coldest that most Tallahassee residents could remember. Mud froze in the streets, and water in the hotel wash basins. Though the sun shone brightly, the day did not warm up much, for the wind remained sharp. Inside the capitol the debate was warm enough, the tempers hot. When the sun went down, leaving briefly an eerie opalescent glow, the Reed forces had yet to get control of the convention. On Friday they failed when they lost a critical motion by one vote. But Reed was not about to give up.[26]

On Monday, Feburary 3, when the convention reassembled in the capitol, the Reed delegates were absent. So the Radicals, all but a few of them black, had things to themselves. By Saturday they had drawn up and signed a constitution and had nominated candidates for offices under the proposed government, with Liberty Billings as the nominee for governor. The absent delegates, practically all of them white, were meeting in the town of Monticello, about twenty-five miles away, and were drafting a different constitution.

This document, as completed, would authorize the governor to appoint most of the state and county officials, and it would limit each county to a maximum of four representatives in the legislature. Thus, offsetting heavy black concentrations in several counties, it would check black power in both state and local government. By contrast, the Radicals' constitution would make most state and county offices elective and would apportion legislative seats according to population. Blacks then could share in politics in proportion to their numbers.

On the following Monday, February 10, the absentees were back from Monticello. About midnight they slipped into the capitol, and during the early morning hours they proceeded to elect officers and adopt rules for carrying on a constitutional convention. For the next several days, while the Reed men continued to occupy the capitol, there was doubt as to which of the two conventions would be recognized as the legitimate one. Billings, Richards, Saunders and their fellow delegates resumed sessions in a Negro church and on the public square. Gathering from the countryside, angry blacks milled around the capitol and threatened to drive out the men they denounced as usurpers. Federal troops arrived, at Governor Walker's request, to patrol the streets and protect the capitol. Then General Meade came from Atlanta to take personal charge.

After a week, on February 17, Meade ordered all the delegates to get back together in a single convention. In it the Reed forces won over enough of the Radicals to gain a majority of the entire number (46) of delegates originally elected—something Billings and his associates had never achieved. The convention then expelled Billings, Saunders, and two others on the grounds that they were not legal residents of Florida. It replaced these four with men friendly to Reed, among them Ossian B. Hart, the prominent ex-Confederate whom Billings had run against and defeated in the fall election. Finally, after one more week, the convention adopted the Monticello constitution by the solid majority of 28 to 16. After adjourning, the majority nominated Reed for governor.

It was Reed's turn to gloat. "The destructors have been overthrown and the state saved to 'law and order,'" he wrote to his conservative friend Yulee. "Under our constitution the judiciary and state officers will be appointed, and the apportionment will prevent a Negro legislature." But Billings, Richards, and Saunders insisted that *their* constitution was the genuine one, and they went to Washington to present their case to the Joint Committee on Reconstruction. Reed went too. He took with him some convincing arguments: his constitution alone had been adopted by a majority of the total of elected delegates, and it alone bore the district commander's stamp of approval. The Joint Committee, the committee of Thaddeus Stevens and his fellow congressional Radicals, decided in favor of the Reed document and against the Radical one.[27]

Back again in Florida to campaign for the constitution and for himself, Reed at first expected the support of conservative Southerners who had been cooperating with him against the Mule Team. He was offering them a constitution that would disfranchise few if any of them. He now also offered them a share of the state patronage, including high offices in his administration, once he was elected with their aid. Nevertheless, most of his recent conservative allies now turned against him and his constitution, reactivated the Democratic party, and nominated their own slate of candidates. The Radical faction of Republicans also ran its ticket, but soon began to fall apart. Saunders, the mulatto member of the Mule Team, defected to Reed's side, and so did Gibbs, the high-principled Afro-American divine. Reed continued to enjoy the backing of the postmasters and mail carriers, the Freedmen's Bureau agents, and the congressional campaign committee. In the May elections he won the governorship and the constitution gained approval by large majorities.

His old antagonist Lyman D. Stickney, who once had got him fired as a United States tax commissioner, now could do no more than reiterate his spite. Reed "is regarded by those who have known him longest as characterless," Stickney wrote after the election. "But for his Mail Agency he could not have figured at all in the politics of the State." Perhaps not. In any event, Reed had nothing more to fear from Stickney. And with the dignity of the governorship about him he might in due time dare to ask Chloe Merrick for her hand.[28]

CHAPTER 5

I Believe in the People
(1867-1868)

During the winter of 1867-68 news followers in the North got the impression that Northerners led—and misled—the constitutional conventions then meeting in the South. "A good deal of bitterness of feeling has been shown in all the conventions in regard to the presence, and great prominence as members, of what the Louisiana people call 'carpet-baggers,'—men, that is, who are newcomers in the [Southern] country." So the high-minded E. L. Godkin, in New York, told the readers of his reformist, purity-in-government weekly, *The Nation*. He added: "Many of these Northern men are fully deserving of the contempt bestowed upon them." But he was merely echoing what the recent rebels were saying.[1]

In truth, of the more than 1,000 delegates to the ten conventions, fewer than 200 were wartime or postwar arrivals from the North. And only about 250 were blacks. The majority were Southern whites, of whom fewer than half were Conservatives, or Democrats. Still, it must be conceded that, whether for good or for ill, the Northerners exerted an influence far out of proportion to their numbers.

Two of the conventions, in North and South Carolina, opened at exactly the same moment, at noon on January 14, 1868, and also adjourned simultaneously on March 17. In North Carolina 88 of the delegates were Southern whites, 19 were other whites, and 13 were blacks. Among them all the most influential (and the youngest, at twenty-nine) was the failed nurseryman from Ohio, Albion W. Tourgee. In South Carolina only 36 were Southern whites and 15 outside whites, but 73 were blacks, who made up the majority in this convention alone. Among the delegates one of the most effective (and far and away the most scholarly) was a thirty-two-year-old alumnus of Yale College and the Harvard Law School—Daniel Henry Chamberlain.[2]

Chamberlain was born on June 23, 1835, on a Massacusetts farm. As a boy, he did his share of the chores on the place and, in winters, attended common school. At fourteen, he was eager to continue his education. Both his stern, strong-minded father and his deeply religious mother were more than willing for him to do so, as they were for all ten of their children, of whom he was the next to youngest. But money was a problem. The parents did manage to send young Henry to Amherst Academy for a few months, and there he acquired a taste for Greek and Latin that was to stay with him the rest of his life. At seventeen he began to teach school while continuing to work on the family farm. After two years he had saved enough to pay for part of a year at the Phillips Academy in Andover.

Not till he was twenty-one did Chamberlain make another attempt at college preparation. He then (1856) enrolled in one of the country's few public secondary schools, the Worcester High School, about fifteen or twenty miles from his home. By that time he was a thin-faced young man with a very sober, earnest look, a man not only older but also more studious than most of his schoolmates. His instructors were so well impressed that, to keep him in school, they enabled him to earn his living expenses by making him a part-time teacher while he was still a student. During vacations he worked and saved to pay his way to college, but when the time came he did not have enough, and before finishing he had to borrow heavily from his high-school instructors, college professors, and other generous and admiring friends.

At Yale, as at other American colleges of the period, much of the intellectual and social life centered on the student literary societies. These maintained libraries and sponsored debates, which constituted the main competitive sport. Into it Chamberlain promptly went with a will. While in high school, he had trained himself by listening to the great orators of the day—in particular, the abolitionists Henry Wilson, Charles Sumner, William Lloyd Garrison, and Wendell Phillips—and in college he continued to do the same. When he himself got up to speak, he might at first betray his background with a bit of a rural Yankee twang, but once he was well under way he stuck to the polished accent of a New England sophisticate. His sober eyes lighted up, his somber face became animated, and though he spoke calmly and clearly, never ranting, his words conveyed fire and feeling as well as logic. At Yale he won the first prize in every debating contest he entered, and on graduating he received the annual medal for excellence in oratory.

As an undergraduate, Chamberlain meanwhile had not neglected either his studies or campus politics. He did very well in the classical languages, and he carried off the top graduation honors in English composition. Among his fellow students he gained a reputation as the ablest politician on the campus. When he left he took with him a letter of recommendation in which the college president described him as "a born leader of men."

With his Yale bachelor's degree in hand, Chamberlain went on directly to the Harvard Law School. That was in 1862, when the Civil War was dragging on with no prospect of an early victory for the Union. A confirmed antislavery Republican, Chamberlain already had felt some embarrassment at staying out of the army, but his friends assured him he could best serve his country by completing his education. Besides, he could not soon repay his college debts (some $2,000) unless he qualified himself to practice law. And he could never repay them if he were to be killed in battle. So he remained at Harvard, helping professors with the writing of their law books, and honing his forensic skills in the legal and political discussions of the student "Parliament."

By November of his second year at Harvard he concluded he could delay no longer—he must leave without a law degree and go to war. "I am told that it is foolish for me to go, that I can do no more in the army than the less educated," he confided to a friend. "I know all that, but years hence I shall be ashamed to have it known that for *any* reason I did not bear a hand in this life-or-death struggle for the Union and for Freedom." He borrowed some more money, to pay for life insurance that would protect his creditors, and early in 1864 he departed from Cambridge and from civilian life.

Through the intercession of one of his professors, Chamberlain obtained from Governor John A. Andrew a commission as lieutenant in the Fifth Massachusetts Cavalry, a black regiment the governor was promoting. Before long Chamberlain took a desk job as an adjutant, keeping records for the regiment's colonel, Charles Francis Adams, Jr. Chamberlain saw little or no action but did get a look at fallen Richmond when his regiment entered the city on Lee's withdrawal. After the surrender he was stationed out West, on the Rio Grande, until late in 1865. He then returned to Boston to be mustered out.

An accident led Chamberlain south again—an accident to one of his Yale classmates, James P. Blake. After serving as a missionary-teacher among the freed people on the South Carolina Sea Islands, young Blake had opened an office for the practice of law in Charleston. Soon afterward word came to his home in New Haven that he had drowned, and his father asked Chamberlain to go to the scene, find and return the body, and dispose of any remaining property and debts. Chamberlain arrived in Charleston early in January 1866 and, after making inquiries there, hired a boatman to take him to Edisto Island. Here he learned that Blake, on a Christmas visit with former missionary associates, had been rowing two young women friends down St. Pierre's Creek in a bateau when it capsized in the strong current of the outgoing tide. Each woman's body had been recovered, but Blake's presumably had been swept out to sea.

While the errand saddened Chamberlain, it also intrigued him. The low, lush, subtropical coast, mild even in January, had a sensuous allure for someone used to the bleak chill of the New England winter. The money-making potential of the area was an even greater attraction to Chamberlain, seeking as he was a way to dispose of the college debts that still hung over him. On the Sea Islands, Northerners were buying or renting plantations and were talking of the fortunes to be made from cotton. For Chamberlain to rent a place and start a crop, he would have to go even more deeply into debt, but the opportunity seemed well worth the risk. He found a likely plantation on Wadmalaw Island, which he had passed on the way from Charleston while looking for the remains of his college friend.

Like most other planters from the North, Chamberlain fell far short of getting rich from cotton. In two seasons of planting on Wadmalaw he did little more than break even. Then, in the fall of 1867, came the chance to supplement his income by gaining a political job—a humble enough one as delegate to the state constitutional convention, but one that might prove a stepping stone to much higher things. And in the convention he could exercise the debating talent and legal training that had gone unused for approximately four years.[3]

On its beautifully landscaped grounds the Charleston Club House reflected the aristocratic taste of the club's former members, all of them high-toned gentlemen. Unable to keep up with expenses after the war, they had disbanded the club and sold the property. Its new owner, the federal marshal for the district, rented the Club House to the military authorities for the use of the constitutional convention that met from January to March 1868.

Handsome though the building was, it provided only a makeshift convention hall. The ballroom lacked a gallery for spectators, so they had to be accommodated on the same floor as the delegates. Temporary wooden railings marked off the official area. On both sides were crude benches on which sat the visitors, nearly all of whom were black. In between were armchairs which the delegates occupied, the white minority in the front rows, the black majority in the rear. In front was a desk on a low platform for the presiding officer, and on each side of it a long table for newspaper reporters.

Some of the reporters were from the distant North, and they gave more or less objective accounts of the proceedings. The local newsmen vied with one another in scurrility. They seemed especially indignant that this "Black and Tan," "Great Unlawful," "Great Ringed-Streaked-Striped," this "Congo Convention" should desecrate an edifice once reserved for gentlemen. The reports made particularly nasty fun of the black delegates. Along with ridicule, the papers offered threats. "I have for some time thought that when negro government went into operation it would be impossible to preserve the peace of the country," the *Charles-*

ton Courier quoted former Governor Benjamin F. Perry as saying. "A war of races must ensue and it will be the most terrific war of extermination that ever desolated the face of the earth in any age or country."[4]

On the convention floor a handful of well-educated and eloquent blacks did most of the talking. Daniel H. Chamberlain was less voluble than they and less so than two or three of the whites, but when he spoke he was conspicuously calm, clear, and to the point. A leading member of the judiciary committee, he championed its proposals but did not confine himself to them. Often he sounded like a schoolmaster, as when he patiently explained that *residence* was a technical term and did not mean mere presence in the state, or when he appealed to his peers to eschew personalities. Early in the proceedings he moved to expel the *Charleston Mercury* editors, who were particularly vicious in the racism of their reporting. The editors' "blackguardism," he said, tended to a breach of the convention's peace. "The members do not want the excitement and disgrace of personal encounters within the walls of this house, or anywhere else, in consequence of articles published in the papers of the city."

Most of what Chamberlain had to say, on this and subsequent occasions, was what the black majority wanted to hear. Though he voted against a debtor stay law and insisted on the sanctity of all "just, legal debts," he opposed requiring the payment of debts owed for the purchase of slaves—debts that some South Carolinians were still trying to collect. He made his longest speech in favor of invalidating all such claims. The war, he insisted, had established two principles: the "perpetuity of the American Union" and the "sacredness before the law of human rights." Now the state constitution must recognize the revolution that had taken place. "Blazon it on that Constitution until the blind shall see and proclaim it, until the deaf shall hear that, hereafter, in no court of South Carolina shall the question ever be raised whether one man has a valid claim to property in another man!" The delegates did blazon it on the constitution.

What the blacks most needed, after emancipation and enfranchisement, was an economic basis for self-dependence—land. The Freedmen's Bureau had been intended to settle freed people on lands that had been abandoned, and Thaddeus Stevens had been talking of confiscating plantations and dividing them among former slaves, but very few blacks had yet realized their dream of owning a farm.

In the South Carolina convention one of the delegates, Richard H. Cain, proposed a plan for making land available. Cain, a mulatto, born free in Virginia, had been educated in the public schools of Ohio and at Wilberforce University, had preached in Brooklyn, New York, and had moved to South Carolina in 1865 to do missionary work among the freed folk. He did not propose that his fellow delegates consider anything so drastic as confiscation but only that they call upon Congress to grant the state $1,000,000 for buying land, dividing it into small farms, and selling these at low prices. "I believe," he declared, "if the same amount of money that has been employed by the Bureau in feeding lazy, worthless men and women, had been expended in purchasing lands, we would to-day have no need of the Bureau."

Rising to second the Cain proposal, Chamberlain said he knew personally the condition of the "loyal majority" of South Carolinians, and he knew they needed some such measure of relief. "They do not own one foot of land. The last two years' disasters to the cotton crop have left them without anything to do. Around them are the greedy, merciless, relentless few who own every foot of the soil." Chamberlain was beginning to sound more radical than the plan he was defending—and more radical than its sponsor. He seemed to be playing the role of the Gracchus brothers, those agrarian revolutionaries of ancient Rome, with whom he would have been quite familiar as an avid student of classical lore. Indicating the newspaper reporters in front of him, he went on:

> I am aware that the pencils at that table are waiting only too eagerly to gibbet to the hatred and scorn of this community any man who dares to say that, as between the landholders and the landless, as between the white and the black, as between the rich and the poor, his sympathies are with the poor, the landless. And I am willing to incur all the odium of saying that I am not only in favor of this measure of positive relief, but when we are told that the sheriff's hammer is about to fall and scatter these hated and unjust monopolists of land, I am ready to take the odium, let the hammer fall, and pray may God speed its way.

After hesitating, Chamberlain asserted he was no politician and was "not apt and experienced in the way of the politician." Then, like a politician on the stump, he resumed with a glance at his black listeners outside the railings on his right and left:

> I shall not expose myself to the rebuke of the Chair by addressing myself to the audience behind the bar. But if it were parliamentary to address a word to my friends who are not members of this Convention, but are within the sound of my voice, I should say to them: Struggle on, be of good cheer, and remember whatever distress, greater if possible than those which are now upon you, shall overtake you, remember there are some men here sent by your votes; there are some men true enough and still brave enough . . . to lift their voices and record their votes for a measure of just and honest relief to your pressing necessities.

Chamberlain concluded by saying there was a constituency that would someday judge the delegates, and those who "stood true" and "defended the loyal majority of this State" would be "able to abide by that judgment." Obviously he was making himself one of those who could abide by it.

Newcomers to the state should be eligible for the gratitude and the reward of that constituency, in Chamberlain's opinion. As for his own chances, a proposed four-year residence requirement for officeholders would disqualify him, though the alternative suggestion of two years would not. But he preferred, in the very first election under the new constitution, to permit any man already in the state to run. He hoped no one would think he was "influenced by any interested motives." It simply seemed to him that South Carolina, for the moment, was "very much in the condition of a territory." In admitting a territory the practice had been to make all its residents full citizens of the newly formed state. "I propose," Chamberlain said, "that nobody now here, who are citizens of the United States, shall be deprived of the opportunity of being a candidate for Governor or any other office within the gift of the people." And he succeeded in putting such a provision in the constitution.

Chamberlain would have liked to see the voters choose the state's judges as well as its governor and other officials. In the meetings of the judiciary committee he argued for the popular election of judges, but other members favored appointment by the governor, and as a compromise he agreed to election by the legislature. When the committee reported to the convention, someone on the floor renewed the idea of gubernatorial appointment. Again addressing the spectators rather than the delegates, Chamberlain repeated his argument for popular election, though he was willing to settle for legislative appointment, and so was the convention majority in the end. "I believe in the people," he declaimed. "I believe they are just as competent to select their Judges as they are to select their Governors." Many of the Northern states, he pointed out, had adopted the elective system, and not only they. "In several of the Southern States in process of reconstruction, the election of Judges, from the highest to the lowest, has been given to the people, and the whole progress of the age is in favor of removing power from the hands of the few, and bestowing it on the many."

Modernization, together with democratization, was the keynote. Chamberlain touched upon the theme again in urging that equity courts be abolished and that equity procedures be left to the regular courts of law. In other states, he said, this had been done with general satisfaction. "I believe that, in retaining the old equity system of South Carolina, we are blindly going against the legal spirit of the age." The convention followed Chamberlain's advice and brought the state up to date in this respect as well as in others.[5]

The completed constitution also provided for the following improvements: A statewide public school system was to be established. Debtors were to be protected from creditors by means of a homestead exemption. Women's property rights were to be extended. Divorces were to be obtainable without special legislative acts. The governor, other state officials, and presidential electors—all of them previously chosen by the legislature—were to be elected by the people (who, for the first time, would be allowed to vote for their governor and their president). And the equality of all citizens, white and black, in political and civil rights was to be recognized. In short, one of the least democratic of all the states was to become one of the most democratic.

Before finishing the constitution, the Republican delegates caucused in the Charleston Club House to nominate candidates for the legislature and state offices. Nearly all the contenders were delegates, and all the top winners proved to be white. The nominee for attorney general was Chamberlain—that bright young man who had quit his law studies four years before and had never argued a case in court.[6] The choice for governor was a man not present in the Club House as a delegate but present in Charleston as the state head of the Freedmen's Bureau. He was Robert Kingston Scott.

General Scott had paid little attention to state politics during the spring and summer of 1867, when South Carolina Republicans were organizing and preparing to elect delegates to the constitutional convention. He was busy with his own affairs and with the Freedmen's Bureau's work. As a well-to-do real-estate speculator, with extensive holdings of farmland and town property in northwestern Ohio and in southern Michigan, he had to keep instructing his agents back home in Napoleon, Ohio, what to buy and what to sell. More continuously and more urgently he had to concern himself with providing relief for South Carolinians both white and black who suffered from crop shortages and other economic ills. The threat of widespread starvation persisted.

"This terrible state of things can only be averted by men of capital of the North coming to the aid of both planter and freedman," Scott thought at first. "Capital can be invested here more profitably than in any part of the United States with security that is undoubted. Planters will give a lien on the growing crop with bond and mortgages on land to secure the payments. And with the Freedmen's Bureau as an auxiliary to see that contracts are kept in good faith there is an absolute certainty that no loss can take place." But Scott failed to find moneyed men to make the kind of loans he considered necessary.

So he turned from Northern capitalists to the federal government. Congress appropriated funds for Southern relief, and he persuaded the Bureau chief, General O. O. Howard, to let him use some of the money for crop-lien loans of a sort. Under Scott's plan the Bureau advanced supplies to planters in the hardest hit parts of the state and took a lien on the anticipated crop as collateral.

Scott also supervised the distribution of immediate relief to the needy. He dispensed rations from the Bureau, cash and goods from Northern charities, and money out of his own pocket. From one white Charlestonian he received thanks for a $100 gift he had forwarded from the Boston Southern Relief Association: "it has been distributed for the benefit of twenty-five persons, sixteen white and nine colored people without regard to their ecclesiastical connection." From another white Charlestonian he learned what had become of $50 he personally had donated. The man divided $30 of it among four dependent women, two of them widows. With the remainder he bought groceries for "a family in the *greatest want*" who had been "rich with every comfort" before the war. "I have had great pleasure in relieving the necessitous from your bounty," this go-between added. "It must gratify you much having the means of dispensing so many blessings amongst our suffering and distressed people."[7]

As Republican politicians lined up voters for the fall elections, Scott showed that he was determined to keep the Freedmen's Bureau out of politics. He voiced his disapproval when some blacks, registering to vote, behaved in what he considered a disorderly way. He disapproved again when leaders of the Union League, the Republicans' secret club, tried to interfere with his Bureau agents. Thus he rebuked Daniel H. Chamberlain after hearing from a semiliterate correspondent on one of the Sea Islands: "i Expect that you Has Received Some Kind of a pertioten [petition] a Gainst Doct McHenry as agent of the Burow on this ilant. Riten by D. H. Chamberlin with the Leage members names all sind to it." When four Bureau employees won election as delegates to the constitutional convention, Scott immediately took steps to dismiss them from their Bureau jobs. In response to the *Charleston Mercury's* accusation that his agency was involved in politics, he averred that not one of its men was a candidate for office or a member of the Union League "or any other organization of a political character." Whether or not this was strictly true, it was no doubt what he wanted to be a fact.[8]

At the moment, in the fall of 1867, Scott had no political ambitions of his own to be realized in South Carolina, nor did he have any personl desire to remain in the army or in the state. His political as well as his economic interests still centered on Ohio. After the October elections there he heard from one of his Napoleon associates that the outlook for Republicans was poor in Ohio and throughout the North. Why were voters turning against the Republican party? "I answer, there are many causes, among others the Negro, taxation of bonds, reconstruction, Freedmen's Bureau, etc. They are tired of radical rule—and want, and will have, a change." From a Toledo friend, Scott received a letter welcoming him back to Ohio's tenth congressional district, which the new Democratic legislature was about to deform with a gerrymander. This friend had read in the paper that Scott was about to be mustered out and, by January 1, 1868, would finally be a civilian once again.

Scott stayed on in South Carolina not because he wanted to stay but because prominent white South Carolinians wanted him to. The conservative *Columbia Phoenix,* though having little good to say about the Bureau, praised him for his "judgment and sound discretion" in administering it. Leading citizens went so far as to petition President Johnson to keep him in charge. One group said his direction of the Bureau had been "beneficial," and another testified: "Genl. Scott is well and favorably known to both freedmen and planters, both of whom have full confidence in his ability and integrity of purpose." Before the end of 1867 Scott received an order revoking the one that would soon have mustered him out. He remained out of a sense of duty.[9]

He was still thinking of his duty when, early in March 1868, he got a letter asking him to allow his name to be used as a candidate for governor. The letter was signed by eight "loyal citizens," all of them outstanding members of the constitutional convention. Six were blacks; one of the whites was a Southerner by birth and the other a Northerner—not Chamberlain. In reply, Scott politely declined to run. He explained that, in his present position, he bore responsibilities so serious he dared not abandon them. But when the president of the convention notified him that the Republicans had gone ahead and chosen him as the "standard bearer of the party," he changed his mind and accepted the nomination.[10]

Scott was the perfect candidate, the perfect governor-to-be, according to a letter he received soon afterward and was to treasure for the rest of his life:

> Allow me to congratulate you upon your nomination as Governor of the ancient State of South Carolina. Had I the opportunity, I would congratulate the people of South Carolina more heartily, for they are more fortunate than you in this matter. The fact is . . . that you are the only man for the position. You will harmonize more effectually the discordant elements amongst both whites and blacks than any other man, and while you will be able to guard this yet comparatively helpless race against any infringement of their rights, you will also be able to wisely restrain them against prejudice in opinion or intemperance in action, and will lead them gradually up to good citizenship. Thus you will bind them with strong chains to the most important issues of the Commonwealth. This has been your character heretofore in your dealings with the colored people. They all cling to you and hang their political faith upon your teachings. The whites recognize in you one who is not controlled by partisan views or biased by personal prejudices, and they trust you. They regard you as a straightforward, honest man, one not easily swayed by any influences other than candid convictions of right. They look upon you, also, as having the interests of the planter at heart, as well as those of the laboring classes. They think you, in short, a man of comprehensive mind, from whom openhanded justice may rightfully be expected toward all classes. . . .
>
> Gen'l, it will be a pretty "big thing" to be Governor of South Carolina—the first Governor under a truly Republican form of government. It will bring with it many responsibilities and annoyances, but it will be a historic position, and will bring much renown to the present nominee. I congratulate Ohio upon having one of her citizens selected for this honorable position.[11]

Now that he was a candidate, Scott counted upon his subordinates in the Freedmen's Bureau to help elect him. He gave money to agents for them to use in campaigning for him. As the chief dispenser of Bureau supplies and rations, he was in a position to gain the support of many party workers without spending much money of his own. In the April voting he and the rest of the Republican slate won handily, and the new constitution easily carried. Still, the Democrats of South Carolina were not about to give up. In a protest to Congress they asserted that a superior race was being "put under the rule of an inferior race" and that "the people of our State will never quietly submit to negro rule." The air was ominous, and there was little prospect that Governor Scott—or anyone else—could do what his admiring correspondent expected of him, could "harmonize . . . the discordant elements among both whites and blacks" in South Carolina.[12]

Albion W. Tourgee was approaching the nadir of his North Carolina existence when, in March 1867, Congress passed the Reconstruction Act, which was to rescue him from economic disaster. One of his recent partners in the nursery near Greensboro had involved the partnership in obligations that Tourgee was unaware of—until the creditors took action to collect. He could not both pay his rent and keep up with his accumulating debts, which in May he tallied up to $1,015. So he quit the nursery business.

For the time being he still had his newspaper, the *Greensboro Register*, but to make it profitable he needed a government printing contract, and he failed to get one even though he went to Washington to lobby for it. "I *do* hope and pray that all may be well with us," he attempted to console his wife, Emma, "and I believe the God we try to trust will not desert us." In June he had to let the paper go. Reduced to poverty, he was now living with Emma in a log cabin, wearing threadbare clothes, and riding a bony white nag that, like him, had a blind eye. Emma panicked when the thought struck her that she might be pregnant.[13]

Politics continued to be Tourgee's obsession, and it proved to be also his salvation. On his old white horse he went from one Republican meeting to another, carrying a pistol. Earlier he had refused to cooperate with W. W. Holden and other Southern whites who, though opposed to Johnson's plan of state restoration, had also been opposed to Negro suffrage. Now the Holdenites were backing the congressional Reconstruction program, and Tourgee was calling for union among all Unionists and was working closely with native white as well as black Republicans. On the Fourth of July he was the main speaker at a gathering of some 70 whites and 1500 blacks. In August he began to serve on the local board of voting registrars—and began thereby to earn a little money.

In September he could hope to earn still more, once the constitutional convention should meet. He was one of the Republican nominees for

Guilford County's two allotted delegates, and he had the endorsement of the Negro community of Warnersville, on the southern edge of Greensboro. He had opposition, for an anti-radical faction of Republicans nominated two other candidates, and the Conservatives (Democrats) endorsed them.

During the campaign Tourgee presented himself as the champion of the common people, black and white, against the landlords, capitalists, and aristocrats. He did not propose confiscation but did call for a more equitable distribution of land. Still, the Conservative *Greensboro Patriot* labeled him and his associates as *"agrarian radical* confiscators" and accused them of trying to rouse the poor against the rich. Apparently Tourgee had quite a few of the common people behind him, for in November he won a place in the constitutional convention, though by a margin of only 43 votes. About one hundred men in the county were temporarily disfranchised under the Reconstruction Act. If they had been able to vote, Tourgee undoubtedly would have lost.[14]

Soon after the election he had a fleeting hope of getting a better-paying job than convention delegate. A vacancy occurred on the state superior court, and the commander of the North and South Carolina military district, General Edward R. S. Canby, was going to appoint someone to fill it. Former Governor Holden recommended Tourgee, but incumbent Governor Jonathan Worth denounced him as a man of "detestable character." Worth still fumed when he recalled the story Tourgee had told and Northern newspapers had published, more than a year before, about the Negro corpses dragged from a Guilford County pond. In correspondence with his cronies, Worth referred to Tourgee as a "mean Yankee adventurer" who had "come among us to traduce us and get office." Worth acquired a new grievence when Tourgee complained to General Canby that local law enforcement officials discriminated against Southern Unionists, and Canby ordered the arrest of the Caswell County sheriff. Before making the judiciary appointment, Canby asked Worth for evidence of Tourgee's bad character. Worth then wrote to leading citizens of Guilford and neighboring counties and urged these men—some of them Tourgee's friends— to join him in disparaging Tourgee. In the end Tourgee failed to get the judgeship, and Worth took credit for depriving him of it.[15]

"I happen to know that Gov. Worth used every inducement to get some of my enemies here to slander me," Tourgee later wrote from Greensboro. "I intend to make the old scoundrel smart for it." Soon Tourgee would get his revenge on Worth and the rest of the "secession bastards," as he called them. Soon he would be a judge with a more regular and more lasting tenure than Canby's appointee would have. Meanwhile, with his salary as a convention delegate, he would be able to maintain Emma and himself on a somewhat improved living standard.[16]

The hall of the House of Commons, where the North Carolina convention began its proceedings on January 14, 1868, was a large square room in the capitol in Raleigh. From the high domed ceiling a chandelier hung down, and curving around the sides and the back of the room was a gallery, the area beneath which was known as the lobby. The seating arrangement on the floor, conforming to the gallery's semicircle overhead, took the shape of a fan. In the third row, just to the right of the center aisle, sat the youngest member of the convention, Albion W. Tourgee.

In a nearby private home he roomed with his considerably older but quite like-minded colleague from Guilford County, the Pennsylvania-born preacher, long a North Carolina resident, George W. Welker. The two were very congenially, comfortably, and reasonably accommodated: "Board lights fuel &c $50 per month." Tourgee's pay as a delegate would take care of his living expenses and leave him a fair income besides, for the convention agreed on a per diem of $8, plus mileage of 20 cents, but the pay was slow in coming. "I will send some money as soon as possible," he reassured Emma. "You know God has never yet forsaken us."

He wrote to Emma whenever he got a chance, even dashing off a letter at his seat in the convention hall while some other delegate held forth. "I am up in the Commons Library today all alone with a good fire now writing to you," he penned one Sunday. "There is more office-getting, wire-pulling than a little," he went on to confide. "I have concluded to do nothing more to secure a nomination for anything whatever." Yet he continued to seek a nomination for Congress, procured the endorsement of a Republican meeting in Guilford County, and expected Emma to serve as a campaign manager by circulating petitions and performing other political chores. "It is a little unfortunate that you are not a man," he joked, "but on the whole I am not a little grateful that you are of the feminine gender." Even though he was providing so little money for her, he instructed her to set aside all she could for campaign expenses.[17]

For the present, Tourgee had little time or energy of his own to devote to politics. He helped persuade the convention to hold night as well as day sessions, and he kept himself busy day and night. He served on the master committee to plan the convention's work and also on three other committees, those on local government, the judiciary, and criminal punishments. On the convention floor he spoke often on these subjects and on other matters as well. Before long he came down with a bad cold, but he kept going despite a congested head, a persisting cough, and after any special exertion an overwhelming sense of fatigue.

He soon made himself the most conspicuous of all the delegates. He became so famous, in the eyes of at least one North Carolinian, that the man wanted to interview him for a biography. Tourgee replied that his life was, he hoped, "still too incomplete to be a proper subject for biographical effort," but he did vouchsafe a few personal revelations. For one thing, he confessed that he had had "ample opportunities to acquire a thorough knowledge of almost every natural science" but had wasted his time "in the classic twaddle of the colleges." Nevertheless, "By this means I have secured an education which I believe finely prepares me to discharge the duties of a member of this Convention."[18]

At the same time, Tourgee became so infamous among North Carolina Conservatives that he received a disproportionate share of the obloquy they directed at what they called the "nigger convention" (though it contained 107 whites and only 13 blacks). "The pillars of the Capitol should be hung in mourning to-day for the murdered sovereignty of North Carolina," the *Raleigh Sentinel* observed when the "Convention (So Called)" opened. "In the seats which have been filled by some of the best and truest sons of North Carolina will be found a number of negroes, a still larger number of men who have no interests or sentiments in common with our people but who were left in our midst by the receding tide of war, and yet others who have proven false to their mother and leagued with her enemies." Subsequently, reporting the proceedings, the *Sentinel* burlesqued them while identifying every black speaker by his race and every Northern white by the state he had come from. Another paper, the *North Carolinian,* referred to the convention as a museum of "Baboons, Monkeys, Mules, Tourgee, and other Jackasses."[19]

Though hopelessly outnumbered, the Conservatives in the convention put up a desperate struggle to keep a white man's government in North Carolina. Despite the requirements of the Reconstruction Act, they argued at length against Negro suffrage, basing their objections on a theory of racial incompetence. "Just now Dr. Ellis . . . is instructing us on anatomical and physiological differences between white and black races," Tourgee noted in the midst of the debate. "One would think that no one had ever been cognizant of any scientific truth before."

When Tourgee himself spoke on the suffrage question, he made it an issue of democracy and human rights, not race. "The war from which we have just emerged," he declared, "was a struggle between Republicanism and Oligarchy, between the rights of the people and the usurpations of Aristocracy, between the elevation of the masses and the exaltation of the few, between feudal theory and free principles." He proposed to exclude from voting and officeholding not the blacks but the whites who refused to avow the political equality of blacks. This proposal failed to carry, and the constitution was to disfranchise neither blacks nor whites.

As chairman of the committee on local government, Tourgee brought about a further democratization of North Carolina. Previously the people of a county had not been allowed to choose the county magistrates; instead, the state legislature had appointed them. Now Tourgee prepared a plan that he based on the Pennsylvania arrangement, with which he was familiar. The North Carolina counties were to be divided into townships, and the voters in each of these were to elect a town clerk and two county commissioners. For the first time, North Carolinians were to enjoy local self-government.[20]

Tourgee also applied democratic and progressive ideas to the judicial system. Adopting his recommendations, the convention agreed to allow the people, instead of the legislature, to elect judges. It also eliminated equity courts and combined law and equity proceedings. On this subject Tourgee was something of an expert. He possessed a first-hand acquaintance with the combined system as it operated in Ohio and New York, two pioneers in the reform, which fifteen other states had adopted. He had corresponded with its greatest advocate, David Dudley Field, who had inscribed and sent him a copy of his pamphlet on the New York legal code. In his own presentation to the North Carolina convention Tourgee described the old-fashioned "distinction between actions at law and suits in equity" as a "distinction accidental in its origin, cumbrous and artificial in its nature, tedious and expensive in practice, and not unfrequently mischievous and unjust in its results."

Tourgee had less success in advocating another legal reform that was dear to his heart—the limitation of the death penalty. He would have preferred its complete abolition but saw no chance for such a proposal. So, as a member of the committee on punishments, he urged only that the death sentence be restricted to cases of "wilful murder." Unable to get enough support for that, he settled for a compromise by which the legislature, in defining capital crimes, would be permitted to include arson, burglary, and rape. He wished the legislature might, for a time, forget to act at all—"in which case we shall have the advantage of a few months without any instance of legal murder," as he told his Quaker friend Dr. Nereus Mendenhall. Tourgee hoped that, when the legislature did act, it would limit capital punishment to murder in the first degree. As soon as the legislators should meet, he urged Mendenhall, the Quakers ought to petition for this partial reform rather than insisting on the Quaker principle of no death penalty at all. "Such another opportunity to humanize our laws may not present itself in half a century."

Consistently the humanitarian, Tourgee tried to give the poor a break in the new constitution. He secured a provision that would spare them, as defendants in criminal proceedings, from having to pay court costs—as they formerly had to do—even when they were adjudged innocent. He failed to put a temporary stay on all debts, but succeeded in delaying foreclosures and exempting homesteads. With his Guilford colleague, Welker, he undertook to relieve the mass of the people further by repudiating the entire state debt. "He would be a fool who would emigrate to North Carolina," Tourgee argued, "if the new State is to be saddled with the debts of the old." Instead of throwing off the state's obligations, however, the delegates added to them by approving the issue of state bonds to aid railroad construction. Tourgee opposed aid to one railroad, the Wilmington, Charlotte and Rutherfordton, which had a Conservative president but enough Radical supporters to get what it wanted. Tourgee relented and approved assisting another line that was to run from Greensboro west to Salem and was so popular among his prospective constituents that, as a would-be congressman, he dared not stand up against it.[21]

Before the convention completed its work, Tourgee was gratified to receive his colleagues' endorsement on two occasions. First, they stood by him when, in a comic-opera sequence, he refused to sit down after the presiding officer ordered him to do so, and the president called upon the sergeant-at-arms to arrest him and bring him before the bar of the house. Almost unanimously the delegates defeated a motion to reprimand him; then they passed a resolution to discharge him as "unlawfully arrested." Next, and much more important, his fellows chose him as one of three commissioners who, in accord with a proposal from his judiciary committee, were to codify the laws of the state. The pay was to be $200 a month, and the term of office three years. "So you see," he promptly wrote to Emma, "I am tolerably well provided for in case I should not get the nomination for Congress or fail of election."

To Conservatives, who thought it a desecration of the capitol for blacks and other Republicans even to sit there, the document that emerged from the sittings seemed the utmost in sacrilege. John A. Graham, a member of the convention and of a most prestigious North Carolina family, complained that a "stranger boy" had done away with the legal system North Carolinians revered. Governor Worth said the judiciary provisions of the new constitution were, by themselves, enough to make him "view it with horror." Others lamented the loss of even the time-honored name of the General Assembly's lower chamber: the House of Commons was henceforth to be known as the House of Representatives. To Tourgee, the complainers were simply old fogies who worshiped the customs, habits, and laws of the "dim and shadowy days of yore" and who were incapable of realizing there was "such a thing as positive progress in government." They and their ancestors had always reviled anyone who "dared to disturb the ancient dust upon the shield of that hide-bound, venerable Rip Van Winkle, North Carolina."[22]

On Tuesday morning, March 17, 1868, the delegates assembled for the last time. The Republicans proceeded with the ceremony of affixing their names to the new constitution, and the Conservatives, refusing to sign it, left the convention hall. Once the ceremony was over, the big bell in the capitol dome rang out. Tourgee opened a Freedmen's Bureau song book and struck up the Union wartime favorite "Rally 'Round the Flag," in which the remaining delegates and visitors joined. Then he and several others made impromptu speeches. One of the most cheered was the handsome, plausible, ingratiating Milton S. Littlefield, formerly a

Union general from Illinois, just now a railroad lobbyist in this convention. More singing followed—"Hang Jeff Davis to a Sour Apple Tree," "Old John Brown," "Yankee Doodle," "Hail Columbia," "The Star-Spangled Banner." Finally, at noon, the convention adjourned.[23]

Tourgee was tired and had a hacking cough as he rode the train to Greensboro at the end of March 1868. A strenuous campaigner for the new constitution, he was returning from a speechmaking tour of the southeastern part of the state. He was suffering from a respiratory infection that persisted after the cold he had caught at the convention. He was also suffering from a political disappointment, for he had failed to get the congressional nomination he wanted.

Nevertheless, he was optimistic, even buoyant. Though not a candidate for Congress, he was a nominee for Seventh District judge of the state superior court, with the promise of a much longer tenure than a congressman would have. And he had high hopes for the success of Reconstruction in North Carolina and throughout the South when he reflected on the news from Washington. One of the main obstacles to that success was, apparently, about to be removed. Andrew Johnson, having been impeached, was on trial and surely would be convicted. "I have hung on here through rain and shine and now it begins to look tolerably fair," Tourgee wrote, after arriving back in Greensboro, to a former army comrade in Ohio, who had inquired about the prospects for a new Republican paper in North Carolina. "I think we shall have a human country here sometime, and when we do, it will be a good place for any *human* journalist. . . . Come down after the impeachment is over and look about some."

As Tourgee and his fellow Republicans saw it, they were carrying on a struggle for the rights of the common man, white as well as black. They were trying to bring about the "education and elevation of the toiling masses," as the North Carolina Union League put it. They were trying to prevent the former masters from keeping the former slaves at the level of serfs or peons. And they aimed to stimulate prosperity by welcoming northern enterprise and capital, instead of complaining about "Northern adventurers" and "Radical emissaries" as the leaders of the late rebellion were doing.

Privately, leading Conservatives recognized the issue of class. "I regard the proposed new constitution as virtual confiscation. No government based on the will of mere numbers, irrespective of intelligence and virtue, can last long." So Governor Worth fretted in confidence. "Civilization consists in the possession and protection of property."[24]

But, drawing the color line, the Conservatives in their public statements made the question primarily one of race. "WHITE MEN, ORGANIZE!" they proclaimed at a meeting in the Guilford County courthouse. Do not vote for "surrendering the State to the negro and his demagoging white office-seekers." The proposed constitutional changes will "bear heavier upon the common people than the more wealthy," so let's "hear no more of 'the rich man's war and the poor man's fight.'" No, "be true to your RACE" and "hand down to your children a white man's government!" Thus, to break up the Republican coalition of poor whites and poor blacks, the Conservatives raised the bogey of Negro rule, though blacks constituted only about 36 percent of the people in North Carolina, a much smaller proportion of those in Guilford County, and a still smaller share of the candidates on the statewide Republican ticket.

When, on April 3, the local Republicans met in the same courthouse, to make nominations for county offices, the main speaker was to have been the party's state leader and gubernatorial candidate, Holden, but he had other things to do. In Holden's absence, Tourgee agreed to deliver the principal speech, though he was quite hoarse, rather short of breath on account of his congested lungs, and almost too weak to stand up. As a crowd filled the courthouse—the pride of Greensboro, with its stuccoed brick walls, its Corinthian columns, and its graceful wooden tower—he could estimate a total of about 200 blacks, some of them women, and perhaps 250 whites, of whom at least 200 were obviously not Republicans. "The whole secesh *élite* of the county were present," it seemed to Tourgee. "I was in very bad condition but I was bound to give them one piece of my mind if I never spoke again." He kept going for nearly two hours, saying things that turned the faces of his Conservative listeners into "seething cauldrons of suppressed wrath."

After Tourgee had finished his harangue and his fellow partisans had agreed on county candidates, an obese and no longer youthful man from among the "secesh *élite*" waddled forward and demanded the right to be heard. This was "Young Jim" Morehead, an ex-colonel of the Confederate army and a member of a very prominent Greensboro family. Morehead announced his own candidacy for the state senate, spoke at length along the Conservative line, and challenged anyone who was "white in the face" to meet him in the various county precincts and debate the merits of the proposed constitution. Angered, Tourgee rose to reply and, according to his own account, "laid on lustily." Afterward he was satisfied he had had much the better of the set-to—though the Conservative *Greensboro Times,* reporting on this "great mass meeting of the negro party," gave the impression that Colonel Morehead had completely outclassed "JUDGE toogee."

Tourgee had intended to take the train to Raleigh that same evening to consult with Holden and then to go on an electioneering trip with him. The party needed Tourgee—"I am counted our best stump speaker"—and he hated to let the party down. But his exertion had done him in, and he was too ill to go, so he decided to stay home and rest a while. He resumed his traveling and speaking before he had fully recovered, and in a week he was back in bed, "an invalid condemned to inordinate rations of whiskey cod-liver-oil, and doing nothing."[25]

To the Conservatives he was a "loathsome, scurvy, low-down Yankee." He was also "the Cain-marked Tourgee," "Tourgee the infamous," and "mean, low, grasping Tourgee." But on the stump, when he was well enough to mount it, he gave as good as he got. He called one of his traducers a "foul-mouthed political pimp," and he blamed his blind eye on his ex-Confederate detractors, saying it was "the result of an ineffectual attempt to stop a particle of Confederate shell." (It was, of course, the result of a boyhood accident.)

The hazards of Southern politics could be more than verbal, as Tourgee was reminded when he read the news of the assassination of George W. Ashburne, a native Georgian, a Union veteran, and a member of the Georgia constitutional convention. Tourgee had become a close friend of Ashburne in the army, had roomed with him at the Philadelphia Loyalist convention in 1866, and had recently heard from him about the glorious future of a reconstructed Georgia. Ashburne was the victim of a persisting rebel spirit, Tourgee believed. "Kindred spirits in North Carolina are now striving to incite revolution and bloodshed among our people"—to incite the murder of men like Ashburne, or Tourgee, in this state.[26]

When the returns of the April 21–23 election were in, they did not quite come up to Tourgee's expectations, for the Republican majority was not larger but somewhat smaller than it had been in the November 1867 election. Still, he won and so did Holden and most of the party's candidates, and the constitution carried. Tourgee could look forward to two salaries from the state, one as code commissioner and the other as judge. Now he and Emma could plan to live a little better, and he arranged for them to eat at a boardinghouse for $35 per month apiece. While awaiting his pay, the two could depend on advances from political friends. He told Emma that, during his absence, she could expect a check for $200 from Milton S. Littlefield, the gracious lobbyist he had met at the convention. Or she could call upon Governor-elect Holden for $100 at any time.

Tourgee was heading north on a mission of charity. Though good times were coming for him, the outlook was less promising for most North Carolinians. "Thousands of poor whites and colored are suffering for want of bread," Holden noted in his commission to Tourgee and James H. Harris, the black vice president of the state Union League. The 1867 grain crop had been short, and the scarcity would not be over until the next harvest was in, if even then. Tourgee and Harris were setting out to appeal to Northerners for money with which to buy grain to feed the hungry in North Carolina.

On the way north Tourgee reached Washington in time to witness a historic event, the rendering of the Senate's verdict in the impeachment trial of Andrew Johnson. It was a perfect spring day, May 16, 1868. That morning a crowd of the curious, some in carriages, some on foot, moved along Pennsylvania Avenue toward the Capitol. Outside the Senate chamber policemen stopped those who did not have admission tickets, while keeping open a narrow passage for those who did. Tourgee showed his pass, squeezed through, and climbed the stairs to the gallery, which extended along each of the four sides of the chamber.

By eleven o'clock the gallery could provide standing room only, and by twelve it was jammed. The Senate floor also was full, with the senators sitting at their desks and representatives and others standing in the rear of the hall. In front, near the presiding officer's platform, was a table at which the House's impeachment managers sat. There was Old Thad Stevens, with his clubfoot, his crooked wig, his thin, taut lips, and his grim expression. And there was Ben Butler with his bald dome, his drooping mustache, and his mismatched eyes. Butler had been expecting the "obstacle"—Johnson—to be removed by apple-blossom time, but he and the other impeachers were not quite so optimistic now.

At noon the statesmanlike-appearing Chief Justice, Salmon P. Chase, took his position in the presiding officer's chair. The Senate promptly passed a motion to vote first on the last of the eleven articles of impeachment that the House had adopted. Stevens, the author of the eleventh article, had thought it would get the most support from the Senate, now sitting as a jury.

None of the eleven charges adequately presented the real grievance of the Radicals against the president, but the final one came the closest to doing so. The real grievance was Johnson's scheming to frustrate the Reconstruction Act, especially by instructing the generals in the South to disregard its provisions and by removing those who insisted on trying to carry them out. But, to many senators, it might not seem quite an impeachable offense for the commander in chief to direct and to assign and reassign those officers as he saw fit. The case called for a presidential action more obviously illegal, one more convincing as a "high crime" or "misdemeanor" in the constitutional sense. President Johnson had appeared to commit the requisite crime when, without the consent of the Senate, he removed Secretary of War Edwin M. Stanton in violation of the Tenure of Office Act, which forbade the president to remove department heads without Senate approval.

The eleventh impeachment article related this presidential offense to other alleged misdeeds. According to the charge, Johnson had pretended that Congress was "a Congress of only part of the States" (since the Southern states were not represented in it) and that hence its legislation was not "obligatory upon him"—despite his oath to "take care that the laws be faithfully executed." In dismissing Stanton, he had violated the oath by attempting to prevent the execution of both the Tenure of Office Act and the Reconstruction Act.

As Chief Justice Chase began the roll call, the suspense was high, the outcome uncertain. Conviction would require a two-thirds majority, and the impeachers could hope, at best, to obtain barely the minimum necessary vote. It all depended on Senator Edmund G. Ross of Kansas, and the rumor ran that Johnson's henchmen, tampering with the jury, had got to Ross as well as several other Republicans, whose support the impeachers had already written off. For Tourgee and all those present, the climax came when Chase, proceeding alphabetically and repeating the cumbersome question in full each time, inquired: "Mr. Senator Ross, how say you? Is the respondent Andrew Johnson, President of the United States, guilty or not guilty of a high misdemeanor as charged in this article?" Ross, having risen to his feet, replied: "Not guilty." The rest was anticlimax.

At the end of the voting, Tourgee noted on a slip of paper: "For conviction 35. For acquittal 19. The President is therefore acquitted upon the eleventh article." As the crowd dispersed, two young black men carried the furiously frowning Stevens out of the room in his chair. Though dying, he was determined to keep pressing the case, but almost nobody thought it had a chance any longer, and soon it too was to be dead. Like other Radicals, Tourgee was thoroughly disgusted. "Ross of Kansas sold out," he was convinced, "getting probably between $500,000 and $1,000,000." That was what Radicals were saying, though in fact there was, and is, no real evidence that Ross or any of the other Republicans voting for acquittal expected or received a bribe.

Tourgee went from Washington to Pittsburgh and then to Cleveland. The sight of familiar country in Pennsylvania and Ohio made him a bit homesick and, with spring well advanced, reminded him of May 1863, five years before, when he and Emma returned to Erie after being married in Columbus. "We should be so happy in this glorious home country renewing our honeymoon," he now wrote to her. "I am so lonesome without you." His health was good and he was taking his medicine regularly, he assured her, yet he was often tired and had caught another cold. He did not expect to succeed very well on his fund raising tour for Southern relief. "People that live here at the North seem to be entirely sick of the words 'South' and 'Give' in conjunction." But what troubled him most were the foreseeable consequences of Johnson's acquittal. "It will have a very bad effect upon the prospect of the Southern States."[27]

The failure of impeachment was, indeed, to mark a turning point in the history of Reconstruction. In making new constitutions and setting up new governments the Republican party had achieved its greatest successes, and Northerners had exerted their greatest influence, in the South. Henceforth the Republicans—the Northern whites along with the blacks and the Southern whites—were to see their power erode as they quarreled among themselves and struggled against their Conservative (and violent) foes.

CHAPTER 6

The Spirit of the Rebellion (1868-1869)

As long as the Andrew Johnson impeachment trial lasted, that spring of 1868, it remained one of Washington's principal diversions. Adelbert Ames attended as often as he could during his brief stay in the capital on military business. Rather slightly built but quite athletic, Ames looked neat and trim in his lieutenant colonel's uniform, and he was fairly handsome with his sharp, aristocratic features and his fashionable drooping mustache. He took a keen interest in the issues of impeachment, and he viewed the most active of its managers, Benjamin F. Butler, as something of a personal friend, for he had served under General Butler in the closing phases of the war.

Still, at the trial, Ames gave most of his attention neither to the proceedings nor to the prosecutor but to the latter's daughter, whom he had just met for the first time. She appeared regularly in the Senate gallery to hear her father present the case against the President. Adelbert Ames was thirty-two, Blanche Butler twenty-one. Those who considered Ben Butler a kind of monster could but wonder at the loveliness of his only child. She was a rare beauty, with splendid auburn hair, a radiant and vibrant personality, and a low, warm voice.

Behind Ames lay a brilliant record in the army. He had stood near the top of his class at West Point and, after his graduation, had shown unusual bravery in the first battle of Bull Run. There, while serving with a battery, he refused to leave the field when he was shot in the thigh; he kept on giving fire commands until he collapsed from loss of blood. For this performance he received the Congressional Medal of Honor. Later he fought in the Peninsular campaign and at Antietam, Fredericksburg, and Gettysburg, and he also took part in the siege of Charleston, the attack on Petersburg, and the capture of Fort Fisher. In the course of the war he was promoted to brigadier general of volunteers and, for gallantry in action, was finally brevetted a major general.

The wartime deeds of Adelbert Ames were impelled and guided by an old-fashioned New England conscience, a stern sense of military duty, and a fastidious standard of personal conduct. He had been born in Rockland, Maine, on October 31, 1835, the son of a sea captain. As a boy he accompanied his father on a number of voyages and thus saw something of the world. He excelled in mathematics and in art, having a certain talent for watercolor sketches. At home and at school he learned of the horrors of slavery and the sins of the slaveholding South. He embodied the traditions of his Pilgrim and Puritan ancestors.[1]

As a young army officer—impeccable in dress, erect in bearing, precise in speech—he seemed a terrible martinet to the raw recruits of the 20th Maine when, in 1862, he returned from the fighting in Virginia to whip the new regiment into shape. The attitude of his soldiers was revealed in letters that one of them sent to a sister: "Col. A. will take the men out to drill & will d'm them up hill and down." "I swear they will shoot him the first battle we are in." "I tell you he is about as savage a man as you ever saw." All this, however, reflected the men's inexperience and Ames's determination rather than any real savagery on his part. In battle, as his aide-de-camp once said, he "never asked men to go where he would not go himself," and "under the hottest fire" he "quietly gave his orders, and generally in the form of a request." Eschewing the common vices of a professional soldier, Ames rarely smoked, drank little, seldom used profanity, and never debauched with women. Indeed, he was about as close an approximation to Sir Galahad as was likely to be found in the Union army.[2]

When the war was over, Ames, like many another career soldier, confronted the choice of remaining in the regular army at reduced rank or seeking better opportunities in civilian life. For about a year he stayed in uniform and served with the occupation forces in South Carolina. "I am still at my duties," he informed his parents, "which consist in little more than aiding the agents of the Treasury Department and the Freedmen's Bureau in trying white men for killing negroes, of which work we have more than we can well do." In South Carolina he liked the winter climate but not the hot summers, nor could he get used to the unfriendliness of the native whites. "Fire still burns in the hearts of the people," he wrote; "and our star-spangled banner or our country's uniform are only needed to fan the flames into wrath."

Ames thought of going into a flour-milling business, which his father had started in Minnesota, and he also considered taking up the profession of law, which he began to study in his spare time. When he was mustered out of the volunteers, though, he accepted an appointment as a lieutenant colonel in the regular army. From the summer of 1866 to the summer of 1867 he took a leave of absence and made a tour of Europe. While abroad, he had second thoughts about continuing his army career. He noted in his diary: "Heretofore, I have had something to look forward to—to my West Point life—to my graduation . . . —to the war—to my advancement and its successful issue. Then, to the day of my departure for Europe and the world there." No longer did he have anything exciting to look forward to—unless, perhaps, he looked to politics.[3]

There was excitement and challenge in the struggle that was developing between President Johnson and the Republicans in Congress. "I must confess," Ames had confided to his parents while he was still in South Carolina, "I think President Johnson is nearer right than the majorities in the two branches of Congress, in the present issue. Yet, I fear he will go too far in his reconstruction and too soon relieve the South from the debt its action during the past four years has brought upon itself. Most truly, the politics of the day is deeply interesting."

While in Europe, Ames followed the American news as best he could, and in his diary he was crtical of both Johnson and the Radicals. Regarding Johnson he wrote: "He may soil his own garments, but I seriously object to his trailing his presidential mantle in the mud." And regarding the Radicals: "In affairs of state, I approve the policy of taking half if the whole is unattainable. Yet, I know many say unless we have all we will take nothing. This is illustrated by those who in the present crisis cry for negro suffrage. Foolishly, they would let such a plank in a platform be a source of great insecurity—fatally so. But I do not believe in negro suffrage."[4]

By the time Ames was back from Europe, the Radicals had prevailed and had passed the Reconstruction Act of 1867. The returning lieutenant colonel (brevet major-general) was assigned to duty with the troops in Mississippi. He now devoted himself to Reconstruction with the same conscientiousness and resolve he had shown in the Civil War. Whatever the reservations he once had held regarding Negro suffrage, the present law required it in the Southern states, and his duty was to see that the law was faithfully carried out. Moreover, he came to sympathize with the freedmen from the knowledge he gained, in Mississippi as well as South Carolina, of the "barbarous treatment" they were receiving "at the hands of some of their white neighbours." He presided over a military commission to try a gang of Mississippi whites who had killed some black men, burned their houses, and driven their families away. Such gangs continued to threaten, beat, and murder black leaders to keep them from exercising their recently acquired political rights, while state and local officials condoned and even incited the outrages.

Hence, by the spring of 1868, Ames would have sided with the impeachers even if he had not been an old associate of Ben Butler and a new admirer of Blanche. She had many other admirers; indeed, she was, in her more youthful and more innocent way, as much the belle of Washington as was Kate Chase Sprague. At the trial Ames managed to be at Blanche's side much of the time—so much that a newspaper artist sketched the two of them together. The artist presented the drawing to her, and she thought enough of Ames to treasure it. After going back on duty in Mississippi, however, he did not feel like continuing to press his attentions upon such a popular young lady. The pair were not to meet again or to communicate in any way for nearly two years. After that, they were to see a great deal of one another.[5]

Soon after his return to Mississippi, General Ames proceeded, under orders, from the army headquarters in Vicksburg to the state capitol in Jackson. Without yet abandoning military life, he was about to take a long step toward his transition to a political career. His orders, dated June 15, 1868, instructed him to assume the office and duties of provisional governor of the state, replacing Benjamin G. Humphreys, a sixty-year-old ex-Confederate brigadier-general, whom the white voters of Mississippi had elected governor under the Johnson plan of restoration in 1865. Ames's orders came from General Irwin McDowell (once the victim of bad luck at Bull Run), who quite recently had taken command of the military district that included Mississippi. McDowell had decided to remove Humphreys because of complaints that Humphreys was trying to sabotage the Reconstruction program.

Ames found Jackson an unprepossessing town of about four thousand, less than half as populous as Vicksburg and much less prosperous. Signs were still to be seen of the conflagration that had occurred with the Union capture of Jackson in 1863. Many of the hastily rebuilt stores, shops, and houses remained unpainted, giving the place a raw, frontierlike appearance. The statehouse, at least, survived in reasonably good condition, and so did the governor's mansion, a large and handsome edifice in the finest classical style, with a half-round portico of Corinthian columns and with wooded grounds occupying an entire block.

Ames sent a messenger to inform Humphreys that he was replacing him. He had to wait a week for a reply. When it finally arrived, it was full of righteous indignation and Mississippi pride. You are a usurper, Humphreys told Ames. In response to a telegram, President Johnson had made it clear that he disapproved of McDowell's removal of Humphreys. "I must, therefore, in view of my duty to the constitutional rights of the people of Mississippi, and the disapproval of the President, refuse to vacate the office of governor." Having read this, Ames detailed a few soldiers to take possession of the governor's office in the statehouse. With pointed bayonets they prevented Humphreys from reentering the office once he had stepped out of it.

Humphreys still refused to give up the governor's mansion. Always the gentleman, Ames tried to accommodate him. "I presume it is because of the difficulty of finding any other fit residence," he responded to Humphrey's refusal. "It is my wish to put you to as little personal inconvenience as possible. Under the above supposition, I have no objection to your occupying a part of the house. Next Monday, by which time you can make the necessary arrangements, I, with others, will take possession of a part of the house. So long as we may remain joint tenants, great care shall be taken not to inconvenience your family." Humphreys replied that such an arrangement would be unsatisfactory for him, so Ames ordered the commander of the Jackson post to take possession of half of the mansion.

Humphreys insisted on holding on until his "constitutional successor" should be chosen. The Mississippi election, to pass on the newly drafted constitution and to choose state officials, legislators, and congressmen, was just getting under way and was to last for several days. Humphreys was the Democrats' candidate for governor. The election followed the lines that McDowell's predecessor as district commander, General Alvan C. Gillem, had laid down. A Tennesseean by birth, Gillem sympathized with reactionary Southern whites on matters of Reconstruction and race. In Mississippi a great many of his appointees as registrars were Conservatives, and at the polling places they were able to discourage blacks from voting. There remained fewer than 2,000 federal troops in the state, too few to assure a full and honest balloting even if they had favored it, but a large proportion of the officers and men sided with the Democrats. In a free and fair election the Republicans would have had a winning margin of at least 17,000—counting only the registered blacks and omitting the white Republicans. In this election, however, the Republicans polled 7,000 votes fewer than the Democrats, who rejected the new constitution and carried their entire slate of state officials.

Republicans complained to General McDowell of gross irregularities in the polling, but he could do nothing, for President Johnson suddenly removed him from the command he had held exactly one month. Restored to the command by Johnson, Gillem reported that each side had accused the other of intimidation and fraud, but he considered the election reasonably reflective of the popular will. Still, the winning Democratic candidates could not take office, since there were, strictly speaking, no offices for them to take. The constitution having failed to pass, Mississippi fell short of the Reconstruction requirements, and so it remained something less than a semi-sovereign state. Its military government would continue, and Ames would stay on as provisional governor.

Having won reelection as regular gcvernor, Humphreys was not about to make way willingly for Ames. The time had come, he insisted, for Ames to leave the entire executive mansion for the occupancy of the duly elected governor and his family. The qualified voters, black as well as white, had unmistakably spoken, Humphreys argued. To Ames, however, it seemed that Humphreys simply did not get the point. "You entirely ignore the reconstruction acts and the action taken by those empowered to act under them," Ames wrote him with finality. "The feeling entertained not only by me but by others not to cause you any personal inconvenience has, through your own action, ceased to exist." Humphreys now would have to get completely out, Ames informed him, while reemphasizing his own wish to avoid unpleasantness. "If," he added, "you desire for political purposes to have a military pantomime, it shall be carried out with all the appearance of a reality, without actual indignity." Apparently Humphreys did desire such a pantomine, and he obtained it, he and his family marching out between two lines of soldiers.[6]

While Ames was installing himself as provisional governor, his future allies in Mississippi politics were less successful in dealing with reactionary obstructionism. They were dispirited by the failure to convict and remove President Johnson, by the defeat of the reconstructed state constitution, and by the widening campaign of anti-black and anti-Republican terrorism. They could hope for eventual succor as they looked ahead to the November national election—even though, as residents of unreconstructed Mississippi, they would have no chance to vote in it. The Republican presidential candidate seemed almost sure to win, and he was none other than the Union's conquering hero Ulysses S. Grant. But inauguration day, March 4, 1869, was months off. In the meantime the Mississippi Republicans would have to survive as best they could.

For Albert and Charles Morgan, those Wisconsinites of Yazoo City, the interval was the worst they were to experience in Mississippi until the climax of terrorism there in the fall of 1875. As the state election approached in the spring of 1868, the Morgans received so many threats they thought it advisable to have a place to hide. They and a few of their fellow "Yankee outcasts" found rooms above a shoemaker's shop in the Negro section of town. They barred the windows, bolted and braced the doors, and equipped themselves with a small arsenal of shotguns, rifles, and revolvers. Eventually the hideaway was discovered, and some of its occupants, including Charles Morgan, were arrested, tried, and convicted on a charge of carrying deadly weapons. Thus the Yazoo City authorities made a mockery of justice, since native whites customarily went about well armed and with impunity.[7]

The local Democratic paper, the *Yazoo Banner*, played upon the humorous (and murderous) inclinations of its readers with some rhyming lines to be sung to the tune of a popular hymn. The verses included the following:

Old Morgan came to the Southern land
With a little carpet-bag in his hand.
Old Morgan thought he would get bigger
By running a saw-mill with a nigger.

The chorus went, in part:

If you belong to the Ku Klux Klan,
Here's my heart and here's my hand.

Democratic newspapers throughout the state advocated the use of economic pressure against black Republicans. The *Vicksburg Times,* for one, promised to publish lists of those to be boycotted. The lists were to include not only merchants, hotels, and other establishments employing black members of Loyal Leagues but also draymen, hackmen, barbers, and other self-employed blacks who were known to be members. Said the editor: "The Southern Democrat who feeds a radical, white or black, is false to his race." The threat of economic reprisal was no idle one. Fairly typical was the case of a Yazoo County tenant farmer who fell behind in his rent because of illness and was evicted. "I have good reason to believe that had I not voted the Republican ticket this would not have been done," he complained to General Gillem after the election; "indeed my land lord informs me that if I had voted the Democratic ticket I would have had no trouble."[8]

In Yazoo County, as elsewhere in the state, the Democrats supplemented threats, propaganda, and economic pressure with outright force. When Republicans carrying the United States flag and party banners paraded through Benton, about ten miles from Yazoo City, a mob of a hundred heavily armed men broke into the procession and tried to make off with the banners, but were repulsed. The next day one of the mob shot a black man, who was expected to die. The Freedmen's Bureau agent in Yazoo City assumed the crime would go unpunished, since the local authorities were used to having things their own way. There was not a big enough military force on hand to do any good; it had dwindled to a total of one sergeant and three privates, the agent reported. He requested that at least twenty cavalrymen be stationed here before the election.

Members of the local establishment took a rather different approach to the question of law and order. Fifteen of the most prominent of them, in their capacity as the grand jury for Yazoo County, sent their own appeal to General Gillem. "The public peace of said county," they maintained, "is likely to be disturbed and broken by armed processions of freedmen banded together as a political organization and carrying banners inscribed with offensive devices and seditious inscriptions marching through and from place to place in said county." These freedmen were incited by "desperate political adventurers and office seekers." Gillem must act. "Your petitioners pray that such orders may be issued and enforced as may effectually prevent all future political processions of all parties of every color from parading in said county until after the ensuing election." This was too much even for Gillem. He answered: "It is believed that if the white people will let the freedmen alone no disturbance will occur."

In response to the urging of the Freedmen's Bureau agent, Gillem did dispatch a contingent of cavalry to Yazoo City, but these troops were of little help to the Morgans and their friends. Indeed, two of the cavalrymen fell upon Charles Morgan on a city street and gave him a savage beating (the two men were later courtmartialed and dishonorably discharged). Charles Morgan and other Republicans, most of them black, petitioned Gillem to remove the mayor as a ringleader of renascent rebels, but the mayor stayed on. The Morgans would not be able to overturn the local establishment until after Johnson had given way to Grant, and Gillem to Ames.[9]

From various points in the state, Republicans appealed to Congress. "The feelings against Northern men who entertain Republican sentiments," Urbain Ozanne wrote from Panola County, in the northwest, "exceed by far those displayed in 1860 & 61 against Union men." A Frenchman by birth, Ozanne had lived in Tennessee before settling in Mississippi; he was eventually to be the Panola County sheriff. In his letter he told how, before and during the election, "gangs of white men, opposed to reconstruction, prowled around, at night, hunting up the leading freedmen who took an active part in the canvass, perpetrating on them gross outrages, and by so doing frightening hundreds and thousands and preventing them from voting if, through threats, they could not be induced or compelled to vote the Democratic ticket." White Republicans from the North and the black men of Mississippi, Ozanne went on, were "on the same footing in the eyes of the Rebels."

These Northerners (such as the Morgans) would have to leave the state, Ozanne believed, unless Congress acted in their behalf. "They came and settled in the South with no desire to meddle in politics, but for the purpose of engaging in agricultural pursuits, and are being grossly and unjustly persecuted, because they have not seen proper to join the hosts of rebels to trample down the flag of our country, and especially because they have upholded Congress in the reconstruction of the State civil government." Congress now ought to reciprocate by assuring protection for these Northerners, by setting up a provisional government for Mississippi, and by seeing that only men loyal to the United States could hold office in the state.[10]

Ozanne addressed his appeal to Thaddeus Stevens, who in the past had been a powerful congressman but who now was gravely ill and had only about a month to live. Other Republicans in Mississippi looked to other prominent senators or representatives, the Republican from the North usually choosing one from his own state of origin. A favorite with some, whether Illinoisans or not, was Representative Elihu B. Washburne of Illinois. Washburne was known to be a very close friend of Grant, who was currently the general in chief and prospectively the commander in chief of the United States army. A word to Washburne could be expected to get to Grant.

One who wrote repeatedly to Washburne was William H. Gibbs, once a fellow Illinoisan, then a major in a Union regiment, and now a resident of Jackson and a candidate for the Mississippi state senate. The state government, Gibbs had been complaining to Washburne, was in the hands of men "bitterly & irreconcilably opposed to reconstruction on the

Congressional plan." General Gillem was a "tool of Andrew Johnson" and was "in sympathy with rebels." Unless changes were made before the election, Gibbs insisted, the new constitution would not have a chance. The complaints Washburne received from Gibbs and other Mississippi Republicans doubtless reached Grant and helped persuade him to replace Gillem with McDowell and Humphreys with Ames, whom he knew well and regarded highly. Gibbs himself was not yet acquainted with Ames but was eventually to become a political crony of his.

After the state election Gibbs gave Washburne his own version of the familiar story. "Threats, intimidations & even violence have been resorted to to force the colored voters to vote Democratic tickets," Gibbs wrote. "Many who have been courageous enough to vote their sentiments have been turned off from employment." The federal troops, few as they were, had failed to provide the necessary protection. "In some localities indeed the soldiers have operated against us by urging & advising the freedmen to vote the Democratic ticket & have actually distributed Democratic tickets among them while on duty." It was beginning to look like civil war again. "The spirit of rebellion is as rampant here now as in the days of 1861."[11]

Another of Washburne's Mississippi correspondents was, like Gibbs, an Illinoisan by birth and a Mississippian by choice but, unlike Gibbs, a former member of the master class and a longtime resident of the state. This was James L. Alcorn, who was to become, temporarily, Ames's strongest Republican ally and, ultimately, his most dangerous factional foe. As an infant, Alcorn had gone with his parents to Kentucky, and at twenty-eight he moved on his own to Mississippi. There he rose from a successful lawyer to one of the state's wealthest planters and largest slaveholders, second only to Jefferson Davis's brother Joseph. The Davises were Democrats and Alcorn was a Whig. A reluctant secessionist, he had no use for Jefferson Davis or the war, and his military career was brief. He was the most prominent of the Mississippi Whigs who joined the Republican party, but he was by no means the only one; perhaps as many as 20 percent of white Mississippians were to go through a Republican phase during Reconstruction.[12]

From his home in Friar's Point, far to the north on the Mississippi River, Alcorn poured forth his feelings after the defeat of the new constitution. "The impeachment failure has revived the spirit of the rebellion," he told Washburne; "it comes with more than its original wrath."

> The proscriptions of 1861 were not so fierce as those of the present day. I was told by a friend but the other day that, but for fear of the military power, I would not be permitted to remain in the state. The statement was true. And the poor negroes, God help them if Democracy [the Democratic party] is to rule in the land. Can it be possible that the northern people have made the negro free but to be returned the slave of society, to bear in such

> slavery the vindictive resentments that the satraps of Davis maintain today towards the people of the North? Better a thousand times for the negro that the government should return him to the custody of his original owner, where he would have a master to look after his well being, than that his neck should be placed under the heel of a society vindictive towards him because he is free. . . .
>
> I am a Southerner. I love peace rather than war. I have hoped for honorable and favorable terms in the settlement of the question of restoration, but I had rather see the country charred by the flames of a ten years war than see the Jeff Davis tyranny again revived in the land. The Republican party has everything staked on the issue; they must play boldly or they are beaten. Has Genl Grant nerve? I think so, have reason to think so; the Congress with Grant to back it ought to be invincible.

Before concluding his long letter, Alcorn protested: "I am no scalawag, or carpet bagger." He was correct in saying he was no carpetbagger, for though Northern-born he had gone south before the war. He had reason for denying also that he was a scalawag, since the term implied membership in the poor white trash. Still, the Democrats applied the word to any Southern white Republican, regardless of his wealth or social standing. Like it or not, Alcorn was a scalawag in the language of contemporary politics.

Alcorn said he did not want "such cruel murderers as Forrest" to rule over him. He was referring to Nathan Bedford Forrest, the onetime slave trader and Mississippi planter who became a Confederate cavalry commander and war hero and then the founder and head of the Ku Klux Klan. From Tennessee, where it originated, the Klan spread to Mississippi and other Southern states. As its Grand Wizard, Forrest launched a kind of guerrilla war against Southern Republicans. But he did not establish or control all the far-flung terrorist bands, most of which arose spontaneously. They were commonly known as Ku Klux Klans whether or not they had any connection with Forrest or his organization.

After Grant's electoral victory in November 1868, Alcorn and other Mississippi Republicans could reasonably expect an early relief from Ku Kluxism. Relief, if it came, would be none too soon. As Alcorn informed Washburne in January 1869:

> The incendiaries burned one of my plantations on the 8th inst. The offence was [due to] political hate, coupled with the fact that I had the day before leased it to freedmen. My loss was about six thousand dollars. I have thought it best to guard the remainder of my plantations as well as I can until I see what Congress may do under Genl Grant's administration. Should there be no improvement, then I will make the best disposition of my estates, and leave the State. Genl Gillem's administration is but little better than a Democratic administration would be. . . .
>
> I observe the Northern newspapers are vying with each other in commending the Southern leaders for the manly style in which they are acqui-

> escing in the election of Genl Grant. Is there a man in Congress so stupid as to believe that there is a Democrat in the South who regards Genl Grant other than with the most intense hatred? who considers the American government other than a stupendous tyranny? who would not hail with joy the overthrow of that government by France, England, or any other power, as a Christian would hail the coming of the Messiah?[13]

Soon after his election as governor of Louisiana, in the spring of 1868, Henry Clay Warmoth received an anonymous warning in the mail: "Villain, beware. Your doom is sealed. *Death* now awaits you. The midnight owl screams: Revenge! Revenge!! Revenge!!! *Ku Klux Klan.*" Only twenty-six, immature and inexperienced as a politician, Warmoth faced the insidious threat of terrorism in addition to the responsibilities, baffling enough in themselves, of governing a bankrupt and backward city and state.

New Orleans, for all its bustle and appeal, was hardly a progressive city, though it was the capital, metropolis, and showplace of Louisiana. Only a few of its streets were paved—with stone blocks brought all the way from Belgium—and only a few had streetcar tracks. Each of the streetcars was pulled by a single mule with a tinkling bell attached to the harness. Until recently, blacks had not been allowed to ride the cars except for special ones marked with a star. But in 1867 some blacks began to force their way into the vehicles reserved for whites, and when General Sheridan refused to help enforce segregation the street railways quit operating "star cars." The city got its drinking water from the Mississippi River, into which slaughterhouses dumped their offal. There were few factories, but plenty of licensed brothels and gambling dens. Levees along the river must be repaired and additional lines of railroad built if New Orleans and Louisiana were ever to enjoy the progress and prosperity that nature seemed to authorize.

"I needed the advice, help, and friendly cooperation of the ablest men of the state," Warmoth was to recall many years afterward. But he could expect the support of practically none of the planters or businessmen among the Louisiana elite. The party he led consisted of a comparative few Northern conquerors like him, a somewhat larger number of Unionist Southern whites, most of the long-free Afro-Americans, and a mass of recent slaves.[14]

With such a following, and with the backing of the United States army, Warmoth took charge of Louisiana even before it was quite readmitted as a state. On June 25 Congress provided for its readmission as soon as its new legislature should have ratified the Fourteenth Amendment. Two days later, through the influence of General Grant, Warmoth received an appointment as provisional governor.

He promptly called the legislature into session. When it met, in the Mechanics' Institute, a total of 49 Democrats claimed membership, along with 88 Republicans, 42 of them black. But the black lieutenant governor, Oscar J. Dunn, refused to admit to the senate, and the black temporary chairman refused to admit to the house, those Democrats who could not or would not take the "ironclad" oath, which required them to swear that they had never willingly borne arms against the United States. A mob gathered to demand that the nonjuring Democrats be given their seats. Still fresh in the minds of Republicans was the New Orleans massacre, which had started at this very building just two years before. Federal troops now arrived to help local policemen protect the legislature, but the Republicans in it still felt too insecure to disregard the mob, and they decided not to insist on the oath of previous loyalty.

Without the support of federal troops, the state government might have a hard time maintaining itself, and Warmoth would not have the federal troops much longer at his beck and call. Once the legislature had ratified the Fourteenth Amendment and Congress had recognized Louisiana as a state, the area would cease to be under military control, and the only federal forces available would be those that the army authorities might, from time to time, choose to provide. In the near future Warmoth and his fellow Republicans would desperately need some kind of force to take the place of the regular army. For the time being, a state militia seemed out of the question, for Congress was yet to repeal a recent act disallowing militias in the former Confederate states.

To help meet the emergency, the legislature hastily passed and Warmoth promptly signed a bill to create a board of metropolitan police, which presumably would see to law enforcement in the city of New Orleans. Warmoth appointed to the board two white and three black commissioners, who were to raise, equip, and oversee the new constabulary.

After two weeks as provisional governor, Warmoth was to be inaugurated as the regular governor on July 13. He delayed informing Congress that the legislature had ratified the Fourteenth Amendment, and so the federal troops remained to preserve order at the inauguration.

When, at half past twelve, Warmoth took his place on the platform for the inaugural ceremony, he was greeted with thundering applause and piercing yells from the mostly black crowd of visitors in the legislative hall. Even some of his enemies conceded that, for all his callowness, he exhibited a certain dignity and charm. Indeed, he made a fine appearance with his tall and sinewy figure and, as one observer noted, his "large nose, full at the nostrils, keen, measuring eyes, superb mustache, and well cut brows and chin." He took pains to avoid antagonizing his opponents in his inaugural address, which he read from a manuscript and in a serious, statesmanlike tone, quite different from his usual extemporaneous buffoonery. "My object will be to enforce the law, protect the people, and aid in advancing the social, material, and political interest of the whole people," he declared. "I believe the epoch has the smiles of Providence."[15]

When the legislature proceeded to the election of United States senators, Warmoth used his influence to see that one of the two places went to a friend and fellow Illinoisan, the thirty-seven-year-old William Pitt Kellogg. Vermont-born, Kellogg as a boy of fifteen had moved with his family to Illinois. There he taught school for a while, then went into law and politics. He was a delegate to the Chicago convention that nominated Lincoln in 1860, and he was a presidential elector pledged to Lincoln on the Republican ticket that fall. For his services in the campaign, he received an appointment as chief justice of Nebraska Territory. Although he briefly served as a messenger for General Grant and was himself commissioned a brigadier general, he saw no real action in the war. At the war's end, with the strong backing of Illinois Republican leaders, he obtained the very last job that Lincoln awarded before his assassination—the collectorship of the port of New Orleans, one of the choicest of all patronage plums. In May 1868 he was again a delegate to a Chicago convention, the one that nominated Grant for President.[16]

Now in Washington as a senator from Louisiana, Kellogg was keeping constantly in touch with Warmoth and cooperating closely with him. It was reassuring to Warmoth to have such a dependable ally in such a strategic place (and it was just as well, perhaps, that Warmoth could not see a few years into the future, when Kellogg was to be his implacable foe). "We all think that you are doing splendidly and our friends believe as I always have that you will make a good Governor and be a credit to the party that elected you," Kellogg assured him. "We know that you have a trying ordeal, but we also know that you are equal to the emergency."

That was a nice enough letter, and here was an even nicer one—from John Hay, formerly President Lincoln's assistant private secretary, at present an employee of the United States legation in Vienna, and eventually to be a famous secretary of state, the sponsor of the Open Door policy. "It is a most cheering indication for the South," Hay had written, "that the fresh young energy of the West is taking so large a share in the management of civil affairs." Truly, if the good wishes of friends could bring success in civil affairs, Warmoth would have been a much more successful governor of Louisiana than he was in fact to be.[17]

At the time of Warmoth's inauguration the Democratic national convention, meeting as usual much later than the Republican, was completing its labors in New York. For President, the Democrats nominated Horatio Seymour, New York's wartime governor and prominent Copperhead. For vice president, after an ex-Confederate general had presented his name, they chose Frank Blair, a former Union general from Missouri and a member of an old Jacksonian family that had supported Lincoln during the war. Before the convention, hoping for the presidential nomination, Blair had asserted in a public letter that the next President must "declare these [Reconstruction] Acts null and void, compel the army to undo its usurpations at the South, dispossess the carpet-bag State governments," and "allow the white people to re-organize their own governments." In their platform the Democrats denounced the acts as "usurpations, unconstitutional, revolutionary, and void."[18]

Of course, no President would have authority to nullify acts of Congress (though that is pretty much what President Johnson had tried to do). Still, the Blair letter and the Democratic platform were incitements to violence in the South, and the party's campaigners there made the most of them. What rights had a Southern Republican, white or black, if he was nothing but a usurper—if he owed his political existence to pretended laws that were in fact unconstitutional, revolutionary, and void? Surely, revolutionary and terroristic means would be justified in countering such a usurpation.

In Louisiana the terrorists were already beginning to stir. Directing the Republican campaign from the governor's rooms in the Mechanics' Institute, Warmoth kept himself informed by means of detectives or spies as well as an extensive correspondence. Some of his men infiltrated the Knights of the White Camellia, which in the New Orleans area was larger and more active than the Ku Klux Klan, and which differed from the Klan mainly in omitting its hoods, robes, and hocus-pocus. Warmoth's informers reported that the Knights were plotting high-level assassinations, and his widespread correspondents wrote of black Republicans already dying at the terrorists' hands. In some parishes Republican officeholders were finding it unsafe to remain and try to hold on to their jobs.

Warmoth was under pressure from national Republican leaders. "Let it be understood that the State must be carried for Grant this fall," Senator Kellogg reminded him from Washington, "and that those that expect official favors, to secure them, must help to secure the success of the party." Federal officeholders in Louisiana, Kellogg said, were expected to contribute generously to the campaign chest. The Republican national committee promised additional funds. All this was well and good, so far as Warmoth was concerned. Doing his part, he used the state patronage to reward dependable Republican workers, and he converted the *New Orleans Republican,* of which he was co-owner, into the state's official journal, the better to propagate sound Republican doctrine.

Still, Warmoth knew that the Republicans' chances in Louisiana would be slim unless he had sufficient military support to deal with the armed bands of roving Democrats. These paramilitary bands would have the field pretty much to themselves once the federal troops in the state were reduced or withdrawn, as they were expected to be. So Warmoth repeatedly asked Kellogg to see that something was done. It would help if Congress would not only authorize but also arm and equip a state militia.

Kellogg replied, at the end of July, that such a bill had passed the Senate but failed in the House. "Some of our people I think did not rightly understand the matter," he explained, "and feared the effect of putting arms into the hands of the colored people of the South." In any event, Kellogg was not sure congressional aid was necessary, and neither were all the colleagues and officials to whom he showed Warmoth's letters. Some of these men suggested that Warmoth buy weapons on credit or borrow them from one of the Northern states. General John M. Schofield, now secretary of war, proposed a way to get around the militia ban: "he says . . . that if you establish a constabulary force in each parish . . . this force if prompt and resolute will be sufficient, provided sufficient troops remain within the State . . . and . . . he promises to leave as large a force as there is now in the State and probably add another regiment."

Though Schofield doubtless meant well, Warmoth could not take him at his word, for the war secretary was but an agent of the President, and any commitment regarding troops, to be valid, would have to come from Johnson himself. So, on August 1, the Louisiana legislature adopted a joint resolution appealing to the President for additional military protection. Warmoth wrote and addressed to Johnson a letter detailing the outrages that the Knights of the White Camellia and other Klan-like groups were committing; he said that in the past month and a half they had murdered 150 persons in the state. He put together a collection of correspondence to document his charges. Then he instructed a friend to carry this correspondence, the governor's letter, and the legislature's resolution to the White House. As Warmoth was later to learn, Johnson received the messenger with scorn.

For a day or two Warmoth enjoyed a respite from the denunciations of local Democrats. They had brought in a token black to make speeches for them, and when this orator tried to speak in front of their Constitution Club he was shouted down by a crowd of Republican blacks, who threatened to attack him. Two Democratic leaders hurried to the governor's office to implore Warmoth to help. Going quickly to the scene, he addressed the crowd from the balcony of the Constitution Club. "My Republican friends," he began, "I come here to ask at your hands that freedom of speech which, as Republicans, we demand for everybody." He went on to make what the Democratic *New Orleans Times* called a "fearless and telling speech to the mob" and "at once scattered it like chaff and restored public order." Democrats generally praised him.

But they changed their tune when news of his recent appeal to Johnson appeared in the press. In an anti-Warmoth diatribe a Democratic state senator said the governor at the Constitution Club had used "words which reflected credit upon him," but in his murder charges against white Louisianans he had slandered them and discredited himself. "Does he represent the white people of Louisiana?" the legislator demanded. No, "he was elected by political demagogues, and adventurers, and mountebanks, who made use of the colored element for the accomplishment of their purposes."[19]

In a word, Warmoth was a carpetbagger, and in the minds and mouths of Democrats the word itself was a sufficient reply to anything he might say or do. He gained national publicity as both Northern and Southern Democrats made a campaign issue of him in particular and his kind of politicians in general—that is, white Northern Republicans in the South. The *New York World,* a leading Democratic paper, thought it quite fit to print such doggerel as the following:

I am a carpet-bagger—
    I've a brother scalawag—
Come South to boast and swagger
    With an empty carpet-bag,
To rob the whites of green-backs
    And with the blacks go bunk
And change my empty satchel
    For a full sole-leather trunk.
I'm *some* on constitution,
    For a late rebellious state,
And I'm *some* on persecution,
    Of disloyal men I hate;
I'm *some* at nigger meetings
    When white folks ain't about,
And I'm *some* among the nigger gals
    When their marms don't know they're out.[20]

Already the Democrats were creating a carpetbagger stereotype, and they were characterizing politicians of the type as plunderers and exploiters even before the men in question had been in office long enough to make much of a record of any kind, either good or bad.

Some Republican spokesmen came to the defense of Warmoth and other so-called carpetbaggers. *Harper's Weekly* said "it is to the class against whose crimes upon loyal citizens Governor Warmouth *[sic]* invokes aid of the President that the Democratic party proposes to give exclusive political power in the State." General Daniel E. Sickles—who had lost a leg at Gettysburg and whom Johnson had removed as Reconstruction commander of the Carolinas—gave what *Harper's Weekly* called an "admirable historical survey of carpet-baggers" in an address to Union veterans on the anniversary of the battle of Antietam.

The West, Sickles related, had been settled by carpetbaggers, that is, by pioneers. The North and East had also been peopled by carpetbaggers, the immigrants. "The *Mayflower* brought a colony of carpet-baggers and landed them on the shores of New England," Sickles went on. "William the Conqueror took some Norman carpet-baggers over to England, and captured it, and founded a nation that has sent its carpet-baggers forth all over the world, most of which they own, or propose to own." Then, after waiting for the laughter and applause to die down, Sickles delivered the punch line: "Our carpet-baggers carry intelligence and civilization and enterprise wherever they go, and they are not to be barred out or excluded from the South at rebel dictation."[21]

Warmoth could derive no encouragement from such rhetorical defiance on the part of a Republican campaigner far from the perilous front in Louisiana. The number of federal troops in the state was not being increased as War Secretary Schofield had so confidently predicted it would be, and those remaining were scattered among a dozen posts. Schofield now was giving vague and noncommittal answers to inquiries regarding possible use of the troops to preserve order among civilians. After the legislature authorized a state militia of 2500 blacks and 2500 whites, Warmoth named Robert E. Lee's former lieutenant James Longstreet as adjutant general and sent a mission to the North to procure arms. But Warmoth did not go through with organizing the militia. He had good reason to hesitate, since the deployment of such a force might lead to a race war, a war in which the militiamen themselves would be fighting one another.

In mid-August he called Democratic and Republican leaders to his office to discuss means of avoiding bloodshed, but his "peace conference" broke up without an agreement. He continued to be more conciliatory toward the Democrats than most of his fellow Republicans were. In late September the legislature passed a bill to punish any owner of a hotel, steamboat, or other public place or vehicle who refused to accommodate blacks in exactly the same way as whites. Warmoth vetoed the bill. He explained that such "class legislation" would be unenforceable, would inflame race feelings, and would defeat its own purpose. Meanwhile he was making no effort to carry out the state constitution's mandate to set up racially integrated schools.

Unappeased, the Democrats stepped up their campaign of violence, especially in and around New Orleans. Inspiring and directing it were various Democratic clubs in addition to the Knights of the White Camellia, the Ku Klux Klan, and the Innocents, an organization of working-class toughs, many of them immigrants from Europe. Rioters lay in wait for Republican parades, then fired upon the marchers, mostly black, and pursued and assaulted them as they fled. As the election approached, the rioting intensified, culminating in late October in bloody affrays in Jefferson, Orleans, and St. Bernard parishes—below the city proper, within it, and across the river from it.

By this time Warmoth and his fellow Republicans were desperate, their position almost hopeless. True, he possessed, on paper, a remarkable degree of control over the electoral process. The legislature had recently given the governor power to appoint a board of registration that could exclude voters it considered unqualified and, in cases of rioting at the polls, could recommend to him that he disallow the returns. Legally, then, Warmoth had the means to guarantee a fair election and, indeed, a Republican victory. But in reality his legal powers would amount to nothing unless he could assure the safety of Republicans both before and during the voting.

So he urged General L. H. Rousseau, now the military commander in New Orleans, to call on the War Department for additional troops. Rousseau had only 550 men available for duty. "The civil authorities in the parishes of Orleans, Jefferson, and St. Bernard are unable to preserve order and protect the lives and property of the people," Warmoth told the general in a written statement. "I am compelled to appeal to you to take charge of the peace of these parishes and use your forces to that end." Rousseau telegraphed the governor's statement to Washington and asked for instructions. He was advised to take appropriate measures to keep order but was given no reinforcements.

Already Warmoth was hastily putting together a kind of army of his own. The legislature had passed an emergency bill to combine Orleans, Jefferson, and St. Bernard parishes in a single police district and to reorganize and enlarge the metropolitan police. Warmoth named black Lieutenant-Governor Dunn to head the new police board, and it soon mustered a force of 130 blacks and 243 whites. These "Metropolitans," completely independent of the mayor and the parish authorities, were the governor's to command. They could make arrests anywhere in the state.

The climax came on Monday, October 26, just over a week before election day. At Rousseau's invitation, Warmoth went with a few other top Republicans to confer with Democratic leaders at the general's headquarters. Fearful of a blood bath at the polls, Warmoth was in an especially conciliatory mood. He suggested that the two parties schedule their mass meetings and parades on different days, and he intimated that, if the Democrats would stop using violence, he would disband the metropolitan police. But the Democrats were unwilling to make any concessions whatsoever. Even without a quid pro quo, Warmoth promised to issue a pacifying proclamation, and he did so, "requesting all good citizens to refrain from assembling in public places" and urging that "no public meetings or processions of either political party be held prior to the coming election."

That evening Warmoth was still fuming at the intransigence of the Democratic politicians when he received an equally angry caller at the governor's office. The visitor, the Democratic mayor of New Orleans, demanded that Warmoth get rid of the metropolitan police board. The mayor said he had a petition from fifty prominent citizens to support his demand. He was confident that, once the police were removed, these citizens and their clubs could do all that was necessary to maintain order. Now more irate than ever, Warmoth gave the mayor a sharp refusal and showed him to the door.

Soon after the mayor's departure Warmoth got word that a mob was descending on the city hall with the object of capturing the police headquarters. Rousseau sent a few officers to the scene, and they persuaded the crowd to break up. Still, it was obvious to Warmoth, as it was to Rousseau, that in a military sense the Republicans were outmanned and outgunned. The only way to save Republican lives on election day was to surrender now.

On Tuesday, October 27, Warmoth saw Rousseau again, along with the editor of the *New Orleans Republican,* the official state newspaper. The three decided that blacks, in places where their safety was in question, should not attempt to vote. Through the *Republican,* Warmoth counseled his followers to stay away from the polls.[22]

At this moment of peril for the Louisiana Republican party Warmoth had to contend not only with the terrorism of the Democrats but also with disaffection in his own ranks. From the party's beginning he had encountered hostility from some Afro-Americans, especially the Roudanez brothers and the New Orleans community of prewar free persons of color. But the black leader Dunn had consented to be his running mate and helped to bring most blacks to his support. Then, when Warmoth vetoed the bill for equal accommodations, Dunn began to turn away from him. And when Warmoth failed to provide protection for black voters, he certainly added nothing to his popularity among Louisiana blacks.

He had also antagonized some of the party's white leaders, particularly Michael Hahn, the long-resident Louisianan from Germany who had served as governor of the "free state" erected during the war. Hahn was aggrieved because, for one thing, Warmoth had not backed him for a United States senatorship but had pushed Kellogg instead. Before the November election Hahn unburdened himself to Congressman Washburne of Illinois:

> Republicans, I am sorry to say, no longer have any hopes of carrying this State. This is owing not only to the brutal conduct of the Confederate mobs, but also to the bad management & weakness of the men who have foisted themselves on the Republican party as office holders and leaders. It is generally believed that one of the officers high in the State government has a personal dislike to General Grant, so great as to prevent him giving any active & sincere support to the party in his election.

The high state official rumored to be anti-Grant was, of course, Warmoth. In fact, he had long since lost any ill-feeling he may once have entertained because of Grant's dismissing him from the army in 1863. Warmoth's willingness to yield the upcoming Louisiana election was due to political realism and prudence, not to personal vindictiveness. But Hahn, writing to Grant's friend, could hope to queer Warmoth with Grant. He continued:

> Early in the fight I canvassed some of the parishes on my own account &

> reported to the [Republican State] Central Committee that the State could be carried by a judicious, bold & energetic campaign. But the Committee, made up principally of men whom our enemies term "Carpet-baggers," was slow, weak & indiscreet in its movements. Instead of extending the Republican fold, old citizens of Union and Republican proclivities were ostracized & only new comers were placed in positions of honor & emolument. They were not satisfied with filling the positions of Governor and other State offices & U. S. Senators with "Carpet-baggers," but went further: in the present campaign every white man on the [presidential] electoral ticket & every one of the five nominations for Congress is a "Carpet-bagger."
>
> This greediness naturally excites & inflames the old rebel population, & disgusts the tried old Union citizens.

Despite Warmoth's proclamation against public demonstrations, the Democratic clubs continued to rove and raid up to and through election day, November 3. By that time, 1,081 persons had been killed, according to the later count of a congressional committee. The tactics of intimidation were quite effective. In several parishes the Republicans cast no votes at all. In New Orleans, where an estimated 18,000 Republicans were registered, exactly 276 of them voted. In the state as a whole the Republicans polled hardly more than half as many as they had done in April, when Warmoth was elected. Grant and the five carpetbag congressional candidates were overwhelmingly defeated in Louisiana.

"The pistol and the knife are more potent than the ballot," one of the five commented the next day. At least he could console himself with the national returns, which made Grant the next President. "Now what do you think will be the course of General Grant towards us in the South?" That question was on the mind of every Louisiana Republican.[23]

While losing the friendship of Dunn the black and gaining the enmity of Hahn the scalawag, Warmoth remained on the best of terms with Kellogg, his fellow carpetbagger. During the Christmas season he and Kellogg exchanged gifts and good wishes. "I wish you a happier & more peaceable New Year than the old has been," Kellogg wrote from Washington. Not long before Grant's inauguration he added this prophetic bit: "I should not be surprised if before the close of his administration Genl Grant should find the Southern Senators his best friends." Kellogg thought of himself as one of those Southern senators. Before the end of President Grant's first term he and Grant would indeed be the best of friends—and Warmoth would be the enemy of both.[24]

CHAPTER 7

Turbulent and Lawless Men (1868-1869)

Powell Clayton came out on the balcony of the Anthony House, the finest hotel in Little Rock, to respond to the crowd that was yelling for him in the street below. It was early April 1868, and the returns, now in, showed that he had won the election and was to be the next governor of Arkansas. When the crowd quieted, he spoke a few words of thanks to all the Republicans who had voted for him. He made an impressive appearance—still youthful at thirty-four, taller than average, with light hair and mustache and a graceful yet decisive manner. His followers considered him a natural leader; his enemies, while granting his courage and combativeness, took exception to his "haughty bearing."[1]

Clayton could justify a certain amount of pride and self-assurance on the basis of both his family background and his own career. He traced his ancestry back to the William Clayton who had come to Pennsylvania with William Penn in 1682. Since then, the Claytons had been prominent in both Pennsylvania and Delaware, one of them becoming a United States senator and another a secretary of state. Powell Clayton himself was born, August 7, 1833, on a farm in southeastern Pennsylvania near the Delaware line. He studied civil engineering at Bristol Military College in Pennsylvania and at an engineering school in Wilmington, Delaware.

When twenty-one, Clayton went west to Kansas Territory, which at the time, in 1855, was "Bleeding Kansas," bleeding from the murderous struggle between proslavery and antislavery settlers. He went there not so much to fight either for or against slavery as to find an opportunity in the engineering profession. He had no use for the free-soilers, though. His father had been a Whig, but he was himself a decided Democrat. He bypassed the town of Lawrence, the free-soil capital of Kansas, and settled in Leavenworth, the nesting place of the Democrats, who wanted to see Kansas become a slave state. Two years later the people of Leavenworth elected him, despite his youth, to the office of city engineer and surveyor.[2]

Though not an abolitionist and, indeed, not even a free-soiler, Clayton was an unequivocal Unionist, and when the Southern states seceded he was ready to fight for his country. He promptly raised a company and, as its captain, went off to war with the very first regiment of Kansas volunteers. Before long he was commanding a cavalry regiment in the campaign to recover Arkansas for the Union. He gained some renown when he led an expedition into the state from Helena on the Mississippi, dispersing guerrilla bands and capturing Confederate stores. But his most famous exploit was his heroic defense of Union-occupied Pine Bluff.

The Jefferson County seat of Pine Bluff was aptly named, located as it was, some forty miles below Little Rock on the Arkansas River, on the edge of a bluff and a thick pine forest. In October 1863, when Union forces controlled most of the state, Colonel Clayton commanded the post at Pine Bluff with a garrison of 550 men. Approaching with an army of 2500, the Confederate General John S. Marmaduke, a West Pointer, sent an aide ahead to demand Clayton's capitulation. The lieutenant who met the aide replied: "Colonel Clayton never surrenders." Clayton quickly set 300 blacks to work rolling cotton bales out of warehouses and piling up the bales so as to block every street leading to the courthouse square. Then he ordered his troops into positions behind the improvised breastworks. When Marmaduke arrived he found it hopeless to storm the works, and he contented himself with shelling the square, setting fire to houses and other buildings outside it, and looting the town. When he withdrew, the courthouse itself lay in ruins, along with most of the rest of Pine Bluff, but the Stars and Stripes still waved above the place.

"The Federals fought like devils," Marmaduke reported. Clayton in his report gave a large share of the credit to the blacks whose help he recognized as indispensable. He was rapidly gaining a new respect for blacks as a people. But he himself deserved considerable credit in the judgment of his superiors; they soon saw to his promotion to brigadier general.

General Clayton kept busy with the pacification of Arkansas until the last of the Confederate armies in the entire South had quit. As winter turned to spring in 1865, he confronted two main tasks: the protection of black refugees and the destruction of guerrilla bands, which continued to roam much of the countryside. To save the refugees, he provided subsistence until he could settle them on abandoned plantations and enable them to support themselves. To destroy the guerrillas, he raided the country they infested between the Arkansas River and the White. He succeeded in "cleaning out the rebels" in that area, but elsewhere others rose from time to time even after Lee's surrender at Appomattox.

Finally, on hearing of Kirby Smith's surrender in Texas, he got the impression that all the rebels remaining in Arkansas were ready to give up. In time he was to realize that, despite the Union victory, neither the rebel spirit nor the bushwhacking urge had entirely disappeared from the state.[3]

For the present, though, Arkansas looked to Clayton like a promising place to live in, and after his more than three years there it had begun to seem like home. He expected no trouble in getting along with the recent rebels; he had already made friends with some of them—and with the daughter of one. Adeline McGraw lived in Helena, where he had first entered the state. Though she belonged to a good pro-Confederate family, she was not above fraternizing with the handsome young officer from the North. A few months after Clayton was mustered out of the Union army, he and Adeline were married, apparently with the blessing of her parents.

Clayton took his bride to what was now the Clayton plantation on the Arkansas River below Pine Bluff. It was one of the largest and finest plantations in the state; the only thing wrong with it was the constant erosion of its land along the riverbank. It had belonged to one of Clayton's Confederate friends, Colonel Willoughby Williams, a Tennesseean who spent most of his time taking care of his properties in Arkansas. For it, Clayton paid $53,000 in cash, a great deal of money in those days. Part of the money came from his brother William and from his own savings as a well-paid army officer and from profits he had made in buying and selling cotton. By the end of 1865 he was prepared to settle down to the peaceful and prosperous life of an Arkansas cotton planter.

As a planter, Clayton had interests and problems in common with his cotton-growing neighbors, including the former slave masters and disunionists. He needed to find black laborers, furnish supplies and equipment for them, and keep them going until they could repay him with a share of the crop. "Niggers are working well; but you can't get only about two thirds as much out of 'em as you could when they were slaves." So said one of the neighbors just as Clayton was getting started. "The nigger is fated: he can't live with the white race, now he's free."[4]

To obtain supplies and to arrange for marketing his crop, Clayton had to make occasional visits to Memphis, the entrepôt for Arkansas. Since the state lacked railroads (except for a total of 45 miles of track) the trip was long and slow. The traveler had to go by steamboat down the meandering Arkansas and up the meandering Mississippi. On a voyage to Memphis in June 1866, when his first cotton plants were beginning to blossom, Clayton fell in with his friend Willoughby Williams, the ex-Confederate colonel who had sold him the plantation. The day was sweltering. To get what breeze they could, the two men sat in the shade of an awning high on the hurricane deck. To cool off further, they steadily sipped mint juleps. And they talked of politics.

For the moment, these onetime enemies saw pretty much eye to eye. Still a Democrat, Clayton had been siding with President Johnson and against the Radical Republicans in Congress, while Williams was growing more and more enthusiastic about Johnson as the President repeatedly struck at the Radicals. Johnson's stand encouraged Williams and other Arkansas Democrats in their hope of recovering control of the state government. Already the Democrats, the former secessionists, dominated the legislature. But they had to contend against an unremitting Unionist in the executive branch—Isaac Murphy, who alone had voted against secession in the Arkansas convention of 1861, and who had been governor since the formation of the free state under President Lincoln's plan in 1864. Williams thought it would be smart tactics to stop denouncing Murphy for the present and to nominate, in the future, congressional and senatorial candidates who had not been conspicuous as secessionists. He hinted that Clayton himself might make an ideal Democratic nominee for Congress.

Clayton, however, was already beginning to lose his enthusiasm for Johnson and Johnson's policy. Home again on his plantation, he was more and more troubled by the growing hostility of his ex-rebel neighbors—a hostility that Johnson's policy helped to foment. At first, these people, along with most Arkansans, had seemed to welcome the thousands of Northerners who remained or arrived in the state after the war. Like Clayton, many others had brought in cash that stimulated the economy and lessened, at least a bit, the prevailing backwardness and poverty. Yet, a year after the war's end, the rebel feelings appeared to be even stronger than at its start.

The ex-rebels took out their feelings on blacks and native Unionist whites as well as Northerners. A new arrival from the North reported an instance that occurred near Pine Bluff on a May night in 1866: "that night the Negroes cabbens were seen to be on fire, the next morning I went to the spot, where I saw a sight that apald me 24 Negro men women and children were hanging to trees all around the cabbens." White Unionists, whether Northern or Southern, had less fear for their lives than did the blacks, but they, too, suffered from personal harassment and property damage.[5]

Clayton had had no intention of going into politics at the time he bought his plantation, and when a delegation of Pine Bluff Democrats invited him to run for Congress, he politely declined. "He continuously resided upon his plantation," as he was to write long afterward, in the third person, "until ill treatment by his ex-Confederate neighbors became so pronounced as to cause him to take a political stand for the preservation of his life and property." And when he took his stand, he did it as a Republican, not a Democrat. After the passage of the Reconstruction Act of 1867 he joined with other Union veterans, loyalist whites, and recent slaves to form the Arkansas Republican party. He soon dominated it, and he was to go on dominating it for an entire decade.

Temporarily he retained the respect and even the admiration of prominent ex-Confederates. Before he was nominated for governor, the local Democratic paper, the *Pine Bluff Dispatch,* suggested that Democrats combine with Republicans in backing such an able man. After his nomination another opposition weekly, the *Fort Smith Herald,* observed that he was an intelligent-looking person—too intelligent to be a Republican. In the eyes of black voters he was not merely able and intelligent; he was a veritable hero. Many of the native white Republicans were much less favorable toward him. They would have preferred James M. Johnson, an old Arkansan who had fought for the Union and who now, as the candidate for lieutenant governor, was relegated to second place on the Republican ticket.[6]

When Governor-elect Clayton responded to his well-wishers, in front of the Anthony House in Little Rock on that April day in 1868, he knew he had no easy task ahead of him. But he could not know quite how rough the work would be and how much resistance he would run into—resistance on the part of James M. Johnson's as well as Andrew Johnson's followers.

On the morning of July 2, 1868, cavalrymen on strutting horses escorted an open carriage down Main Street in Little Rock. In the back seat sat the incoming governor, Powell Clayton, not yet thirty-five, and on his right the outgoing governor, Isaac Murphy, almost twice as old. Clayton was in full dress, with a top hat, a swallow-tail coat, and fancy gloves. Murphy had on the simple homespun of the Ozark mountaineer he was. After eyeing Clayton he said to him: "Why do you wear gloves in July? Only dudes wear gloves in summertime." Clayton replied: "Governor, it is not the garb that makes the man, yet in deference to your opinion, and especially in view of the character of the work I am about to enter upon today, which will doubtless require 'handling without gloves,' I now remove mine." As the two men cordially shook hands, Murphy exclaimed: "May God help you!"

At about ten o'clock the carriage turned into the crowded statehouse grounds, which bordered the Arkansas River. Soon Clayton took his place on the temporary platform in front of the capitol, a long, low, graceful Greek Revival building with a central pediment and two pedimented wings. As he delivered his inaugural—on the new era for Arkansas—he took in a scene that he was never to forget. Immediately before him, colorfully dressed white women sat on benches and constantly fanned themselves as they listened to him. Behind them stood a much larger number of white men, whose interested expressions revealed their Republicanism. At one side, in the shade of oaks, clustered some scowling whites, obviously Democrats. And on the fringes of the crowd were the blacks, keeping a respectful distance, apparently not yet sure what citizenship and suffrage were going to mean for them.

Once the ceremonies were over, Governor Clayton followed ex-Governor Murphy on a tour of the statehouse. Clayton found the executive chambers unprepossessing. Here was a large room with its floor uncarpeted, its walls bare except for a portrait of George Washington over the fireplace, and its only furniture a long table, a case of pigeonholes on top of the table, and a couple of dozen homemade split-bottom chairs. Adjoining was a small room containing a barrel filled with straw. From the barrel Murphy lifted a jug of mountain dew, and the two men drank to one another's health. As they proceeded on their tour, Clayton noticed that the building as a whole was in bad repair and that the corridors and legislative halls, like the grounds, were littered with trash. He must mention the need to fix up and clean up when he addressed the legislature the next day.

When he appeared before the legislature he faced a large majority of Republicans, most of whom were white. In his message he elaborated on themes he had set in his inaugural. "It was surely a strange frenzy," he began, "that drove the people to cut loose from the safe moorings of the Union and launch out amid the rocks and breakers of rebellion." But now the people must look to the future. The legislators must act to set up a militia, to encourage in-migration, to promote railroads, and to establish public schools.

Arkansas, its new governor declared, had the potential for becoming a populous and prosperous state. "Yet in the midst of this great age of progress and improvements, our primeval forests, as of yore, rear their arms to Heaven and seem to defy the hand of man." An influx of industrious settlers would help unlock the hidden wealth, and so would the construction of railroads. "Wherever the shrill voice of the 'iron horse' is heard every branch of industry is stimulated; along the tracks upon which he courses the forests disappear, the rough face of nature is smoothed down, and farms, villages, towns, and cities spring up as if by magic." Education not only would contribute to prosperity but also would assure freedom to the recently freed. The need was urgent, for, as voter registration lists showed, nearly a third of the white men and nearly all the black were illiterate. But the schools must be strictly segregated; if they were mixed the cause of education itself would be in jeopardy.[7]

Within a few weeks the legislature had passed all the laws that Governor Clayton requested. But he could not carry out his program until he had demonstrated his capacity to enforce the laws and govern the state. And he was soon to have a rebellion on his hands. The first sign of impending trouble appeared when, just three weeks after his inauguration, the Republicans rallied in Little Rock to start the Grant-for-President campaign.

Once again Clayton was to address his followers from the balcony of the Anthony House. It was already dark when a torchlight procession of a few thousand blacks approached on foot. Leading them on horseback was James Hinds, a Union veteran from New York, lawyer, and congressman—and the only white man in the procession. Hinds took his place on the balcony beside Clayton and Joseph Brooks, an Ohio native, once a Methodist minister and an army chaplain, now an Arkansas planter and state legislator. Clayton had concluded his remarks and Hinds was speaking when the fire bell began to clang on top of the nearby city hall. Horse-drawn fire engines rolled down the street and through the crowd. As torch-bearers beat their torches over the horses' heads, men here and there drew pistols and started to shoot, and then someone set off bunch after bunch of firecrackers. Several firemen and members of the crowd were wounded. Remaining on the balcony, Clayton angrily denounced the Democrats (who, as he pointed out, had met the night before without interruption) for what was obviously a false alarm intended to break up the Republican meeting.

People of the old master class felt uneasy—or professed to do so—at the assembling of ex-slaves for such a political demonstration. "They have left us our lives," a planter's widow sarcastically remarked as she watched them; "I suppose they now propose to put us to the torture." For some time, Arkansas planters had been complaining that blacks were stealing and slaughtering cattle and hogs, were growing insolent, and were plotting to rise up and seize the planters' land. Now the state's leading Democratic newspaper called for the utmost in violence against the imagined threat. "The negro element in the South is like a gangrene upon the body politic," the *Arkansas Gazette* warned, "and the first drop of blood shed in a servile war will be the signal for the extermination of the whole race. The white men of the Southern States will not always permit their land to be the scene of the successive depredations of Yankee bummers, carpet-baggers, and truculent negroes." Ku Kluxism clearly had the sanction of prominent Arkansas Democrats as they faced the state's Republicans in the presidential campaign of 1868.

To Clayton it made no sense to talk of the danger of Negro domination, as the Democrats continually did, since blacks constituted only about 25 percent of the state's population and held a much smaller proportion of the political jobs—including no really high positions. But by August he had reason to suspect that the Democrats would go to almost any length to keep blacks from voting. The thought of blacks voting was especially repugnant to whites who could not swear to past loyalty and therefore could not themselves vote.[8]

From Lewisburg, about forty miles north of Little Rock, word came to Clayton, in the statehouse chambers he was refurbishing, that a clash of races impended as whites obstructed blacks who tried to register. He persuaded several local Democrats to go with him to Lewisburg and join him in appealing to its citizens for a fair and peaceful registration. He returned with the satisfaction of having calmed the town, but reports of serious disorders began to pour in from other points in the state. Masked night riders were making the rounds of plantations and terrorizing black tenants—whipping them, driving them off, shooting and killing them. Sheriffs were unable to raise posses, some were even afraid to go on holding office, and local governments seemed to be losing the power to govern. Then came a telegram informing Clayton that Dr. A. M. Johnson had been assassinated just as he was about to start on an electioneering trip. Dr. Johnson was white. He had been a member of the legislature and a friend of Clayton's.[9]

Clayton now decided to strike back. His plan of action was twofold: he would call out the state militia to fight the Ku Klux Klan, and he would use undercover agents to penetrate the Klan and find out its secrets. But he faced tremendous difficulties in both undertakings. Though he could expect to raise enough militiamen—blacks from the lowlands and whites from the hill country, Southern whites who were veterans of the Union army—he would have to find some way to equip and arm them. As for the undercover agents, he would need men, preferably ex-Confederate soldiers, who could worm their way into the confidence of Klansmen, yet they must be men on whom he could absolutely rely.

In the midst of his preparations Clayton took time out, on a September day, for a bit of recreation with dog and gun. While out hunting, not far from Little Rock, he accidentally shot himself in the left hand. He had gone through four years of war without a scratch—and now this! His hand was so badly mangled that it had to be cut off.

He was still recovering from the amputation when, one night, a stranger called at the governor's house (the state did not provide an official residence but only a rental allowance) and demanded to see the governor in private. Clayton admitted him to his bedside. The man said he was the cyclops of a Ku Klux den but could not stomach the Klan's increasing use of violence and would tell what he knew about the organization if the governor would enable him and his family to relocate outside the state. From him Clayton learned enough to help his secret agents, a dozen of them, gain entrance to KKK dens. One of the agents, posing as a cattle buyer, disappeared from Searcy in neighboring White County. The local paper reported that the cattle buyer had absconded to avoid paying his hotel bill. Only later was Clayton to find out the truth: Klansmen had shot the agent and thrown the body into an abandoned well. The rest of the detectives were luckier, and from them Clayton obtained a good deal of information about the Klan's membership and activities.[10]

Still, he could not organize and arm the state troops fast enough to keep up with the Klan. Its depredatons continued and expanded. Its members threatened to take down the names and shoot on sight all blacks who signed up for the militia. A band of some two hundred masked men rode through one county to take guns away from individual recruits. Though nameless blacks were killed and wounded in large numbers, prominent whites also were victims—voting registrars, a state representative, and other officeholders.

When someone murdered a leading Democratic politician, a former Confederate general, Clayton offered a $10,000 reward for the arrest of the assassin. Only the one Democrat died, but Republicans continued to fall. The most prominent to die was Congressman James Hinds, who a few months earlier had stood at Clayton's side on the balcony of the Anthony House. State Representative Joseph Brooks, also present at the August rally, survived the shotgun blast that brought Hinds down. At the report of Hinds's murder and Brooks's wounding, the *Arkansas Gazette* cynically commented: "If true at all, we believe that the deed was perpetrated by the radicals themselves for effect in the presidential election north." Democrats continued to deny that they were carrying on a campaign of terror or that such an organization as the KKK existed—even when a white Republican deputy sheriff was found dead with his body tied to a black man's in such a way that the two corpses appeared to be embracing and kissing.

No Republican could feel safe any longer from the Democratic assassins, and certainly not the number one Republican, Governor Clayton. He gave the danger little thought until, late one October night, he started to walk home from his office in the capitol and, fatigued after the long day, stopped at a saloon "to get a stimulant." Three young men came in, sat down at a distance, eyed him, and whispered together. When he left they followed him. He dodged out of the bright moonlight and hid in the shadow of a board fence, where, with his revolver cocked, he listened to them talk of heading him off. While they ran on he went back to the police station and obtained bodyguards. At home he learned from his excited black servants that a mysterious horseman had been watching the house, that three men on foot had joined him, and that, upon his firing three shots in the air, all the men had scattered. Thereafter, when going to and from the office, Clayton always had an escort of militiamen, the "Governor's Guard." Masked men continued to prowl around the capitol at night, and so he had the building barricaded.[11]

Clayton's enemies, practically all of them Confederate veterans, were quite well armed and well mounted, having been generously allowed to keep their guns and horses at the time of their surrender. To buy arms and ammunition, Clayton borrowed money and sent an agent northward. When the shipment reached Memphis he hired a steamboat, the *Hesper,* to bring it on to Little Rock. Several days later he received distressing news from the *Hesper*'s captain. Twenty miles below Memphis the tug *Netty Jones,* much larger and more powerful than the *Hesper,* had overtaken her. From the tug sixty or seventy masked men, firing pistols, had leaped aboard the *Hesper* and proceeded to throw the cargo overboard.

Still, there were sufficient weapons right in Little Rock—if Clayton could only get his hands on them. They lay in the federal arsenal, and to borrow them he would need permission from the Johnson Administration. So he wrote to General John M. Schofield, now the secretary of war.

Schofield read Clayton's letter at a cabinet meeting and urged that the request be granted. He said the reconstructed state governments in the South would have to be propped up by military force until they could establish themselves. "Do you mean by that," Navy Secretary Gideon Welles sarcastically inquired, "until the black and ignorant element controls the intelligent white population?" Schofield replied: "There is no other way to keep down the Rebels." But Welles, an old Democrat from Connecticut, was sure that Clayton wanted to use the militia only for party purposes. "One after another of the scalawag and carpet-bag governers is calling for arms and troops to help him in the elections," Welles thought. And President Johnson, the old Democrat from Tennessee, agreed with Welles to the extent of turning down Clayton's appeal.[12]

Despite Welles's insinuations and allegations, Clayton was not about to use the militia for overawing the Democrats at the polls, though he certainly had reason to use the militia for protecting Republicans, since he received numerous reports of the KKK's intimidating both voting registrars and prospective voters. He also received urgent pleas that he declare martial law. Instead of immediately doing so, he reminded all the registrars in a form letter: "The whole principle of the ballot is a free expression of the public will, and the use of a military force, either at the registration or election, is not desirable." He added that such a free expression could be had only in places where the citizens respected the law and protected the registrar. Where the citizens did not do so, he would not provide a military force "for the purpose of enabling them to enjoy the privileges of an election." In other words, he was, in effect, recalling the registrars and calling off the election in those counties where the Klan made voting unsafe for Republicans.

Thus the Republicans managed to carry Arkansas for Grant on November 3. With him in the White House, Clayton could expect the support of the federal government, but Grant would not be inaugurated for four months. Meanwhile Clayton would have to continue on his own.

On the day after the election he proclaimed martial law for certain counties of the state and asked for additional volunteers to enforce it. "I passed some very anxious days and nights," he later recollected, "as it was far from certain that the militia, in the face of such a situation, would respond to my call." Before long he was relieved to learn how whites from the hill country and blacks from the lowlands were flocking to his support, accumulating to a total of about two thousand men.

They constituted a motley force. As the *Arkansas Gazette* sniffed, they were "dressed in citizen's clothes, with red flannel bands to their hats," were "mounted on anything that could be picked up, from a poor mule to a superb horse," and were "armed with pretty much every weapon known in civilized or uncivilized warfare." They proceeded to live off the land, despoiling their enemies. As Clayton explained, "My men must eat, and sleep, and be clothed, and if they take what they need, the losers only get what they deserve."[13]

The "militia war" lasted nearly four months. The state troops, as they saw it, were contending not against a legitimate army but against "rebels," "insurgents," "desperadoes," and "outlaws"—hence were justified in resorting to fairly severe measures. One of Clayton's commanders, facing the threat of a counterattack after occupying a hostile town, arrested fifteen local leaders and announced that he would kill them and burn the town if he were attacked. Still, the officers maintained fairly good discipline, seeing to the execution of five black militiamen whom courts martial convicted of rape.

Rough tactics paid off. State forces broke up Ku Klux dens and apprehended dozens of Klansmen. They tried, convicted, and hanged several for murder, among them the man who had killed and trussed up together the white deputy sheriff and the unoffending black man. When Clayton traveled by riverboat to the combat zone of eastern Arkansas, and a fellow passenger stalked him with gun in hand, one of his detectives disarmed and arrested the would-be assassin, and (without Clayton's prior knowledge) the man eventually went to the gallows. Finally the governor's men seized the *Netty Jones* and captured her piratical captain, the one who had boarded the *Hesper* and disposed of Clayton's arms shipment. By the end of February 1869 the whole of Arkansas seemed to have been pacified.[14]

The militia war gave Clayton favorable notice far beyond the borders of his state. Some Arkansans accused him of perpetrating a "reign of terror," *The Nation* of New York observed, and he had indeed put to flight some "distinguished citizens" of Arkansas, but before he did so, "twenty leading Republicans had been killed or wounded by assassins, and about two hundred colored Republicans had been murdered, to say nothing of the wounded and whipped." The militia might have been rough with murderers, but on the whole the campaign was in the interest of law and order. Or so *The Nation* said. And letters and telegrams from Washington assured Clayton that he had the wholehearted approval of Republican congressmen and senators and President-elect Grant.

At home, in Arkansas, Republicans were not so unanimous in their praise. A majority of those in the legislature did sustain the governor, but a large minority complained of what they considered high-handed policy. These critical Republicans were scalawags, white Southerners, followers of the scalawag lieutenant governor, James M. Johnson. They were to cause increasing trouble for the carpetbagger Clayton, now that the militia war had widened the party rift.[15]

The outlook seemed promising for Robert K. Scott as he took the train for Columbia, in July 1868, to be inaugurated as the first Republican governor of South Carolina. In some quarters at least he appeared to be the ablest of the newly elected carpetbag governors in the South. Four of the six governors (in the states being readmitted to the Union that summer) were Northern-born and were viewed as "Western" men: Warmoth from Illinois, Clayton from Kansas, Scott from Ohio, and Reed from Wisconsin. "General Scott, of South Carolina, a clear-headed, practical man, in the prime of life, a good soldier, and as sensible in political ideas as he was in the field, is a Westerner of the Westerners," *The Nation* had recently editorialized, quite unaware of his opium habit. "He, at any rate, will disappoint us if he does not turn out a good governor."[16]

His arrival in Columbia—after a rather tedious ten-hour, 130-mile ride from Charleston—could only have been sobering. There was nothing but track and dirt and open sky where he stepped off the train, the depot having not yet been rebuilt after the great fire. All around were other reminders of the conflagration that had occurred three and a half years earlier when he was here with Sherman's army. The once beautiful city, with its broad, tree-shaded avenues and its colorful flower gardens, was only slowly recovering. Nickerson's Hotel, the city's finest, had been restored, and Scott had an invitation from its proprietor to stay there, free of charge, until he could make other living arrangements.

To carry on the state's business, the governor and the legislature would have to make do with temporary official quarters. The old capitol was in ruins, and the new one, an imposing mass of granite, under construction at the start of the war, was not yet completed. The University of South Carolina had not escaped the flames, but Jainey Hall on the park-like campus was in usable condition. There the legislature was already meeting when the governor-elect arrived. In the senate sat 20 whites and 10 blacks; in the house, 46 whites and 78 blacks. Thus the blacks constituted a sizable majority in the General Assembly as a whole.

When Scott appeared in Jainey Hall for his inauguration on July 9, the visitors as well as the legislators were mostly black. He repeated the oath of office and the invocation "God save the state of South Carolina." Then the blacks stood up and began to chant those words while rhythmically stamping their feet and clapping their hands or waving their hats and handkerchiefs. Some of the whites in the crowd joined in. The spectacle disgusted conservative Carolinians who read about it in the local Democratic paper, the *Columbia Phoenix*. Still, the new governor's inaugural, with its themes of compromise and moderation, was well designed to assuage the feelings of the former ruling class.

In his message to the legislature the next day, Scott spelled out a program for appeasing the ex-Confederates. He made four recommendations (only one of them, the fourth, within the legislature's power): restore political rights to all citizens, discontinue the Freedmen's Bureau, remove the federal troops, and set up separate schools for whites and blacks.

Segregated schools were contrary to the intent of the new constitution, but Scott had no difficulty in justifying them. "While the moralist and the philanthropist cheerfully recognize the fact that 'God hath made of one blood all nations of men,' yet the statesman, in legislating for . . . two distinct and, in some measure, antagonistic races . . . must, as far as the law of equal rights will permit, take cognizance of existing prejudices among both." So argued the statesman Scott. "Let us therefore recognize facts as they are, and rely upon time and the elevating influence of popular education to dispel any unjust prejudices that may exist among the two races of our fellow citizens."

This message was "reassuringly moderate in sentiment," according to the *Charleston Daily News,* a voice of coastal conservatism. Scott seemed to be "anxious to gain the good will of the respectability and intelligence of the State." He indicated his concern by deed as well as word, many of his early appointments being quite acceptable to conservatives. From a former Confederate soldier, one who belonged to "the proscribed class of the Southern people," he received a letter heartily approving the message and promising to support him as long as he followed the policies he had set forth in it. If the signs of approval were also signs of a political honeymoon, it was to be an extremely brief one.[17]

For several weeks after becoming governor of South Carolina, Scott remained the head of the Freedmen's Bureau in the state. He continued even longer to administer the federal program of lending supplies to planters. Thus for a time he could exert political influence by collecting or postponing debts when due. He also had the political support of Bureau agents. One of them, the busy politician T. J. Mackey, reportedly had "done no duty in the Bureau since his appointment in S. C.," a Washington official of the Bureau complained to Scott. The dual position of Scott occasioned a sarcastic retort when he accused planters in one county of ejecting laborers for refusing to join Democratic clubs. "You write as Assistant Commissioner of the Freedmen's Bureau; you also claim to be Governor of this State," a local magistrate replied, denying the charge. "It will be no satisfaction to the people of South Carolina to know that you extend over them two protecting arms, either of which you can drop at pleasure, according to the exigencies and circumstances of the case."[18]

While getting used to his gubernatorial duties, Scott was making preparations for himself and his family to live in a style appropriate to his status and his wealth. At forty-two, he was already a rich man, worth nearly a third of a million dollars, a fortune for that time. He had just two dependents: his wife, Rebecca, thirty-five; and his son, Robert K., Jr., only three. Having acquired a suitable house, he bought new furniture for it through his friend F. A. Sawyer, the Northern-born United States senator recently sent to Washington from South Carolina. All the furniture was in the best of contemporary taste, including the marble-topped bureau, washstand, and bedroom table. He also obtained a set of "very fine harness" for his carriage horses, and he hired a contractor to build a stable and carriage house with a groom's apartment overhead.

Now he could maintain as splendid a turnout as could be seen on the broad thoroughfares of Columbia.

Known for generosity as well as affluence, Scott received more than a governor's usual allotment of begging letters. Not only did friends and relatives request jobs and other political favors; fellow politicians besought him for loans, and though annoyed he doled out various sums to members of the legislature to tide them over. One of his supplicants was Franklin J. Moses, Jr., descendant of a prominent South Carolina Jewish family, once a Confederate enthusiast, then a Republican delegate to the recent constitutional convention, and now the speaker of the house. Only "dire necessity," Moses assured Scott, had induced him to ask for help; he had "the most urgent need" for $400. (His gratitude was to be considerably less than permanent.) Though "short of funds" because of the demands made on him, Scott found money to help reelect Congressman James M. Ashley from Scott's home district in Ohio.[19]

Much more important than reelecting Ashley was electing Grant. Scott procured $4,000 from Republicans in Congress to help finance the presidential campaign in South Carolina. But he needed more than money: he would be hard pressed to make it physically possible for Republicans to campaign at all. For him and his fellow partisans—as for Republicans in other states of the South—the practice of politics required the enforcement of law and order, since for their opponents the practice of politics meant lawlessness and terrorism.

Early in the summer Scott received reports that white men throughout the state were arming, organizing, drilling, and "threatening the public peace." At first he tried to deal with the threat by exhorting all citizens, black as well as white, to obey the laws and "resist those prejudices and passions" that could "only result in violence, suspend progress, and interfere with the material and social welfare of the State." He undertook to allay the fear and anger of blacks by assuring them of the falsity of rumors that the lives of legislators were "in the most imminent danger." But the rumors proved to be only too true as the political (and on the Democratic side, the military) campaign intensified during August, September, and October. At least four black Republicans and a white one were murdered, among them two members of the legislature. "Sir," Scott heard from a Republican newspaper editor in Charleston, "your own life—the party, the country, humanity—demand prompt, stern, thorough action."

Scott blamed the top Democratic leaders, state and national, for the violence. He had in mind, for one, the Democratic vice-presidential candidate, Frank Blair, whom he had known personally as his superior in Sherman's army, and who recently had called for the overthrow of the carpetbag governments in the South. "Blair has in advance declared war!" Scott expostulated privately. "He has plainly told us that the Reconstruction [program] of Congress is revolutionary and must be set aside. The leading men in the Rebellion understand him to mean that it must be done by force if need be and they are prepared to act on his declaration."[20]

Scott also had in mind the great South Carolina hero of the Confederacy—Wade Hampton. Scion of one of the state's wealthiest families (one grandfather had been reputedly the largest slaveholder in the entire country), Hampton was now more than $1,000,000 in debt and was soon to lose his remaining plantations in South Carolina and Mississippi. But his devotion to the Confederate cause was undiminished; he continued habitually to wear gray. A graduate of South Carolina College (as the university was known before the war), he felt a sentimental attachment to the city of Columbia.

At the time of Sherman's approach to Columbia in February 1865, Hampton commanded the cavalry rearguard in the city. A year later he accused Sherman of having "burned it to the ground, deliberately, systematically and atrociously," though Hampton's own men had started the fire by ripping open cotton bales and lighting them to keep them from falling into Sherman's hands. Hampton's charge of incendiarism, an article of faith with most white South Carolinians, had exacerbated their anti-Yankee bitterness.

Hampton again exercised his rabble-rousing talent in the presidential campaign of 1868. At the Democratic convention in New York he was a member of the platform committee, and afterward in a speech at Charleston he claimed as his own contribution the plank that denounced the Reconstruction acts as "unconstitutional, revolutionary, and void." He added, before his South Carolina audience, that once the Democrats were back in power they would "do their utmost to relieve the Southern States and restore to us the Union and the Constitution as it existed before the war." And the prewar Constitution and Union had, of course, permitted slavery in the Southern states.

Scott was addressing Hampton in particular when, in one of his early proclamations, he said: "I . . . earnestly and respectfully appeal to all good citizens, and especially to those whose position and character enable them to exercise a salutary influence upon public opinion, to aid me in my efforts to maintain the supremacy of the laws and preserve the peace and dignity of the Commonwealth." When neither Hampton nor any other Democrat responded with assistance, Scott reluctantly considered answering illegal violence with legal armed force. All he had at hand was a mounted constabulary of some 150 men, about two-thirds of them Northern whites and one-sixth of them native blacks. To raise an adequate militia, he would have to rely on black recruits and he would have to find the means to arm them. He did order 1500 rapid-fire rifles from a Massachusetts manufacturer, only to learn that there were none in stock. He heard that War Secretary Schofield favored declaring martial law in parts of the state, but nothing came of that proposal.[21]

In the *Columbia Phoenix* of October 18, Scott could see all too plainly the cynicism of Democratic leaders who denied that party members were doing anything except "treating with great kindness and forbearance the colored population of the State." "We have no doubt you will make manifest the untruth of the malicious charge that by force you have compelled their votes or by intimidation kept them from the polls," the address from the Central Democratic Club to rank-and-file Democrats continued. "Their minds are rapidly opening to the truth, that the vagrant white man of the North, as well as the renegade of the South, who live by deceiving and plundering them, and who have been driving them to destruction, are not true friends and are unworthy of confidence and support."

Scott knew that these statements were farcical, as their authors themselves must have known. He announced that if "turbulent and lawless men resisting executive authority" should persist in infringing the rights of citizens, white or black, he would be compelled to "arm and organize a sufficient force of loyal citizens to overcome the resistance." At about the same time he happened to meet a couple of ex-Confederate colonels, named Gibbs and Childs, in a local bank. As he was to recall two years later:

> I spoke to them concerning the numerous murders and outrages then being perpetrated throughout the State, and I said that unless they were stopped, I would no longer use my influence to prevent the colored people from retaliating upon the leaders of the Democratic Party, as the people held them responsible for the outrages committed. That Wade Hampton was the recognized leader of the Democratic Party, and that he had inaugurated this reign of terror . . . by his speech at Charleston. . . . They wished to know in what way Gen. Hampton could put a stop to the numerous outrages committed. I replied that if Gen. Hampton would issue an address as Chairman of the Democratic State Central Committee, repudiating the murders and advising that they cease, that it would have the desired effect. Then Col. Gibbs asked if I would follow Hampton's address by a proclamation to the public recognizing Hampton's services. I said emphatically that I would do so.

Before long Scott had a call from Hampton, then about fifty, well formed, muscular, with a heavy mustache and mutton-chop whiskers, and with all the grace and charm of a true Southern cavalier. Scott repeated to him his conviction that *he* was responsible for the "reign of terror" and that he alone could put a stop to it. Hampton replied that Colonel Childs had spoken to him about the matter and that he, Hampton, had already acted on the governor's suggestion by preparing an address to the people of the state. A copy of it was in the office of the *Columbia Phoenix,* he said, and would appear in the paper the next day, October 23, 1868. On the morrow Scott was able to read it for himself. "Fellow-citizens," Hampton had written, " . . . we feel it our duty to invoke your earnest efforts in the cause of peace and the preservation of order. We beg you to unite with us in reprobating these recent acts of violence. . . . No cause can prosper which calls murder to its assistance, or which looks to assassination for success."[22]

Scott could feel that this public statement had pretty much the effect for which he had hoped. At any rate, election day in South Carolina proved to be quiet enough that the Republicans could carry the state for Grant. But the future was to show that Hampton's cause, despite his words on this occasion, could indeed prosper by means of murder and could suceed quite well through recourse to assassination.

The live oaks were still green, as they would be all winter, on the capitol square in Tallahassee. The sun was warm, the breeze mild. How different from Wisconsin in November! Yet, as Harrison Reed sat in his office, gazing out the window from time to time, he had cause to wonder about the wisdom of going into politics in Florida. No matter how often he stroked his bushy beard or his bald head, his troubles refused to go away. He had been governor for only five months, and already the legislature was in revolt against him, threatening to throw him out and terminate his political career.

The predicament in which Reed now found himself was rather ironic. At the time he took office, even his bitterest foes among the Radical Republicans had predicted no such outcome. On the contrary, they were describing Reed as practically a dictator, one who would be unbeatable if Congress should sanction his regime. They said he had imposed a fraudulent constitution on the state and had got himself elected by catering to ex-Confederates and by misusing his powers as federal postal agent. "You know the history of that Constitution," the Mule Team leader and one-time Unitarian preacher Liberty Billings protested to Congressman Elihu B. Washburne of Illinois: "Rebel Herods & Johnson office-holding Copperhead-Pilates combining to crucify Radical Republicanism." Another of the Radicals wrote Washburne: "It is plain that the legislature under that constitution will not be the Representatives of the people but the tools of the Governor."

Reed appeared to be in complete command when the legislature first got down to business and turned to the election of United States senators. "The apparent party harmony which brought about the choice of Senators by the so-called Legislature," it seemed to one of his Radical critics, "was like the concord of a gang of slaves lashed by the whip of the enormous appointing power of the Governor." Named to the short term in the Senate was a man from Michigan and to the long term one from New Jersey. The former was to have little influence in Florida politics; the latter, Thomas W. Osborn, was to contest powerfully for the control of state politics. As the erstwhile state commissioner of the Freedmen's Bureau, Osborn retained a following among the Bureau's beneficiaries, mostly black. More recently, as a federal register of bankruptcy, he showed he had the backing of the Treasury Department and its former head, Salmon P. Chase. Reed, anti-Chase and pro-Johnson, had no reason to rely on Senator Osborn, despite the appearance of party harmony at the time of Osborn's election.[23]

Governor Reed did have a great deal of state patronage to dispose of, whether or not his appointing power was as enormous or as "imperial" as his Radical foes alleged. Under the new constitution, designed as it was to offset the Negro vote, he appointed not only state but also county officeholders, except constables. The Mule Team member Daniel Richards accused him of giving high places to some of the "vilest and bitterest rebels" in the state. "News of the failure to convict Johnson will be like Greek fire throughout the entire South," Richards had predicted at the end of the impeachment trial. "The eyes of rebels sparkle like those of the fiery serpent. They hope they have found their 'Lost Cause,' and they think they see it." Now, the Radicals feared, Reed was giving further encouragement to Florida ex-rebels. He did, in fact, appoint former Confederates and present Democrats to some judgeships and to two of the eight cabinet posts, but he divided most of the jobs among carpetbaggers, scalawags, and blacks. He assigned blacks to lowly positions such as justice of the peace; he elevated none of them to his original cabinet. All together, Governor Reed (with the consent of the state senate) had about five hundred appointments to make.

Senator Osborn, however, was beginning to wield an even more effective patronage power. He controlled federal appointments in the state. These were less numerous—about one hundred postmasters, fifty customs employees, six judges, two public land and two internal revenue officers, one register of bankruptcy, and one marshal—but they paid much better than state jobs. Formerly, as U.S. postal agent, Reed had had behind him the Post Office Department (under his friend Alexander Randall, onetime governor of Wisconsin) and the department's patronage. Now, as governor, he no longer held that advantage.[24]

Before the first legislative session ended, on August 6, Reed had succeeded in antagonizing at least some members of not only the Osborn faction but practically every political group in Florida. He did this by trying to check the special interests and give the state a responsible and businesslike government. He proposed to raise taxes for individual property owners and also for railroads (hitherto untaxed), telegraph companies, and other corporations. He vetoed a bill to incorporate a bank that he considered the dishonest project of New York "money sharks." He refused to authorize the state to aid Osborn and Osborn's friends in some financial schemes of theirs. When the legislature presented him a bill requiring hotels and railroads to treat blacks exactly like whites, he faced a dilemma: he was bound to lose support among either blacks or native whites. He promptly vetoed the bill.

On one issue, at least, the governor and the Republicans in the legislature agreed. Something must be done to put down the spreading lawlessness and enable the majority to rule. Otherwise the state could never be carried for Grant in the fall. Night riders—Ku Klux Klansmen, Regulators, or simply Democratic clubs—were threatening, whipping, and killing black Republicans. Federal troops, though some were still stationed in Jacksonville and other Florida towns, failed to stop the depredations. Reed got authorization from the legislature to raise and arm a militia, which of necessity would be mostly black. Still, he and other Republicans doubted whether they could create a force strong enough to put down the terrorist menace.

So the governor recommended and the legislators passed a law giving the choice of presidential electors to the legislature. There was nothing unconstitutional about this: at one time all the states had allowed their legislatures to choose the President. Anyhow, Reed remarked, Florida could not afford another election so soon. Considering the large Republican majority in the legislature, the electoral vote of Florida now seemed safely in the bag for Grant—three months before election day.

Short of overthrowing the legislature, there was little the Democrats could do to carry the state for Seymour and Blair. They did mount a campaign of protest, and they persisted in their terrorist tactics. To counter these, Reed traveled north after the legislature's adjournment to seek arms for his militia. Stopping in Washington, he had no luck with his former patron Andrew Johnson. Proceeding to Boston and Albany, he tried unsuccessfully to borrow arms from the governors of Massachusetts and New York. In New York City he finally managed to buy, on credit, two thousand rifles and ammunition for them. These were to go to Jacksonville by ship and on to Tallahassee by rail.[25]

On November 3, election day, the legislature reassembled in Tallahassee to choose three electors who would cast the state's three votes for Grant. Remaining in session, the legislators passed a bill to give themselves extra pay, and Reed vetoed it. Immediately one of the representatives proposed to impeach him on charges of "falsehood and lying," appointing incompetent officials, trying to oust legislators, and embezzling state funds. On November 7 the house passed a resolution for impeachment. Radicals in Congress had set an example with President Johnson; now those in the Florida assembly were following it with Governor Reed.

It was a critical moment for Reed as he sat in his capitol office and pondered his options. He knew he was innocent of the charges, but he also knew his guilt or innocence was irrelevant. "A conspiracy was formed by Osborn and his military satraps to depose me by violence and take possession of the Capitol," he recalled long afterward. "It embraced all the prominent Federal office-holders in the State, from the marshal down."

And now came more bad news. The arms Reed had bought in New York would never reach his militia. Between Jacksonville and Tallahassee men had boarded the train and, apparently with the connivance of railroad employees, had broken up the guns and scattered the fragments along the right of way. On second thought, perhaps this news was not quite so bad as it seemed at first. Reed's plan to arm the blacks had counteracted his effort to woo conservative whites; the frustration of this plan might appease some of the conservative hostility.

Reed needed all the help he could get. Lieutenant-Governor William H. Gleason, Reed's fellow Wisconsinite but Osborn's follower, proceeded to proclaim himself acting governor. The new constitution provided for the suspension of an impeached oficial, and Gleason's proclamation seemed authoritative enough: it bore the imprint of the great seal of the state of Florida. Reed's appointee as secretary of state and keeper of the seal, George R. Alden, had defected to the Osborn-Gleason side.

But Reed believed himself entitled to his office, and he certainly did not intend to give it up. He reasoned that, legally, there was no impeachment, for the senate had lacked a quorum at the time the house presented the charges. The senate lacked a quorum because Reed earlier had declared the seats of some of its members vacant—members who unconstitutionally held other state jobs. He now asked the state supreme court for an advisory opinion.

Reed and his friends feared that the Osborn-Gleason men might attempt to seize his office. So his friends armed themselves and formed a guard, under the command of an army captain on leave, to protect him and the capitol. When Gleason tried to pick up some personal papers, he was turned away at gunpoint. Unable to occupy the executive chambers in the capitol, Gleason set up his headquarters in the hotel across the street. To his room came job-seekers and other hangers-on who expected him to win the contest for the governorship.

Besieged in his office, Reed had reason to continue fearing an attack. Mobs roamed around the capitol, and rockets flared at night, like signals for the attack to begin. A rumor ran that Ku Kluxers, or possibly Radical Republicans masquerading as Klansmen, were plotting to assassinate Reed. If his enemies thought to frighten him into resigning, they misjudged their man, a man whom many of them condemned as old-womanish. He reacted decisively and forcefuly.

First, he fired the turncoat Alden and put in Alden's place as secretary of state the eloquent and well-educated black, Jonathan C. Gibbs. Earlier, to win back friends he had lost by vetoing the equal-accommodations bill, Reed had called in C. H. Pearce, a state senator and also a minister of the African Methodist Episcopal church. He persuaded Pearce, and gave him expense money, to go out among his fellow black preachers and assure them that the governor was not really in league with ex-rebels and Democrats. Now, by appointing Gibbs to the cabinet, Reed could expect to regain still more support among blacks.

Next, through his loyal attorney general, Reed charged Gleason and Alden with conspiring to interfere with the operation of the government. A circuit court judge, the onetime slaveowner William A. Cocke, issued a warrant, and a faithful sheriff arrested the two men but left them at liberty while awaiting trial. Then Reed and his attorney general sought from the supreme court a writ of *quo warranto* calling on Gleason to prove his right to hold even the office of lieutenant governor. After all, the new constitution required three years of Florida residence, and Gleason had not resided in the state that long. Eventually two of the three supreme court justices, both of them ex-Confederates, decided against Gleason, who then had to vacate the lieutenant-governorship.

When the supreme court came out with the advisory opinion Reed had requested, the majority upheld his point of view. There was no senate quorum when the house brought its charges against the governor, the judges ruled, and therefore he was not legally impeached and should not be tried. Thus Reed succeeded in staving off impeachment by shifting the contest to the courts—a method that Johnson had hoped in vain to use.[26]

CHAPTER 8

Some Good and Some Bad (1868-1872)

Willard Warner, now a United States senator, was in Washington for the session beginning in December 1868. As recently as the previous January he had been an Ohio state senator—only about six months before the Alabama legislature elected him to his present position. Still, he was no stranger to Alabama, having operated a plantation there since 1865.

He continued to revisit Ohio from time to time, to see his motherless children—Willard III ("Willie"), now eleven, and May ("Ezzie"), two years younger—who were being raised by their mother's parents. He always had interesting things to tell the children about life on the plantation, with its cotton and corn, its melons, plums, and peaches, its fish that Mose the black man caught in baskets, and its six-foot-long alligators in the creek. Willie and Ezzie usually spent part of their summers on the plantation. Now, with winter coming on, Willie was helping his grandfather kill rats on the Ohio farm and was asking his father for permission to skate on the canal as soon as it froze over. Senator Warner was shortly to leave for Ohio again, for Christmas.

For the moment, his political future looked very good. In less than three months Ulysses S. Grant would be President, and Grant was a personal friend of General William Tecumseh Sherman and his young brother, Senator John Sherman, both of whom were personal friends of Warner's. General Sherman, on whose staff Warner had served during the war, had congratulated him most warmly on his election to the Senate. "Your greatest difficulty will be to reconcile the ambitious men of Alabama, who must be jealous of the newcomers," Sherman had advised him. "I suppose you are classed as a Carpetbagger, but this is not so, as you made purchase of a plantation and are as much a citizen as if you were born there." In fact, Warner was to have less to fear politically from leading Alabama whites than from a fellow Northerner, his Senate colleague George E. Spencer, and from Spencer's black allies and followers.[1]

Despite his Alabama property, Warner certainly fit the classification of a carpetbagger, at least in the view of Alabama Democrats. "He is a nigger Senator," the Democratic *Montgomery Advertiser* declared, "and the people of Alabama had nothing to do with his ridiculous so-called election." Campaigning for Grant, in the town of Eutaw, Warner had come up against gun-toting hecklers who insisted that no damned carpetbagger was going to speak there. His very clothing marked him as a Northerner and heightened the ire of the mob. He wore a silk top hat and a less than knee-length coat; the well-dressed Southerner preferred a soft felt, broad-brimmed hat and swallow tails. "God damn him, his coat-tail is too short!" one man in Eutaw yelled, and another cursed him on account of his "plug hat." Finally Warner gave up. Never before had he been compelled to yield his freedom of speech, and he now felt almost as if he were "running away from battle in time of war."[2]

When, on December 15, he rose to speak on the Senate floor, he took occasion to avow and defend his role as a carpetbagger, though the subject of debate was a bill to authorize the formation of militia in the reconstructed states. He was only too well aware of anti-Republican atrocities in Alabama—"the rebel yell is still heard in the caves of the Ku Klux," he had noted—and he favored the use of state militia as well as federal troops to preserve order. But, like some of the new governors in the South, he thought no congressional action was needed, since the reconstructed states had the same rights as others in the Union, including the right under the Second Amendment of the federal Constitution to organize a militia. We "intend to maintain these governments," he went on, "native and carpet-bag Union men" standing shoulder to shoulder. "I glory in the progressive spirit which made me a carpet-bagger," he dared to proclaim. "We are in these States by virtue of the Constitution of the United States; we are there as citizens, and we intend to remain there."

After the Christmas recess the Senate took up a resolution honoring the late Congressman Hinds of Arkansas, the victim of a political murder the previous autumn. Warner, who had known Hinds personally, lauded him as "an earnest and a sincere man," hence a true hero of the kind Thomas Carlyle described in *Heroes and Hero-Worship* (1841). Hinds's assassination was "not a singular occurrence"; political murders were all too common in the South. "Two of the men who sheltered me in my campaign in Alabama last summer, two of those who gave me hospitable welcome under their roofs, within a week afterward were assassinated," Warner said. "Now let the impression be left upon our minds by this sad event that we shall protect everywhere American citizens in the exercise of their constitutional and natural rights."

To help protect citizens in the exercise of their rights, the Senate was discussing a joint resolution for a constitutional amendment, which would be the fifteenth. Warner himself had presented to the Senate the original resolution coming from the House. But he did not like the wording that his more cautious colleagues agreed upon: negative and limited wording that would merely forbid the state and federal governments to deprive citizens of the vote on account of race, color, or previous condition of servitude. Warner pointed out, prophetically, that such an amendment would not prevent states from disfranchising citizens on other grounds, such as an educational or property requirement.

He pleaded in vain for a positive guarantee of the right of both blacks and whites to vote and hold office. "I would admit woman, the most beautiful, the purest and best of God's creatures, to an equal voice with us in the Government." But to add woman's suffrage would only defeat the measure. "Besides, whenever the women of this country ask with anything like unanimity for the ballot they will get it." Most urgent was preventing the disfranchisement of "the poor and the ignorant" and protecting "the great laboring, industrial classes of the country."

The Democrats of Alabama did not think much of Warner's speech. "He is of the opinion that negro women as well as negro men ought to vote," the *Montgomery Advertiser* misleadingly reported. Nor were most of his Republican colleagues much impressed. Before the end of the session, the last session during the presidency of Andrew Johnson, Congress (on February 27, 1869) approved the suffrage resolution without the changes that Warner had urged. In a little more than a year the requisite number of states would ratify it and it would become the Fifteenth Amendment.[3]

March 4, 1869. Grant was inaugurated as President and the new Congress began its first session. The day marked a fresh start, with better times at hand, or so it seemed to Republicans and especially to those in the South. Under the Grant Administration the carpetbaggers, scalawags, and blacks could expect greater support from the federal government than they had received under the Johnson Administration. More immediately, the Republicans in Congress could look forward to distributing lots of spoils, since the change at the top would mean wholesale removals and replacements of federal jobholders at all levels.

In the case of Alabama's senators, Warner and Spencer, there was some question as to just how the two should share in the disposing of patronage within the state. Traditionally, when both senators from a state belonged to the party in power, the senior one had his choice of the juiciest plums to give away. But, as between Warner and Spencer, which was the senior senator? Warner had been elected only to the short term, ending in 1871, and Spencer to the long term, ending in 1873. (When the seceded states rejoined the union, Senate terms did not begin anew at six years, but resumed at the point they would have reached if the seats had been occupied all along.) But the two men had been admitted to the Senate on exactly the same day. And, forty-two at that time, Warner was the elder by all of ten years. Besides, he would be close to General Sherman, whom President Grant was bringing to Washington as his general in chief, and who could be expected to have Grant's ear.

At first, all was harmony between the two senators from Alabama. Warner desired an appointment as federal circuit judge for his brother-in-law William B. Woods, the former Union general and present Alabama planter. Spencer obliged his colleague by recommending Woods. But both Spencer and Warner wanted to name the collector of customs for the port of Mobile. To settle the quarrel, Grant's aides proposed a compromise: Warner could pick the Mobile collector, and Spencer the Mobile postmaster. Neither Warner nor Spencer was quite satisfied with this arrangement, and the two began to disagree more and more stridently, on policy as well as patronage.

While antagonizing some Alabama Republicans—the followers of Spencer—Warner urged one federal appointment that pleased Alabama Democrats. For surveyor of customs at Mobile, Grant nominated his friend of the old army days, best man at his wedding, James Longstreet. Many Northerners were shocked at the idea of giving a federal job to such a conspicuous ex-Confederate. A number of Republican senators objected to confirming Longstreet. Standing out as one of Longstreet's foremost advocates, Warner could claim much of the credit when the Senate finally consented to the appointment. Even his continual critic the *Montgomery Advertiser* now had at least a qualified good word for him. "Warner O. K.—outside political circle," ran the headline of one article, which said he bore "the character of a respectable gentleman," and no one would insult him by calling him a carpetbagger "but for his unfortunate political ambition."[4]

On questions of economic policy, Warner found himself in agreement with General Sherman, whom he saw from time to time either in the General's War Department office or in the palatial residence his wealthy admirers had given him. With regard to the people of the South, the aim should be to "turn their minds from politics into material channels," Sherman believed. "Once get prosperity restored [and] men will soon reconcile themselves to the changes that war has brought about."[5] As a member of the committee on finance, in the Senate Warner elaborated on the same theme. He appealed to his fellow senators:

> The South now needs your aid. Dig out her harbors; give her the share of bank circulation which belongs to her; aid to build her railroads, and in every way by your practical legislation aid to upbuild her material interests, and to give encouragement to her enterprises, and you will not simply have benefited your common country, but you will have done a wise work in the matter of the reconstruction of these States.

Again and again, during 1869 and 1870, Warner argued for economic policies that would be fair to the South. The national banking system, set up during the war, had not been extended as it ought to have been to the Southern states. Hence national banks and banknotes were unfairly distributed, "Massachusetts having thirty-five dollars per capita and my State having thirty-five cents." Warner introduced a bill to lessen the disparity.

Also discriminatory against the South was the annual appropriation for the improvement of rivers and harbors. Of the 1869 river-and-harbor bill Warner said its drafters had never looked southward. "I see that Sheboygan harbor, Wisconsin, and Saugatuck harbor in Michigan, and little Conneaut harbor in Ohio—a place that I do not remember ever to have heard of although I am accused of representing or misrepresenting that State in the Senate—and Little Sodus in New York are provided for." But there was nothing for the vastly more important harbor of Mobile or for any of the other "great harbors" of the South. The 1870 appropriation, thanks to the efforts of Warner and other carpetbag and scalawag senators, included nearly $1,000,000 for Southern rivers and harbors. "While this bill is not as liberal to the South as I should be glad to have it," Warner remarked, "I am very glad to find in it some very considerable recognition of the fact that the late rebel States have been restored to the Union."

Like other Republican senators from the South, Warner advocated federal aid for railways as well as waterways. What the railroads wanted from the federal government was its conferral of new land grants or renewal of old ones. As a member of the committee on public lands, Warner was in a strategic position to assist Alabama companies. He interested himself particularly in the Selma, Rome and Dalton line, running eastward into Georgia, and the Alabama and Chattanooga, running southwestward from Tennessee across Alabama and into Mississippi. This line was expected to link up with the Texas and Pacific, a planned transcontinental railroad whose sponsors were confident that it would do wonders for Southern commerce.

Spencer, too, supported land grants and other measures to promote the economic development of the South, though he spent less time on such projects than Warner did. While agreeing on the principle, the two senators occasionally disagreed on its application. During the discussion of the Texas and Pacific aid bill, Spencer offered an amendment to give equal privileges and grants to the Decatur, Aberdeen and Vicksburg, another projected link with the transcontinental road. Warner objected that Spencer's amendment was not germane to the bill before the Senate. "It certainly is germane to this bill," Spencer replied, but when he called for yeas and nays his amendment was voted down. Warner still appeared to hold the upper hand.[6]

Warner and Spencer disagreed more basically, and more bitterly, on the question of restoring political rights to ex-Confederate military officers and civilian officials. Most of these men could hold no state or federal office, because the Fourteenth Amendment prohibited it, but in Alabama and some of the other reconstructed states they were allowed to vote. In early 1870 the Congress considered proposals to restrict their right to vote in Virginia, Mississippi, and Georgia, all three of which were still awaiting permission to be restored to the Union.

President Grant was known to oppose restrictions, and Senator Warner argued repeatedly and forcefully against the imposition of political disabilities. "I want to repel that old idea that only the men with white skins are to be called 'the people,'" he remarked in discussing the Mississippi bill. Yet he did not want to exclude whites of the old master class, either. To restrict their rights, he said, would imply a "suspicion of bad faith," which would tend to provoke the very attitude suspected. "I have more faith in the reconstruction of these States, a faith based upon five years of actual knowledge and intercourse with these people," he continued. "I do not desire to doubt their honesty and good faith."

After the Georgia bill had come up, Senator Spencer joined the debate with an argument in favor of "imposing fundamental conditions" on the state. He began by saying that Congress had already been too generous with the defeated South, that this generosity had been "productive of almost irreparable mischief," and that it had been much more than "the rebellious element" had deserved or even expected.

> It [the rebellious element] fully understood that this "arbitrament of arms" . . . brought with it certain inevitable penalties which always follow unsuccessful revolutions, and it was prepared to receive them. Contrary to what had been the prevailing idea of the confederates, we exacted no penalties of person or property, and to-day, for the first time in the history of all revolutions, the leaders of the rebellion walk the streets unmolested and enjoy the privileges of citizenship, wholly unrestricted in their estates and persons—an unprecedented example of national liberality and magnanimity. Before the ink had scarcely dried upon their written paroles, these revolutionists commenced the formation of combinations to secure again power and place, and they have been and are now unceasing in their unscrupulous efforts to regain political strength and to consecrate the *bona fides* of the "lost cause."

Given these facts, Spencer went on, he was quite surprised that his colleague from Alabama should have taken the position he took, espousing the cause of the "rebellious element."

> If the consent of the disloyal governed were alone indispensable in the State of Alabama, I am satisfied that neither he nor I would be here to-day. . . . I favor protection to those now governing the Southern States, the Unionists. My desire is to strengthen them to maintain a loyal government, not to assist the rebellious element to oust this loyal element, and to invoke if possible in the Senate a mischievous sentimentality to the injury of the country. . . .
>
> My honorable colleague, with a zeal worthy of a better cause, proposes to

> leave this very element of rebellion free and untrammeled to upturn free constitutions, usurp government, and work its unholy will upon the loyal people. . . .
>
> Take the State of Alabama, for instance. No sooner had we begun to tinker with and remove limitations and restrictions imposed by the reconstruction acts than, mistaking our clemency for cowardice, . . . the secession element resorted to the dagger and the rope, the lash and the torch, to frighten Union men from the polls, with the view of recovering the political supremacy they had held so long. . . .
>
> Contrast this chivalry with the poor men of Alabama, her mountain boys who gathered under the old flag of the country, their fathers' flag, and on many a weary march and cheerless bivouac and hard-fought field, under my immediate command, attested their devotion to the Union. I can assure the Senate that these soldiers do not agree with the suicidal policy advocated by those Senators who oppose fundamental conditions. . . .
>
> I utterly and entirely disagree with him [Warner] upon the questions at issue.

After waiting a month, Warner replied to Spencer in a set speech of his own. To some extent he agreed with his Alabama colleague. He said:

> The country [at the end of the war] was naturally and properly distrustful of the power of the governing class of the South, of the white people. They might have placed confidence in them and reconstructed by putting the Government back into their hands, and there might have been peace upon such conditions at the South; but it would have been peace at the sacrifice of every right which made life and liberty desirable to the colored people of the South, who had been liberated by the national Government.

Warner went on to say that Radical Reconstruction had been necessary and—here he began to diverge from Spencer's views—that it was adequate and a success. In all history, he elaborated, "you cannot find an instance where so great a revolution has been wrought, where all the institutions and habits and customs of a people have been so completely overturned, where so many people have been elevated to their just rights." To pacify the South, Warner argued, the federal government should use a combination of power and kindness. It should employ military force where needed to put down crime, but it should rely mainly on fostering the prosperity of the people and making them feel truly a part of the country. The future of Southern Republicanism depended on such a policy.

> Now, the political problem of the South is this: the Union or Republican party of the South must draw to its ranks an additional element of the old white population in order to [secure] its permanent maintenance. They are needed to sustain the colored friends of the Union and to give good government. . . . To do that it is not necessary to modify in the slightest degree our policy of reconstruction or . . . the principle of political equality and equal

> rights to all. The only thing that is needed to be done now is to put the party on a basis of respectability and character that will make it invulnerable to the attacks of its enemies, on account of the personal fitness and character of its leaders, its representative men, and its office-holders. When that is done, as is fast being done, . . . the great Republican party . . . will . . . be sustained not only by the colored people as a unit, but by a majority in many of the States of the white people.
>
> We have in the Southern States as much to fear from bad men in our own ranks as we have from the rebels themselves. . . . It was unavoidable that, in a political revolution like the one we have had, many such men should have come to the surface. Time will cure these defects. . . .
>
> We have vindicated them [the principles of Reconstruction] very thoroughly and completely in my own State. While there have been deplorable outrages committed there in certain localities, while there are assassins going at large unpunished, yet it is still true that the general condition of the State is peaceable and prosperous.

Warner took specific issue with this statement of Spencer's: "Our generosity has been mistaken for cowardice and has been productive of almost irreparable mischief." Warner insisted that "if a vindictive policy of confiscation and hanging had been adopted, . . . things would have been vastly worse."[7]

Whether or not he won the argument with Spencer, Warner turned out to be on the winning side, for Congress did not require the kind of restrictions that Spencer demanded for Virginia, Mississippi, and Georgia. Both of the Alabama senators favored the enforcement act of May 31, 1870, which authorized the President to use the military, when necessary, to make the Fifteenth (and the Fourteenth) Amendment effective. But personal relations between the two were extremely poor when Congress adjourned that summer to enable its members to go home and mend their fences.

At home on his plantation near Montgomery, Warner felt positively euphoric as he looked ahead to the fall campaign. His chances for reelection to the Senate, for a regular six-year term this time, seemed almost certain. The Republicans would surely maintain their control in the next Alabama legislature, which would decide Warner's fate. They could count on an overwhelming majority in the state senate, for its members had two more years to serve, and the Republicans outnumbered the Democrats by thirty-two to one. Though the entire house was up for reelection, it also appeared to be safe enough. All but a few of the 100 representatives elected in 1868 were Republicans, and if the Republicans could hold on to no more than thirty-five house seats, they would still have a majority in the assembly as a whole.

True, there were potential troublemakers in the party—Senator

Spencer and his followers—but what could they do? Spencer was at outs not only with Warner but also with William H. Smith, the former Confederate (a Georgian by birth) who had defected to the Union side in 1862 and for whom Spencer had tried to get the provisional state governorship in 1865. Recently Spencer had been claiming he had "placed Smith where he was" as Alabama's first Republican governor, but Spencer had also been criticizing the Smith administration as both conservative and weak. Governor Smith was now Warner's friend.

There seemed less to fear from Republican dissidents than from Democratic terrorists. Continuing Ku Klux activity had been reported from time to time. Still, at the moment, the Klan was quiescent, and if it should come alive during the campaign it could be kept in bounds by the federal troops already in the state plus reinforcements to come. Remaining in Alabama was an infantry regiment of 631 men, with contingents of them deployed at five locations. They were under the command of General Samuel W. Crawford, a graduate of the University of Pennsylvania medical school who, after becoming a professional soldier, had served throughout the war, beginning with the defense of Fort Sumter.

On August 23, just seven days before the Republican state convention was to meet and make nominations for the 1870 campaign, Warner expatiated on his glorious prospects in a letter to Senator Sherman. He had no inkling of the political disaster that lay ahead for him. He wrote:

> I was welcomed home by all parties. Everybody here is really & professionally my friend. In our County Convention which met on the 13 inst. no man could get anything except by avowing himself my friend. And all over the State the feeling is very kind towards me. My friends are in the ascendant in two thirds of the State and will nominate and elect the four [incumbent] Republican members of Congress and perhaps five. All Republicans elected will be my friends, as well as the Democrats.
>
> It is conceded that I have, through my friends, the nomination of Governor in my hands and both the leading candidates have made offers of alliance. I shall harmonize the two perfectly and try to nominate our present Gov. Smith who has always sustained me and my course in the Senate. His nomination ends Spencer and his policy of bitterness and rascality. Smith and his friends pledge to support me for the Senate.
>
> Now the question is Can we carry the State [ticket] and enough members of the [Alabama] House to give us a majority in joint ballot with the Senate, all Republicans but one [and] holding over. Of this there is no doubt. We shall have a majority of the House, four of the six members of Congress and State ticket by 5000 to 10000 majority.
>
> But to do this we must have help in troops, money and speakers. With Smith for our candidate I hope for a tolerably quiet election, as he is conservative and not unpopular with the moderate Democrats, but the presence of troops in a few counties will assure what otherwise might be doubtful. Grant and the General must send Crawford another regiment early in October.[8]

When the state convention met, in the Selma opera house, the proceedings at first seemed to justify Warner's optimism. His friends secured the adoption of a platform commending the Smith administration and endorsing the Warner principles of universal amnesty and no political disabilities. But when one of Warner's friends proposed Smith's renomination, Spencer and some of his followers objected, complaining that Smith had favored Democrats, including former secessionists, but had done little or nothing for blacks.

Two days of wrangling followed, with tempers aggravated by the 95-degree heat. Finally the Spencer delegates offered a compromise: they would accept Smith if (for the first time in Alabama history) a black man should be placed on the state ticket. The Warner-Smith forces agreed, and the convention settled upon a slate that included James T. Rapier as the candidate for secretary of state.

Alabama-born, son of a free Negro barber, the thirty-three-year-old Rapier had gained an excellent education in American and Canadian schools. He had beeen a delegate to the 1868 constitutional convention (and in 1872 he was to be elected to Congress). At the Selma convention he made an impressive appearance with his tall figure, full beard, fashionable clothes, and dignified bearing. He was equally impressive when he spoke. Still, his nomination horrified most native white Republicans in the Selma gathering and throughout the state. One said it would kill the Alabama Republican party. Certainly it would help to kill the hopes of Warner, though he was not yet aware of the consequences.

Nor was he yet aware of the even more deadly scheming of his rivalrous colleague Spencer. As the campaign got underway, it became obvious enough that Spencer had little interest in backing Republican candidates all along the line. In a confidential letter he explained that he was campaigning only for certain candidates for the Alabama house and that he had a specific aim in doing so—to prevent Warner's reelection to the United States Senate. "In close contests I am trying to help my friends," he confided, "for I wish a colleague that will render me some assistance." Before election day the rumor spread that he was secretly working to assist certain Democratic candidates. In a published letter Smith charged that Spencer's gestures of support for him were only pretense: "only to enable him to stab me more effectually than if he told the truth of his real opposition to me." If the Democrats should gain not only the governorship but also a large number of house seats, the Democrats along with a few Republicans in the assembly could prevent Warner's reelection. For Spencer, a Democrat would be a better colleague than Warner, since he would not have to divide the patronage with a Democrat.[9]

Thus the Democrats were benefiting from the disaffection of white Republicans who could not support a ticket with a black man on it. They were getting surreptitious aid from Spencer. And they had the additional advantage of revived Ku Klux activity, which could be expected to cut down the black Republican vote.

"To say there is no danger with the facts that have been developed here and which almost every breeze brings to our ears, would be to talk like simpletons." So Warner heard early in the campaign from a party worker in the field. In response to such reports, Warner begged the War Department to send extra troops, put them under the command of General Crawford, and authorize him to move them about as he saw fit. By mid-October Crawford had received companies from here and there containing nearly four hundred men and bringing the total in Alabama to about one thousand, all of them white. He dispersed them among ten (as compared with the previous five) locations. From these, after consultation with Governor Smith, he sent details out to thirty other places. He cautioned the soldiers that they must behave not as partisans but strictly as "conservators of the peace."[10]

On the stump, Smith performed in keeping with the reality that a black running mate was an asset with blacks and a liability with whites. In predominantly black counties he endorsed the entire Republican ticket, including Rapier, but he tried to avoid mentioning him in predominantly white areas. He was reported, however, as saying in Florence, Rapier's home town, that to become governor of Alabama one unfortunately had to "run on a ticket with a nigger." At another stop a white heckler compelled him to declare that he was going to vote for Rapier.[11]

Warner engaged in no such equivocations, and he even spoke on the same platform with Rapier, as he did on other occasions with Smith. For Warner, the campaign trail was a fairly long one, taking him through northern and central Alabama, with appearances in Talladega, Huntsville, Decatur, Tuscumbia, Florence, Moulton, Courtland, Selma, Demopolis, Livingston, Eutaw, Tuscaloosa, and other politically important towns. All went well enough in the north, but when he reached Eutaw, a Ku Klux stronghold in the west central part of the state, he ran into serious trouble.

He was then traveling with Smith and Lewis E. Parsons, whom President Johnson had appointed provisional governor instead of Smith in 1865. When the three men got off the train in Eutaw on the morning of October 25, they saw posters announcing a Democratic meeting to be held at the courthouse at the same time as the previously scheduled Republican meeting. As they walked through town they noticed around the saloons knots of surly white youths with revolvers in plain sight. Warner, Smith, and Parsons were worried, and so was Congressman Charles Hays, who soon joined them. Hays was a Eutaw native, a very large planter, owning more than 10,000 acres, and a former Confederate officer (who had beaten a Democratic Union veteran in the 1868 race for Congress). Still, as a local scalawag, Hays had perhaps more to fear from the white townspeople than the three visitors did.

Governor Smith sent for the sheriff, a Democrat, and for General Crawford, who happened to be nearby, with a contingent of men only half a mile from the courthouse. Smith and his associates told the sheriff and the general they expected a riot. The sheriff objected to the bringing in of soldiers, arguing that their presence would be more likely to provoke than to prevent violence. He said he had sworn in a hundred deputies and they could keep the peace. So the Republican campaigners did not insist that Crawford be on hand with his troops. Instead, they made a conciliatory gesture to the Democratic leaders, inviting them to a joint discussion. There came back a written reply declining the proposal on the ground that the questions of the hour, "both as to men and measures," were "not debatable."

That afternoon Smith stayed in his hotel room instead of going to the meeting. He was not feeling well, he said. When Warner, Parsons, and Hays arrived at the courthouse, about two hundred Democrats had already gathered and were being harangued by a speaker who stood on a stile over the paling fence that surrounded the courthouse square. After conferring with the sheriff again, Warner and his companions went to the other side of the building, completely out of the way of the Democrats. Here a crowd of some two thousand collected, only about a dozen of them white.

In front of a courthouse window the Republicans set up a small table, with a top about three feet square. Senator Warner stood on this to deliver his speech. As he spoke he noticed young whites from the Democratic rally edging around the corners of the building. Though he was careful to say nothing that might offend anyone, they started to hoot and to shout: "You're a damned liar!" "Why don't you go back where you came from?" "We don't want any damned carpetbaggers around here!" Warner kept on despite the interruptions, talking for approximately an hour.

While Ex-Governor Parsons was speaking from the table, the hecklers became both more numerous and more noisy, though he tried to appease them by honoring the memory of Robert E. Lee. One young man drew a pistol and said: "Let me kill the God-damned old son of a bitch." Others restrained him, telling him it was not yet time to shoot.

Congressman Hays had not planned to speak. Warner had advised him not to, since the local feeling was so strong against him. Besides, Hays had his young son with him and did not want to do anything that might bring harm to the boy. When Parsons had finished, the Democrats mockingly called for Hays, and he got up on the table, intending only to adjourn the meeting and not to give an address. The Democrats, the whites, now howled louder than ever; the Republicans, the blacks, stood motionless and silent. Hays waited for a chance to be heard. Suddenly a man grabbed him and yanked him off the table while two others tipped it over—almost on top of Warner, who had been sitting beside the table, his hand resting on it.

Out of the window above the table now came gunshots, the bullets passing over the heads of Warner and his companions and directly into the crowd of blacks. Soon Warner saw white men with pistols advancing from the corners of the courthouse and firing point blank at the crowd. Fleeing in a panic, the blacks broke down the fence in their effort to escape. Warner could see them falling down and trying to scramble up and move on. He walked over to a group of whites, raised his hand in a disapproving gesture, and pleaded: "For God's sake, stop this!" One of them threatened to shoot Hays, but the sheriff dissuaded him. From a distance a few of the Negroes began to fire back, ineffectually.

Warner started for the nearby hotel, walking as deliberately as he could. He was almost away from the rioters when one of them struck him in the head from behind and knocked off his high silk hat—that hated symbol of Yankeeism. He turned around to pick it up, but one of the men kicked it and then another and another until the whole bunch was playing football with it. A friendly Democrat advised him to get away before he got hurt, but he would not leave without his hat. Finally one of the pranksters returned it, battered and dusty. Just as Warner reached the hotel he looked back and saw soldiers marching into the courthouse yard. At last the shooting stopped. Four or five blacks had been killed and more than fifty wounded, Warner heard afterward.[12]

Home again on his plantation, Warner waited for returns from the election on November 8. He could no longer feel confident of a sweeping victory for the Republicans and a six-year Senate term for himself. The party seemed to be losing most of its white adherents. "They cannot vote for a negro," the *Montgomery Daily Mail* observed with satisfaction, "nor for a party which puts negroes in nomination for office." And the party could hardly expect a full turnout of its usual black voters, since Democratic ruffians were stepping up their activities despite the presence of General Crawford's thousand scattered infantrymen.

Once the returns were in, Warner could still see more than a glimmer of hope for himself, even though his party had suffered devastating losses. Rapier, trailing the state ticket, ran five thousand votes behind his Democratic opponent. Smith, too, apparently had lost, though by a much smaller margin, but he was refusing to admit defeat. He barricaded himself in his office in the Montgomery capitol, obtained food supplies through a window, and called for federal troops, who took possession of the building. They allowed the Democratic candidate, Robert B. Lindsay, to set up his gubernatorial office in another room. For the time being, Alabama enjoyed the luxury of having two governors. In the house of representatives, meanwhile, the Democrats would increase from three to fifty-seven, but since they had only one member in the holdover senate, they would still constitute slightly less than a majority of the assembly as a whole.

If the Republicans in the legislature should stick together and stand behind Warner, he would be reelected. If even a few of them should desert him, a Democrat could win. So he appealed to his friends in Washington to persuade Grant to intercede for him. Reluctantly and cautiously, Grant composed a note for Alabama carpetbag Congressman C. W. Buckley to show legislators but not to publish. The note read:

> It is not my desire as a usual thing to indicate a preference among republicans for office, when the choice is not with myself, but seeing how close the Legislature of the State of Ala. is, and how the defection of two or three republicans might defeat the party altogether in the Senatorial Contest, I drop a line to express my appreciation of the services of Senator Warner. He has been a true representative of his party and his adopted State. I know that it would please his many friends in Congress and out of it if he could be returned again.
>
> Disclaiming any desire to dictate, or to express a preference for one Candidate of the party over another, but believing Senator Warner to be the choice of the great majority of the republicans in the Legislature, I write this.

For Warner, Grant's good word was of course encouraging, but it soon proved ineffective. When the assembly met in joint session on December 7, the Republicans divided their votes not only between Warner and a scalawag but among them and a Democrat. Thus the Democrat won by the margin of a single vote.

A day or two later Warner received a copy of a public statement, addressed to him, which his supporters in the legislature had prepared. "Your defeat," they had written, " . . . was brought about by the treachery of those who called themselves members of our party, but who in fact were Judases." Warner did not need to guess who the foremost of the Judases was. He and his friends were convinced that Spencer had betrayed the party by inducing Republican legislators to defect. On December 10 Smith conceded the governorship and left the capitol, but Warner continued to insist that the senatorship rightfully belonged to him. No matter. All that remained of his senatorial career was one three-month session as a lame duck.[13]

At least, Warner could hope for a good federal job as a consolation prize. He would go to Washington "fierce as a hornet after his defeat," the friendly *Mobile Register* predicted on December 22, but at the end of his term he would be "comfortably taken care of by the president."

In the Senate, angry as a hornet all right, Warner recounted the horrors of the Eutaw riot for the edification of his colleagues and the country. He was speaking in favor of setting up a committee to investigate the alleged political crimes in the South. He had been in battle and had seen men fall around him, he said, but never had he beheld quite such a spectacle as the one in Eutaw—"man after man in that crowd falling and scrambling away with wounds, while a set of demons stood deliberately firing and shooting them down."

On March 3, 1871, his last day in the Senate, Warner presented a kind of swan song. The Senate was debating the repeal of the duty on coal, and to get the floor he offered the following amendment: "And that all political disabilities imposed by law or by the Constitution of the United States upon citizens of the United States on account of the rebellion are hereby removed." Despite his recent experience with Southern terrorism, he still favored lifting the Fourteenth Amendment ban on officeholding by former Confederate leaders (which Congress could do by a two-thirds vote of both houses). In support of his proposal he made much the longest of his Senate speeches, this one ranging widely over the problems and prospects of Reconstruction.

The Reconstruction program of Congress, Warner said, was neither vindictive nor unfair; rather, it showed the "unparalleled liberality of the Government." It did not punish the rebels except to the extent that it freed and enfranchised their slaves and temporarily disqualified their leaders for voting and holding office. Unfortunately, it did not begin soon enough, and for a time a "faithless President" led these men of the master class to expect to get back into power immediately. Thus that President rekindled the "passions of the war." Still, it would have been better if Congress had extended general amnesty; then "the best men of the South would have at once taken hold of the work of reconstruction."

Democrats were making much of the "failures and corruptions" in the reconstructed states, Warner continued, and such scandals did occur, exacerbating the bitterness of Southern whites. But corruption was neither a Republican nor a Southern monopoly. Look at the Tweed Ring and other Northern machines for which Democrats were responsible. "And when they shall purify the government of the city and State of New York, where they have ample power, I will agree that they may cast stones at our southern State governments."

Democrats also were charging that these governments were maintained at the point of a bayonet. This was absolutely untrue, Warner insisted. The army had never been used "to intimidate or to control voters, or to influence their votes in favor of the Republican party."

Here Frank Blair, the recent Democratic vice-presidential candidate, now a senator from Missouri, interrupted Warner to ask him whether "the military did not occupy the State-house in his own State to keep out the regularly elected Governor in the interest of one who was defeated by the people."

Warner answered with an emphatic "No." The army had not undertaken to influence, and had not influenced, the outcome of the recent election in Alabama.

Blair having called attention to himself, Warner took occasion to respond to Blair's continual aspersion of carpetbaggers. He reminded the Senate that, at the end of the war, Blair had invited his troops to follow the example of the ancient Romans, who "made their conquering soldiers freeholders of the lands they had conquered." Warner noted that

Blair had then gone to Louisiana to raise cotton for a while. "I think he has been something of a carpet-bagger himself." In any event, carpetbaggers "are like men everywhere; there are some good and some bad among them."

As for the Alabama election that Blair had referred to, the result was "due mainly to Democratic violence and intimidation" but also to "the opposition of Senator Spencer and his particular friends"—that is, to both "Republican 'thieves and fools' and Democratic Ku Klux." Thus Warner left no doubt as to who he thought were the good men and the bad men among the carpetbaggers, at least in Alabama.

In concluding his final words to the Senate, Warner made clear that he wished to conciliate but not to capitulate. He advocated "forgiving the rebel" but not "asking his forgiveness for having been a Union man." Justice must go along with mercy: the federal government must see to the maintenance of law and order in the South. If the government should fail to do so, Warner declared with the voice of prophecy, the result would be the "nullification of the fifteenth amendment" and the "reduction of the negro at the South to a serfdom nearly as bad as slavery."[14]

Congress was advancing toward the twofold policy of kindness and sternness that Warner asked for. Eventually, in 1871 and 1872, it was to repeal in stages the Fourteenth Amendment ban on officeholding (for all except a handful of ex-rebels who, like Jefferson Davis, refused to take an oath of loyalty to the United States). Already Congress had passed a second act for the enforcement of the Fifteenth Amendment and had set up an investigating committee to see if still further legislation was necessary.

A couple of months after leaving the Senate, Warner appeared before the investigating committee (the "Ku Klux committee") in Washington, to engage in another confrontation with Blair, a committee member. Warner recounted in detail the Eutaw riot of the previous fall. Despite the political hostility toward him, he was not disposed to complain about his personal treatment during his five years' residence in Alabama. "While a great many people, nearly all the people, let me alone socially very severely, yet I have always been treated courteously." He thought the Democratic politicians and newspaper editors were mostly to blame for the ill-feeling that erupted in violence.

Blair asked whether the people of Ohio would not "have been bitter and hostile, and have made a noise at meetings, if they had had such a condition of affairs forced upon them." Warner replied that "if Ohio had gone into a rebellion against the General Government and had got whipped," he hoped the people "would have given up and accepted the situation." Blair retorted that the Southerners might have done the same if "they had not been gouged after they were down."[15]

Meanwhile, going home to Alabama and then back to Washington repeatedly, Warner pursued the government job he considered his due.

En route, he stopped in Chattanooga when he could, to see his son, who was now attending a school at Lookout Mountain. From the plantation he would send Willie homilies such as the following:

> Latin will come easy by and by. I never studied Latin and have always regretted it, have felt the loss of the knowledge of it. . . . Be careful to bathe all over at least once a week and rub your body *hard* every morning with a coarse towel, and wash your teeth every day and after each meal and keep a quill toothpick in your pocket to use whenever you eat anything. Don't forget or fail to say your prayers. Papa prays for you daily. Be a good noble *boy* and you will make a noble and successful *man.* I mean to give you as good an education as possible and much better than I had.[16]

The federal job Warner had set his heart upon was the Mobile collectorship. His own appointee as collector, the scalawag William Miller, was willing to resign, especially since he was tired of Spencer's efforts to dictate personnel changes within the customhouse. Spencer wanted Miller removed but did not want Warner to replace him, nor did Rapier, who, thanks to Spencer, now held a federal job as assessor of internal revenue in Montgomery.

Spencer and Rapier wrote to Treasury Secretary George S. Boutwell, and induced others to write to him, opposing Warner's appointment. "From the time he took his seat in the U. S. Senate," a carpetbag member of the Alabama senate complained of Warner, "he was continually talking about the 'change of heart' of the people of this [Southern] country, and never missed an opportunity to contradict Senator Spencer when he represented the lawless condition of the country." Another Alabama Republican based his opposition strictly on grounds of partisan expediency. "I recognize in Mr. Warner a gentleman of ability & education," this man wrote from Mobile. "But to send him here at this time would be suicidal to the interest and harmony of the Republican Party of this section of the State & would open up anew the bitter internal strife in our political organization."

Cleverly Spencer suggested to President Grant that he could "reconcile all conflicts" by offering Warner some other post, such as that of minister to Venezuela or governor of New Mexico, either of which ought to "suffice a moderate ambition." Grant responded by nominating Warner for the New Mexico governorship. Spencer moved that the Senate confirm the appointment, and, out of courtesy to the one Republican member from Alabama, the Senate quickly complied.

"Will you accept? Can't you get along awhile without any office?" These questions came to Warner from Senator Sherman, who added that he would be glad to do whatever he could to help. Warner pondered the offer at least to the extent of asking the advice of another Ohio friend, J. D. Cox, who had resigned from Grant's cabinet and gone back to practice law in Cincinnati. After about a week, without waiting for Cox to reply, Warner informed the President: "I respectfully decline."

When Cox's answer came, it reaffirmed Warner's decision. "Santa Fé I have understood to be a dirty village of one story adobe houses, with a rough frontier population of greasers, frontiersmen & Indians, a little Indian trading & whiskey drinking being the only business, & the whole country in as utter a stagnation as possible," Cox had written. "Don't go. You can make a better living on your plantation, or in making your way into trade in Alabama, & surely there never was an emptier honor than the Governorship of N. Mexico." A little later Warner received another letter from Cox, who had read the news of Warner's refusal and now congratulated him on it. "You ought to let Grant know in some polite but unmistakable form," Cox advised, "that you do not think you were complimented in the attempt to send you into exile."[17]

But Warner did not wish to offend Grant, for he still hoped to land the Mobile collectorship, and he and his friends resumed the struggle to get it for him. Spencer and Rapier intensified their efforts to prevent his obtaining it. Ex-Governor Parsons and two other Alabama friends of Warner called on both Secretary Boutwell and President Grant to press Warner's case. When Rapier learned of this, he protested to Boutwell that the split in the Alabama party would have been healed if only Warner had gone to New Mexico, but the party would be hopelessly divided and utterly ruined if he should go to Mobile. Spencer collected from Boutwell and turned over to Grant all the letters in the Treasury Department favoring and opposing Warner, to show that those opposing greatly outnumbered those favoring. In a covering letter Spencer assured the President that he himself, Congressman Charles Hays, and indeed all but one of the Republican congressional delegation from Alabama "earnestly opposed" the appointment. "It certainly does appear marvellous," Spencer told Grant, "that a single Congressman" should "outweigh the influence and overcome the protests of the only Republican Senator and the other Republican Representatives" from the state.[18]

Temporarily at least, the influence of Warner's backers, including the Shermans, did outweigh the influence of Spencer and overcome his protests. Early in August 1871 the President removed the Mobile collector and replaced him with Warner. Congress had recessed for the summer; the Senate would have no chance to confirm or deny the appointment until it met in December.

Warner went confidently to Mobile and took up his duties at the customhouse, handling large sums of money which, as he told his aunt in Ohio, he had to watch carefully to see that nothing went wrong. When he could he visited the plantation, where he was building two new frame houses for his hands; he expected to be working a dozen of them the next season. Before Christmas he planned to go to Chattanooga and meet a female relative who was to bring his daughter, Ezzie, with her. Willie and Ezzie were to go on south with their father for a long midwinter vacation.

All through the fall and winter Spencer and Rapier kept up a campaign against Warner's confirmation. Rapier wrote to Spencer, for Boutwell's benefit, that Warner had no followers in Alabama except for "a few Federal office holders and some *quasi* Republicans" like Parsons and that Warner suffered from extreme *"unpopularity among the leading colored men"* of the state. Warner countered by corresponding with some of the senators he thought were leaning his way. It would be a victory for the spoils system, he assured Carl Schurz, a civil-service reformer from Missouri, if a man like himself should be deprived of office by a man like Spencer.

Some Alabama Democrats saw little to choose as between the two carpetbaggers. Testifying before a congressional Ku Klux subcommittee, which held hearings in Huntsville in November, a Democrat defined the term *carpetbagger* to mean a man "of an ignorant or bad character" who came from the North to seek office by arraying blacks against whites. Question: "Is Senator Warner an ignorant man of bad character?" Answer: "Well, we have Senator Spencer's word for it." What about Senator Spencer? Well, he might not be ignorant, but he certainly was unprincipled. Did he attempt to stir up blacks against whites? "Yes, sir." Did Senator Warner ever try to do so? "I have no personal knowledge. . . . "[19]

Congress had not been back in session long before Spencer made it clear to Grant that there was no possibility of the Senate's approving the Warner appointment. Early in January 1872 the President withdrew the nomination. Spencer was making good his recent boast that he was going to have "everything his own way" and would "run the machine with an iron rule."

As for Warner, he could find little comfort in the efforts of his friends to console him. Senator Sherman was as disgusted as he was surprised by the President's action. "I could not talk with Grant about this without showing a feeling that may do you injury, but in a day or two I probably will," Sherman explained to Warner. "My advice is that you . . . come directly here and fight this thing out. It is humiliating and annoying that such men as Spencer . . . should control all the patronage of a State, and that such men as you should be made the victims of a plainly malicious opposition." But, at home once more on the plantation, Warner could only wonder what good it would do to go back to Washington and resume the fight. One thing was certain: he could no longer consider Grant much of a friend.[20]

CHAPTER 9

The War Still Exists
(1869-1872)

At the time of Ulysses S. Grant's inauguration Adelbert Ames was still provisional governor of Mississippi, which was yet to be restored as a state. His responsibilities for its restoration were now to be greatly enlarged. On March 5, 1869, Grant's first full day in office, word came by wire to Jackson that the new President had appointed Ames to the command of the military district embracing Mississippi. For almost a year he was to play a dual role as provisional governor and military commander.

Even the Democratic newspapers welcomed Ames to his new position. "The appointment should be acceptable to the people," the *Jackson Clarion* commented. "In the discharge of the duties of provisional governor, General Ames has commanded the respect and won the esteem of all classes." Barely eight months had gone by since the Democrats were cursing him for evicting the ex-Confederate Governor Humphreys from the gubernatorial mansion, but they seemed to have forgotten or at least forgiven that. Before long they were to be accusing him of worse instances of the high-handed use of military power.

Ames antagonized most white Mississippians when, as provisional governor, he proceeded to remove state and local officeholders by the hundreds and replace them with his own appointees. He was only doing what the law required him to do, a recent act of Congress having specified that no one should hold office in Mississippi who could not take the "ironclad oath" (or had not received congressional exemption from it). This oath required a man to swear that he had never willingly borne arms against the United States. Very few prominent Mississippians could honestly make such a declaration.

So Ames had to look mainly to men who had never held office in the state, that is, to comparatively recent white arrivals from the North and to former slaves and freeborn blacks. Day after day he made removals and appointments until the changes totaled about two thousand—sheriffs, judges, prosecuting attorneys, county clerks and treasurers and assessors, mayors, aldermen, constables, and many others, including justices of the peace. Only to such lower posts as those of constables and justices did he appoint blacks. Still, these were the first of their race to hold any public offices in Mississippi.

In other ways, too, Ames undertook to give black Mississippians a fairer deal than they had been getting. The existing poll tax of $4.00 fell far more heavily upon poor freedmen than upon comparatively well-to-do planters. Ames directed that the tax be cut to $1.50. While lowering the tax, he applied it to disabled Confederate veterans, who previously had been exempt from it. So blacks could "protect themselves from much oppression and injustice," he ordered that "all persons, without respect to race, color or previous condition of servitude," who were qualified under the existing code, should be competent to serve as jurors. Blacks in Mississippi needed more than ever some means to help and protect themselves since, like blacks in other Southern states, they no longer had the assistance and protection of the Freedmen's Bureau, which had terminated most of its functions at the beginning of 1869.[1]

While the Freedmen's Bureau was being phased out, the number of federal troops in the South had been decreased. In the spring of 1869 some reinforcements came from Virginia to Mississippi, to bring the infantry regiment there up to considerably less than full strength. Cavalrymen would have been more useful, but they could not be spared from the Indian wars on the Great Plains. Thus, as military commander, Ames did not have much of an army to command.

To him, as to others in the occupation force, the hazards of the military life were demonstrated by the fate of Lieutenant Colonel Joseph G. Crane. As provisional mayor of Jackson, Ames's appointee, the tall, mild-mannered officer, son of a former Ohio congressman, seemed to be well liked even by the townspeople. In the line of duty he auctioned for delinquent taxes a piano belonging to Edward M. Yerger, a member of a notable Mississippi family. Yerger confronted Crane outside the capitol, pulled out a knife, and stabbed him to death. Ames had Yerger arrested and court-martialed.

Native whites thought Yerger emotionally unstable and hence unfit for trial, but Northerners in Mississippi were inclined to view him as typifying the local hostility toward them. "The people are sullen and brutal, with little regard for human life, and none at all for law," an Ohio soldier wrote from Jackson to his congressman friend James A. Garfield. "The murder of poor Col. Crane, a month since, was only a fair example of the lawless spirit here. Of course that touched us more nearly because he was one of our best, and a man whom everybody loved, but we have had as many as seven murders in a week, in a single county of the State." The feelings of Ames and his soldiers were not assuaged when, after the United States Supreme Court objected to the military trial, Yerger eventually went scot-free.[2]

The Yerger case made Ames all the more suspicious of conservative politicians as they began to prepare for the fall elections. Democrats talked of running Louis Dent as their gubernatorial candidate. A Northerner residing in Mississippi, Dent had one outstanding qualification: he was a brother-in-law of President Grant. The Democrats could hope, with a relative heading their ticket, to get the President's support. Conservative Republicans also favored the Dent movement. "Some Northern men (carpet-baggers in very truth) are supporting the movement, but only for the sake of office," Garfield's soldier friend believed. Bipartisan backers of Dent got together to form the National Republican party. They avowed their willingness to accept the Fifteenth Amendment, which the state would now have to ratify in addition to the Fourteenth Amendment before it could be fully restored to the Union.

Nevertheless, it seemed to Ames that a victory for the conservatives would be a defeat for Reconstruction. He looked for better things from the regular Republicans, the Radicals, when they met in Jackson on July 1. As expected, the Radicals produced a thoroughgoing platform. They favored not only the Fifteenth Amendment but also free schools, free speech, tax reform, and racial equality. They endorsed the administration of Ames, commending him especially for having reduced the poll tax and opened juries to blacks. He responded in kind. Making a dramatic appearance at the convention, he assured the delegates (most of them black) that they had his sympathy and would have his support.

As good as his word, Ames proceeded to remove from state and local offices his appointees who had joined the movement for Dent. He replaced them with Radicals. The conservatives, Republicans and Democrats alike, now charged him with using his military authority for partisan ends. They contended that, like Caesar, he was tyrannical and ambitious. Not that he aspired to be emperor but, they said, he wanted to be a United States senator, and he was scheming to elect a legislature that would make him one. His critics appealed to the Sherman brothers and to Grant.[3]

From both of the Shermans came rebukes to Ames. The senator could not understand why a professional soldier like Ames would use his military position to gain political office. The general in chief, thoroughly disgusted, considered removing him from command. Ames reassured Senator Sherman: "A moment's reflection should show that I could not leave a lifelong position in a profession I love for a temporary honor the very holding of which might reflect discredit upon me."

To General Sherman he explained that, in backing the Radicals, he was not engaging in party politics in the ordinary sense. "The contest [in Mississippi] is not between two established parties, as they are elsewhere, but between loyal men and a class of men who are disloyal." Success for "the men who took this State from the Union" would lead to a "reign of terror." Union men, especially Northerners, would be compelled to leave the state, and blacks would be "reduced to a condition bordering on serfdom." The frequent murders were not the "usual events of ordinary times" but were "Ku-Klux outrages mainly based on political enmity and hatred." As military commander, Ames had a duty to protect the loyal people from their enemies. "The war still exists in a very important phase here."[4]

Ames could take comfort in the response of the commander in chief, a response quite different from that of the general in chief. The conservatives had been assuming that Grant, like Sherman, was on their side, and as late as August 10 the *Jackson Clarion* trumpeted that Grant "unquestionably desired the success of the Dent ticket." In fact, Grant had already told his wife's brother politely and confidentially: "I must throw the weight of my influence in favor of the party opposed to you." When a Mississippi carpetbagger called at the White House, Grant made his position publicly clear. He said, for publication, that he approved of Ames's removing disloyal officeholders and that he favored the Radicals in the coming campaign, since the real purpose of the conservatives was to frustrate the congressional plan of Reconstruction.

Despite Grant's repudiation of Dent, the National Union Republicans went ahead and, early in September, nominated him for governor. They divided the rest of the state ticket between Republicans and Democrats. At the end of the month the Radicals chose the large planter and former large slaveowner James L. Alcorn to run against Dent. Altogether, their slate consisted of three scalawags (including Alcorn), three carpetbaggers, and one black.

It was up to Ames, as military commander, to oversee the election, which Grant had scheduled for November 30 and December 1. To be elected, besides state officials, were congressmen and members of the legislature (but not local officials; Ames's appointees could expect to continue in office for two more years). Also to be voted on was the proposed state constitution. This time the voters would have a chance to reject the proscriptive clauses—without rejecting the document as a whole.

Ames not only appointed voting registrars but, to be sure of a fair election, he also directed that each party should provide two poll watchers, one white and one black. To prevent intimidation at the polls, he had to depend on his troops, of which he feared he did not have enough. Democrats continued to protest to Washington that he was planning to carry the election by military force. He responded to an inquiry from the adjutant general: "Three hundred and twenty two men, including the regimental band, non-commissioned staff, clerks and orderlies . . . &c. &c. are all I have with which to force a state to vote against its will!" His subordinates at the several Mississippi posts begged for additional men, and shortly before the election five more companies arrived in the state.[5]

At the polls the troops served not to intimidate voters but to prevent their intimidation. The election proved to be quite fair and quite peaceful, though there were disorders at a few places. Blacks voted more freely than ever before in Mississippi. The result was an overwhelming victory for the regular Republicans, Alcorn defeating Dent by two to one, and all the congressional and a large majority of the legislative candidates winning.

"They are men who have canvassed the state with their lives in their hands," Garfield's soldier friend wrote, "and have made speeches to six-shooters & bowie knives with very desperate characters behind them. Less real outrage has been committed just while the election was being held, than we had expected, but order was generally kept through fear of troops, and not from any love of the same."

The constitution won almost unanimous approval without the proscriptive clauses, which were voted down. So, at last, Mississippi would rejoin the Union, and the winning candidates would be allowed to take office.

Alcorn's inauguration as governor was set for March 10, 1870. Before Christmas, Ames issued an order appointing Alcorn immediately as provisional governor in Ames's place. Alcorn refused to obey the order. He explained that he could not accept office from the military authority since he was soon to have it from a higher authority, the people. Alcorn was asserting his independence from Ames. "I have thus far dictated my terms," he confided to his wife, "and will continue to do so."

Ames, then, would still be provisional governor as well as military commander when the newly elected legislature met. In his order announcing the official returns he had directed that the legislators assemble on January 11, 1870.[6]

One of the leading members of the legislature was to be Albert T. Morgan, who more than four years earlier had moved from Wisconsin to Mississippi, then had failed as a planter and as a lumberman before deciding to become a lawyer. Though not yet twenty-eight, Morgan looked like a man who did not have long to live. Still sallow and underweight, he limped from his war wounds and suffered recurring chills and fever from the malaria he had caught while in the army. He continued to wear a truss and to treat himself with liberal doses of quinine. The quinine bottle was the only one he kept on hand: he avoided alcoholic drinks but was addicted to cigars. Despite his infirmities he had energy to spare for politics.[7]

For the Morgans, Albert and Charles, and their Republican friends in Yazoo County, new opportunities in politics had arisen with the installation of Grant as President and Ames as military commander. Ames relied heavily on Albert Morgan's advice in selecting men for Yazoo offices. Albert himself could probably have obtained the choicest job of all, that of sheriff and tax collector, a position that could pay as much as $10,000 a year. His brother Charles did accept the sheriff's job in neighboring Washington County, but Albert contented himself with appointment as a member of the Yazoo County board of supervisors, at an annual salary of less than $100. He could serve on the county board and in the state legislature at the same time; he was mainly interested in becoming a state lawmaker.

At last the revolution in Yazoo appeared to be really underway. Not only could Albert Morgan and his associates come out of hiding and walk the Yazoo City streets without arms and without fear. He was close to the center of power as a friend of Ames and was about to become boss of the city and the county. His political associates—Northerners, native white Unionists, and blacks—held all the local offices. The old Yazoo establishment had been completely overthrown.[8]

Morgan's onetime landlord, James J. B. White, who two years earlier had evicted him and his brother from Tokeba plantation, seemed powerless to do him further harm. White continued to insist that he and his wife, not the Morgans, had been wronged in the Tokeba transaction. He now complained to Ames that the Whites had "sustained a heavy loss of several thousand dollars" when the sheriff, after the interposition of the military commander, repeatedly postponed the sale of the Morgans' possessions, which the Whites claimed for debts due them. "In the meantime the Morgans had made way with nearly all the available property subject to our claims." Whatever the merits of the case—and the Whites had at best a dubious argument—they could get no help from Ames.

When the newly appointed county supervisors met, they elected Albert Morgan president of the board. This group had greater powers than a county board in Wisconsin, since there was here no township government to share the authority. Morgan, as president, held the most important local policy-making position.

Morgan and his fellow supervisors faced tasks that would have daunted less idealistic and enthusiastic men—and that their predecessors had left undone. The county poorhouse, as Morgan saw it, was no better than a hovel. The poor farm had gone uncultivated. There was no courthouse; the courts were held in a rented hall above a storeroom. The jail, in Morgan's words, "was a rickety old brick contrivance, with a board fence, half rotted down, and toppling over in places." Roads and bridges had been neglected, and at times of high water the people in some areas could get to the county seat only by taking a circuitous land route and then waiting for one of the irregular river packets. Not a single public schoolhouse was to be found in the entire county.

When Morgan looked into the county's financial records, he discovered that the treasury was bare. Worse than that, the county was in debt, but what the total indebtedness was he could not ascertain, for the records were incomplete. The debt consisted of county warrants, or promises to pay, which were circulating at a discount of from 45 to 65 cents on the dollar.

The first thing to do, then, it seemed to Morgan, was to increase the county's revenue, and the way to do that, without raising tax rates, was to raise property assessments. He found the existing ones ridiculously low.

For example, the land at Tokeba plantation was assessed, some of it, as low as $1.00 an acre, and none of it higher than $8.00. This was the land for which the Morgans had been paying $7.00 an acre in annual rent! The county board increased the tax value of the Tokeba land to $2.00, $8.00, and $12.00 an acre, and the value of other plantations correspondingly.[9]

With his influence in the local party organization, Morgan easily secured his nomination for the state senate, and with his popularity among the blacks he could be sure of an easy election if the vote was free and fair. On the election days, November 30 and December 1, 1869, the sheriff saw that a deputy was vigilant at each polling place. A small detachment of soldiers remained at their quarters in a small house in the center of the city, ready to respond to any emergency, but none arose. "The election in this county," the captain in command of the detachment reported afterward, "is pronounced by some of the oldest citizens as the quietest and most peaceful that has ever taken place here."

Morgan's hold upon the black voters remained intact even after some newly arrived blacks from the North challenged his leadership. "One of them," he later recalled,

> was a quite intelligent colored man, whose parents had passed through the color crucible at the North and still felt the pain of the burn. By way of illustrating the fact that he had inherited their remembrance of Yankee prejudices and their secret contempt of the Yankee character, he began, almost immediately upon his arrival at Yazoo, an effort to gather the freed people into a separate political organization. To accomplish this purpose, he gravely assured them that their liberties did not depend upon the leadership of any man or set of men, but upon themselves; that they were under no obligations whatever to any person or to any party for their freedom, because freedom was the natural state of man, and their emancipation was evidence merely that the country had come to the point of recognizing the fact. The obligation, therefore, was all on the other side, and could not be discharged until the white man, who had always lived upon the negro's toil, went a step farther and made some sort of restitution.

The newcomer denounced Morgan as a false friend of the colored people (certainly Morgan did not agree with the restitution idea) and then suddenly disappeared. Back in the North he spread the word that carpetbaggers were deluding the freed people throughout the South. Morgan, he said, feared the presence of "intelligent gentlemen of color" and hence had incited the Yazoo blacks to drive him away.[10]

In the legislature, once it had met in Jackson on January 11, 1870, Senator Morgan proved himself on the whole an effective spokesman for his black constituents. Blacks were underrepresented if only legislators of their own race were counted. Though blacks constituted more than 50 percent of the state's population, they made up less than 28 percent of the legislature's membership.

The purpose of the January session was specifically the ratification of the Fourteenth and Fifteenth Amendments, which quickly received overwhelming approval, and the election of United States senators. Three were to be chosen: one for the term expiring in 1871, another for that expiring in 1875, and a third for the full six years beginning in 1871. For the full term, Governor Alcorn was an avowed candidate, and he was almost unanimously elected. For the longer of the unexpired terms, the favorite of Morgan and other carpetbaggers was General Ames, but some Republicans hesitated to elect him to a civil office while he still held a military command. Ames won only after two rivals, a black and a scalawag, had withdrawn from the contest. For the one-year term the legislature finally agreed on Hiram R. Revels, a preacher and state senator of African and American Indian ancestry, freeborn in North Carolina. Having completed these labors, the legislators were glad to adjourn and get away from the cold, drafty statehouse.

Resuming their sittings in March, after repairs had made the capitol more nearly weathertight, the members kept themselves busy until late in July. They set up a new court system. They carved out new counties and gave them such names as Union, Lincoln, Sumner, and Colfax (after Schuyler Colfax, who had been elected vice president on the ticket with Grant). They repealed the black code, which the immediate postwar legislature had adopted to control the behavior of blacks.

But when it came to positive assurances of black rights, the Republicans disagreed among themselves. A black senator, William H. Gray, introduced a bill to prohibit and punish discrimination on account of race, whether occurring in public conveyances or in any other public situation. Morgan rose to object. That kind of legislation had hurt Republicans in Louisiana, he said, and the Gray bill could do the same to Republicans in Mississippi. He no longer objected after the senate judiciary committee had lopped off the reference to public places and had reduced the offense to a mere misdemeanor. The amended bill passed the senate without a nay vote from any white Republican. In the house of representatives, however, the blacks secured the passage of a measure making discrimination on railroads a crime. The senate added its approval, but Governor Alcorn vetoed the bill.

Public education also was a subject of considerable debate. Morgan, along with other carpetbaggers, did not insist on immediate integration of the schools, yet he opposed any legal prohibition of racial mixing. Governor Alcorn maintained, for a time, that without such a prohibition the school system could not possibly get the popular support it needed for success. Finally the legislature passed a bill neither requiring nor prohibiting mixed schools, and the governor signed it.[11]

Morgan left his mark on legislation most notably when he brought about the repeal of a law against the intermarriage of blacks and whites. He had a personal interest in the matter. He was planning to marry a woman of (partly) African descent. Having removed the legal hindrance, he had only one other obstacle to dispose of. He had promised his betrothed to give up, before their wedding day, the filthy habit of smoking cigars.

He could never forget the first time he saw her. One day in the previous fall he had happened to be in Jackson on campaign business when a politician friend invited him to visit a school that Northern charities maintained for black boys and girls. As he and his companion approached the building he heard the children singing a hymn, and he was captivated by a clear, pure voice that accompanied and guided the children's voices. Restraining his friend, he stopped to listen as the singers went on to "John Brown's Body" and then to an unfamiliar number containing the words "We are rising as a people." The voice of the woman somehow magnetized him and pulled him toward her. He could no longer wait to make her acquaintance.

Inside the building the two men discovered, in front of her flock of pupils, a pretty, shapely, light-skinned mulatto who appeared to be no older than some of the teenagers in her care. She impressed Morgan as a "veritable queen" as she came down the aisle with simple grace and greeted her visitors with a spontaneous smile. She welcomed such distinguished gentlemen, she said, because their presence and interest encouraged the children. She invited these guests to interrogate the students, and after both had done so, to their immense satisfaction, she dismissed her charges. The two men then walked home with her.

Morgan learned that her name was Carrie V. Highgate, that she was twenty years old, born in Syracuse, New York, had been in Mississippi two years, and lived with her widowed mother and two sisters. An older brother had died in action near Petersburg as the war was about to end. The mother and all her surviving children, four of them, were teaching in the South. Carrie not only taught her hundred weekday pupils but also superintended a Sunday school, led a temperance society, and found time for other good works on behalf of the freed people. She had the love of the former slaves and the respect of the former masters. One of these described her a few years later as "a rather large, stout woman" (Morgan had seen her as a girl "of slender figure," smaller than many of her students) and "a woman of very good qualities, of fine education."

On August 3, 1870, three weeks after the end of the legislative session, Carrie and Albert were married in Jackson. Presiding was the Reverend J. Aaron Moore, a Negro blacksmith and legislator as well as minister of the gospel. The bride and groom took a train to honeymoon in Syracuse and to see her friends. Then they set up housekeeping in Yazoo City. In less than a week two fancily dressed and gaudily painted black women called to pay their respects and to welcome "Mrs. Senator Morgan" to Yazoo. The Morgans afterward learned that some white ladies of the city's elite had prompted the two black ladies to make the call.

About a month after the wedding Carrie found herself pregnant, and on June 5, 1871, she gave birth to a son, Albert T., Jr. In six months she was pregnant again, and on September 9, 1872, a daughter arrived, to be named Carrie V. after her mother.[12]

Meanwhile Morgan continued to be active in the state senate, on the political stump, and on the county board. In the senate he helped to thwart a group of speculators from England and the Northeast who had bought up defaulted antebellum bonds cheaply and were lobbying to induce the legislature to redeem the bonds at par. At Republican rallies he addressed black crowds, listened to brass bands, marched in parades, and, with his family, joined in festive picnics. As president of the county supervisors, he took pride in the organization of (segregated) public schools, of which the county could boast sixty-six by the time classes began in the fall of 1871. "The citizens of the county, without reference to politics, have manfully supported the free school system," the *Vicksburg Times and Republican* reported. There were also other signs of progress, among them the construction of a handsome, stylish, red-brick courthouse.[13]

Despite his ailments, Morgan could face the future with confidence and even joy. Or so he thought.

Senator-elect Ames was comfortably settled in lodgings on McPherson Square. Only a few blocks away was the White House, where he promptly went to pay his respects to President and Mrs. Grant. Much closer, within sight at 15th and I streets, was the elegant home of Representative Benjamin F. Butler, under whom he had served in the ill-fated Fort Fisher campaign. Butler invited him to dinner, and there he met the congressman's beautiful wife and renewed acquaintance with the still more beautiful daughter, whom he had not seen since the Johnson impeachment trial nearly two years before.

Blanche, a frequent visitor at that trial, still liked to visit the Senate or the House when something interesting was going on there. On the schedule now was business that certainly interested Ames—the admission of Mississippi as a state and the seating of its two senators-elect. From the Butlers' to the Capitol was a distance of nearly two miles, but it did not seem that far when Ames and Blanche walked it together, as they often did. Day after day the two watched the proceedings from the Senate gallery.

Mississippi was promptly readmitted, on February 3, 1870. But when Hiram R. Revels was proposed for a seat, one of the senators raised an objection. The problem was not that Revels was black or that he was lacking in accomplishment. He had been educated at a Quaker seminary in Indiana, had become a Methodist minister, had helped to organize two black regiments, had gone with the army to Mississippi, and there had been elected to the state senate. No, the question concerned his credentials. These were signed by Ames as military commander and provisional governor of Mississippi. The objecting senator argued that Ames had not been a bona fide governor and that, as a military officer, he had not been competent to sign such credentials. Some debate ensued, but before the end of February the Senate accepted Revels. Its first black member, he appropriately enough took the place that Jefferson Davis had vacated in 1861.[14]

If it was somewhat anomalous for a military officer to sign a senator's credentials, it was perhaps even more so for him to sign his own. And though Revels could easily qualify as a resident of Mississippi after living there for five years, Ames could anticipate some difficulty in qualifying after military service there for two. The Constitution requires that a senator be an "inhabitant" of the state he represents. Was Ames, who owned no property in Mississippi, an inhabitant of the state?

Invited to present his case to the Senate judiciary committee, Ames testified before its members and also submitted a written statement to them. He explained that, after the Republican victory in Mississippi, party leaders had repeatedly urged him to let them nominate him. At first he flatly declined and then he hesitated, not quite willing to give up his military career.

> Finally, for personal and public reasons, I decided to become a candidate and leave the Army. My intentions were publicly declared and sincere. (The intentions thus declared were not only to become a candidate for the Senate, but to remain and reside in Mississippi.) I even made arrangements, almost final and permanent, with a person to manage property I intended to buy. This was before I left Mississippi [to come to Washington and join the Senate]. My resignation was accepted by the President before he signed the bill to admit the State.

In his presentation to the committee Ames did not elaborate on his "personal and public reasons." The personal ones could be summarized as ambition. No doubt Ames had meant it when, only six months earlier, he had assured Senator Sherman: "I could not leave a lifelong position in a profession I love for a temporary honor the very holding of which might reflect discredit upon me." Still, the prospects for advancement in the army were uncertain, and it would be rather gratifying, especially for a man so young and so inexperienced in politics, to make the leap directly into such a lofty position as a Senate seat.

As for the public reasons, he made them clear on other occasions. He said he had done what he could, as provisional governor and military commander, for the advancement of Mississippi blacks, but he believed he could do much more as senator. "I felt that I had a mission to perform in their interest, and I hesitatingly consented to represent them and unite my fortune with theirs."

After appearing before the judiciary committee, Ames waited for it to report to the Senate. Days passed, then weeks, and nothing happened. Ames and Blanche had to find other diversions than Senate watching. The two visited museums and art galleries, went on carriage drives and horseback rides. At the Butler home Ames played billiards and talked politics with the congressman, took tea and conversed about everything under the sun with Mrs. Butler. He learned more and more about Blanche, including the fact that she had studied French, Latin, voice, piano, drawing, and painting and had received much of her education at a Roman Catholic convent in Georgetown, though the Butlers were Episcopalians. Other would-be courters called at the Butler house, and Ames more and more disliked to see them there, for he was beginning to realize that he was in love with Blanche.

On March 18 the judiciary committee was finally ready with its report, and Ames and Blanche could resume their places in the Senate gallery. The Senate delayed almost a week before taking up the report. Then the secretary read the credentials: "I, Adelbert Ames, Brevet Major General, United States Army, provisional governor of the State of Mississippi, do hereby certify that Adelbert Ames was elected United States Senator on the 18th day of January, 1870." Next the secretary read the committee's argument and conclusions. These were, first, that Ames was not an inhabitant of Mississippi when elected and, second, that he was therefore ineligible for the Senate seat.

A long and acrimonious debate began. Not only Democrats but some Republicans, foremost among them the Radical Roscoe Conkling of New York, agreed with the committee that Ames should be excluded. Conkling argued that it was harder to become an "inhabitant" than to become a "resident" and that mere presence on army duty was not enough. He conceded that, if Ames had been a married man and had taken his wife and family with him, that might have helped to establish "inhabitancy." Democrat Allen G. Thurman of Ohio reiterated: "Did he buy a homestead? No. Did he settle a family? He had none to settle." Ames himself could have replied that, well, he might soon have a wife and family to settle in Mississippi.

Some of the Democrats raved with indignation. Garrett Davis of Kentucky described Ames as a "military dictator" and "autocrat" who had filled the Mississippi legislature with his "creatures" and had "commanded whom he pleased to vote." George Vickers of Maryland declaimed: "Never before in the history of our country has a military commander descended to compromise his high position and use it for selfish, ambitious, and political purposes."

Most of the leading Republicans were for seating Ames—among them John Sherman of Ohio, Charles Sumner of Massachusetts, and Lot M. Morrill of Ames's native state of Maine. One of his defenders pointed out that, according to the Mississippi constitution, all citizens of the United States residing in Mississippi were citizens of the state. Morrill read a resolution which the Mississippi legislature had just passed to urge the State to seat Ames without further delay.

At last, on April 1, Sumner moved to strike the word "not" from the phrase "not eligible" in the judiciary committee's proposed resolution.

The motion carried, and the amended resolution then passed by a vote of 40 to 12, with many senators pairing or abstaining. Morrill immediately escorted Ames to the chair for him to take the oath of office.[15]

Though now a United States senator, Ames sometimes wondered whether he was worthy of Blanche, whether he could provide the luxuries she was used to. Nevertheless, on an April evening about three weeks after being seated, he offered her an engagement ring. She accepted it and gave him a gold locket containing a tiny picture of her and a lock of her hair. The next morning she left for a long visit in New York.

In her absence Ames could hardly concentrate on Senate business. On the afternoon of her departure he left his colleagues to communicate with her. "I will close my first letter to you," he finished, "and go back to my seat to assume that dignified (?), indifferent air, just as though I had not been having a chat with my Love, so far away." He found it hard to entertain himself. Treasury Secretary Boutwell insisted that he play billiards with him, and Ames was growing tired of it. As his letters followed one another, he apologized for their monotony. "But you must remember, my days are just the same. Senate—dinner—billiards—and more billiards—and more."

One thing he found worth doing, and that was reading *General Butler in New Orleans,* by the popular biographer James Parton. Ames confessed to Blanche that he thoroughly approved of her father's course as wartime commander of occupied New Orleans. "His great genius—his resources, his tact, his courage strike me as something remarkable and worthy of the highest admiration. Of his gifts I have only the honesty of purpose and courage."

In her letters Blanche indicated that she was very much a person in her own right and, even when a senator's wife, intended to retain her identity. "I wonder if you will ever succeed in inspiring me with that awe and reverence which some wives feel for the 'Lords of Creation,'" she wrote. "I think not." She was not just engaging in banter with her beloved. The word "obey," she insisted, must be omitted from her part in the marriage ceremony. "Love me and honor me," Ames replied, "and I will be content."

Once they knew when Congress would adjourn, the couple set the date of their wedding at July 21 and the place at St. Ann's Episcopal Church in Lowell, Massachusetts, the Butlers' hometown. On the marriage certificate Ames described himself as thirty-four years old and, rather imaginatively, as a "planter" of Jackson, Mississippi. Blanche gave her age as twenty-three. Six hundred guests looked on as, at the appointed hour, Butler escorted his daughter and Ames her mother under a floral arch to the altar.

In September, after a honeymoon in Lowell, Mr. and Mrs. Ames started on a long and slow wedding trip, which was to take them by a roundabout route to their adopted home state. They stopped at West

Point, where they "attended two hops" and talked with Mrs. Grant. Then, in Detroit, they visited the home of Senator Zachariah Chandler, whose daughter Minnie had been one of Blanche's bridesmaids. Next, they spent some time with Ames's parents, who had moved from Maine to Northfield, Minnesota. Finally heading south, they paused at Fort Atkinson, Iowa, to look over a mill property that Ames thought he might like to buy.

"You must not go to Mississippi till there have been frosts there," Mrs. Butler had cautioned Blanche. "You must not encounter a double danger—the fever and the rebels." Obediently, the Ameses delayed their arrival until the beginning of November, when they found the Mississippi weather still mild. In Vicksburg, Blanche noted in her diary:

> To me, the only redeeming feature of the South is the climate. But that is not sufficient to cover its multitudinous disadvantages. The malarious atmosphere, with its baleful influence upon mind and body, the red, clayey, turfless soil, filled with watercourses and gullies, the slothful indolence of all its people, would be insurmountable reasons why I could never regard it with favor, as a permanent place of residence. Yet we are to think of it, speak of it, as home for at least the next five years.

But Natchez at least momentarily "redeemed the South" for Blanche. After four days there, she wrote excitedly:

> What a glorious home, glorious in its beauty I mean, a man could make here. One half the pains bestowed upon an Eastern garden would make a bower of roses, jasmine, magnolias, orange blossoms, in fact all that the North or the tropics can furnish of fragrance and loveliness. . . . As we ride through the country and I think of this I begin to regret that Gen'l Ames is not ready to decide upon purchasing a home here.

Before heading for Washington, Ames decided to meet with some of his constituents. Blanche advised him to have a speech ready and persuaded him to practice it on her as they rode through the countryside. "Poor Del," she thought. "It was an effort for him, before me. His dear face flushed to the eyes. He is so little used to public speaking." Still, he managed to address his "colored friends," urging them to take advantage of their opportunities and reminding them of the progress they made since he "took control of the destinies of the State."

"These have been happy months," Blanche recorded after three months of married life. "No unkind words or thoughts. No forced affection or want of adaptability." Yet she was not entirely content. "Men always seem to have the advantage—in dress, in law, in politics—everything," she wrote after the end of the wedding trip. "Will the time ever come when it will be equally easy for women to exist?"[16]

As for Ames, he had no complaints about his marriage or his bride. Certainly Blanche was to prove an asset to him even in politics, as she had already begun to do in advising and coaching him. Indeed, she was a smarter politician than he. Yet she was also to be something of a political liability. With a strong-minded wife, who could stand very little of Mississippi living, he would find it harder than ever to establish himself as a true inhabitant of the state. And among white Mississippians it was no advantage for him to be known as the son-in-law of Ben Butler—"Beast" Butler—the man whom, of all living Yankees, Southern whites hated the most.

The Ameses were back in Washington before the meeting of Congress on the first Monday of December 1870. They now made their home with the Butlers—in an apartment and office that had been added onto the house. This arrangement made it easy for the senator and the congressman to confer, as they frequently did. About the time the Ameses moved in, Blanche discovered that she was pregnant.

In the Senate chamber Ames sat on the front row, next to Morrill of Maine at the extreme left. Ames was a member of the committee on military affairs. In this lame-duck session he was one of 11 carpetbaggers, who constituted exactly 50 percent of the senatorial representation from the ex-Confederate states. In the next Congress, beginning on March 4, 1871, he was one of 10 carpetbaggers, among a total of 74 senators, only 17 of whom were Democrats. During the first session of the new Congress, from March to July, he was the lone senator from Mississippi. Senator-elect Alcorn, instead of coming to Washington to replace Revels, chose for the time being to remain in Jackson as governor of the state.

No sooner had the new session begun than bad news came from Mississippi. For some time Ku Kluxism had been endemic in and around Meridian, a rail center near the Alabama line. When the English traveler Robert Somers stopped there in January 1871, he got the impression that Confederate veterans had resumed the war. He wrote: "the remains of the Confederate armies—swept, after a long and heroic day of fair fight, from the field—flitted before the eyes of the people in their weird and midnight shape of a 'Ku-Klux-Klan.'" The Klan sprang into action in the Meridian riot on March 6 and 7.

After a Meridian rally to protest against terrorism, three black speakers had been jailed for "creating disorder." One of the three was J. Aaron Moore, the state representative from Meridian who the previous summer had officiated at the wedding of Carrie Highgate and Albert Morgan. While the three defendants were appearing in the courtroom for arraignment, pistol shots suddenly rang out, clearing the room of blacks except for the dead and wounded. Moore escaped by pretending to be dead and lying on the floor until he had a chance to flee. Vigilantes tracked down other survivors, and by the time federal troops arrived, a few days later, unnumbered blacks had suffered wounds and approximately thirty had lost their lives.[17]

Soon afterward, on March 10, the Senate committee investigating the Ku Klux conspiracy made a preliminary report. The committee had gathered a great deal of testimony to show that atrocities were continuing in much of the South and were increasing in Mississippi. This evidence convinced the Republican majority on the committee and the Republican majority in the Senate as a whole that Congress needed to take further steps for the enforcement of the Fourteenth and Fifteenth Amendments. News of the Meridian riot seemed to underscore the point.

Ames prepared to speak in favor of a new enforcement bill. Lacking confidence in his forensic ability, he had not yet participated in any debate, though he had been a senator for almost a year. "General Ames is in great tribulation today," Blanche noted on March 21, "—for he is to make his maiden speech this afternoon." Once on his feet, he did pretty well.

He pointed out that blacks outnumbered whites in Mississippi. "Because the majority dare strive to exercise its lawful rights, and in doing so keep from place and power a minority, a false cry of injustice and wrong is sounded from one end of the country to the other." We must not suppose that "all the evils of slavery and rebellion vanished on the day of surrender at Appomattox." We still have to deal with those evils, and the federal government must act, for the states cannot do it alone. Look at the Meridian riot: Governor Alcorn, when calling for federal troops, admitted that he could not enforce the law.

Two weeks later the hard-bitten Frank Blair got up to make a reply. He talked for three and a half hours one day and continued the next with what turned into a personal attack on Ames. As a member of the committee investigating conditions in the South, Blair said, he knew that the disorders there had been grossly exaggerated. Such crimes as did occur were offenses against state law and should be punished by the state authorities. The alleged mistreatment of blacks was only a pretext for depriving the people of self-government, putting them under the rule of major generals, and plundering them. It meant turning away from the Senate such fine men as William Sharkey (elected in 1865 by the Mississippi legislature restored under the Johnson plan) "to give place to one of these major generals and a vagrant negro, the twin emblems of Radical supremacy in this country."

"What a remarkable spectacle," Ames retorted the following week. "He who wore the blue in the days of rebellion now leading the rebel gray!" Blair had spoken like the ex-Confederates who wanted to take the vote away from blacks and drive out carpetbaggers. "The colored man deprived of the ballot would be in a condition worse than slavery," Ames declared, "for he would not even have a master's interest in him to the amount of his coin value." As for the carpetbaggers and their "crusades" that Blair had referred to, the European crusades to the Near East had done a good deal to disseminate Christianity and stimulate civilization. "So would great blessings and benefits result from northern crusades, necessitated by the rebellion, into benighted regions, were not violence and murder now working their defeat."

Blair had alluded flatteringly to Governor Alcorn, who insisted that no further enforcement legislation was necessary. Ames held in his hand a telegram from the governor claiming that sixty-two murders had occurred during twelve months of Ames's governorship and exactly the same number during twelve months of Alcorn's. "The civil power," Alcorn's message concluded, "has been fully as successful as the bayonet in protecting life." After reading that telegram, Ames picked up another, this one dated one day later and signed by four members of the legislature, who disputed Alcorn's figures. "Instead of nineteen murders in the last six months," the legislators maintained, "there have been at least sixty-three in the last three months."

Blair had spoken of the Mississippi senator as a major general. "Let him bear in mind the fact that the Senator from Mississippi is not a member of Congress and a major general at one and the same time, as was the Senator from Missouri, in defiance of the Constitution of the United States" (Blair had served, for a time during the war, in both the army and the House of Representatives). Blair would rather see Mississippi represented by William Sharkey, "a man who as judge [chief justice of the state, 1832-1851] decided that by the common law of Mississippi a master could not set free his own slaves, his children, by a valid will!" According to Blair, Mississippi had sent, instead, a "vagrant negro" to the Senate. "As to his insult to my late colleague I have only to say that in all those attributes which constitute the honorable, high-minded Christian gentleman Mr. Revels is in no degree the honorable Senator's inferior."

Ames had spoken for about an hour, while Blanche proudly looked on from the gallery, observing the audience as well as the speaker. His speech was "really remarkably good," she thought. "Everybody listened with marked attention." Senator George F. Edmunds of Vermont said it was a "magnificent" speech. Senator Chandler told Ames: "Frank Blair feels pretty cross—he knows he has found his master."

Ames and Blanche expected Blair to retaliate, and in a couple of days he did, saying there was no disputing tastes and he would not object if Ames wanted to consort with Negroes. As for Revels, "I do not suppose that any other race of people could ever have discovered senatorial timber in that gentleman except the negro race." The *New York Times* published a letter from Alcorn accusing Ames of misstatements. "So," Blanche informed her mother, "there are two opponents on hand to be disposed of."[18]

Ames could feel that he had scored a point on his opponents when the Senate and the House approved the bill he was advocating. This Ku

Klux Act of 1871 authorized the use of troops and, if necessary, military trials to deal with violators. In the course of the year several hundred were to be arrested and brought before civil courts in Mississippi. Many were indicted, but nearly all were let off with suspended sentences or, at worst, small fines. Terror itself made it almost impossible to convict and impose stiff penalties on terrorists.

After the passage of the bill, in late April, Blanche left for Lowell to stay with her mother and, now five months pregnant, wait for her baby. Lonely in Washington, Ames visited Blanche in Lowell and his parents in Northfield before the end of the session. From Northfield he wrote to Blanche in June: "Father has just come with the morning's paper wherein I see Mr. Alcorn has removed some of my friends in Mississippi." Two days later: "Alcorn has removed the Mayor of Vicksburg and taken the state printing from my friends." Before long, Alcorn had replaced practically all the local officials that Ames, as provisional governor, had appointed. Of Alcorn's 536 appointees, 217 were Democrats, and among the Republicans few were carpetbaggers and still fewer blacks.

At the end of July, after the Senate's adjournment, Ames went to Lowell to remain with Blanche until the baby came. On August 22 she gave birth to a boy, whom they named Butler. When Butler was three weeks old his father left for Mississippi, again by way of Minnesota. "I am admonished," he wrote from Northfield, "that I should be in a more Southern latitude among my political friends—my constituents. I shall make no delay."

Once in Mississippi, he began "mule riding"—that is, in local parlance, traveling around to campaign for his party's candidates in the fall elections. "Speaking to colored audiences is not the highest order of oratory," he remarked in one of his frequent letters to Blanche. "Stories and jokes please them much, and of such material I have but little." Still, he thought he was doing pretty well and was developing "confidence and ease." He feared that the Democrats would get many more votes than in 1869, because of the "Andrew Johnson policy" of Alcorn as governor. On election day, November 7, the Democrats did make sizable gains, even though the Republicans polled their largest total yet and blacks won more local offices than they had lost through Alcorn's recent removals.[19]

For Ames, it proved to be a rather dubious victory. The Republican party of Mississippi was splitting between his followers and Alcorn's. Alcorn had the greater appeal for native whites, Ames for carpetbaggers and blacks. But Alcorn held on to some important carpetbag and black allies. The lieutenant governor, Ridgely C. Powers, an Ohioan by birth and a former captain in the Union army, now stood by him, though at first he was unfriendly. So did ex-Senator Revels, whom Alcorn had made president of Alcorn University, the new state university for blacks.

The question remained as to which of the two factions was the winner.

"Although Mr. Alcorn has been fighting hard for his own personal adherents he has uniformly been beaten everywhere," Ames professed to believe. Through Alcorn's "warfare" on carpetbaggers he had driven nearly all of them over to Ames's side, it seemed, and certainly a couple of prominent ones had recently switched to supporting Ames—"a long step toward unanimity among carpet-baggers—a thing earnestly to be wished." But as the post-election weeks passed, the prospect for Ames dimmed somewhat. "Our party majority over the Democracy is so small that a few bolters from us will hold the balance of power," he feared. And Alcorn would no doubt order his followers to join the Democrats, if necessary, to beat the Ames faction.

Now that Lieutenant Governor Powers was safely on Alcorn's side, Alcorn could turn the governorship over to him and, at last, occupy the Senate seat that Revels had vacated in March. Conservative Mississippians urged Alcorn to stay on in Jackson and keep a restraining hand on the Radicals in the legislature, but on November 30, Thanksgiving Day, he resigned as governor. "Now as he is to go to Washington he and I will have 'a row,'" Ames assumed. "Shall he whip me or I him in Washington?" Nevertheless, when Alcorn appeared in the Senate, Ames greeted him cordially enough. Alcorn was sure the recent elections had strengthened *his* faction, and he misinterpreted Ames's politeness. He gloated to his wife: "He sees how the land lies and surrenders like a man."[20]

Outwardly the relations between Ames and Alcorn remained fairly calm for several months, and then, on the evening of May 20, 1872, the "row" that Ames had anticipated suddenly erupted. Alcorn took the Senate floor to discuss a bill extending the Ku Klux Act and also to make a "personal explanation" or defense. Well dressed, well groomed, he was the very picture of a Southern gentleman, and he was a master of the Southern style of orotund oratory. A far more effective speaker than Ames, he could think quickly on his feet, make apt remarks off the cuff, draw laughs—and blood—with sarcastic humor, and all the while keep in rapport with his audience.

When, twelve months earlier, the Senate was considering the present Ku Klux law, he began, he had "apprehended that Congress might be misled by the exaggerated accounts of violence" and, as Mississippi governor, had "sent a dispatch to the delegation from Mississippi." The lone senator from the state "saw proper to arraign me." That gentleman would not have been in the Senate if it had not been for the war. "The senatorial toga flung upon his shoulders before he had taken off his soldier's coat, he was admitted here, sir, an exceptional precedent—a sort of brevet brigadier Senator." He was not a citizen of Mississippi, had never paid a dollar in taxes there, and did not have "even a technical residence" in the state. True, an "official fiction" in the congressional directory assigned him a home in Natchez, but he had never been "identified with its interests to the extent of even the washing of a shirt."

Alcorn made it clear that he himself, by contrast, was an old resident of the state and owned a plantation in Coahoma County. "When the Republicans were beaten [in 1868] . . . when they saw . . . that the cause of Republicanism in Mississippi was hopeless without a moderation that would give it a footing among the old citizens of the State, they offered me the candidacy on the Republican ticket for Governor." He then "met violence at nearly every stump" despite Ames's control of troops.

Here Ames interrupted to say he had sent a bodyguard to protect Alcorn on the campaign trail because of Mrs. Alcorn's concern for his safety. Somewhat taken aback, Alcorn confessed he had not known of this, but said he did know that his wife was a "timid southern woman" and had implored him "not to go into the canvass."

Recovering his aplomb, Alcorn launched into a tirade against the "hordes of northern adventurers" who, once the Negro had been given the vote, "had caught a scent of strife and prey from afar off." They were to blame for such race conflict as existed in Mississippi and other Southern states. "The kindliness between the two races at the South had been maintained at its old cordiality up to the close of the war." Then the Freedmen's Bureau interposed and formed a "wall of separation between the two." Next, under "military rule," the "Northern camp followers" and soldiers remaining in the South, "conquerors among the conquered, did much to make the wall separating the two races of the southern people a wall of fire!"

(Alcorn was forgetting how, just a few years earlier, he had been thankful for the presence of the Northern "military power" and had pitied the poor Negro "under the heel of a society vindictive towards him because he is free.")

When Alcorn had finished, Ames got to his feet and replied with some of his own brand of sarcasm. His colleague, he said, had been "pronouncing the personal pronoun 'I'" and bragging of his plantation, his state, and his people as if only he and his kind had a right to be in Mississippi and as if Ames "had no business here" in the Senate. True, if there had been no war he would not be here, but neither would Alcorn. "He stayed in the war some two or three or four months, and then retired to this plantation in Coahoma county and remained there the rest of the time." But "I found my way to Mississippi through much blood and over many battle-fields. I had the right to go there. I have the right to stay there even if I do not own a plantation in Coahoma county."

> And now my colleague comes here, as I say, to represent the Republican Party of the State of Mississippi. Does he talk like a Republican? Has he ever uttered a Republican sentiment? Does he vote for anything that is Republican, Ku Klux law or civil rights bill, anything that the Republicans of the State ask? No. He comes here simply or in part to abuse the very men who sent him here. It is a fact that the carpet-baggers and the colored men are the controlling element of the Republican Party of that State. They con-

> trolled it when he was nominated and when he was elected to the Senate, and they control it now.

Alcorn was more like a Democrat than like a Republican, Ames contended. Indeed, while governor, he had filled many county offices with "Democrats of the Ku Klux order." Now, as senator, he could not speak for the Republicans of the state. "Mr. President, I can speak for the Republican Party of the State of Mississippi, and I do assert that they desire the continuation of the operation of this law."

The Senate passed the bill for extending the law, but the House failed to do so. The House did pass a general amnesty bill, one that Representative Butler had introduced. Earlier Ames had proposed a similar measure in the Senate, where it had died, but the Senate now gave its approval to the Butler bill. This act completely removed the Fourteenth Amendment prohibition of officeholding by former rebel leaders. Hereafter they could not only vote in Mississippi but could seek election there (and in other Southern states). On the part of Ames, Butler, and other Radicals, it was a peace offering to the country's late enemies, but it failed to mollify them with regard to Reconstruction.[21]

CHAPTER 10

Juries Are All Ku Klux
(1869-1872)

Prosperity had come to Albion and Emma Tourgee by the beginning of 1869. As a code commissioner and a superior court judge, he drew from the state of North Carolina two salaries totaling $5,000 a year, enough for comfortable affluence in those days. Though only thirty, he could feel that he had arrived.

The Tourgees were starting to live in a style appropriate to their new station. They bought a red-brick, two-storied house and enlarged and remodeled it, giving it the most up-to-date Gothic trim. The house and its spacious oak-shaded yard were well located in a fashionable, newly developing area just outside the southeast edge of Greensboro. Emma selected brand-new, made-to-order furniture. "We were glad to hear that you were well pleased with your chairs and that you are settled in your new home," she heard from a Lincolnton furniture manufacturer; "nothing like home a great deal can be said on that one word." The Tourgees also found other words for the place; they came to refer to it affectionately as Carpet Bag Lodge.

Not content with one house and lot, Tourgee proceeded to buy up other property southeast of Greensboro, and Emma acquired some parcels for her Pennsylvania kin. Before long the Tourgees owned approximately 150 acres. Much of this was farmland, which they hired men to cultivate for corn, vegetables, grapes, and other fruit. They invested in cows and pigs, churned their own butter and peddled some of it.

A fancier of horseflesh, Tourgee took a special interest in its acquisition. No longer could he be expected to ride around on a half-blind nag. His recently acquired Billy was a spirited animal, not the best for riding but excellent for driving and usable for plowing. Though Billy alone was more than adequate for pulling a buggy, Tourgee needed a team for heavier work. He found a horse that would "make a splendid match" except for one defect—one that Tourgee would be acutely conscious of—"a very bad eye." Eventually he teamed Billy with Fan. He shopped around for a buggy until he discovered a model, made in Fayetteville, that exactly suited him.[1]

These many purchases ran into a lot of money, and Tourgee had no savings and not enough income to pay cash for everything. Creditors were still dunning him for debts left over from the failure of his nursery business. Some of his real estate he could buy on time, and pieces of it he could resell for more than they had cost him. He also had a pair of flush friends upon whom he—and many other Republican politicians—could and did rely. These two were Milton S. Littlefield and George W. Swepson.

The handsome, prepossessing Littlefield, a former Union general from Illinois, had lobbied for railroad enterprises at the state constitutional convention early in 1868. Tourgee had made his acquaintance there and had joined him in leading the celebration at the convention's close. Through Littlefield he had met Swepson, a slight, mild-mannered banker who was both a North Carolina native and a lifelong Democrat. Littlefield and Swepson were partners in schemes to obtain railroad-aid bonds from the legislature and sell them for a generous commission.

Tourgee was not in a position to help Littlefield and Swepson with their schemes. Still, he was a politician of some influence, and the partners were glad to do favors for him. On one occasion, Littlefield allowed Tourgee to draw on him for $1500. Later Littlefield presented him with a draft on Swepson for $3500. When Tourgee tried to cash these notes, they were protested, and he had to keep after Littlefield and Swepson to make good. The two financiers were hard to catch up with, for they were constantly on the go—from Raleigh to New York, Florida, and other places.

There would be a chance to see Littlefield at the Raleigh memorial ceremonies scheduled for May 29, 1869. The arrangements, which Littlefield had helped to prepare, called for a procession with a brass band in the lead; followed by Union veterans (members of the Grand Army of the Republic) and soldiers of the U.S. army marching in formation; next, the mayor, governor, other dignitaries, and their ladies riding in carriages; and finally schoolchildren, representatives of charitable and other societies, and miscellaneous citizens following on foot. The parade was to move through the Raleigh streets to the national cemetery. There General Littlefield would deliver the oration of the day, and the participants would proceed to the decoration of soldier graves.

Tourgee hoped to arrange for a friend's private railroad car to take carpetbaggers and their wives from Greensboro to Raleigh for the ceremonies, but his plans fell through. In time, though, he did manage to realize the proceeds from the Littlefield-Swepson loans. Or were they loans? Neither Littlefield nor Swepson ever bothered to ask for repayment. "I never heard Genl Littlefield say one word as to the terms or conditions upon which he loaned you or let you have that thirty five hundred dollars or any other sum whatsoever," the obliging Swepson confided to Tourgee. "He has never transferred to me your notes or said anything to me about them in any way. I did not know you gave him any note whatever."[2]

As a superior court judge, Tourgee spent a good deal of time traveling from courthouse to courthouse within his judicial district, which comprised a block of eight counties in the north central part of the state. Three of the county seats, including Greensboro, were on the railroad, so it was easy enough to get to them. To reach the others, Tourgee went in his own buggy or by public stage or by some combination of horse-drawn conveyance and steam train. About thirty miles from Greensboro lay the tiny, forest-hidden hamlet of Wentworth, county seat of Rockingham and home of Tourgee's good friend Thomas Settle, a native Unionist and state supreme court justice. "The pleasantest way to come or go is by buggy," Tourgee wrote his wife from Wentworth on a March day. "The train leaves late you know and one has to go 8 miles to it and then sit in a comfortless depot till the 'fire-horse' comes along and get to Greensboro at midnight. I can leave here at, say, 12:30 and get home by sun-down easy, if the roads continue good."

Touring the circuit had its dull and difficult moments (and before long it was to offer real hazards to life and limb). Tourgee might arrive, as he did one night at Roxboro, "very weary after an all-day's journey from Hillsboro, horrible roads and slow team." Occasionally his buggy broke down, and he had to patch it together with hickory withes until he could stop for more professional repairs. Sometimes the lodging was uncomfortable and the meals unpalatable or worse, leading to headaches or diarrhea.

But on the whole Tourgee found the itinerant life most enjoyable. En route he usually had the company of a court official, a lawyer, or at least his dog Bruno. "Billy is in splendid spirits and Bruno ditto," he once reported. Most of the time he was ditto, too. Frequently he spent the night as the guest of some genial and hospitable friend, such as Judge Settle. On his travels he confirmed his love for the Carolina countryside and climate. "Is not this beautiful *glorious* weather?" he wrote Emma from Hillsboro one April evening, as he looked out the window at a range of flowering hills "just in their glory," which reminded him of the Berkshire Hills as he had known them during the Massachusetts phase of his boyhood.[3]

Besides the eight county seats, Tourgee had frequent occasion to visit the state capital, to confer with his fellow code commissioners or to attend to political or other business. The other two commissioners were native North Carolinians and former Confederate officers, the one a Whig and the other a Democrat. Tourgee got along well with both. By the beginning of 1869 the three had completed a code of civil procedure, and by the end of the year a code of criminal procedure and a penal code. Most North Carolina lawyers resented the elimination of legal complexities they had mastered as arcane lore. A Conservative newspaper sneered that the commissioners had undertaken to "do away with the necessity of legal learning, so that negroes and carpetbaggers might be qualified to come to the bar, or sit upon the bench." But in time an expert in legal history was to praise their work—or those parts of it that the legislature approved—as "the most sweeping legislative contribution in the nineteenth century to the law of private relations."[4]

The trustees of the University of North Carolina met from time to time in Raleigh, and as a faithful member of the board Tourgee attended the meetings. The president of the board was his friend the governor of the state, W. W. Holden, and the president of the university was another friend and fellow Republican, the Reverend Solomon Pool. On behalf of the faculty, Pool once invited Tourgee to deliver an evening lecture on a subject of his own choice. Tourgee readily accepted, and Pool arranged for him to be met at Durham's Station (near the place where General Joseph E. Johnston had surrendered to General William T. Sherman only a little more than four years earlier). "The driver will bring you to my house," Pool wrote him, "and Mrs. Pool will be happy to offer you the hospitality of our home upon the occasion."

While Tourgee was traveling about—and now and then enjoying the hospitality of someone's home—Emma stayed in Greensboro. He wrote to her almost every day, and sometimes he said it would be nice if she could come along with him, but she seldom if ever did. In his letters he constantly reassured her of his love, as when he wrote on May 14, 1869, from Pittsboro:

> This is our anniversary! And I must pass the day, not in pleasant association with you, but amid the turmoil of a court—briefs, motions, exceptions and the trial of two persons for their lives are the wearisome and ghastly duties which contrast themselves so broadly with the bright memories of six years ago! Oh Darling, what do I not owe to that day!

During her husband's frequent absences Emma had to look after the house and the yard, the grapevines, fruit trees, and planted fields. She was not entirely alone. Her father and some of her other relatives lived nearby, and servants and hired hands continually came and went. Among the servants were a light-complexioned mulatto cook and her bright, attractive, nearly white teen-aged daughter Adaline.

As the child of slaves, Adaline had had little or no opportunity to develop either social graces or intellectual skills. Tourgee took notice. Once the principal of an Ohio academy, he remained something of a pedagogue. He was beginning to think that Southerners, both black and white, must be reeducated if the persisting taint of slavery was ever to be removed from their minds. He was about to propose that the federal government take over the schools of the South. Meanwhile, he could make a modest start, himself, by tutoring one of slavery's offspring, Adaline.

He became her legal guardian and persuaded Emma to let her live with them. Never enthusiastic about the plan, Emma quickly found Adaline something of an annoyance and began to wonder a bit about her husband's interest in the girl, expressing what he dismissed as a "somewhat romantic supposition of possibilities." Soon the neighbors were talking. Then the Democratic *Raleigh Sentinel* noticed the adoption of Adaline and commented nastily: "This is generous of the Judge—very generous! Is Tourgee a married man?" But he refused to be deflected by either his wife's misgivings or the local and statewide gossip. "I know that the course I have marked out—in the main—is for Ada's benefit, and *is right,*" he assured Emma. "I shall not ask my neighbors to define my duty for me, nor to dictate my course."[5]

Musing on Adaline and slavery, Tourgee got the idea for a novel, and in such moments as he could snatch from his busy schedule he began to write out the story in bits and pieces. In it Toinette (like Adaline) is something of a Pygmalion character. A young planter, Geoffrey Hunter, takes the beautiful, nearly white slave girl and molds her into an educated and accomplished lady. Just before the Civil War, Hunter frees Toinette in accordance with the wishes of his parents, now dead. He settles her in a cottage in Oberlin, Ohio, where she lives as a respectable white widow and raises their son. Still in love with Hunter, she becomes a Union nurse, looks for him, locates him as a wounded prisoner of war, and takes care of him. He is still attached to her, but insists on something like the old master-slave relationship.

This novel, *Toinette,* Tourgee was later to say, "concerns itself with Slavery only to mark the growth of character under that influence." "It carefully traces only those unconscious influences which shape and mold mental and moral qualities, and through which *Slavery still lives and dominates.*" But the story is not entirely consistent with such a theme. As Tourgee told it, the white people of Oberlin, an outpost of abolitionism where slavery had never existed, were really no better than those of Greensboro in their attitude toward Toinette. "Educated and refined Christian ladies and gentlemen were her familiar friends. Of course, it was all upon the hypothesis of an unmixed Caucasian descent." The ladies and gentlemen of Oberlin—most of them, at any rate—would have shunned Toinette if they had had any inkling of her Negro blood, infinitesimal though it was. "With this revealed, and her descent known, she would have been as much a Pariah in that part of the nation, which boasted of its freedom and equality, and even in a community of the most ardent fanatics, as in the very hotbed of slavery."

Tourgee was in no hurry to finish or publish *Toinette.* He was, however, writing shorter pieces for publication. In 1869 an editor of *Harper's Magazine* accepted some of his anecdotes and assured him: "Anything else of the same sort will always be *welcome.*" That year a Rochester University classmate, now running the Hornellsville, New York, *Valley Times,* was glad to accept a contribution from Tourgee. "Had thought of asking you for sketches of scenes and incidents around you, but, had you time to devote to it, I presumed you could find an organ of wider fame and influence, to publish your contributions," the *Valley Times* editor confessed in thanking Tourgee for the piece. "But anything which illustrates the *Renaissance* period of the South has both a present interest and a historical value, and is gladly published." Thus Tourgee was encouraged to believe there was a market in the North for fictional or factual reporting about the South. A decade was to pass, though, before he gained wealth and renown as a novelist of Reconstruction.[6]

In writing *Toinette* he intended to show the evil and almost ineradicable effects of slavery on human characer. But he did not think its consequences wholly bad—at least, not for the slaves. This he made clear, to the former slaves themselves, when he addressed the freed people of Greensboro at their observance of the seventh anniversary of the Emancipation Proclamation, January 1, 1870. He took "The Slave's Wages" as his topic. Northerners, he said, had sympathized with the slave because he was an unpaid laborer. Some concluded that he was owed back pay for "two centuries and a half of unrequited toil." The freedman himself had "come to regard the past as an inexhaustible fountain of grievances, from which at any time may be drawn a sufficient excuse for present remissness or future delinquency."

> This view is eminently hurtful to the freedman as tending to make him less regardful of his present opportunity and less inclined to rely upon himself for the amelioration of the future. Like the feeling that the world owes one a living, it is well calculated to prevent its possessor from getting one in a legitimate way. . . .
>
> It imparts to the freedman the role of a perpetual mendicant, asking for that which could never be paid if it were actually his due. . . .
>
> What did two and a half centuries do for the slave? Compare the American freedman of today with his congener of the African coast, and you have the answer from a physical standpoint. "Hyperion to a satyr." Slavery brought to our shores the weak, unskilled, barbarous ancestor, incapable of continued exertion, enervated and degraded by centuries of sloth and ignorance. His enforced exertion brought wealth and leisure to the white man, it is true, but it brought a far richer reward to the slave, strength, endurance, power. Year by year he rose above his brutish origin. Skill came to his hand and life to his brain.

So slavery did the slave more good than it did the master. Two objections might be made, Tourgee conceded, but he had answers for both of them. "1. *These are the arguments by which Slavery sought to defend itself.*" Yes, but they are true. "2. *If the results of Slavery were beneficial, why was not the institution preserved?*" The institution was no longer necessary or desirable once it had performed its function as an "apprenticeship" and had instilled in the blacks a sensitivity to suffering and a desire for freedom.[7]

In thus addressing North Carolina blacks, Tourgee may unwittingly have misinformed them, but he certainly had their best interests at heart. He demonstrated his sympathy with them on many occasions and never more convincingly than in his resistance to their—and his—Ku Klux tormentors.

Judicial and presumably impartial though he was, Tourgee could not ignore politics. With his six-year term as judge, he did not have to be immediately concerned about his own reelection. He had to concern himself with the continued success of the Republican party, however, for on it depended the success of Reconstruction. Of course, he also had to take cognizance of crime. On the part of the opposition, political activity and criminal activity were pretty much the same thing.

During the recent election, in 1868, the Conservatives (as the Democrats called themselves to attract former Whigs) had threatened to punish anyone who voted against them. "They are exhibiting more bitterness by far than they did in 1860-61 when they got up the other rebellion," Tourgee heard from Judge Settle in Wentworth. "These organizations are holding meetings all over this section of the State & they boldly proclaim that no republican, white or black, shall work or live on their lands." Afterward a number of blacks who had dared to vote found themselves without a place to live or work.[8]

The election resulted in a qualified victory for the Republicans. While they won the governorship and a majority in the legislature, the Conservatives got control of many local governments, including some of the counties in Tourgee's judicial district. In only one of these counties, Caswell, did blacks outnumber whites. In North Carolina as a whole, Negroes constituted only about a third of the population. The Republican party could maintain itself in power only with the support of a great many whites in addition to practically all blacks.

The next test of strength would come in the summer of 1870, when elections were to be held for local offices and for legislative seats, though not for the governorship, which had a four-year term. If the Conservatives should continue and enlarge their Ku Klux activity, they could expect to dominate still more localities and even the state legislature. And waves of intensifying terrorism did ensue, particularly within the judicial district of Tourgee. This terrorism formed much of the background—and much of the substance—for his decisions in court.

From the beginning the Conservative newspapers had fomented disrespect for the court by abusing the judge. When, in his opening address, he suggested that an increase in crime could be expected from the dislocations of the war, the *Greensboro Patriot* commented that to say the war led to crime was a "slur upon the Confederate soldiery" by a veteran from the army corps "of one of the most noted pillagers that ever robbed a henroost or made war upon the smokehouses and pantries of defenseless women."

But from other quarters Tourgee received compliments that immensely gratified him. "They say everybody is praising your spouse and that old 'rebs' are coming around and asking to be excused for what they have said of me," he wrote Emma from Asheboro. Again, from Pittsboro: "You cannot imagine how funny it is to hear the people come to me and say in genuine solemn style, 'I think you have been misrepresented!'" An army captain and former schoolmate told him he had overheard lawyers talking about him in the supreme court library in Raleigh. One said the bar of his district, "as a general thing, *were all highly pleased* with you. Said you was prompt, clear in your instructions to juries—a good judge of law—*and an excellent court disciplinarian.*" A fellow code commissioner congratulated Tourgee after hearing comments from his district. "Both sides concur in your ability and fairness; and this is high praise in these times."[9]

Not all the attorneys practicing before Tourgee approved of him. One notable exception was Josiah Turner, Jr., who figured prominently not only as a lawyer but also as a state senator, as the editor of the state's leading Democratic (or Conservative) newspaper, the *Raleigh Sentinel,* and as the reputed "King of the Ku Klux." Turner was described as being of "revolutionary proportions" and as having "a forehead not unlike some cathedral dome, eyes deep set, a cavernous mouth and a voice that carried conviction." His "presence was masterful." Certainly he was a master of vituperation.

Turner seemed often to teeter on the edge of insanity. He may have been mentally and emotionally unbalanced as a result of his war wound. A Minié ball had struck him on the top of the head, fracturing his skull, knocking him off his horse, and leaving him with unbearable headaches. He could not stand the presence of his wife, Sophia, once she had acquired the morphine habit. After enduring "torture and torment" for several years, he had her committed to an insane asylum in Raleigh. He was left with their four young boys and a still younger daughter, who Sophia's family complained were receiving inadequate care.

Turner was nearly eighteen years older than Tourgee. Born in Hillsboro, he had studied at the University of North Carolina, then read law and practiced it. As a Whig, he repeatedly won election to the legislature. In 1861 he opposed secession—unlike Holden, as he afterward liked to point out—but enlisted and served as a captain in the Confederate army until he became wounded in 1862. As a member of the Confederate Congress from 1862 to 1865, he denounced Jefferson Davis and demanded an early peace. He was one of those Southern representatives whom the U.S. Congress refused to seat in 1865. Three years later he was elected to the state senate and, with a secret loan from George W. Swepson, bought the *Raleigh Sentinel.*

In the *Sentinel* and in the senate Turner at first pretended there was no such secret organization as the Ku Klux Klan. Then he began to justify Klan violence by blaming its victims. He charged they had joined the Republican's secret organizations, the Union Leagues, and in their dark-of-the-night meetings had plotted barn burnings and other crimes. The Klan was a necessary and natural response, he said. Privately, he praised the Klan as a means of throwing Republicans out of office. Whether or not he was the King of the Ku Klux, as Holden and Tourgee believed, whether or not he was even a member of the Klan, Turner was without question its most effective champion, the man who did the most to promote the Ku Klux conspiracy in North Carolina.[10]

In the courtroom Turner made life as miserable as he could for Tourgee. He resented Tourgee's insisting that blacks be impaneled on juries and his reproving and fining lawyers for using the term "nigger." Turner showed his special displeasure whenever a decision went against his client. On one occasion he showed it in an editorial he published in his *Sentinel* under the heading "Judge Tourgee's Revenge," accusing the judge of personal bias against him. After one of Turner's courtroom tantrums, Tourgee could only wonder at "the ceaseless hate, the unscrupulous daring and astonishingly fertile mendacity of this truly remarkable man." Tourgee was delighted to write Emma from Hillsboro one evening: "Joe Turner was scared almost to a 'jelly' in court today by stepping on a parlor match which exploded under his foot."

As Klan violence intensified, Turner and other Conservatives alleged that Tourgee provoked it by showing favoritism to blacks in his court. "A partisan judge upon the bench—administering laws made by partisans, for party purposes," the *Greensboro Patriot* editorialized. "A *white* boy is sentenced to the penitentiary for ten years for defending himself against a man: a *colored* boy, for wantonly killing another, is neither fined nor imprisoned." Nothing infuriated Tourgee more than this kind of misleading journalism. In a letter to the *Greeensboro Register*, a Republican paper, he flayed the offending editor and set the record straight. The *white* boy was sixteen years old. The evidence leaving no possibility of acquittal, the boy's counsel had plea-bargained for a manslaughter verdict, and "out of pity for the youth" Tourgee had agreed to it. The *black* boy was only nine years old; "a jury *more than two-thirds of which were conservatives*" had "rendered a verdict of 'Not Guilty.'"

In the state senate John W. Graham of Hillsboro characterized one series of particularly horrible lynchings as "a species of wild justice." He said the vigilantes had taken matters in their own hands because they could not trust the court under Tourgee, who had "*twice* granted a new trial to a colored man found guilty of larceny." In a letter to Holden's *North Carolina Standard* Tourgee demolished Graham's argument by pointing out that the murders "committed by 'wild' men in that county" had begun even before the *first* trial of the accused black man. "Believing that the evidence was legally insufficient for conviction, I acted accordingly," Tourgee ended. "I prize my own self respect too highly to do otherwise, and believing, as I do, that justice should at least be 'color-blind,' I shall know no man by the hue of his skin."[11]

There was no truth whatever in the assertion that Tourgee tilted the scales of justice in favor of blacks. Despite his best efforts to keep the scales even, they were usually tilted the other way. He did not hesitate to sentence two blacks to death after a racially mixed jury had found them guilty of murder. He gave each of three blacks six years at hard labor for disguising themselves and whipping another black, and he gave three others five years for merely wearing masks to frighten—in violation of a new anti-Klan state law prohibiting anyone from going about in disguise with intent to frighten or commit trespass or violence. He imposed long prison terms on several blacks for retaliating against Klansmen by burning their barns. For want of convictions, however, he had been unable to sentence a single member of the Klan. As he once wrote Emma in exasperation, from Alamance County:

> The juries are all Ku Klux, or at least a controlling element of them are so. There is no crime can be committed by a *white* conservative. Yesterday three men were tried for cutting a colored man in pieces almost—stabbing and beating and maltreating in every possible manner—but it was all to no avail. "Not Guilty" was the verdict.[12]

Ku Kluxery flared up in Rockingham County in May 1869. "Men in disguise, at night," Settle informed Tourgee, had "inflicted cruel whipping upon several of our colored citizens." In one instance Klansmen compelled one of the citizens to have sex, or try to, with a young black woman while they whipped him. "This state of affairs is simply intolerable," Settle said, "and must be stopped." Settle induced Governor Holden and Judge Tourgee to arrange for a special term of court in the county, so that the offenders could be brought promptly to justice. "There must be no delay," Tourgee argreed after charging the grand jury of six blacks and twelve whites in Wentworth. "Our only chance to avoid a widespread and bloody turmoil—in my opinion—is to put an iron heel upon these things at once *here* and *now*." But no convictions followed.

Much worse trouble broke out in Orange County during the summer. Between midnight and one o'clock on August 7, the mayor of Hillsboro wrote Tourgee later that morning, 75 to 100 armed men, "dressed all in white and something over their faces," seized the jail keys from the sheriff, "took out 2 colored boys" in jail for alleged barn burning, led them out on the Chapel Hill road, questioned them, turned them loose, and then fired on them as they fled. One died the next day from his wounds; the other was eventually acquitted of the arson charge. Soon after the shooting, a gang of masked and robed men hanged the dead youth's father and uncle from trees near Hillsboro and then another black man from a tree not far away.

Tourgee wrote an account of the disorders in his district, and Republicans in the legislature used the account as an argument for strengthening the militia law. The new act of January 1870 gave little additional power to the governor: he could already call out the militia to suppress disorders; now he could also proclaim an insurrection in any county where disorders prevailed. But he could not suspend the writ of habeas corpus and impose martial law; the state constitution prohibited that. Violence soon spread to Alamance and Caswell, which became the most lawless counties in Tourgee's district.

On the night of February 26, 1870, a howling mob of Klansmen rode into Graham, the county seat of Alamance. They dragged Wyatt Outlaw out of his house and left him hanging from a branch of a large oak, a branch pointing at the door of Tourgee's courthouse just thirty yards away. Outlaw, a town councilman and the president of the local Union League, had been the most prominent black in the county. Tourgee remembered him as "a quiet, peaceable, orderly colored mechanic against whom there was no evil report . . . except the fact that he was a Republican."

Two weeks after the hanging of Outlaw, the body of William Puryear, weighted down with stones, was found in a mill pond. Puryear, a mentally unstable black man, had recognized and was willing to testify against a couple of the Klansmen who had taken part in the Outlaw lynching. Governor Holden now proclaimed an insurrection in Alamance. Instead of calling out the state militia, he asked for federal troops, and a small detachment of them was stationed in the county for a while. No arrests, no trials ensued. There were no witnesses.[13]

"Meantime the County of Caswell seemed to have suddenly become the seat of war," Tourgee noted soon afterward. "Then Mr. J. M. Jones, a white Justice of the Peace, a man of irreproachable character, a church member and an ex-Confederate soldier who was wounded at Gettysburg, was taken from his bed at midnight, one of his children being seriously injured in his removal,—stripped and bound and beaten to a jelly with hickory rods. His recovery at all is simply wonderful to any one who witnessed as I did the lacerations and bruises upon his person." In Caswell, things went from bad to worse, culminating in the murder of State Senator John W. Stephens, also white, on May 21, 1870.

Stephens, about thirty-seven at the time of his death, had been born to impoverished parents in Guilford County. He worked as a harnessmaker before the war, and during it he managed to dodge the draft. Afterward he blamed rich landowners for both the war and the plight of the poor. In the reconstructed state he became the leader of Caswell Republicans, much to the disgust of his fellow Methodists, who expelled him from their church. Conservatives hated and feared and yet belittled him, accusing him of being a common chicken-thief. In the *Sentinel* Turner always referred to him as Chicken Stephens.

Tourgee often saw Senator Stephens when holding court in Yanceyville, the Caswell county seat. The two men became close friends. Tourgee gave Stephens the bar exam, passed him, and qualified him as a lawyer. He often advised him on legal, political, and financial matters. When Stephens expected a Klan attack on his house (an attack that never materialized) Tourgee joined him and other friends, black and white, in arming themselves and lying in wait for the attackers. After Stephens had taken out life insurance to provide for his wife and two children, Tourgee helped him make out his will—about a month before his death. "Since you left," Stephens then wrote Tourgee, "the K. K.s has still bin committing their helish deeds. They have taken out of his house another white man Mr. Wm. I. Ward and tied him to a tree and beat him, & a col. man by the name of Young Richmond and in addition to their usual barbarianism they castrated him it is thought that he will die."

On the morning of May 22 apprehensive black followers of Stephens discovered his body on a pile of firewood in a storage room of the Yanceyville courthouse. He had been strangled and repeatedly stabbed. In the courthouse the previous evening the Conservatives had met to make plans for the upcoming political campaign. Republicans were sure that the murderer or murderers had been attending that meeting. In particular they suspected the sheriff, Frank A. Wiley, and two other men. But Conservatives put the blame on disaffected blacks. Turner said in the *Sentinel* that really Governor Holden was at fault: he had urged Caswell Republicans to "kill off" Stephens; he had meant it in a political sense but they had taken him literally! Turner grew indignant at attempts to cast suspicion on Sheriff Wiley and his associates. "We say positively, after having known Messrs. Wiley, Mitchell, and Roan for years, that they are as innocent of the charge of murdering Stephens as their children three years old."

Not till after more than two years was Tourgee to get confirmation of Wiley's guilt. He then received a statement from a female servant who, immediately after the crime, had overheard Wiley describe it to her employer. According to her statement, Wiley lured Stephens from the courtroom to the "wood room" on the pretext of talking confidentially with him. (Stephens had hoped to conciliate the opposition by persuading Wiley to run for reelection as both the Republican and the Democratic candidate.) About a dozen well-known Conservatives took part in the murder—and a great many others, undoubtedly including Turner, were accessories after the fact. Long after Tourgee's life was over, further confirmation and additional details were to be revealed when the confession of one of the participants was made public.

"Mr. Stephens' murder sent a thrill of horror and alarm through the breast of every republican in the State," it seemed to Tourgee. "For the first time the conviction forced itself upon the mind of every reasoning man that the Conservative party in the State were bound to control it, if by no other means, at least by the cord and dagger. If they could not outvote the republican party, they were bound to out murder it."

In his own thrill of horror and alarm, Tourgee dashed off an excited letter to his friend Joseph C. Abbott, the carpetbag U.S. senator from North Carolina. In it he provided some statistics on the number of killings, beatings, housebreakings, scarings, and other evildoings that had come to his attention. He estimated that, in his judicial district, the outrages of all kinds totaled at least a thousand. Both Abbott and his scalawag colleague from North Carolina, Senator John Pool, were deeply impressed by Tourgee's letter. "I think it a most important and terrible disclosure," Pool wrote him. "The country ought to see it." Other Republican senators and congressmen did see it, and it no doubt helped to speed the passage, ten days after Stephens' death, of the first Enforcement Act, which made Ku Kluxism a federal crime and authorized the use of federal troops to deal with it.

The Enforcement Act could not apply, of course, to atrocities already committed. To enforce the law in the Klan-ridden counties, Governor Holden would have to assert his own powers. Republicans urged him to follow the example of Arkansas Governor Powell Clayton and make war on the Klan. North Carolina was not Arkansas, and Holden was no Clayton, but he nevertheless decided to take bold action. He not only proclaimed the counties of Caswell and Alamance to be in insurrection but he also called for enlistments in the militia—not for local men either white or black but for mountaineers who had served in the Union army. To command them he appointed George W. Kirk, a Tennesseean, the wartime colonel of the Third North Carolina United States Volunteers. With two regiments of rather obstreperous state troops, Kirk quickly pacified the two counties and arrested a number of suspected Klansmen, including Wiley and some of his accomplices in the Stephens assassination. He also apprehended Turner. On Holden's orders, he held the prisoners without formal charges or a trial.

On the whole, Tourgee approved of what Holden was doing, though he had some misgivings. "Governor Holden has done well to put these counties under law," he wrote to the *National Standard* of New York at the height of the military operation. "If he shall ever be arraigned, whether at the bar of any tribunal or by public opinion, for his acts in this emergency, thus far, he can proudly answer with the noble Roman, 'I have saved the republic.'" A little later Tourgee wrote to the *New York Tribune:*

> I have never had any idea that the members of this [Ku Klux] organization could be brought to justice by the *ordinary* machinery of justice here and have constantly for months urged upon the Governor the necessity of employing a sufficient force of *competent professional detectives* to ferret out their acts and ascertain their identity. I have also urged upon him to have parties whom he has had arrested brought before a proper judicial tribunal for examination and commitment or acquittal. I hope, however, that the course which he has adopted, though it did not meet with my entire approval, may

result in the disclosure of their crimes and the utter disruption and obliteration of this bloody and ruthless organization in this State.

Tourgee soon was badly disappointed. Appealing first to a state judge and then to a federal one, the prisoners obtained from the latter a writ of habeas corpus. Holden finally yielded and turned the men loose. What Conservatives called the Kirk-Holden War was over.

Also over was Republican rule in North Carolina, only two years after the readmission of the state. On August 6, election day, Kirk's militiamen were still patrolling Caswell and Alamance, and with the freedom of the ballot assured, these two counties went Republican. But the Conservatives carried most of the state. Henceforth they would control the legislature, and as soon as possible they disallowed the election in Caswell and Alamance.[14]

Carpet Bag Lodge was hardly a happy home that summer of 1870. True, the Tourgees had what ought to be a happy event to look forward to. By election day, Emma was already more than five months along toward having a baby. But she had suffered a miscarriage once before; the worry and strain of the Ku Klux terror could easily induce another one. And the Tourgees had reason to fear that, for them, the worst of the terror might be yet to come.

Ever since the Stephens murder Tourgee had wondered whether he might be next on the assassins' list. At one time or another they did conspire to get him, but each time they somehow bungled the attempt. Once they plotted to seize him boldly on a Greensboro street and hang him to the nearest tree, another time to waylay him as he rode the circuit alone in his buggy at night, and yet again to provoke a courtroom brawl, then shoot him in the midst of it. He did not know about these perils until long after they were past. The present danger, the one he feared in advance, was coming to a head, he thought, in consequence of the publication of a confidential letter of his.

Here it was in the *New York Tribune* for August 3—the letter Tourgee had sent to Senator Abbott in May, just a few days after Stephens's death. It was embarrassing to see the thing in print, particularly in a paper of national circulation like the *Tribune*. In the haste and excitement of writing the letter, Tourgee had made a few little errors of fact, and in transcribing or setting it up someone had further garbled it. For instance, he had attributed thirteen murders to the Klan in his district, whereas one of them had occurred outside it. He had mentioned four arsons, not fourteen as the *Tribune* said, and 400 or 500 housebreakings, not 4,000 or 5,000. He remained convinced that he was right on the main points, however, and that the total of Ku Klux outrages in the district was, as he had written, at least 1,000.

It was worse than embarrassing for Tourgee to find himself thus quoted and misquoted in the *Tribune*. It was downright alarming. History, bad history, seemed to be repeating itself. Four years earlier a New York paper had quoted Tourgee on the mistreatment and murder of blacks in Guilford County, and with dire warnings and death threats some of the local citizens had made life miserable for both him and Emma. Now the two could expect an even more murderous reaction on the part of the Klan.

Tourgee promptly sent the *Tribune* a letter to protest the use, without his permission, of his correspondence with Abbott; to correct the inaccuracies in that correspondence; and to reaffirm his estimate of at least 1,000 outrages. He demanded that the *Tribune* publish this letter of explanation and correction, and the paper did so. On the same day he wrote to the *Tribune,* he also wrote Abbott and Holden, to whom he knew Abbott had given a copy of the earlier letter, and rebuked both men for their "breach of confidence." After both had denied responsibility he concluded that Holden must be to blame. "Holden made a series of egregious blunders," he explained to an old acquaintance in the North, "and then tried to push it off on me by publishing my letter which had been put into his hands under a promise, express, of secrecy."

To Abbott he wrote back, under the conspicuous heading "Strictly Private and Confidential," to say he was in desperate straits and needed help. He explained:

> . . . it has become very evident that I cannot stay in the State. The publication of the letter has enraged every K. K. in the State against me, to an extent almost inconceivable. It will be necessary for me to quit soon. Can you secure me any position under the Government, out of the State, where I can stay a year or two until it will be safe to come back. I have no intention of giving up my hold but must let go for a time to get a new one.
>
> I don't care where, nor what I do, if I can only get a tolerable situation to pay expenses for a year or two. I can leave my property here and it will take care of itself while I am gone. I cannot sell now as all values are depreciated and will go still lower. . . .
>
> P. S. If you cannot get me a place in the U. S. can you get me one out of the country? I don't mean a place whose salary won't pay expenses, but I would as lief have a tolerable one that will, as anything at home. I can *do* French, Spanish, Italian and almost any other modern language except *Servian.*

Desperate though he was, Tourgee could joke about his plight. A carpetbag acquaintance in Goldsboro had offered him a device for converting quills into pens. Asking the man to send it, Tourgee quipped: "Now that the Kuklux are to rule the State without let or hindrance, I want a good pen to write my will with."[15]

Before long Tourgee received an ominous missive from a committee of three members of the Guilford bar, one of whom was his former Quaker landlord Cyrus P. Mendenhall. Readers of the *Raleigh Sentinel* and the *Greensboro Patriot* had been able to see, reprinted from the *New York Tribune,* Tourgee's correspondence on Ku Klux activity in his district. Members of the local bar had seen his two letters "with surprise & regret," the committee said. They would consider it a "dereliction of their duty to the Country, to let such communications pass without their notice, and condemnation." They wished to know whether Tourgee acknowledged himself the author of the letters and whether he still affirmed their contents. "An answer in writing is requested at as early a day as convenient."

Tourgee found it convenient to sit down immediately and pen a spirited reply. Yes, he acknowledged, he had written the two letters and he stood by them—except, of course, for the inaccuracies in the first that he had pointed out in the second. He knew of the outrages largely from the first-hand reports of victims. "Ignorant of the extent of judicial power these persons have flocked to me from every county [in the district] in the hope of legal redress." Why had the lawyers of Guilford never said or done anything against the barbarity all around them?

> They have no "duty to the country" to perform when men are whipped, women beaten almost to a jelly, white women too, children made imbecile by fright, and other outrages perpetrated upon the persons of citizens dwelling "in the peace of God and the State" within the limits of the county. But no sooner does a Judge utter a cry of warning, a call for help, a protest against these fearful enormities, wrung from his very soul by their frequency and horror, than the "bar of Guilford" has a duty to the country and must not let this cry escape its notice and condemnation.

This reply was a "classic," close friends assured Tourgee when he showed them a copy of it. Quite pleased with it himself, he thought it almost unanswerable, and the members of the bar must have thought so, too, for they never got around to answering it. When he held a special term of the Guilford court, he and they stood on their "respective dignities." He heard that some of them were talking of refusing to appear in his court if they should ask for his resignation and he should decline to give it. He was not about to gratify them by offering it, though he still thought that sooner or later he would have to resign.

During the next several weeks he kept on looking for another job. He appealed for aid to other friends in addition to Abbott. Judge Settle assured him he would be sorry to lose his services in the district—"for all must admit that you have stood up like a hero"—but would do what he could for him. He advised him to "run to Washington" and look around. To another correspondent Tourgee reiterated that he would accept any reasonably paying position, even some remote foreign post. "I wouldn't mind yellow fever, cholera, fleas, earthquakes, vertigo, smallpox, cannibalism, icebergs, sharks, or any other name or shape of horror—provided always there are no K. K. K." The very thought of having to move, together with his frantic search for somewhere to go, left Tourgee so enfeebled by asthma and insomnia that for several days he could not even write. Despite his efforts and those of his friends, nothing suitable turned up except the post of minister to Peru, and Judge Settle himself took that when it was offered to him.[16]

So Tourgee did not let go of his judgeship, but he did resign as a code commissioner. All along the Conservatives had been hostile both to him and to the idea of codifying and simplifying the laws. The new legislature, with the Conservatives in control, was to meet on November 21. By leaving the commission before then, Tourgee could hope to lessen their antagonism toward it and thus keep the legislature from terminating its work. Governor Holden accepted his resignation exactly one week before the legislature opened. Unappeased, the Conservative legislators proceeded to treat the commission pretty much as if it had already been abolished. Without his commissioner's salary, Tourgee faced the loss of nearly half of his income.

Resuming the rounds of his circuit, he gradually lost his fear for his life as Klan violence fell off. The Conservatives no longer needed Ku Kluxery, now that they controlled the state. When holding court in Yanceyville, Tourgee usually stopped to see Stephens's widow. Frequently ill, and lame from a sore foot, Mrs. Stephens was having a hard time trying to care for herself and her two children. "I feel under many obligations to you for taking an interest in my welfare," she told Tourgee. He did what he could to help her but could not see that justice was done in her case. She kept hoping, in vain, for an investigation that would lead to the arrest, conviction, and punishment of her husband's murderers.

The man who had helped to inspire and to protect those murderers—Josiah Turner, Jr.—was seeking justice for himself and was again being a nuisance in Tourgee's court. Furious with Governor Holden for having had him taken prisoner during the Kirk-Holden War, Turner was seeking a bench warrant for Holden's apprehension "for an assault committed on the person of said Turner and the false arrest and imprisonment of the same." "Joe Turner is after me for a warrant," Tourgee wrote Emma from Hillsboro, "and has all Raleigh, and not a few from the outer world, here as witnesses." Turner engaged Ralph Gorrell of the Guilford bar to apply to Tourgee. Gorrell was one of the committee of three who had reprimanded Tourgee for his *Tribune* letters, and Tourgee now had the immense satisfaction of replying to him: "As members of the bar, both yourself and Mr. Turner must be aware of the fact that sufficient grounds for the issuing of a warrant against any citizen of the State, under any circumstances, has not been properly shown before me, and any such action upon my part would be manifestly irregular."

Poor Holden! Had it not been for his invitation and welcome back in 1865, Tourgee would not be living in North Carolina in 1870. And had it not been for Holden's recent indiscretion, Tourgee would not be thinking now of leaving the state. Though he had mixed feelings toward the governor, he could not help sympathizing with him when the Conservatives in the legislature went ahead with his impeachment. He called on him to cheer him up. It was no use. Holden was to be convicted, removed from office, and stripped of all rights of North Carolina citizenship. He was to be remembered as a kind of traitor to the state—not as the man whom Tourgee had commended, not as the noble Roman who saved the republic.[17]

During Tourgee's absences Emma continued to look after the farm work while she waited for the arrival of her baby. She supervised men as they weeded the strawberry beds and planted beans, cucumbers, and other crops while the growing season lasted. In the fall she saw to such chores as storing the corn, hay, and firewood. From time to time she was sick. One night, with severe cramping and vomiting, she had no one to help her, "as Ada did not come in at all that night." Emma expected the baby earlier than it came. Relatives in Pennsylvania wondered about the delay, Tourgee's sister writing: "I daily look to hear good news from the south of a new *Carpet-bagger* making his appearance at your 'Lodge.'" When the event at last occurred, on November 19, 1870, it was not his but *her* appearance. The Tourgees christened her Lodolska, which was Emma's mother's family name, and they called her Lodie.

As soon as Emma felt well enough to travel, she took the infant and went home to Erie, Pennsylvania. She seemed to be suffering from postpartum melancholia, or perhaps she had simply had enough of living in the South. Tourgee was left to face Christmas alone in Greensboro. With him it was a cold time for both the body and the spirit. Night after night the temperature dropped far under the normal low. Tourgee was sleepless, worrying about Emma's estrangement, while painfully missing her and Lodie.

He stayed up late one night writing Emma a letter, then tearing it up and writing another, which he did not finish until three in the morning. "Please do not ever intimate again that I desire your death," he pleaded. His only happiness was to see her happy, and his greatest sorrow was to think she could be happy only when away from him. "Darling, I thank God I shall see you again, as I believe, and our hearts and lives will be one once more." He had to finish what he was working on—a digest of North Carolina laws—and then he would be free to leave. "I will go to Erie, to the West, anywhere, anywhere for your sake, your sweet love's sake, as gaily and happily as I first came to your arms." Some day in the spring, he assured her before closing, he would show up in Erie.[18]

Before the end of January 1871 Emma and Lodie were back in Greensboro, and the Tourgees were reunited. No longer was Tourgee eager to leave the South. Instead, he was excited about a new business project that would mean staying in Greensboro and investing more money there. He had in mind the manufacture of spokes, handles, and other woodenware. In the vicinity were abundant stands of hardwood, and in the neighboring black community of Warnersville a more than adequate labor supply. Part of the land that Tourgee already owned, along the railroad tracks, would make an ideal location for the factory.

The problem was to find capital with which to build the plant and get it started. Tourgee naturally thought of the financier Swepson, who previously had provided him with funds and now was neglecting to charge him interest or remind him of the principal. And Swepson was even more anxious to obtain help from Tourgee.

Along with Littlefield, Swepson had been indicted for embezzlement on account of their handling of state railroad-aid bonds. Littlefield, just back from Europe, had gone on to Florida after leaving "several most important messages" for Swepson to deliver to Tourgee "in *person* only." Swepson was returning from Washington to his home in Haw River (between Greensboro and Raleigh) and was lying low.

He sent Tourgee a note: "You will please write me to Haw River at once and arrange in some way for me to meet you without the knowledge of *any* one." The two managed to get together inconspicuously on a train. One asked for legal advice, the other for a loan. But Swepson, now disappointingly businesslike, expected 2 percent a month in interest, which was more than Tourgee was willing to pay.

Tourgee then thought of selling stock to local investors, telling one prospect that this would be better than relying on "some Northern capitalist," for it would "awaken a more certain and beneficial interest in manufactures among our people." When nothing came of the proposal, Tourgee turned to the black-run Freedmen's Bank, which had branches throughout the South, but the response was no better. "If I cannot raise the money in some manner," he swore, "I am going to 'dig out' of North Carolina as speedily as possible."

Instead, he decided to enlist a partner, his carpetbag friend W. H. Snow, and go ahead with their own resources, trusting to luck. Soon three teams and more than a dozen carpenters and laborers were at work. Before the end of February an office was up, a well dug, a "dry-house" and a temporary workshop framed, and "the foundation wall nearly laid for the main building." Snow then went north to arrange for the purchase of a steam engine and milling machinery. By summer, the Greensboro Spoke and Handle Factory was in full swing.

Though Tourgee was responding to the profit motive, he also had a humanitarian aim—to give employment to needy blacks. He showed his humanitarianism in another way when he protested the conditions in North Carolina jails. He had fought to see that stoves were put in them, but now the commissioners in some counties were neglecting to furnish fuel. After the extreme cold spell of the previous December, he received a scrawled complaint from a Caswell County inmate, which led him to exclaim: "It is horrible! damnable! Think of . . . those poor devils, half clad in a room as exposed as our jails are, *without fire!*" He sent a protest to the Caswell County commissioners and an appeal to his friend and neighbor the Reverend George W. Welker, chairman of the state board of public charities: "Do, for God's sake, make a special report to the Legislature asking for a stringent law compelling the County Commrs to provide fuel and the means for warming our jails."[19]

Throughout 1871, on and off the bench, Tourgee continued his efforts to expose and punish the Klan. Early in the year he began to expect confessions. "I sent you a list of the Alamance Kuklux who are willing to puke the thing up," he told Senator Abbott, a member of the congressional committee investigating the Klan, but he was reluctant to testify before the committee. "You know that I know nothing except at second hand and it seems to me that it would be better to examine the victims themselves."

By the end of the year Tourgee thought he was about to crack the Wyatt Outlaw murder case. In Alamance County two men finally confessed to having taken part, nearly two years earlier, in hanging Outlaw from a tree in the courthouse square. More than a hundred men hastily left the county or took to the woods. A grand jury, composed largely of Klan members, indicted 63 men for the felonious wearing of disguises and 18 for murder. Many of those indicted were "of the most respectable families in the County." Often before, Tourgee had tried unsuccessfully to penetrate the secrets of the Klan, securing a few indictments but no convictions. Now, at last, there seemed to be a chance for justice to prevail.

So Tourgee assured President Grant during a White House visit in January 1872. Tourgee was on a trip—for business, politics, and pleasure—to Washington and New York. He hoped, for one thing, to get a federal appointment, preferably one as a district attorney. Grant admitted him at once, even though a great many people were waiting to see the President. Tourgee related his progress against the Klan and said it would have been impossible without Grant's support (under the Enforcement Act Grant had sent troops to southwestern North Carolina, though not to Tourgee's district). The United States had won a great victory, Tourgee believed, over "foes more bitter and dangerous than those which yielded at Appomattox." As he left the White House, he sensed that he had had a "very full and pleasant interview" with the President, but no federal appointment was to be forthcoming.

While away from home, Tourgee tried to amuse Emma with accounts of urban society and femininity. From Washington he wrote: "The city doesn't seem to be so gay as last winter and the styles of dress are not nearly so attractive. Indeed they are sloppy and grotesque . . . they not only conceal the person but disguize and travesty its grace and proportion." From New York he sent his impressions of the long-running operetta *The Black Crook*. He did not think much of it except for "some of the transformation scenes and the trained dogs." "The rest of the piece is just a mere maze of bare legs and arms and almost all the rest which female humanity has to show."

His letters were full of affection for Emma and for Lodie, now a bright-eyed, rosy-cheeked, mischief-loving fourteen-month-old. "Kiss the prodi*gal* for me and tell her her papa will come back some day," he wrote, "and take good care of *yourself* and her until my return." In Greensboro, Emma was lonely for her husband and Lodie's father. "I have talked to her so much of her Papa," Emma wrote to Tourgee's sister in Erie, "that every picture she finds in the papers, she runs to me and calls it '*Papa*' and every time the hall door is open she runs out and knocks on the door of our room and calls 'Papa Papa,' seeming to think he must be there."

After returning to North Carolina, Tourgee tendered his resignation as a university trustee. He would have done so long before, "had it not been for the rancour of a partizan press which assailed me in that capacity before I had even accepted the appointment." He was resigning now in response to a hint from the new superintendent of public instruction, who had expressed the hope that party politics might be removed from the university. "I seriously fear that it will result in removing the politics of one party and putting in that of the other," he informed the superintendent. Sure enough. Hereafter the university would be in the hands of the Conservatives.

Tourgee felt a much greater sense of defeat when, in February 1872, the Conservatives repealed the state law making it a misdemeanor to go about disguised with intent to terrify and a felony to do so with intent to do bodily harm. This left him without a case against the 63 Alamance Klansmen indicted under that law. He still hoped to see murder charges pressed in Alamance and also in Caswell and Rockingham counties. In Wentworth, "the most desolate town in the known world," where he was holding court in the "cold, cheerless, windy days of a late spring," he uncovered evidence of various Ku Klux conspiracies, including the earlier plots against his own life. He also heard of a new threat "that the prosecutions must be stopped or there would be another Stephens affair in Wentworth." For all his efforts, he was to have no opportunity to sentence any of the Wentworth defendants. As for the murderers of Stephens, they were to remain at large, and the murderers of Outlaw were soon to go free.[20]

CHAPTER 11

The Best-Abused Man
(1869-1872)

On a rainy April day in 1871 a *New York Times* correspondent made his way to the South Carolina statehouse to interview the governor, "perhaps the best-abused man in the country." Until recently the capitol square had looked something like a junkyard, littered as it was with pieces of rusted iron, piles of broken brick and tile, and odd blocks of marble and granite, much of it blackened by the fire that had destroyed a large part of Columbia in 1865. Though the refuse had been cleaned up, the capitol remained unfinished, with makeshift wooden steps at the four entrances, and without the planned cupola or dome on top. Still, the massive gray stone building impressed even the big-city reporter as "magnificent."

Accompanying him was a rather slight, prematurely balding, neatly dressed, thirty-five-year-old man who had a professorial air. This was Daniel H. Chamberlain, the Massachusetts native with degrees from both Harvard and Yale, now attorney general of South Carolina. He had been brought up a strict, Calvinistic Congregationalist but, for more than a year, had been married to a Unitarian, the young and pretty Alice Ingersoll of Bangor, Maine, and was leaning toward her faith—though hers had even less standing than his in this part of the country. Chamberlain made an excellent impression on the visiting journalist, who gathered that he was "a Northern man universally respected and popular throughout the State for his ability" and for the "just manner" in which he performed the duties of his office.

Climbing the rickety wooden steps, the two men entered the capitol and walked down a dimly lighted corridor to the governor's office at the southeastern corner of the building. His room was bright and cheerful but (unlike other offices and the legislative halls) quite plainly furnished. Sitting at his desk, Robert K. Scott quickly rose and cordially shook hands with his colleague and the correspondent. Scott, now forty-four, was a rather large and well-built man with rugged features and a heavy mustache. His ready smile and friendly gray eyes exerted a certain masculine charm. The *New York Times* man, expecting some kind of ogre, was favorably surprised. For an hour or so Scott talked freely with him about the state's affairs—about the Ku Klux Klan, the black militia, black politicians, debts, taxes, and resistance to paying them. He vigorously defended his own administration. "Socially he is an exceedingly pleasant and entertaining gentleman," it seemed to the reporter. "His fault is lack of capacity rather than lack of intention."

From Scott's office the reporter and the attorney general went to Chamberlain's, where the two had a conversation without Scott. Chamberlain now conceded that, "although a warm Republican, and sympathizing in general with the policy of that party," he "could not quite agree with the Governor's views." Things were not going well in South Carolina. "The last Legislature was ignorant and openly corrupt to a degree that was disgraceful." It was time for a change. The condition of the state "should be understood at the North, and with the undercurrent of discontent and disaffection which rendered everything uneasy, disquiet, and unpleasant." Clearly, Chamberlain wanted *New York Times* readers to get the message that he and not Scott was the one the future of South Carolina demanded.

At the time of his election Scott had been hailed as the most able, the most promising, of all the carpetbag governors. Now, before the end of the third of his four years in office, he already had a badly sagging reputation. Much if not most of South Carolina's trouble seemed to be his fault. He did not appear capable of providing good, clean government—as Chamberlain professed to be. But perhaps Scott was at least as much a hero as anyone else among the many villains, Republican and Democratic, in South Carolina politics.[1]

Everyone who knew Scott agreed that he was affable, kind-hearted, and well-meaning, though sometimes forgetful and ineffective. "There is no hardness of heart in you . . . you really abound in kindness for your fellow-man," a Columbia lawyer and former Confederate once assured him. "You have it in such a degree that this kindness of disposition is charged by some as your weakness." An Ohio friend wrote him: "You and myself are troubled with a common infirmity. A kind of heedlessness or absent mindedness."

He had another weakness, another infirmity, which his friends and acquaintances knew nothing about. That was his drug habit. Ever since the wartime injury to his spine, he had lived under the threat of recurring and excruciating pain. Only opium enabled him to stay cheerful and charming. Only opium made life even tolerable for him.

Another physical handicap, less serious but nevertheless troublesome, was a peculiarity of eyesight that made it difficult for him to read. He had to hold reading matter close to his eyes, but the problem was not nearsightedness. It was, rather, an inability to see more than one word at a time. This was a great misfortune for a politician, since it meant he could not speak from a manuscript or even from notes. He had to speak from memory or not at all, and so he avoided public speaking as much as he could. He was no orator like Chamberlain.

Considerably younger than Scott was his wife, née Rebecca Jane Lowry and known as Jane, the daughter of an Ohio pioneer. She had borne a son and a daughter. The little girl having died, both Mr. and Mrs. Scott were especially attentive to the boy, Robert K., Jr., or R. K. ("Arky"), who would be six in October 1871. As soon as he was old enough to ride it, little R. K. had a pony of his own. His mother was inclined to be sickly; two servants took care of the household chores. She was also inclined to be alcoholic, so Scott had to be careful to keep wine and spirits away from her.

This was rather hard to do, since the governor was expected to carry on a certain amount of entertaining, and both grateful constituents and expectant liquor dealers were constantly presenting him with bottles and whole cases of whiskey, brandy, champagne and other expensive wines. Official entertaining was sometimes a perplexing task, even for such a genial host as Scott. The *New York Times* criticized him when he gave a ball for state officeholders and invited no blacks. Thereafter he held weekly receptions that were open to all, but few except blacks ever came.[2]

Scott kept up his friendships and his interests in his hometown of Napoleon, Ohio, and on a few occasions he managed to revisit the place. He did not get there for his father's eighty-sixth birthday, on December 6, 1871, but he heard that the old man, though quite feeble, had attended a party with his old cronies. "We had a fine old fashioned time and a great dinner," one of them reported to Scott, "—it would have done you good to have been there." Scott contributed to the support not only of his father but also of other needy people in Napoleon. "You may think it a small matter," said one pensioner, already under "great obligation" for past favors, in thanking him for an "allowance" of $100. "But to me a hundred dollars is a larger amount probably than one hundred thousand to you." That may have been something of an exaggeration, though Scott was indeed a wealthy man as a result of his prewar successes in medicine, merchandising, and land speculation.

Scott's house in Napoleon had burned down in a fire that destroyed a whole block. A new house was being built of brick with stone trim and the finest factory-made door and window frames. As he had done for years, Scott continued to invest in real estate, railroads, and other properties in northwestern Ohio. He was just as glad not to be there when, sitting in mild Columbia on a winter day, he read of subzero temperatures and drifting snow in Napoleon. Yet Napoleon was home to him.[3]

So was Columbia, for that matter. He had many friends and many interests in South Carolina as well as in Ohio. In South Carolina, too, he invested in real estate, railroads, and other enterprises, among them a brick-making business, a monthly magazine, two newspapers, and a patent for a sewing-machine motor. "Just think," the inventor wrote him from Georgetown, D. C., "there are in the U. S. over five million sewing machines in use and . . . when we get one million [motors] made we will clear ten millions."

Scott held mortgages on several plantations to whose owners he had made loans. As a moneylender he was generous, easily persuaded to postpone collection. "We would have paid you, but the caterpillars killed the cotton, and the drought burned up the rice," black tenants reported to him from a plantation near Charleston. "We feel grateful to you for your past kindness." He offered a prize to anyone who could find a way to cultivate sea-island cotton so that the caterpillars would not eat it up. As he had done earlier, he lent money to or endorsed notes for Republican politicians, among them three leaders of the legislature—the ex-Confederate Franklin J. Moses and the Negroes W. J. Whipper and Robert B. Elliott. He was not giving them money: he required security or collateral from these as well as from other borrowers.[4]

But he did make donations to, and do other favors for, persons and institutions he considered worthy. He contributed money to Erskine College, Furman University, the Chester Methodist church, and other institutions in South Carolina. He served as a trustee of Wilberforce University, a school for blacks in Xenia, Ohio, and he gave his collection of Confederate bonds and paper money to the Historical and Philosophical Society of Ohio in Cincinnati. A husband and wife in Anderson, South Carolina, thanked him for his "*special* kindness" to them and sent him in return a bottle of brandy, a jar of honey, and a pair of home-raised mockingbirds.

On behalf of a constituent whose heifer had been killed by a train, Scott took the trouble to intercede with the superintendent of the Charlotte, Columbia and Augusta Railroad Company. He managed to obtain from the company only half of what the heifer was worth. "We . . . have been compelled to adopt the principle of never paying the *full* value of stock killed," the superintendent explained, "to prevent persons from getting their stock killed purposely, by driving them in cuts just before train time." Scott could understand the company's position, since he was himself deeply involved in the complexities of South Carolina railroading.[5]

Scott shared a dream that had intrigued John C. Calhoun and other South Carolinians as early as the 1830s and that continued to intrigue many of them in the 1860s and 1870s. It was the dream of connecting Charleston with Cincinnati, the Atlantic Ocean with the Ohio River, by rail. The idea also appealed to a number of Ohioans in addition to Scott. A Cincinnati banker assured him that local capitalists were interested and would help to finance the project. Surely it would stimulate the economy at each end of the line.

The state of South Carolina had been promoting such a railroad since the 1850s. It chartered the Blue Ridge Railroad Company, guaranteed its bonds, and bought $1,310,000 of its stock, while the city of Charleston purchased $1,049,000 worth and individual investors $500,000. By the time the war came, the company had spent all its money and could boast only thirty-three miles of track, running from Anderson to Walhalla in the northwestern part of the state. The really difficult and costly construction, tunneling through the Blue Ridge Mountains, still lay ahead.

After the war the directors of the company were eager to extend the track. To do so, they would have to get additional aid from the state. Governor James L. Orr, Scott's Democratic predecessor, urged the legislature to act, and so did Scott. In 1868 the legislature, with its Republican and black majority, authorized the state to endorse and thus guarantee payment of $4,000,000 in new issues of Blue Ridge railroad bonds. "The Road when completed will be worth all that it shall properly cost," Scott predicted in an excess of optimism, "and from its great superiority in shortness of distance between the great commercial points alluded to, must yield a heavy income from freight and passengers." He was the more confident, he said, because the undertaking was "sustained and advocated by the leading men of all parties in this State." Certainly, Democrats as well as Republicans involved themselves in the enterprise, and the officers and stockholders of the company were predominantly Southerners.

When the Republicans adopted the bankrupt railroad, they had already inherited a bankrupt state. There was a bonded debt of $5,407,306.27 and there was exactly $45 in the treasury. Means had to be found to pay the interest on the existing debt and to meet the day-to-day expenses of the government. This task was up to the financial board, consisting of Governor Scott, Attorney General Chamberlain, and Treasurer Niles J. Parker, another carpetbagger.[6]

To obtain expert assistance, the board employed as financial agent, at Chamberlain's suggestion, a Yale classmate of his, Hiram H. Kimpton. The "cherubic" Kimpton, as he was often described, came with glowing recommendations from New York bankers and businessmen and from prominent Republican politicians, among them the governor and the treasurer of New York and Congressman Thaddeus Stevens of Pennsylvania. Kimpton was said to be "a very correct man and a consistent supporter of Republican principles," "an educated and accomplished gentleman occupying a high social position," and a man who enjoyed "the confidence of capitalists" in New York City. With Kimpton's credentials at hand, Scott could hope for an early solution to South Carolina's financial problem.

Setting out to reform the state's fiscal system, Scott turned to Ohio authorities for advice, obtaining information on the Ohio tax and revenue laws. At his urging, the legislature approved a bill for assessing all property at a fair and uniform rate. The revised taxes would fall more heavily on landowners than did the traditional ones, which had spared the large planters and slaveowners while hitting bankers, merchants, and professional men. The revised taxes also promised to increase revenue. Still, to meet expenditures for schools and other improvements, the state would have to do more long-term borrowing, and the legislature provided for new issues of general revenue bonds.

As financial agent, Kimpton was to sell these and other bonds of the state, for a fat commission. To be near the money market, he set up his headquarters in New York City. He soon found it difficult to dispose of the state's new bonds, except at a ruinous discount, when its old ones were worth no more than forty cents on the dollar. Things did not improve even though Scott, in the spring of 1869, visited the city to talk personally with bankers and brokers. Kimpton encouraged him to believe that better times were on the way. And, that summer, Chamberlain assured the *New York Times* that his friend Kimpton, "a young man of much ability and promise," was making it possible for the city's financiers to help bring about the recovery of South Carolina.[7]

The financial board and the financial agent had to contend with the efforts of Democrats to frighten away Northern investors. Ominously the *Charleston News* had asked at the outset: "Would New York or Boston touch these bonds, issued by authority of a horde of Negroes, and in the face of the protest of the white people of the State?" Then, shifting about, the *News* argued for a while that the state's finances were basically sound and that people ought to back Scott in his fight to restore the state's credit. Later, however, the *News* and other Democratic papers began to hint at repudiating the debt. Kimpton informed Scott that such talk could only result in higher interest rates for South Carolinians. "If they think that they can afford it," Kimpton wrote, "I am sure Wall St. can, and the Charleston News may rest assured that we can have all the money we want, in spite of all their efforts."

Yet bond sales continued to lag. Scott and his colleagues on the financial board resorted to short-term borrowing to pay the government's operating expenses and the interest on the state debt. The interest on these short-term loans was high—as high as 3 percent a month—and collateral was hard to find. Bills receivable, to the extent that they accumulated, could be used with local banks. New York bankers were reluctant to take the state's general revenue bonds as security, but they would accept the state-guaranteed bonds of the Blue Ridge railroad, once these had come off the presses of the American Banknote Company.[8]

Scott believed that the state had more than enough obligations without taking on additional ones. Some native South Carolinians had other ideas. The director of the Greenville and Columbia railroad wanted the state to endorse a new issue of its bonds. This company, which had completed its line in 1853, needed help to restore the line after the war. In 1866 the state government (while under native white, Democratic control) gave the company new loan guarantees, which made the state's total liability to it $1,500,000.

In early 1869 Scott vetoed a bill to increase the state's liability to the Greenville and Columbia. If, he said, a corporation like this one could get what it wanted "by assiduous lobbying and other questionable means," the capitol would be continually "infested with the paid agents and advocates of every conceivable project by which speculators may hope to obtain control of the people's money." Nevertheless, the lobbyists got their way when the legislature repassed the bill over the governor's veto.

For Scott, the Blue Ridge railroad was quite a different matter. He was himself an officer of the company, a member of its executive committee along with the company's president, the native Southerner James W. Harrison. In the summer of 1869 the executive committee awarded a contract for railroad construction to three Pennsylvanians whom Kimpton recommended to Scott as *"our friends."* It was agreed that Scott's brother-in-law George W. Waterman, "for a valuable consideration," would "receive one eighth of all profits arising out of said contract."

Of the three Pennsylvanians, much the most important was John J. Patterson, previously a newspaper publisher, a state legislator, an army captain, and a small-town banker, but never a railroad contractor. Patterson inquired whether he would have to move to South Carolina by October 1869 if he was to vote in October 1870. When Scott replied in the affirmative, Patterson made immediate preparations for him and his family to leave Pennsylvania. As things turned out, Patterson was not to engage in any actual railroad construction, but he was soon to play a conspicuous role in the finances and politics of South Carolina. And Scott was to have cause to regret welcoming him to the state.

Construction on the Blue Ridge railroad could not begin because Blue Ridge bonds could not be sold except at a discount so great as to make them hardly worth selling. The state's credit would first have to be restored. Kimpton and the New York banking firm with which he dealt, Henry Clews & Company, had their moments of exultation when they thought they were going to find eager buyers in Europe. But the most they could do with the bonds was to hypothecate them for temporary loans, which helped to pay the state's operating expenses in anticipation of tax collections. As late as September 1870, two years after the legislature had agreed to endorse the Blue Ridge bonds, the entire issue of $4,000,000 remained in the possession of Kimpton and Clews.[9]

If railroading in South Carolina was depressed for the moment, it nevertheless held great promise for the future, or so it seemed to two members of the financial board, Treasurer Parker and Attorney General Chamberlain. Why not monopolize the railroads of the state? The undertaking could begin with acquisition of the Greenville and Columbia. From that point on, the prospect was quite heady. As Chamberlain wrote his old chum Kimpton on January 5, 1870:

> Parker arrived last evening, and spoke of the G. & C. matter, etc. . . .
>
> Do you understand fully the plan of the G. & C. enterprise? It is proposed to buy $350,000 worth of the G. & C. stock. This with the $433,000 of stock held by the State will give entire control to us. The Laurens branch will be sold in February by decree of court, and will cost us not more than $50,000, and probably not more than $40,000. The Spartanburg and Union can also be got without difficulty.
>
> We shall then have in G. & C. 168 miles, in Laurens 31, and S. & U. 70 miles—in all 269 miles—equipped and running. Put a first mortgage of $20,000 a mile on this—sell the bonds at 85 or 90, and the balance, after paying all outlays for cost and repairs, is immense, over $2,000,000. There is a mint of money in this or I am a fool.
>
> Then we will soon compel the South Carolina Railroad to fall into our hands and complete the connection to Asheville, N. C.
>
> There is an infinite verge for expansion of power before us.

This was pretty much a pipe dream. It made little sense to talk of clearing millions through the sale of new railroad bonds at a time when existing ones, guaranteed by the state, could not be sold for anything close to 85 or 90 percent of par.

In any event, Chamberlain, Parker, Kimpton, and their associates, including Southerners and Democrats, did manage to get control of the Greenville and Columbia. They did so by means of an act they induced the legislature to pass and the governor to sign on March 1, 1870. According to this act, a sinking fund commission was to oversee the sale of unproductive state property and put the proceeds into a fund for redeeming state bonds. The commission was to consist of the governor, attorney general, comptroller general, and chairmen of the house and senate finance committees. At their first meeting the commission members, except for Scott, voted over his objections to sell the state's G. & C. stock, for which the state had paid $20 a share, to John H. Moore for $2.75 a share. Scott found out later that Moore was a dummy for the Kimpton-Parker-Chamberlain group.

The sinking fund did nothing to raise the price of South Carolina bonds. Through their sale at a drastic discount, the state's debt increased nearly three times as fast as its income. As the South Carolina election of 1870 approached, the Democrats used their national organ, the *New York World,* as well as their local papers to point with alarm at the rising debt. From Treasurer Parker, in New York to consult with Kimpton, Scott learned: "The entire democracy of S. Carolina, aided by that of the whole country and a portion of the Republicans, are doing their best to break us down." In thus playing politics with the financial problem, the Democrats and the disaffected Republicans were only making it worse.[10]

Along with other state expenditures, those of the land commission were to figure in the election of 1870. This commission had come into existence in March 1869 to buy land and resell it in parcels of 25 to 100 acres to freedmen (and also to poor whites) who would settle on it, with eight years in which to pay. The land commissioner, originally Charles P. Leslie, a carpetbagger from New York, could make no purchase without the approval of three of the five members of an advisory board. The five were Governor Scott; Attorney General Chamberlain; Treasurer Parker; Comptroller John L. Neagle, a scalawag from North Carolina; and Secretary of State Francis L. Cardozo, who, born to a Jewish economist and a free black woman in Charleston, had graduated with honors from the University of Glasgow.

From the outset the commissioner and his advisers were beset by planters with land they wanted to unload. Commissioner Leslie did not bother to inspect personally the tracts that the advisory board approved and he arranged to buy. As an experienced dealer in real estate, Scott knew, as he was later to say, that "no man could buy lands with any hope of having property that would be desirable without giving it some personal attention." He himself, having "numerous and onerous" other duties, could not give much time to the commission's activities. So, in October 1869, he resigned as chairman of the board and, for the time being, stayed away from its meetings.

Before the end of the year, the commission had spent more than twice its appropriation and needed a new one. Scott appealed to the legislature, but its Negro leaders refused to appropriate any more money for land acquisitions until the carpetbagger Leslie was removed as commissioner and replaced by a Negro. Cardozo refused to attend board meetings until Leslie resigned. Finally the board members persuaded him to quit, on March 1, 1870, and they agreed upon Robert C. De Large as his successor. Like Cardozo, De Large was a Charleston native and a mulatto, his mother a black, his father a Jew. "This appears in his face," a *New York Times* correspondent asserted. A former tailor, self-educated, De Large had a facile tongue and a ready wit. Though only twenty-eight, he was one of Scott's most effective allies.[11]

While Leslie was still land commissioner, board members Chamberlain, Parker, and Neagle had agreed to buy from a Charleston real estate broker half a dozen plantations, including a tract known as Hell-Hole Swamp. As attorney general, Chamberlain was responsible for seeing that the land titles were good. As treasurer, Parker was responsible for making the actual payment. It soon appeared that the title to some of the land was defective, the land being encumbered by a mortgage, and it also appeared that the price paid was exorbitant. According to rumor, the excess went in part to Leslie to compensate him for giving up his job.

Scott and Cardozo, again attending board meetings after De Large became commissioner, undertook to clear up the mess. The board named Cardozo and Chamberlain as a committee to investigate the Hell-Hole Swamp affair. They began to look in Parker's direction. Scott wired Kimpton, who had charge of the state's bank deposits in New York: "Pay no money on account of Land Commission on the State Treasurer's order until you are notified that the Land Commission [matter] is satisfactorily settled." Scott proposed that Chamberlain and Cardozo employ special legal counsel, and he himself consulted a Columbia lawyer, only to learn that it would be difficult to prove wrongdoing since the seller of the land would have to testify to it.

Parker secured legal counsel in his own behalf. Chamberlain wrote to Parker's attorney in New York, intimating that he was going to take action against Parker. He received a kind of blackmailing letter in reply. The land commission had bought real estate from the prominent black politicians William J. Whipper and Robert B. Elliott. "You may instance yourself Whipper & Elliott's land last winter," the New York lawyer now advised Chamberlain. "Your connection with that was the same as my client's with the other and so on." It made no difference whether the mortgage was paid before or after the land was deeded to the state, the attorney told Chamberlain, and he counseled Parker to see that the seller promptly paid the mortgage. Chamberlain refrained from pressing the case against Parker.

Scott, too, cooperated at times with friends who had property they wanted the state to buy. When Benjamin F. Bates, once a Confederate, now a Republican, asked Scott to help him out of financial difficulties, Scott induced the commission to pay Bates $16,620 for 1,976 acres. When John R. Cochran needed aid, Scott was equally obliging, though Cochran was a Democrat. Cochran, Scott, and their railroad associate James W. Harrison jointly owned a 4,157-acre tract. Scott and Harrison conveyed their undivided two-thirds to Cochran, and Cochran then sold the property to the land commission.

As the 1870 election approached, critics of the Scott administration harped increasingly upon the commission's alleged misdeeds. Scott urged De Large to speed up the commission's work, so that as many black voters as possible could acquire farms before election day. As of June 1, only twenty-four tracts had been subdivided, yielding but 654 homesteads. The state surveyor encouraged Scott and De Large to believe that, by the end of 1870, at least 3,000 families or a total of 15,000 persons would be settled on farms of their own.[12]

In South Carolina the black voters outnumbered the white by more than 30,000. Hence the Republicans should be able to win the next election easily—if they remained united and if the election was free and fair. But some Republicans both north and south complained of the existing carpetbag regimes, and Northern as well as Southern Democrats considered violence as something of a necessary evil in dealing with such regimes. In the circumstances, Scott opposed lifting the Fourteenth Amendment ban on officeholding by leaders of the late rebellion. He wrote in January 1869 to carpetbag Congressman B. F. Whittemore:

> Our so called Democrats of the South have the faculty of completely hoodwinking our Northern Republicans into the belief that they are the men who have been sinned against and then misrepresented to the public. I am willing that every Democrat or Rebel shall be placed in office who has been . . . fairly elected. . . . But when they openly and defiantly declare that they will permit no man to vote unless he votes their ticket—and enforce their declaration with arms in their hands by murdering those who have the courage to attempt to exercise the rights of an American citizen—and thereby have what they may desire to palm off on the people as an election—[I say] keep them out of office until they are conscious that the American people intend the ballot box to be the medium through which their will must be expressed.

To secure obedience to the laws, Scott needed an armed force. The legislature responded, before spring, by authorizing him to form a constabulary and a militia and to use, in supporting them and keeping the peace, any funds in the treasury not appropriated for other purposes. Scott, as commander in chief, appointed the scalawag speaker of the house, Fanklin J. Moses, Jr., as adjutant, inspector general, and quartermaster general to assist in organizing the militia and to procure arms for it. During the summer Moses went to Ilion, New York, bought five thousand obsolete Springfield muskets from E. Remington & Sons and had them shipped to New York City to be converted into modern breechloading rifles. He also arranged to have musket cartridges changed into rifle shells. Thus preparations for the 1870 election were well under way more than a year in advance.

By the fall of 1870 the militia consisted of fourteen regiments of infantry, each containing nearly a thousand men. Most of these troops carried muskets, since there were not enough rifles to go around. Except for some of the officers, all the militiamen were black. Scott started to arm a few white companies, but blacks objected so strongly that he soon desisted. The carpetbag colonel of the fourteenth regiment wrote him from Chester County, north of Columbia, to protest against a white cavalry company's being accepted as part of the militia. "The present companies," the colonel explained to the chief constable of the state, " . . . are incensed over the prospect . . . and say if the Governor is going to arm the white K. K.'s to operate against them, he, the Gov., can take back the guns and commissions that has been already sent to this County." Even at best, these raw infantrymen would be no match for veteran cavalrymen of the Confederacy. "Does he [the governor] think a lot of ignorant colored men with clumsy muskets in their hands can catch a squad of experienced soldiers on blooded horses?"

The Democratic whites in the upcountry proceeded to organize, arm, and train their own military companies. Some justified this on the grounds that race war was about to begin. "The coloured population of this section & in Newberry have recently become so utterly lawless & threatening in conduct, that it becomes necessary to be constantly on the watch to prevent incendiarism & bloodshed," Scott heard from an Edgefield County man about three weeks before election day. "*They mean war.* I learn, reliably, that they threaten to kill our women & children & sack & plunder the country."[13]

The constables, several dozen of them, and the militia constituted an electioneering as well as a peacekeeping force. The armed force fund was also a campaign fund. In addition, the Republicans had the benefit (as did the party in power everywhere in the country) of state expenditures for public printing. These helped to finance the *Columbia Union* and the *Charleston Republican,* two newspapers owned by a firm of which both Scott and Chamberlain were directors. The editor of the *Charleston News,* the leading Democratic paper of the low country, wanted a share of the public printing and, to get it, was willing to give qualified support to the Scott administration. The editor did not receive enough to keep the *News* from becoming one of Scott's most scurrilous critics by election time. Scott obtained further campaign financing by serving as a special Freedman's Bureau agent to collect, for a 10 percent commission, debts due the Bureau for corn and bacon supplied to South Carolina farmers in 1867 and 1868.

Scott needed these political assets to balance potential liabilities. As summer approached in 1870, he was facing the possibility of defections from two elements of the party—the more militant of the blacks and the less radical of the whites.

He had a large and loyal following among rank-and-file blacks, who remembered him as their Freedmen's Bureau benefactor and who in many instances knew him as an unpretentious friend. One, recalling the old days when he and Scott together "tapped the ivory balls" in a Charleston billiard saloon, said the "lamented Thad. Stevens" used to be his favorite but Scott now was. "I feel, I see, I *know* that you has endeavored to promote the well-being of my race from the moment 'twere in your province." Some of the black leaders, however, were demanding an increased share of offices and were talking of forming a separate black party, if necessary, in order to get them.

Some leading white Republicans, with various grievances against Scott, considered deserting him and combining with the Democrats. Seeing no other hope, Democratic leaders were willing to join with Republican bolters and try to cultivate black support. These anti-Scott elements organized what they called at first the Citizens' and then the Union Reform party. They got a head start by holding their convention in mid-June. For governor, they nominated Richard B. Carpenter, a native of Vermont, a prewar resident of Kentucky, and a former Democrat who had been elected a state circuit judge as a Republican. For lieutenant governor, they picked Matthew C. Butler, who was once the owner of seventy slaves and who, as a Confederate general, had lost a leg in the war.

Instead of catering to conservative sentiment, Scott determined to appease the discontented black leaders and make sure of their support. He decided to see that the Republicans increased the number of blacks on their ticket and, in particular, to see that they nominated Robert C. De Large and Robert B. Elliott for Congress. The *New York Times* described Elliott as "a full negro" from Massachusetts, "a bitter enemy of the white race," and a man "bold, ambitious, and ready at speech." De Large would be running against Christopher C. Bowen, the scalawag incumbent. Congressman Bowen resented Scott's program, and so did Bowen's friends, including carpetbag U.S. Senator Frederick A. Sawyer. They toyed with the idea of persuading the Union Reform leaders to run Chamberlain for governor and thus split the Republican party and defeat Scott. But before they could put the idea into practice the Union Reform convention met and made its commitment to Carpenter.[14]

When the Republicans assembled for their state convention, late in July, they easily renominated both Scott and Chamberlain. They gave the number-two position on their slate, that of lieutenant-governor, to the Charleston mulatto A. J. Ransier in place of the incumbent scalawag Lemuel Boozer. Congressional district conventions then named non-whites for three of the four congressional seats, all of which were occupied by white Republicans. The three non-whites were the black Elliott, the mulatto De Large, and another mulatto, Joseph H. Rainey, a one-time Charleston barber.

In the campaign the Union Reform politicians did their best, or their worst, to attract Negro votes. Congressman Whittemore warned Scott that Democrats in Washington were sending a "colored man"—"an illiterate and yet insinuating speaker" who had "great influence with his race"—to South Carolina to work for the Union Reform party. "He took $1500 with him and is to be furnished with all the funds he will need. The prominent colored men here say he is a dangerous man. So look out for him." The party's candidate for lieutenant governor, the one-legged Confederate veteran Butler, went so far in appealing to blacks as to alienate some conservative whites. The *Sumter Watchman* criticized Butler for saying "blacks and whites are a common people" and complained: "[He] berates the Scott administration because they have not given the negroes offices enough!"

Butler and other opposition campaigners concentrated on the Republicans' alleged extravagance, corruption, and misgovernment. Butler pointed an accusing finger at the land commission in particular, though he neglected to mention that the commission had turned him down when he tried to foist off upon it 650 acres of his Edgefield land. An opposition newspaper described the Republicans as "vultures, harpies, jackals, and vampires" who were "sucking to repletion the very life blood of the State," Scott being the "king of the beasts."

Scott refrained from taking the stump in his own behalf, but Ransier, Elliott, Chamberlain, and others toured the state for him and for the ticket as a whole. Chamberlain, calmly eloquent in his professorial way, conceded that "excesses and crimes" had occurred. He insisted, however, that on the whole the Republicans were providing honest and economical government. The increase in the public debt, he said, was due not to extravagance but to the cost of providing new services to an enlarged citizenry, one made up of blacks as well as whites. And, speaking of debts, the "debt which this State, its property and its present intelligence, owes to the colored race, to all her uneducated children, can never be fully discharged."

The carpetbag and black campaigners received a boost when a prominent native white suddenly joined them. This was ex-Governor James L. Orr. He declared the Union Reform movement hopeless, for it could not lure blacks from the party that had given them their freedom and political rights. The Republicans, he said, also had "done much to ameliorate the condition of the white people" and had succeeded in "raising the price of state bonds from 26 in January 1868, to 90 at the present time. All "good and true men" ought to accept the reality of Reconstruction. "If they will affiliate with the Republican organization . . . much can be done to correct abuse and malfeasance that may have grown up in the anomalous state of affairs surrounding us."

Election day, October 16, proved quieter than Scott had any reason to expect. The Ku Klux Klan kept a few Republicans from the polls, but the militia and the constabulary enabled the rest to cast their ballots. Scott and his state ticket won by nearly 35,000 votes—somewhat more than the margin by which black voters outnumbered white. Three of the four Republican candidates were elected to Congress. The fourth, Scott's favorite, De Large, also claimed victory, but Congress questioned his majority and refused to seat him.[15]

Not long after his decisive reelection Scott confronted a twofold revolt on the part of South Carolina whites. In the upcountry, where blacks were in the minority, Klansmen were riding again. In both the upcountry and the low country, planters and businessmen were threatening to stop paying taxes. Either movement could eventuate in the overthrow of the Republican regime.

In mid-November 1870 Scott put on a show of optimism when the traveling Englishman Robert Somers stopped to interview him. Somers, who liked to hobnob with Southern aristocrats, had heard bad things about the governor and was somewhat surprised to find him so courteous and communicative. Scott told him it was necessary for the state to protect its black citizens because so many South Carolinians still acted in accordance with Chief Justice Roger B. Taney's dictum in the Dred Scott case (1857) that "a negro had no rights which a white man was bound to respect." Waxing enthusiastic about the Blue Ridge railroad, Scott pointed out its projected route on a map, readily convincing his visitor of the line's importance. "To get into direct and continuous communication by rail with the great West is a common object of ambition to all the Atlantic Cotton States," Somers was to report in his travel book, "and may be said to have become an absolute necessity for South Carolina if she is to keep pace with the progress made in this direction by her sister States."

The Ku Klux rampage had begun the very day after the election, when Klansmen attacked hundreds and killed several who had voted Republican. In January 1871, Klansmen took from jail and shot to death six of thirteen black militiamen who had been arrested on a murder charge. To protect the remaining seven, Scott ordered them brought to Columbia, but they too were taken out and shot. He appealed to President Grant for troops, and Grant sent him twelve infantry and four cavalry companies. When disorders continued, Chamberlain went to Washington to request additional aid. Grant assured him he would use all the power he had to put down the disturbers of the peace.[16]

The Blue Ridge railroad continued to languish, its bonds unsalable. Its president, James W. Harrison, and its promoter ex-Governor Orr thought the aborted project would benefit from consolidation with the Greenville and Columbia, a going concern. Scott came to agree. He told a New York banker the merger would "inspire confidence on the part of capitalists," who then would "feel disposed to invest in the bonds of the road." On his recommendation the legislature passed a consolidation act in March 1871.

Later Scott, Chamberlain, and the other members of the sinking fund commission sold the state-owned stock of the Blue Ridge to Harrison and associates of his. The state had paid $100 apiece for the shares; it now received $1 apiece for them. They were probably not worth much more than that, for the company had squandered the state's money and had become insolvent—before the Republicans ever came into power. In any case, the would-be beneficiaries of the transaction included Southerners as well as Northerners, Democrats as well as Republicans. Interested in the rail project were not only Scott, Chamberlain, Parker, Patterson, and other carpetbaggers but also Matthew C. Butler, Martin W. Gary, and other native Democrats, in addition to such scalawags as Harrison and Orr. Gary, a Harvard graduate, ex-Confederate general, and upcountry planter and lawyer, was to mastermind the strategy by which the Democrats eventually "redeemed" South Carolina through violence.[17]

Some of the Southerners who cooperated with Scott in railroad promotion were inclined to cooperate with him, at least to a certain degee, in politics. Harrison, the Blue Ridge president, hoped to wean him from his dependence on blacks. Before the recent election he had advised him to avoid the error of going to war against the Klan, as Governor Holden of North Carolina had done to his sorrow. Writing from New York, where he was trying to help Kimpton sell bonds, Harrison had continued:

> You will certainly be reelected; but you must be supported in your next two years by more of the old citizens of the State, or your administration (in my judgment) cannot be such a success as I know you desire. Be very cautious, and if you can conciliate good white citizens do so in every instance. The colored people, from ignorance and a vain lust for office and brief power, are going to bring swift destruction on their race. There is not only no sympathy for them here, but actual hostility and contempt. I don't allude to this city, but all through the North and West. In other words, the *Negro is played out,* and other more practical and exciting subjects will soon be brought on the political boards. . . .
>
> I of course want you to succeed, but at the same time I, as you know, desire the State gradually to go into the hands of the good and virtuous of our own people, and I will help to the extent of my means and influence to stop the corruption and stock jobbing so prevalent up to this time.

But Scott, himself now at war with the Klan, had declined to follow Harrison's advice. So he had fallen still farther in the esteem of the "good white citizens" of South Carolina. One of these was Benjamin Franklin Perry, a thoroughly unreconstructed rebel who, as provisional governor in 1865, had resisted even President Johnson's mild terms for the restoration of the state. Perry addressed to Scott a public letter, dated March 13, 1871, in which he said:

> There are two things which you can do, and should do, the sooner the better. Disarm your militia and appoint good and intelligent men to office. All the lawlessness and violence which has disgraced the State has been owing to these two sources of mischief. Never was there a more fatal mistake nor a more diabolical wrong committed than when you organized colored troops throughout the State and put arms in their hands with powder and ball, and denied the same to the white people. . . .
>
> The colored people of South Carolina behaved well during the war and would have continued to do so but for the unprincipled carpet-bagger, who came among them and stirred up hatred to the white race by the most artful and devilish appeals to their fears and bad passions. . . . The public officers and the Legislature are charged with the most shameful corruption, bribery and roguery. It is impossible for the industry of the State to pay the taxes.

In March the Charleston Chamber of Commerce called a taxpayers' convention to meet in Columbia in May. The Chamber laid out an agenda for the convention by adopting the following resolutions: that a majority of property owners and taxpayers were excluded from the legislative power, that the tax revenues were being corruptly used, that bonds had been illegally issued, and that the Chamber would "by all legitimate means" resist the collection of taxes for the payment of such bonds.

Scott had a chance to defend himself and his administration before the country when the *New York Times* correspondent interviewed him in April. Why, the reporter asked, do you need federal intervention and martial law to deal with the Klan? Because juries refuse to convict Klansmen in the state courts. What about the oppressive taxation? All the talk is for political effect; the planters are much better off than they pretend to be; I pay higher taxes on my properties in Ohio than they do on theirs here. Ought you to keep on arming the blacks? Well, some people ask me to disband the militia, and at the same time they threaten revolution! They must be made to understand that the laws *will* be enforced and the taxes *will* be collected. Why do the Negroes elect to office the least intelligent of their race? I don't think they necessarily do. Of course, the freeborn Negroes are better educated and more conservative than the former slaves, who often prefer to elect men of their own kind, though these may be relatively ignorant. Anyhow, the Constitution, with the Fifteenth Amendment, gives them the right to vote as they please, and I wouldn't think much of a constitution that didn't do so.

In an interview with a *Cincinnati Gazette* reporter, Scott drew a distinction between men like himself, who had fought the Confederates, and recently arrived "northern adventurers, who came here solely to make money out of these people's misfortunes." Though he mentioned no names, he had in mind John J. Patterson and other late arrivals like him. These men, with black support, had "pushed themselves into the control of political affairs" and were, "doubtless, working greater evils to the State."

On balance, Scott remained optimistic about the future of South Carolina under Republican rule. Chamberlain publicly disagreed with him, dissociated himself from the administration, and cultivated the good will of native Democrats. He gave every sign of being ready to seek higher office with their support.

Chamberlain told the *New York Times* correspondent it was "still an unanswered question whether Republicanism in South Carolina must not be considered as a failure so far." The last legislature, consisting mostly of ignorant men, had been brazenly corrupt. "Adventurers in search of office, unprincipled men left behind by the dissolution of the Freedmen's Bureau, and who thus acquired an influence among the negroes, plundered the State Treasury for their own benefit, and cared little or nothing for the weal of the commonwealth." (Scott, of course, had been the state head of the Freedmen's Bureau.) According to Chamberlain, the state needed the brains of the "intelligent portion of the citizens." These people could vote but many could not hold office because of the Fourteenth Amendment ban. Congress should promptly lift it, Chamberlain declared.

Just before the taxpayers' convention met, Chamberlain wrote for publication in the *Charleston Republican* a long letter to Colonel W. L. Trenholm, who belonged to a wealthy mercantile family of Charleston. Reconstruction, he said, had resulted in absolute political control on the part of one race, a race "devoid of political experience" and dependent for it mainly on those who "chanced to have drifted here from other States." The consequences were incompetence, dishonesty, corruption, and lawlessness. He himself was one of the outsiders. "I profess, however, to be not behind the foremost in my desire to do all that lies in my power to serve and benefit the State, with which all my interests are now identified."

Chamberlain had a sovereign remedy to offer. It was a system of proportional representation, or cumulative voting. Take the example of Charleston County, which had eighteen representatives in the lower house of the legislature. Give each voter eighteen votes and allow him to cast them as he sees fit—all eighteen for one candidate if he wishes. This system would assure the decent, intelligent citizens (the Democrats) of enough representation to check the worst of the abuses. Other reforms, Chamberlain said, would also help: a change in the election law, a limit on expenditures and the debt, the removal (by the governor) of corrupt and incompetent local officers, especially tax collectors, and the appointment of honest, capable men in their places. But Ku Kluxism was not the way to go about reform. It was "simply horrible, infamous, diabolical," a threat to the very existence of society.[18]

While openly offering to work with conservatives, Chamberlain was confidentially confirming the offer. Some of the conservatives worried about the upcoming taxpayers' convention because they owned South Carolina bonds, which presumably would lose value if the convention should declare them void. Northern investors in the bonds had the same concern. So financiers in New York, Charleston, and Columbia agreed to employ men to keep the convention from disavowing the debt. Chosen for the task were two prominent delegates—Matthew C. Butler and Martin W. Gary—who were secretly associated with Chamberlain, Scott, and other Republicans in railroad ventures and who, as Confederate veterans and solid Democrats, would have the confidence of their fellow delegates. "*I will cooperate* with Butler and Gary," Chamberlain assured Kimpton, "*in any possible way.*"

When the convention met, its proceedings turned partly into a charade that Butler, Gary, and Chamberlain together carried out. Chamberlain, after being elected third vice president, started the proceedings by introducing two resolutions: 1. that a special committee examine the accounts of the financial agent, Kimpton; 2. that the executive committee inquire into the prevailing violence and recommend ways to protect the lives and property of all citizens. Gary and Chamberlain served on another committee, the one on cumulative voting.

Addressing the convention, Gary indicated he would approve the proportional representation scheme with no enthusiasm but with the attitude that half a loaf was better than none. The real problem, he thought, was universal suffrage. "It is the subterfuge of the politician who caters to ignorant masses for personal aggrandizement." Chamberlain treated the delegates to a bit of oratory in which he advocated government by the "property and intelligence" of the state and opposed the rule of the "mere numerical majority"—familiar phrases of the old nullifier John C. Calhoun, whom Chamberlain obviously had been reading. He estimated that cumulative voting would bring at least forty-seven Democrats into the house of representatives, and he drew applause when he went on to ask: "Do you believe for a moment, then, when you put into an ignorant assembly, many of whom can neither read nor write, forty-seven gentlemen, whom I might select in this body, that you would not shame them into decency, or frighten them from crime?" After listening to Chamberlain, the convention endorsed his proportional representation plan.

But Chamberlain could take no satisfaction in the executive committee's report on the cause and cure of violence. According to the report, the cause lay in the "larcenies and incendiarism practiced by ignorant, deluded, and bad men," which had led to "instances of corporal punishments and homicides, perpetrated by unknown persons." The cure was simply good government.

Butler headed a committee of eleven who called on the governor to inspect the financial records of the state. Scott assured the committee that he had signed no bonds other than those on the comptroller's list. He also promised to do what he could to bring about certain reforms—to reduce the number of state offices, replace incompetent appointees, adopt cumulative voting, change the election laws, and postpone the collection of taxes. Butler recommended to the convention that "a cheerful response be made to this effort of his excellency to secure retrenchment and reform."

The upshot was a compromise on the crucial point, the validity of the state debt. The delegates agreed to the following: "*Resolved,* That we deem it our duty to warn all persons not to receive . . . any bond or obligation hereafter issued by the present State government or by any subsequent government in which the property-holders of the State are not represented." In other words, the convention would put a cloud upon *future* bond issues by the Republicans but would not question the issues they had already made.[19]

So the Scott administration survived the taxpayers' revolt, but the Ku Klux uprising remained a menace. In June, testifying before the Ku Klux investigating committee in Washington, Chamberlain said that he personally had suffered no outrages and had seen none. He thought the motives were largely political, to put an end to Republican rule, but the victims were mostly bad, corrupt officeholders. The majority of the committee took a more serious view of Ku Klux terrorism, and so did President Grant.

In June, Grant sent federal detectives to South Carolina to gather evidence against the Klan. In July he directed that prosecutions begin under the enforcement acts, and later he proclaimed martial law in nine upcountry counties. Eagerly cooperating, Scott hired a special state prosecutor who, along with the attorney general, was to assist the federal prosecutors. He also offered a reward of $200 for each arrest and conviction (a federal detective claimed $18,600 for the apprehension of 93 who were convicted). Before the end of November Scott could tally 600 arrests. At last he and his administration were fairly safe from the Klan.[20]

Scott still had to deal with revolters inside the party. During 1871 the Republicans in the legislature carried on three investigations—of the Blue Ridge railroad, the land commission, and the financial board—with the governor as a conspicuous target. The findings led to an attempt to impeach him.

That there was corruption in the government, no one in South Carolina seemed to doubt. The only question was who was responsible for it. Everywhere was heard the rumor that legislators were taking bribes and state officials were making private use of public funds. In testimony before the committee on the Blue Ridge railroad, Scott himself declared that few bills could pass the legislature without bribery. He said that, if Jesus Christ were to come down and try to pass a bill for reform, He would not only fail but would be crucified unless He paid the expected bribes.

Scott suspected some of his close associates of corruption and fraud, though he refrained from publicly accusing them. One of the prime suspects was John J. Patterson, the Pennsylvanian who had come to South Carolina to build the Blue Ridge railroad and now was president of the company, of which Scott was one of the directors. Another suspect was Niles G. Parker, the state treasurer.

Since the state-guaranteed Blue Ridge bonds were not selling, Patterson wanted the legislature to make a direct loan to the railroad, but Scott opposed the scheme. He believed that Patterson and Parker were conspiring together. In October he heard that Parker had signed and sent to Kimpton some bonds of a new issue known as the Sterling loan. Only the governor could legally execute such bonds. He wrote to Kimpton to warn that, if his information was correct, he would consider it his duty "to notify the public of the fact and caution all parties against purchasing said bonds," since they would have been "fraudulently issued." He went to New York again to look personally into financial affairs. Afterward he did not expose the attempted fraud—which he was sure involved Patterson as well as Parker—but he did instruct the president of the American Banknote Company to print no more bonds or stock certificates for South Carolina and to hold back all those already printed until further notice from him.[21]

In a December message to the legislature Scott blamed others than himself for the deplorable financial condition of the state. He did not mention Kimpton, though he privately was criticizing him for mismanagement. He denounced the legislature for extravagance. But he accused South Carolina Democrats of primary responsibility for the depreciation of state securities, since the Democrats continually fomented doubts about the state's ability to pay its debt. Such propaganda, he said, was "simply Kukluxism applied to the state credit."

Scott's message pleased his friends in Ohio—"'twill give people to understand that some one else besides yourself is responsible for the condition of things in S. C."—but did not appease his enemies in the legislature. Its investigating committees reported that he must share the guilt along with the financial agent and with other members of the financial board, the land commission, and the sinking fund commission. Two of his bitterest enemies in the legislature were the black W. J. Whipper and the scalawag C. C. Bowen, the man whose hope of reelection to Congress he had frustrated by backing De Large against him.

On December 17 Bowen introduced a resolution for the impeachment of both Parker and Scott. On December 22 the legislature was scheduled to adjourn for the Christmas holiday. The impeachers knew they did not have the two-thirds majority needed to pass the resolution. They aimed to prevent a vote on it for the time being and to leave the charges hanging until after the vacation, in the hope of gaining sufficient votes to impeach or at least to embarrass Scott. Whipper planned to hold the floor for the impeachers until the scheduled recess.

On December 21 Scott held a strategy conference at his home. Among those present was Franklin J. Moses, who, as speaker of the house, could possibly arrange to interrupt Whipper's filibuster. So far as Scott could tell, Moses had an equivocal attitude, and Scott half suspected both him and Patterson of favoring impeachment. But Moses promised to cooperate with the Scott faction in the assembly if Scott would cancel a debt of a few thousand dollars that Moses owed him. Scott said he would consider it once Moses had done his duty. The next day, while Whipper was haranguing the house, Moses by prearrangement recognized a black member who rose to a question of privilege. Whipper having thus been deprived of the floor, the house proceeded to vote down the impeachment resolution by 63 to 27.

Rumors later circulated to the effect that Scott had bribed legislators to defeat the resolution. Eventually there came to light three vouchers bearing his signature and drawing on the armed force fund to pay tens of thousands of dollars to three persons designated by phony names.

Opponents of the Scott administration charged that this was the money distributed as bribes. But Scott had no reason to pay legislators to vote against impeachment, since there was never a majority willing to vote for it. When he heard of the faked vouchers, he assumed that Parker must have stolen some of the pre-signed forms that were kept on hand in the governor's office. He believed that all the money went to Parker and Patterson and that they kept it for themselves.[22]

Patterson apparently did bribe legislators, however, to induce them to pass a series of bills early in 1872. Two of these called in the $4,000,000 worth of state-guaranteed Blue Ridge bonds and gave the railroad instead a direct loan of $1,800,000 in state scrip. Patterson wanted $4,000,000 in scrip, but neither Scott nor the legislative majority would go along with that. Another law authorized the financial board to make a settlement with Kimpton and award him, for his ineffective labors, a very large sum.

In June 1872 one of the large stockholders in the Blue Ridge railroad brought suit against Patterson, Scott, and other officers and directors of the company, as well as against Parker in his capacity as state treasurer. The complainant charged that Patterson was using the scrip and the proceeds from it "for his own purposes, instead of applying it for the benefit of the said Road and the Stockholders thereof."[23]

Little was left of the dream of a railroad that would connect Ohio and South Carolina and bring prosperity to both states. Little was left, for that matter, of any of the great expectations that once had been aroused by the governorship of Robert K. Scott.

CHAPTER 12

The Leprous Hands Upraised (1869-1872)

Across the street from the Florida capitol stood the governor's residence, a rather pleasant if unimposing house. It was occupied by a widower from Wisconsin, the slightly built, bushy-bearded, bald-headed, bespectacled Harrison Reed. Though once described as a "fussy old granny," Reed had won the heart of an attractive and capable woman young enough to be his daughter. In August 1869, shortly before his fifty-sixth birthday, he and Chloe Merrick were wed in Wilmington, North Carolina, where she was conducting one of her schools for black children. As Florida's first lady, Chloe made the official residence an even more pleasant house and provided the governor with emotional support he sorely needed.

Opposite the capitol on another side of the square stood the Capitol Hotel, the best in Tallahassee. Lobbyists crowded the hotel when the legislature was in session. They flourished about town in fancy carriages, and they entertained legislators with oyster suppers, whiskey, champagne, and cigars. Among the lobbyists, the most conspicuous and most persuasive was Milton S. Littlefield, the debonair Union veteran from Illinois, whom both Mr. and Mrs. Reed knew from their wartime days together in Union-occupied Florida. Here, as in North Carolina, Littlefield and his associate the native Tar Heel George W. Swepson were interested in the financing of railroads. Here, too, they were willing to do favors for their friends.[1]

Governor Reed desperately needed financial help, not for himself but for the state. Its treasury had been bare when he took office, and though its acknowledged debt was not extremely large its credit was very poor, prewar administrations having failed to make good on some $3,000,000 in bonds. Consequently new issues were hard to dispose of. Going to New York himself, Reed managed to find buyers for some bonds, then spent the proceeds on a state seal and other official equipment and supplies. Back home, waiting for tax revenue to come in, he borrowed on personal notes to help meet the state's current expenses. Littlefield and Swepson obliged him with loans.

Reed hoped to get adequate revenue not by raising tax rates but by equalizing and increasing assessments. Previously landowners had been allowed to assess their own property. An assessment board was set up, but the state comptroller, a Democrat, permitted planters to continue the old practice, and some of them set the taxable value of their land as low as 80 cents an acre. Taxes could be paid in the scrip that the state issued in payment of salaries and other expenses. Though the scrip rapidly depreciated, the state accepted it at par. Tax collectors kept such cash as they received; in place of it they turned in scrip. After two years in office Reed persuaded the legislature to economize, and he accepted a salary cut from $5,000 to $3,500. This, paid in scrip, did not allow for very high living.

It was hard enough at best to reestablish the state's credit, and the Democrats made it still harder by their opposition to increases in either taxes or the debt. "Our only hope," one of them confessed in the *Tallahassee Floridian*, "is in the State's utter financial bankruptcy . . . in having the State's financial credit so low that Reed & Co. can't sell State bonds so as to raise money with which to perpetuate their hold on office."

Nevertheless, Reed could boast near the end of his four-year term that Florida was in much better shape financially than it had been under the Democrats. It now supported institutions unknown to them—a school system, a university, and a penitentiary—yet the debt under his administration had risen by only $240,000 (to a total of $1,311,694.97). Under his predecessors from 1848 to 1860, he pointed out, the state had not even accounted for the money that was spent. "That was during the halcyon days of peace, prosperity and harmony 'before the war,'" he sarcastically noted. "There were no 'scalawags' or 'carpet-baggers' or 'freedmen' to disturb the political sea."[2]

In his summary of the 1872 state debt, Reed did not include the $4,000,000 in state bonds that had been given to railroad companies in exchange for railroad bonds. Supposedly, these corporate obligations in the possession of the state amounted to an asset that balanced the state's liability. Reed assumed that interest from the railroad bonds would enable the state to pay interest on the bonds it exchanged for them.

Now devoted to Florida's economic development, as he once had been to Wisconsin's, Reed sincerely believed in public aid to private enterprise. He tried to persuade Congress to restore the federal land grants it had given—and then revoked on account of secession—for the encouragement of railroad and canal construction. In proposing state assistance, he had particularly in mind an extension of the rail line from Tallahassee west to Pensacola and Mobile, so as to connect with a line stretching on to New Orleans and, prospectively, to the Pacific coast. The connection with Pensacola seemed especially urgent as a means of holding the state together. It could be expected to appease discontented

West Floridians and quiet their agitation for combining West Florida with Alabama.

But Reed did not originate the policy of railroad aid in Florida, nor did he introduce the railroad financiers Littlefield and Swepson to the state. In 1855 the legislature had set up an Internal Improvement Fund, which helped to finance the construction of railroads by buying their securities. Before Reed's inauguration in 1868 a group of Democratic Floridians invited Swepson to help them acquire railroad stock from the Internal Improvement Fund, consolidate several companies, and finance the completion of the track. Littlefield and Swepson, through their lobbying, secured acts for consolidation and state aid. These men and their Florida associates thenceforth controlled the Jacksonville, Pensacola and Mobile, the east-west route that Reed considered most important for the development of the state.

Nevertheless, Reed hesitated to issue state bonds to the company. There had been some hanky-panky between Swepson and the trustees of the Internal Improvement Fund, and there was some question as to whether he held a valid title to the railroad stock he had obtained from them. Even if that matter were cleared up, Reed was willing to release the bonds only in stages as sections of track were completed—not all at once, as the promoters demanded. So Littlefield lobbied through a new law, but Reed still held back the bonds, denouncing the "disappointed corruptionists" who had "sought to fasten themselves" on the Florida railroads for "personal aggrandizement." He yielded, however, when Littlefield's attorneys, two Florida Democrats, advised him to do so.

Later, while launching his economy drive, Reed cautioned the legislature against further assistance to railroads and suggested the repeal of some aid laws already passed. His warning was wise, though late. From the $3,000,000 (face value) in bonds he had issued to the Jacksonville, Pensacola and Mobile, only about $300,000 went into the actual purchase of equipment and laying of track. Such waste and extravagance were distressing to Reed. Though a friend to enterprise, he was (for the time) a fiscal conservative as well as a conservative Republican.[3]

This did not keep the Democrats from charging him with extravagance and waste, nor did it deter them from carrying on their Ku Klux activity. Terrorism went to the worst extremes in Jackson County, adjacent to the corner where Florida, Georgia, and Alabama meet. Bloodshed began in February 1869 when a sniper killed the scalawag county clerk and wounded a carpetbag assemblyman as the two crossed the courthouse square in Marianna late at night. When the assemblyman, W. J. Purman, appeared in Tallahassee with an ugly scar on his neck, Reed advised him to stay away from Marianna. Purman was for taking punitive action, but Reed—who thought Purman had been asking for trouble—preferred to temporize.

Reports from Jackson County indicated continuing violence there. After the murder of a white farmer, the bloated bodies of blacks could be seen floating down the placid Chipola River from time to time. Then, in September and October 1869, a new and greater wave of terror swept the county. Reed learned the details in letters he received from J. Q. Dickinson, a Harvard graduate and former army captain from Maine whom he had appointed as county clerk to replace the assassinated scalawag. In retaliation for an attack on a Negro picnic, in which two people died, a shot was fired at the local chief of the Ku Klux Klan. It missed him but killed a young white woman and wounded her father. The Klan now declared an open season on leading blacks. A Jewish merchant in Marianna protested the killings. Klansmen took him outside the county and warned him never to come back. A week later he was found dead on the road to Marianna.

Purman and other Republicans in Tallahassee urged Reed to declare martial law in Jackson County and send (black) militia there. From Marianna he received two letters, one signed by Dickinson and two Democrats and expressing confidence that local authorities could restore law and order; the other signed by Dickinson alone and suggesting the possible need for martial law. Reed feared that declaring martial law and sending militia to enforce it might lead to race war. Instead, he appointed a local Democrat as sheriff and sent two white Southerners to conciliate the Jackson County whites. The federal government stationed a small detachment of troops in Marianna and another in Tallahassee. A degree of calm was temporarily restored.

"In several counties organized bands of lawless men have combined to override the civil authorities, and many acts of violence have occurred," Reed told the legislature; "but these have been incidental to the State in all its past history, and arise less, perhaps, from special enmity to the present form of government than from opposition to the restraints of law in general." In so saying, Reed endorsed the view of many Southern conservatives, who argued that Klan violence was a manifestation of endemic lawlessness and, for the most part, was not racially or politically motivated.

Dickinson, the Jackson County clerk, did not look at it that way. When Ku Klux activity resumed in and around Marianna early in 1871, he wrote to Jonathan C. Gibbs, Reed's black secretary of state: "Since reconstruction there have been seventy-five persons violently killed in this county; and more than nine-tenths were republicans, and nearly nine-tenths colored." The sheriff resigned after being mobbed and beaten almost to death. He was powerless to enforce the law, he explained to Reed. Then Dickinson was shot and killed while crossing the courthouse square at night, almost exactly as his predecessor had been.

The black Republican Charles Pearce, praising Dickinson as a "martyr, saint, hero," proposed that Florida honor him as one of its two most distinguished citizens by putting his statue in the U.S. Capitol's Statuary Hall. Reed did not second this proposal but, after conferring with Jackson County Democrats, appointed a sheriff and a county clerk acceptable to them. Several months later, federal marshals, deputies, detectives, and troops arrived in Florida to enforce the Ku Klux Act, and Reed no longer felt compelled to appease the Klansmen and their apologists.[4]

Politically, Reed had less to fear from Klansmen and Democrats than from some members of his own party, including fellow carpetbaggers. Democrats would have no opportunity to vote him out of office before his four-year term was up, in 1872, but hostile Republicans could try to remove him any year through impeachment. After having failed in 1868, they made three more attempts—in 1869, 1870, and 1872.

Among Reed's Republican foes the most determined continued to be carpetbag U.S. Senator Thomas W. Osborn and his faction of federal officeholders, several of whom were also state legislators. Osborn's allies included State Senator Purman and house speaker M. L. Stearns, a former Freedmen's Bureau agent who had lost an arm in the war. As for Reed's adherents, he had few he could consistently depend upon. Gone to pieces was the coalition that had elected him. He must look for support wherever he could find it—among blacks, unattached radicals from the North, conservative scalawags, and even Democrats.

In the 1869 impeachment attempt, its sponsors charged Reed with accepting bribes and misusing money obtained from bond sales. He explained that he had used this money plus his own and that of a friend (the alleged "bribe") for official expenses. He called on blacks to stand by him if they thought he was trying to provide an honest administration. He got the backing of Liberty Billings and Daniel Richards of the old Mule Team by giving Richards to believe he favored him for a U.S. senatorship. Richards said of Reed: "He may be guilty but my God look at the leprous hands upraised against him." The house voted 45 to 3 that there were no grounds for impeaching him.

When the legislature met in January 1870, Reed made an overture to Southern whites by recommending that Congress be asked to remove the Fourteenth Amendment bar to officeholding whenever anyone applied for such relief. He also tried to mollify the legislators, particularly those newly "admitted to the rights of freemen," by congratulating them upon their resistance to bribery. "You," he said, "have preserved the State from the incubus of a corrupt and corrupting power, which has fastened itself upon so many of the States now struggling to rise from the ruins of war." But some of the legislators thought *he* was guilty of corruption.

This time his enemies claimed to have positive proof. It consisted of a letter that Swepson purportedly had written to Reed on May 31, 1869, shortly before the legislature met in a special session that Reed had called. The letter read in part:

> General Littlefield has the bill, etc., and will fully explain everything to you; we expect him to prevent any difficulty being made with you by Osborn's

> friends. I write hastily and to the point. You remember, when in New York, our agreement was this: You were to call the Legislature together, and use your influence to have our bills passed as drawn by us, and if you were successful in this you were to be paid twelve thousand five hundred dollars in cash, out of which amount was to be deducted the seventy-five hundred (7500) dollars you have heretofore received, leaving a balance of five thousand dollars to be paid at an early day.

Reed could only gasp at the brazenness of this forgery. Of course, he had received money from Littlefield and Swepson, but only in the form of loans to himself and to the state. He certainly did not have to be bribed to favor the bills in question. They were meant to assist the construction of the great east-west railroad, a project dear to his own heart. If he had suspected Littlefield of attempting to bribe him—or of conspiring to make it appear that he had accepted bribes—he would have disowned him, despite his and Chloe's long and pleasant acquaintance with him. But Reed did no such thing. And he refused to comply when the govenor of North Carolina asked him to extradite Littlefield to face charges of conspiracy and embezzlement in that state. Reed and his friends were sure that Osborn was responsible for the fabrication of the incriminating letter. In any event, the letter fell short of convincing the house, which voted 27 to 22 against impeachment.

Finally, on the fourth attempt, in February 1872, the Osborn men induced the house to adopt articles of impeachment by a unanimous vote. The sixteen articles accused him not only of accepting bribes but also of illegally issuing bonds, conniving with railroads to defraud the state, and embezzling public funds. According to the state constitution, when the governor was impeached the powers and duties of his office were to devolve upon the lieutenant governor until the governor was acquitted or his term was over. So the lieutenant governor, an anti-Reed Republican, occupied the office, and Reed and his wife went home to their orange grove just south of Jacksonville.

Reed was eager for his trial to get under way, knowing as he did that the impeachers had no evidence to sustain their charges. But word soon came that the legislature had adjourned *sine die*. Obviously the enemies of Reed were plotting to leave him in limbo for the remaining ten months of his term. He took the position, however, that by adjourning without trying him the senate had, in effect, acquitted him. He waited for a chance to act on that principle and reassert his authority.

His chance came in April when he learned that the lieutenant governor had arrived in Jacksonville for a political meeting. Reed promptly took the train in the opposite direction, to Tallahassee. There he reoccupied the gubernatorial office, proclaimed himself governor, and asked the state supreme court to rule in his favor. Secretary of State Gibbs authenticated Reed's proclamation with the great seal of Florida, but the court held that only the senate could decide to whom the governorship rightfully belonged.

The lieutenant governor now made the mistake of calling the legislature into special session. He wanted to impeach Gibbs as well as Reed. While Purman and other Osborn allies tried to adjourn the legislature again, two Democrats argued that Reed deserved a trial, and the majority concurred. So the senate sat as an impeachment court, but not for long. Reed's counsel quickly moved to dismiss the charges. Six Democrats and four Republicans voted aye, three Democrats and four Republicans no. The motion carried.[5]

Tourists in New Orleans liked to visit the Mechanics Institute building, still the temporary state capitol, to view one of the local curiosities that white citizens jokingly recommended—the "Negro legislature." The traveling Englishman Robert Somers went to see it while he was in town in 1871. Along the hallway leading to the chamber of representatives he found Negro women selling cakes, oranges, and lollipops. Inside the chamber he discovered, seated in a semicircle, "a body of men as sedate and civilized in appearance as a convention of miners' delegates in Scotland or the North of England. On closer inspection, a few Africans were visible, but yellow men seemed to predominate." The senate looked much the same as the house, but presiding over it was the lieutenant governor, Oscar J. Dunn, "a really black man." Dunn, a former slave, was a plasterer by trade.

The governor, Henry Clay Warmoth, struck Somers as "a young man of spirit and ability" who had obtained his office by manipulating the Negro vote. "The outcry against him has been loud and deep; but all that can be said is that, whereas he was once poor, he is now very rich, and that his wealth, if the wages of corruption, has been so deftly acquired that no one can lay his finger on the foul spot." Some people, Somers heard, believed that Dunn was "a more trustworthy man."

But Warmoth, after three years in office, still had his admirers and even his adulators. After interviewing him a correspondent for the *Cincinnati Commercial* wrote:

> Governor Warmoth is a man of striking presence and decided ability. He is but twenty-nine years of age, and but for that he would be in the [U.S.] Senate. In person he is very tall and very slender, being considerably over six feet, and weighing not more than one hundred and forty pounds. His eyes, eyebrows, mustache and hair are brown, while his skin is as fair and smooth as a woman's. Through the pale, clear, smooth skin of his face shines his soul and the ability that is in him. He is the ablest Republican in Louisiana, and this, together with his youth, makes him a mark for envious darts.

Warmoth clipped and saved this tribute after his own paper, the *New Orleans Republican*, reprinted it.[6]

Henry Clay Warmoth
Southern Historical Collection, University of North Carolina at Chapel Hill

Harrison Reed
State Historical Society of Wisconsin

Willard Warner
Mathew B. Brady Collection, National Archives

George Eliphaz Spencer
Mathew B. Brady Collection, National Archives

Robert Kingston Scott
Ohio Historical Society

Albion Winegar Tourgee
Chautauqua County Historical Society, Westfield, N.Y.

Daniel Henry Chamberlain
Yale University Library

Adelbert Ames
Mathew B. Brady Collection, National Archives

Powell Clayton
Mathew B. Brady Collection, National Archives

Still a bachelor, Warmoth continued to get around a lot, associating with some of the most prestigious people and managing often to be where the excitement was. He could never forget the dinner given for him by Dr. W. Newton Mercier, who lived in a "palatial residence" and who was "perhaps the first man in social life in the city of New Orleans." Present were "twenty-five or thirty of the leading men of the State," among them ex-Confederate General Richard Taylor (son of Zachary Taylor and brother-in-law of Jefferson Davis) and ex-Governor P. O. Hebert. Nor could Warmoth ever forget the time he was a guest on board the winning steamboat in the famous race between the *Natchez* and the *Robert E. Lee.* After handing out diplomas at the state university in Baton Rouge, he had disembarked at New Orleans on the day the race was to begin (June 30, 1870). With him was a friend of the *Robert E. Lee*'s captain, who invited both men along.[7]

While Warmoth liked to remember his association with prominent Louisianans, he did not get the political cooperation of as many of them as he hoped. Some of them complained of corruption in the government, and after a mass meeting in Lafayette Square a delegation came to him with resolutions of protest. He replied:

> You charge the Legislature with passing, corruptly, many bills looking to the personal aggrandizement of individuals and corporations. Let me suggest to you that these individuals and corporations are your very best people. For instance, this bank bill that is being lobbied through the Legislature now by the hardest kind of work. We have been able to defeat this bill twice in the House, and now it is up again. Who are doing it? Your bank presidents. The best people of the City of New Orleans are crowding the lobby of the Legislature continually, whispering bribes into these men's ears to pass this measure. How are we to defend the State against the interposition of these people who are potent in their influence in this community?
>
> I make this complaint to you as an individual; I make it as a citizen of Louisiana. I came here to settle among you, although by accident I have been elevated to the position I now occupy, and if you and the 2,500 citizens who were present at the meeting which sent you here would only give their support to me and the honest members of the Legislature, there will be no difficulty in restraining improvident legislation.

Enemies of Warmoth maintained that *he,* as the head of a ring of crooks, was corrupting the legislature for his own and the ring's benefit. Specific charges appeared in a letter, signed "Metaire," which the *New York Sun* published in 1870 under the heading "The Louisiana Thieves." According to the writer, Warmoth and his accomplices had swindled the public the worst in the following ways: They paid themselves $1,000,000 for state printing that might have been done profitably for $50,000. They gave one company the exclusive right to operate a slaughterhouse, the monopoly profits of which they shared. And in return for a huge bribe they sold the state-owned and city-owned stock of the New Orleans and Jackson Railroad for only about a third of its market value.

After seeing this epistolary attack, Warmoth composed a letter of defense and sent it to New York in the custody of Thomas W. Conway, former state head of the Freedmen's Bureau and present superintendent of education. As Warmoth soon heard from Conway, the *New York Sun* editor Charles A. Dana had received him pleasantrly but refused to publish the letter. "We cannot defend Warmoth," Dana said, repeating the charges against him and adding that he had been paid $100,000 for his influence in "the Jackson R. R. job." "I protested in the strongest terms and told Dana that he was doing an outrageous wrong," Conway reported to Warmoth. "I espoused your case in '67 and have no knowledge yet that you have become the dishonest man they tell about."

The letter defending Warmoth did appear in his official newspaper, the *New Orleans Republican.* Instead of "The Louisiana Thieves," the heading was "Honest Men of Louisiana." The *Republican,* this letter asserted, "has received about $100,000 per annum for all the printing it has done, and the quantity has been unusually great." The slaughtering of animals was now confined to one place, downriver from the city, for reasons of health. Formerly the slaughtering had been done "in the upper part of the city, and the offal was poured into the river, which, in consequence, reeked with putridity." (The Louisiana supreme court and eventually the United States Supreme Court were to uphold the granting of the slaughterhouse monopoly as a legitimate exercise of the state's police power.) As for the New Orleans and Jackson Railroad, its stock "was not worth one dollar to the State" as long as the state continued to hold it. "The city authorities, *while under Democratic rule,* sold the portion owned by the city for three dollars and fifty cents per share, and the State stock, after being thoroughly advertised, was sold by our Republican Governor for four dollars per share, and by so doing placed the corporation in the hands of gentlemen who will infuse new life into the concern and [make it] of some practical benefit to the State."[8]

Foremost among the gentlemen who were infusing new life into the New Orleans and Jackson Railroad was Henry S. McComb, once a Union officer, now a leading capitalist of Wilmington, Delaware. Warmoth expected McComb also to take control of and infuse new life into the Louisiana Levee Company, which the state had encouraged with loans to improve and maintain the embankments confining the Mississippi River. But McComb proposed that Warmoth assume responsibility for the portion of the levee company's stock and bonds intended for McComb. Reluctantly Warmoth agreed. "God bless you," my dear friend," McComb responded. "I learn you are getting it [the levee company] resuscitated, and infusing new life into it, which I sincerely hope may end in good to you and to the State."

Like other Louisiana governors before him, Warmoth advocated state aid for internal improvements of various kinds. He shared his predecessors' dream of a railroad from New Orleans to Houston (and ultimately to the Pacific), which became the destination of the New Orleans, Mobile

& Chattanooga, one of the more successful of the state-assisted projects. Corruption attended the passage of many improvement bills, as Warmoth himself recognized. He listed eighty legislators who he thought had been bribed to vote for the Louisiana Levee Company bill. These men were beyond his reach, but he removed a state auditor for forging and selling state warrants, and he suspended a secretary of state for bribery and for the misappropriation of funds. Despite frequent accusations, no one ever produced convincing evidence that he himself gave or received bribes.

He did not need to sell his influence in order to acquire wealth. As a lawyer from 1864 to 1868 he had earned some fairly large fees, so that, by the time he took office, he already possessed something of a nest egg. Then, as governor, he found ways to enlarge it. "He made his money in the depreciated State bonds, by an investment based upon his knowledge of the time fixed to resume paying interest upon them," his good friend the railroad promoter McComb explained. "Warmoth bought Louisiana bonds standing at thirty-five; by funding the coupons and resuming interest they rose more than one hundred per cent." After this windfall he had still more capital with which to make speculations that, from his vantage point as an insider, he could expect to pay unusually well.

There was some question as to how long he would continue to influence policy in such a way as to benefit both himself and the state. To many he seemed a veritable dictator, and a shockingly flamboyant one at that, but in fact he had passed the peak of his power by the time he was halfway through his four-year term. It was not easy to keep control of the factious Republican party of Louisiana, and in one way or another he had managed to turn all too many friends into enemies, one of the most dangerous of whom was Lieutenant-Governor Dunn.[9]

To maintain his position as leader of Louisiana Republicans, Warmoth needed the continuing support of President U. S. Grant. And, to be sure of Grant's support, he needed to keep on good terms with James F. Casey, husband of Mrs. Grant's sister and collector of the port of New Orleans. As collector, Casey had a number of customhouse jobs at his disposal—and large sums of money to handle. His patronage power made him a key figure in the politics of the state.

Casey had held the office for less than a year when some of the Louisiana Republicans undertook to get rid of him. Heading the anti-Casey movement were the two carpetbag senators from Louisiana: J. S. Harris, from New York, and William Pitt Kellogg, the former collector of the New Orleans port, from Illinois. Harris and Kellogg assured Grant that the state's Republican leaders were unanimous in opposing Casey's retention. But Warmoth refused to go along with Harris and Kellogg. He sent them a telegram—and Grant a telegram and a letter—to say he was perfectly satisfied with Casey.

Warmoth heard from Harris and Kellogg that they were sorry he took the stand he did. Surely he must know, as they knew, that Casey was a poor manager and, what was worse, was keeping Democrats in customhouse jobs. The interests of the party demanded that "Casey give way to some good and efficient man & Republican." The two senators feared that Warmoth was hurting his own as well as the party's interests. But Warmoth was unconcerned. He learned from another correspondent, a friend who had interviewed Grant three times in the recent past: "Grant was much gratified at the reception of your letter and spoke very kindly of you. I am certain you have gained a good point for yourself in standing by Casey." [10]

While Warmoth held on to the support of Casey and Grant, he was losing the support of a number of prominent Louisiana Republicans. He offended Lieutenant-Governor Dunn and many other blacks (though by no means all of them) by failing to enforce legislation for equal rights and by vetoing a bill to make discrimination a crime. He antagonized two leading carpetbaggers by vetoing bills for projects in which they had a stake. One was Stephen B. Packard, a Union veteran from Maine, a United States marshal, and the chairman of the Republican state central committee. The other was Charles W. Lowell, also a Union veteran from Maine and a federal officeholder, the postmaster of New Orleans.

When the Republican state convention met in August 1870 to make nominations for the fall campaign, Warmoth suffered a bit of a setback: the convention chose Dunn instead of him as its permanent president. Still, most of the nominees for the legislature proved to be pro-Warmoth men. To be voted on, in addition to the candidates, were four constitutional amendments. One would give the suffrage back to those ex-rebels whom the state constitution had deprived of it. Another would make the governor eligible for a second term. Warmoth (whose first term would not end until 1872) wanted to be governor again if the people wanted him to be. As he later said, it was gratifying to be able to "wield power and do good."

Though not yet up for reelection himself, Warmoth that fall campaigned vigorously for the constitutional amendments and for the party's ticket. He was too busy to meet all the requests for a personal appearance. From a carpetbagger in Opelousas, in the Cajun country of southwestern Louisiana, came an urgent appeal: Warmoth must be on hand for a Republican rally, to encourage the blacks to vote. "The colored people in this parish are still to a great extent under the influence of fear, created by the riots of '68." The Democrats might again win by intimidation, as they had done at the last election. But Warmoth chose to concentrate on the white voters of northern and northwestern Louisiana.

On a stumping tour he and his fellow carpetbagger George A. Sheridan, traveling by carriage, took the ferry across the Red River to Shreveport at dawn on October 23. They were mystified and a little worried to discover that all the buildings were draped in black. At the hotel their bellboy told them that Robert E. Lee had died the day before. "Sheridan looked at me, and I looked at Sheridan, and we both felt great regret at the death of General Lee," Warmoth was to recall; "but we were much relieved to find it was 'not our funeral.'" They rented a brass band from John Robinson's circus, which happened to be in town, and they got permission to hold their meeting on a huge platform in front of the market house.

As Warmoth rose to speak he faced a crowd he estimated at three thousand, nearly all of them white. He proceeded to stroke their Southern sensibilities. His own blood was Southern, he declared, his father having been born in Tennessee. He had not "forced the race issue" in regard to the public schools. One of the constitutional amendments he was advocating would "strike the shackles from the limbs of every ex-Confederate in the State." In the militia he had enrolled 2500 "young rebels," and to positions of command he had appointed several ex-Confederates, most notably General Lee's former right hand man Lieutenant-General James Longstreet. After Warmoth sat down, the circus band played "Dixie," and then Sheridan delivered a eulogy of Lee that moved the audience to both tears and cheers.

At election time Warmoth was better prepared than in 1868 to deal with the disruptive tactics of the Democrats. In each parish his appointees as registrars and supervisors were ready to report to him as chairman of a returning board, which could throw out returns from polling places where he and his colleagues suspected intimidation or fraud. But the election proved to be relatively quiet, and he and the board did not have to reject any of the polls. The Republicans elected their state ticket, their congressional candidates, and majorities in both houses of the legislature. All the constitutional amendments carried, including the one making Warmoth eligible for a second term.[11]

After the election he went to Washington and called at the White House. Grant, receiving him cordially, invited him to dinner with the family—the rather plain-looking Julia Dent Grant; her elderly father; the two younger of the three boys, eighteen-year-old Buck and twelve-year-old Jesse; and the budding beauty and darling of the household, fifteen-year-old Nellie. Grant and Warmoth talked pleasantly of old friends and old times—but not of the time in 1863 when Grant removed Warmoth from command and Warmoth persuaded Lincoln to reinstate him. After dinner the two retired to the library and discussed politics until late that night. Warmoth had arrived with a purpose—to induce Grant to remove Charles W. Lowell from the New Orleans postmastership—and Warmoth left the White House with a sense that he and the President were in complete agreement.

Back in New Orleans, Warmoth waited for Lowell's head to roll. Eventually he learned that Grant had, indeed, named a new man for the job. Then Lowell's ally Dunn hurried to Washington and talked with Grant. After that, Grant withdrew the nomination of a successor, and Lowell remained in office, to continue causing trouble for Warmoth.

Warmoth had failed in this test of strength between himself and his factional foes, but another test offered itself when the newly elected legislature met in January 1871. His followers constituted a majority in the house, his Republican opponents a majority in the senate. The senate contained only seven Democrats, but if he could get their cooperation he would control both houses. The showdown would come when the legislature balloted on candidates for the U.S. Senate.

Since he was not yet thirty, the minimum age for a U.S. senator, Warmoth could not seek the office for himself, but if he should succeed in controlling the legislature he could decide who else would get it. One of the hopefuls was Pinckney Benton Stewart Pinchback, a rival of Lieutenant-Governor Dunn for leadership among Louisiana Negroes. Pinchback, a "fancy mulatto" in the view of conservative whites, differed from the coal-black Dunn in background as well as appearance. Never a slave, Pinchback was the son of a freed woman and a Mississippi planter, who sent him to school in Cincinnati. A caucus of black Republicans chose Pinchback over Dunn for the senatorship.

Another contender was Collector Casey. The deputy collector, P. F. Herwig, came to Warmoth and asked him to use his influence in Casey's behalf. Herwig told Warmoth "that Mrs. Casey was the favorite sister of Mrs. Grant; that she was not very well and that our climate was too hot for her; and that the President would like to have Collector Casey sent to the Senate so that his wife might be near Mrs. Grant." Warmoth replied that he had recently dined with the Grants and they had said nothing about Casey and the senatorship, but he would do what he could for Casey if Grant would give him the word. No word came from Grant, so Warmoth concluded that Deputy Collector Herwig was only trying to eliminate Collector Casey and take over his job.

Warmoth favored a different customhouse official, Joseph R. West, the auditor of customs. Born in New Orleans but brought up in Philadelphia, West had served as a major general in the Union army. He was a business associate and close friend of Warmoth. The Democrats much preferred him to Pinchback, and with their vote in addition to the Warmoth Republicans' he was elected.

Thus Warmoth made an enemy of Casey, who up to this time had supported him in gratitude for his standing by him when Senator Kellogg, Lieutenant-Governor Dunn, and other Republican leaders tried to have him removed. Now Casey switched to the anti-Warmoth faction, and so did Kellogg, reconciling himself to Casey. Henceforth Warmoth faced the hostility of a "customhouse ring" that also included his antagonists Packard and Lowell. At least fifteen customhouse jobholders belonging to the ring were also members of the legislature.[12]

While making an enemy of Casey, Warmoth did not yet make an enemy of Grant. At first he wondered about Grant's reaction to the senatorial election. To make sure of Grant's continued friendship—and to renew the attack on Postmaster Lowell—he sent Longstreet on a diplomatic mission to Washington. Longstreet was an ideal go-between, having been a prewar army buddy of Grant's and the best man at his wedding. He reported to Warmoth on January 19:

> I arrived last night. Had an extended interview with the President to-day and explained your views as to the political prospects of La. and your apprehension that designing parties might have misrepresented you, to him, and stated that you only needed his confidence and support to insure satisfactory results in the future.
>
> He says that such reports as have reached him have been made in such a way as to indicate intentions to prejudice your purposes and interests, and that therefore they have made no impression upon him. That your recommendations will have great weight, and probably controlling influence. . . .
>
> He seems fully prepared to renew his nomination of your choice for P. M. as soon as it is probable that the nomination will be confirmed.
>
> In short he only asks that you, or those who make recommendations, will only select the best men for the positions.
>
> He expressed the hope that Gen West will not come here pledged against San Domingo [which Grant wanted to annex but Charles Sumner and other senators did not].

Senator West, whom Grant welcomed, did not oppose the annexation of Santo Domingo but did oppose the retention of Lowell in the postmastership. He alleged, at Warmoth's prompting, that Lowell was living in sin with a "nigger woman."

To make up for the defection of Republicans, Warmoth sought allies among the Democrats. With those in the legislature he made a secret agreement, according to which he would cooperate with them in "administering the government wisely and frugally," making appointments in Democratic parishes, and limiting the power of Dunn, as the senate's presiding officer, to name senate committee members and chairmen.[13]

As spring approached in 1871, with Grant apparently well disposed and the Democratic legislators cooperative, Warmoth could look forward to completing a first and possibly a second term as a powerful governor. Then, suddenly, his luck turned bad.

It was only a small misstep but it was to have large consequences. With a "party of prominent gentlemen," Warmoth was making an excursion downriver in a small steamboat when he caught his right foot in a part of the boat's machinery. Though no bones were broken, the foot was badly bruised. According to the doctor who examined him at Charity Hospital, he would be confined for at least a few days to his room at the St. Charles Hotel.

Despite the doctor's orders for complete quiet, Warmoth could hardly relax a moment from politics. He must get Lowell out of the post office and his own man in, but there was no sign that Grant had taken the promised action. Warmoth consulted with his friends and with them sent a joint telegram to Senator West for presentation to Grant. Soon came a dispiriting reply from West. Grant had sent the name of Warmoth's man to the Senate, had withdrawn it after a visit from Kellogg, and then had promised to withdraw the withdrawal, but had failed to do so. "We need never expect to hear of Grant's support again," West advised. "It is all gone, or rather never was worth a cent. Bottle your wrath, draw your own inferences—lay out your plans and *stand alone* for you have got to."

In a literal sense, Warmoth could not stand alone. Weeks passed and his injured foot grew worse instead of better, becoming infected and making him seriously ill. More than three months after the accident, his physician took him back to the hospital and operated on him, removing part of a toe. On June 24 he left to recuperate at Pass Christian, a coastal resort just beyond the state line in Mississippi.

Disquieting news soon arrived from New Orleans. Lieutenant-Governor Dunn had moved into the governor's office and begun to assume the governor's prerogatives, justifying his action on the grounds that Warmoth had temporarily disqualified himself by leaving the state. On June 26, Dunn presided at a mass meeting to welcome Senator Kellogg, who now made public his break with Warmoth. "Among the faithless, faithful only he," Dunn said of Kellogg. Dunn and other speakers denounced Warmoth and lauded Grant.

At Pass Christian, Warmoth rapidly improved as he took a daily drive on the beach and breathed the invigorating sea air. Politicians and others made the short trip by train from New Orleans to cheer him and counsel him. None of them was more welcome than James Longstreet, whom he needed again to intercede with Grant. "He gives me now the assurance he has often repeated, that he will . . . support the present national administration," Longstreet wrote to his old friend in the White House.

> Whilst he has no doubt of his ability to hold the greater portion of the party, and to overcome these combined efforts against him, he thinks it due to you and to himself that an explanation should be made, and that he should appeal to you to exercise such influence as you may think proper, and necessary, to cause these gentlemen to abandon their violent efforts against him.

This was a rather desperate appeal, but Warmoth's position in Louisiana politics was becoming desperate. He heard that Dunn, playing the governor's role as he was, intended to remove Warmoth's appointees and replace them with his own. So, on July 18, Warmoth took the morning train to New Orleans and entered the governor's office, to find Dunn sitting in the governor's chair. According to a witness, Warmoth "stood revealed leaning upon his crutches, with an arch smile playing around the corners of his mouth." Dunn, startled and embarrassed, rose and after a brief conversation left the room. Warmoth went back to Pass Christian.[14]

Soon the news from New Orleans foreshadowed a plot to reorganize the Republican party and leave Warmoth out of it. The party chairman, U.S. Marshal Stephen B. Packard, was calling a convention to choose a new state central committee. Warmoth wanted the convention postponed to November, when he could hope to be fully recovered, but Packard set August 9 as the date. He did not specify the hour or indicate the place.

On August 8, still crippled and somewhat feverish, Warmoth arrived in the city to make plans for attending the convention with his delegates. They would constitute a majority if all were admitted, but the opposing faction also claimed a majority. Not till the next morning did the Warmothites learn that the proceedings were to begin at noon and were to be held not in the usual place, the Mechanics' Institute, but in the federal courtroom in the customhouse. According to Packard's announcement, delegates would have to get tickets at the post office. Postmaster Lowell allotted tickets to only about half of the Warmoth delegates.

Before eleven o'clock a curious procession moved down Canal Street toward the customhouse. Riding in a carriage were a white man and a mulatto, Warmoth and Pinchback, and marching behind were dozens of their black and white followers. Once at the customhouse—one of the largest public buildings in the country, occupying an entire block—the paraders made their way into the rotunda. There they encountered, among the hostile politicians, forty or fifty deputy marshals with badges and pistols. With friends assisting him, Warmoth led his entourage through the crowd and up the great wooden staircase, toward the courtroom, only to confront a company of U.S. troops and two Gatling guns at the top. Despite his crutches, Warmoth managed to stand on a chair and deliver a tirade against the presence of the troops, until the captain stopped him.

Surrounded and supported by the faithful, Warmoth crutched back down the steep stairs and out to his carriage. Some of the men unhitched the horses and, themselves, pulled the carriage back up Canal Street, while the rest followed, shouting their defiance. Assembling at Turners' Hall, the delegates cheered the flag, sang "The Star Spangled Banner," and listened to Warmoth as he condemned the tactics of the customhouse ring and declared that all Louisiana Republicans were for Grant. After electing Pinchback as the new party chairman, they adopted a resolution calling on Grant to investigate the use of a federal building and federal troops for political skulduggery.

At Turners' Hall the next day, having seen reports of the Dunn or

"Gatling gun" convention, in which he was the object of scurrility, Warmoth excoriated his enemies one by one in a long, impromptu, and self-revealing philippic as he stood between his crutches. He showed special bitterness in disposing of Charles W. Lowell:

> What has he done for the colored people of this State? What has Charles W. Lowell ever done for anybody but Charles W. Lowell? [Loud cheers.] He seems to be the peculiar champion of the black people. He goes further than Dunn, or Pinchback, or anybody else goes, but when it comes to something practical he is not there. [Cheers.] You would think from his speeches he would not have anything to do with a man not as black as the ace of spades, but when you go down to the post office what do you find? Every important office filled by a white man. Now I don't object to his appointing white men to office. I am a white man, and have all the sympathies of a white man in favor of his race. I believe I am not without some prejudices, but I mean to make them apply to white men or black men according to their virtues and the good they can do in the country without regard to race or color. [Cheers.] But I do not like to see a white man get so enthusiastic on the negro question in public, and perhaps in extreme privacy. [Laughter.] And yet when he comes before the world with his acts, he prefers miserable white trash to these colored men whom he takes into his arms in private or talks so loud about in public. [Cheers.]

After a while, growing even more sarcastic, Warmoth took up the case of James F. Casey in a manner that was not likely to win the favor of Casey's brother-in-law, President Grant:

> There is yet another one—the intelligent individual [laughter], that bright specimen of God's creation [renewed laughter] who goes lumbering around these streets from side to side like a great big boy just turned out of school, where he hadn't studied enough to learn his geography lesson [continued laughter], who makes it a *sine qua non* that everybody shall be for Grant, and if there is any doubt about his being for Grant, he considers him a Democrat, not entitled to any confidence, not entitled to any position in the customhouse, and not entitled to any rights at all. [Laughter and applause.] My friend Jim Casey is a clever fellow. He hasn't sense enough to be a bad fellow. [Laughter.] A man to be a bad fellow must have some character—he hasn't any. [Much laughter.]

The longer Warmoth stood, the worse the pain in his foot, yet he managed one more tongue-lashing before sitting down—one that was to provoke the victim to challenge him to a duel:

> I have expended a good deal of strength on these leading characters. [Laughter.] I won't attempt to disturb the small fry, for though not very numerous they smell very badly. [Laughter.] I don't want to take up John A. Walsh, who is the editor of the New Orleans *Patriot;* a man who denounces me because I would not sign the Civil Rights bill, although it was unconstitu-

> tional, and would have been inoperative—a man who attacks me because he says I am not in favor of mixed schools. When I asked him if he would send his children to a mixed school, he said no; he would not send them to any public school. This model Republican—this enlightened advocate of the mixed school system—deems his own children so much better than the balance of the children of this country that they ought to be educated in some monastery or private institution, where they would not come in contact with little dirty children, black or white.
>
> I won't tell you the reason that he is indignant with me now, nor how mad he became when Packard and that crowd sent him to me to offer me fifty thousand dollars cash if I would sign the Nicholson pavement bill. I refused and he made up his mind immediately that I was not for Grant! [Laughter and cheers.]

These remarks of Warmoth's were published at length in the *New Orleans Republican.*[15]

A couple of days later Warmoth received a note in which Packard asked him to retract the statement that Packard had sent Walsh to bribe him. "You know," Packard wrote, "there has never been any transaction between you and myself not strictly honorable." The day after that a letter came from Walsh, who said the reference to his children was "unkind, uncalled for and in every sense of the word unmanly and ungentlemanly." Considering Warmoth's physical condition, Walsh would "let the matter pass" for the present, but would demand satisfaction if Warmoth made any further references of the kind.

Walsh also published a "card" (in Southern lingo, a signed statement in a newspaper) in which he admitted offering Warmoth a $50,000 bribe and said Warmoth refused to accept less than $75,000. Then, issuing a card of his own, Warmoth denied having asked for a larger bribe than Walsh had offered. He insisted he had told Walsh that *"no pecuniary consideration whatever"* could induce him to sign the bill in question. "I assert Mr. Walsh's statement to be a willful and malicious falsehood."

This brought a quick response from Walsh. He noted that "differences of opinion, involving a question of veracity," had occurred, and using the euphemisms of the duello he invited Warmoth to send two friends "with the view of properly adjusting those differences." Warmoth pretended not to get the point. "In reply I have to say," he wrote, "that I am perfectly willing to submit the question of veracity between us to the determination of two respectable gentlemen to be selected by yourself and two chosen by me, a fifth to be selected by these four in case they cannot agree."

Walsh retorted that he could not permit his veracity to "be made the subject of arbitration." He insisted: " . . . an apology or retraction is absolutely necessary; or in the absence thereof such an adjustment as usually obtains among gentlemen."

"This means, I suppose, *apologize, retract* or *fight,"* Warmoth answered. He did not see how he could retract or apologize, since Walsh's allegation was in fact "a wilful & malicious falsehood." As for fighting, Walsh knew when he made the challenge that Warmoth could not accept it. "If I should accept it & go out with you to fight, when we returned, whether dead or alive, the question of veracity would still be unsettled," Warmoth now explained. "If you were to kill me it would not prove that I stated a falsehood or that you told the truth or *vice versa.*" Besides, dueling was illegal in the state. "As Chief Magistrate of this Great Commonwealth I am charged with the faithful execution of the laws."

"High tone is declining even in Louisiana," the *New York Tribune* commented. "A man can refuse to fight in that State, and if he does it neatly and cleverly, his neighbors still continue to recognize him."[16]

All this was exhilarating and in the end gratifying for Warmoth, but it hardly made up for the erosion of his relationship with Grant. While the *New York Tribune* approved of Warmoth, the *New York Times* condemned him and left the impression that he was ceasing to be loyal to the President or even to the party. "Overtures have passed between Warmoth and certain Democratic leaders," a *Times* correspondent reported from New Orleans. "Warmoth is to surrender the State to the Democracy, and he is to be re-elected Governor and then United States Senator." The writer said he did not know whether the President had authorized the use of troops at the customhouse convention. He was sure, though, that only their presence had prevented Warmoth—with the backing of the militia, the police, and a mob of "'plug uglies' and unwashed rebels"—from perpetrating a massacre like the one at the Mechanics' Institute in 1866!

"We are loth to believe that Grant has ordered United States bayonets to be pointed in a hostile manner toward a Republican State administration," Warmoth's *New Orleans Republican* editorialized. Grant had been led to believe that, with Warmoth in command, the party could not hold on to the Negro vote in Louisiana (though Pinchback and his black followers were remaining loyal to Warmoth). Warmoth was unaware of this, but he gained little reassurance when a delegation from the Turners' Hall convention returned after visiting Grant at his summer home in Long Branch, New Jersey. The delegates reported that Grant had given them a chilly reception. He told them he could not see what harm there was in having United States soldiers at a Republican gathering. He did not object to that, but he did resent some of the things that had been said about his brother-in-law, Collector Casey.

After getting this report, Warmoth could have no doubt that, by slurring Casey, he was further queering himself with Grant. Yet he now told a *Cincinnati Commercial* correspondent that Casey was an "ass" who had filled the customhouse with his Democratic relatives and who ought to be removed. At the same time Warmoth insisted he was not against Grant but would support him if he were nominated again.

Warmoth gained an advantage over his factional foes when, on November 21, Lieutenant-Governor Dunn suddenly died—poisoned, his friends said. Calling the senate into special session, Warmoth (now without crutches but with a slight limp) persuaded the majority to elect Pinchback as president pro tem, thus making him Dunn's successor in effect. But at the regular session in January 1872 the members of the customhouse faction were ready to unseat Pinchback and impeach Warmoth. Federal troops arrived and arrested Warmoth, Pinchback, and twenty-two pro-Warmoth legislators on charges of conspiring to obstruct state and federal laws. As soon as the men were freed on bail, Warmoth stealthily occupied the statehouse with his followers and ordered General Longstreet to call out the militia. Under Longstreet's command, 1,000 white and 1,000 black militiamen, 700 metropolitan police, and a battery of artillery took up positions near the Mechanics' Institute. The heavily outnumbered U.S. soldiers stood off. For the time being, Warmoth prevailed.

A congressional committee came to investigate the goings on, and Warmoth testified before it for three days. When he had finished, a committee member said to him: "We cannot determine whether you are an angel from Heaven or a devil from Hell." Warmoth liked that.[17]

Business boomed in Little Rock, Arkansas, during the years 1869-72. Even the *Arkansas Gazette*, hostile though it was to the Republican administration, joined in the booster spirit and applauded the capital's progress and improvement. New enterprises were constantly appearing—sawmills, foundries, brick kilns, banks, and stores of all kinds, not to mention peanut stands and bootblack stalls. The city's population grew to several times what it had been before the war. New houses and other buildings kept springing up, to the accompaniment of the sound of hammer and saw.

Some of the finest new houses stood on a high bluff overlooking the Arkansas River. Carpetbag officeholders owned and occupied several of them, and Democratic rivermen referred to the ridge as "Robbers' Roost." One of the mansions belonged to Governor Powell Clayton, for whom the state provided no official residence but only a housing allowance. The governor lived there with his wife, while his younger brother John M. Clayton, a Union veteran from Pennsylvania, looked after the governor's plantation below Pine Bluff.

"For the general satisfaction, peace, quiet, and prosperity that exist in our State, we are much indebted to the wise and considerate administration of Governor Clayton," one of his fellow Republicans wrote to the *New York Times*. "Even the rebel leaders are participating in the health and wealth-giving race of individual energy and enterprise that we Yankee 'carpet-baggers' have set before them."[18]

Certainly the economic development of Arkansas owed a great deal to Clayton. Prosperity was due largely to the railroad construction (and the anticipation of railroad construction) that he advocated as a means of bringing a "New Era" to the state. State aid to railroads was approved by the people in a referendum; Clayton was ready to issue state bonds to certain companies as soon as he could reestablish the state's credit and thus make the bonds marketable.

Arkansas suffered from a very low credit rating because it had failed to pay interest on some of its previously issued bonds. It had sold an 1840 issue of bonds to the American Trust and Banking Company, which illegally transferred them to the English bankers Holford and Company. The face value of these "Holford" bonds was $500,000, but their original, heavily discounted purchase price was only $121,336.59, and the state had refused to redeem them for a cent more. Now they could be exchanged for more than ten times as much in new bonds—for $1,370,000—if Clayton should follow the letter of the funding act of 1869, which provided for replacing old bonds with new at par plus accumulated interest.

Clayton faced a dilemma. If, on the one hand, he were to include the Holford bonds in the refunding, he would antagonize citizens who did not want to be taxed to pay what they considered a fraudulent claim. If, on the other hand, he were to exclude the Holford bonds, he would not only violate the law but also leave the state's credit impaired, as Holford's Democratic lobbyists and the Democratic *Arkansas Gazette* insistently pointed out. After thinking over the alternatives, he decided to fund the Holford bonds in exactly the same way as all the rest. Then he went to New York City to supervise the funding.

As chairman of the board of railroad commissioners, Clayton could veto state aid to any applicant. Some forty companies aspired to build railroads; he and his fellow commissioners granted assistance to only six. Rejected applicants accused him of favoritism, but only two of the six railroads receiving aid belonged to political friends of his. He had a personal interest in one of the two—the Little Rock, Pine Bluff and New Orleans, which would run across his plantation on land he donated to the company. He was careful to see that no company received state bonds until it had qualified for them by constructing a roadbed and preparing it for rails.

At the time Clayton became governor, there were in all of Arkansas only forty-five miles of track, running east from Little Rock about a third of the way to Memphis. When he left the governorship, in 1871, he could boast that this line had been completed and, all together, nearly two hundred miles of new track laid. The trip from Little Rock to Memphis used to take as much as six days by riverboat; it now took about twelve hours by railroad train. Even the Democrats rejoiced. "In spite of the ignorance and corruption of the despotic regime of Clayton," one Democratic editor said, "Arkansas makes most rapid prograss in railroad construction."

Clayton could also claim that under his regime there had been a great advance in public education. Between 1869 and 1870 the number of children attending the (segregated) schools, he reported to the legislature, rose from 67,412 to 107,906, while the number of school-age children increased only from 176,910 to 180,274. That is to say, the enrollment rate improved from 38 percent to 60 percent in just one year.

Regarding the financial condition of the state, Clayton had less to brag about. True, the state's credit was much better when he left office than when he took it, but both taxation and indebtedness were considerably higher. Clayton had tried to maintain the price of bonds by holding them back until there was revenue enough for servicing them. Still, he could not avoid issuing scrip for revenue in advance of taxes—scrip that tax collectors then bought at a discount and turned in instead of cash—nor could he avoid selling bonds at a large discount. He put much of the blame on the Democrats, who he said did their worst to ruin the state's credit by trying to destroy confidence in him and his administration.[19]

Troublesome though the Democrats were, they constituted less of a political hazard to Clayton than did some of his fellow Republicans. The Democrats had attracted comparatively few voters even among whites. In Arkansas as a whole, whites outnumbered blacks by four to one. In some of the lowland counties blacks made up a majority—65 percent in Jefferson County, where Clayton's plantation was located—but in the highland counties of the west and north the black percentage ran as low as one or less. According to the reconstructed constitution, men could not vote if they had ever taken an oath of loyalty to the United States and then had violated that oath by supporting the Confederacy. Though this provision disqualified several thousand, the white voters greatly outnumbered the black in 1868. Nevertheless, the Republicans elected 103 and the Democrats only two members of the first legislature in the reconstructed state.

From the outset the Republicans were divided between the followers of Governor Clayton and those of Lieutenant-Governor Johnson, a native white. Soon the anti-Clayton Republicans, mostly scalawags, got control of the lower house. In April 1869 they caucused to denounce Clayton for his "bad management" and his "unwise administration" and to discuss the prospects for leaving the Clayton party and combining with the Democrats.

That summer, when Clayton went to New York to arrange for funding the debt, the Johnson men plotted a coup d'etat. While starting a rumor that Clayton had absconded with the state's money, two messengers made their way to the northwestern corner of the state where Johnson, unaware of Clayton's absence, was passing the time quietly at home. He readily agreed to occupy and hold the governor's ofice on the pretext that Clayton had abandoned it. But the trip up the Arkansas River and into the Ozark hills, then down again, was difficult and slow. Clayton, having received a warning telegram, was back in Little Rock before Johnson got there.

Johnson and his followers had to content themselves with an anti-Clayton rally. Speaking from a balcony to a serenading crowd in front of the Anthony House—where Clayton himself had addressed the multitudes on previous occasions—Johnson accused him and his associates of filling their own pockets with railroad aid money. A voice in the crowd: "Fill up their carpet bags!" Johnson: "A carpet bag will not hold it—it will take a goods box." He went on to urge removing the political disabilities from "the down-trodden people of Arkansas" and thus appealing to the Democrats. But they need not call themselves Democrats. "If we organize another party, it will not be necessary to give it another name than anti-Clayton, anti-radical, and we will be sure to win."[20]

The Clayton men retaliated by asking the state supreme court for a writ of *quo warranto,* which would compel Johnson to prove his right to the lieutenant-governorship, a right they now questioned on a technicality. Before the court could hear the case, the Johnsonites held a convention, organized what they termed the Liberal Republican party, and adopted a platform demanding universal amnesty, universal suffrage, governmental economy, and an end to "one man rule." That was on October 14, 1869.

The very next night Clayton made a dramatic counter-move. Having arranged for a group to serenade him in front of the capitol, he responded with a speech in which he offered his own concessions to the Democrats. He now advocated cutting expenditures, lowering taxes, and restoring full political rights to former rebels. Of course, he cautioned, it would take time to eliminate the disfranchisement clause from the constitution, for the legislature would have to pass an amendment twice and then the people would have to ratify it. But if the existing peace and quiet should continue, he pledged, he would recommend the change to the next session of the legislature.

This speech was a bombshell. As reflected in the party presses, the Democrats at first expressed amazement and then adopted a wait-and-see attitude. The Liberal Republicans (who actually were conservative Republicans) showed some embarrassment at Clayton's having pulled the rug out from under them. They could only assert that he was muddling the issues and misleading the public. The extreme radicals accused him of having sold out to the Democrats.

Clayton heard this charge from an old friend when, on the morning after the speech, he met Robert F. Catterson at the entrance to the governor's office. Formerly a Union general, now a United States marshal, Catterson had given outstanding service as a commander of Clayton's militia in the recent war against the Klan. When he accused Clayton of conspiring with the Democrats, Clayton called him a liar, and Catterson retorted that Clayton was a damned liar. Instantaneously Clayton slapped him on the cheek with his right hand, the only hand he had. Catterson, saying he would not strike a one-armed man, simply walked away. Clayton was left to regret his quick temper. He had lost not only a close friend but also a powerful ally.[21]

By mid-1870 the Arkansas Republican party had broken into three bickering and seemingly irreconcilable factions. The largest consisted of Clayton's followers, the regular Republicans, who were coming to be known as "Minstrels." Next in numbers were the radicals or "Brindletails," whose leader was Joseph Brooks, a minister of the gospel from Iowa. Fewest were the so-called Liberal Republicans, the followers of Lieutenant-Governor Johnson. The three factions vied for the support of Democrats, who could not yet hope to carry the state on their own and who therefore sought the best terms they could get from each of the Republican groups.

At the start of the fall campaign for legislators and congressmen, Clayton announced that he hoped the next legislature would elect him to the U.S. Senate. His candidacy became a campaign issue. As he electioneered, he had the advantages of the Grant Administration's backing, his own control of state patronage, including the appointment of election officials, and the power of his dominant (his opponents said "domineering") personality. His campaigning intensified the factional bitterness in his party but resulted in the election of more friendly than hostile Republicans to the legislature.

The Democrats were willing to see Clayton go off to the Senate, for they expected to control Johnson, who presumably would succeed him in the governorship. On January 10, 1871, the legislature almost unanimously chose Clayton as U.S. senator. But he was determined that Johnson should not succeed him, and he refused to leave the governorship until he had made sure that Johnson would not succeed him. He renewed the *quo warranto* proceedings that he had discontinued.

In reply, the anti-Clayton men mustered enough votes to impeach and suspend Clayton, but the impeachment managers soon confessed they could find no evidence against him, and they dropped the case. Then Johnson agreed to a compromise: he would resign as lieutenant governor and accept appointment as secretary of state. The duties of the lieutenant governor would fall to the senate president, a carpetbagger on Clayton's side. Again the legislature elected Clayton to the Senate, this time by a narrower vote (60 to 40), and he soon left for Washington.[22]

His Republican foes were not ready to give up. Through the efforts of U.S. Marshal Catterson, U.S. District Attorney William G. Whipple, and Brindletails on a federal grand jury, he was indicted on a charge of falsely certifying the election of a Democrat to Congress. There was no basis for the charge—except a desire to harass Clayton—and the case was shortly dismissed. Clayton got his revenge by persuading Grant to remove Catterson, Whipple, and other Brindletails holding federal office.

Once more the Brindletails attacked, challenging Clayton's fitness for a Senate seat, They enlisted Francis P. Blair, the Missouri Democrat on the Ku Klux investigating committee, and Blair made a one-sided report to the Senate. Clayton demanded and obtained a complete investigation. Eventually he was exonerated, as he knew he would be.

Once admitted to the Senate, Clayton joined a circle of poker-playing cronies that included the speaker of the House of Representatives, James G. Blaine, who shared with him an interest in Arkansas railroads. Blaine became very fond of him. "He is a man of character," Blaine was to write, "—quiet and undemonstrative in manner, but with extraordinary qualities of firmness and endurance."[23]

CHAPTER 13

Guttersnipes from the North (1872)

The reputation of carpetbaggers suffered from presidential politics in 1872. Opponents of U. S. Grant attacked him by attacking them. His opponents now included not only Democrats but also dissident Republicans, who referred to themselves as Liberals. The Liberal Republicans nominated the famous editor of the *New York Tribune,* Horace Greeley, as their candidate to unseat Grant, and the Democrats seconded the nomination. Greeley's adherents made up a miscellaneous lot: former Radicals and former rebels, free-traders and high-tariffites, civil-service reformers and disappointed spoilsmen. All of them could agree on one thing: Grant was to blame for the horrors of Reconstruction, and those horrors consisted in the activities of the carpetbaggers (not in those of the Ku Klux Klan). Hence the carpetbagger served as a whipping boy for Liberal Republicans as well as Democrats.

Greeley had set the theme when, in 1871, he returned to New York from a tour of the South. In a widely published speech he declared:

> The thieving carpet-baggers are a mournful fact; they do exist there, and I have seen them. They are fellows who crawled down South in the track of our armies, generally at a very safe distance in the rear; some of them in sutler's wagons; some bearing cotton permits; some of them looking sharply to see what might turn up; and they remained there. They at once ingratiated themselves with the blacks, simple, credulous, ignorant men, very glad to welcome and to follow any whites who professed to be the champions of their rights. Some of them got elected Senators, others Representatives, some Sheriffs, some Judges, and so on. And there they stand, right in the public eye, stealing and plundering, many of them with both arms around negroes, and their hands in their rear pockets, seeing if they cannot pick a paltry dollar out of them. . . . What the Southern people see of us are these thieves, who represent the North to their jaundiced vision, and, represent-

ing it, they disgrace it. *They are the greatest obstacle to the triumph and permanent ascendancy of Republican principles at the South, and as such I denounce them.*

During the 1872 campaign the *Chicago Tribune*, second only to the *New York Tribune* as a Liberal Republican newspaper, reprinted the Greeley speech and editorialized: "The great point in this campaign is, Shall the President maintain and perpetuate these adventurers, or shall the people be free to elect their own Governments?" When the *Nation* objected that the President could not remove the carpetbaggers, since they held their positions by virtue of the state legislatures and the popular vote, the *Chicago Tribune* replied that presidential patronage had fastened the carpetbag regimes upon the South. "It was the official patronage which gave Clayton in Arkansas, Casey in Louisiana, Spencer in Alabama, Scott in South Carolina, and Perry [!] in North Carolina, their power for mischief."

The Liberal Republicans were rewriting history with little regard for fact. Or, rather, they were endorsing and elaborating upon the interpretation of postwar events that Democrats in the North as well as the South had already put forth. Democrats and Liberal Republicans now cast upon carpetbaggers the aspersions that Democrats formerly had thrown at Republicans in general.

According to the Greeley partisans' version of the recent past, the carpetbaggers were responsible for disturbing what, without their presence, would have been ideal race relations in the South. "At the close of the war, the North Carolinians stood ready to accept the result," a Greeleyite reported from Raleigh. "Good order prevailed, and it was not until the Union Leagues were formed, and the negroes, ignorant and liable to tumult, were inflamed to acts of passion and incendiarism, that counter-demonstrations of violence followed, and many acts of crime were perpetrated. But for the presence of the foreign adventurers, now well known to the country as carpet-baggers, it is doubtful whether there would have been any turbulence or conflict of races in North Carolina."

In their campaign propaganda the Liberal Republicans appealed to racism in a way only slightly more subtle than the Democrats had been doing for some time. There is a question, the *Chicago Tribune* said, "whether the political power wielded by the negro element in the South is not a serious menace to Republican institutions." It was not a question of the right of black men to vote, but of the wisdom of allowing the black vote to be "managed by designing men, bent upon public plunder." Responsibility lay with the Republicans who had brought about Radical Reconstruction in the first place. Now "it becomes those in the North who have invested these negroes with such dangerous powers to put them under better influences, and this can only be done by turning out the carpet-bag tribe."

While making carpetbaggers the villains, Greeley campaigners made ex-rebels the heroes of the Southern melodrama. The alien adventurers had brought ruin, but the respectable native whites were looking to Greeley's election for the region's recovery, one journalist wrote. "Such are the conditions and aspirations of the South after eight years of piratical rule [actually, Radical Reconstruction had been in effect for only five years]—all dignity, emulation, and hope being taken from people of character and property there, in order that a set of guttersnipes from the North shall riot under the protection of the American flag."[1]

Grant Republicans denied that the President himself was to blame for carpetbag misgovernment, but none of the leaders stepped forward to defend carpetbaggers as a class. The most the pro-Grant *New York Times* could say for them was that they were not much worse than Democrats. "Though the earliest, and some of the worst, corruptionists in the South were Republicans, that was owing to the peculiar constitution of the voting population, which made it impossible for Southern Democrats to make much headway, and gave the offices in the main to professed Republicans, most of whom, of white complexion, were Northern born." So the *Times* explained. "But the Republican corruptionists from the North found ready and skillful partners in the South, and in some of the blackest chapters of the recent humiliating history of the Southern States, the names of native Democrats occur with unpleasant frequency."

The defense of carpetbaggers as a class was left to an obscure author, the Georgia-born Republican Albert Griffin, writing in an obscure periodical, the *Kansas Magazine* of Topeka. "If we were to take the New York and Chicago *Tribunes* of to-day as authority," Griffin observed, "we would believe that most of those holding office in the reconstructed States are Northern men, utterly devoid of honor and honesty, and that the State governments have been brought by them so near financial ruin that they can only be saved by restoring the ex-Rebels to power." In fact, Griffin pointed out, the great majority of Republican officeholders in the South were natives or old residents, nearly all of them "men of good character." As for the financial condition of the reconstructed states, their "real indebtedness" had been grossly exaggerated.

Greeley's followers argued that improvement could come only from letting the "Southern people control their own governments," Griffin continued. But the Southern people had always controlled them.

> The negroes are Southern people—natives, mostly—and even the so-called carpet-baggers are as much entitled to be considered a part of the people as are a majority of the inhabitants of this State [Kansas] to be called Kansans, or Carl Schurz [a leading Liberal, born in Germany, formerly a Wisconsinite] a Missourian. It seems strange indeed to hear recent settlers in the West quietly assume that those who have gone South since the war are not a part of the people where they reside, and have no political rights, except to pay taxes and vote for those who despise and revile them. But it is stranger still to try to realize that Horace Greeley, Theodore Tilton, and others with like record, in looking South for "the people," can now see none but ex-Rebels and their allies; that in their eyes the colored men they have pleaded

> for so eloquently, and the union soldiers they have so often, so justly and so highly praised, have suddenly become nobodys merely because the Republican party refused to be dictated to by a cabal of malcontents respecting the renomination of President Grant.

Only a small proportion of Republicans in the South, Griffin insisted, were corrupt. "Nineteen-twentieths of those who are denounced as thieving carpet-baggers and scallawags [*sic*] are upright men, and known to be such by those who malign them." But the Greeley backers did not distinguish between the good and the bad. Indeed, they were collaborating with "the most infamous of all carpet-baggers, but now a white-washed Liberal'"—Henry Clay Warmoth.[2]

Warmoth was not the only prominent carpetbagger to join the Liberal ranks. The party split heightened tensions among blacks and scalawags as well as carpetbaggers and further demoralized state organizations that were already fragmenting as a result of differences within and between the three constituent groups. Not only blacks but also whites of old antislavery principle faced a dilemma in choosing between Grant, their protector against the Klan, and his opponents, who included the greatest of living Radicals, Charles Sumner.

Southern Republicans encountered another new disadvantage in the campaign of 1872. Hitherto most of the ex-Confederate leaders had been allowed to vote, by virtue of state laws, but not to hold office, because of the Fourteenth Amendment ban. Some carpetbaggers turned to advocating the removal of this ban, while others continued to insist on retaining it. By acts of 1871 and 1872 Congress lifted it with respect to all but a handful of former rebels. Practically all could now return to full participation in politics.

In the election the Greeleyites did not come close to defeating Grant. In the course of trying to do so, however, they helped to fix the reputation of carpetbaggers as villains of the most despicable sort. Years after the 1872 election the man who then had been the *Chicago Tribune* editor, Horace White, privately conceded that the "sins" of the carpetbaggers and the blacks had been "much magnified and lied about."[3] But he never said so publicly, and later historians were left to infer that, when Republicans and Democrats agreed with regard to the carpetbagger, what they said about him must be true.

Readers of the *Chicago Tribune* got a grotesquely distorted view of politics in Arkansas, as indeed readers of this and other Liberal Republican and Democratic papers did of politics in all the Southern states. Visiting Arkansas in the summer of 1872, to report for the *Tribune,* was the budding poet and novelist as well as veteran war correspondent George Alfred Townsend, who often signed his articles "Gath." Townsend deprecated most of what he saw and heard on the trip.

The train, Townsend noted, took twelve hours and a quarter to cover the 134 miles from Memphis to Little Rock. For the first forty-one miles, crossing the Mississippi bottom land, the train crept along at seven miles an hour with a continual "squeaking of screws and bolts and wail of rolling stock." At Brinkley it stopped for passengers to get off and eat their midday meal, which included something resembling "boiled cotton stalk" (apparently okra). After "passing over mile upon mile of trestle-work," the train at dusk reached the station opposite Little Rock. There the passengers boarded a horse-drawn omnibus, which crossed the Arkansas River on a steam ferry and climbed a hill on the other side "in the midst of clouds of dust."

Little Rock struck Townsend as an up-and-coming place, one that had recently boomed to a population of 20,000 and could boast of many beautiful houses and such modern improvements as gas lights. Still, he doubted whether the city's future growth would be as great as its boosters predicted, and he was sure the resources of the state as a whole were far less than they claimed. What was worse, most of the people seemed to lack the refinements of civilization. "The domesticated carpet baggers have learned the Southern habits, carry their side-arms to the dinner table, and out-Herod the natives in desperation." Obviously, "since the war we have grown no closer to these Southwestern people than before, but have simply barbarized, so to speak, our Northern population which has ventured amongst them." The worst of the lot was Powell Clayton, "as reckless a man as John A. Murrell." (Murrell was the notorious and murderous leader of an antebellum gang of slave-stealers and horse-thieves.)

Townsend did not interview Clayton but did talk with such "old citizens" as John D. Adams, a proprietor of the Democratic *Arkansas Gazette*. From the conversations Townsend had, he drew the inference that Clayton and Grant were partners in a criminal conspiracy, and he elaborated on the theme in an account that the *Chicago Tribune* printed under the headlines "Operations of Clayton and His Myrmidons—The President's Bargain with the Corruptionists." According to this account, when Clayton had "accomplished his wicked and unhallowed design—that of forcing himself into the Senate of the United States," he turned to Grant for help. He promised that, "if the President would become his friend and protector," he would work for the President's reelection. Grant obligingly "removed United States officers who had commenced to prosecute Clayton" and then replaced them with men "suggested by Clayton and his associates in crime."[4]

It was true that after Clayton's election to the Senate his factional foes accused him of falsifying returns in a congressional race. It was also true that Grant removed two federal officials who had been pressing the case against Clayton. In doing so, however, Grant had not interfered with the course of justice; there was no valid evidence against Clayton in the first place. The contest between him and his political enemies was not one between the wicked and the righteous. It was one between the ambitious on both sides.

True it certainly was that Grant and Clayton were cooperating, though only on the basis of mutual interest and not on the basis of some corrupt bargain. Clayton's Senate colleague Benjamin F. Rice, a former Union army captain from New York, had defected to Greeley. Clayton led the Arkansas delegation to the Philadelphia convention that nominated Grant. Thereafter Clayton was, in his own words, "solid with the Administration and with the Republican United States Senators." He now had complete control of federal patronage in Arkansas. He became chairman of the Republican state central committee and a member of the Republican national committee, to remain a member for nearly all the rest of his life.

The anti-Clayton Republicans, the Brindletails, had little choice but to go for Greeley, anomalous though he was as a candidate with whom to appeal to Democrats. The Brindletails' candidate for governor, Joseph Brooks, was just as anomalous, having come from Iowa as a Methodist minister and army chaplain and having been a friend and follower of Clayton's, one who during the Ku Klux terror had survived the shotgun blast that killed Congressman James Hinds. Though the Arkansas Democrats had given Brooks their nomination too, few of them could muster much enthusiasm for him. Most of them sneered at him as the "Carpet-Bag Cardinal" and distrusted him as lately the most extreme Radical in the state.

It occurred to Clayton that, by nominating someone acceptable to Democrats, the regular Republicans might attract a number of them. He had in mind Elisha Baxter, whom he had appointed to a state circuit judgeship. A wartime Unionist, Baxter could not boast a record of Confederate service, but he was a former slaveowner and a Southerner by birth, a native of North Carolina. As compared with Brooks, he ought to seem to Democrats the lesser of evils.

When the Republican convention met in the statehouse in August, Clayton was ready with a plan of action. After calling the convention to order, he allowed delegates black and white to use up the afternoon with oratory, lauding Grant and Clayton, condemning Greeley and Brooks. At the evening session, the convention having turned to choosing a gubernatorial candidate, Clayton announced that he was authorized to withdraw the name of the incumbent governor. A Clayton confidant did the same with respect to another contender, and a third withdrew his own name. Then the convention nominated Baxter by acclamation.

By the time Baxter began his campaign, Brooks had already been stumping for several weeks, and Clayton had been meeting him in debate. The two had a rather dramatic encounter, before the end of June, at Lewisburg on the Arkansas River about fifty miles above Little Rock.

Lewisburg was a decaying town, with a "tumble-down worm fence" along the road and no building more imposing than an "old, weather-beaten, two-story jail." Gullies ran down to the muddy river, and beyond it cotton fields stretched away to a distant blue ridge, the Petit Jean Mountain. Here in Lewisburg, less than three years earlier, Clayton's militia had executed a popular leader of the Ku Klux Klan. The motley crowd, now awaiting the performance in a grove on the edge of town, included both ex-Klansmen and ex-militiamen who remembered all too well the recent militia war.

Brooks stepped up on the wooden stand to make the first speech. He had the sallow look and irritable manner of a dyspeptic, and he proceeded to arraign his adversaries like a Methodist minister dealing with sinners. After charging the Clayton administration with corruption and fraud, he promised to cleanse the state government and introduce the reforms that Liberal Republicans advocated, in particular the reduction of taxes and the removal of political disabilities from former Confederates. His motto, he said, was the same as Greeley's: "Honest men for office, thieves to the rear!" Both he and Greeley, he added, were proud of their long service in the cause of Negro rights.

While Brooks was speaking, Clayton watched him intently, and when his own turn came he undertook to present a reasoned and dignified reply. He began by comparing the party platforms, then apologized for his Democratic background, a topic on which he was sensitive, since his opponents often accused him of having been proslavery and pro-secession. "I was accustomed to labor from my boyhood in the eighty-two acre farm of my father, who raised a family of ten children," he said. "I am here to defend that party which made labor honorable and rendered it possible for the colored man to enjoy the fruits of his honest toil. My father never voted the Democratic ticket. But I thought I was wiser than he, and when I came of age I acted with the Democracy for a time."

At this point a heckler interrupted to ask: "How about that secession cockade?" Quickly abandoning his dignified pose. Clayton retorted:

> The man that said that is a liar! The man who says I ever wore a secession cockade, or any other kind of cockade, is an unmitigated, infamous, damnable liar! I have heard that before and other lies about my being a "border ruffian," and sending colored men back into slavery from Kansas. They are all infamous lies.

Recovering his aplomb, Clayton pointed out that *he* had proposed eliminating political disabilities and cutting state expenditures long before Brooks ever thought of doing so. Clayton then turned the tables on Brooks and his associates by accusing *them* of "robbery and peculation" and of being "thieves and scoundrels, reeking with corruption!" He concluded: "They are a nice set of fellows to talk of 'honest men for office, and thieves to the rear!'"

Even the Democrats admired Clayton for his gameness and pluck, and many of them cheered him when he finished. But the blacks remained silent. They seemed perplexed at hearing the two Republican leaders accuse one another of crimes.

When Brooks and Clayton appeared together at Van Buren in August, Brooks was accompanied by the Liberal candidate for congressman-at-large, an Irishman named Hynes, who displayed side whiskers and a receding chin and who wore a seersucker jacket, a white tie, and a high silk hat. After Brooks and Clayton had spoken, Hynes excoriated Clayton and his "myrmidons." Sitting in an open carriage, Clayton listened calmly until Hynes referred to the "secession cockade." Clayton immediately sprang from the carriage and rushed to the speakers' stand. Hynes jumped from the rear of the platform, ran off, and stayed away until Brooks brought him back, bareheaded and panting. While Hynes adjusted his tie and wiped his hat with his handkerchief, Clayton disposed of him as the "henchman of as scurvy a set of knaves as ever eluded the State's prison."

After the nomination of Baxter, he and Clayton traveled about in the same buggy, to meet Brooks and Hynes at various stops. In the course of the campaigning Clayton began to be suspicious of Baxter. "He worked with me during the day and at night he was having secret conferences with the Democrats," Clayton was to recall. "It then dawned on me that we had made a bad political deal." The regular Republicans would be the losers, he feared, whether Baxter won or lost. Their victory was indeed to prove a Pyrrhic one, and before long Clayton was to be opposing Baxter and, once again, supporting Brooks.[5]

A brass band in the gallery played "Shoo Fly," "Dixie," and other popular numbers while black and white delegates crowded the floor of the South Carolina senate chamber amid the August heat. The main business of this convention was to nominate a Republican for governor.

Robert K. Scott, the incumbent, was declining to seek a second term, preferring to take his chances on election to the United States Senate. The preconvention favorites for the governorship were Franklin J. Moses, Jr., and John L. Neagle, both of them scalawags. "Great God!" exclaimed the Columbia and Charlotte Railroad president, another scalawag. "If either of those men should be elected, the whole State will be given over to pillage, like a city taken by storm. It would be far better to have Scott for governor, even if everything that has been said about him were true."

Moses saw his name placed before the convention, but Neagle did not choose to run. Instead, he proposed Daniel H. Chamberlain as the candidate who could best hold the party together. Carpetbag Senator Frederick A. Sawyer had brought word from Washington that Grant favored Chamberlain on the ground that Moses, if nominated, would disrupt the party. But Robert B. Elliott, the black leader chairing the convention, stepped down from the podium to speak in Moses's behalf. He denied that Chamberlain's nomination would have a harmonizing effect, and he intimated that Chamberlain was attempting to bribe delegates. The majority of them went for Moses.

Moses's nomination certainly split the party, whether or not Chamberlain's would have done so. James L. Orr, ex-Confederate and ex-governor, led a group of bolters, including a number of blacks, who held a separate convention. But Chamberlain refused to join them, for he could see no future in going for Greeley and alienating Grant. Better to stay with the regular Republicans even if it meant waiting two years for another chance at the governorship. Meanwhile he would campaign loyally for Moses and the rest of the regular ticket.

So would Scott. If he could make no eloquent speeches, he could at least appear at barbecues to shake hands and chat. "You are the same good friend to the colored man now," a follower reminded him, "that you were years ago when you had charge of the Freedman's Bureau." He could also use his patronage powers in the interests of the ticket, especially his power of appointing constables, ostensibly to keep the peace at election time. He was advised to appoint, as constables, "representative republicans of great personal influence and active organizers."[6]

Scott figured as the worst of a gang of corruptionists in the campaign propaganda of the *Chicago Tribune* and the *New York Tribune*. According to the Chicago paper, "the corner which the carpet-baggers had on the public funds" of South Carolina was coming to an end, as the thieves "commenced quarreling over the plunder." The governor was fighting with some of his associates, and charges and countercharges were flying, but one thing stood out clearly enough: the financial board, of which he was head, had "put upon the market nearly $7,000,000 in fraudulent bonds."

That kind of scurrility Scott was used to, and he could find nothing actionable in it. The case was different with the personal attack that appeared in the *New York Tribune*. This article accused Scott not only "of leading the State officers in thefts from the State" but also "of having acquired a fortune of $2,000,000, all of which he had stolen from the State, and of being paid large sums for approving bills passed by the Legislature." In response, Scott prepared to sue Greeley and his *Tribune* for libel, seeking damages of $100,000. He explained in a statement the *New York Times* published:

> I have no vindictive motive in this matter, but simply desire to invoke the decision of the Court upon the question whether a public journalist is autho-

> rized to pass sentence of outlawry against the character of a citizen . . . without being held responsible in law. I invoke the most searching examination into my conduct, and prepare to subject my acts to the most severe legal tests.

As Scott's attorney, the scalawag state judge T. J. Mackey left for New York to institute both civil and criminal proceedings in the federal district court. There Mackey enlisted George Bliss, Jr., as associate counsel. Bliss, he informed Scott, was "eminent as a jurist," was "the leading member of the Republican Executive Committee of the State of New York," and was "in the most intimate personal relations with President Grant." Such an eminent jurist would hardly have considered taking the case, except for a fee several times as large as he was asking, had it not been for his "personal and political feeling in the matter."

Mackey and Bliss promptly started the civil suit, about a month before election day, and expected the case to come up around the second Monday in December. The attorneys decided to wait until after the election to institute criminal proceedings. They did so on the advice of the prominent New York Republican politicians Alonzo B. Cornell and Thurlow Weed, who thought that "to arrest Greeley & Co. now might create a reaction in his favor, as it would look like an attempt to suppress the candidate." But Greeley died on November 29, just a few weeks after his devastating defeat. To Scott, there no longer seemed to be any point in going ahead with either the civil or the criminal prosecution.

If either suit had ever come to trial, his lawyers could have presented a cogent brief in behalf of Scott. Attorneys for the defense would have had a hard time demonstrating that he ever stole a penny from the state of South Carolina or that he ever accepted a cent in bribes for signing bills. In fact, he was doing his best to put a stop to thievery and bribery. He believed the recent "Revenue Bond Scrip" act was unconstitutional, but he could not stop this kind of bribe-assisted legislation with his veto, for the apparently bought majorities were large enough to repass vetoed bills. So, at his own expense, he engaged a Columbia law firm to look into the possibilities of legal action. He told the firm's senior partner that "if it became necessary the Bond Scrip case must be taken to the Supreme Court of the United States." He also hoped to prosecute the state treasurer, Niles G. Parker, but he was unable to find any of the legal remedies he sought.[7]

After the regular Republicans had won at the polls, electing a large majority to the legislature, Scott could hope that the legislature would send him to the United States Senate. He heard from one of his black friends: "I feel that for you victory is easy and certain." But Scott did not view it as either certain or easy. He would need to use his persuasive powers on the legislators, and to facilitate this he rented for his campaign headquarters a backyard cottage near the capitol. It seemed reasonable to expect that he could at least count on the votes of those who had not repaid his earlier loans.

Scott was not generally considered the front-runner. Elliott was. According to the reporter Townsend ("Gath"), Elliott had early put other contenders *hors de combat.* This congressman and senator-to-be was, as Townsend described him, a "full-blooded negro," "educated, low, and clever," who had "carpet-bagged it" from Massachusetts to South Carolina. "He affects to despise white men, and to covet a Government where only the black shall have offices and honors," Townsend reported. "Some think he is the ablest negro, intellectually, in the South."

There was a third man in the race—John J. Patterson, the Pennsylvanian whom Scott a few years previously had invited to South Carolina to build the Blue Ridge railroad and who now, as president of the Blue Ridge company, was facing a stockholders' lawsuit for misuse of the company's funds. Patterson was conducting his campaign from a plush suite where he and his manager, H. C. Worthington, plied members of the legislature with cigars, drinks, cash, and promises of more cash. One black member told Worthington he was pledged to Scott, who had lent him $175. Overhearing, Patterson said he would pay off the debt if the man would switch to him.

Scott later received from Patterson repayment of the $175 note. That was small compensation for the loss of the vote, and still less for the loss of the senatorial election. On the first ballot Patterson got only a plurality. Then one of the chief backers of Scott, the man who had nominated him, deserted to Patterson, and Patterson gained a narrow majority. He was said to have offered $1,000 for the deciding vote.

A couple of hours later Patterson was arrested for bribery but was promptly freed on a writ of habeas corpus from Scott's friend and attorney Judge Mackey (and was never to be tried). Patterson then joined a victory celebration, where Governor-elect Moses and his defeated opponent Chamberlain, along with other politicians, carried him on their shoulders and sang "When Johnny Comes Marching Home Again."

Elliott was not there and neither was Scott. With the expiration of his gubernatorial term, Scott left public office for good. He and his family remained in Columbia, though moving out of the governor's residence. Citizens seeking official favors—whether lucrative jobs or only a few goldfish from the governor's pond—could no longer look to him.[8]

As late as June, when the Republican convention met in Philadelphia, Willard Warner had not yet made up his mind to come out for Greeley. For some time he had found himself agreeing more and more with him and becoming increasingly disgusted with Grant. In August 1871 he congratulated Greeley for exposing the carpetbagger thieves and scoundrels in the South, and Greeley responded: "It was necessary that *someone* should speak out or the thieves would have ruined us."

Warner was thinking particularly of Senator George E. Spencer, who was about to ruin *him*. Spencer was keeping the Senate from confirming Warner's appointment as collector of the port of Mobile—thus leaving Grant with little choice except to withdraw the appointment, as he finally did in January 1872. Warner was left in a dilemma. Bitter though he felt toward both the Republican President and the Republican Senate, he could not easily pull himself away from the Republican party. And he received conflicting advice from his friends.

While still in Mobile, Warner heard from Jacob D. Cox, of Cincinnati, who was now even more decidedly anti-Grant than he had been when he quit the Grant cabinet. "I long since made up my mind that professions of friendship made by Grant were of no real meaning or value, & that the slightest supposed interest on his part is sufficient to make him sacrifice the friends to whom he has avowed the warmest attachment." So Warner read in the letter from Cox. "He perfectly knows you & he knows Spencer, & he cannot but respect you & despise him, but he thinks Spencer can be of use to him, & does not hesitate to throw you over in behalf of a man of no character or principle." Warner must face up to "the question whether the good men of the reconstructed States will not necessarily unite with the Liberal Republican movement."[9]

From Senator John Sherman, however, came a note of concern that Warner might break with Grant and line up with the disaffected Liberals. He must not, Sherman counseled, let himself be guided by the feelings of the moment, by personal irritation or pique. Certainly he must not, as he had hinted he might, propose Sherman as the alternative to Grant. Warner replied to Sherman:

> I hope you do not think me foolish enough to use your name as a candidate for President without your consent and knowledge nor without large organization for success and . . . considerations of the fitting time.
>
> You fear that I intend to make a breach between myself and Gen. Grant. I do not know that I will do any such thing, but permit me to say in cool sincerity that I do not fear to oppose Gen. Grant nor shall I hesitate on account of any possible consequences to me personally, when I am convinced that he is but a political trader, intent on nothing so much as his own re-election and mischievously using the power of his office to that low end. . . . That his nomination would be much weaker than several that might be made, I have not a doubt. The people demand and *will* have, before long, a *higher tone* in politics and government than now prevails, either at the White House or in the Senate. There is little moral virtue at either end of the Avenue. . . .
>
> Do not fear that I shall make any blunders because of personal "irritation." The danger rather is that the embarrassment of my personal wrong may keep me silent when I ought to speak. I shall try to act from conscience and judgement in the future as in the past, and to be able to give a valid

> reason for what I may do. I have never yet made a political mistake, though I have generally been in advance of my party. Of course, I feel keenly the cool slight of Grant, but not much more than I do the action of the Senate in permitting my nomination to be held in Committee for six weeks to the end that a known and infamous scoundrel might have full opportunity to do just what he did do. I am mortified to think that I was mistaken in believing that I had, by honest well doing, made a character in the Senate that would protect me against such treatment. As in battle few care to be first in mounting the enemy's works, so Senators did not want to be conspicuous in antagonizing Spencer lest he might sometime in a pinch vote against them. The country is ringing with just charges of incompetency and corruption in the Republican Party, South. I have made a bold fight against both, but neither the President [n]or the Senate has sustained me. Politically I was master of the situation, mainly because I was right. I will win the fight yet but it will require much harder work and more time. . . . [10]

Already Warner was displaying the Liberal Republican mentality, which automatically transformed a grudge into the grandeur of high principle and a disappointed office seeker into a paragon of purity in government.

Still, Warner hesitated to declare himself one of them after the Liberal Republicans had organized their party and nominated Greeley in May. He remained on the fence despite a personal appeal from Greeley's assistant at the *New York Tribune,* Whitelaw Reid, who hoped to hear from him soon "both directly and on the stump." In Philadelphia, during the regular Republican convention there in June, Warner talked politics with the *Chicago Tribune* reporter Townsend but left him with the impression that he was not in politics and was not a Greeley man. He predicted, nevertheless, that Greeley would carry every Southern state except South Carolina and Mississippi. As for the Philadelphia convention, he said the delegates from Alabama did not really represent their districts but only represented the "Spencer gang" of carpetbag federal officeholders in the state. The reporter described Warner as reputedly "the only decent carpet-bagger in the South" and Spencer as one of the worst of the "guttersnipes from the North."

By July, Warner was campaigning for the combined Liberal Republican and Democratic ticket, both state and national. This meant cooperating with ex-Confederates as well as Democrats. Congratulating Warner, the ex-rebel editor of the *Louisville Courier-Journal,* Henry Watterson, reminded him of the time in 1864 when the two had met as members of opposing truce teams outside Atlanta. "You will recall that I was then quite ready to clasp hands across the bloody chasm." This—"to clasp hands across the bloody chasm"—was now a catch-phrase of Democratic and Liberal campaigners. The spirit was noble enough, perhaps, but campaigning for Democratic state and local candidates was an embarrassment to Warner. He confided to Carl Schurz that the Democrats had put together a "straight Ku-Klux" ticket in Alabama and that it was a "great hindrance to the progress of liberalism in this State."

The regular Republicans' main organ, the *Alabama State Journal,* dismissed Warner as a sorehead who owed a great deal to Grant and the party but who now was telling the people that Grant was "a corrupt demagogue and a nepotist" and that the party was "a band of carpet-bag scoundrels and corrupt office seekers." The newspaper warned that, if Greeley should win, Warner would control the federal patronage in Alabama and would rule the state. The unexpressed corollary was that Greeley's defeat would mean oblivion for Warner.[11]

Though the November election in Alabama resulted in a clear victory for Grant, the consequences for Spencer were at first uncertain. The regular Republicans had unquestionably elected their state and congressional tickets (consisting mostly of scalawags) as well as their presidential ticket. But the Democrats and Liberals disputed the Republican claim to a majority in the next legislature, which was shortly to meet and presumably to decide whether Spencer would go back to the Senate, this time with a full, six-year term.

A week or two before the legislature was to meet, Spencer arrived in Montgomery and set up his headquarters in the Madison House. He was well prepared for the senatorial contest. In the First National Bank of Montgomery he had deposited funds left over from the fall campaign. The money came from the Republican national committee and from federal officeholders in Alabama, whom he had heavily assessed. He had already spent considerable sums to elect legislators favorable to him, but a large amount was still available in the bank. Besides money, he could offer federal jobs.

Spencer could count on the loyalty of most black politicians, who much preferred him to Warner; most carpetbaggers, for many of whom he had already secured federal offices; and most scalawags, including such prominent ones as William H. Smith, the former governor, and (no relative) James Q. Smith, the incumbent judge of the state circuit in which Montgomery lay. Spencer could also depend upon the faithfulness and skill of his right-hand man, Jerome J. Hinds, a carpetbagger and mail contractor who had served as an officer in the First Alabama Federal Cavalry, which Spencer had commanded during the war. According to a Liberal Republican reporter, Hinds was a "tall, forbidding, black-haired follower of fortune" with a reputation as "the meanest white man in Alabama." An adherent of Spencer's described him thus: "The most active man, I think, I ever saw in my life; the most energetic, untiring, and hard worker, night and day."

Spencer and his assistants soon needed all their energy and ingenuity as well as their political assets. When the legislature assembled in the capitol, he could not be sure that his followers would get enough of the contested seats to have a clear majority. Some of his advisers thought he and his men ought to stay in the legislative hall and fight for control of it. He decided, instead, to withdraw his men from the capitol and reassemble them in the federal courthouse. Here they claimed to function as the legitimate body, the one with a legal quorum. For the time being, Alabama had both a "capitol legislature" and a "courthouse legislature."[12]

The courthouse legislature scheduled its senatorial election for Tuesday, December 3, at noon. Meanwhile, to be sure of a quorum at that time, Spencer must prevent his legislators from defecting to the other side or simply wandering away. He and his assistants, especially the energetic Hinds, kept busy at the Madison House. They closely watched members who showed signs of straying. They used their powers of persuasion on them, regaled them with food and drink, promised them federal jobs, and offered them unsecured (and unrecorded) loans to tide them over until they could begin collecting legislative pay.

A couple of days before the election Spencer heard that Hales Ellsworth was grumbling. Hitherto Ellsworth, a black member, had been a faithful follower. Spencer, much excited, called at a liquor and grocery store to ask the owner, a mutual friend, what the hell was the matter with that fellow Ellsworth. After talking with Ellsworth, the grocer told Spencer that the man gave no specific reason for his dissatisfaction but said "that he would not be driven around like a damned horse, or like dumb cattle, or something like that; that he did not belong to anybody, that he was a free man." Spencer then talked with him and succeeded in mollifying him.

The night preceding the election was critical. That evening the Spencer men caucused in the courtroom and nominated him by acclamation. He must still make sure that a quorum would be on hand at noon the next day to elect him. The Democrats were making last-ditch efforts to detach some members of his legislature. He heard that they were offering to bribe one of them and were trying to hire another to go on an errand twenty miles away, too far for him to be back in time for the voting.

Spencer, Hinds, and their associates got little or no sleep that night. They maintained a vigil at their rooms in the Madison House, where party workers reported to them from time to time. They provided a free supper at a saloon for blacks, with baskets of shrimp from Savannah, plenty of wine and liquor, and expensive cigars. Then, taking an occasional nip themselves, since it was a nippy night, the workers guarded the rooming houses of doubtful members—and a dance hall where one member was preparing for the next day's responsibilities—to prevent escapes. Shortly after daybreak they escorted the doubtful legislators to a sumptuous breakfast at the Madison House.

These efforts paid off. At noon the legislators in the courtroom totaled fifty-two, one more than enough for a quorum. They voted unanimously for Spencer. That evening he attended a champagne party in his honor at Judge Smith's home. He had something to celebrate: he would continue as senator for six more years.

Or would he? The other legislature, the one sitting in the capitol, might yet elect a senator to contest the seat. For the present, no candidate could command a majority in the capitol legislature, and even if some candidate should do so, that body lacked a quorum. To keep it from getting a quorum, Spencer and his allies managed to dissuade a few of its members from attending its sessions. After about a week the capitol legislature nevertheless claimed a sufficient number and elected Francis W. Sykes, a scalawag.

Grant's attorney general, George H. Williams, in Montgomery to act for the President, proposed a settlement of the senatorial dispute. Let the two legislatures meet as one and hold another election. Assuming that Williams could compel agreement by the use of federal troops, the Democrats and Liberals assented to the proposal. On December 17 the combined legislature decided in Spencer's favor by the margin of a single vote. His election was later to be investigated by Democrats in the Alabama legislature and by Republicans in the United States Senate. The Democrats were to condemn him, but the Republicans were to clear him, and he was to hold his Senate seat until 1879.[13]

Governor Henry Clay Warmoth did not know he was creating his own nemesis when he arranged to have the mulatto P. B. S. Pinchback elected president pro tem of the Louisiana senate, to act in place of the deceased lieutenant governor, the black Oscar J. Dunn. Before the year 1872 was out, Pinchback was to take not only Dunn's position but also Warmoth's. He did so with Grant's blessing and support, which Warmoth had lost even before the start of the presidential campaign.

"Your wise course," a friend had advised Warmoth as early as August 1871, "is to go for Horace Greeley for president and let Grant office holders go to *Hell.*" That was when Greeley, having toured the South and denounced carpetbag corruption there, was first being mentioned as a possible candidate. The *New York Tribune* was beginning to make approving references to Warmoth, and Dunn protested to Greeley: "the young man who now occupies the executive chair of Louisiana . . . whose championship you so boldly assume, is pre-eminently the prototype and prince of the tribe of carpet-baggers who seem to be your pet aversion."

Dunn's protest did not prevent the *Tribune* and its editors from continuing to cultivate Warmoth. One of them, Whitelaw Reid, asked him for an interview in March 1872 when he was in New York City to attend a stockholders' meeting of the New Orleans, Mobile and Texas Railroad Company, in which the state of Louisiana held a large amount of stock. A *Tribune* reporter, with a list of easy questions from Reid, talked with Warmoth in the Fifth Avenue Hotel. "Gov. Warmoth is a tall, keen-eyed, dark-mustached man," the reporter wrote, "with a quiet air of clear-headed determination and a straightforward but temperate manner of expressing himself." He expressed himself as determined to "make no overtures of conciliation to the President." The interviewer asked: "Is corruption really as prevalent in Louisiana as people at the North generally suppose?" Warmoth replied:

> The general belief here, I think, is much exaggerated, though undoubtedly there has been a frightful amount of corruption. The negro legislators have held out against bribery quite as well as the white Republicans, and at least as well as the Democrats. We have no law in our State against bribery. . . . I proposed a law against it . . . and it passed the Senate unanimously, but in the House it mysteriously disappeared. . . . All the bills with money in them were voted for by a very large majority, and sometimes by all of the Democratic members of both houses. There is no doubt that reform is greatly needed in our State among all classes of society.

Warmoth was talking like a reformer, and he had perhaps as good a claim to be one as did any other Louisiana politician of the time. While governor, he vetoed approximately seventy bills and refused to sign forty others on the grounds that they had been improperly or corruptly passed. Thanks largely to him, the state's credit remained at least as good as it had been under the Democrats before him. Taxes and the public debt rose much less during his administration than his critics maintained. Even the *New York Herald*, which seldom had anything but a scurrilous word for carpetbaggers, commended him for his economy. Though "politically unscrupulous," he was "socially the best of fellows," the *Herald* said, and he had "for some time back earnestly labored to lighten the burdens upon the people."[14]

That was just before the May assembling of the Liberal Republican convention in Cincinnati. Warmoth led to Cincinnati a delegation of 125 Louisianans, a third of them black. He preferred Senator Lyman Trumbull, from his native state of Illinois, but after Greeley's nomination he returned to Louisiana to organize the Liberal Republican party there and to support the party's candidate.

Warmoth knew the Liberals had little hope of carrying the state without allies, but at first he hardly knew which way to look for them. The political scene in Louisiana was confusing. Parties were breaking up and re-forming; by summer a total of five were in the field. Besides Liberal Republicans, there were Custom House Republicans, Pinchback Republicans, Reform Democrats, and regular Democrats. Pinchback offered Warmoth his party's nomination for governor, but Warmoth declined it, suspecting that he would be a pawn for Pinchback to sacrifice in exchange for an alliance with the Custom House group. Warmoth preferred a fusion with the Reform Democrats. He could not expect any Democrats to support him for governor, but he could hope they would help elect him United States senator, now that he would be old enough to qualify.

Before the end of August he and his Liberal Republicans had managed to combine with both of the Democratic factions and with them were backing John McEnery, a Democrat and an ex-Confederate, for governor. The Pinchback and Custom House Republicans, now united, were running William Pitt Kellogg, who was completing his term as United States senator. Over the years Warmoth had parted from many of his political friends, and in declaring for McEnery he parted from most of the rest, among them James Longstreet, who remained loyal to his old army buddy Grant. The *New Orleans Republican,* once Warmoth's journalistic voice, repudiated him and the Fusion ticket, which it said represented the "negro-hating, schoolhouse-burning, fire-eating Bourbonists."

At a September mass meeting of Liberal and Democratic fusionists, Warmoth reminded the crowd that on his recommendation the legislature had passed bills to revise the election laws. The new laws would, in general, reduce the governor's power over the electoral process. In particular, they would let the senate appoint members of a new returning board, which could decide whether returns were valid. Warmoth was delaying to sign the bills (he could wait until the assembling of the next legislature, in December 1872, to do so). He now announced that he was not going to sign them. He explained: "we intend to take all the legal, all the righteous, all the honest and fair advantages in this election that our position authorizes us to take."[15]

Warmoth was in no mood to respond when Pinchback appealed to him for a reconciliation. Writing from Boston, where he was campaigning for the Grant ticket, Pinchback urged him not to ruin his future by continuing to oppose Grant, who was sure to be reelected. He could expect nothing from the Democrats once they were through with him, Pinchback went on. But if he would help elect a Republican legislature, he would have a chance of going to the United States Senate. At the moment, Pinchback seemed more eager for Warmoth's aid than Warmoth was for Pinchback's.

That September Warmoth was in New York City again on state business and, as usual, was staying at the Fifth Avenue Hotel. There he met Pinchback, who was returning from his New England campaign tour. Between these two clever politicians there was still an old spirit of camaraderie as well as a new one of rivalry. The pair agreed to go out to a fancy restaurant together on Saturday evening. That evening Warmoth waited in his room until eleven o'clock and then went to bed, assuming that Pinchback had found more attractive means of big-city entertainment. Next morning he learned that Pinchback had been seen boarding a train in Jersey City on Saturday night.

Warmoth immediately suspected what Pinchback was up to. By sneaking back to New Orleans, Pinchback could sign the election-law bills as acting governor during Warmoth's absence from the state. In fact, Pinchback had been conferring with Senator Henry Wilson of Massachusetts, vice-presidential candidate on the Grant ticket, and Senator William E. Chandler of New Hampshire, chairman of the Republican national committee, at the committee's headquarters in the Fifth Avenue

Hotel. Pinchback told them Grant had no chance of carrying Louisiana because of the existing election laws. Chandler advised him to hurry back and authorize the new ones.

Telegraphing to E. A. Burke, state chairman of the Liberal Republican campaign committee and New Orleans manager of the Illinois Central Railroad, Warmoth arranged to have a special car waiting for him in Kentucky. As soon as possible he took a fast Pennsylvania Railroad train out of New York. After making his connection with the Illinois Central, he was standing on the front platform of his special car when it arrived in Canton, Mississippi. There, in the station, waiting for the train, was Pinchback. The two rode the rest of the way together, joshing one another. When, after his arrival, Warmoth spoke at a Democratic rally, the crowd responded with great enthusiasm to the shout: "Three cheers for the race horse of Louisiana!"

In the election Warmoth made the most of the laws that enabled him to influence the balloting. He and his fellow Fusionists scheduled registration at times made known only to their own followers. They arranged to have a larger number of polling places in precincts predominantly Democratic than in those predominantly Republican. When it came to voting they used various tactics, short of violence, to discourage blacks. And they stuffed a number of ballot boxes. The returns, according to Warmoth's count, added up to 65,579 for the Fusion ticket and 55,973 for the regular Republican.

But the returns had to be validated by the returning board, and a majority of its members were partisans of Kellogg and Grant. So Warmoth now took out one of the unsigned election bills and signed it. This law would terminate the existing board and set up the new one with members to be named by the senate. As governor, Warmoth could fill vacancies occurring while the legislature was not in session, and it was not to be in session, according to his call, until December 9. On December 3 he appointed members of the new board, and the next day they certified that the Greeley and McEnery slate had been duly elected. But the old board had reconstituted itself, with Longstreet as a leading member. Though Longstreet and his colleagues possessed no returns, they held affidavits from a number of citizens who testified that, by one device or another, they had been kept from voting. The Longstreet board declared the Grant and Kellogg ticket victorious.[16]

After conferring with the President and the attorney general in Washington, Kellogg, back again in New Orleans, applied to United States Circuit Judge E. H. Durell for an injunction against Warmoth and his associates. Warmoth and McEnery were in the courtroom, along with about 350 others, most of them black, to hear the judge's decision on the morning of December 5. Pronouncing the Longstreet board the legal one, the judge enjoined the Warmoth board from having anything to do with the returns. Warmoth, according to a newspaperman on the spot, "appeared to be in no wise surprised or dismayed." Actually, he was in a plight already desperate and soon to get worse.

That night, on Judge Durell's order, two companies of United States soldiers occupied the Mechanics' Institute, which was still serving as the statehouse. The soldiers were to admit only those legislators whose names were on the judge's approved list. So Warmoth arranged for his legislature to meet in the City Hall. "There is no law fixing the State house in any building in the State of Louisiana," he said, and he added that the state's lease on the Mechanics' Institute had expired on November 20. "Whatever may be Warmoth's next step," the *New York Times* editorialized, "it is plain that he is not the absolute dictator he assumes to be in Louisiana."

He had hardly been a real dictator at any time, but he had certainly not been a supplicant, and that was what he was temporarily reduced to. At midnight before the day both legislatures were to meet, he called at the home of Pinchback, woke him up, and proposed to join forces with him. Early the next morning Warmoth sent a messenger to him with the following note: "Come as soon as you can. Before 9 if possible. I must see you, whatever may have been your determination." The messenger returned with this reply from Pinchback: "I have slept on the proposition you made last night, and have resolved to do my duty to my State, party, and race, and I therefore respectfully decline to accept your proposition. I am truly sorry for you, but I cannot help you."

When the legislature met that day in the Mechanics' Institute, Pinchback took the chair as presiding officer of the senate. He announced that, at "the dead hour of midnight last night," Warmoth had approached him with an offer of $50,000 and he had rejected the tendered bribe. The house quickly impeached Warmoth and thus suspended him from the governorship. Pinchback, who had been acting as lieutenant governor, broke into Warmoth's office, occupied it, and assumed the title and authority of governor. His claim to the succession rested on his position as president pro tem of the senate—the only position to which he had been elected—and his senate term had already expired!

Warmoth applied to the United States Supreme Court for a writ overruling Judge Durell, then appealed to Grant in a long telegram:

> Under an order from the judge of the United States district court, investing James Longstreet, Jacob Hawkins, and others with the powers and duties of returning-officers under State election law, and charging them with the duty of completing the legal returns and declaring the result in accordance therewith, those persons have promulgated results based upon no returns whatever, and no evidence except *ex parte* statements. They have constructed a pretended general assembly, composed mainly of candidates defeated at the election, and those candidates, protected by United States military forces, have taken possession of the State-house and have organized a pretended legislature, which to-day passed pretended articles of impeach-

> ment against the governor; in pursuance of which the person claiming to be lieutenant-governor, broke into the executive office under the protection of United States soldiers and took possession of the archives. In the mean-time the general assembly has met at the city-hall and organized for business with . . . more than a quorum. . . . I ask . . . that no violent action be taken, and no force used by the Government, at least until the supreme court shall have passed final judgement on the case.

Then, referring to himself as "I, Henry Clay Warmoth, Governor of the State of Louisiana," he issued a proclamation denouncing the "revolutionary and fraudulent assemblage" in the Mechanics' Institute and cautioning "all good citizens" to disregard its actions and those of the person who "falsely and fraudulently" was pretending to act as governor of the state.

Local representatives of forty-eight Northern firms doing business in New Orleans met and signed an address to the people of the North, asking them to protest to Congress and the President against the "arbitrary usurpation of power and place, by political adventurers backed by a United States Judge." A committee of one hundred citizens prepared to go to Washington and protest in person, with McEnery in the lead. But Attorney General Williams warned McEnery: "Your visit with a hundred citizens will be unavailing so far as the President is concerned. His decision is made and will not be changed, and the sooner it is acquiesced in the sooner good order and peace will be restored."

For the moment, Warmoth could count on the state militia at least. When Pinchback ordered the militia officers to report to Longstreet as their commander, they indicated that they would obey no orders except those emanating from Warmoth, whom they still regarded as their commander in chief. They again refused when ordered to surrender their arms and their armory to Longstreet. Warmoth could not similarly depend on the metropolitan police, which once had been virtually his palace guard. A force of a hundred policemen, under orders to take the armory, moved to within half a block of it and then withdrew after a parley. Though willing to stand up to the metropolitans, the militia officers hardly dared to resist the federal troops. And on December 14 General W. H. Emory, in command of the federal troops in New Orleans, received the following wire from the adjutant general in Washington: "You may use all force necessary to preserve the peace, and will recognize the authority of Governor Pinchback. By order of the President."[17]

CHAPTER 14

The Leopard Don't Change His Spots (1873-1875)

"As a general thing the leopard don't change his spots and I had rather a leopard with a sheepskin than a Kuklux disguized as a Liberal Republican and shouting—Reform, Reform!" So Albion W. Tourgee had declaimed, in Rochester, New York, while campaigning for Ulysses S. Grant in 1872. If the Greeleyites should win, Tourgee then predicted, the South would be "under the control of the same party and spirit that sustained slavery, supported the Rebellion, opposed Reconstruction, and constituted the Kuklux." But now that he was back home in Greensboro, North Carolina, and was resuming his rounds as a circuit judge, he was beginning to realize that, even with Grant reelected, the South was going to rise again—the South of slavery, rebellion, and the Ku Klux Klan.

Once reinaugurated, Grant pardoned the Klansmen whom the federal government had imprisoned in various Southern states. That same year, 1873, the Conservatives (Democrats) having strengthened their control of the North Carolina legislature in the recent election, they extended a blanket pardon to members of secret orders who, under state law, were being held for various crimes, including murder. Thus the killers of the black leader Wyatt Outlaw, men whom Tourgee had hoped to see convicted in his Alamance County court, never came to trial. He had to give up his long effort to bring the white terrorists to justice, yet the black arsonists whom he had already sentenced remained in jail.[1]

Besides hearing cases in his own circuit, Tourgee accepted assignments to duty in other courts as far away as Greenville, in the eastern part of the state. Though dockets were often heavy, he occasionally had time to loaf, walk, write, or join others in a game of whist. Invitations to dinner parties fortunately were rare, for "dinings and tea-ings" were "dreadful ogres" to him. "All my self-consciousness comes to the surface then and I cannot even breathe without fear of a *faux pas*." So he told Emma, at any rate. He gave repeated assurances that he loved her and missed her—especially after overhearing a lovers' quarrel on the other side of a thin hotel-room partition and then having to listen to the lovers make up "with the tell-tale clinking of the iron bedstead." He feared that, by neglecting his own wife, he was responsible for her "careworn" appearance with "crow's feet" around the eyes. "Your face has gathered a fixed patient look as if you were all the time carrying some burden."

Well, Emma *was* carrying the burden of the Greensboro household while her husband traveled around the state. She had to oversee such womanly chores as the spring house cleaning. "I have a most fearful headache today," she complained in the midst of it, "and the house is torn up all over." As in previous years, she also had to see to such manly work as the harvesting of grain and the repair of a broken buggy. Besides, she had the daily care of little Lodie, who in 1873 was in her third year. Of course, Lodie was a comfort as well as a care, and she "behaved admirably" the first time her mother took her to church. "She sang when the choir did and continued through the interlude much to our amusement. She looked very chagrined when she found no one else was singing and hid her head in my lap."[2]

Another day, at home, Lodie began to cry when she overheard her mother say her father was going to have his eye taken out. Emma, leaving Lodie with a relative, went to Philadelphia to be present during the operation. For some time, Tourgee had been suffering from an irritation of his blind eye and a seemingly related disturbance of his good one. The good one, he was glad to find, did improve after the "butchering" of the other, but it took him a long time to get used to wearing a glass eye.

Tourgee was in Greensboro just recovering from the surgery when in September 1873 a financial panic began with the failure of the nation's largest investment banking firm, Jay Cooke & Company, of Philadelphia. Not for several years was either Tourgee or the country to recover from the business depression that ensued. "It caught me bad—'mighty bad' as we say down here—with rapidly maturing liabilities amounting to $30,000, and only bad debts and a big lot of unsalable stock to meet it with," he informed a Northern friend, a professor at Tourgee's alma mater, the University of Rochester. (Tourgee sent the professor's wife some Confederate money for her collection. "The Southern people are a little sore about Confederate money going into museums &c," he observed, but he nevertheless expected soon to have "the pick of a large amount.") For the moment he was satisfying his creditors with mortgages on his real estate. His North Carolina Handle Company was bankrupt.

"I have the consolation of knowing that I did not hold money and let it rust and canker but so used it that others received good from it though I lost," he mused at Christmastide. "I can sit by my window and see scores of snug homes that would never have been built but for the steady work and good wages which their owners derived from my enterprise." Those were the homes of the black workers whom he had employed in the nearby plant. He could also console himself with the knowledge that he and his family, despite their calamitous financial straits, were in excellent physical condition. Emma enjoyed "good health and unquenchable faith in the future," and Lodie was growing "brighter and fairer and wickeder—quite as fast as anyone could wish." As for Tourgee himself, he had at least the appearance of prosperity. "The operation of last summer seemed to remove an *incubus* upon my health and despite the panic I have been fattening till I hardly know myself."[3]

From time to time Tourgee saw hope of sizable income from his writing, but it was a rather faint and flickering hope. In early 1873 he looked again at the pages of the novel he had begun in 1868—the story of Toinette, that nearly white girl who, as a slave, was the mistress of a wealthy and handsome young planter but who, once freed, refused to be less than his wife. "I must say, my dear," Tourgee confided to Emma, "there are some splendid things in it, but I am satisfied it will never 'take.' I could write one that would, though, I think." Despite the faults he found in "Toinette," he determined to finish it. He took the manuscript with him as he made the rounds from one county seat to another, and he worked at it whenever he had the inclination and the time.

At first, the panic seemed to have killed his literary venture as well as his industrial enterprise. One publisher agreed to take his manuscript but demanded an author's subsidy of $500, which Tourgee "did not feel justified in risking" when he could not pay his creditors. Another publisher, J. B. Ford & Company of New York, accepted the manuscript at the publisher's risk. By April 1874 Tourgee was reading proof sheets of *Toinette* as he traveled the circuit. He found the printing good. "I am becoming well satisfied however that poor 'Toinette' will not be a success in a pecuniary point of view," he told Emma. "It will not be an utter failure but will have only a moderate sale." His prediction was to prove all too accurate.

When the book appeared, it bore not Tourgee's name but the pseudonym Henry Churton, the name of a planter who once owned the site of Hillsborough, North Carolina. Tourgee's authorship became known, however, when the editor of a village newspaper in Lee, Massachusetts, where Tourgee had once lived, ran a review with a local-boy-makes-good theme. The *Charlotte Observer* was now inspired to deplore the book, shrieking: *"The real purpose of Tourgee was TO POPULARIZE INTER-MARRIAGE BETWEEN THE RACES IN NORTH CAROLINA."*

Offsetting the denunciation to some extent was a batch of favorable notices that Tourgee's publisher clipped from Northern periodicals and sent him. "The style is so bright, terse, and clear that you prove by it your *vocation for literature,*" his Rochester professor friend assured him. "I venture the suggestion that the plot of your story as a whole is hardly equal to the style of writing and the dramatic power displayed in the separate scenes," the professor added with discernment. "Let me say that your army and judicial experience ought to [be] recorded while the facts and coloring of the scenes are fresh in your mind." Indeed, Tourgee would someday use his judicial experience as the basis for a best-selling novel about a carpetbagger and the Ku Klux Klan.[4]

Toinette was bringing in a little money, but nothing like the fortune that the later book was to bring in. Before the end of 1874 Tourgee's term as a judge would end and, with it, his judicial salary. He would have little chance of being reelected to the judgeship, or of being elected to Congress, unless the Republicans should stage a comeback in the fall. And he would have no chance at all if the Democrats should continue to dominate. His need for a paying job made him especially sensitive to what the Republicans in Congress were doing, for it was sure to alienate Southern whites and hurt the political prospects of Republicans in North Carolina and elsewhere in the South.

In the Senate, Charles Sumner had long advocated a thoroughgoing civil rights act, one that would prohibit racial discrimination not only in jury selection and in public transportation and accommodations of all kinds but also in public schools. A couple of months after Sumner's death, as a kind of memorial to him, the Senate in May 1874 passed his civil rights bill. Privately, Tourgee protested:

> The worst thing will be the Civil Rights Bill—Sumner's Supplementary. I know the maxim *De mortuis nihil* &c but I have no use for those who prescribe for diseases without knowing their nature. Sumner knew no more of the actual condition of the colored man here than he realized his condition on the Gold Coast. The bill, with all respect to its author, is just like a blister plaster put on a dozing man whom it is desirable to soothe to sleep. The most important thing in the world is to let the South forget the negro for a bit: let him acquire property, stability, and self-respect; let as many as possible be educated; in short, let the race itself get used to freedom, self-dependence and proper self-assertion; and then let the bill come little by little if necessary. Of course, if it becomes law, it will be constantly avoided. No man can frame a statute which some other cannot avoid. For all its benevolent purposes it will be a dead letter. For its evil influences it will be vivid and active. It will be like the fire-brands between the tails of Samson's foxes. It is just pure folly and results from what I have so long claimed, that the people of the North and our Legislators will not study the people of the South, reasonably. They will not remember that a prejudice 250 years old (at least) should only be legislated against when *positively harmful*, and should always be let alone when it only conflicts with good doctrine, fine theory. It will utterly destroy the bulk of our common schools at the South. These States will throw them aside at once, and the people, except in those where there is a colored majority, will approve. They are not overfond of education here at the best. . . . If we get this fool's notion imposed on us, good bye schools in the South. It simply delays—puts back—the thorough and complete rehabilitation of the South ten or twenty years. It is the idea of a visionary quack who prescribes for the disease without having made a diagnosis.

The House of Representatives struck out the reference to public schools before passing the civil rights bill in February 1875—too late to be of any help to Southern Republicans in the fall elections of 1874.

Tourgee was not running for any office that fall. Even if the Republicans had nominated him for congressman or judge, he would have had little chance as the Democrats again swept the state. So, with the collapse of his woodworking business and the termination of his judgeship, he no longer had a source of income except for the uncertain sales of his novel *Toinette*. His first period of prosperity was over.[5]

Tourgee could hope to get a livelihood once again as an attorney, and after forming a partnership with another Greensboro lawyer he began to practice in the familiar courthouses of the Seventh Judicial District. "I have . . . but little prospect it seems to me for getting any or much business," he confessed to Emma. He felt "pretty blue" but tried to cheer up his wife and himself by saying: "I have no doubt I shall get my share of the practice as soon as they get over being rather afraid of me as having lately been a Judge."

His fellow lawyers of the Guilford Bar Association were no longer particularly hostile, but Democratic politicians and journalists continued to stir up prejudices against him. When he and his partner won the acquittal of a black woman charged with slaying her child, the *Greensboro Patriot* said the skill of the lawyers and the "over generous sympathies of twelve men" had produced a verdict that could "only have the effect of lessening the dread of punishment and encouraging indulgence in vice." Such cases did not yield big fees, and after three months Tourgee was still receiving pay only in driblets.

Then came discouraging news from his publisher: "I fear there will not be much coming from Toinette, as we have advertised it so much, hoping to drive it into a large sale, that its profits have been eaten into." Tourgee had been expecting at least a modest accumulation of royalties. "Well, God only can help us out now and I fear nothing can save us from complete wreck—as to estate and prospects," he lamented to Emma. "If Toinette had only been a success we could have pulled out and I might have seen you happy again."

Despite his difficulties, Tourgee as yet had no thought of leaving the South or even of leaving Greensboro. When he received an inquiry from a Northerner about the desirability of settling in the South, he responded with several pages of disillusioning advice. Ignorance of the region, he said, "has led very many good men from the North to incur the odium of being termed carpet-baggers and build an illusory hope of bettering their conditions by a removal hither." Newcomers should realize that farming in the South is quite different from farming in the North or the West, that Southerners know much more about it than Northerners do, and that planters combine egregious flattery with shrewd bargaining in a way that leaves most Yankees helpless. Having said all this, Tourgee avowed: "*I* like living here."

He had the promise of a little money from short stories he was writing, and he gained an opportunity to make a few dollars per diem when he won election to the new constitutional convention, which met in the capitol in Raleigh from September 5 to October 11, 1875. To supplement his meager earnings, he took along a batch of his books to peddle among his fellow delegates and other likely customers. He did fairly well. After less than a week he informed Emma: "I have ordered 4 Doz. Toinettes by telegraph, having sold what I have and having application[s] for 20 more."

Still, he could not send Emma enough money for her to keep up with her expenses. "If I had but $5.00, it would relieve the present necessity," she wrote him. "I expect one reason of my feeling so blue this week, has been because my cows have failed so much in their milk that I have been unable to supply much more than half the quantity needed, and representing as it did all the income I had I could not see what I was going to do, for I had steadfastly determined not to run the risk of insult by asking any one 'to trust' for necessaries."[6]

Among the 119 delegates at the 1875 convention, only Tourgee and five others had been delegates at the 1868 convention. He had dominated the proceedings in that earlier assemblage, in which the Republicans had held a large majority. Again he was the most conspicuous of the Republicans, but this time the Democrats possessed a slight edge, as became apparent when they succeeded in electing the Republican defector Edward Ransom as the convention's president. Tourgee immediately moved that the convention adjourn *sine die;* his motion lost by 57 to 59. He and the rest of the Republicans had no desire to tinker with the constitution. They had opposed the calling of the convention in the first place, and during its sessions they tried repeatedly to bring about an adjournment.

The most distinguished of the Democratic delegates, the onetime governor and Confederate senator William A. Graham, had died just before the convention met. "Today the resolutions upon the death of Governor Graham came up and I made *the* speech of the occasion as is admitted by all," Tourgee boasted to Emma on September 10. "I had a large portion of the auditory in tears much of the time and have been overburdened with compliments ever since." In regard to another ex-governor, William W. Holden, Tourgee two weeks later spoke eloquently again but with less effect. A resolution called for restoring to Holden the political rights as a North Carolina citizen that he had lost by his impeachment and removal from office. "It must be admitted by every honest man," Tourgee pleaded, "that his error was one of the head and not of the heart." The resolution, in a close vote, failed to carry.

Later on the day that Tourgee spoke in Holden's behalf, while he was at supper in the hotel, a man warned him that Ransom, the convention president, was waiting for him in the lobby and swearing to shoot him on sight. "I finished my supper and came sauntering out with my hands in my pockets," Tourgee related to Emma.

> The office was all alive with excited groups who were evidently looking for something to occur. Ransom was standing just at the left of the entrance talking excitedly with one or two Democrats and looking toward me. The Republicans were swarming around like bees and everybody looking at me and Ransom. I stopped by the counter and spoke to a friend. Some one came up and slipped a revolver into my hand. After waiting a short time to give him [Ransom] a good chance I went on through to my room. After a time I went back and walked along in front of where he was then sitting, stopped, looked at him and waited a minute or so for his attack. He did not make it but continues to tell what he will do. There is no sort of danger in him.
>
> My friends stood up for me splendidly, and I was much gratified that they did so. The cause of his wrath was that Cunningham of Persons [County] had told him some thing I said about his (R's) photograph. I was in the [photographer's] gallery and was laughing about all our pictures but especially my own. Finally I put it up beside his and said, "Lord what a pair for the Rogue's Gallery."

Tourgee soon got into a noisier altercation with his old antagonist Josiah Turner, recently the provoker and apologist of the Klan, now a Democratic delegate to the convention. The Democrats were proposing and the Republicans opposing a reduction of the supreme court from five to three members. In the debate the Democrats made nasty remarks about carpetbaggers, and Tourgee rose to say a good word about them. He remarked that the Democrats would no doubt have reviled Columbus, the Pilgrims, and even Jesus Christ as carpetbaggers. After the window shades had been lowered at Tourgee's request, to keep out the glare of the setting sun, Turner got the floor. He declared that the convention needed all the light it could get, and he demanded that the shades be raised again. While Tourgee sat with the sun in his eyes, Turner made a speech in which he insisted that the original carpetbagger was not Jesus Christ but Judas Iscariot.

The Democrats also advocated a constitutional amendment that would prohibit marriage between a white and a Negro "to the third degree," that is, between a white and a person with one black great-grandparent. Objecting to this, Tourgee proposed as an alternative an amendment stating "that any act of *illicit* sexual intercourse between a white person and a negro, or a person of negro blood to the third degree, shall be a misdemeanor." Presumably the existing laws against fornication and adultery would apply to interracial sex, making Tourgee's amendment unnecessary, but he wanted to emphasize the point that white men should be discouraged from debasing black women. The planter paramour of Toinette should not be allowed to cohabit with her, but she should be permitted to become his wife.

For Tourgee and his fellow Republicans, the convention ended in utter defeat. Several of the thirty newly adopted amendments, including the ban on interracial marriage, had the effect of lowering the status and influence of blacks. Segregated schools, already prescribed by statute, were now required by the constitution. To vote in any county, a man henceforth had to reside there for ninety rather than sixty days preceding an election. And, white or black, he could no longer choose his local officials, not even justices of the peace. All would be appointed by the legislature. Thus the 1875 constitution took away the local self-government that the 1868 constitution had brought. The object was, of course, to deprive blacks of political control in counties where they made up a majority. It was a shocking setback for Reconstruction in North Carolina.[7]

Back home in Greensboro, Tourgee planned to eke out his income by appearing on the lecture platform. In a printed circular he advertised the topics on which he was prepared to speak: "The Ben Adhemite Era," "The Next Crusade," "Out of the Strong—Sweetness," "Southern Humor," and "To-day in Account with Yesterday." He offered testimonials from several friends, including the native Tar Heels William W. Holden, Thomas Settle, and R. P. Dick, the last of whom attested to Tourgee's "originality of thought, rich literary attainments, forcible and brilliant style and delivery."

Tourgee could get a more dependable living, however, from a government job, and before Thanksgiving he went to Washington to look for one. He succeeded in obtaining an appointment as pension agent at Raleigh, but Senator A. G. Merrimon from North Carolina objected to his confirmation on the grounds that his character was not good enough. In a statement Tourgee prepared for the Senate committee on pensions, he cited his war record, especially his part in the first battle of Bull Run, "losing an eye as the result of one wound and being unable to walk for more than ten months as the result of another." (It will be remembered that, in fact, he had lost the eye in a boyhood accident long before the war.) He denied the charge that George W. Swepson had given him $3500 "to secure the passage of certain bills"; he said it was a loan made "openly and above board" for the purchase of a house (and indeed it was, but he neglected to mention that he had never repaid it). After several months the Senate was to confirm the appointment, and the Tourgees were to move to Raleigh and sell their home in Greensboro.[8]

On January 13, 1873, two men took the governor's oath in New Orleans—William Pitt Kellogg in the Mechanics' Institute and John McEnery in Lafayette Square. Each of the two delivered an inaugural before the legislature that recognized and supported him, the McEnery legislature assembling in Odd Fellows Hall. Which was the true governor and which the real legislature of Louisiana? The decision was up to the President and the Congress of the United States.

No one was more interested in the outcome than ex-Governor Henry Clay Warmoth. He hoped for the repudiation of Kellogg and the vindication of McEnery. Kellogg was a fellow Illinoisan, Union veteran, and Republican; McEnery a native Louisianan, ex-Confederate, and Democrat; but Warmoth, for the moment, saw his own political future as dependent on McEnery's success. In the 1872 election he had helped to bring about McEnery's victory—or claim to victory—by "fusing" the Liberal Republicans with the Democrats and by reorganizing the returning board. As a reward for his services to the common cause, he expected the Fusionists in the McEnery legislature, Democrats as well as Republicans, to send him to the United States Senate.

Warmoth quickly discovered that he was expecting a bit too much. Just a few days after the dual inauguration, while he was conferring with McEnery in the latter's makeshift office, a delegation of some two hundred of the "best citizens" of New Orleans appeared outside the door. The group's spokesman, T. A. Adams, a leading Democrat, requested that Warmoth withdraw from the senatorial race. Adams explained that the Senate would never admit Warmoth, since Grant was so hostile to him. Grant and his adherents in the Senate, Adams went on, believed the charge that Warmoth had tried to deprive Grant of Louisiana's electoral vote by manipulating the returns. "Don't you know," Warmoth replied, "that by throwing me overboard you give a virtual acknowledgment to all these charges, and lead the country to believe that you believe them?" He refused to withdraw.[9]

To lobby for recognition of the McEnery government, Warmoth went to Washington, where, in response to a request from Grant, the Senate committee on privileges and elections was looking into Louisiana affairs. The committee's chairman, Oliver P. Morton of Indiana, presumably could be counted on to see that Grant's will be done, and so could a majority of the members. Only Lyman Trumbull of Illinois, recently a Greeleyite, could be expected to listen sympathetically to Warmoth. But Warmoth found a champion also in one of the regular Grant Republicans—Matthew H. Carpenter of Wisconsin—who enabled him to get much more of a hearing than otherwise would have been possible.

Though born in Vermont, Carpenter was no New England puritan. He enjoyed good eating and good drinking, took a cynical view of political reform, and made fun of moralists and hypocrites. With him, no one could have been more congenial than Warmoth, who was immediately welcomed into Carpenter's circle of poker-playing cronies. Carpenter and two others of the group begged for copies of Warmoth's photograph after he had his picture taken at Matthew B. Brady's Washington studio. (Warmoth ordered, for himself, an expensive "life size crayon" to be made from the photo.) The eloquent Carpenter did not hesitate to tell the entire Senate what he thought of Warmoth:

> There is in Louisiana, and has been for several years, a very remarkable young man, dignified in mien, of elegant presence and agreeable conversation; a man full of resources, political and social—gallant, daring, and with a genius for politics; such a man as would rise to power in any great civil disturbance, embodying in himself the elements of revolution, and delighting in the exercise of his natural gifts in the midst of political excitement.

Among themselves, the new chums of Warmoth liked to refer to him as "the Cataline of Louisiana," but one of them assured him: "I don't believe you are as arch a scoundrel as your opponents say. In short, Governor, there is a high career before you, if you will take advantage of your circumstances." Amid such pleasant company, Warmoth enjoyed trying to take advantage of his circumstances, though he was never to realize the high career that supposedly lay before him.

Under Carpenter's influence, the majority of the committee on privileges and elections reported that Louisiana had no legitimate government and recommended that a new election be held. Carpenter introduced a bill providing for a supervised polling, Warmoth to remain in office as governor until a successor had been properly chosen. Both Morton and Trumbull opposed the bill—though Trumbull argued that Grant ought to recognize the McEnery government—and after an all-night debate it lost by two votes. Congress having declined to do anything at all about the Louisiana imbroglio, the President announced: it is "my duty" to "adhere to that government heretofore recognized by me . . . that government which is recognized and upheld by the courts of the State." He was referring, of course, to the Kellogg government.[10]

Now, at the end of February 1873, it appeared that no senator elected by the McEnery legislature could possibly be seated. In any case, the senator elected by that legislature would not be Warmoth. While he was still in Washington, at the beginning of March, the legislature in New Orleans proceeded to ballot—despite his telegram asking them to wait until he got home. Warmoth heard from an intimate that the "last ditch" Democrats had insisted on going ahead and that the senator-elect was William L. McMillan, a friend and fellow carpetbagger of Warmoth's but one less obnoxious to the Democrats. "Governor," Warmoth's informant wrote, "my faith in man has vanished; I thought woman was inconstant alone, now I include both sexes. You have been beaten by treachery."

Warmoth returned to a Louisiana that seemed on the verge of civil war. On March 5, McEnery's militia tried to seize some stations of Kellogg's metropolitan police; several men were wounded. The next day a force of one hundred police invaded the Odd Fellows Hall, arrested all the McEnery legislators, and held them until Kellogg ordered their release. Some of the associates of Warmoth looked to him to "do something to relieve the State from its unhappy condition."

So Warmoth went to see Kellogg. He found him apparently "anxious for a compromise" and willing to procure the resignation of forty-nine members of his house of representatives and an unspecified number of his senate, so that they could be replaced by Fusionists. But Warmoth soon realized that Kellogg would do nothing without instructions from Grant's attorney general, George H. Williams. Warmoth also sensed that Kellogg hesitated to make a deal with him—"he distrusts me and expects constantly one of those 'Coup de Etats' which my enemies say I am always concocting." No wonder Kellogg was suspicious, for Warmoth had frankly told him that the Fusionists would overthrow the Kellogg regime if they only had the power to do so.

After leaving Kellogg, Warmoth consulted with McEnery and other allies. He confided to them that he thought it "a waste of time to attempt a settlement" with Kellogg. At best, it would be undignified and indeed dishonorable to compromise with a "usurpation" so villainous. And there was nothing to be gained from Kellogg's proposal to seat Fusionists in the legislature, for his own men would be in the majority and could pass any legislation they wanted. McEnery and his associates agreed with Warmoth: the Fusionists must simply "await events."

Events did not improve during that spring of 1873. At Colfax in Grant parish (places renamed for President Grant and his first-term Vice President, Schuyler Colfax), seventy-odd blacks died in an Easter clash with whites—a considerably larger number than died in the New Orleans riot of 1866. Fusionists resolved to pay no taxes to the Kellogg government and to resist tax collection by force of arms. Some localities insisted on keeping Warmoth's appointees in office and keeping Kellogg's appointees out. A would-be assassin shot at Kellogg and missed. Kellogg proclaimed a policy of no compromise, denied rumors of a deal with Warmoth, blamed him for an era of corruption, and promised to bring about reform. On May 22 Grant issued a proclamation in which he confirmed his recognition of the Kellogg regime and commanded "certain turbulent and disorderly persons" to disperse.[11]

Warmoth and his Liberal Republicans advocated tax resistance but did not approve of the violence that last-ditch Democrats were resorting to. He was being estranged from many of his allies of 1872, and he was further estranged from them when, on his invitation, his friend Senator Carpenter spoke in New Orleans. On a night of heavy rain three thousand drenched but eager citizens crowded into Exposition Hall to hear the renowned orator of Wisconsin, the "Webster of the West." He provoked them to frequent interruptions as he denounced both Kellogg men and McEnery men but blamed Louisiana's troubles mainly on the native whites. Some carpetbaggers, he conceded, were an "infernal lot," but he insisted that most were worthy men whose enterprise was an asset to the South. After three hours of this kind of talk, the "last ditchers" in the audience were furious—at Warmoth as well as Carpenter.

In his New Orleans speech Carpenter had promised to try again to get a new election for Louisiana, and he did repeatedly try again at the next session of Congress, in 1873-74, but with no more success than previously. Still, Warmoth could find some gratification, by the end of the session, in the non-action of Congress. While the Senate would not accept the McEnery government's senator, neither would it accept the Kellogg government's, who was the black leader, P. B. S. Pinchback. For six years the seat was to remain unoccupied.[12]

As the autumn of 1874 approached, with its regularly scheduled election, the need for a special election decreased as far as legislators and congressmen were concerned. But it would be two years more before the governor's term would end. Louisiana Democrats became more and more incensed at the continuance of Kellogg in office. For a short time in 1873 some of them, under the lead of ex-Confederate General P. G. T. Beauregard, had expressed a willingness to recognize the civil rights of blacks and to cooperate with them in politics. In the summer and fall of 1874, however, the Democrats resorted increasingly to racism and violence. The White League, more like an army than the Klan was, shot and killed six local officeholders in the "Coushatta massacre." It defeated General James Longstreet's black militia in a pitched battle in New Orleans, then took control of the state government for a few days, while Kellogg hid out in the Custom House.

Warmoth had nothing to do with either the military or the political campaigning of the Democrats. Indeed, he had nothing to do with the election of 1874—except to watch it from a distance. For months he stayed away from Louisiana, spending most of his time in New York City and attending to his business affairs. From loyal followers in New Orleans he received disquieting accounts of the course of politics. The White Leaguers and "last ditchers" expected, through intimidation, to carry the state and threatened warfare in case Kellogg should use his returning board to take away the anticipated majority at the polls.

"Just at this time all parties imagine if you were here you would be with them," Warmoth heard from one of his friends in New Orleans a few weeks before election day. "The Negroes, Kellogg & the Democrats all think you would be with them. If here you would have to take sides with one & make enemies of the other two parties." Therefore Warmoth had best prolong his absence until after the election. "There is nothing in sight now for you except the U. States Senate, which is remotely possible, but your presence here now would do more to kill that off than anything else in the world."

Remaining in New York, Warmoth read with some concern the election news from the various states. From Massachusetts the word was that his friend Ben Butler had lost his race for reelection to the House of Representatives. From other states, too, came reports of Republicans defeated for Congress—so many of them defeated that at the next session, beginning in December 1875, the Democrats would control the House for the first time since secession. "People here seem to have lost their breath and can hardly realize the full extent of the ruin that has been wrought," a comrade wrote Warmoth from Chicago, "for I believe it ruin with the democracy returning to power."

From Louisiana the news was uncertain but ominous. The Democrats were convinced of victory, and on election night they celebrated with a torchlight parade in New Orleans. But Kellogg's returning board had yet to make its official count of the returns. Another election dispute appeared to be in the making.[13]

Warmoth would probably have done well to stay away from New Orleans even longer than he did. He might then have avoided the necessity of killing the man he was about to kill. As it was, he went back to find the White Leaguers again threatening to take over the city, and the "last ditchers" becoming more and more murderous in their hostility to all blacks and all Republicans—including him.

Republicans in Congress were hoping that Kellogg's returning board would give no cause for another Louisiana election dispute. The existing controversy had embarrassed the party and turned voters away in the North, thus adding to the recent disaster at the polls. So it was widely believed. "The opinion is universal among Republicans," Warmoth heard from a Louisiana friend in Washington, "that it would be sheer folly and add still further to Republican (national) embarrassment for the Board to make a false count. Better, say the Republicans, that the State should be handed over to the Democrats than to furnish unending material for Democratic assaults."

But Republicans in Congress were expecting the worst in Louisiana, as Warmoth learned from his Washington mail. Morton, Grant's right-hand man in the Senate, was saying that the leaders of the White League ought to be shot and that they had "better let Kellogg alone." Warmoth's Senate champion Carpenter was saying that, even if the Democrats should win a majority in the new legislature, they "could not reverse the action of the Legislature declaring Kellogg elected." Nor could they likely obtain a Senate seat for Warmoth or for anyone else. Carpenter "doubted very much whether the Senate would consider the credentials of another Senator from Louisiana, but if you were elected you would have his full active hearty support for admission."

Suspense mounted in New Orleans as weeks passed and the returning board made no announcement. Their rage intensifying with their frustration, the last-ditch Democrats demanded the removal of the remaining vestiges of civil rights for blacks. For a time, some black children had attended racially integrated schools in the city, but no longer; nor did blacks continue to mix with whites in other places—except on the mule-drawn streetcars. The old segregated, blacks-only cars, marked with a star, had been eliminated for seven years, and the last-ditchers now determined to bring them back. "Having succeeded, then, in obtaining the purification of the public schools, the inviolability of the places of public amusement and resort," the *New Orleans Bulletin* editorialized on December 20, 1874, "we have now but one duty to perform, and that is to secure a return to the system of 'star' cars on our street railways."

Warmoth read this editorial with a rising sense of disappointment and disgust. After thinking about it for a few days, he sat down and wrote out a long reply. He had agreed with the *Bulletin,* he began, taking care to avoid offense, in its denunciations of the men who had "usurped power by means of midnight orders, Gatling guns, and ingenious frauds." However, "I must respectfully but firmly remonstrate against the suggestion, in your issue of Sunday last, concerning the rights of colored citizens." The constitution and laws of the state prohibited racial discrimination, Warmoth reminded the editor, and conservative leaders such as McEnery in the Fusion platform of 1872 and Beauregard in the "unification" program of 1873 had promised equal privileges and immunities for blacks. "In conclusion, Mr. Editor, let me ask you if at such a time as this we can afford to go back on the pledges we repeatedly made."

Warmoth took this letter to the *Bulletin* office. There he found D. C. Byerly, the founder and manager of the paper, and E. L. Jewell, the editor who had written the piece on "star" cars. Forty-eight years old, a Pennsylvania native but for thirty years a Louisiana resident, Byerly was a big, heavy-set, bearded man with a useless left arm six inches shorter than the right. As a lieutenant of Louisiana infantry, he had been wounded in the defense of Atlanta, and the army surgeon had saved as much of the arm as he could by resection of the bone. Both Byerly and Jewell, furious after reading Warmoth's letter, gave him to understand that they would ruin him if he allowed it to be published.

That same day the *Bulletin* ran the letter and accompanied it with several paragraphs aspersing Warmoth. The next morning, in an anti-Warmoth screed a column and a half long, the *Bulletin* raked up stale charges of corruption and blamed Warmoth for originating "every objectionable and outrageous feature" of the state government that Kellogg, in his "usurpation," was perpetuating. Warmoth had launched his Louisiana career by playing up to blacks, the paper said, and then had tried, without success, to gain respectability by cultivating whites. "Like the 'dog returning to his vomit and the sow to her wallowing in the mire,' so does the ex-Governor return to the fond and loving embrace of his former disreputable associates."

On December 24 Warmoth wrote and the *Bulletin* published a reply vigorously refuting the charges of corruption and inquiring: "If these charges are true which Mr. Jewell makes against me, will he explain how it was that he was such a violent advocate of my nomination for Governor by the Liberal Convention in 1872?" Jewell seemed to be forgetting, Warmoth went on, how he had hobnobbed with Radicals of the Custom House faction in 1871. "It is said that 'a good liar ought to have a good memory,'" Warmoth concluded. "Even if I had aspired to social distinction, as you say, such aspirations have never turned in the direction of the manager of the New Orleans *Bulletin* or Mr. E. L. Jewell."

On that same December 24, more than six weeks after the 1874 election, the returning board at last made its report. According to the board's count, the Kellogg party had again elected a majority to the legislature. Once more an election was being stolen, Democrats believed, and now they lost what little patience they had left. It was not to be a very merry Christmas for most of them, as they continued to curse the returning board and consider ways to undo what it had done.

Christmas was not a happy day for Warmoth, either. Early in the morning two friends of Jewell's called at Warmoth's house and, in Jewell's behalf, demanded an apology. When he refused to give one, they asked if he was willing to meet Jewell, and he indicated that he would be glad to meet him for a friendly talk. The two men then left. Soon they were back with a peremptory challenge. Warmoth said he would reply that night through friends.

Duelling still seemed to Warmoth a stupid way to settle disagreements. Recently John A. Walsh had tried to provoke anew the fight that Warmoth, in 1871, had talked him out of. "Don't you really think you have done about enough to vindicate your wounded honor and to heal your lacerated feelings?" Warmoth responded this time in a note to Walsh. "Now I propose that neither of us make fools of ourselves, but let by gones be by gones." Warmoth did not have to send the note, for Walsh changed his mind and told him to "let it go."

But now, discussing the Jewell challenge with friends, Warmoth did not see how he could turn it aside and still maintain his self-respect. He decided on duelling pistols at ten paces. His and Jewell's seconds scheduled the encounter for Monday morning, December 28, at some out-of-state location yet to be agreed on.

On the morning after Christmas Warmoth left his house at about half-past ten to see his lawyer and make a will. An hour later, walking up Canal Street, he happened to meet Jewell's partner Byerly. Without a word, Byerly with his one good arm suddenly began to beat Warmoth over the head with a heavy cane. Warmoth, grappling with him, thought he was reaching for a pistol. He himself carried no gun, but he had in his pocket a patented knife with a spring blade he could release by pulling on a ring at the end of the handle. With this knife he stabbed Byerly again and again as the two men fell to the sidewalk, the bulky Byerly on top. A large crowd gathered to watch, and finally some of the bystanders separated the two as police arrived. Byerly was taken to the Orleans Infirmary, Warmoth to the Parish Prison.[14]

"The news of the tragedy spread with lightning rapidity," according to a *New York Herald* correspondent in New Orleans. "The excitement became intense, and for ten hours at least the Returning Board gave way as a prominent topic of interest and conversation."

At the prison, Warmoth was put into a cell that, for five days and five nights, he was to share with a convicted murderer, a professional gambler who was waiting to be hanged for a woman's death. A physician had cleaned and dressed a gash on Warmoth's left temple and had pronounced his injuries not serious, but the cut on his head and the bruises on his arms and back were nevertheless quite painful.

Before long, the *New York Herald* reporter called to see him. "In a few moments the tall form of the Governor appeared behind the bars, the grated door was opened by a turnkey, and the inmate stepped out into a bare, unfurnished, dismal room in the basement of the building." Warmoth, "neatly dressed, perfectly calm and collected," recounted in detail the disagreement, the Jewell challenge, and the Byerly affray. "I am no fighting man but, on the contrary, have always had the greatest distaste and horror of personal altercations," he said in ending the interview. "I sincerely hope and trust that Mr. Byerly's condition may not be so bad as reported, and that his days in the land may yet be long and prosperously happy ones."

At the infirmary it was not clear for some time just how serious the patient's wounds were. "The doctors were not able to probe or fully investigate them, owing to Mr. Byerly's restless condition, he having been drinking considerably." Eventually it became apparent that his internal hemorrhaging was severe, and at about ten-thirty that night he died.

While Warmoth was in prison, hundreds of well-wishers came to see him, among them both "Governor" McEnery and Governor Kellogg. The Episcopal bishop, paying him a visit, reproved him for accepting the challenge but assured him he was perfectly justified in defending himself against his assailant. Warmoth "jumped up, seized him by the hand and said to him: 'My dear, dear Bishop, I shall join your church as soon as I get out of this jail!'" And Warmoth was indeed to be a member of the Episcopal church for the rest of his life.

Not even Jewell or any other friend of Byerly could justify what he had done. He had not only offended common decency but, what was worse, had grossly violated the duelling code. In the country as a whole, Warmoth was viewed as more sinned against than sinning. "This encounter . . . shows the utter and uncompromising ultraism of the Southern Democrats, which is worse, if possible, than the opposing ultraism of the carpet-baggers," the *Chicago Tribune* commented. "Warmoth has been acting with the so-called Conservatives since 1872, but this could not save him from brutal assault simply because he refused to join in a general war against 'the niggers.'"

The municipal courtroom was packed when Warmoth, "pale but composed," was brought in for the inquest into Byerly's death. After hearing testimony, the judge told Warmoth he had acted in self-defense. "I therefore dismiss you. You can go." From the spectators came a burst of applause.

In a few days, on January 4, 1875, the new Kellogg legislature was to meet, and the rumor ran that the White League was going to prevent its doing so. On January 4 federal troops and state militia surrounded the Mechanics' Institute. In command was General Philip H. Sheridan, hero of the Shenandoah Valley campaign of 1864-65. Sheridan announced that he was ready, if President Grant would authorize him, to treat the White Leaguers as "banditti." The Kellogg government remained in power, and Warmoth's chances of becoming a United States senator, very slim at best, completely disappeared.[15]

The next Sunday, recovering from his cuts and bruises, Warmoth had a chance to show off the proudest of his possessions—Magnolia plantation, in which he recently had acquired a one-third interest. The co-owner was his good friend Effingham Lawrence, once a colonel in the Confederate army, then (after the Union occupation of Louisiana) a loyal Unionist, and more recently a Republican ally of Warmoth's. Warmoth paid for his share of the plantation with state bonds and cash. He still owned several pieces of property in New Orleans and, after selling one "palatial residence" there, had bought another. Financially he was doing quite well despite the panic of '73.

Now Warmoth and Lawrence were playing hosts to a congressional committee and a few other men. It was a cold morning even for January—barely above freezing—when the party left the city, but somewhat warmer when their boat put in at the Magnolia wharf after a downriver trip of four hours and forty-seven miles, to be greeted by "a dozen coal-black little darkeys." Warmoth and Lawrence immediately took their guests on a walking tour of the place. At the sugar house, huge carts drawn by teams of three mules abreast were bringing in cane, which a continuous, sloping elevator carried up to the rollers overhead. The two hosts explained in detail the process by which sugar was made—750,000 pounds of it from this year's crop, plus 750 barrels of syrup. But not all the 2,700 acres of the plantation were devoted to growing cane. The group next went through the orange orchard, extending for a mile along the river, containing 7,000 trees, and producing this season more than 1,100,000 oranges. "It is the finest plantation of its kind in the world," a newspaperman with the party gathered.

After the tour, the men—twenty of them—sat down to dinner in the mansion, Colonel Lawrence at one end of the table and his brother Henry at the other, "both gentlemen of the old school." Elegant was the hundred-year-old silver plate, delicious the homegrown mutton, unforgettable the wine and the wit. Serving were black women, former slaves on the place, who made "sprightly waiters, as well as jolly ones." The colonel's womenfolk, his wife and two daughters, were back in the city, where he and they made their home. His eighteen-year-old son ran the sugar refinery.

After the emancipation proclamation, January 1, 1863, Effingham Lawrence had freed his slaves and divided among them a large tract several miles below Magnolia plantation. There they now lived, about three hundred of them, on their own farms. "Colonel Lawrence is one of the few men in this section who has accepted the results of the war in good faith," the reporter wrote after the visit. "He has done so, and notwithstanding his wealth and generous impulses, he has been compelled to suffer in a grievous manner, socially, for his patriotism."[16]

Warmoth could make himself at home here at Magnolia. If he could not be a United States senator, at least he could be a sugar planter and an orange grower.

In March 1874, Senator Powell Clayton arrived in Little Rock, along with his junior colleague, Senator Stephen W. Dorsey, to face worsening financial and political troubles. Spring was arriving at the same time, and the azalea were about to blossom, the peach trees already in full bloom. Little Rock was beginning to look its best, and the Greek Revival statehouse, its back to the Arkansas River, was still handsome in its proportions, shabby though it had become. This hardly seemed like the setting for a bloody clash between political parties, a clash that was to break out very soon and was to go down in Arkansas history as the Brooks-Baxter War.

Arkansas had a reputation as the most backward of all the states. Yet its capital, despite the recent onset of a nationwide depression, still gave an appearance of progress and civilization. After visiting Little Rock that spring of 1874, the traveling reporter Edward King wrote for *Scribner's Magazine:* It "has a flourishing library, several well-ordered banks, and fine streets; society and schools are as good as in Eastern towns of the same size." Blacks shared in the general advance, according to King. Among them were "many gentlemen of education and refinement," a number of state and city officials, and graduates of Harvard, Oberlin, and other excellent schools. "A large proportion of the colored people of Little Rock own their own homes."

To be sure, conditions remained primitive in most of Arkansas, but railroads were bringing improvement to the state as a whole. One line ran from the northwest corner to the southwest corner and "placed Arkansas on the direct high road to Texas." Another crossed from east to west. The river now having been "handsomely bridged for the railroad's convenience," passengers from St. Louis or from Memphis could get into Little Rock without taking a ferry. Several projected railroads remained incomplete, however, the depression having brought construction to a halt.

Railroading was a subject of immediate concern to both Senator Clayton and Senator Dorsey. A native of Vermont and a prewar resident of Oberlin, Ohio, Dorsey had served in both the Army of the Tennessee and the Army of the Potomac, then returned to Ohio to become president of a Sandusky tool works. Elected president of the Arkansas Central Railroad, he moved to Helena to oversee the construction of the road between Helena and Little Rock. His company received $300,000 worth of railroad-aid bonds from the state.

Clayton also was president of a railroad company, the Little Rock, Mississippi and Texas, a consolidation of the Mississippi, Ouachita and Red River with the Little Rock, Pine Bluff and New Orleans. This Pine Bluff route was of special interest to Clayton, since it ran through his plantation on a strip of land he had donated to the company. The track from Pine Bluff to the Mississippi (at a point below the mouth of the Arkansas) had been laid before the Panic of '73. It gave Clayton much faster and more dependable shipping than the Arkansas River had provided. From Linwood, the new station in the midst of his property, he could ship to the New Orleans market not only his cotton but also the cypress lumber he now could afford to cut at his sawmill.

Once the forty-three-mile stretch from Pine Bluff to Little Rock was completed, Clayton would also have good access to Little Rock, Memphis, and other upriver markets. He was negotiating with men who in turn were negotiating with a European syndicate for funds to pay for the project—when the financial crash occurred. His company went bankrupt. Eventually the new owners were to finish the road, but he would no longer be its president.[17]

To Clayton, politics was more urgent than business when he revisited the Arkansas capital in the spring of 1874. Political control of the state seemed to be slipping from his grasp. And only a little more than a year had passed since he reconfirmed his position as Republican boss of Arkansas!

When the legislature met in January 1873, his brother John M. Clayton was elected president pro tem of the senate. Another brother, W. H. H. Clayton, was already a state circuit judge. The legislature sent Clayton's man Dorsey to the United States Senate. It awarded the governorship to Clayton's candidate, the scalawag Elisha Baxter, and not to the Liberal Republican and Democratic candidate, the carpetbagger Joseph Brooks, who disputed the election.

Brooks continued to dispute it. He started *quo warranto* proceedings in the Pulaski County (Little Rock) circuit court, and Baxter replied with a demurrer. Clayton, in New York on railroad business, sent to Baxter on June 3, 1873, a telegram advising him to "stand firm." The judge, John Whytock, soon discontinued the case. For the time being, Baxter remained governor de jure as well as de facto.

But Clayton began to wonder whether Baxter ought to remain. Though Baxter owed his nomination and election to Clayton, he was looking to Democrats for counsel and was rewarding them with state jobs. He favored them particularly in appointing officers for the large militia that he began to build up. Clayton and Dorsey urged him, in the interest of "harmony," to disband the militia. He agreed to do so, but he suggested that, if real harmony were to prevail, John M. Clayton should quit as president of the senate and all other state officials in the line of succession to the governorship should also resign. Apparently Baxter feared that the Clayton forces might try to remove him by impeachment and replace him with Clayton's brother John.

By March 1874, when Clayton and Dorsey returned to Little Rock, they were losing all influence with Baxter. He now refused to issue state bonds to railroads; he said he had no constitutional or legal authority to do so. Dorsey's Arkansas Central was one of the companies applying for additional aid, and Dorsey thus acquired a new grievance against Baxter. Clayton agreed with Baxter in opposing further state assistance, but he could hardly approve the grounds on which Baxter was basing his refusal. If it was unconstitutional for Baxter to issue railroad-aid bonds, it was equally unconstitutional for Clayton, as governor, to have issued them. Not only was Baxter implying malfeasance on Clayton's part; he was also threatening the interests of bondholders and undermining the state's credit.[18]

A few days later Clayton chaired and Dorsey attended a meeting of the Republican state central committee in Little Rock. The committeemen agreed that they must take drastic steps to prevent Baxter from turning Arkansas over to the Democrats. Indeed, they must get rid of him. But how? Well, they could arrange a coup d'état—a perfectly legal one—by which to eject Baxter and install Brooks in his place. Brooks had been a loyal Claytonite before the rise of the Liberal Republican heresy and the split in the party in 1872. Baxter was hopeless, but there was hope for Brooks. Clayton and his co-conspirators needed the cooperation of three men: Brooks, Circuit Judge John Whytock, and Chief Justice John McClure of the state supreme court.

By the time the plan eventuated in action, on April 15, 1874, both Clayton and Dorsey were back in Washington, but they were ready for events in Arkansas and followed them as closely as they could. On that April 15, without informing Baxter or his attorneys, Judge Whytock quietly reconsidered Brooks's application for a writ of *quo warranto* and quickly granted it, thus giving Brooks a legal title to the governorship. Then Chief Justice McClure secretly administered the oath of office to him. Immediately a dozen or more armed men accompanied Brooks to the statehouse, compelled Baxter to leave the executive chambers, and installed Brooks as governor. As his first official act, "Governor" Brooks telegraphed President Grant to ask for recognition and for arms from the federal arsenal in Little Rock.

From Washington that same day Senators Clayton and Dorsey by telegram urged Brooks to hold on. The two senators and three of the four Arkansas congressmen telegraphed messages to the *Little Rock Republican* to say that the federal government undoubtedly would recognize and support the man whom the state courts had just recognized. But Grant hesitated to take the side of either Baxter or Brooks. Instead, he that day ordered the commander of the federal troops in Little Rock to use them only for keeping the peace and preventing bloodshed.

Two days after the Brooks takeover a telegram came to Washington from Devalls Bluff, about fifty miles east of Little Rock on the railroad to Memphis. The telegram was addressed to either Dorsey or Clayton and was sent by McClure, the Arkansas chief justice who had sworn Brooks in. It read:

> Can not send dispatches from Little Rock as the telegraph office is in the hands of Baxter's militia. Baxter has placed the country under martial law. We are likely to have trouble. The [U.S. military] officer here is not disposed to do his duty [is not siding with the Brooks government]. Have him instructed definitely. None of the State officers recognize Baxter.

With this telegram in hand, the two senators and three congressmen from Arkansas called on President Grant and Attorney General Williams to protest. They argued that the Grant Administration ought to make the same decision the state courts had already made. From Grant and Williams they gathered that the Administration would indeed do so, and Clayton and Dorsey promptly sent Brooks new assurances of federal support.

Receiving from Grant no promise of military aid, Brooks on April 20 sent him another appeal and, along with it, a statement from Chief Justice McClure and both of the associate justices of the state supreme court declaring that they recognized Brooks as governor. While waiting for a response—which never came—Brooks saw to the readying of his militia and the erection of earthworks and barricades around the capitol. Baxter, from his headquarters at the Anthony House a few blocks away, made his military preparations while consulting with the state's top Democrats. Federal troops were lined up between the opposing forces with the intention of keeping them apart.

Nevertheless, a clash soon occurred. On April 20, Baxter augmented his forces with five hundred black militiamen from Jefferson County, where Clayton's plantation was located. Commanding these men was Ferd Havis, a black leader who formerly had been a Claytonite but now was a colonel in Baxter's army. On April 21, Havis and his regiment marched toward the capitol while the Brooks militia were on dress parade in front of it. Shots rang out. One man was killed and several wounded. (During the month the "war" was to last, a total of about twenty were to die and many more were to be scarred or maimed.)

The next day Baxter proposed to Grant that the legislature meet and decide who had the better claim to the governorship. Back came the reply that the President would "heartily approve any adjustment, peaceably, of the pending difficulty in Arkansas—by means of the legislative assembly, the courts, or otherwise." Accordingly, Baxter convoked the legislature for a session to begin on May 11. If the decision were to be made by that "assembly"—and not by "the courts or otherwise"—Baxter would be sure to win. A special election to fill vacancies in the legislature had been held the previous autumn. All ex-Confederates could then vote and run for office by virtue of a state constitutional amendment that both Clayton and his opponents had advocated. As a result, the Democrats would have a majority in the legislature when it next met.

Clayton was unwilling to concede that Brooks's claim could even be questioned. In a public statement, which appeared in Arkansas newspapers, he declared: "Brooks was fairly elected in 1872; he was kept out of office by fraud." This, of course, contradicted what Clayton had been saying in 1872 and 1873. But in 1874, the two parties having switched loyalties, the Democrats as well as the Republicans were, in effect, repudiating their earlier statements as the most incredible of lies.

On May Day the attorney general allowed lawyers and other advocates of Brooks and Baxter, in Washington, to present oral and written arguments. After about a week the attorney general suggested a compromise: when, in a few days, the legislature assembled, it should not merely pick a winner but should investigate and report on the merits of Brooks's claim. Clayton and the other Brooks spokesmen in Washington reluctantly agreed to this proposal, and so did Brooks himself. But Baxter refused to accept any arrangement that would appear even temporarily to recognize Brooks.

When the legislature at its May session declared Baxter to be governor, Attorney General Williams advised President Grant to recognize him. After all, the legislature had now endorsed him twice—once when it was under Republican control and now again when under Democratic control. So Grant by proclamation recognized Baxter and ordered Brooks to disband his militia.[19]

Though this was a crushing blow to Clayton, it did not completely destroy his hopes. He could still appeal from the President to the Congress. The House of Representatives soon set up a committee to investigate the Brooks-Baxter contest, and he had a chance to testify before the committee. But he was discouraged when he entered the committee room. There sat the chairman, Luke Poland of Vermont, who he felt was "distinctly antagonistic" to him. There, as Brooks's counsel, was the brother of ex-Senator B. F. Rice, a Republican but a bitterly anti-Clayton one. And there, as Baxter's attorney, was the chairman of the Democratic state central committee. Baxter, Clayton now learned, had appointed as brigadier-general of his militia a former Klansman who had been implicated in the 1868 murder of Clayton's detective Albert Parker. Clayton decided not to testify.

Still, he could examine the witnesses appearing before the Poland committee, and he was eager to question Baxter when it held hearings in Little Rock in July and again in November. Baxter had been vituperating him in interviews with correspondents of the *New York Herald* and the *New York Times*. The *Times* reported:

> Governor Baxter is particularly bitter in his expressions regarding Clayton. It almost seems as if he could forgive Brooks for his share in the contest. But of Clayton he speaks with a hatred and a violence that cannot well be described. To-day, in the presence of the writer and several well-known Arkansas politicians, he said: "Clayton is a rascal of the worst kind; and should he ever dare return to this State, I am not so sure that I will not have him arrested and tried for treason in having attempted to overthrow the State government." He further stated: "Such crimes could be proven against him as would cause his immediate expulsion from the Senate, if not his imprisonment as a common felon."

Baxter backed down considerably when Clayton confronted him. He was vague and evasive in regard to most of Clayton's "crimes" but did insist: "I think you have been guilty of treason in the late rebellion." Clayton: "In what respect?" Baxter: "In aiding and abetting and encouraging it." Clayton: "Was I here at the time?" Baxter: "You were not here at the time, but you did aid and abet it."[20]

In July, while the Poland committee was in Little Rock, the Baxter people were holding a constitutional convention there. They reduced the governor's powers and shortened his term from four to two years. They also decreased the representation of the southeastern lowland counties in the legislature, thereby lessening black influence, and they increased the representation of the northwestern hill counties, thereby enlarging white influence. The convention set October 13 as the date for a popular vote to ratify the new constitution and elect men to office under it.

Meanwhile, in mid-September, the Republicans held a party conclave in Little Rock. Clayton denounced the Baxter men in a vitriolic speech, but he was careful to say nothing against the Poland committee. Under his leadership the assembled Republicans adopted a resolution thanking the committee for its work— and thus, they hoped, influencing the committee's final report. They also agreed to make no nominations for the October 13 election, but simply to ignore it and hold an election of their own at the regular time in November.

In the October 13 election Augustus H. Garland won the governorship. Tennessee-born, a former Confederate congressman and senator, now the foremost of Arkansas Democrats, Garland had recently been the chief strategist in Baxter's war with Brooks. Elected to the state senate were thirty-one Democrats and two Republicans; to the house of representatives, eighty Democrats and ten Republicans. The Clayton men never got around to electing candidates to contest the October results.

At the time of the October election in Arkansas, Clayton was attending a convention of Southern Republicans in Chattanooga, Tennessee. The Southern Republicans had much to preoccupy them, but could do little about it except talk. Of the ten states reconstructed under the congressional act of 1867, five had already fallen to the Democrats. If Arkansas should now follow them, only four would be left under Republican control—Mississippi, South Carolina, Florida, and Louisiana. A *New York Times* correspondent covering the Chattanooga convention could not help sympathizing with the carpetbaggers and scalawags. He wrote:

> I frankly confess that Senator Clayton, of Arkansas, from private conversations I had with him, seemed to me the most of all entitled to sympathy and regard. I will own I was prejudiced against Clayton. In common with everyone else acquainted with the outlines of his history, I considered him a political adventurer of incomparable shrewdness, pluck, and unscrupulousness. I am still convinced that he is all that, but I have now discovered that only by strong provocation was he induced to enter upon that political career which has made him notorious, or, as some would say, infamous.

Clayton had been telling the reporter how, after the war, his Jefferson County neighbors made life so miserable for him that his only alternatives were to flee the state or to govern and improve it.[21]

On December 8, 1874, the Poland committee published a preliminary report of its hearings. Clayton's spirits rose when, in January 1875, responding to his Senate resolution asking the executive for information on Arkansas affairs, Grant in a special message said the evidence seemed to uphold Brooks's claim. All along, Grant had been inclined to the Brooks and Clayton side but had been restrained by the advice of his attorney general and by his unhappy experience in regard to Louisiana, where his commitment to the Republican claimant Kellogg had led to endless controversy. So Clayton could still entertain a little hope that Congress might take action to replace Baxter with Brooks.

Then, in February, the Poland committee gave its final report. A four-to-one majority recommended that the United States government refrain from interference with the existing Arkansas government. And Congress, in March, overwhelmingly approved the committee's recommendation. Clayton finally had to concede defeat, and he did it as gracefully as he could. "The action of Congress on Arkansas affairs is conclusive," he advised his followers in a telegram to the *Little Rock Republican*. "It is the duty of Republicans to accept the verdict, and to render the same acquiescence which we would have demanded had the case been reversed."

Democrats would henceforth control the state, but Republicans could still count on majorities in Jefferson and several other counties along the Mississippi River, where the population was predominantly black. If nothing were done to prevent it, however, the blacks might monopolize the county offices. So local Democratic leaders proposed to local Republican leaders that the two parties agree on a single ticket dividing the offices between them. Clayton reasoned that such an arrangement would stop the Democrats from raising the "negro domination" cry. "I was visiting my brother John on my plantation when the question was brought up," he recalled long afterward, "and I advised him to adopt the plan."[22]

CHAPTER 15

Political Death of the Negro (1873-1876)

"I do not think I am a politician by nature," Adelbert Ames once mused, "but rather by necessity." Certainly he did not consider himself a typical Mississippi politician. He never had been a drinking man, and he no longer smoked, not even an occasional cigar. He not only refrained from profanity himself; he expected others to refrain from it in his presence. With such a creature as Henry Clay Warmoth, he hoped he shared nothing more than the carpetbagger tag.

Just before the recent election of 1872, while campaigning in Mississippi for Grant, Ames had crossed the Mississippi River to observe the events on the Louisiana side. "Gov. Warmoth has sold the state to the Democracy," he inferred. He was disgusted at what he saw. "It causes two different and conflicting emotions to rise up within me—the one, to abandon a life of politics where such things alone find place, and another, to buckle on my armor anew that I may better fight the battle of the poor and oppressed colored man." A knight in shining armor—that was how he saw himself.

And now, in January 1873, he was tilting against oppression from his place in the United States Senate. Speaking for a bill he had introduced to desegregate the army, he pointed out that a black could serve as a soldier in only four of forty existing regiments. The law providing for segregated units had been passed before the ratification of the Fourteenth Amendment, which gave citizenship to the colored man. "Now that he is a citizen . . . he ought to be permitted to serve in one regiment or another, as he sees fit, as the white man or an Indian or a man of any other race is permitted to do." But Ames was more than seventy years ahead of time in his attempt to repeal the army's color bar.[1]

He could remain in the Senate, as the blacks' champion there, until the end of his term, in 1875, when the Mississippi legislature might choose him for a second term. But he would improve his chances for another term if he first demonstrated his popularity by winning a statewide election. Besides, he would thereby remove the stigma of the charge that he had gained his senatorship—and could only have gained it—through his own military influence. When the legislature last chose him, he was both provisional governor and military governor of the state. Now he aspired to be the regular governor. Once he had made his point, he would resign the governorship and again accept the senatorship.

To get the Republican nomination, he would have to defeat the incumbent, Governor Ridgley C. Powers, an Ohio-born carpetbagger but a follower of the scalawag Senator James L. Alcorn. In eliminating Powers, he would be humiliating Alcorn, his great rival for Republican leadership in the state. It would require the election of pro-Ames delegates to the county conventions, which would choose delegates to the state nominating convention. So Ames must go to Mississippi and begin taking part in local politics as soon as possible after the congressional session ended.

He must take his family with him to Mississippi. True, the presence of his wife, the daughter of Ben Butler, would underscore the fact that he himself was the son-in-law of the same man—whom Southerners often called "Spoon" or "Spoons" Butler, alleging that, as wartime commander of occupied New Orleans, he had seized as booty the silverware of some of the best families in town. This Butler-Ames relationship was one of two defects that Mississippians continually attributed to Ames. But the other of the two defects was much more serious, and the presence of Blanche would help to counteract it. This was the charge that he possessed no domicile in the state. In fact, he now owned—and had owned since the previous November—a house in Natchez, the one place in Mississippi that Blanche considered habitable. By bringing his family to live in the house awhile, he could demonstrate that he did indeed have a Mississippi home.[2]

Blanche gave birth to her second child — a daughter, Edith—on March 4, 1873, the day of U. S. Grant's second inauguration. On May 2, when Edith at two months seemed old enough to travel, the Ameses set out with her and her nursemaid, Mary. They left their son Butler, not yet two years old, with his grandparents in Lowell, Massachusetts. The last leg of the trip to Natchez was by a steamboat on the Mississippi, and Edith attracted a good deal of attention from fellow passengers. "A woman on the boat wanted to take her—and said, 'What a fine child! Whose is it?' When Mary told her Gen'l Ames'—'Oh, take it, take it,—It is a Yankee baby, take it.'" The reaction of Natchez neighbors was much the same. "Everyone asks on the street 'Oh, whose baby is that?' When they learned it is Gen'l Ames' the noses fly up and they start back as from an adder."

After about a month of this, with heat and humidity rising at the approach of summer, Blanche decided the Mississippi climate was not good for Edith. Ames accompanied his wife and daughter to Massachusetts, then quickly returned to Mississippi without them for the political campaign. He cultivated black support not only at party rallies but also at black gatherings of all kinds, including a revivalistic "camp meeting" and a "colored ball" at a "colored hotel." Blacks assured him they would "go for" him. "Youse de man," they said. And, sure enough, at the state convention in August he received 187 votes and Governor Powers only forty.

Nominated on the ticket with Ames—for lieutenant governor, secretary of state, and superintendent of education—were three blacks. He had anticipated that at least the candidate for lieutenant governor would be a Negro, but he had hoped for a better representative of the race than A. K. Davis. With Davis as his prospective successor, Ames could not expect enough white votes in the legislature to send him back to the Senate in 1875. He would have to wait till 1877, when his and Davis's terms would be over—and so would Alcorn's term in the Senate. He could then complete his rout of Alcorn by taking Alcorn's Senate seat away from him.

Alcorn decided to challenge Ames immediately. He announced himself as an Independent Republican candidate for governor, and held a rump convention ("or more properly, a caucus," as Ames contemptuously described it) to declare himself the nominee. Supporting him were a few carpetbaggers, among them Henry R. Pease, the superintendent of education, whom one of the blacks was replacing on the Ames ticket. Also supporting Alcorn, at least passively, were the Democrats, who refrained from nominating a gubernatorial candidate of their own.

Back in Mississippi for the fall campaign, Ames received letters of encouragement and advice from Blanche, who remained in Lowell with the children, while her father campaigned (unsuccessfully) for governor of Massachusetts. Not all of Blanche's letters were as pleasing as Ames might have wished. In one of them she told how her parents had met Warmoth and two pals on a train and had brought them home. "Gov. Warmouth [*sic*] is quite good-looking. I remember that I used to know him years ago—when he was attentive to Miss Harlan." So Blanche wrote, in a spirit that, considering the subject, must have been a bit too effervescent for Ames. "The Governor said they were all going into Mississippi to vote for you. I replied there could be no doubt of your success with such able allies."[3]

There would be doubt of Ames's success if Governor Powers should get away with his scheme to postpone the election. Powers asserted that, according to the constitution, the election should be held in 1874, not in 1873. Hoping to obtain legislative confirmation, he called the legislature into special session. On October 31, Ames's thirty-eighth birthday, the legislature finally decided that the voting should go ahead as scheduled, on November 4.

Meanwhile, despite the possibility that he might be wasting his time, Ames exhausted himself in a determined effort to bring out the votes as he traveled through the state by horseback, carriage, riverboat, and train. One Sunday, in Holly Springs, he addressed a crowd of two thousand for two hours. "It seemed as if every colored man in the county had presented himself. There were two four-horse carriages decorated with flags, one having my name in large letters pasted in every conspicuous place. Even the rough, country wagons had on their sides my name—and the colored people had it tied or fastened on their hats—hundreds of them." The crowd was so large that the courthouse could not contain it, and so Ames spoke from the courthouse steps.

At Vicksburg he and Alcorn met in debate. Going first, Alcorn used up the afternoon by speaking for four hours, so that Ames had to wait till evening to reply. At Greenville, where Ames insisted on speaking first, Alcorn held a separate meeting at the same time, with a brass band. That attracted a crowd, but soon most of Alcorn's audience drifted over to Ames. He took pride in what a Democratic paper said of his speech at Winona:

> Gen. Ames has been misrepresented by the Press; he is anything but "addle-pated" or foolish. His speech was extremely deliberate, his enunciation remarkably clear and distinct, his grammatical construction faultless, his manner calm and dispassionate, his rhetoric chaste, his sarcasm abundant, polished and cutting; there was no sign of haste or confusion, every sentence had the complete finish, the correctness and polish, of an epigram.
>
> We have heard no Republican speaker who has so favorably impressed us as a *speaker*. His speech was certainly, in a literary point, superior to Gen. Alcorn's speech made here some time back.

This was quite an accolade for one who, only a few years earlier, could hardly open his mouth in public without blushing and who, quite recently, seemed envious of Alcorn's persuasive oratory, of his "crazy, insane, drunken speeches."

On election day, after campaigning up to the last minute, Ames in an open buggy rode forty miles through rain and mud to reach Natchez in time to cast his ballot. It was only the second time in his entire life that he had voted, the first time having been the previous year. Now his vote helped to give the ticket a majority of approximately 70,000 to 50,000.[1]

On January 10, 1874, Ames resigned from the Senate and, with his wife and two children, soon left Washington for Jackson, where they stayed in a hotel beside the railroad tracks awaiting his inauguration as Mississippi governor. The incumbent, Powers, was still trying desperately to hold on to the job for another year. He had appealed to the state supreme court to invalidate the recent election on the grounds that it should not have been held until the fall of 1874. On January 19 the court ruled that the election was valid, and on January 22 Ames was duly inaugurated.

It was raining very hard that day, but the Ameses were, as Blanche said, "very anxious to make any change which would take us away from the confinement of the hotel and the noise of the cars which kept passing and repassing under the windows, night and day." So, in the afternoon, they moved right into the executive mansion, which Powers had finally vacated that morning. There was plenty of room—indeed, too much of it—here in this "great barn of a house," as Blanche irreverently called the imposing classical edifice. And certainly the grounds were spacious enough, occupying, as they did, an entire block. "The walks are brick with grass growing between," Blanche sniffed, "so that the grounds have a weedy appearance."

In the ensuing weeks Blanche did what she could to put things to rights. She had to teach the cook that "lard is not the staff of life" and that servants must show respect for their superiors. "Oh! gal Oh! gal," the cook once addressed her in some excitement. Sternly Blanche replied: "What did you call me—you are to say Madame when you want anything of me." She had to give instructions to a prison guard who, with a large pistol in his belt, stood over three convicts from the penitentiary while they cleaned the carpets and washed the windows. By March 4 she could report: "The house is in nice order, the curtains washed and in place, and a regular system established by which the work goes on easily."

Blanche took seriously her duties as Mississippi's first lady. "Yours is a difficult part," her mother advised her, "for while it is far better that you should lead or bear your part with those of your own color and station, yet your real strength of position is elsewhere." So remember this: "When there comes a pressure either socially or politically, you belong to the colored people." Yet, socially, Blanche was rather cautious. She received visits from white ladies of Jackson—most of them "lynx-eyed"—and she repaid their calls. But she and Ames thought it best not to hold weekly receptions at which both races and both sexes would have to mingle. For carpetbag friends, she put on occasional teas, dinners, and croquet parties.

Then, at the adjournment of the legislature, in April, she and the governor entertained all the 140 state officials and members of the legislature, without their wives, at a tremendous bash, though a quite temperate one. On such an occasion it had been customary to serve only boughten cake and cheap wine—known locally as "nigger champagne"—which "led to a great deal of rowdyism and drunkenness." Ames determined to have none of that. So Blanche served no alcoholic beverages but lots of fine food (the supplies coming mostly from New Orleans, more than 200 miles away): 36 chickens and 24 pounds of lobster, both made into salad, 6 large roast turkeys, 4 baked hams, 10 large frosted cakes, and 27 loaves of bread "nicely sliced and buttered," not to mention olives, sardines, oranges, bananas, strawberries, ice cream, coffee, and choice cigars (of which "some *gentlemen* took three or four").

The next day the grounds were "littered with orange peel and banana skins."

After the cleanup the Ameses could relax somewhat. The governor had less to do, now that the legislature was no longer in session, and he could spend more time at home, where he occupied himself with studying law. Blanche, pregnant again, sewed or painted, finishing a portrait of three-year-old Butler that she considered pretty good. She was beginning to think that life in Jackson was rather pleasant, with its mild winter and delightful spring, its many days when Butler and even one-year-old Edith could play outdoors. But her mother insisted that she and the children must come North well before the "debilitating heat" should begin. Mrs. Butler knew about the Southern summer, having spent some time in New Orleans during the war. "If you stay there till the heat sets in you will lose your bright color and never regain it," she warned. "A sallow, Southern woman cannot compare with the bright, glowing color of a Northern one."[5]

Ames had not been able to get from the legislature all that he had asked of it. In his inaugural, on January 22, he proposed that steps be taken to eliminate illiteracy, to provide land for blacks and thus keep them from "tenantry or peasantry," and to make Mississippi a great manufacturing state. At the same time he urged "retrenchment in expenditures" and adherence to "rigid economy." In a special message on February 7 he renewed his plea for economy and reform. This kind of talk pleased conservative Mississippi whites, but when little action followed they lost some of their tolerance for Ames, though his administration proved to be, on the whole, a very frugal one.

He made some progress toward equalizing taxes and assuring their collection. Railroads had been tax-exempt, but by executive orders he brought about the assessment and taxation of their property. He called, in vain, for the repeal of an act that would lend to the Vicksburg and Nashville Railroad a federal land grant intended for an agricultural college. He refused to turn the land-grant scrip over to the railroad until the state supreme court directed him to do so. While Ames was opposing public largesse for private enterprise, Nathan Bedford Forrest, the founder of the Ku Klux Klan, was favoring it, at least for the railroad he was promoting in Mississippi. The advocate of governmental extravagance was not the carpetbagger but the Klansman!

As a fiscal conservative, Ames vetoed bills for the relief of farmers suffering from the depression—one bill to postpone the collection of debts, another to deny creditors a crop lien. When spring floods threatened starvation in some of the river counties, and the legislature was no longer in session, he appealed to the Mississippi delegation in Congress for federal aid. Over the objections of Senator Alcorn, whose plantation was free from flooding, Congress provided $100,000 worth of military rations, and Ames appointed committees to distribute them.

As a teetotaler and a native of Maine, the prohibitionist state, Ames would have liked to see a "Maine law" for Mississippi. But that was out of the question, so he contented himself with requesting and obtaining a local-option law. This required a person applying for a liquor license to present a petition bearing the signatures of both a majority of the voters and a majority of the women in the locality. "One of the finest features of the law," Ames declared, "is its recognition of the voices of the women of the State. It recognizes their equal ability with male counterparts."

This New England puritanism of Ames's did not, of course, improve his popularity among white Mississippians. Most of them did consider him the lesser of evils, however, as compared with the lieutenant governor, the black A. K. Davis. In Mississippi the lieutenant governor became the governor whenever the latter left the state. In February and again in May, Ames went to southern Mississippi by way of New Orleans, and both times Davis immediately took over the gubernatorial office, to embarrass Ames by issuing pardons and making appointments and removals. By June, when Ames departed for the North with his family, most Democrats were afraid of what might happen in his absence. A few chose to embarrass him further by preferring Davis to him—or pretending to do so. One paper remarked: "As Davis, though a molasses-colored pet of the nation, is a better man than Ames, we hope little Bullet-head will spend the summer with his pappy-in-law, old Spoons Butler."

Of the grievances the Democrats were accumulating against Ames, the worst was the charge that he had conspired to free a friend and fellow carpetbagger who had been jailed for murder. This man was Albert T. Morgan, the Republican leader of Yazoo County.[6]

The new courthouse in Yazoo City was the pride of local Republicans. It was a substantial brick building with a tall bell-tower, all done in up-to-date Gothic style. Surrounding it was a high, sturdy, iron picket fence. As president of the county board of supervisors, Morgan had overseen the construction of the building. As sheriff-elect, he looked forward to occupying the sheriff's room, off the central hallway on the first floor. But January 1874 came and the incumbent, F. P. Hilliard, persisted in occupying the quarters and claiming the title of sheriff.

Hilliard, a prewar resident and wartime refugee, had received an appointment as sheriff from Provisional Governor Ames in 1869. Morgan could have had the appointment at that time but, instead, had recommended Hilliard as a Southern Unionist and a personal friend. Hilliard won election to another term in 1871. Then, in 1873, Morgan decided to run for sheriff instead of running again for state senator. He needed the money. He had accumulated no property, not even a house or lot, while Hilliard was well-to-do, his wife having inherited a plantation and he himself having enjoyed the emoluments of office for four years. The sheriff was also tax collector, and from his salary and fees he could make as much as $10,000 a year (the equivalent of more than ten times that much in the dollars of the 1980s). After Morgan took from him the Republican nomination for sheriff, Hilliard ran as an independent, with Democratic support. Morgan defeated him by a vote of 2,365 to 431.

Then Governor Powers started his suit before the state supreme court to try and prolong his own term for a year. If the court should decide in Powers's favor, the effect would be to extend also the terms of Hilliard and other state and local officeholders. So Hilliard refused to give up the sheriff's ofice when, on January 5, Morgan went to him and demanded possession of it.

At a meeting of the board of supervisors the next day, Hilliard and his lawyer argued his right to keep the job at least until the court should make its decision. But Morgan presented his certificate of election and his receipt for having given bond. Then he took the oath of office. It was "*Ordered,* That this board do recognize the said A. T. Morgan as the only person legally entitled to exercise the functions and perform the duties of the office of sheriff of Yazoo County." Nevertheless, Hilliard persisted in holding the sheriff's room, posting armed guards at the door.[7]

His frustration growing, Morgan spent a sleepless night while his wife, Carrie, wondered and worried. What was wrong? Had her husband not been duly installed as sheriff? She had, besides him, three children (all of them almost white) to be concerned about. Albert, Jr., was two and a half years old, Carrie a little more than a year, and Nina not quite four months. The baby was colicky that night, and both she and her parents were feeling cross when daylight finally appeared.

Early that morning, when Morgan went to check the situation at the courthouse, he found the sheriff's room unguarded except for one man, a young relative of Hilliard's. Morgan quickly got together his brother William and three black deputies. At about seven o'clock they hurried to the courthouse, told the young man on guard to leave, and took possession of the office. In a few minutes a black follower of Hilliard's pounded on the door and demanded admittance, then rang the courthouse bell and left.

An hour or so later Morgan saw Hilliard and a few dozen men come around a corner two blocks away and head for the courthouse. Morgan, with one of his deputies, went out to meet the hastily assembled posse. Telling Hilliard his own men had charge of the office, he warned him not to go in. Hilliard and his posse ignored Morgan and strode on past him.

Morgan followed them. When he reached the gate of the courthouse fence, he heard, from inside the building, the crash of splintering wood and then the popping of repeated gunfire. Pistol in hand, he ran to the courthouse steps. A bullet whizzed past him; he fired two or three shots in return. Hilliard staggered toward him and fell at the entrance, bleeding profusely from the head. He did not live long. One of Morgan's deputies, wounded when Hilliard's men broke into the office, also was expected to die, but survived.

Promptly Morgan surrendered himself to the mayor, who allowed him to to remain at home while awaiting a hearing before the chancellor, that is, the local judge. The *Yazoo City Democrat* provocatively accused him not only of murder but also of fiendish brutality, alleging falsely that he had shot Hilliard at close range while Hilliard, already wounded, was trying to escape. After a hearing, the chancellor, a man named Drennan, remanded Morgan to jail—for protection from a potential mob, he told him. Even the jail seemed unsafe, so Morgan was removed to the one in Jackson. He arrived there at about the time that Ames was inaugurated as governor.

In Morgan's absence Judge Drennan named a leading Yazoo Democrat as sheriff and tax collector, though a chancellor had no legal authority to do such a thing. Yazoo Republicans protested to Ames that Drennan was conspiring with local Democrats to "revolutionize" the county government and take control of it. Morgan concurred when Ames visited him in jail. So Ames removed Drennan, who held at best a dubious tenure, since the state senate had never confirmed his appointment by Powers. Ames replaced him with Thomas Walton, a professor of law at the University of Mississippi. Judge Walton released Morgan, after nearly three months of confinement, on $5,000 bail.

Morgan returned to Yazoo City to rejoin his wife and children and to reassume the title and role of sheriff, taking over from his brother William, who had been holding the office on an interim appointment from Ames. Later a grand jury declined to indict Morgan. The evidence was confusing, and the jury could not be sure which of the several men engaging in gunfire on that fatal morning was responsible for the shot that killed Hilliard. (It might have been one of Hilliard's own men.) Undeterred by the evidence, or by the lack of it, Democrats continued to vilify Sheriff Morgan as a murderer—and Governor Ames as a kind of accessory after the fact.[8]

In July 1874, Ames had to leave his pregnant wife and his children in Massachusetts and hurry back to Mississippi. There was ominous news from Vicksburg, where in preparation for a local election the "White Liners" were arming themselves and patrolling the streets to overawe the blacks.

No longer could Ames deal with these Ku Klux tactics as he had done when he was military governor. At that time he had had at least a thousand troops under his immediate command, but now there were only about half that many in the state, and he had no authority over them. To secure military aid, he must appeal to the President in accordance with the Ku Klux Acts that he himself, as a senator, had helped to pass. On July 29 and again on August 1 he wrote to Grant and asked for troops to keep the peace at the August 4 election, but Grant only sent a man to Vicksburg to investigate. This man reported that a riot was unlikely.

"The election at Vicksburg passed off quietly only because the Democrats, or white man's party, had both intimidated the blacks and perpetrated frauds of registration, so, of course, they had no cause to commit murder," Ames explained to Blanche. "The whites are organized to carry the state as thay have carried V." Certainly the Democrats had shown how, by pre-election terrorism, they could carry the state with a minimum of violence on election day. By this strategy they were to gain control of the legislature and the local governments in the fall of 1875.

Ames was beginning to foresee his own political doom. He was losing both his hope and his ambition of being sent back to the Senate. Lonely without his wife, he poured out his feelings in letter after letter to her. One evening, while he was at a neighbor's house for dinner, another guest's boy, Warren, came into the yard crying. "The cause of which was," Ames related, "that a Negro boy, larger than he, had kicked him in the stomach—and really for no cause. Upon inquiry I learned that it is a common practice for the Negro boys to lick white boys whenever they catch them out after dark, and Warren was only getting his regular allowance!" Ames could not help thinking of his own little boy, Butler. "We will not raise our boy here, will we?" Then, a few days later:

> The North seems the place for us. . . . Why is it, Beloved I dwell so much on a different occupation than that I am now devoting myself to? Is it because I love you so much and find so little contentment away from you—or is it the fact that our own latitude is the best for us? Slavery blighted this people [the Southern whites]—then the war—then reconstruction—all piled on such a base destroyed the minds—at least impaired their judgment and consciousness to that extent that we cannot live among them.

Ames was further discouraged by news of Democratic victories in the 1874 congressional elections in the North—one of which was costing his father-in-law his seat in the House. "A Democratic Congress! And the war not yet over." The Democrats of Mississippi were "made wild by the news." For Ames, it was depressing, but the governor's mansion became a cheerier place when, late in November, Blanche arrived with all three of the children—the third one, Sarah Hildreth (named for Blanche's mother), not yet two months old.[9]

Before long, though, Ames was preoccupied by reports of new and more serious trouble in Vicksburg. While the Democrats (the whites) now controlled the government of Vicksburg itself, the Republicans (the blacks) still dominated the government of Warren County, and there was growing hostility between the city hall and the courthouse. Several county officials, including the sheriff, Peter Crosby, had been indicted (by a predominantly black grand jury) for embezzlement. Delegates attending a taxpayers' convention demanded Crosby's resignation, then marched to the courthouse in a body, some five hundred strong, and compelled him to resign. He fled to Jackson to consult with Ames.

Ames had been embarrassed by the allegations of malfeasance against Crosby and his colleagues (and also by those against Thomas W. Cardozo, the state superintendent of education elected on the Ames ticket). But he firmly believed that the law should be allowed to take its course and that Crosby should be permitted to hold office until convicted of wrongdoing. He gave him to understand that he ought to go back to Warren County, raise a posse, and reinstate himself as sheriff. A massacre resulted—the bloodiest in Reconstruction history. As Crosby marched toward Vicksburg at the head of his black posse, on December 7, he was met by an armed mob of whites. They took him prisoner, fired into the backs of his retreating followers, and then swept the county in search of additional victims. The death toll: for whites, exactly two; for blacks, perhaps as many as three hundred.

Calling the legislature into special session, Ames told its members that what had happened in Vicksburg was "insurrection in its fullest sense"; that if permitted to succeed, it would "reduce a majority to the will of the minority"; and that "one race of our people" would be "deprived of their rights and remanded back to as unfortunate a condition" as they had ever known. The legislature appealed to the President, and on January 5, 1875, Grant sent to Vicksburg a company of troops, who restored Crosby to the position of sheriff.[10]

By that time the legislature was meeting in its regular session, and a taxpayers' convention in Jackson was demanding a reduction of taxes on real estate. As military governor, Ames had lowered the poll tax, and since then the Republicans had reduced the levies on artisans, professionals, and businessmen, but had increased property taxes, thus shifting the burden to planters, who had been paying very little after the end of slavery and the disappearance of the tax on slaves. Ames urged the legislature to cut both taxes and expenses and to maintain a balanced budget. The legislature did lower the rate on real property from 14 to 9.75 mills.

This did nothing to appease the Democrats. They were infuriated by other legislation that Ames secured—a law authorizing him to reorganize the militia and to purchase rapid-fire, multiple barrel Gatling guns—which they denounced as the "Gatling Gun Bill." The anti-Republican *Brandon Republican* advised "Mr. Adelbert Ames to pack his carpet bag and take his wife and babies to Massachusetts before he issues an order to his 'melish' to turn his Gatling guns on the white people of Mississippi." Regarding Ames and his prospective "negro regiments," the Mississippi congressman Lucius Quintus Cincinnatus Lamar wrote to his own wife: "He will get them killed up, and then Grant will take possession for him." Lamar was to mastermind the strategy by which the Democrats, having learned their lesson from events in Vicksburg, would get enough blacks killed to carry the state election in the fall—and would do it in such a way as to keep Grant from taking possession for Ames.[11]

Ames meanwhile was led to believe he could depend on Grant to intervene if necessary and frustrate the Democrats. In a letter of March 3 from his father-in-law he read of a conversation between Butler and Grant in which Grant said

> that he thought as Congress had not interfered and would not interfere in the Arkansas matter, it was quite probable that you might have trouble and . . . that he wished you to check in the very beginning anything that looked like a revolution after the manner of Arkansas, such as calling a constitutional convention, otherwise than as provided by law, or any movement of conspiracy or fraud, to overturn the government, and to assure you that he will stand by you in every emergency to the full extent of his power.

Ames was further reassured when, in July, he stopped at the White House on his way back to Mississippi after a month's vacation in Massachusetts, where he left his family. He now had a long and satisfying talk with Grant. "He showed his old interest in me, I judged," Ames boasted to Blanche.

When the Democrats held their nominating convention, early in August, Lamar addressed them with what Ames understood was a "very bitter" speech. They seemed determined to regain control of the state at whatever cost. "The only thing which will do us harm," Ames believed, "will be the intimidation and murdering of the poor negroes. If they [the Democrats] extend their savage policy [as] in Vicksburg we cannot predict the results." At the Republican convention, later in the month, opposition to Ames's influence arose not only from the scalawag Alcorn and the black Revels but also from prominent carpetbaggers, notably Henry R. Pease, who had been sent to the Senate to finish out Ames's term. Ames dismissed them as "soreheads," and he took satisfaction in retaining his hold on the black rank and file.

Suffering from the summer heat and from the strain of his position, Ames looked rather haggard; he had been losing weight. "Though I dislike ale and beer, I have taken to beer," he informed Blanche, "and drink a glass every day at dinner with the hope that it may be fattening." His room in the mansion was like "a moderately heated furnace" when, on September 2, he received a telegram from Yazoo City indicating that the Democrats' campaign of terror was already underway. They had attacked a Republican meeting at which Albert T. Morgan was speaking; apparently one or two men had been killed and a large number wounded. On September 3, before dawn, a woman called at the governor's mansion after arriving in Jackson on the night train from the north. She, the wife of Morgan's brother William, had come as a messenger from the Yazoo Republicans, they having now no other way to communicate with the governor. From her he learned: "The Democracy are organized into military companies and have assumed control—taken military possession of the county."[12]

Whites in Yazoo County had been organizing, arming, and training as unofficial cavalry companies ever since the disturbances in neighboring Warren County during the previous summer. The leaders said they had nothing more in mind than to protect the white people in case of a Negro uprising. Rumors of such an uprising used to circulate every now and then in slavery days, and they continued to do so—especially at election times. Sheriff Morgan sent three deputies (two native Southern whites and a black) to investigate both the rumors and the reaction to them. The deputies found ample evidence that whites were preparing for violence, but no evidence that blacks were doing the same.

To reassure the whites, Morgan and other Republican leaders invited them to an open meeting. It was held, one Saturday night, in the African Methodist Episcopal church, a modest frame structure on a hill outside of town. Morgan and his fellow sponsors were disappointed when only two or three white people (besides the usual Republicans) appeared. After first the A.M.E. preacher, next a black politician, and then the carpetbag postmaster had spoken, Morgan made the principal speech. He said, as the *Yazoo City Herald*, the local Republican paper, paraphrased him:

> . . . he would assure his hearers that he would be as ready and as prompt to put down a mob of colored men as he would of white men. He hoped he would never be called upon to do either. He warned the colored men to give no cause of offense, that it was wholly unnecessary for them to organize in opposition to the secret bands of white men, that their greatest strength had always been, and was likely to be for some time yet, in their weakness. The civilized world would be arrayed on the side of those who upheld and obeyed the law. He trusted the bad example set for them by a few white men would not be followed. Then if the "war of races" should come, it would not be a war, not a slaughter of white men, women, and children by colored men, but of colored people by the white people. Christendom would revolt at this, and the future [would] be full of hope and peace for the colored people through their long suffering and martyrdom.

After Morgan's plea for passive resistance, the meeting unanimously adopted the black minister's resolutions to "continue in this attitude of good-will and peace, and to rely upon the law."[13]

That was in the summer of 1874. In the local election that fall, the Democrats won control in Yazoo City, as they did at the same time in Vicksburg. But Yazoo County, like Warren County, remained in the hands of the Republicans. The county offices would not be up for grabs until the fall election of 1875.

As Morgan saw it, the record of the Republicans more than justified their continuance in power. By the beginning of 1875 they could boast of a great many city and county improvements: not only a new courthouse but also a jail with safe iron cells; a poor-farm reorganized and almost paying for itself; new bridges built and old roads and bridges repaired; new sidewalks, pavements, and gutters; and a steam fire-engine of the latest model. True, there was no railroad yet, the depression having halted construction on the one that had been planned. The Republicans took special pride in the progress the schools had made since William Morgan's becoming superintendent in 1872. At that time there had been 41 schools for whites and only 25 for blacks, though black children outnumbered white by almost two to one. Now there were 45 schools for whites and 63 for blacks. Despite the cost of these improvements, the county treasury showed a healthy surplus of $30,000.

The Democrats, however, did not intend to rely on a discussion of schools or other public improvements in seeking control of the county government. They had not needed to use overt violence in the city, where the two races were numerically more or less even, but they would have to resort to extreme violence if they were to carry the county, where blacks heavily outnumbered whites.

Looking back afterwards, Morgan could find some consolation in the fact that his wife and children did not have to live through the local terror. They were at the family's summer home in Holly Springs, in the hill country of northern Mississippi, where people who could afford it went to escape the miasmatic heat of the Yazoo Valley swamplands.[14]

Morgan's nemesis was to be Henry M. Dixon, a Yazoo County planter, top leader of the local Democrats, and captain of a mounted troop known as Dixon's Scouts. Morgan once described Dixon as "a small, slim, wiry nervous man, 'quick as a cat.'" The man buzzed around so menacingly that Morgan thought of him as the "human hornet." As late as January 1875, when Dixon sent Morgan a note to thank him graciously for a personal favor, the two men were on fairly good terms. But Dixon turned hostile as campaigning season approached.

By late August the electoral tactics of Dixon and his followers were becoming fairly obvious. Democratic newspapers played upon the theme that the blacks were, in the words of one headline, "preparing to take the war-path." These papers published a letter purportedly written and signed by two blacks who bragged in confidence: "The colored folk have got 1600 Army guns All prepared for Business." Morgan concluded that the letter was a forgery after having ascertained that one of the pretended authors was an illiterate fieldhand in Dixon's employ. "But," commented the *Yazoo City Democrat*, drawing a very different conclusion, "as the dapper little son-in-law of the national spoon-thief, Ben Butler, religiously believes that the death of twenty-five negroes is really necessary to the success of the radical party in the present canvass, perhaps it is his emissaries who are putting mischief in the heads of these black people, in the hope that radicalism would in the end be benefitted thereby."[15]

This revelation of supposed Republican plotting came out shortly before the Republicans, on the evening of September 1, were to hold a rally in Wilson's Hall, with Morgan as the speaker. That afternoon the A.M.E. pastor and other black leaders, anticipating trouble, urged him to have a large number of armed deputies on hand and to see that all Republicans attending the rally carried arms. But, again arguing that their weakness was their strength, Morgan insisted that they leave their weapons at home. He himself, as sheriff, took his pistol with him to the meeting.

From the platform in Wilson's Hall, when Morgan got up to speak, he could barely see the crowd in the tiers of seat that sloped up in front of him. Only a dim light came from the candles in widely spaced wall-holders, but the platform itself was well illuminated by a chandelier and a lamp. Morgan estimated that perhaps a hundred blacks along with a handful of white Republicans were present. In the very first row, as he could see all too clearly, sat several prominent Democrats. Near the doorway stood Dixon and two or three others.

No sooner had Morgan begin to speak than Dixon brought in a black man who held a grudge against county officials, they having gone after him for delinquent taxes. The irate citizen interrupted Morgan with a speech of his own. Dixon and a couple of others, standing near the heckler, drew their pistols when members of the audience yelled for him to shut up and sit down. Morgan, after waiting for a chance to resume his own remarks, made a complimentary reference to the president of the board of supervisors. Dixon shouted: "He's a thief! He's a thief!" A voice from the crowd replied: "That's a lie!"

Instantly, guns went off. Smoke from the firing drifted through the room, obscuring most of it, but the platform where Morgan stood remained brightly lit, exposing him as a target. He drew his pistol, stepped forward, and commanded peace. Now bullets came in his direction. He fired back, then ran to a window at the back of the platform and climbed out. A ladder at the window slipped, and he fell ten or twelve feet to the brick pavement below. After making his way back upstairs to the auditorium, he found several of his black followers bleeding from their wounds and one of the native white Republicans dying from his.

Some blacks arrived to warn him the main street was full of armed whites who were looking for him. He proceeded cautiously to his house and there talked with the A.M.E. minister and other leading blacks. He decided against summoning a posse, for it would have to consist mainly of black men, and he feared "it would be taken as a pretext for the slaughter generally of the colored people."

That night he could hear the sound of horseshoes and men's boots on the pavement as mounted and unmounted squads patrolled the street. In the morning Dixon, at the head of his Scouts, knocked at the door.

Morgan's black hostler, who was staying with him, answered by saying Morgan had left town. During the day the numbers of gun-toting horsemen steadily increased as fresh contingents arrived from the countryside. Very few blacks were to be seen; patrollers stopped those few, questioned them, searched them. "The city keeps up its warlike appearance," newspapers reported the following day. Fearing discovery at home, Morgan under the cover of darkness moved to his brother's house, two blocks away.

He was now being hunted as a fugitive from justice. Dixon had sworn out a warrant for his arrest—he was accusing Morgan of having attempted to murder *him!* Dixon made the allegation an excuse for putting one of his men in the sheriff's office.

One day a friend brought Morgan a warning that his enemies suspected his hiding place and were going to search it. That night he stayed out in the yard, concealing himself behind a board fence, where he overhead patrollers talk of hanging him. At dark the next day—his twelfth in hiding—he sneaked back to his own house, mounted his sorrel mare, and rode off in the direction of Jackson. By ten o'clock the following morning he was at the governor's mansion.[16]

From day to day Republican politicians had been gathering anxiously in the mansion to ask the governor's advice, and refugees had been flocking to Jackson to seek relative safety under the protection of a company of United States soldiers. The worst of the recent outrages had occurred at Clinton, a village about ten miles away. In the Clinton massacre, shooting broke out at a Republican barbecue attended by more than a thousand blacks. Several of them were killed and many more wounded, but also killed were three of their white assailants. Vengeful whites, having descended upon the village with their guns, were soon "scouring the county killing Negroes," as Ames was informed. They killed at least twenty or thirty of them.

Ames telegraphed to President Grant for additional troops. The new attorney general, Edwards Pierrepont, replied with a telegram that quoted Grant as saying: "The whole public are tired out with these annual autumnal outbreaks in the South, and the great majority are now ready to condemn any interference on the part of the government." The President would act, Pierrepont said, but only if he absolutely must to prevent disorders and protect the state government itself from attack. Pierrepont advised Ames and his black followers to fight their own battle in the Mississippi arena, with the Northern people as spectators. As Pierrepont put it, "I suggest that you take all lawful means and all needed measures to preserve the peace by the forces in your own state, and let the country see that the citizens of Mississippi, who are largely favorable to good order, and are largely Republican, have the courage and manhood to *fight* for their rights and to destroy the bloody ruffians who murder the innocent and unoffending freedmen."

Ames was thoroughly exasperated by this response from the Grant Administration. What did he have to fight with? Besides the company of federal troops in Jackson, there was one in Vicksburg and there were two in Holly Springs—a total of fewer than five hundred men. They would act only on orders from others than Ames. He himself could legally organize, arm, and command state militia, but he could not depend on the loyalty of white militiamen and he hesitated to build up an exclusively black force. Black leaders themselves counseled against this as likely to lead to a race war that would decimate their people.[17]

L. Q. C. Lamar, the Democratic Mississippi congressman, and John B. Gordon, former head of the Georgia Ku Klux Klan, were visiting the state and making what seemed to Ames "most incendiary" speeches. "The language they use is not of itself violent, but the conclusions they reach are that this election must be carried, even if violence be resorted to." Regardless, the chairman of the Democratic state central committee, James Z. George, sent Attorney General Pierrepont a telegram, bearing the signatures of several leading Democrats, to assure him that "everywhere, throughout the State, the most profound peace and good order" prevailed. A delegation of anti-Ames Republicans—who accused him of alienating whites by showing partiality to blacks—went to Washington and gave the same assurance, thus undercutting a committee of Ames Republicans who were renewing the appeal for military aid. Northerners got the impression that Ames was the villain and Mississippians, black as well as white, his victims. "The belief is coming to be quite general," the *New York Tribune* loftily announced, "that except for the constant interference of such men as Gov. Ames between the two races there would be not only no occasion for troops but no disturbance whatever of their friendly relations."[18]

Despite the bland assurances of both Democrats and anti-Ames Republicans, Mississippians continued to perish in political confrontations. Senator Alcorn, in his home county of Coahoma, put together a ticket to oppose the pro-Ames incumbents, especially the sheriff, John Brown, a black man from Oberlin, Ohio. When Brown held a meeting at Friar's Point, to reply to Alcorn's charges of "plundering," Alcorn arrived with a band of gun-wielders and ordered the assembled blacks to disperse. Shots were exchanged; six blacks and two or three whites lay dead or dying. Without bloodshed, Alcorn could not have hoped to elect his anti-Ames ticket, for the county was overwhelmingly black and had given Ames a landslide victory over Alcorn in the gubernatorial election of 1873. Now Alcorn was to be "First in Coahoma" again.

Having been repeatedly rebuffed by the commander in chief in Washington, Ames thought of dealing directly with the commander of the Department of the Gulf in New Orleans. He dispatched Morgan to New Orleans with a message for General William H. Emory. Morgan undertook to "represent the true condition of things in Mississippi" and delivered a letter in which Ames asked that "a company of troops be sent to Yazoo, and some to Jackson, as the latter would be the chief seat of war, if war we have." Morgan came back empty-handed.

So Ames proceeded with the organization of a few militia companies. He offered three of them—two black, one white—to Morgan for him to use in reestablishing his authority in Yazoo County. Morgan had reason to believe that the white company would defect and the black ones would be destroyed. He decided not to make the attempt. But the rumor got out that he and his militiamen were taking a special train to Vaughan's Station, the railroad stop nearest Yazoo City. According to the *Yazoo City Democrat*, nearly a thousand armed and mounted men, with "the intrepid Capt. Henry M. Dixon" in the forefront, prepared to meet the train. "And we venture the opinion that had Morgan and his invaders attempted a landing in our county, Vaughan's Station would have been known in the future annals of Mississippi as the Bloody Ground."

The election was three weeks away, and Ames was beginning to consider the war already lost. "Yes, a *revolution* has taken place—by force of arms—and a race are disfranchised—they are to be returned to a condition of serfdom—an era of second slavery," he wrote despondently and prophetically to Blanche. "Now it is too late. The nation should have acted but *it* was '*tired* of the annual autumnal outbreaks in the South'—see Grant's and Pierrepont's letter to me. The political death of the Negro will forever release the nation from the weariness from such 'political outbreaks.'"[19]

Ames was greatly encouraged the next day, October 13, when the Democrats agreed to a "treaty of peace." This was largely the work of a Justice Department agent, C. K. Chase, whom Pierrepont had sent to Mississippi as a conciliator. Chase feared that, with Ames organizing the militia, large-scale bloodshed was imminent, so he brought J. Z. George with a group of other prominent Democrats to the governor's mansion for an interview with Ames. George and his associates now promised to "do all in their power to preserve the peace and secure a fair election" if Ames would disarm and disband the militia. Ames agreed to send home the two companies still on active duty and to put their arms in storage.

"Through the timely intervention of Mr. C. K. Chase," Ames wrote Pierrepont, "a bloody revolution has been averted." He kept his part of the bargain and at first he trusted the Democrats to keep theirs; he had "full faith in their honor," he said. Pierrepont responded with his and Grant's approval and with this assurance: "You will be advised of preparations made to aid you, in case the opposition violate their honor and break their faith."

Morgan now thought it possible to put up a Republican ticket in Yazoo County. But, negotiating with Yazoo Republicans by mail, he could find few who were willing to see their names on the ballot. Since the Wilson's Hall shoot-out, three local leaders of the party—a carpetbagger and two blacks—had been murdered. Nevertheless, Morgan managed to put together a slate, with himself the candidate for reelection as sheriff.

Ames and Morgan were disillusioned when, only a week or so after the understanding with George, the outrages began again. Chase, as peacemaker, was disillusioned also. Ames, expecting him to see that the agreement was observed, sent him frequent complaints, which he relayed to George. But George, as Chase later testified, also responded promptly with "statements to prove that no such thing occurred, or if it did occur that the party killed or the party outraged was the aggressor." The Mississippi Democrats of 1875 were masters of the Big Lie.

By election day, Republican leaders in many localities were hiding out in woods and swamps. It was a time for revolution. In 1873 Ames had carried the state by 70,000 to 50,000. Now the Democrats claimed victory by a margin of 50,000, which would have required a switch of about half of the Republican votes. In 1873 Morgan had won by 2,365 to 431. According to the Democrats' official returns, he now lost by exactly two votes to more than 4,000. There were not that many registered voters in Yazoo County.[20]

After the election Ames visited his parents in Northfield, Minnesota, and then rejoined his wife and children at her parents' home in Lowell, Massachusetts. With her and the children he returned to Mississippi in time to face the new, hostile, Democratic legislature at its convening in January 1876. "At night in the town here," she wrote home, "the crack of the pistol or gun is as frequent as the barking of dogs." Some shots were fired at the mansion itself. Undeterred by this, Ames in his first message to the legislature denounced it as an illegal body, the product of force and fraud.

Promptly the legislature responded with the first steps toward an impeachment of the governor. The impeachers had no difficulty in trumping up charges against him—that he absented himself from the state, enabled criminals to go free, degraded the judiciary, and so on. They did not accuse him of corruption. "Nothing is charged beyond political sins," Ames explained to a New York friend; "of course, with them that is a sin which to Republicans is of the highest virtue. Their object is to restore the Confederacy and reduce the colored people to a state of serfdom. I am in their way, consequently they impeach me."[21]

From his father-in-law, Ames received mixed reports concerning the possibility of aid from Washington. "The President," Butler wrote, "still professes, and I think meaningly, that he has faith in you . . . but he is very much troubled what to do." There was no reason to expect help from Senator Alcorn, but the case was different with Blanche K. Bruce, the junior senator from Mississippi. Born in slavery, educated briefly at Oberlin College, the mulatto Bruce had been elected with Ames's support to serve the six-year term that Ames himself might have been serving if things had gone his way. Butler further advised Ames: "With Alcorn here in the Senate, and Bruce, who doesn't stand up like a man anywhere, I don't think the delegation amounts to much."

As Butler saw it, the most helpful member of the Mississippi delegation would be Congressman Lamar—the very head and inspiration of the revolt that had put Ames into the predicament in which he now found himself. Lamar "is against impeachment," Butler gathered; he "has undertaken to stop the procedure as well as he can." But Butler's daughter, Ames's wife, had no faith in Lamar. "The warmest friends of Lamar here are the most violent for impeachment—and Mr. Lamar is a double dealer on whom no dependence can be placed, as it is well known that in all matters political he does not hesitate to be false." So wrote Blanche Ames to her mother. "If he really wishes to be of service, let him call off the dogs—which he can easily do, as they are trained to hound or retreat at the word of command."[22]

Lamar did not call off the dogs, who went ahead and scheduled the impeachment trial to begin on March 29. "There is but little suspense," Blanche noted, "as we can anticipate but one result—conviction." The Mississippi spring had arrived, and it was as lovely as ever, but Ames remained in rather poor health, the situation weighing heavily upon him. Some Republicans urged him to resign. That would be the easy way out, but to do so while under charges would seem like a confession of guilt.

Blanche conceived of a possible compromise: let the Democrats dismiss the charges, and Ames would give them his resignation (the black lieutenant governor having been already persuaded to resign). She proposed this to Roger A. Pryor, one of the two attorneys whom Butler had secured for Ames. Pryor was a smart choice, for he was a Southern Democrat of impeccable credentials—a Virginian who, as a fire-eating secessionist, had urged South Carolinians to attack and take Fort Sumter even before the approach of Lincoln's relief expedition. Pryor now got credit for the deal that Blanche had thought up. On March 28, the day before the trial was to start, the governor agreed to quit if the charges were dropped, and that same day the legislature directed the impeachment managers to "dismiss the said Articles against the said Adelbert Ames." On March 29 he resigned.

Once more, however, his enemies went back on their word, as they had done when they disregarded the "treaty of peace" during the recent political campaign. They now violated the spirit of the new agreement when the legislature published the charges against Ames with the implication that these would have justified removing him. So much for Southern honor!

In April the Ameses left Mississippi, never to return. While they were in Minnesota, and Ames's father was urging him to join him in the flour-milling business, they learned by telegram that Blanche's mother had died, at the age of fifty-eight, after an operation for a malignant growth on her throat. They were in Lowell in time for the funeral.

Before the end of the month, Ames went to Washington to testify before the Senate committee investigating the Mississippi election of 1875. Democrats on the committee tried to divert attention from their fellow Democrats' atrocities in that election by questioning Ames about his status as a Mississippi resident. He answered in the same (somewhat equivocal) way as he had done five years earlier, when he was seeking admission to the Senate and was responding to similar questions. He now insisted that Mississippi Democrats had wanted to remove him as governor not because he was an outsider but because he was an advocate of "the rights of the negro to citizenship."

His testimony before the Senate committee was secret for the time being, but he got immediate publicity for his opinions when a *New York Times* correspondent intervewed him in Washington. He told the *Times* man that the Mississippi Democrats would try to get rid of anyone, Northerner or Southerner, who stood by the Fourteenth and Fifteenth Amendments. They were determined, he said, to control or neutralize the blacks in politics.

"Does not Lamar oppose this policy?" the reporter asked incredulously. Lamar, now Alcorn's successor in the Senate, enjoyed throughout the North a reputation as the foremost Southern advocate of reconciliation between the sections and between the races. He was remembered for the eloquence of his eulogy of Charles Sumner after Sumner's death. "No; Lamar makes very different speeches in Mississippi from those he delivers for the Northern market," Ames replied to the newsman's query. "He made the most vituperative speeches during the last campaign, and he owes his election as United States Senator to that fact. He explained away his eulogy to Sumner as being a political necessity—to give the South a hearing in the North."

A couple of months later, in July, Ames's Yazoo County ally Albert T. Morgan appeared before the same Senate committee. Morgan was now living in Washington with his wife and three children and was supporting them as best he could by practicing law. At the moment he was representing a Yazoo County woman who had a claim against the federal government for cotton, horses, and mules the Union army had seized from her, a Unionist, during the war. The Democrats in control of the county had indicted Morgan for murder in the Hilliard case, and it would have been unsafe for him to go back there. For the benefit of the investigating committee, he recounted in detail his Mississippi career from his arival as would-be cotton planter in 1865 through his defeat in the "revolution" of 1875. Then he declared:

> I willingly assume the responsibility of the utter overthrow of government in Yazoo County last fall. It is not to be charged to the ignorance or cowardice of the colored people there. Like the colored people, I was unused to

guerrilla warfare. When the general arming of the whites became first known to me, I communicated the fact to the governor. Colored men in the county, many of them, consulted with me as to what republicans ought to do. In every instance I counseled against irregular arming, advising all to rely upon the law and its officers. I hoped by steadfastly pursuing this course, by offering no pretext for violence, we might pass the ordeal I saw approaching. I knew there was no just ground in high taxes or corrupt local government for a violent revolution.[24]

CHAPTER 16

This Pathway of Political Reform (1873-1876)

Daniel H. Chamberlain could look ahead with optimism as summer came to South Carolina in 1874. Franklin J. Moses, Jr., was governor and Robert K. Scott ex-governor, but he himself was surely governor-to-be. Of the three men, all of them contenders for the Republican nomination this year, he was the preconvention favorite. In state politics the magic word now was "reform." Neither Scott nor Moses could pose with much plausibility as a reformer, each having presided over a government notoriously corrupt. Chamberlain approached the campaign comparatively fresh and clean. True, he had been part of the Scott administration, as attorney general from 1868 to 1872, but since then he had remained in private life as a Columbia lawyer, unbesmirched by the scandals of the Moses regime.

At the same time he had strengthened his hold upon the black electorate. He was serving as a trustee of the University of South Carolina, and in 1873 he and his fellow trustees decided to integrate the university. When the first Negro enrolled—a man who happened to be the secretary of state—most of the students withdrew and most of the faculty resigned. Chamberlain drafted the trustees' statement accepting the resignations without regret and declaring the university "the common property of all our citizens without distinction of race." Soon the student body was predominantly black.

Chamberlain could count on the support of the state's most influential black politician, Congressman Robert B. Elliott, who the last time had backed Moses, thus helping to make him governor. And this time Chamberlain could expect Moses, in return for a favor, to stand aside for him. Chamberlain and Elliott were cooperating as attorneys for Moses, who had got himself into trouble that threatened to cost him his job. In return for Chamberlain's help, Moses appeared willing to forgo a second term.

The recently impecunious Moses was now living high. Not content with the governor's official residence on Arsenal Hill, he was buying and occupying the most elegant mansion in Columbia. He ran up a huge personal debt and was accused of diverting public funds to pay for it. To prevent his arrest and protect his home and office, he called out four companies of black militia. When the case went to court, Chamberlain and Elliott argued that the chief executive of a state, like the chief executive of the United States, could not be indicted until he had been impeached and removed from office. The judge agreed.[1]

As for ex-Governor Scott, his chances of regaining the governorship seemed no better than Moses's—if as good as his. Scott still lived in Columbia, and lived quite well, but in no such extravagant style as Moses did. After leaving office, Scott had thought of moving back to Napoleon, Ohio, and had arranged for the construction of another new residence there, one that local people said would be "the finest house in town." He did go back for a reunion of his army comrades in Toledo, but soon put the Napoleon house up for sale.

In Columbia he and his family occupied an antebellum mansion that he had bought, enlarged, and remodeled with a two-story piazza and a "first class front door with side lights." He was to be congratulated, a friend wrote him from New York during a late March snowstorm there, for choosing to remain "in a part of the world where freezing is almost unknown." Here he continued his money-lending, his dealing in real estate, and his investments in banks and other businesses, all the while trying to unload his large holding of Blue Ridge Railroad bonds, which became less and less salable after the bankruptcy of the company and the onset of the depression following the Panic of '73.

Scott received encouragement for his gubernatorial ambition in the spring of 1874. One adherent wrote him: "My Dear Gov: As such I address you, and such I hope you will be again, as I told you on the 19th August, 1872, when Frank Moses was nominated—that he would soon run wild, would serve his two years and then would be buried in oblivion—perhaps it would be better to say, in the walls of the penitentiary." But, as this correspondent added, "Chamberlain is pushing like the devil." Another well-wisher, to counter Chamberlain's pushing and to rebut the charges against Scott, asked him to make it known that such "mismanagement" as occurred during his administration was "directly and indirectly due to Hon. D. H. Chamberlain, then Atty General."[2]

Scott was put on the defensive, however, when another taxpayers' convention (like the one of 1871) met in Columbia, drew up resolutions of protest, and sent a copy to Congress and to President Grant. The taxpayers complained that Scott, as assistant commissioner of the Freedmen's Bureau, had distributed relief supplies in such a way as to gain Republican votes. The protesters also alleged that "the last two Governors were without estates, and their expensive mode of living established beyond a doubt that the money must have come from some irregular or illegal source."

These falsehoods about him vexed Scott, and to correct them he dictated a long and indignant letter and addressed it to Congress and to Grant. The corn, bacon, and other supplies for hungry South Carolinians, he pointed out, had been issued mostly to native white men, to factors and planters, for them to distribute among the needy, and it was nonsensical to suppose that those men had used their influence with black employees and tenants for his political benefit. Nor had the food gone only to recent slaves. "Hundreds of the proud and once wealthy families of the State who were subsisted by these charities will doubtless feel surprised when they learn that bread was furnished them for expected services in securing the election of the nominees of the Republican party."

It was equally vicious and equally ridiculous to insinuate that Scott had come to South Carolina "without any estate" and had got rich from the plunder of public office. He was already quite well-to-do when he arrived. In fact, "there probably was not a half dozen members of the 'tax payers' Convention whose estates were worth more than mine was at that time." As for the intimation that, as governor, he had lived beyond his means, he could truthfully say: "[M]y manner of living was not better than I had been accustomed to for years." He would welcome a congressional investigation. "If Congress is to take action in connection with these alleged evils, I would most earnestly and respectfully beg that a Committee of its members inquire minutely into these charges against myself, so that their falsity may be established beyond cavil." But he was to have no such opportunity to clear his name.

Scott's reputation was not helped when, in June, a *New York Times* correspondent interviewed the three Republican contenders for the governorship. Chamberlain came off as the "best fitted" for the job. In his remarks he did not fault Scott alone for the alarming increase in the state debt during Scott's two terms, nor did he put all the blame on the blacks who dominated the legislature. In time "they would correct their own mistakes, and forever discard the leaders by whom they had been brought into disgrace." Meanwhile, the next governor and legislature ought to see that expenditures were cut by at least one-third.

Moses insisted, without presenting any kind of proof, that he himself was "a much-injured man," one guilty of no public wrongdoing whatsoever, though he "admitted that his private character had been very bad." He struck the reporters as "quick and impulsive" in speech, "most agreeable" in manner, and rather dissipated in appearance. "He is not yet forty years old, yet his face is careworn and wrinkled, and his long hair almost white."

Scott impressed the reporter still less favorably. While blaming the existing troubles on the incumbent, he did not account for the extravagance during his own tenure. "He could suggest no remedy for the present difficulties."

Scott responded to these criticisms in speeches he made to Republican gatherings at Newberry and Jenkinsville in July. During his governorship, he now conceded, the legislature had indulged in "reckless and profligate expenditures," but he contended that he had been powerless to stop it. When he tried to do so, he was impeached, and when impeachment failed, the legislature changed the law so that money could be paid out of the treasury without the approval of the governor. He could, indeed, offer a remedy: "elect a better class of men to office" in the future. "When you elect colored men to office take the honest and hardworking men, who are naturally honest, instead of those who have been coachmen or upper servants, and who have learned by contact the vices of the white man without his virtues." This would mean—though Scott did not say so—electing poor dark-skinned, pure African, illiterate former field hands in preference to relatively well-off, light-skinned, mixed-blooded, more or less educated former house servants and skilled artisans, many of them freeborn.

Despite his preconvention campaigning, Scott improved his prospects little if at all. By mid-August, men could congratulate him on his speeches and still consider him out of the running. "Moses & Chamberlain are both fiercely contending for the office of governor & the 'Party' is not looking beyond them," one of his black admirers wrote him. "You know them both—will you not tell the poor ignorant negroes whether there is any possibility of 'reform' by voting for either of them?" But Scott refrained from endorsing the one or the other; he took no part in the contest between them.[3]

So it was Chamberlain against Moses—who seemed to have forgotten his earlier hint that he would oblige Chamberlain by not seeking reelection if Chamberlain would oblige him by defending him in the embezzlement case. The two men were equally bad in the view of South Carolina conservatives, and the better Chamberlain's chances appeared, the more the opposition newspapers concentrated their fire on him. He could not deter them in the slightest by the public statement he issued: "To every specific and general charge involving moral delinquency or conscious wrong in my official action in this State I give my absolute and solemn denial."

Nor could he soften the wrath of his journalistic critics by playing up to them with a humorous touch. "I knew I was not in favor with the Editors of the *News and Courier*, but I did not imagine you would go to the extent of refusing to *sell* me your paper," he wrote to the men who, in Charleston, ran the state's most influential daily and his most lacerating critic. He begged them to renew his subscription. "The *News & C.* is like surgery to me, painful but necessary!" he said. "I wish I could add, healthful!" (He did not explain that, at the moment, he was ill enough to be confined to his bed.)

Undeterred, the *News and Courier* kept on with its attack. According to its editorials, Chamberlain might lack the "vulgar audacity" of Moses, but he was "more culpable as well as more adroit than that profligate debauchee" and "even less worthy than he" to "fill the executive chair." After all, Chamberlain had been attorney general during four years of the worst misgovernment. "As the highest law officer of the State . . . either he stole, or allowed others to steal; either he saw others steal and said nothing, or he was the only man in the State who did not see the stealing."[4]

Whatever the Democrats thought of him, Chamberlain was still the favorite among Republicans when their state convention met in the capitol on September 8. They put off the nominations for four days while the committee on credentials weighed the claims of contesting delegations from several counties. On the second day there was, as one of the delegates recorded, "great excitement and quite a big row" when a "number of rowdies with sticks and other weapons, believed to be in the interest of Moses, entered the Convention without tickets." Even if they had been allowed to stay, the gate-crashers could not have revived the chances of Moses, since he had lost the support of the two most important Negro leaders—the coal-black Elliott and the light-complexioned Francis L. Cardozo. Elliott, chairman of the credentials committee as well as the state executive committee, had a large say in the settling of the delegation disputes.

Cardozo, state treasurer in the Moses administration, presented Chamberlain's name when the convention finally got down to business. Cardozo said "the party was sick and needed a physician like Chamberlain." Moses was no longer in the running, but two other native white Republicans were proposed for the gubernatorial nomination. Together, these two received only fifty votes to Chamberlain's seventy-two. Nominated on the ticket with him were Cardozo for another term as treasurer and Samuel W. Melton, Chamberlain's scalawag law partner, for attorney general.

Using a sentence so long that, skilled orator though he was, it must have left him breathless, Chamberlain declared in his acceptance speech:

> . . . no platform which does not commit us irrevocably and solemnly to the duty of reducing public expenditures to their lowest limits; of administering the public funds honestly in the public interest; of electing competent public officers; of filling the local offices of our counties and townships with honest and faithful incumbents; of guarding our language and our action so as to allay rather than rekindle the flames of past controversies; of directing the attention of our fellow-citizens to the hopes of the future rather than the memories of the past, can bring to us party success or political honor.

Though the platform did commit the party to retrenchment and reform, the *News and Courier* did not let up for a moment. "The supporters of D. H. Chamberlain, those who procured him the nomination on Saturday night," the Charleston paper alleged, "are the men who devised and carried into execution every fraud of magnitude which has been committed in South Carolina during the past six years." Chamberlain,

Melton, and Cardozo replied through a journal of their own, the *Columbia Union Herald*, which served well enough to carry their message to South Carolina Republicans but could boast no such wide circulation and influence as the *Charleston News and Courier*. The latter's point of view prevailed in the Republican as well as the Democratic press of the North. The *Washington Post*, for example, was led to say: "If there is any abiding sense of justice left in the Palmetto State, Mr. Chamberlain or any other person connected with the Moses ring will be left out of office."

For South Carolina voters, the alternative in 1874 was the Independent Republican slate, which had the backing of Democrats as well as dissident Republicans. The candidates had lost out in the regular Republican convention and then bolted—a scalawag for governor and a black (opposing another black on the Chamberlain ticket) for lieutenant governor. On election day in November, the voters gave Chamberlain a majority of 11,585. That was a much smaller margin than either Scott or Moses had received, but it was large enough.[5]

After his election and before his inauguration Chamberlain received a visit from the man who recently had been his most assiduous maligner and who was about to become—and was to remain for nearly two years—his most enthusiastic laudator. This was Francis W. Dawson, the editor and part owner of the *Charleston News and Courier*.

Now thirty-four (five years younger than Chamberlain), lean, muscular, and handsome, Dawson spoke with an upper-class British accent and dressed immaculately in the best British fashion, with a black cutaway, a matching waistcoat, gray-striped trousers, and a silk ascot in black and white. He had been born in London to well-to-do Catholic parents and had been raised by an aunt after his father lost the family fortune by speculating in wheat. At twenty-two he enlisted in the Confederate navy, then transferred to the Army of Northern Virginia, in which he saw a good deal of action while rising to the rank of captain. After the war he remained a devotee of the Lost Cause.

During the summer and fall of 1874 Dawson did his damnedest to keep Chamberlain from being nominated and elected governor. He not only lambasted him in the columns of the *News and Courier*. He also bribed delegates at the Republican nominating convention in an attempt to defeat him, and he tried to persuade President Grant to come out against him. (His emissary to Grant's summer home at Long Branch, New Jersey, reported back: "Grant is thoroughly committed to Chamberlain. I can accomplish nothing.") Dawson was quite sincere in these efforts, for he really believed that Chamberlain, though superficially respectable, was rotten at the core. He was a "whited sepulchre."

As the governor-elect greeted his visitor, he was quite unaware of this behind-the-scenes hostility, though he was all too familiar with the journalistic attack. Months earlier he had made his overture to the *News and Courier* with his plea that the proprietors at least deign to sell him their paper. At last, one of the proprietors appeared to be responding. Certainly the man was friendly enough. The two now had a very long and, to both of them, a very pleasant talk. Afterward Dawson announced in the *News and Courier:* "I must put on record my own belief that Governor Chamberlain will make a much better Governor than has been predicted, or his antecedents would lead one to believe."[6]

But Chamberlain could hardly please both Dawson and Elliott, and to the latter he owed a political debt, which he partially repaid in a couple of days, when the legislature met and Elliott ran for speaker of the house. "Mr. Chamberlain and Attorney General Melton supported Elliott," Dawson commented, "and the consequence is that the worst man that could have been found has been chosen to preside over the deliberations of the lower branch of the General Assembly." The sad conclusion was hard to avoid: "the victory of Elliott is the defeat of reform."

Chamberlain again raised Dawson's hopes when, in his inaugural on December 2, he gave definiteness and detail to his reform program. Dawson responded: "Mr. Chamberlain has placed his foot on the rock of a living principle, with the eye of a great nation upon him, and the light of a great future breaking all around him." Other ex-Confederates also approved of the course the new governor laid out, and some of them personally told him so. "Accept my warm thanks," he wrote to one of them, ". . . for your kind expressions of confidence in my purpose to serve *all* our people in my present office."

When a state judgeship in Charleston fell vacant, Chamberlain got another chance to cultivate the good will of Democrats. He could not appoint the new judge—that was up to the legislature—but he could sway many of its members. Of those in the house, seventy-five were black and fifty white. The favorite of Speaker Elliott and of most representatives was William J. Whipper, a black attorney from the North, formerly Elliott's law partner, who had served in the Freedmen's Bureau under Scott. The planters and businessmen of the Charleston area were horrified at the thought of Whipper's presiding over *their* circuit court. They wanted J. P. Reed, once a Confederate colonel, now a conservative Republican. To urge Reed's election, Chamberlain attended a legislators' caucus—not as governor, he said, but only as a "private citizen" and a "simple member of the Republican party." With the assistance of State Treasurer Cardozo he won over enough of the Negroes to elect Reed by a (combined senate and house) vote of 103 to 40.

Dawson rejoiced at the size of Reed's majority. "It may be taken for granted, therefore, that, in every measure which is clearly for the benefit of the State, Mr. Chamberlain can count on pretty nearly a two-thirds vote in each house." Indeed, Chamberlain had succeeded in putting together a new coalition of conservative legislators. It consisted of Democrats, Independent Republicans, and the Negro followers of Cardozo—men who mostly were, like him, relatively light-skinned, more or less propertied, and fairly well educated.

Elliott could derive no joy from this development, which would leave him with a following of poorer blacks. Those were men of the kind that Scott had preferred as the more trustworthy, and Elliott certainly had nothing against them, but he aspired to the leadership of Negro Republicans as a whole. He still hoped to avert the permanent party rift that Dawson was encouraging. According to Dawson, Elliott was "reported to have foully cursed Mr. Chamberlain on the floor of the House on Friday when the election of Mr. Reed was announced." "I supported Mr. Chamberlain when those who are now lavish in their praise renounced and traduced him," Elliott retorted in a letter to the editor. "I trust that long after the *News and Courier* shall have ceased to find anything good or noble in him, I shall still be at his side supporting his every effort to give the people of the State good government." Here was a prophecy and a warning which Chamberlain ignored.[7]

As the legislature got down to business during the winter of 1874-75, Chamberlain further endeared himself to Dawson and further alienated Elliott by reiterating the economy plea of the inaugural and by slashing at would-be spenders with the veto. He vetoed twenty bills. While doing so, he brought the pressure of publicity to bear upon the legislators both through the state's leading Republican journal, his own, and through its leading Democratic one, Dawson's. In a letter carefully marked "Private," he advised Dawson:

> You will find in the Union-Herald of this morning a letter of mine to the Senate Finance Committee, on the pending appropriation bill.
>
> I think it important for the public good that all who are moved by public considerations should hold this Legislature—and especially the Regular Republicans in it—to a sharp and strict accountability to the people on this question.
>
> You can do much, and I write, primarily, to ask you to do all in your power to help keep down appropriations to the limits of our income. Members should be moved to feel that they will be watched and their names paraded and remembered if they fail of their duty in this respect.
>
> You know better than I how to make your paper felt, and so I say no more on this.
>
> My sole object is to give good government to S. C. and I know that is yours too.

Dawson was more than willing to cooperate. He reprinted items from the *Union Herald* (which returned the compliment), and he incorporated Chamberlain's ideas and even his words in his own editorials. Once Chamberlain confided that most of his fellow Republicans did not really have reform at heart. "My inaugural chilled them, my special message enraged them," he wrote, "and nothing keeps them from attacking me . . . except the power of my office and the support which the Conservatives and the country at large give me in my efforts at reform." This inspired Dawson to editorialize that the governor's inaugural had "chilled" the political hypocrites. "Only their knowledge of Governor Chamberlain's strength in and out of the state prevented the chagrined corruptionists from framing articles of impeachment against him."

While Dawson praised the "wise, prudent and just Governor Chamberlain," Elliott grew more and more disgusted with the governor's budget-balancing program. It involved cutting, or trying to cut, salaries of state employees and appropriations for public schools, the state university, the lunatic asylum, and the penitentiary (by reinstating the convict-lease system). From the viewpoint of Elliott and his black followers, the new "reform" policy actually meant the sacrifice of reforms already achieved. But he could not muster the two-thirds majority required to override the governor's vetoes.

Elliott did manage to get around the veto of one appropriation bill. As speaker, he ruled that the vetoed bill had not been returned to the house within the constitutional limit of three days. He needed only a simple majority to sustain his ruling, and he got it. So the bill became law. Those who had brought this about were "plunderers" of the state treasury, according to the *Union Herald*. "No pack of jackals scenting the carcass ever made night so hideous." Elliott had the editor arrested for using "scandalous and malicious language to defame the House of Representatives." The house of representatives quickly let him go.

In a more serious attempt at retaliation, Speaker Elliott backed a movement to impeach State Treasurer Cardozo. By discrediting Cardozo, he could hope to weaken Cardozo's hold on his black (or rather, brown) followers—and also to weaken Chamberlain's hold on them. The charge was the familiar one of misusing state funds. Chamberlain stood by the accused. "Mr. Cardozo has certainly impressed me with the belief that he is doing all in his power to administer the affairs of his office with honesty and economy," he assured Dawson. He explained: "The rabble, the average Republican politician is simply assailing him because there is nothing this winter in the way of plunder here in Columbia. All this is of course *doubly* confidential." Chamberlain's law partner Melton, as attorney general, defended Cardozo at the impeachment trial. Elliott gave a two-hour speech for the prosecution, but the house voted 63 to 45 to acquit.[8]

While exculpating his own (and Moses's) state treasurer, Chamberlain demanded punishment for Scott's—Niles G. Parker. This man had been not only Chamberlain's colleague in the Scott administration but also his associate in a scheme to monopolize South Carolina railroads. At present he was on trial for embezzlement. Before his conviction (and flight from the state) he threatened to expose the past misdeeds of his accuser Chamberlain.

Insinuations against Chamberlain did begin to appear in Northern newspapers, particularly the *Washington Star*. "The *fact* is that Parker has nothing which he can injure me with, and I don't think he has ever thought of trying it," Chamberlain told Dawson's partner B. R. Riordan, who had sent him a *Star* clipping.

> My evils have heretofore come from the *friendship* of bad men. Perhaps I shall fare better if I now have their *hatred*. At any rate I am ready to try it. You can speak broadly and positively in denial of any and all such surmises or reports as the Star contains. I do not, however, want you to speak by my authority in the paper. . . .
>
> By the way, whenever you see these items, you will, I think, be able to trace their inspiration to Kirk, Patterson and those men who hate me now because my words last fall [about corruption among Republicans] have not been proved *lies*. Patterson is now in Washn [*sic*] pouring his venom on me, "squat like a toad," at the ear of the President and spitting his venomous filth on me at every chance. He no doubt put the item into the Star. Scott (old R. R.) is also busy at the same work and is believed to be paying Kirk to write his various letters. One of Kirk's letters has appeared in Napoleon, O., where Scott once peddled pills. They are all doing their level best to punish me for being more discreet than they.

So it was Chamberlain's misfortune to have had the friendship of "bad men" such as Scott—"old R. R." Scott, the contemptible pill-peddler from Napoleon, Ohio! All along, Chamberlain was beholden to this same Scott for a large loan, one that he could not conveniently repay. He kept on begging Scott to renew the note each time it fell due, and Scott kept on obliging him by doing so.[9]

The biggest of the anti-Chamberlain journalistic bombshells exploded on June 5, 1875, when the *New York Sun* published the letter that Chamberlain had written to his chum H. H. Kimpton on Januray 5, 1870, telling him about Chamberlain's and Parker's scheme to make a killing by buying up the railroads of South Carolina. Again Dawson and Riordan sent Chamberlain a clipping. He informed them he could not say for sure whether the letter was genuine or not—he had no recollection of it—but in any case it concerned a mere "business venture" with "nothing sinister" about it. "That I hoped to make money—dreamed of thousands—there is no doubt, but I never knew of or consented to any transaction, even in that connection, which involved any injury to the State as I then understood it."

And again the *News and Courier* cleared his name, assuring its readers that he had had a "legitimate business speculation" in mind. (Legitimate it may well have been by the standards of the time, though by subsequent standards it would seem reprehensible, a case of conflict of interest, since in it state officials were to buy state-owned railroad securities and were to do so at a bargain price.) The *News and Courier* saw no reason to retract its recently expressed opinion that, when all the facts were in, "the record of Attorney General Chamberlain" would be found "every whit as clean as the record of Governor Chamberlain."

The governor was rapidly gaining respectability among the most respectable people of South Carolina and the country as a whole. He was deeply gratified. "My thanks for your generous treatment of my official conduct," he wrote to Samuel Bowles, editor of the *Springfield Republican* in Chamberlain's home state of Massachusetts. "I long bore a load of reproach which I rejoice now to see falling away."

Invitations to speak came to him from reputable institutions near and far. He was unable to attend the centennial banquet of the German Fusiliers, a social-military organization of the elite of Charleston, but he declined with such exquisite regret that the *News and Courier* could not refrain from lauding him for his "savoire faire"—which the paper defined as "the knack, and the habit, of saying and doing the right thing, at the right time, and in the right way." Chamberlain requested half a dozen extra copies of that issue.

He was also compelled to decline an invitation from Erskine College, because he had already agreed to deliver, on June 30, the commencement address at the law school of his alma mater, Yale. On the way to New Haven he took with him his family—his wife, Alice, and his two small boys—to leave them in New England for the summer. After his return he had another visit from the dapper Englishman Dawson. He wanted Dawson to read the Yale oration as soon as printed copies were available. "You will find one feature, the allusions to reconstruction, on which you can criticize me justly from your point of view and opinion,—and that will enable you to commend me the more kindly for the other points on which I know you will agree with me." It was a pleasure to be with the genial Dawson, a representative of the finest folk of Charleston and the low country. But it would not be politic for him and Dawson to appear to be as close as they actually were. "You know we must not be *too good* friends."[10]

As he neared the midpoint of his two-year term, Governor Chamberlain could anticipate a second go at the governorship and, after that, possibly a seat in the United States Senate. Was he not gaining a following among Democrats while maintaining his leadership among Republicans? Indeed, under Dawson's tutelage, conservatives were beginning to look upon him as the white hope of South Carolina politics.

Dawson had a chance to show him off to Charleston friends when the governor accepted an invitation to address the local Chamber of Commerce in November 1875. This meeting, according to Dawson's report of it, was "the largest and most influential that had been seen for some time, and among those present were most of the oldest and most prominent merchants and business men in the city." Chamberlain thanked them for their support. "You may rest assured," he told them, "that my best services shall be devoted to the commercial interests of Charleston."

Chamberlain was glad to accommodate Dawson and the Democrats in appointing men to state positions. These positions included the empty but honorific ones of representing South Carolina at the Centennial Exposition set for Philadelphia in 1876. "We must make the appointments from that class who can do some good," Chamberlain confided to Dawson, "—and that of course will require the larger part to be from the conservatives [that is, the Democrats], but that is no objection with me." Meanwhile he tossed an honorary sop to the Radical Republicans by naming Scott—"old R. R." Scott—as a delegate to the Southwestern Pacific Railroad convention, which was to meet in St. Louis on November 23 and 24 and agitate for a new transcontinental route.

After the legislature reconvened that November, Chamberlain congratulated himself that he was still in command of it. The house unanimously sustained him in vetoing a money bill, and he easily persuaded his fellow partisans to cooperate in keeping taxes down. "Have told the House of Reps. that I cannot approve tax bills levying more than eleven mills—in any event," he wrote to Dawson. "I met a large Repub. caucus and went carefully over the whole field and showed them how it could be done and that it *must* be done or they would have a *veto*."[11]

The legislature seemed so docile that Chamberlain was quite unprepared for the revolt about to come. The issue was not fiscal legislation but judiciary elections. Suddenly, on Tuesday, December 14, the senate resolved that the legislature should elect circuit-court judges in just two days, on Thursday. By that time Chamberlain would be in Greenville to speak on the occasion of Furman University's awarding student prizes for excellence in Greek. He did not want the circuit-court judges chosen while he was away. Only his presence and his lobbying had kept the legislature from picking the Northern black Whipper instead of the Southern white Reed the previous year.

The house had yet to concur in the senate resolution. On Tuesday evening Chamberlain spoke to both Republican and Democratic friends among the representatives, and he sent a note to Speaker Elliott, urging them all to postpone the elections. On Wednesday morning Elliott appeared at the governor's office and said he thought there would be no difficulty in arranging a postponement. Later that day the house did vote to table the senate resolution rather than to concur in it.

So Chamberlain went confidently off to Greenville for his Thursday engagement. He was proud of the oration he delivered there on the importance of liberal education in general and classical studies in particular. Regarding the address, he afterward remarked to Dawson: "I value it chiefly, if you will allow me the be frank, for its testimony to the calming and strengthening influence of letters on a man who is forced into a rough and tumble fight with men who never heard of Socrates or

Cicero." As things turned out, he needed immediately all the help that Socrates or Cicero could give him.

On his return to Columbia he was horrified to discover that, during his absence, the house had met with the senate, and the joint session had gone ahead with the election of the judges. One of the eight chosen was the egregious Franklin J. Moses, Jr. Even worse, Whipper had defeated Reed for the Charleston circuit. Elliott had insisted on the election of Whipper, who he said had been a victim of discrimination on account of his race. There was a rumor "that Judge Reed complained of Chamberlain's absence and that he had been wounded in the house of his friends."

Conservatives all over South Carolina and especially in Charleston were shocked by what they were to remember as "Black Thursday." The *News and Courier* blamed the Elliott forces. "Their plan is to Africanize the State and put the white man under the splay foot of the negro and hold him there." (In fact, the Negroes, who constituted a majority of the state's population, continued to hold a far less than proportionate share of important state offices.) Chamberlain's *Union Herald* agreed that black Republicans were to blame. Actually, sixteen of the blacks had voted against Whipper, but the rest had abandoned the governor's coalition. Political insiders were saying that the election of Whipper and Moses amounted to "a triumph over Chamberlain."[12]

It was time for Chamberlain and Dawson to consult again, and on Sunday they met privately in Columbia. Why, Dawson wondered, had Chamberlain gone to Greenville when, by staying at home, he could have prevented Whipper's election as he had done before? Chamberlain, while explaining how Elliott had doublecrossed him, doubted whether his own presence would have made any difference this time, for Elliott's plot had been too well matured. "The color line, the party line, and the line of antagonism to my Administration, all were sharply drawn." His greatest fear now was that he might lose support among conservative whites. "One immediate effect will obviously be the reorganization of the Democratic party within the State as the only means left for opposing . . . this terrible crevasse of misgovernment and public debauchery." Until now—ever since the start of Radical Reconstruction—the Democratic party in the state had been moribund.

There was one thing Chamberlain could do to preserve both purity in government and his own political chances. In the course of their tête-à-tête Dawson suggested to him that he need not honor the election of unqualified judges. Without the governor's signature, those elected could not constitutionally take office. Chamberlain could refuse to sign the commissions of Whipper and Moses. He agreed.

This interview reconfirmed Dawson's faith in Chamberlain, and the next day the editor published an account highly favorable to the governor. He quoted him as saying: "I do not allow myself to think that the good and honest men of South Carolina will find it impossible, because they are organized as Democrats, to give their help to whomsoever [*sic*] shall be best able to undo the terrible wrongs of last Thursday." Here was an appeal to Dawson's fellow partisans to stick with the reform Republican as the man who could most effectively safeguard their interests.

On Tuesday, Chamberlain proclaimed his decision not to sign the two commissions. He said he need not to do so, because the terms of the incumbent judges would not expire until after the next legislature had been elected, and so the next legislature rather than the existing one should choose the new judges. But he saw nothing objectionable in the rest of the eight commissions, since these would not put such grossly unsuitable persons on the bench, and so he was signing the other six.

That was on December 21, the anniversary of the landing of the Pilgrims on Plymouth Rock in 1620. The New England Society of Charleston, another of the city's high-toned organizations, was celebrating the occasion with its annual dinner. Chamberlain sent the celebrants a telegram in which he said the civilization of the Puritan, the Cavalier, and the Huguenot had been imperiled. He did not have to add that it was he who had come to the rescue.

In the *News and Courier* Dawson praised him as the savior, if not of civilization, at least of South Carolina. The governor had pulled off a beautiful "coup d'état"; he had carried the war "into Africa"; he had stood his ground while the "Radical hounds" yelped at his feet. By mail Dawson wished him and his family a Merry Christmas. "Thanks," Chamberlain replied, ". . . and a warm, deep, hearty return of your wish to *you* and *yours*." Thanks also from Mrs. Chamberlain for Dawson's having recommended a certain romantic novel to her, the best she had read for a long time, one so good it reminded her of Sir Walter Scott.[13]

It looked like a Happy New Year, too, for both the Chamberlains and the Dawsons. One thing did cause Dawson a bit of worry—the possibility that Elliott and his accomplices might try to remove Chamberlain from office. "I don't at present think impeachment is much thought of," Chamberlain reassured the editor. "It will require 83 votes to do it, in the House, and I don't think they can *hope* even to get them, but we must watch them."

For the moment, Elliott had to content himself with trying further to embarrass Chamberlain. He appointed a committee to investigate the board of land commissioners, the state agency that had undertaken to buy up land, divide it into small farms, and sell these cheaply to landless blacks. Chamberlain, as attorney general, had been ex officio a member of the board. The investigating committee now called on him to testify. He denied having acted carelessly or dishonestly while a land commissioner, though he admitted that improper if not fraudulent deals had taken place. The investigators found no proof that he had done any wrong.

But Whipper, defending himself before the house, insisted that Chamberlain had indeed done wrong as governor. Whipper said that in striking at *him* Chamberlain was striking at blacks in general. "The real thrust was aimed at the negro," he declared. "So far as Daniel H. Chamberlain is concerned, I regard him as unfit for earth; to heaven he cannot ascend, and were he to make his advent in hell, I fear he would incur the displeasure of his Satanic majesty."

Most white people—and even some of the "best elements" of the colored people—took a different view of the Whipper and Moses affair. At meetings all over the state they were denouncing the action of the legislature and endorsing that of the governor.[14]

On New Year's Eve he was not feeling well, and throughout the winter and spring of 1876 he suffered from frequent attacks of migraine. Apparently the calming influence of the classics was not enough to soothe the nerves of the scholarly Chamberlain, torn as he was by the conflicting demands of politics. He needed to hold the support of both Democrats and Republicans, but the more he appealed to either group, the more he alienated the other. No man can serve two masters—without considerable nervous strain.

By replacing state and local jobholders, Chamberlain kept on trying to please the Democrats, but there were limits beyond which he could not go without antagonizing Republicans. Some Democratic newspapers of the upcountry, particularly the *Greenville News* and the *Spartanburg Herald*, complained about the Democratic appointments that he did make. In regard to one jury commissioner whom the critics objected to, he protested to Dawson that he believed the man to be "a fine, honest Conservative citizen," and he promised to remove him on proof of bad behavior. "But I swear I think I have earned the right to be trusted to do this, and to be believed to have acted honestly in the appointment."

"I am deuced weak just now—hardly able to hold my pen," he wrote to Dawson on another occasion, but he was not too weak to answer the charge from Marion County that he was not putting in enough good officers there. "The Conservatives now have an unusual number of Trial Justices in Marion—*four* and perhaps five out of the *nine*," he pointed out. He went on:

> In regard to the *Marion* appointments I do not understand that I have made any pledges which I have not kept. . . . What I have done I have done from a desire to do the most good *ultimately*. My friends in Marion ought to understand that unless I throw away all my influence with my own party, then I must manage things so as to keep my hold on the party. If they are not willing to accept my acts and interpret them in that light, then they ought not to have any confidence in me. To urge me to try to get the nomination of my party and then to denounce me for taking only a small step in that direction, and one which does no harm to them, is idle. I cannot play that part. I must stop, or I must act in such a way as a sensible politician would act.

For the time being, Chamberlain managed to hold the support of a majority of South Carolina Democrats. In January the Democratic state executive committee announced that Democrats had "watched with growing confidence" the course of the present governor. "And they declare their belief that the Democracy of the State, rising above party as he has done, will give an unfaltering support to his efforts, as Governor, for the redress of wrongs." At the same time, however, the executive committee urged the people to "reorganize thoroughly the Democratic party."

When Democrats convened in May, the majority still preferred to rise above party and go along with Chamberlain. But a minority insisted that Democrats ought to be Democrats and ought to decide now that their next gubernatorial candidate must be a "true conservative moderate son of South Carolina—a native." The dissenting delegates came mostly from the upcountry, where blacks were less numerous than in the low country, and where Democrats could expect more feasibly, by means of intimidation and force, to carry a straight-out ticket of their own.

A straight-out program might be practicable for the upcountry, Dawson objected in the *News and Courier*, but it would be disastrous for the Charleston area, if not for the state as a whole. "Straight-outism, with its threat and bluster, with its possible disturbances and certain turmoil, is the foe of mercantile security and commercial prosperity." Anyhow, such a campaign was bound to lose, Dawson argued, because of the overwhelming number of blacks in the lower counties. And a ticket with Chamberlain at the head of it was sure to win. Chamberlain would have "the solid Republican vote," the control of election officials, and the ability to call in federal troops. So "what prospect is there that he could be defeated? It could be done in only one way: by *armed force*. For that the people are not ready, and if they were ready such a course would end in disaster and ruin."

But Dawson had little credibility among the extreme straight-outers of the upcountry, and he was losing what little he had. Distrusting both him and Chamberlain, the *Edgefield Advertiser* had previously asserted: "All the beautiful resolutions and newspaper puffs that South Carolina people have showered on this man lately are to the end that he might keep South Carolina Republican." The Edgefield editor now accused the *News and Courier* publishers of being "Northerners and Radicals" and of having "no more understanding of the feelings, hopes and aspirations of the people of South Carolina than a hog of heaven."

Despite Dawson's opinion, many upcountry whites and especially those in Edgefield County were indeed ready to use violence. They knew perfectly well how selective violence had recently worked in Mississippi, and they were eager to try, in the South Carolina election this fall, their own version of the Mississippi plan.

Some could not wait till autumn to begin it. In May an Edgefield County mob took from the sheriff and shot to death six blacks suspected of complicity in the murder of a white couple. This murder was "cold-blooded and fiendish," Chamberlain declared, but the subsequent killing rendered "every person engaged in the killing a murderer in the eyes of the law." He could only plead with the county law officers to see that justice was done. More than a year earlier he had ordered the disbanding of the Edgefield black militia after clashes occurred between it and the white rifle clubs. He could not call the militia back into service now without jeopardizing his relationship with the Democratic party.[15]

Already, on other grounds, he was jeopardizing his relationship with the Republican party. Almost the only white men in the party who remained friends of his were natives such as Thomas Jefferson Robertson, the wealthy and conservative United States senator. Not even all the native whites stayed with Chamberlain. His own law partner, Melton, sold his share in the *Union Herald* and resigned as attorney general. Melton was quoted as saying "that if Chamberlain's measures were not checked he would eventually bring disaster and defeat to the Republican party, and that if he presumed to be a candidate for re-election as Governor he [Melton] would feel obligated to sever his legal relations with him."

The other United States senator from South Carolina, John J. Patterson, the railroad promoter from Pennsylvania, led the anti-Chamberlain Republicans, among them the scalawag circuit judge in Edgefield County, Robert B. Carpenter, and the scalawag comptroller general in Chamberlain's administration, Thomas C. Dunn. In part the factional opposition was "a piece of Frank Moses' deviltry. Dunn is in it too. He has become a candidate for Gov. with Judge Carpenter as alternate." So Chamberlain, in the midst of one of his sick headaches, confided to Dawson. "Patterson is here openly fighting me, and with him are Dunn, Carpenter (L. C. & R. B.), Hardy Solomon, but *not* Sam Melton," Chamberlain added a little later. "I really think Melton does not intend to act with them."

Though Chamberlain did not wish Melton's hostility, he did want Patterson's—or at least the appearance of it. He needed to distance himself from the alleged "corruptionists" so as to maintain his reputation as a sincere reformer. Hence he was annoyed to read in the *New York Herald* that he and Patterson had reconciled. From Spartanburg, where he was about to address the student literary societies of Wofford College, he mailed Dawson a denial for him to send out as an Associated Press dispatch. He suggested that Dawson paraphrase him this way: "He says no terms of reconciliation have been offered to or by him, and that he would regard any settlement of existing differences in the Republican party of this State which sacrificed or compromised in any degree the cause of reform or good government as worse than utter defeat."

With his bipartisan reformist line, Chamberlain was causing some concern to leaders of the national Republican party as they calculated their chances in the upcoming presidential election. Whoever the party's candidate might be, the candidate could hardly count on carrying South Carolina if the state ticket should consist of one Republican—Chamberlain—and all the rest Democrats. Senator Oliver P. Morton of Indiana, one of President Grant's right-hand men, was an early front-runner among contenders for the Republican nomination.

"Mr. Morton looks on your attitude as in practical identification with the Democrats," Chamberlain heard from a friend in Washington, "and already gives up the State to the opposition." Chamberlain answered in a letter to the President and another to the senator, both of which letters were eventually published. "For you or me, as Republicans, to countenance the election of Moses and Whipper," he wrote rather presumptuously to Grant, "is as impossible as it would be for [the reformist New York] Governor [Samuel J.] Tilden, as a Democrat, to countenance the election of William M. Tweed" to a judgeship in that state—Boss Tweed, the notoriously corrupt chief of Tammany Hall. "To try to save the seven electoral votes of South Carolina at the price of silence under this infliction will cost us, in my judgment, many times that number of votes elsewhere." In his letter to Morton he said he was merely keeping his pledges of good government. "Of course those who dislike practical reform cried out: 'He is going over to the Democrats!'"

Reform was the watchword in national politics, too. Now that the Democrats controlled the House of Representatives, they were busily investigating the Grant Administration and were uncovering one scandal after another. The Democrats were expected to nominate as their presidential candidate the man who was gaining fame as a great reformer in New York—Samuel J. Tilden. The Republicans, some of them thought, should run a reformer of their own. A likely one seemed to be Grant's secretary of the treasury, Benjamin H. Bristow, who was completing his self-imposed task of breaking up the whiskey ring (in which distillers in collusion with treasury agents had been evading excise taxes).

A few of the Liberal Republicans, the anti-Grant reformers of 1872, were still trying to maintain their independence from the regular party. They were ready to cooperate with the Democrats again if the Democrats should have the better candidate in 1876. Samuel Bowles, a leader of this movement, invited Chamberlain to a conference of good-government people both Republican and Democratic. Chamberlain, while expressing sympathy and admiration, begged off. "In order to do good and really control things here," he explained, "I must have a pretty large contingent of colored Republicans at my back. These colored Republicans are morbidly afraid of the name or idea of 'Democrats,' and the most effective cry yet raised against me is the cry of *Democrat*."[16]

Having raised this cry, Senator Morton hoped to keep Chamberlain and his friends away from the Republican national convention, which was to meet in Cincinnati in June. When the South Carolina Republicans gathered in the statehouse in April to choose delegates at large, Senator

Patterson was on hand to act in Senator Morton's interest. Chamberlain faced a powerful combination of Patterson, Carpenter, and Elliott—a carpetbagger, a scalawag, and a black.

At the opening of the state convention Elliott tried to prevent the seating of pro-Chamberlain delegates. One of these, the scalawag E. W. Mackey, protested: "We are met here today face to face and eye to eye with the banded robbers who have plundered the State." Elliott went up to Mackey and asked who the "banded robbers" were. "You are one of them," Mackey replied. "You are a liar," Elliott retorted. The two threatened one another with pistols, one delegate threw an inkstand, and others wielded chairs as weapons. Chamberlain sat calmly through the brawl, even when a chair was waved over his head. Women screamed, among them Elliott's wife, Grace, whom a female reporter once described as a "quadroon with a complexion of the creamy hue of Southern magnolia, just tinted with the suggestion of primroses on cheeks and lips." Eventually the pro-Chamberlain delegates were seated.

When, after another day of wrangling, the convention got around to balloting in an all-night session, Elliott was the first to be elected. Next, the voting was between Patterson and Chamberlain. Speaking in Patterson's behalf, Carpenter charged that Chamberlain, from the time he entered the governor's office, had "sought only to advance himself at the cost of his allegiance to the party." Carpenter spoke effectively and drew loud and frequent applause. It was after four o'clock when he finished, and the faint light of dawn was already showing in the windows of the assembly hall.

Chamberlain, as he got up to reply, was participating in the most crucial oratorical contest yet in his career. Unless he could turn the audience around, he was sure to lose the election—and with it the leadership of the Republican party in the state. By now, most of the men in front of him were dozing; he had to wake them up. A nervous shudder ran through his slight frame and drops of sweat stood out on his high forehead as he began to speak.

> Mr. Chairman: Frequent allusion has been made to my coolness. I sometimes feel that nothing could be further from the truth . . . but I am happy to say that as I stand here to-night amongst the Republicans of South Carolina, the touch of whose elbows I have never failed to feel since 1868, I feel as calm and cool as a May morning, and as ready to meet the sweet kisses of my wife and children this morning. . . .
>
> I can tell you, gentlemen, that there have been times in my Administration when, had it not been for the tender counsels and support of the wife of my love, I should have faltered on the way, and stained the record that I would lay down my life for, rather than tarnish, for the sake of the dear children that now lie sleeping at home. As weary as I am, I must come here to take up this new cross. . . .

Suddenly Chamberlain struck at Carpenter's most vulnerable point.

As a bolter in 1870, Carpenter had run with Democratic support against the regular Republican candidate for governor (Scott). Chamberlain now recalled debating Carpenter in that campaign. "I went to Chester," he said. "I met there the chosen leader of the Democracy of South Carolina, the man who now assails me with the charge of want of fealty to the Republican party!" Of such a man it could be said: "*Falsus in uno, falsus in omnibus.* False in one statement, false in all." He himself was guiltless. "Let me say that the only sin that I can lay to my door is that I have not stood still firmer in this pathway of political reform."

After nearly two hours, as Chamberlain sat down pale and exhausted, roars of approval echoed through the capitol. The roll was called, and the tally showed Chamberlain 89, Patterson 32. This result was not due to Chamberlain's eloquence alone. Cardozo and others had been quietly using their powers of persuasion on black members of the convention. But Cardozo could not get himself elected; he was twice defeated, the second time by Patterson. Nor could Chamberlain secure the passage of a resolution endorsing his administration.

Among the fourteen South Carolina delegates at the Cincinnati convention (the four at large plus ten from the five congressional districts) Chamberlain alone voted consistently for Bristow, the crusader against the whiskey ring, on the first six ballots. The other thirteen at first voted for Morton and then scattered their votes. On the seventh ballot, after Bristow and Morton had withdrawn, Chamberlain and six others voted for Rutherford B. Hayes, who now won the nomination. Morton could not have made a worse President than Hayes, so far as Chamberlain's future was concerned.[17]

Soon after his return from Cincinnati, Chamberlain went to Charleston to join, on June 28, in commemorating the Revolutionary War victory at Fort Moultrie a hundred years before. It was the hottest day anyone could remember. Old and prestigious social-military clubs from several states, including Massachusetts, marched in the parade, men in uniform here and there collapsing from the heat. Wade Hampton, astride a charger at the head of the procession, still had the air of the great cavalry commander he once had been, though now a bit portlier and grayer. Cheer after cheer came from the crowds along the streets as he passed by. Chamberlain, at last recovered from his off-and-on illness, managed to look trim and graceful in the carriage in which he rode. There were also cheers for him.

It was an occasion for extending hands across the chasm left over from the Civil War—if there still existed a chasm to divide these joint heirs of the Revolutionary War. "We desire that this celebration shall promote peace, fraternity, good-will among all Americans," Chamberlain declaimed, opening the program from a gaily decorated stand in a city park.

"The day of wrong and misrule, I fully believe, is passing away—the day of deliverance is at hand," predicted the main speaker on the program, the ex-Confederate General J. B. Kershaw, one of the foremost proponents of Democratic support for Chamberlain. After Kershaw had concluded his oration and the applause had subsided, he stepped forward to make clear that in speaking of the "sad condition" of South Carolina he had been referring, of course, to the period *before* Chamberlain was governor.

Chamberlain promptly rose from his chair and, with an ingratiating smile, demonstrated that he had lost none of his savoir-faire, his knack for doing and saying just the right thing. "Gentlemen, it is needless for me to say that I have detected nothing in the words of General Kershaw that I do not recognize as the sincere utterance of a true heart," he averred. "I could not expect, indeed it is impossible, that General Kershaw, so brave upon the battlefield of war, could be unjust upon the peaceful field of this day." The cheering was immense.

At a banquet that evening in Hibernian Hall—where the Palmetto Rifle club was the host and the only blacks present were waiters or other servants—Hampton and Chamberlain were the honored guests, Hampton sitting at the right of the master of ceremonies and Chamberlain at the left. Chamberlain offered a toast: "South Carolina, let her future only be worthy of her past." Hampton responded: "I declare to you to-night, on the honor of a soldier and gentleman, that we consider the decision of the war as final, and we accept the Constitution as it is"—meaning, presumably, the Constitution with the Thirteenth, Fourteenth, and Fifteenth Amendments.

At the end of the dinner the Charleston Riflemen appeared at the dining-room door and gave three cheers and a tiger for Chamberlain. He responded: "This compliment from the citizen soldiery of South Carolina to a man who is not a South Carolinian nerves me to say that I pledge myself to support that candidate for Governor of the State who will carry the banner of reform." He was assuming that he himself would be carrying that banner for both Republicans and Democrats.[18]

This occasion was to mark the high point of cooperation between Governor Chamberlain and the Democrats of South Carolina. Within a week, events were to start an estrangement that would soon be utterly complete. Chamberlain was to carry the banner for Republicans, but Hampton for the Democrats, and no longer was there to be a peaceful field like the one in Charleston on June 28.

CHAPTER 17

The Abandonment of Southern Republicans (1876-1879)

July 4, 1876: the hundredth anniversary of the Declaration of Independence, which proclaimed the equality of all human beings in their right to life, liberty, and the pursuit of happiness. In Hamburg, South Carolina (on the Savannah River opposite Augusta, Georgia), members of a black militia company were observing the occasion with a parade. Two young white men came along in a carriage and demanded that the militiamen make way for them. In refusing, the captain of the company pointed out that there was plenty of room to pass on either side. The street, so little used that it was overgrown with grass, had a width of more than a hundred feet. But the two white men insisted on following the carriage tracks down the middle, and so the captain reluctantly allowed them to go through.

Angered at such black insolence, the two white men had the captain charged with obstructing a public thoroughfare. At the hearing a few days later, their attorney, Matthew C. Butler, ordered him to surrender the company's arms. When the captain declined to do so, two or three hundred white men took up positions outside a building where the militiamen had gathered in their second-floor drill room. Shots were fired at the building, and a return shot hit and killed one of the besiegers. Now thoroughly enraged, the whites brought up a cannon and blasted away with it, so as to drive the blacks outside. The whites then shot one of them to death, captured twenty-five others, executed five in succession, and targeted the rest as they ran off, severely wounding three of them.

Governor Daniel H. Chamberlain was appalled when he learned the details from his attorney general, whom he sent from Columbia to Hamburg to investigate. Only a few weeks earlier, in faraway Montana, the Sioux had wiped out General George A. Custer and his immediate command, to the horror of most of those who read of the "Custer massacre," but to Chamberlain the affair at Hamburg seemed far worse. "It presents a darker picture of human cruelty than the slaughter of Custer and his soldiers, as they were shot in open battle," he wrote to South Carolina's Senator T. J. Robertson in Washington. "The victims at Hamburg were murdered in cold blood after they had surrendered and were utterly defenceless." Such barbarity could only move a civilized person to shame and disgust.

Chamberlain did not hide his feelings. He deplored the Hamburg massacre in a speech at Beaufort, on one of the Sea Islands below Charleston. Then, in search of support from the Grant Administration, he went to Washington and conferred with Secretary of War J. D. Cameron and Attorney General Alphonso Taft. These men told him the President and the cabinet would insist that the state of South Carolina enforce its own laws and bring the murderers promptly to trial and punishment. But Chamberlain needed more help than that.

On his return to Columbia the governor dispatched a long letter to the President, enclosing documents that detailed the brutality of the Hamburg mob. Such occurrences, he pointed out, worked to the advantage of the Democratic party. Hence South Carolina Republicans looked on the affair as "only the beginning of a series of similar race and party collisions," the aim of which was Democratic control of the state. "They see, therefore, in this event what foreshadows a campaign of blood and violence . . . a campaign conducted on the 'Mississippi plan.'" The question was, would the federal government step in if the violence should become too much for the state authorities to handle? Grant replied: "I will give every aid for which I can find law or constitutional power."[1]

At the moment, advocates of a "straight-out" campaign for the Democratic party were putting into practice exactly the strategy that Chamberlain described to Grant. The chief of these strategists was Martin W. Gary, and second only to him was Matthew C. Butler, the instigator of the Hamburg riot. Both of them, ex-Confederate generals, were well known to Chamberlain, having been associated with him in railroad enterprises and having cooperated with him to protect the interests of state bondholders.

Gary had been in Charleston on June 28, when Chamberlain and Wade Hampton shared honors at the ceremonies marking the Fort Moultrie centennial. Gary was there to head off the Democrats-for-Chamberlain movement and to start a Democrats-for-Butler drive instead. The next day he happened to meet Hampton on the train departing from Charleston. Hampton, though Gary disliked him, would make a much more appealing candidate than would Gary's friend and neighbor Butler. In conversation on the train Hampton indicated that, despite his camaraderie with Chamberlain the night before, he would rather see a Democrat at the head of the ticket. He finally agreed to run.

The pro-Hampton straight-outers shrewdly waited until the excitement over the Hamburg murders was at its height before making a public move. Then, on July 12, the Democratic state executive committee issued a call for a nominating convention to meet on August 15. Meanwhile, sentiment for a straight-out ticket increased when Chamberlain condemned the murderers.[2]

He knew he risked losing white support by speaking out, but he also knew he would alienate his black followers if he kept silent. For the time being, he still seemed to have a chance to head a fusion ticket, win the governorship, resign in favor of a Democratic lieutenant governor, and then go on to the United States Senate. Francis W. Dawson and the *Charleston News and Courier* remained on his side. The paper regretted the massacre, blamed it on Gary and Butler, and ran a series of ten articles, the last of them on July 18, elaborating on the governor's praiseworthy record of reform. Gary felt his "honor" so seriously impugned that he challenged Dawson to a duel.

But Chamberlain was soon to lose what little hope he had left for a Democratic nomination. On August 12 he made bold to enter the Gary and Butler stronghold of Edgefield, not far from Hamburg, to address a Republican rally, along with the scalawag Judge T. J. Mackey and the black Congressman Robert Smalls. Before noon the speakers in a carriage followed a parade of marching blacks that a black band led down a dusty red clay road to a grove outside the hilly town. Awaiting them at the grove, Gary sat astride his steed at the head of several hundred armed and mounted men.

Gary was of more or less the same age as Chamberlain, who was now forty-one. Both men were prematurely bald, Gary being "as bald as a billiard ball" and Chamberlain having only a fringe of hair around his ears and the back of his head. Each wore a mustache, but Gary also a pointed goatee, which with his deepset eyes and habitual scowl gave him a forbidding, almost demonic look. While Chamberlain had the pallid face of a scholar, Gary displayed the tanned and ruddy features of an outdoorsman, though he too was a lawyer and an alumnus of Harvard. Financially, he had done much better than Chamberlain since the war. Returning penniless from Appomattox, he had managed to acquire three thousand Edgefield acres and an imposing mansion, Oakly Park, where as a bachelor he lived in a style approximating that of an antebellum planter.

When, on that August morning, Chamberlain stepped upon the temporary wooden stand, Gary and Butler joined him there, and so many of Gary's and Butler's followers crowded onto the structure that one end of it collapsed. Others swarmed around the stand or climbed into the trees overhanging it and trained their pistols on it. These men cheered as Butler took it upon himself to open the proceedings. When Chamberlain tried to speak, there was so much yelling he could not make himself heard. His associates fared no better. Butler and Gary, however, proceeded to harangue the audience at great length, calling Chamberlain a liar (for his remarks about the Hamburg massacre) and a man unworthy of even the votes of blacks. Chamberlain was aghast. He was not used to this kind of political debate.

That same day the *News and Courier* made plain that Dawson was turning against Chamberlain. Headlines read: "The truth about Hamburg . . . lawlessness of the black soldiery . . . a militia company organized to kill the whites." Dawson now apologized for ever having criticized the whites at Hamburg, but he made no mention of their behavior at Edgefield, though he had a reporter on the scene. He was yielding to the pressure of straight-out opinion, which was costing his paper advertisements and subscriptions. Three days after the Edgefield imbroglio the state Democratic convention, meeting in Charleston, nominated Hampton for governor. "Wade Hampton and Victory!" the *News and Courier* proclaimed.[3]

There was nothing left for Chamberlain to do except to give up or else to go on campaigning—for the top position on a Republican rather than a Democratic slate. In his subsequent appearances he ran into the same kind of heckling by gun-toting horsemen as in his appearance at Edgefield. At Newberry one of the uninvited speakers recommended lynching for white as well as black Republicans. At Abbeville some of the mounted men, firing pistols into the air, tried to tear a United States flag from the black paraders who were carrying it. At a stop in Barnwell County the intruders cursed Chamberlain as a "God-damn Son-of-a-bitch" and cheered a Democrat who took over the platform to deliver a tirade against carpetbaggers.

Still, Chamberlain persisted with his campaign. He had to continue demonstrating his devotion to the Republican cause if he were to gain the votes of a majority of the delegates at the nominating convention. He was compelled to cultivate the good will of Republicans both black and white with whom he recently had been exchanging insults.

When the convention met in the representatives' hall of the state capitol in mid-September, his foremost advocate was John J. Patterson, the same reputedly corrupt carpetbagger he had been trying hardest, until lately, to dissociate himself from. Patterson explained to the delegates that he and Chamberlain had never really disagreed. "I was opposed to him for none of his reforms, but because he was too thick with the Democrats, and I got suspicious of him." Here Chamberlain interrupted: "Well, do you think so now?" Patterson: "No, I see that you have thrown off your new friends, and Daniel is all right again."

But the black leader Robert B. Elliott did not consider Chamberlain all right again, despite Chamberlain's courageous, unequivocal, and reiterated condemnation of the Hamburg massacre. In a speech to the convention Elliott resurrected old evidence of racial prejudice on Chamberlain's part. He read from a copy of a letter Chamberlain had written six years earlier, when, having heard that two blacks were interested in running for the United States Senate, he offered himself as a candidate "to keep the party from going over to negroism." Elliott also reminded the delegates how Chamberlain had deprived William J. Whipper and Franklin J. Moses, Jr., of the judgeships to which the legislature had elected them. Elliott added that he possessed information—

but would not divulge it—which could send Chamberlain to the penitentiary.

After speaking in his own defense, Chamberlain had the satisfaction of winning the nomination by a vote of 88 to 36. He then left the legislative hall and went to his office in the capitol. After a while he learned that Elliott had been nominated for attorney general (by a vote of 115 to 1). He disliked the prospect of having Elliott as a running mate, and the thought crossed his mind that he ought to go back to the delegates and threaten to withdraw his own name unless they retracted Elliott's nomination. But he also disliked the prospect of losing the votes of Elliott's black followers on election day. When he returned to the convention hall, he and Elliott made a show of being the best of friends. Beaming, they strode down the aisle arm in arm.

This gave Dawson his cue for rebuking Chamberlain. In the *News and Courier* he described the Elliott nomination as "iniquitous and infamous," and he called on Chamberlain to show his sincerity as a reformer by leaving the Republican ticket and coming to the support of the Democratic. Chamberlain replied in an anonymous editorial he wrote for his own paper, the *Columbia Union Herald.* Dawson, he said, was going against his own better judgment in endorsing the Democrats' "Edgefield policy" of terror and intimidation. Elliott was now a true convert to the reform cause, and Chamberlain would stand by the Republican party. "It is his mission again to rescue the people of this state who oppose him from their own madness and folly."[4]

So the contest was to be between the carpetbagger and the ex-Confederate, between the volunteer spokesman for the black majority and the acclaimed champion of the white minority. The Democrats pretended to stand for "home rule." In fact, they could not hope to win if all natives were to have a free and unhindered vote. The Democrats pictured Chamberlain as an interloper. In fact, he owned property in South Carolina and had made the state his home continuously for almost a decade. Hampton, a Mississippi planter, no longer possessed so much as a square foot of land in South Carolina and, though an occasional visitor since the war, was not even a resident of the state.

As a public speaker, Hampton could not compare with Chamberlain, but the contest was not to be decided by forensic skill. Chamberlain, having spoken repeatedly in pursuit of the nomination, refrained from stumping at all in pursuit of the election. He left that to others and especially to Elliott, who as party chairman managed the Republican campaign. Hampton did make speaking tours through the state and thought he was having a persuasive effect on black voters. His influence on them was negligible, however, in comparison with Gary's influence.

Gary continued the campaign of intimidation that he had begun at

Edgefield in August. It was much like a guerrilla campaign. Under Gary's carefully worked-out strategy, the Democrats formed what he called "Military Clubs." Uniformed in red shirts, they rode about with rifles and revolvers to frighten blacks and disrupt Republican meetings. "Every Democrat," Gary secretly admonished his Red Shirt followers, "must feel honor bound to control the vote of at least one negro, by intimidation, purchase, keeping him away, or as each individual may determine how best he may accomplish it." Democrats also agreed among themselves to accept as tenants or employees no blacks who voted Republican.[5]

No sooner was Chamberlain renominated than the Red Shirts went into action with their bloodiest forays of the campaign. On September 16, rifle clubs from various places descended upon Ellenton, about twenty miles from Hamburg, avowedly to avenge the rape and robbery of a white woman. For three days and nights the mounted gunmen, their numbers growing to several hundred, roved the countryside in search of potential victims. The blacks, as Chamberlain summarized the story, "were shot down wherever found: in fields and woods, on highways and in cabins, along the railroad tracks and at the railroad stations." By the time a company of United States troops arrived to stop the killing, two whites and thirty blacks lay dead according to Democrats, one white and forty to fifty blacks according to Republicans. Weeks afterward other blacks were still missing, and large areas from which people had fled were still depopulated. The Ellenton massacre was even worse—far worse—than the Hamburg massacre had been.

Democrats did not apologize. They contended that whites were in constant danger from the possibility of black uprisings. There had been strikes in the rice fields of the low country and rioting in Charleston where the blacks appeared to be the aggressors. (No Red Shirts rode in that part of the state, where whites were hopelessly outnumbered.) Chamberlain and the Republican local authorities had managed to put down those troubles, but Democrats continued to criticize him for failing to maintain law and order throughout the state.[6]

The Democratic party chairman, Alexander C. Haskell, declared that Chamberlain, instead of depending on the federal government, ought to ask for the cooperation of the Democrats. Chamberlain replied in a public letter:

> It is made the occasion of constant reproach that I am Governor of the State and yet cannot and do not preserve the public peace. General Hampton and his followers are seeking to profit politically by uttering this reproach and declaring their easy ability to maintain the peace of the State. I shall answer your demand with perfect plainness of speech. The reason I cannot and do not maintain the peace of the State and suppress lawlessness and prevent terrorism is solely because the Democratic party are the authors of the disturbances of the peace, the lawlessness and terrorism which they now reproach me with, and demand that I shall allow or invite them to suppress.

> *Quis custodes custodiet?* [Who will guard the guards?] To entrust the protection of those who are to-day endangered by the present disturbances to the armed, mounted, unlawful Democratic Rifle Clubs would, in my sober judgment, be as unnatural and unfaithful in me as to set kites to watch doves, or wolves to guard sheep.

Instead of appealing to the Red Shirts for help, Chamberlain on October 7 issued a proclamation calling on them to disband and disperse. Otherwise, he said, he would have to ask the President for additional troops. Some of the riflemen greeted the proclamation with a hillbilly sense of the comic. They held meetings on horseback, dissolved their rifle clubs, and instantly reorganized under such names as "Allendale Mounted Base Ball Club," "Mother's Little Helpers," and "First Baptist Church Sewing Circle." Gary himself responded with a new threat. "We must warn the leaders that 'the tall poppies will fall first,'" he told a Red Shirt gathering. "I for one would shoot first Chamberlain, Elliott, Patterson, and such carpet-baggers; second, the miserable white native scalawags; and, lastly, the black leaders generally."

The Red Shirt activity continuing, Chamberlain made the expected request of Grant, and on October 17 the President ordered all available troops in the military district of the Atlantic to report to General Thomas H. Ruger in Columbia. By election day, November 7, there were about five thousand federal soldiers in the state. General Ruger scattered them among as many localities as he could—five or ten here and five or ten there—but did not station them right at the polling places. There was nevertheless little violence at the polls. The Democrats relied, for the most part, on the residual effect of their pre-election terrorism.[7]

So confident were the Democrats that immediately after the election they began to celebrate. One night Chamberlain sat in the governor's office with a newspaperman who remembered him as being "calm and collected as ever, but with a pale face and quivering lip," while "a great crowd of yelling red-shirted rifle-club Democrats, drunk like the rest of those in the town, came about the building and under the Governor's windows cursing, shouting, discharging their guns and pistols, and calling upon Chamberlain to show his Radical head that they might blow it off." He was not primarily concerned about the danger to himself. "My poor wife! my poor wife!" he kept exclaiming. She was only days away from giving birth to their third child.

The state board of canvassers had yet to announce the official returns. The canvassers were finding conclusive evidence of intimidation and fraud in Edgefield and Laurens counties. In the town of Edgefield a Red Shirt patrol had stood in the way of blacks attempting to vote, and in other places the ballot boxes had been hidden from black voters. If the canvassers were to accept the ballots from these two counties, Hampton would come out ahead in the total vote; if not, Chamberlain would.

After two weeks the canvassers reached a decision to exclude the Edgefield and Laurens returns. Then the state supreme court, whose chief justice was the father of Chamberlain's enemy Moses, declared that the canvassers had no power to do so. In a dispute of this sort, it was up to the legislature to say who was rightfully the governor-elect, but the legislature's composition—and hence its conclusion—would itself depend on the disputed returns. If these were rejected, there would be two vacancies in the senate and eight in the house, and the Republicans would fill a slight majority of the remaining seats in both chambers.

The legislature was to meet at noon on November 28. From day to day "white men in red shirts swaggered in the streets . . . displaying their revolvers," the *New York Times* reported. Fearing a Democratic coup, Chamberlain telegraphed to Washington for military protection. President Grant instructed Secretary Cameron to "sustain Governor Chamberlain," and Secretary Cameron told General Ruger to "advise with the Governor" in carrying out this order. At midnight, just twelve hours before the convening of the legislature, a company of United States soldiers marched into the statehouse.[8]

At noon, when the Democratic members-elect, with Hampton accompanying them, arrived at the door of the representatives' hall, the sergeant at arms with the backing of the troops refused to admit the claimants from Edgefield and Laurens. Angry whites crowded around the front entrance of the capitol to protest this "barefaced usurpation," as one of the Edgefield men called it. From the windows of the governor's office Chamberlain and Ruger watched the surging mass outside. It looked as if the mob might attempt to storm the building. So Chamberlain spoke to Ruger, and Ruger sent an officer to ask Hampton to quiet his followers. Hampton, knowing that a clash would hurt his cause in Washington, appeared at the entrance and persuaded the demonstrators to leave. Then the Democratic members-elect withdrew to Carolina Hall, the headquarters of the local rifle club, and organized their own house of representatives.

Meanwhile, in the capitol, the Republican members-elect organized both a senate and a house. They held the advantage of possessing the official legislative chambers—but not for long. On Thanksgiving Day, November 30, at half-past eleven in the morning, the Democrats managed to slip into the representatives' hall while the Republicans were enjoying a recess. Ruger, though ordering the men from Edgefield and Laurens to take no part in the proceedings, made no attempt to evict the Democrats. Chamberlain telegraphed to Cameron:

> Members from Edgefield and Laurens who have no pretence of membership are now taking part in legislative proceedings. Ruger has ordered them not to do so, but does not enforce his orders. I do not propose to yield one inch or compromise one right. . . . We are fighting with our lives in our hands and unless we are sustained fully we can fight no longer. Personally

> you know I was reluct[ant] to enter upon this fight but duty compelled me and now I will never yield till I am deprived of support. We are right morally, legally, and politically and all claims to the contrary are lying pretences.

For four days and four nights the contending groups shared the same room. Then the Democrats suddenly left and went back to Carolina Hall. The reason, Hampton said, was that Chamberlain was plotting to bring in a gang of roughs to throw the Democrats out and was going to call in the troops if the Democrats resisted!

The legislators remaining in the statehouse proceeded to recount the gubernatorial vote. Omitting the returns from Edgefield and Laurens, they declared Chamberlain the winner by 86,216 to 83,071. On December 7 he delivered his inaugural address before them. "If we fail now," he said, "our government—the government of South Carolina—will no longer rest on the consent of the governed, expressed by a free vote of majority of our people." He stood "appalled at the crimes against freedom" that had recently occurred, and he was still more appalled to see the North, even the Republican party itself, "divided in its sympathies and judgment upon such questions."

One week later, the Democratic legislators having declared Hampton the winner by 92,261 to 91,127, he was inaugurated in front of his makeshift capitol, Carolina Hall, as cannon boomed and Red Shirts shouted in the street. He immediately sent a messenger to demand that Chamberlain deliver up to him the great seal of the state and possession of the statehouse. Chamberlain could afford to be curt in his refusal. For the moment at least, he had the military power of the United States to back it up.[9]

Chamberlain could expect to continue enjoying federal support when—and if—the Republican Rutherford B. Hayes succeeded the Republican Ulysses S. Grant in the presidency. But the outcome of the presidential election remained in doubt, the Democrats claiming victory for their candidate, Samuel J. Tilden. The presidential vote, like the gubernatorial vote, was under dispute in South Carolina and also in Louisiana and Florida (besides Oregon, where one of the electoral votes was being contested). Tilden needed just one of the disputed votes to have a majority in the electoral college; Hayes needed *all* of them. And if Hayes deserved those of South Carolina, surely Chamberlain did also.

On the day of Hampton's inauguration a friend of Chamberlain's, the carpetbag federal collector of internal revenue in Columbia, undertook to convince Hayes of the falsity of Hampton's claim to have been legally elected. The collector wrote:

> Hampton's plan all through the late campaign was to have armed democrats

attend and break up republican meetings at the places where he (Hampton) did not expect to be present; while at *his* meetings he would prate of peace and good order . . . which he has done more to subvert than any other man in the state. . . .

The census of 1875 (State) shows that there were in round numbers 94,000 colored voters and 68,000 white voters. At the late election the republicans polled 92,000 and the democrats 91,000 votes. Now if "colored men" can be put down as republicans, and the white as democrats, it will be seen that the republicans polled within 2,000 of their entire voting strength . . . while the democrats polled 23,000 *more* than their entire voting strength. The question now is, where did this surplus of votes come from? . . . Fraud, intimidation, and villainy of the most outrageous character can only explain the matter.

Chamberlain shared these convictions, and he assumed that Hayes shared them, too. As the weeks passed, however, Chamberlain found it more and more difficult to demonstrate that he could, in fact, govern the state of South Carolina. To enforce his authority, he had only the soldiers in the statehouse, who amounted to no more than a corporal's guard. Hampton had on hand in Columbia four or five thousand trigger-happy Red Shirts. To finance his government, Chamberlain could collect little in the way of taxes, and the state supreme court forbade him to draw on existing funds, while Hampton received tens of thousands of dollars in voluntary contributions.

To assert his pardoning power—and thus to establish his legal right to govern—Chamberlain issued a pardon to one of the convicts. When the warden of the penitentiary refused to let the man go, the question of the pardon's validity went to the local county court. The judges decided that neither Chamberlain nor Hampton was legally governor, since neither had received his qualification from a legislature with a quorum in both chambers. But the judges declared that Chamberlain could lawfully act as governor until a successor should be properly qualified. He did not long enjoy the satisfaction of thus being partially sustained, for Hampton had pardoned another prisoner, and the state supreme court soon upheld his power to do so.[10]

Christmas came—not a very merry one for either Chamberlain or his wife, who was worrying about his safety—and still he had no way of knowing whether Hayes would be the next President and, if so, whether he would stand behind the Republicans in the South. Though Hayes would be beholden to them for his own election, they were becoming more and more an embarrassment to him as they continued to lose popularity in the North.

Chamberlain was somewhat relieved to see the *Chicago Tribune* publish an interview in which he had a chance to gain a hearing in the North. "It is quite too much the custom on speaking of what are called the 'carpetbag' Governments of the South to present only one side of the picture," he had told the interviewer. True, there had been extravagance, waste, incompetence, and dishonesty in his own state. Yet the Republicans had introduced, for the first time there, fair representation, real self-government, and a system of public schools. "Republicanism, with all its faults, has made South Carolina its debtor." So Chamberlain argued, with conviction but without much hope of changing the minds of many Northerners.

Other things that Chamberlain read in the newspapers caused him additional concern about Hayes's attitude. T. J. Mackey had gone from Columbia to Columbus to see Hayes, who continued to hold the office of governor of Ohio while waiting to see if he was ever to be President of the United States. During the past eight years the scalawag Mackey had attached himself to Scott, Moses, and Chamberlain in succession as each of the three became governor of South Carolina. At the beginning of the 1876 campaign he still supported Chamberlain and, indeed, was on the platform with him at Edgefield when Gary, Butler, and their gunmen interrupted the meeting. Later he went over to Hampton, to join numerous other scalawags who were deserting the Republican party.

Mackey, acting as a go-between for Hampton, was now pleading his case with Hayes. He intimated that during the campaign he himself had been "for Hayes and Hampton" and that since the election Hampton too had come to prefer Hayes to Tilden. Mackey brought along a copy of Hampton's inaugural, with its assurances that Hampton and his followers would not use force but would appeal to the "proper legal tribunals" and to the "patriotism and public sentiments of the whole country" in dealing with the "usurped power" which was defying the "Supreme Judicial authority of the State."

The purport of Mackey's errand Chamberlain could guess accurately enough. "I felt very much like sending you a word of condolence," he promptly wrote Hayes, "when the papers announced that Mackey had called on you and remained *till 1 o'clock at night.*" The man was as untrustworthy as he was tedious. "He deserted the Republican party here and supported Hampton *and Tilden* in his public speeches," Chamberlain elaborated. "He doubtless says he supported you, and this will give you an idea of his veracity."[11]

Chamberlain would have become much more apprehensive if he had known what kind of advice prominent Republicans soon were giving Hayes. Joseph Medill of the *Chicago Tribune,* for one, wrote for Hayes's benefit:

> The old Whig feeling in the South [the Whigs were the prewar opponents of the Democrats] is beginning to crop out in spots, and if carpetbaggery can be got rid of, and "home rule" in state affairs be substituted, a Southern white Republican party can be organized down there which, with the aid of the blacks, will give us control of half the South. . . .
>
> Chamberlain is a pretty good man for a Carpet-bagger . . . still it would be vastly better if he would retire. We have tried for eight years to uphold

> negro rule in the South officered by Carpet baggers, but without exception it has resulted in failure and almost ruin to our party.

Self-appointed advisers of Hayes assured him that, by making concessions to Southern conservatives, he could induce Hampton's followers in South Carolina and Democrats in other Southern states to concede his own election.

To decide the winner of the presidential race, Congress finally appointed a special commission of five congressmen, five senators, and five Supreme Court justices. The fifteen-man group turned out to consist of eight Republicans and seven Democrats. Predictably, by a vote of eight to seven each time, the commission awarded Hayes the disputed electoral votes of South Carolina, Louisiana, Florida, and Oregon. The commission did not complete its work until February 23, 1877, and March 4 was inauguration day.

The inauguration of Hayes gave Chamberlain no reason to rejoice. Two days later a messenger arrived with a letter for him from one of Hayes's close friends. The messenger was none other than A. C. Haskell, the chairman of the South Carolina Democratic party, and the message was to the effect that, for the good of the country, Chamberlain ought to yield to Hampton! "This is embarrassing beyond belief," Chamberlain confessed to an associate. He replied to Hayes's friend that, much as he desired to "aid and relieve President Hayes," he simply could not "permit Hampton to reap the fruits of a campaign of murder and fraud." Perhaps he could make Hayes see the situation as it actually was if he could have "the privilege of a personal conversation" with him.[12]

In a few weeks Chamberlain received an invitation to confer in person with the President—and with it a notice that exactly the same invitation was going to Hampton. On March 28 Chamberlain in Washington talked with Hayes and with members of the new cabinet. "He has found them all more than favorably disposed toward him" a reporter gathered from Chamberlain afterward, "and he felt much more confident of ultimate recognition and success than he did some days ago." Chamberlain remained in Washington to wait for a decision while Hampton had his interview. Then, on request, each of the two wrote out a detailed statement of his own case.

Chamberlain lost his confidence in success as quickly as he had regained it. Friends of Hayes came to him with the strong hint that if he would give up the contest he could have the vacant post of minister to Switzerland. Obviously the Administration was not about to decide the contest in his favor. He had agreed to dine with the President on April 1, but he no longer felt like facing him. "I accepted the invitation in complete forgetfulness of a previous acceptance by me of an invitation to dine this evening in Baltimore," he apologized to Hayes in a hurried note. "I beg that you will pardon my strange lapse of memory. . . ." Sure enough, the very next day the President and his cabinet unanimously decided to remove the troops from the South Carolina statehouse, and to do it in just over a week, on April 10.

Back home Chamberlain went with mixed emotions: a sense of outrage and a feeling of relief. "For months his devoted wife has lived in daily and nightly dread that the hand of an assassin would take her husband," a *Cincinnati Commercial* correspondent revealed. "What satisfaction is such a life to a cultivated, quiet, domestic man, a natural scholar and student, having little in common with South Carolina politics and pistols?" For the past four months he had been serving without pay. Now he could think of his personal finances and of his law practice, which he had neglected for more than two years. "But," he confided to a son of the famous abolitionist William Lloyd Garrison, "personal considerations are so overshadowed by the sad fate that awaits the innocent thousands of colored people who are now to be left 'naked to their enemies.'"[13]

On the morning of April 10, Chamberlain and his colleagues in the capitol formally expressed their acceptance of fate. Elliott, Cardozo, and other state officials addressed to Chamberlain a public letter in which they praised him for his "intelligent and unselfish service" and agreed with him that it was pointless to continue the struggle "in view of the disastrous odds." Chamberlain issued a statement in which he told the Republicans of South Carolina: "Today—April 10, 1877—by the order of the President whom your votes alone rescued from overwhelming defeat, the Government of the United States abandons you, deliberately withdraws from you its support, with the full knowledge that the lawful government of the State will be speedily overthrown."

At 11:55 that morning the lieutenant commanding the nineteen soldiers inside the statehouse gave them the order of parade rest. At noon, as soon as the town hall bell began to strike, he ordered: "Shoulder arms! Right face! Forward, march!" The men filed out the rear door while spectators, a hundred or so of them, silently looked on. "There was," as one of them remarked, "nothing dramatic in the scene."

Chamberlain had arranged for his private secretary to turn the executive chamber over to Hampton's agent the following noon. He himself left the office, for the last time, shortly after eleven. As he rode home in his carriage, the streets were crowded, but the people paid no attention to him; they were watching a circus parade. If any of them had noticed the "cold, handsome face of the ex-governor," commented his onetime trumpeter the *Charleston News and Courier*, they would have detected no emotion in "the expression of his pale, quiet features." One detail they could hardly have missed: "The familiar portfolio, without which he has never, or seldom, been seen, in his daily journey to and from the Statehouse, was as usual under his arm."

Two weeks later came the news that federal troops had departed from the statehouse in New Orleans and the ex-Confederates were taking possession of it—on precisely the fifteenth anniversary of the wartime surrender of the city to the forces of the United States. In Louisiana and Florida, as in South Carolina, the Republican governments fell when the forces of the United States were finally withdrawn. Reconstruction was over, and the Lost Cause was not wholly lost.

As for Chamberlain, he had no political future in South Carolina, if he had one anywhere, though rumors were again circulating that he could have the Swiss job. The senatorship he had once set his heart upon was now going to the choice of the Hampton legislature. That choice was Matthew C. Butler—the man who had given one of his legs to the cause of slavery and disunion—the man who, more recently, had started at Hamburg and Edgefield the terrorist campaign for white supremacy and state rights. Chamberlain considered resuming his legal career in Columbia but decided, instead, to move to New York City. There, on May 17, he was admitted to the New York bar.

On July 4, just one year after the incident that led to the Hamburg massacre, a very different celebration was underway in Woodstock, Connecticut. People from miles around had gathered for the dedication of a public park. Scheduled to speak were nationally known figures, among them Maine's Senator James G. Blaine, the Massachusetts physician-poet Oliver Wendell Holmes, and South Carolina's recent Governor Daniel H. Chamberlain. A few hundred of the thousands present waited in front of the speaker's stand, and they gave Chamberlain hearty applause and three cheers when he got to his feet.

He bowed gravely, then launched into a philippic against Hayes and his Southern policy. That policy "consists in the abandonment of Southern Republicans, and especially the colored race." Hayes "stood by, willing to see men risking, by day and night, for months that seemed longer than years, their lives by hundreds, to lift him to the Presidency, upon the lying assurances . . . that he would protect and rescue them by the great powers of the office he should receive." All the men around Hayes joined in the assurances and the deception. "When I think of these things, my heart grows hot with indignation, and a curse comes unbidden to my lips, for the men who thus played with the blood of brave men and women as the gambler plays with the dice. Such treachery . . ."

For more than two hours Chamberlain kept this up, while his hearers showed signs of growing restlessness. Some wandered off in apparent boredom and others muttered in disagreement, one of them saying Chamberlain was nothing but a "sorehead." When he finished, the applause was perfunctory, and a young preacher immediately jumped onto the platform to obtain a hearing. The man said that he, for one, did not agree with the speaker, and he did not want the country to think New England did. So he led the crowd in three cheers for President Hayes.[14]

No longer could Chamberlain expect any sort of patronage from the Hayes Administration. That did not trouble him, for he did not want any. What was distressing was the apparent fact that not even his own people, his fellow New Englanders, were particularly interested in hearing what he had to say.

From his law office in New York City, Chamberlain could follow South Carolina events by reading his mail and the *New York Times*. "Wade Hampton's Domain. Persecutions in the Name of the Law. The Recent Arrests of South Carolina Republicans." So ran the eye-catching headlines of the *Times* on August 25, 1877. The front-page article elaborated: "When the legally elected Republican State officers of South Carolina relinquished their positions in April last, it was the general understanding that they should not meet with any further persecution from the shot-gun Democracy." But now a legislative committee was investigating not only the most recent Republican officeholders but all of them for eight years back. Hampton's attorney general was subpoenaing witnesses and making arrests. The Democratic leaders seemed especially eager to incriminate Chamberlain. Why did they want to "blacken the character" of men who had let them have complete control of the government and had even left the state? The motive of the Democrats was political. "They will not rest content until the Republican Party is buried beyond even a hope of resurrection."

The *Times* reporter could not have described the Democrats' aim more accurately if he had been reading their private correspondence. "Briefly & all this in confidence," the attorney general was writing to the lieutenant governor, "I think our course is to get the Indi[c]tments & not issue requisitions [for extraditing men like Chamberlain from other states], but publish in Shape of a Report, the testimony the Committee has taken: an immense deal of it . . . would not stand test as legal evidence, but the moral evidence would be crushing." Except in a very few cases, there would be little chance of securing convictions in a court of law. But that was beside the point. The object was mainly to accumulate and disseminate ex parte testimony against the Republicans. "The press would revel in it," the attorney general accurately predicted, "& would politically guillotine every man of them."[15]

To obscure the politics in the proceedings, the Democrats tried to make them look bipartisan by assigning key roles to men they identified as Republicans. These were mostly scalawags, some of whom had already defected to the Democratic party. The chairman of the investigating committee, John M. Cochran, was a defector of that kind. The star witness was the egregious Franklin J. Moses, Jr., who still bragged of having raised the Confederate flag over fallen Fort Sumter in 1861.

Moses testified that Chamberlain once had given him money with which to bribe Jonathan J. Wright, a black justice of the state supreme court. That supposedly occurred in April 1874, when Moses was governor and Chamberlain a lawyer in private practice. Moses, according to his story, took $2500 from Chamberlain and gave it to Judge Wright, who then swung the court in favor of Chamberlain's client. As corroboration, Moses exhibited a letter in which Chamberlain had instructed him: "Please arrange that matter at 2,000 or 3,000 as may be necessary." But the letter failed to specify the "matter" or the way that Moses was to "arrange" it.

As usual, the committee released this testimony to the press. When ex-Judge Wright saw it he protested his innocence in a petition to both houses of the legislature. He prayed that they would cause him either to be promptly tried or to be "relieved of the scandalous imputation." But the Democrats would give him no opportunity to clear his name. The investigating committee merely concluded that Chamberlain was guilty whether Wright was or not.

The committee believed, however, that it could make a stronger case against Chamberlain by accusing him of fraud as legal adviser to the ill-fated state land commission. The allegation of overpayment for lands, especially for the tract known as Hell-Hole Swamp, was of course an old one, which his political opponents had repeatedly brought up and he had repeatedly answered. Nevertheless, on November 6, 1878, eighteen months after his leaving South Carolina, a Columbia grand jury indicted him (and the rest of the ex-members of the commission) for conspiracy to defraud the state. He let the attorney general know at once that he would voluntarily appear in Columbia to stand trial. Then he requested a postponement on account of the death of one of his three little boys.[16]

Indicted along with Chamberlain was his former colleague and rival Robert K. Scott. While a reform governor, Chamberlain intimated that Scott had been an incompetent governor if not a corrupt one. Consequently, Scott could not bring himself to back Chamberlain in the campaign of 1876. He sat out the election and afterward visited President Hayes to urge the recognition of Hampton and the removal of the troops. Once Hampton had the governorship all to himself, Scott continued publicly to endorse him. "Hampton is honestly carrying out the promises he made during the campaign," an interviewer reported Scott as saying in August 1877. "He has already appointed more colored men to office than were appointed during the first two years that I was governor."

Scott therefore found it hard to understand why the Hampton administration should threaten to prosecute him as a criminal. He was called before the investigating committee to testify briefly on two occasions in July. Up to this time he had continued to reside in Columbia with his family and to carry on his real-estate operations both in South Carolina and in Ohio. He now went back to Napoleon, Ohio, on business and, to avoid possible arrest, decided to stay there for the time being.[17]

From Columbia he received conflicting advice. At first, he got a reassuring letter from his old hanger-on and Hampton's new hanger-on T. J. Mackey. "I have full faith in your speedy and triumphant vindication," Mackey wrote. "I shall stand your friend at all hazards, having perfect confidence that a judicial investigation will fully demonstrate your official and personal integrity. You should return to Columbia without delay." Later, however, Scott heard differently from a Columbia businessman whom he had queried about the "intentions" of the Democrats. "The conclusion myself and others have come to," this man replied, "is that if you do not return to this country matters will be in time dropped as far as you are concerned but should you return your presence here would cause certain bitter Democrats to assail Hampton and force him to take action in your case. Therefore by no means think of returning here."

So Scott stayed on in Napoleon, leaving his wife, Jane, temporarily in Columbia to look after their business interests there. He depended on a Columbia lawyer, the former Confederate Colonel Fitz W. McMaster, to counsel and defend him in any legal action that might arise. McMaster was "striving in different ways to obtain a general act of amnesty," as he informed Scott. Though failing in that, he did persuade the legislature to empower Hampton to nol-pros the anticipated cases except perhaps those of Chamberlain, Patterson, Kimpton, Parker, and Cardozo. He assured Scott that he believed his protestations of innocence.

And, for McMaster's benefit, Scott wrote out his protestations laboriously and at great length as he learned of the charges that the investigating committee was eliciting from some of its witnesses. It was ridiculous to suppose that he had accepted bribes while governor, as Parker and others were accusing him of having done. "I was a man of fair respectability," he pointed out, "and entirely above the necessity of resorting to any unfair means to make money." It was equally absurd to believe he had given bribes to save himself from his impeachers, for the "impeachment rascals" never had the two-thirds vote they needed to pass their resolution.

To Scott, it was sad but not surprising to see John Cochran at the head of the inquisitorial committee. "I did him many acts of kindness," Scott recalled, "and he would now make fair weather for himself at my expence." Scott could have added that Cochran had been associated with him in the sale of property to the land commission and that, if his own conduct was questionable, so was Cochran's. "The only thing that grieves me," Scott complained to his attorney, "is that I cannot have a fair chance to vindicate myself before an impartial set of men who did not feel it a duty to convict me of some crime."[18]

Scott was never to have a chance to vindicate himself before an impartial jury—or any other jury—even though he was indicted for his alleged misdeeds as a member of the land commission. His onetime comptroller general, the scalawag John L. Neagle, offered to secure his release from present and future indictments for $500 cash plus a contingent fee of $2,000. Scott responded with the money and a conditional promissory note. Considering the hostile atmosphere in South Carolina, he could not hope for a fair trial there, nor could he expect to resume his business there in peace.

So he and his wife decided to abandon their South Carolina residence and make Napoleon, Ohio, once more their home. They had to sell their Columbia house at a considerable loss. "You can form no idea of the depression of every thing here," their Columbia broker wailed; "you can't sell real estate, you have to give it away; your house is rapidly depreciating from non occupancy & the fence is falling & looks bad inside; there is no one here to buy your place [and] pay anything like its worth & you will have to submit to a sacrifice." Despite the depressed market, the broker also advised the Scotts to sell a farm on which they had black tenants: "negroes will eventually ruin a place renting from year to year."

Scott tried to liquidate other South Carolina investments as well. He was willing to let his City of Columbia bonds go for as little as thirty-five cents on the dollar, but the most he could get was thirty cents. He was as anxious as ever to dispose of his Blue Ridge Railroad bonds, and H. H. Kimpton was still optimistic about the prospects. Kimpton was under indictment in South Carolina for his role as the state's financial agent. He and Chamberlain, his Yale chum, were good friends again and were seeing one another in New York. Chamberlain, as Kimpton's attorney, was helping both with the litigation over the railroad bonds and with maneuvers to counter the Democratic indictments.[19]

"The S. C. Republicans will be troubled no more," Scott happily learned from Kimpton in a note of May 3, 1879. "We have made settlement, but in such a way that I can't explain by letter." The gist of the settlement was this: The Hayes Administration would drop charges against South Carolina Democrats for interfering in the 1876 election in such a way as to violate federal laws. The Hampton administration would pardon Cardozo and Smalls, who had been convicted and imprisoned, and it would "continue" (refrain from bringing to trial) the cases against Chamberlain, Scott, and others named in the indictments. Eventually all of these cases were nol-prossed.

Only four Republicans had been tried and convicted. One of these was the former state treasurer Niles G. Parker, who had already been tried and convicted by the reform Republicans under Governor Chamberlain. But the 1700-page report of the investigating committee, chock-full of testimony from unexamined witnesses, gave the impression that the rest of the accused, if ever brought to trial, would also have been proven guilty. The report had nothing to say, however, about Gary, Butler, and other Democrats who had been involved in railroad and similar "rings" along with the allegedly corrupt Republicans.[20]

CHAPTER 18

A Fool's Errand
(1877-1881)

He could not sleep that July night in 1877. His mind kept going over events that had occurred since he first walked the streets of this town, Raleigh, North Carolina. That was exactly twelve years ago. What had he, Albion W. Tourgee, accomplished in all that time? What had Reconstruction achieved?

It was frustrating and exasperating to think how things had turned out, especially since the inauguration of Rutherford B. Hayes. Recently the Northern people, Republicans as well as Democrats, had seemed more and more disposed to "let the South alone," and now President Hayes *was* letting the South alone. Apparently few Northerners cared about the consequences, such as the disfranchisement of blacks and the end of real self-government in the region. Or, rather, few Northerners understood the true nature of the struggle over Reconstruction. They assumed that all Southern Republicans were lying thieves and all Southern Democrats were honest gentlemen.

Even the most well-meaning Northerners shared the widespread illusion concerning Hayes's Southern policy. A Brooklyn preacher, a lifelong friend of Tourgee, had written to congratulate him: "Prospects are brightening for men of your stamp in the South"; "times are growing better there as the President's policy is developed and the Southern people see that it means—peace." Bitterly Tourgee reflected: "Times are better here, for such men as I am, only in the sense that Hell is better than Purgatory." Hayes's surrender to the South had not appeased the Southerners. Ex-Confederates were less pacified now than a dozen years before. "All of the time I have lived here yet I have never seen an hour when political bitterness has been so fierce as it is today."

People in the North failed to realize that the great majority of carpetbaggers, like Tourgee himself, were veterans of the Union army—four-fifths of them, he estimated. "It is rare indeed that you meet one who has not this badge of worthiness or folly on his person." Folly? Yes, the

Hayes program would make fools of all those in the South who had stood by the federal government in the past. "Everyone who fought for the country's integrity or favored the policy of reconstruction will have reason to curse the day he did so."

Both the North and the South needed to be reeducated, it seemed to Tourgee as he lay awake that July night. In recent years he had urged repeatedly—and futilely—a federal system of education in the South. The Southern people black and white, mistaught by slavery, must relearn the meaning of democracy. Only then would Reconstruction have a chance to succeed. But, before such an educational program could get government support, the Northern people would have to be convinced of the program's necessity. They would have to be shown the truth about Reconstruction and the reasons for its failure.

It occurred to Tourgee, as he tossed and turned, that there was something he could do about the problem—something that would give him at least a bit of relief from his frustration. He could write another novel, one in which he told the story of Reconstruction as it actually had happened, basing the story on his own experiences. In the morning he woke his wife, Emma, who had been asleep beside him. "I am going to write a book," he told her, "and call it 'A Fool's Errand.'"

He immediately got up, went into another room, and began to write. It was Sunday and he had no other obligations. Before the day was over, he had dashed off three brief chapters.

In them a young Midwesterner with a French ancestry and name (Servosse) comparable to Tourgee's and with a wife (Metta) much like Emma, patriotically volunteers at the outbreak of the rebellion. "So, in a few days, he marched forth in the foolish foppery of war, avoiding his wife's tearful gaze." He becomes a captain in an infantry regiment made up mostly of men who, like him, exhibit a "species of mental alienation" in their enthusiasm for their cause.

> The persons acutely affected received different names in different localities. In some they were called "Boys in Blue," "The Country's Hope," and "Our Brave Soldier-Boys"; while in others they were termed "Lincoln's Hirelings," "Abolition Hordes," and "Yankee Vandals." It may be observed, too, that the former method of distinguishing them prevailed generally in the States lying to the north, and the latter in those lying to the south, of what used to be called "Mason and Dixon's line." Both meant the same thing. The difference was only in the form of expression peculiar to the respective regions. All these names, when properly translated, signified *Fools*.

Thus ended chapter three.[1]

Not for some time was Tourgee to resume the story. He was soon preoccupied with other things, with the inescapable chore of making a living and with a rather desperate try at a new political career.

For the moment, Tourgee was making a living from his federal job as pension agent in Raleigh. He refrained from openly criticizing the Hayes Administration for fear he would lose the job. He soon lost it anyhow when the pension bureau was reorganized and many of the agencies eliminated. With Emma and their daughter, Lodie, now going on seven, he moved back to Greensboro, where the family could live with Emma's mother in a house belonging to Emma's sister Angie.

Tourgee still had a law partner and something of a law practice in Raleigh, and he had frequent occasion to go there on legal or political errands. He ran into trouble there one day in the spring of 1878 after he had published in a Greensboro newspaper a series of anonymous articles ridiculing four Democrats who were angling for the chief justiceship of the state supreme court. One of the four, D. G. Fowle, was particularly incensed. Ex-Judge Fowle confronted ex-Judge Tourgee at the Raleigh railroad station and wanted to know if he was the author of the so-called "C" letters. When Tourgee declined to say, Fowle swung at him with a cane, and Tourgee countered with a fist. Bystanders separated the two combatants before either of them could do much damage. Reporting the incident under the front-page headline "Brawling Southern Politicians," the *New York Times* commented: "From present appearances, a number of street fights, with duels in the background, may be expected."[2]

No such affrays ensued, though "bad blood" persisted among North Carolina politicians. They looked to the fall elections to settle some of the scores with one another. The outlook was discouraging for Republicans. Now that Hayes was President, they could no longer count on the national Administration for support. Nor could they depend on the state administration, since the Republicans had lost the governorship in 1876, when the wartime governor Zebulon Vance defeated Tourgee's good friend Thomas Settle. Previously, the already Democratic legislature had gerrymandered the state, throwing the most overwhelmingly black counties into a single congressional district, which was the only one of the eight districts left with a Republican congressman.

Among the seven Democrats in Congress was Alfred M. Scales, the representative of the Fifth District, which included Guilford County. Once a Confederate brigadier-general, Scales had since prospered as a Greensboro lawyer. "He is a very strong man, and cannot be beaten without great effort," a political observer declared at the end of June. "Gen. Scales will be renominated by acclamation. It is not probable that the Republicans will run a candidate."

If the Republicans should run a candidate, the man apparently would have to offer himself as a kind of political sacrifice. Tourgee was nevertheless willing and eager to accept the nomination. If elected, he would have a dependable income for at least two years—and possibly for much longer. He would also hold a position that would reaffirm his prestige and his pride.

He decided to run despite Emma's strong objections. She wanted no part in another of those exhausting campaigns in which the duties of manager and factotum inevitably fell to her. She was already unhappy at having to live in the same house as her mother and having to compete with her in the management of household affairs. She was sick of the house, sick of the state, sick of the South. She was not going to put up with it any more. She was going to go home to Erie, Pennsylvania, and take Lodie with her. Tourgee could do nothing except give his consent and even his encouragement for her to go and stay away at least for the duration of the campaign. As cheerfully as he could, he saw her and Lodie off.

"I have got through an awful lonesome day," he wrote her the next night. "I know that it is all for the best for you and Lodie." Ten days later he changed his tune somewhat. "The campaign has opened and matters would look very favorable to me if it were not for your having gone North," he now complained. "I shall lose 500 votes by that, and I have no reasonable prospect of overcoming the difficulty." Many voters did not understand Emma's absence. "They are so suspicious that they believe I am going away as soon as I can get a chance."[3]

Actually, Tourgee was running under much more serious handicaps than that. For one thing, he was getting little support from Republican leaders outside Guilford County, most of them native whites who were jealous of him both as a carpetbagger and as a member of the "Greensboro Ring." Besides, he was taking the unpopular side on the hottest issue of the moment—the question whether Congress should authorize the printing of additional paper money.

Wartime laws had empowered the Treasury Department to put out large quantities of greenbacks, but an act of 1875 required a drastic contraction of the amount still circulating. Farmers and other debtors suffering from the economic depression objected; they thought an inflationary policy would mean higher prices for farm products and easier repayment of existing debts. Now, in 1878, a Greenback party was running candidates in much of the country, among them a congressional candidate in the Fifth District of North Carolina. Scales endorsed the Greenbackers' demand for inflation, but Tourgee opposed it. He took the orthodox view that it would be dishonest to cheapen the currency and thus enable the government as well as individuals to satisfy creditors with devalued dollars.

During September and October he spoke almost every day, making his way by buggy through the counties that formed the congressional district. Most of the counties were familiar to him, since most of them also belonged to his former judicial circuit, but not Stokes County with its rough, broken terrain to the east of Pilot Mountain. Here, at the start of his stumping tour, he found "hot murky weather after numerous rains," sticky mud of red clay, and steep, almost impassable roads. "I am the first G. B. ever seen in this country," he told Emma in one of his frequent letters to her, "and am a curiosity, of course."

Here, at the outset, Tourgee contrived to meet Scales in debate by showing up in Danbury at the time Scales had scheduled for his own appearance there. The two later arranged other debates, where each man knew in advance pretty well what the other was going to say. "He [Scales] takes the old cry of abuse—Swepson, carpet-baggers, Bondholders, &c.," Tourgee informed Emma. The audiences could readily understand what Scales was talking about. George W. Swepson was, of course, Tourgee's friend and benefactor who had been indicted (though not convicted) on charges of defrauding the state. As for bondholders, whether owning corporate or government securities, they presumably stood to benefit from Tourgee's and others' stand against Greenbackism.

From time to time Tourgee varied and enlivened his presentation with touches of humor. When a sudden downpour interrupted a debate, he remarked that Scales's arguments did not hold water so well as his carriage did. Another time, after Scales had concluded with a slur on carpetbaggers, Tourgee began by asking him if he was proud to be a North Carolinian. Scales quickly replied: "Yes, of course." Tourgee: "Well, remember that I became one from inclination, you by accident." Scales: "But you came here a beggar, to make money." Tourgee: "Yes, but had I come in with only rags upon my back, I brought more into the state than you did."[4]

While Tourgee proclaimed himself the best kind of North Carolinian—a North Carolinian by choice—he was becoming less and less sure that he wanted to keep on being a North Carolinian of any kind. At times he longed to get away from "this weary land of strife and hate," as he wrote Emma in one of his downcast moods. "Oh, my Darling, why did I ever bring you here to experience sorrow?" he wrote again. "How happy we should always have been, if we had remained in Erie. I do think it was the very greatest mistake of my mistaken life."

Tourgee tried to cheer himself with predictions of victory. He was not quite satisfied with his performances on the stump. "Yet *I believe I shall win,*" he assured Emma in mid-campaign. "The hard, honest money idea is hitting the people and making friends where I did not dream that it would." Then, just two days later: "There is no estimating how the election will go. The Greenback craze comes and goes in spots and streaks. I think the general notion is in my favor and people think I will win." But the Republican leader of Alamance County, a scalawag whom Scales had beaten in 1876, was saying openly that Scales would also beat Tourgee. The nearer the election came, the more Tourgee dreaded it.

The results proved to be worse, much worse, than his gloomiest forebodings. He lost every county in the district, even his home county of Guilford, and all of them by wide margins. He was crushed. "I can see nothing to look forward to, nothing to hope for," he lamented to Emma. "I have ended a life of bright promise in utter ruin." He wished he were dead, and he knew he *was* dead politically.[5]

To overcome his despondency, Tourgee got immediately to work on one of his writing projects, a digest of North Carolina court cases. He also resolved to complete two novels he previously had begun. One of them needed only a few finishing touches. It was the story of Jacob Churr, a man who rose from poverty to power in the North. The other, "A Fool's Errand," Tourgee had done little with since composing the first three chapters. If he could somehow have seen just a year ahead—when this novel was to be published—he would have had no cause for continued dejection.

As it was, he had to suffer the torments of self-doubt and indecision all through the winter of 1878-79. Emma and Lodie remained in Pennsylvania, and he missed them terribly. But he did not want them to come back to North Carolina, for he feared that Emma would be as unhappy as she had been before. Nor did he really want to join her in Erie, though he would consider doing so if he could discover any kind of opportunity there. "You know it would hurt my pride terribly to go back there but I will put that aside if need be," he wrote on one occasion, and on another: "I believe I hate Erie about as bad as you do N. C."

Somehow, somewhere, he had to make a living. But where? How? If he stayed in North Carolina, he could continue to earn an occasional fee from his rather desultory law practice. He received a little income from his *Code of Civil Procedure in North Carolina,* which had recently come from the press. He could expect a fair amount of money from his digest of law cases, once it was completed and in print. From time to time he heard of a new opportunity—the editorship of a projected Republican paper at $1200 a year, full-time legal service for Swepson at the same salary—but anything of this sort would require him to stay in North Carolina.[6]

He also considered possibilities outside the state. Anywhere but Erie! For a while he thought of moving to Chicago and practicing law there in partnership with Stephen A. Douglas, Jr., his twenty-eight-year-old neighbor and new-found friend. Stephen and his older brother Robert, both native North Carolinians, were seeking damages from the federal Court of Claims on account of property that they, as Southern loyalists, had lost to the depredations of the Union army during the war. The brothers got only a fraction of what they were expecting, though, and young Stephen's share was not enough to finance the move to Chicago and the launching of the partnership. Emma disapproved of the idea, anyhow.

While trying to make up his mind about his future, Tourgee kept doggedly at work on his legal digest. It was a prodigious undertaking—

5600 cases to summarize, 16,000 index slips to note, sort, and arrange—and it would have been even more formidable without the aid of Steve Douglas, a "magnificent fellow." The two of them worked as long as fifteen hours a day, analyzing cases and writing summaries or reading proof as late as two o'clock in the morning. Tourgee let up only when the strain on his eye and the neuralgia in it became too much for him. A person who wrote as extensively as he did—and had a "sole luminary" to see with—needed one of the new writing machines that had been on the market for a few years. He considered buying a typewriter but decided he could not afford it.

Until the digest was done, he had little time for his novels except for odd hours during the week and all day on Sundays. He no longer went to church or belonged to one. If Christianity was the religion of Ku Kluxers, it was not the religion for him. His attitude left his Sundays free but complicated his relationship with Emma, who retained her old piety.

Tourgee sent Harper & Brothers the unfinished manuscript of his Jacob Churr novel, with the tentative title "Figs of Thistles," and the famous publishers sent it back. He planned to revise it in the light of their criticisms and meanwhile to submit one of the chapters to the *Atlantic Monthly* as a short story. But on looking over the manuscript he concluded that, "Harper to the contrary notwithstanding," it did not require any drastic changes. "I set Steve to reading it and watched him all the way through with it. He could not leave it for a moment. I am sure I can put it in a taking shape. He thinks it splendid."[7]

Working so hard in Greensboro, Tourgee was too tired for passion, but during a stay at a hotel in Raleigh he could not help being aroused when "Mrs. H." attempted to seduce him. He confessed the affair to Emma, describing it more realistically than he ever did a love scene in any of his novels. One evening Mrs. H., occupying the room across the hall from his, invited him in and fluttered about him while giving him to understand that her husband was impotent. Tourgee kissed her repeatedly but did nothing more. The next evening she asked him in again and, dressed in a filmy negligee, snuggled up to him on the sofa. Still, he managed to resist temptation, he assured Emma.

This experience made Tourgee more acutely conscious than ever that he could not live without the presence and the love of his wife. According to North Carolina gossip, the two were permanently separated and she was in the process of obtaining a divorce. He relayed the rumor to her. "I see you have made up your mind not to come back to N. C. knowing full well that I will not stay without you," he said. "You never got so much of a home feeling here as I have though."[8]

That was his dilemma. He loved his wife and, for all his disappointments and defeats, he loved the state of North Carolina. He could not hold on to both. So he must leave the state and must leave the South, but for a long time he could not bring himself to make the decision. He kept reminding himself—and his wife and daughter—of the state's physical attractiveness. "Remember that you are not in the balmy old North State where you need pay no attention to wind or storm or wet or cloudy weather," he cautioned Lodie in November. "The harsh North is so treacherous and cruel!" In January he told Emma he was enjoying "that beautiful balmy weather" which she used to like so much. In early March he reported the arrival of spring and a "day of intoxicating loveliness."

By mid-April 1879 he had finally made the decision, which left him with a sense of both relief and regret. "There is nothing for me here—and yet I hate to leave," he confessed. "I do like the old region and I have strung so many sweet hopes on bright dreams here that I seem almost to have knit my heart into the land."[9]

He did not yet know where he was going to go or what he was going to do. After a job search in Washington and New York, he could count on nothing more than a couple of uncertain prospects. He could probably get an appointment as third auditor in the Treasury Department—if he wanted to spend the rest of his life as a petty bureaucrat. Having met the managing editor of the *New York Times,* he thought he had a chance to work his way into a "quasi connection" with the paper. Or he could look to the West. He and his Raleigh law partner talked of relocating their firm in Denver, Colorado, and Tourgee also thought of working as a journalist out there.

Denver was far off and unfamiliar, but perhaps that was all to the good. "It is to us a *new* field," Tourgee wrote hopefully to Emma, "and will do more to get our minds off from old matters and start us on a new life." He was somewhat taken aback when he received reports that Denver was "not a point of such business importance" as he had anticipated and that Colorado was "terribly cold" in winter, extremely dry in summer, and on the whole "pretty desolate." But he did not abandon the idea of starting a new life there.

To finance the venture, he could sell his Greensboro property, though he would probably have to do so at a sacrifice, since the country had not recovered from the economic depression, and real estate was still hard to dispose of. He prepared an advertisement and had it printed as a circular, with a map of "Tourgee's Plan" of eighty-five lots plus an unplatted tract of thirty-five acres and a house with a six-acre yard. All this lay, as he described it, "in one of the most prosperous, attractive and promising localities in the South." Greensboro, a developing rail center, could already boast 3,000 inhabitants, eight churches, two colleges, and not a single barroom. "It is destined to be the heart of the Piedmont region of North Carolina,—that broken upland full of brawling streams, which must very soon become the seat of vast and valuable manufactures." In Tourgee's vision, Greensboro possessed much more of a future than Denver seemed to possess. How sad to have to exchange the one place for the other![10]

Before departing, Tourgee wanted to finish the manuscripts of the two novels he was working on. He now had a publisher for both of them, the same firm that had issued his *Toinette*—Fords, Howard & Hulbert, of New York. The partners were willing to consider a second edition of *Toinette,* but were much more interested in the new novels. They already had in their hands the manuscript of what was to be *Figs and Thistles.* "I am going to tackle your ms. book when Hulbert gets through with it," Howard informed Tourgee at the end of April, "and perhaps we can get that out, if you can spend a few days on it for pruning, &c. Then we can swing 'Toinette' again. And the sooner you get your 'Fool's Errand' into shape (even though Anonymous) the better."

By the beginning of summer the Tourgees were reunited in Greensboro, Emma and Lodie having arrived to stay until Tourgee was ready to go. Then the family could set out together on the trek to the new life. Meanwhile Tourgee rapidly penned the story of the fool that he had been himself. As he wrote, he alternated melodrama with preachment, making his main point most explicitly when he had his protagonist, the carpetbagger Servosse, declare:

> The North and the South are simply convenient names for two distinct, hostile, and irreconcilable ideas,—two civilizations they are sometimes called, especially at the South. At the North there is somewhat more of intellectual arrogance; and we are apt to speak of the one as civilization, and of the other as species of barbarism. These two must always be in conflict until the one prevails, and the other falls. To uproot the one, and plant the other in its stead, is not the work of a moment or a day. That was our mistake. We tried to superimpose the civilization, the idea of the North, upon the South at a moment's warning. We presumed that, by the suppression of rebellion, the Southern white man had become identical with the Caucasian of the north in thought and sentiment; and that the slave, by emancipation, had become a saint and a Solomon at once. So we tried to build up communites there which should be identical in thought, sentiment, growth, and development, with those of the North. It was A FOOL'S ERRAND.[11]

On August 25, 1879, Tourgee along with his wife, daughter, and mother-in-law took the night train northbound from Greensboro. He carried with him several letters of introduction and recommendation from lawyers, judges, and other prominent North Carolinians, all of them natives. "It affords me pleasure to ask for him the kindness and courtesy of strangers," Robert P. Dick had written, with praise of Tourgee's record as a lawgiver and judge, and with a personal note: "Good-bye my friend. We have been through stormy times together and I sincerely hope that you may find a home where you will always be treated with justice and highly and fully appreciated." Among those wishing Tourgee well at his departure was the William W. Holden who, as governor, had welcomed him on his arrival fourteen years before.

The local Republican paper, the *Greensboro North State*, also gave Tourgee a most kindly and complimentary send-off. "He believed in the elevation of the colored race," and this had "greatly prejudiced the white people" against him, the paper said. He had invested and lost thousands of dollars in a manufacturing enterprise, but his loss was Greensboro's gain. "The 'North Carolina Handle Works,' which owes its origin to Judge Tourgee, is now the property of other parties—purchased after the panic of 1873—doing a prosperous business, and giving employment to many of our people." Probably he had "made a greater impress upon the history of this State" than any other man during his fourteen years in it. Yet Democrats had continually slandered him as a "vile 'carpet-bagger,' not identified with the State." So, "with many regrets," he had finally "turned his back on his adopted State, to go forth and find a new home."

The Tourgees headed for New York City, where he was to spend some time helping to prepare his manuscripts for publication. He had not been there long when a reporter for the *New York Tribune* called to interview him. Tourgee talked freely about his reasons for leaving the South. A Northerner of independent mind, he explained, could not reside there in comfort. Though no longer "bulldozed"—that is, subjected to physical abuse—the Northerner was constantly discriminated against. For example, a Southern juryman was overheard to say he would never give a verdict in favor of someone who had a carpetbagger for an attorney.

> I thought I could live South. In 1865 there was less bitterness than now. The rebel soldiers were yet alive who respected their late foes and remembered the earlier days. But since then a new generation has grown up, nurtured in hostility. I have hundreds of the best kind of friends at the South, and have received countless hospitalities there, and am now receiving expressions of regret at my departure. . . .
>
> In all except the actual results of the physical struggle, I consider the South to have been the real victors in the war. I am filled with admiration and amazement at the masterly way in which they have brought about these results. The way in which they have neutralized the results of the war and reversed the verdict of Appomattox is the grandest thing in American politics. . . .
>
> The Northern man felt that the idea—the civilization of the North, for which he had fought and in which he was nurtured—was true, and he had a positive pleasure in supporting and maintaining it as against a hostile and, as he believed, dwarfed and defective development. When, however, the North joined in heaping infamy upon him, because he happened to have been born in her borders, he soon lost the missionary spirit.

How, the reporter asked, could this state of things be remedied? "If at all, possibly by education," Tourgee answered.

The *Tribune* gave its most prominent display to this interview, beginning it at the top of the center column on the front page. But the article said nothing about Tourgee's reason for being in New York, nothing about the forthcoming book in which he would elaborate on themes he had just now alluded to—conflict between civilization and barbarism, the necessity of reeducating and desouthernizing the South.[12]

Figs and Thistles came out on October 4 and *A Fool's Errand* on November 15, almost exactly a year after the political defeat that had made Tourgee feel like a hopeless failure. He was not yet counting on either of these books as the means of his salvation. That other work of his also appeared that fall—*A Digest of Cited Cases in the North Carolina Reports*. He had already paid for the production of 600 copies, was pricing the book at $12.00 and allowing the Raleigh printer a commission of $2.00 for selling it, and could therefore expect to realize a total of $6,000 when and if the printing was sold out. This unimaginative kind of writing, tedious though it was, seemed like a more dependable moneymaker than fiction did. So Tourgee was preparing to begin "A Universal Digest of Cited Cases" on the same plan, covering decisions of the United States Supreme Court and all the state courts. This tremendous undertaking would have kept him busy for the rest of his life.[13]

In December the Tourgees traveled on to Denver, leaving Emma's mother in Erie. Tourgee had a position as editor of the evening edition of the *Denver Times*. But he did not remain long at that job, nor did he give any further thought to the "Universal Digest." *Figs and Thistles* was moving quite well, and *A Fool's Errand* was turning into a runaway best-seller. Royalties were beginning to pour in for Tourgee, profits for the publishers. In January 1880 they called him back to New York to produce additional titles for the eager market.

A Fool's Errand being anonymous, the newspapers of the country were "trying their wits at tracking the author," as the *Chicago Tribune* observed. Some critics were comparing it to *Uncle Tom's Cabin*, and so this paper suggested that it be attributed to the same author, Harriet Beecher Stowe.

Tourgee's friends and relatives knew, of course, who had written the book, and they recognized it as a *roman à clef*, in which Tourgee himself was the model for Colonel Servosse, but they wondered who the other originals were. When Robert M. Douglas inquired about one of them, Tourgee readily identified the man for him. Tourgee's father was impatient with the questioners. "The greatest difficulty with me is the wish of half the readers to know who such & such a character means," the father wrote from Tourgee's boyhood home in Kingsville, Ohio, where the local bookseller could not keep up with the demand. "I tell them they may look on it as a political romance founded on actual facts . . . and that the slave holding element in the South and the democratic party at the North is one and the same thing now and always."

Few Democrats North or South bothered to read the book. "Your recent publication entitled 'A Fool's Errand' is not for sale at the bookstores," a New Orleans carpetbagger informed the publishers, "and Southern sentiment is such that I doubt if the dealers care to make any effort to sell the work." He offered to peddle it among his fellow Republicans. From the title, Democrats gathered that the point of the novel was the foolishness of even attempting to reconstruct the South, and they could readily agree with that. But some critics complained that the book slanderously misrepresented the nature and activities of the Ku Klux Klan.[14]

In New York the author was at work on a project that would refute the critics, restate his thesis, and reveal his identity. He was preparing a factual supplement to verify his fictional account—much as Harriet Beecher Stowe had done with *A Key to Uncle Tom's Cabin* to verify her story. The evidence he brought together would prove the Klan responsible for the horrors he had narrated. What could be done to eliminate Ku Kluxism? He now made his point explicit. "The opinion has been ventured in 'A Fool's Errand' that only GENERAL EDUCATION—*universal enlightenment of whites and blacks alike*—can be relied upon to change the spirit which moved these horrors, and that it is the first great duty of the Nation to provide for such enlightenment." So the foolishness lay not in trying to remake the South but in trying to do it all at once. Reconstruction had not gone too far; it had not gone far enough. In May 1880 appeared *The Invisible Empire: Part I. A New, Illustrated, and Enlarged Edition of A Fool's Errand . . . Part II. A Concise Review of Recent Events . . . .* Tourgee's name was on the title page.

Tourgee remained in New York to complete another Reconstruction novel, one in which he elaborated further on the theme he had suggested in *A Fool's Errand.* Near the end of that story a native white Republican speaks to his son at the grave of Colonel Servosse: "He come from the North right after the war, an' went in with us Union men and the niggers to try and make this a free country accordin' to Northern notions. It was a grand idee; but there wa'n't material enough to build of, on hand here at that time." The architects of Reconstruction were asking for "bricks without furnishin' any straw." *Bricks Without Straw* (Reconstruction without reeducation) was the title and theme of the new novel.

Left behind in Denver were Emma and Lodie. At first, Emma found a church with a revival meeting that was "very pleasant." Hoping to move out of her hotel room, she looked for a house and furniture and was delighted to discover that furniture was cheap and there were "several very desirable places for sale," though no satisfactory ones for rent. "I wish we could buy." People were friendly. "The ladies that have called on me have been so elegantly attired that I feel quite as though I needed an elegant costume and nothing is nicer than black silk." Rather wistfully she asked her husband to get her a black silk dress in New York.

After six months of separation, Tourgee decided he could no longer live without his family and would never live in Colorado. In July 1880 he telegraphed to Emma to come east and join him. They rented a fine house near Broadway in a fashionable section of Manhattan. He did his writing in the living room, where he could look out on a well-landscaped garden. Emma helped by taking pages of the manuscript to the publishers and bringing back printed proofs. The book, *Bricks Without Straw,* was ready in October.

It started off with even faster sales than *A Fool's Errand* had done, but *Errand* continued to sell well, too, both in the original edition and in *The Invisible Empire,* and even *Toinette* found an occasional buyer. *Bricks* sold for $1.50, *Empire* for $2.00, and the other three for $1.00 apiece. Thus the author's royalty, 10 percent of the list price, amounted to 10, 15, and 20 cents per copy. In a little more than a year, a total of approximately 250,000 of all the titles were sold. Tourgee's earnings for the period exceeded $25,000 (the equivalent of at least $250,000 in the monetary terms of a century later), and there was more, much more, to come. At last, he was on the way to wealth.[15]

His books brought him fame along with fortune. From his alma mater, the University of Rochester, he received the honorary degree of LL.D. He was the guest of honor at a dinner of the prestigious Union League Club. Along with lesser notabilities of New York, he and Emma celebrated the seventieth birthday of that other famous writer of novels about blacks and whites in the South—Harriet Beecher Stowe. Emma reveled in the attention her husband got and in the parties to which the pair were invited, besides the plays, operas, and concerts they attended.

As if he did not have enough to do or enough to spend, Tourgee went on a lecture tour to augment his income and reinforce the message of his books. While traveling in western New York State in the spring of 1881, he was taken with a house he discovered for sale in the village of Mayville. It was an imposing brick mansion—in the Italian villa style that had been a favorite of the rich before the war—with thirty-five acres of land and a magnificent view of Lake Chautauqua. Tourgee brought Emma to see it, and she too was charmed. How nice, after these last few homeless years, to have this as a permanent residence! Once the property of a Tweed Ring politician, it was expensive, but Tourgee had more than enough money in the bank. He bought the place and presented it to Emma. She gave it the German name of *Thorheim,* signifying "Fool's Home."[16]

Along with fame and fortune, Tourgee acquired a considerable though momentary influence in national politics. This began when he stopped off in Chicago during the 1880 Republican national convention and persuaded the platform-makers to include a plank for federal aid to education in the South. He also talked with James A. Garfield, the leader of the Ohio delegation. Garfield was an old acquaintance, Tourgee having first met him when he himself was a boy of ten visiting relatives in Chester, Ohio, and Garfield was a teenager studying at the academy there. Since then, they had seen each other from time to time, and Garfield had read *A Fool's Errand.* After long balloting in Chicago, he emerged as the party's dark-horse nominee. In accepting the nomination he stressed his endorsement of the educational plank.

Tourgee campaigned hard for Garfield and, after the victory, wired him: "The family of fools send greeting." The President-elect wrote back: "Dear Judge: I thank you for your kind greeting from the 'Family of Fools,' and in return express the hope that the day may come when our country will be a paradise for all such fools." Later he asked Tourgee for advice about policy with respect to the South. Tourgee urged him to discontinue Hayes's policy—which had led to the creation of the Solid South, which the Democrats dominated—and to appoint only good, sound Republicans to all offices.

Tourgee also reemphasized his educational idea. "This matter of education as the remedy for the Southern ill—the true solution of the Southern question—has been my hobby for a good while and I have offered it to a good many," he wrote. He said he had approached some congressmen in 1870, the Republican platform committee in 1872, and the congressional campaign committee in 1876, all to no avail. "Then I quit putting my trust in princes and went to work on my own hook trying to make the people think my thoughts about the matter. The fact that a quarter of a million copies of my books have been bought and read in the short space of fifteen months shows that somebody has been thinking about the subject besides me." He was still trying to make the people think his thoughts. With his fourteen-page letter he enclosed proofs of an article of his on "National Education" that was soon to appear in the *North American Review.*[17]

He did not have the propaganda field all to himself. In the midst of the recent presidential campaign the *New York Sun* had attempted to smear him by printing excerpts from a North Carolina Frauds Commission report. The Democratic commissioners—and the Democratic newspaper—made a great deal of the fact that Swepson had once lent Tourgee money and Tourgee had never repaid it. The plain implication was that Tourgee had been bribed to do Swepson's and Littlefield's dirty work. In a letter to the editor he explained in elaborate detail how Swepson, a friend and legal client (Tourgee's very first one after his settling in North Carolina), had given him a small amount of money as a campaign contribution and a much larger amount as a loan for the purchase of his Greensboro house, a loan Swepson eventually canceled after Tourgee was unable to repay it in consequence of the Panic of 1873. The *Sun* printed this letter but also ran an editorial ridiculing it.

Then, in January 1881, a book appeared with the title *A Reply to "A Fool's Errand, by One of the Fools."* The author, William L. Royall, a New York City lawyer, was a kind of carpetbagger in reverse—one of the many ex-Confederates who had migrated North in search of opportunities. In his *Reply,* after repeating the testimony in regard to the Swepson loan, Royall commented: "Little matters of this sort are quite sufficient to account for the people of North Carolina having made Mr. Tourgee's stay there quite disagreeable to him, without resorting to the presumption that he was unpopular by reason of being a Northern man."

Royall presented a version of Reconstruction that had little resemblance to Tourgee's. "Now, from the very ending of the war," he related, ignoring the two years (1865-67) of Johnsonian policy, "the Federal Government exhibited a fixed determination to force the white people of the South to bow their necks to the negroes' yoke."

> From the very ending of the war the edict went forth from Washington that no man could hold office in the Southern States who could not swear that he had had no sympathy with the Confederacy. As the entire white population had been in earnest sympathy with the Confederacy, this confined the possibility of governmental agencies to the negroes and such strangers as might happen to come there. . . . The whole South was at once overrun with the larvae of the North. Wherever there dwelt a scoundrel, who feared that his neighbors would give him his deserts in the form of a coat of tar and feathers, that neighborhood lost a citizen, and the South gained an apostle of reconstruction.

These "vultures and harpies," Royall continued, proceeded to "use the negroes' ballots to put themselves into all the offices in each State" and began "swindling and plundering the people in every possible way." So long as these carpetbaggers were "egging the negroes on," there was "bound to be hostility" between the Negroes and the whites. Now, with the disappearance of the carpetbag governments, "the utmost cordiality and amity have come to exist between the two races."

Tourgee replied to Royall's *Reply* with a letter that filled four columns of the *New York Tribune.* He made a powerful case in the letter, as he had done in the books and articles he had written, and as he was to do in the many others he was yet to write. Nevertheless, before the end of his life he was to find himself the loser of the argument. Not his version of events but Royall's was to prevail in public opinion, North as well as South. Grandchildren of Union veterans were to be taught the history of Reconstruction with precisely the interpretation that the ex-Confederate was giving it.

For the time being, however, Tourgee could feel like a winner. He might be a bit embarrassed by the wide publicity given to that loan that had become a gift, but he could enjoy the satisfaction of knowing that, though perhaps careless in the matter, he was utterly innocent. Never had he done—never had he been asked to do—anything to further the railroad-aid schemes of Swepson and Littlefield. Besides, his books continued to sell, doing much better and gaining much more attention than

Royall's screed, though this sold well enough to go into a second edition.[18]

In the immediate future Tourgee could look forward to helping make federal policy with respect to the South. On March 4, 1881, the misguided Hayes would be out and the perceptive Garfield in. President Garfield devoted almost a third of his inaugural to the subject of education, repeating Tourgee's opinions as his own. In due course Tourgee received a presidential telegram summoning him to Washington.

Early in June he spent an afternoon at the White House talking with Garfield while the scent of honeysuckle drifted in through an open window. Before serving as a Union general and a Radical Republican congressman, Garfield had been a college professor and a college president, and he retained a personal interest in educational matters as well as a political interest in the aims of Reconstruction. Affable, always eager to please, he listened attentively as Tourgee again elucidated his program. It would not provide federal money for the Southern states to spend as they saw fit. Instead, it would require federal control as well as federal financing of Southern schools. Occasionally Garfield had a question or an objection, to which Tourgee patiently undertook to give a persuasive response.

> "I see," said the President, laying his hand heavily on the other's shoulder as he stood beside him, "I see all that you urge, and admit that it seems reasonable; but it will take so long—*so very long*."
>
> "It will require a long time," replied the other, seriously.
>
> "How long do you think—ten years?" asked the President as he turned away and began to pace hurriedly to and fro in the narrow room.
>
> "Suppose it should require a century?"
>
> "You do not mean to say that it will take that time to cure the evil?"
>
> "I do not say it will require a decade or a century. I only know that it is the growth of centuries and cannot be extirpated in an hour. Peoples—races—change only by the slowest of processes; a little in one generation and a little more in another."

Thus went part of the conversation, according to notes that Tourgee made soon after he left the White House. He left with the conviction that, while not necessarily agreeing with him on every detail, the President was committed to the principle of reeducating the South. Surely Garfield would get from Congress the legislation and appropriation needed to begin the long, long process. Without him, there would not be much hope, but with him in office for four years the program ought to get off to a good start.

Less than a month later Tourgee was preparing to celebrate the Fourth of July at Thorheim when the news came that Garfield had been shot. The wounded President lingered for eleven weeks, then died. Tourgee wrote a memorial and read it to the citizens of Mayville and vicinity who assembled to "express their profound sorrow." None of the others could have felt a sorrow quite so profound as his.[19]

CHAPTER 19

Only a Carpetbagger
(1877-1907)

George Eliphaz Spencer, the senior United States senator from Alabama, after being elected for a second term, continued to wield some power among Alabama Republicans by virtue of senatorial courtesy, that is, the privilege of naming important federal officeholders within his state. After Hayes's nomination, however, Spencer could expect to lose much of his influence on presidential appointments, since he had been conspicuous as an anti-Hayes man. Momentarily, he was so disgusted that he threatened to resign his seat and quit Alabama politics.

During the electoral dispute between Hayes and Tilden, some of the anti-Spencer Republicans of Alabama seemed willing to let Tilden win. Then, in the words of one of them, Tilden could "clear the house of Spencer," who would try to keep Hayes from appointing good men if Hayes should become President. These Republicans were as thoroughly convinced as were the Democrats that Spencer had procured his reelection by means of bribery and fraud. In the view of his opponents, he had not established a just claim to the senatorship merely because he had frustrated them in their attempt to oust him. The Senate investigation had been "little more than a farce," the prosecutors displaying "an evident lack of information and direction," and the witnesses making "statements directly contradictory of what they were expected to prove."

Once Hayes was President, Spencer ceased to have his own way with the patronage. At the outset Hayes removed some of Spencer's protégés and replaced them with anti-Spencer men. In accord with his policy of conciliating the conservative South, he gave preference to scalawags—even those acting like Democrats—in Alabama and in other Southern states. Spencer resisted this practice and recovered some of his influence. He kept much of it even though he had no chance of reelection in 1878 and became thereafter a lame duck.

After the end of his term, on March 3, 1879, Spencer hoped to regain a place in politics by joining the movement for a third term for Ulysses S. Grant. The Grant movement soon collapsed, and so did the Spencer faction of Alabama Republicans, dependent as it was on federal patronage. Having lost their jobs, the leaders of the faction soon left the state, and Spencer himself did not return to it to live. His political career was over.[1]

For a couple of years Spencer remained in Washington, keeping busy as a lobbyist. He agitated for two-cent postage and an eight-hour day. He also helped to expose the "star-route frauds," in which postal officials conspired with mail contractors to gouge the government. His old army friend Grenville Dodge was a fellow lobbyist and also a railroad magnate. Blessed with influential friends, Spencer finally managed to land a choice bit of patronage himself. A vacancy occuring in 1881, he received an appointment as one of the five federal commissioners who, according to the 1862 act of Congress incorporating the Union Pacific Railroad, shared in the direction of the company.

For the remaining twelve years of his life he lived quite well. Most of this time he spent in Nevada, where he invested in silver mines and a ranch. With him was his wife "Major," whom he had married in 1877, ten years after the death of his first wife, Bella Zilfa. Major Spencer had been Miss William Loring Nunez, named for her uncle William W. Loring, a colonel in the United States army, then a major general in the Confederate States army, and finally a general in the army of the Khedive of Egypt. Like the first Mrs. Spencer, the second one wrote books: *Salt Lake Fruit* (1883), *Story of Mary* (1884, republished with the title *Dennis Day, Carpet-Bagger*, 1887), *A Plucky One* (1887), and *Calamity Jane* (1887).

The Spencers also had a home in Washington, D.C., and there Spencer died on February 19, 1893, at the age of fifty-six, leaving his widow and a son, George Eliphaz, Jr. He was buried in Arlington National Cemetery, the resting place for Union veterans on the grounds of what once had been the home of Robert E. Lee.[2]

Willard Warner, staying on in Alabama, gained power in the state's Republican party as his factional foe Spencer lost it, but the party no longer amounted to much. For several years Warner kept hoping to revive the party, then gave up the effort and concentrated on trying to make his iron business pay.

Warner blamed the party's disintegration on Spencer and on Grant for backing him with the patronage. "Yes, it is true," he assured his old friend Senator John Sherman on January 10, 1877, "that, had President Grant (and others) sustained me and the class of men whom I represented, Alabama would have remained as surely Republican as Ohio."

He looked to his and Sherman's fellow Ohioan Hayes for a "wise administration" that would correct the political errors of the Grant Administration. To President Hayes he intimated that, though not an office seeker, he would accept the collectorship of the port of Mobile so as to even the score with Spencer and Grant, who together were responsible for his removal from the collectorship in 1872. Hayes did not offer him any job but did appoint his brother-in-law William B. Woods as an associate justice of the Supreme Court. Though pleased by this appointment, Warner disapproved of Hayes's appointments on the whole. Too many of them, he thought, went to ex-Confederates and Democrats.[3]

After Garfield's election Warner was "very much flattered by and very grateful for" his political friends' recommending him for a place in the new cabinet. He wondered whether he should accept an offer if one came. The position would pay less than he would make by staying at home and tending to his business, and, anyhow, he was not sure he was qualified for such a post. "Ought I to accept?" he inquired of Justice Woods, who assured him that he ought to indeed. "But for my Ohio origins I should think my selection probable," Warner said. Garfield, Ohioan that he was himself, chose not to unbalance his cabinet by putting another Ohioan in it.

Still, Warner hoped that Garfield would not repeat Hayes's mistakes. Hayes had appointed a Southern Democrat, David M. Key, as his postmaster general. No wonder the South had since gone Democratic! Ohio would have done likewise if a Republican President had taken an Ohio Democrat into his cabinet. Warner saw signs of better sense in Garfield's use of the patronage. "Your course makes you strong in the South, and Alabama, North Carolina, and Florida may be carried for the Republicans in 1884, with a fighting chance for Tennessee and Mississippi," he wrote optimistically to the new President. "But I advise you . . . to treat Southern Republicans . . . as others are treated at the North. To do otherwise, is to throw away the South."

After Garfield was shot, Warner refrained from pressing him in regard to federal jobs. "I can now only pray for his recovery" he said in rebuking an applicant who sought a recommendation from him. By 1884 he was disillusioned with Alabama Republicans, who had been reduced to a palace guard of federal officeholders. "Better no party than such a one as we now have in Ala.," he wrote. He continued to be a close observer of national politics, and he was a delegate to the Republican national convention in 1888 (as he had been in 1860, 1868, 1876, and 1880), but he ceased to be a really active politician.[4]

He remained a very active businessman. His chief preoccupation was the Tecumseh Iron Company, of which he was president and general manager. The company, as its letterhead proclaimed, manufactured "Superior Charcoal Pig Iron from Brown Hematite Limestone Ore" in Cherokee County near the northeastern corner of Alabama. Founding the company in 1873, just before the onset of the depression, Warner had named it for William Tecumseh Sherman, on whose staff he had served during the war. Sherman lent money to Warner to help tide him over the difficult early years of the enterprise.

"Eleven out of fourteen furnaces in this region were wrecked and capital all lost in the Panic," Warner reminded his brother-in-law Woods, a fellow stockholder, when Woods complained about the paucity of dividends. "Going through the six hardest years yet known in this country, I have paid eight per cent on nearly half of our capital stock—bonds—exclusive of $10,000.00 in putting furnaces in better condition than when built and show a surplus of $25,000.00" At last, after ten years, the company had something to distribute among its stockholders, one of the largest of whom was Warner himself. As manager, he was also due a salary of $5,000 a year, but he sometimes delayed collecting it lest he run short of funds with which to pay interest on the bonded debt.

Warner managed the company quite ably, considering the fact that the charcoal-iron industry as a whole was obsolescent. Even after the general economic recovery, old-fashioned furnaces burning wood could hardly compete with more modern ones using coal, coke, or even electricity. Only the $7-per-ton duty on pig iron, Warner told a tariff commissioner in 1882, enabled ironmakers like him to survive. He argued that lower labor costs rather than superior technology allowed English producers to make cheaper iron. The following year he again testified to the difficulties of the Alabama industry when a Senate committee held hearings in Birmingham.

Writing to Warner and visiting him, General Sherman gave him psychological as well as pecuniary encouragement. "I feel confident that you have a most valuable property in those beds of iron ore," Sherman wrote him after a visit in 1879. "The only doubt I feel is in the fact that in burning [char]coal, you are consuming wood which one day not very remote will be worth more than your iron products." But, whatever its most valuable resource, the Appalachian hill country of northern Alabama and Georgia and eastern Tennessee seemed to Sherman the most promising area of the United States for future settlement and development. "Your country is not Southern but Northern—where water freezes, and wheat grows—where hickory, oak and chestnut grow is Northern, and it is a misnomer to call it Southern." With immigration from the North and from abroad, the area would become still more Northern and still more productive, Sherman believed.

"I hope you are prospering," Sherman wrote Warner in 1880, after Warner had "paid up the last cent" he owed him. "Indeed, I know of no class of men who deserve more sympathy and praise than such as you, who went boldly to the South to make profit out of their mines and land too long neglected." Warner, too, believed he was doing something for the South as well as for himself. "All classes in our region have been benefitted by manufactures," he declared in 1882, "and none less than the capitalists . . . of iron,—laborers by employment and higher wages, farmers by a home market for all their productions except cotton, merchants, mechanics, lawyers, and doctors by increased business." Land had "doubled and tripled in value in this vicinity" since the construction of the charcoal furnaces.[5]

Warner thought of himself as an Alabama businessman and benefactor, not as a carpetbagger. He did thank Grant for saying a "brave word" in 1880 "for the Carpet-Baggers, so called," though he did not consider himself really one of them. He could not help reminding Grant of his 1872 grievance against him—"General, you sorely wounded and humiliated me in the matter of the Mobile Collectorship"—and he wanted him to know that *he* was not in the same class as Spencer, whom Grant had obliged in that matter. "The *real* Carpet-Baggers who fought me *then*, have mostly left the State, and the remainder will soon follow." In 1881 he rebuked a former Spencer man: "You have traveled with and sustained for ten years or more a little crowd of unprincipled adventurers and Carpet-Baggers who have helped to bring the Republican Party of this State and the South in odious disrepute."

Feeling as he did about such "unprincipled adventurers," Warner was understandably offended and angered when, in September 1882, the nearby *Rome Courier*, just across the state line in Georgia, referred to him as a carpetbagger. He protested:

> I see that the Courier calls me a "Carpet-Bagger." Does not this support the charge so often made that Northern men are not welcome in the South, but are considered as aliens or interlopers . . . ?
>
> I have been in Alabama since 1865 and have been a bona fide resident of the State since 1867. My family and my every dollar are here and if this is not my home I have none. I own more land, pay more taxes and do more business than all the Courier crowd put together and yet I am denounced as a Carpet-Bagger.
>
> The Tecumseh Iron Company which I organized and of which I have been President and Manager for ten years, and of which I am also one of the largest Stockholders, owns 10,000 acres of land in Alabama and Georgia and pays out annually $50,000.00 for labor—and yet I am only a Carpet-Bagger. . . .
>
> All of the $250,000.00 which our Company has invested in its business was brought to Alabama from other States and all of it from north of Mason and Dixon's line and yet I am a Carpet-Bagger.
>
> Let Northern men note this when proposing to come South with their money and their families and when reading the glowing periods of the pamphlet published to advertize Rome and to invite emigration [in-migration].
>
> The United States Association of Charcoal Iron Workers, with a membership of 300 in 27 States, and representing $50,000,000.00 of capital invested in the charcoal iron industry, of which I have the honor to be President, holds its annual meeting at Chattanooga on the 16th proximo and comes South partly through my influence. Shall they be told that in Rome after seventeen years' residence, with family & means, an emigrant is still a Carpet-Bagger?

Indignant though he was, Warner could not convince himself that he had made a mistake in investing his money and his life in the South. Nor did he want to discourage other Northerners from doing as he had done. As Sherman had repeatedly pointed out, enterprising newcomers would add not only to the population but also to the prosperity and the property values of the region. So Warner managed to give an upbeat ending to his letter of protest:

> The New South has its face to the Rising Sun, and in its rapid march in material prosperity and social progress will soon be able to leave the Courier class, with their faces turned to the times "before the war," far behind.
>
> I say to the Northern men and Capitalists, come South with your money and your families. You do not need the association of the Courier class to find pleasant homes here. Come with your energy and skill, your love of schools, and churches, and free speech, and bring your political opinions . . . whatever they may be.[6]

In his own career Warner illustrated the possibilities open to "Northern men and Capitalists" in the South. Certainly he made a successful and satisfying life for himself. Besides serving as president and manager of the Tecumseh Iron Company, he became president of the Alabama Improvement Company, vice president of the Tennessee Coal and Iron Company, and president and manager of the Lawhon Iron Company, with charcoal furnaces in Tennessee.

To help finance his iron business, he had sold his plantation near Montgomery and a farm of his in Muskingum County, Ohio, but he continued to own an Alabama home with 350 acres of land in addition to his interest in the 10,000 acres belonging to the Tecumseh Iron Company. His home, as he described it in 1887, contained twelve rooms "including bath and servants rooms" and had an indoor water supply piped from a spring. On the property were also a barn and a "detached wash house" besides "150 fruit trees of best varieties, 103 best grape vines," and a "raspberry and strawberry bed." Warner eventually offered all this for sale, along with "2 fine cows" and his buggy.

In 1890 he moved to Tennessee and made his home in Chattanooga. He acquired a farm nearby, which he found time to operate while continuing to direct the manufacture of iron.[7]

After recovering from the Panic of '73 he was prosperous enough to afford the best in education for both of his children. He felt keenly his responsibility for their mental and moral upbringing in the absence of their mother, dead since 1864. "I trust we may all meet her in 'the better country,'" he wrote his daughter, May, when she was nearly eighteen. On her eighteenth birthday he presented her a gold watch as a token of his love and a reminder of her duty to "make the world better and happier" for having lived in it. Delighted when she graduated as valedictorian from a girls' school in Ohio, he sent her to a young ladies' seminary in New York. He rejoiced again when, at twenty-two, she was baptized and confirmed an Episcopalian. "Thus," he wrote her, "you add authority to the solemn responsibility of holy living & doing which rests upon all of us always." Later he made it possible for her to make a grand tour of Europe.

Her brother, Willard, Jr., a few years older, had had some difficulties with school, but he too became a member of the Episcopal church, and he graduated from Dartmouth College. He then went to work for his father. Before long he concluded that he would, as his father said, "not pursue the furnace business for a life business." Though "deeply pained by his determination to leave," Warner was glad to recommend his son as a young man of "good business capacity," a "mechanical & engineering turn," excellent habits, a "quiet disposition," and complete trustworthiness.[8]

As Warner grew older, he was gratified to receive recognition above and beyond the monetary rewards of business success. His alma mater, Marietta College, honored him with an LL.D. degree. The *Historical and Biographical Cyclopedia of Ohio* included his biography and portrait. After twice declining the honor of a nomination, he was elected a member of the Tennessee house of representatives. Meanwhile he enjoyed the esteem of his old comrades in arms as they gathered for their annual reunions. When the Army of the Tennessee veterans met in Cincinnati in 1881, he was chosen to respond to the toast "The Citizen Soldier" at the banquet. As late as 1903, when he was seventy-six, he joined his fellows at Vicksburg to relive the siege of forty years before.

Warner was past eighty when, on November 23, 1906, he died in Chattanooga. He was not buried there. His permanent home was to be in his native state of Ohio. Inscribed on his tombstone, in Cedar Hill Cemetery, Newark, Ohio, were his words: "I tried to do right and to do my best."[9]

Harrison Reed, like Willard Warner, chose to remain in the South for the rest of his life. He made Florida his permanent home, and he continued to identify himself with the substantial men, Northern and Southern, who sought to develop the state's resources and enrich themselves in the process. In Florida he was trying to do essentially what he had already tried and failed to do in Wisconsin. He was to fail again.

Despite the depression of the 1870s, Florida remained a land of bright promise and irresistible charm. "There the Northerner . . . finds his past experience outdone," one traveler rhapsodized. "In the winter months, soft breezes come caressingly; the whole peninsula is carpeted with blossoms, and the birds sing sweetly in the untrodden thickets." At least half of Jacksonville's residents were postwar arrivals from the North, and visitors from the North doubled the town's total population during the winter months. Orange groves lined the St. John's River, most of them the property of Northerners who had transplanted wild orange trees from the neighboring swamps.

One of these groves, just south of Jacksonville, belonged to Harrison Reed, and to it he and his wife Chloe had returned at the end of his term as governor of the state. From his four years in office he had acquired no fortune; instead, he had accumulated enduring debts.

In 1874 he petitioned the legislature to reimburse him for money he had spent out of his own pocket, and for bills he had run up on his personal account, during his governorship. He requested $10,000 for attorney's fees he had paid in defending himself against unjustifiable impeachment charges, and $30,000 for "extraordinary expenses" for which he had obligated himself in maintaining peace and order (as, for example, in hiring secret agents and in procuring arms for the militia, the arms that Klansmen intercepted and destroyed). His petition further set forth: "That he is now largely indebted and his property encumbered, on account of his expenditures, and he is now subject to a heavy interest which, if not speedily arrested, will absorb the accumulation of years of frugal industry." The state never repaid him a cent.

To supplement his income, Reed turned once more to journalism. He began to edit *The Semi-Tropical*, a monthly magazine which he filled with Florida promotional literature. He dedicated the magazine to "dispersing the gloom of the lost cause" and "infusing new energy and courage by instilling the real advantages and recuperative powers we possess." This venture lasted only three years, from 1875 to 1878.

Even after the nation's recovery from the depression, Reed and other orange growers continued to face difficulties. The main problem was how to get the oranges to distant markets in good condition and at reasonable cost. As an active member of the Florida Fruit Growers' Association, Reed joined in agitating for transportation improvements, in particular for the removal (at federal expense) of the sand bar at the mouth of the St. John's River, so that ships could steam directly from Jacksonville to New York. Reed also sought state aid during a term in the Florida legislature. But the transportation problem was not to be completely solved within his lifetime.[10]

During the 1880s Reed found himself in increasingly dire financial straits. Until late in the decade he could expect little or no help from his relatives. His older brother George died in 1883 in a fire that razed Milwaukee's once deluxe but now dilapidated Newhall House and killed a total of seventy-one people (making it the worst hotel fire in American history up to that time and for sixty-three years afterward). His younger brother Curtis was poor in health and not much better in wealth. His surviving sister, the wife of Alexander Mitchell, reputedly the wealthiest man in Wisconsin, spent lavishly to collect the paintings of contemporary European and American artists, including James McNeill Whistler, but she was not likely to spend much on her brother Harrison so long as her husband was alive, since he had no use for Reed. Mitchell was a confirmed Democrat, as was his son and, for that matter, were Reed's brothers.[11]

After Mitchell's death in 1887, Reed hoped to persuade his sister to come to Florida and live with him and Chloe. But Mrs. Mitchell, ill and under the care of a woman friend, refused to have anything to do with Reed when he went to Wisconsin and tried to visit her. "I see no way that I can enter the barrier so carefully guarded by the designing & unprincipled woman who holds the key to her purse," Reed complained to her son, his own nephew, John L. Mitchell. "My good wife yearns to be by her bedside & would be a 'ministering' angel of spiritual & bodily comfort, from the promptings of a warm, unselfish & loving heart." But Reed's "estranged & misguided sister" had been led to distrust his and Chloe's interest in her, "even perverting" it "into a purpose of selfish greed."

Though Reed finally persuaded his sister to move to Jacksonville, he could not prevail upon her to give or lend him money. So he appealed to her son, explaining to him that a mortgage on his thirty-two-acre farm was about to fall due and that he was unable to get an extension of the loan. "The place has cost $20,000 & the orange crop the current year will probably net $2000 on the place," he wrote. "I want you to find me a loan of $5000 on it to clear off the old mortgage & enable me to meet the controversy which now seeks to crush me personally & financially."

That was in 1889, the year the Republicans returned to power in Washington with the inauguration of Benjamin Harrison as President, following a term for the Democrat Grover Cleveland. The Harrison Administration brought some relief to Reed by awarding him the job of Jacksonville postmaster. This lasted until 1893, when Cleveland came back into office and another depression began. Then, in the winter of 1894-95, a terrible freeze hit northern Florida, ruining much of the orange crop.

Before many more years, the Reeds' worries were over. Chloe died in Jacksonville on August 5, 1897. Reed's three sons—two by his first wife and one by Chloe—were to outlast him, as was Mrs. Mitchell, the only one left of the seven siblings. Reed was nearly eighty-six when, on May 25, 1899, twenty-seven years after leaving the Florida governorship, he breathed his last.[12]

Robert Kingston Scott, after leaving the South Carolina governorship, might also have spent the rest of his life in the South had it not been for the vengefulness of the state's Democrats after their seizure of power. As it was, he lived out his remaining years in Ohio—years that were to be shadowed by the memory of having shot and killed a man. Scott kept busy buying and selling land in Ohio and neighboring states, while disposing of his properties in South Carolina. One of these was his mortgage on a Columbia house and lot belonging to Robert B. Elliott, once the state's top black Republican leader. In 1877, Elliott having failed to repay the loan, Scott filed for a decree of foreclosure, and in 1880 the property was sold to satisfy his claim.

When the killing for which he was responsible occurred, Scott and his family were rooming temporarily at a boardinghouse in downtown Napoleon. Then fifty-four years old, he still relied on opium to dull the back pain resulting from his wartime injury. His wife, Jane, a semi-invalid, also took laudanum from day to day, along with citrate of magnesia to offset the constipating effect of the opiate, and Bingham's Red Cordial as a restorative and tonic. The cordial worked its wonders by virtue of its high alcoholic content, but neither of the Scotts would touch a drop of beer, wine, whiskey, or any other liquor. Scott had sworn off while still in South Carolina.

As always, the Scotts doted on their son and only living child, Robert K., Jr., or "Arky" (R. K.), as they usually called him. No matter what Arky did, his father could not bear to punish him, but he did hope the boy would never take to drink. In the summer of 1879, when Arky was going on fourteen, his mother accompanied him to Orchard Lake, near Pontiac, Michigan, to enroll him in a military academy where he might continue his education under wholesome discipline. She stayed in the vicinity to see that he got a proper start. "Adieu for a short time, my own Noble Lord," she concluded one of her letters to her husband. "Your forever loving Jane."[13]

One April day in 1880, while Arky was in Napoleon for the Easter vacation, Scott was sitting and reading in the lobby of the boardinghouse when a local saloonkeeper entered to tell him Arky and two schoolmates, in their soldierlike uniforms, had drunk beer at the saloon. The man said he had refused them seconds when he realized they were under age. Having learned Arky's identity, he was now apologizing to Arky's father. Scott, according to his later recollection, thanked his visitor and said to him: "I would rather any man would shoot my son than give him whiskey and make him drunk." The saloonkeeper remembered him as saying something a bit different, to the effect that anyone who gave liquor to his son ought to be shot.

By the end of the school year Scott had decided that the Michigan Military Academy was not a suitable place for Arky. The following year he sent him to the preparatory school of Kenyon College, the Episcopal institution in Gambier, Ohio. In December 1880, Arky was home again for the holidays. On Christmas Eve he wanted to go out and see a new friend. The hour was late—about ten-thirty—and his mother thought he ought to stay in, but he promised to be back in a few minutes, and his father said they might as well let him enjoy himself on such an evening as this. So out he went.

Scott climbed two flights of stairs on his way to the room where his wife was already lying down. He felt exhausted from the climb, and even after some rest he kept gasping, yawning, and perspiring, while his eyes watered and shivers of anxiety shook him. He was suffering the symptoms of withdrawal from opium, having had none of the drug for several days. For the third or fourth time, he was trying to kick the habit.

Once in bed, he quickly went to sleep, but he soon awoke to hear his wife telling him there was a lot of noise outdoors, Arky was still out there somewhere, and she was concerned about him. Scott got up in something of a daze, hastily put on trousers and shoes, threw a coat over his nightshirt, and went out into the cold. Drunken youths were reveling in the street. From one of them Scott learned that Arky had gone into Kneeland's drugstore with a man who clerked and slept there—twenty-three-year-old Warren G. Drury.

The drugstore was dark when Scott got there, but through the glass in the front door he could see a dim light inside in the rear. He tried to open the door, then rattled it and kicked it. Finally Drury appeared. He was a short, slight fellow, and he was only half dressed. He insisted Arky was not there, but reluctantly let Scott come in and look around. When the two reached a closed door at the back of the store, however, Drury refused to let Scott go through. He said it led to his private quarters. Then he made a movement that, to Scott, seemed threatening.

Suddenly a shot rang out. Scott turned his head to see where it came from. When he looked ahead again he saw the young man slumped on the floor in front of him, blood streaming from a hole near his temple. In his own hand Scott held a pistol, he now realized, and its barrel was hot. The gun must have been in the pocket of the long-unused overcoat he had put on in his confusion and haste. Everything seemed rather dreamlike.

Like the physician he once had been, Scott automatically checked the man's pulse, praying that what he felt was not just a deathly twitch. Then he heard the muffled voice of his son, crying "Papa!" Stepping over the body, he went into the adjoining room and up the stairs to where the voice came from. The door was locked. Returning, he reached over the body to a set of keys on the counter, went back upstairs, unlocked the door, and supported Arky as the boy staggered out, thoroughly drunk and almost hysterical.

On Christmas Day the sheriff took Scott by train to jail in Defiance, some twenty-five miles away, the jail in Napoleon having recently burned down. Two days later Scott was brought back to Napoleon for a preliminary hearing, which eventuated in a charge of murder in the first degree.

That evening, waiting at the Napoleon depot for a train to take him to Defiance again, he was surrounded by friends who commiserated with him. How strange—and what a pity!—that this fate should have befallen him now, in a time of utter peace, after his coming through the violence of war and Reconstruction with no such personal tragedy. It was not really so strange, Scott replied. It was an accident, and accidents could happen to anybody. Besides, he could not help thinking that Drury, by his misconduct, had brought his death upon himself. Still, he feared that people would blame him rather than Drury, that they would be prejudiced against him because they thought him rich.

Before boarding the train, he asked one friend to take a message to Mrs. Scott and try to cheer her up. He arranged with a couple of others to look after some of his real-estate transactions that were underway. Still another friend was going along with him, to stay in Defiance and serve as his amanuensis and messenger.[14]

That same day—under the headlines "Was It Murder? Napoleon Thrown into a Great State of Excitement"—the *Toledo Blade* came out with a detailed and more or less accurate account of the tragic event. The callous reporter had gone to the boardinghouse to interview Mrs. Scott. "He was met very pleasantly by the lady until he explained the nature of his visit, when she politely but firmly refused to talk upon the subject," he recounted. "Mrs. Scott is a pleasant looking lady, of medium height, dark hair and eyes, and is said to be a very estimable person. She takes the trouble very much to heart." The reporter also saw Arky but did not get his name straight. "Archy is a hardy looking young fellow for his age but his face plainly shows the dissipation he participated in at the expense of an indulgent parent. Residents of the place . . . state that he had become a very reckless young person, being allowed to do about as he pleased." Picking up the story from the *Toledo Blade*, the Associated Press disseminated it throughout the country.

Scott greeted the New Year, 1881, in his Defiance cell, where he was confined for several weeks. Good wishes came to him in repeated visits from nearby friends and in numerous letters from distant friends—in Ohio, Indiana, South Carolina, and elsewhere. His correspondents included blacks and whites, carpetbaggers and ex-Confederates.

They expressed themselves with variations on a single theme. "We know you too well, not to be assured that you are innocent *of intent* to commit the unfortunate act." "We *all* feel certain you did not intend to take . . . what none of us can give." "We who know you here know full well there is no hardness of heart in you." "A man with more kindness in his heart does not live in Ohio, or anywhere else." Those words were gratifying enough, but the most touching of all the letters came from William J. Whipper, the black man from Massachusetts whom Governor Chamberlain had considered unfit to be a judge in South Carolina and who was now practicing as a lawyer in that state. Whipper had written on January 1:

> I wish I could send you Greeting on this New Year morning, but instead I must send you Condolence and heartfelt sympathy. I can readily understand the parental anxiety and affection that led and prompted you to leave the comforts of your bed-chamber and breast a bleak winter's night in search of your son—and only child. I wish I had some way that I could fully express my own feelings . . . on this which must be a sad day to you, as it is to

> myself and others for your sake. . . . I am made to feel more particularly in your case, for although we have differed most decidedly in matters of state at times, yet I always believed they were honest differences and [they] never broke, and so far as [I] was concerned, [never] even jarred a personal friendship that dates from our earliest acquaintance. . . . With my wife [I] most earnestly pray that the God of immutable Justice will be with you in the shadow of misfortune and will restore you to the bosom of your family and friends.[15]

In February a grand jury indicted Scott, and he was released on bail, to wait until October to be tried. His attorneys suggested a change of venue, but he refused to consider it, despite his belief that many of the local people were prejudiced against him on account of his wealth. The attorneys also proposed to call Arky as a witness and let him tell how he had been misled by a man eight years older than he. Again Scott objected. He said he would rather spend the rest of his life in the penitentiary than submit the boy to such an ordeal.

At the trial, in the Henry County courthouse in Napoleon, Scott himself testified at great length, insisting under severe cross-examination that the shooting had been unintentional. The prosecutors let no one forget the irreparable loss that two women had suffered—Drury's mother and his betrothed, whom he had planned to marry in the near future. The mother sat in the courtoom day after day, weeping. In summing up for the defense, one of Scott's attorneys reminded the jurors that they could not bring Drury back to life by sending Scott to prison. "Are you going to put Scott in the penitentiary to teach someone a lesson,—to furnish a warning example?" the lawyer demanded. "If so, that means that, hereafter, when an anxious mother requests the father to get up on Christmas eve, or Christmas morning, and go out and bring home the young man who happens to be out late in bad company,—don't you get up, but remember that Scott is in the penitentiary!"

The jury of twelve men retired at 3:50 on the afternoon of November 4. They did not reappear until 8:45 the following morning, and then only to ask the judge for further instructions on the law of homicide and the meaning of "reasonable doubt." At 11 a.m. they came into the courtroom, which quickly filled, to announce their verdict: "not guilty." One by one the jurors went up to Scott to congratulate him, and he warmly thanked each of them.[16]

Letters of congratulation soon arrived from his friends around the country. "If there is any compensation for the griefs and afflictions of life," he replied to the ex-Confederate Colonel F. W. McMaster in Columbia, "it is in such expressions of friendly sympathy as yours. I hope that you will believe me when I assure you that no man was ever injured or wronged by any deliberate act of mine." Nearly fifteen years afterward, in the spring of 1896, Scott revisited South Carolina, and McMaster handed him that letter as a token of unforgotten friendship.

After the passage of three more years, in the spring of 1899, Scott suffered a stroke of "apoplexy" (a cerebral hemorrhage), which left him partially paralyzed. Now, at the age of seventy-three, he decided to join a church, the Methodist. It was none too soon. He died the next year, on August 13, 1900, leaving his forever-loving Jane and his not-wisely-but-too-well-loved Arky to mourn.[17]

Daniel Henry Chamberlain, that other carpetbag governor of South Carolina, had a post-Reconstruction career much more notable than Scott's. Attaining the utmost in respectability, Chamberlain succeeded eminently as a Wall Street lawyer, a legal scholar, and a writer and speaker on topics of the times. He wrote and spoke on the race question in particular, a subject on which he considered himself a leading authority, one ideally qualified by his personal experiences. From these, however, he drew no abiding lesson: he spent his later years contradicting what he had said at the start.

In two decades, 1877-97, he made enough from his law practice to retire from it and devote himself to his intellectual hobbies. Already these were occupying much of his time. Year after year, as a nonresident professor, he gave a course in American constitutional law at the Cornell University law school. He composed learned disquisitions on such subjects as "Relation of Federal and State Judiciary," "Constitutional History as Seen in American Law," and "Doctrine of Stare Decisis: Its Reasons and Its Extent," the last of which won the New York State Bar Association's coveted essay prize. He contributed articles to the leading law journals and to other prestigious periodicals, among them the *North American Review*, the *Yale Review*, the *Atlantic Monthly*, and the *American Historical Review*. Many of his speeches and essays also appeared in pamphlet form.

Chamberlain interested himself not merely in legal education but in higher education as a whole. Once a student and always a lover of the classics, he resented and resisted the trend toward eliminating Greek as a college requirement. He disparaged the new free-elective system of his alma mater Harvard and extolled the old-fashioned curriculum of his alma mater Yale. As a proud member of Phi Beta Kappa since his undergraduate days, he was horrified when, speaking to the Harvard chapter, Charles Francis Adams, Jr., dismissed the study of Greek as "a college fetich." Chamberlain delivered an indignant reply to the Phi Betes at Amherst and then to those at Vermont. Later he addressed his own chapter at Yale, but this time he took as his topic "Education at the South." He was glad to give a commencement address at Northwestern University; indeed, he was always happy, always at home, around the ivied halls of higher learning.[18]

At first, as ex-governor of South Carolina, Chamberlain eloquently defended Reconstruction and the role of blacks in it. In an 1879 article he declared that Reconstruction had involved a "strict question of moral right and wrong," the "question whether the colored race should be treated as men or as brutes, as brethren or as aliens and outcasts from the human family." This was an issue of the "moral convictions of the North" against the "stubborn and fanatical bigotry of the South." Despite what many people now were saying, Negro suffrage had been no mistake. The "colored race gave to the Southern States wise, liberal, and just constitutions." The "colored voters of the South never sustained public men whom they believed to be corrupt." In "those States in which the colored race had most complete control," there had been a "steady progress toward good government."

> The fact of the present suppression and overthrow of colored suffrage at the South is now made the ground of the argument that the race was not equal to the duties of self-government. . . . It is said that the inability of a people to cope, in physical and material resources, with its enemies, is proof that such a people is not entitled to retain its political power. Such conclusions are as illogical as they are immoral. Under the principles of our Government and of all just government, rights are not dependent on numbers or physical strength or material resources. The right to vote, and to have that vote honestly counted—the right to hold and exercise the political power conferred by a majority of the votes when honestly counted—these are rights, under our Government, totally independent of the power or wealth or education of the voters.

That was nobly said, and it made Chamberlain appear to be one of the foremost champions of black rights. No wonder he was taken to be the author of *A Fool's Errand* while that best-seller was still anonymous. He was flattered by the surmise. "I might wish it were not mistaken, but I am not the writer of the 'Fool's Errand,' but Judge Albion W. Tourgee, late of Greensboro, N.C., and now I believe of Denver, Col., is," he responded when asked about it. "It is a wonderful story—but most wonderful because *true*."[19]

That was Chamberlain in 1879. By 1886 he was regretting that the ballot had been "bestowed on those who were not qualified to use it or able to defend it" and who therefore had found "their legal right to vote a mockery and snare." In 1890 he declared: "The rule of the numerical majority at the South from 1867 to 1876, wherever it prevailed, resulted in intolerable misgovernment." In 1901 he queried: "Ought it not to have been as clear then as now that good government, or even tolerable administration, could not be had from such an aggregation of ignorance and inexperience and incapacity?" By 1904 he had concluded that, "with a preponderating electorate of negroes, it never was within the bounds of possibility to keep up a bearable government."[20]

While changing his opinions on Reconstruction and race, Chamberlain underwent another transformation: he ceased to be a Republican. He looked with disgust on President Chester A. Arthur, Garfield's successor, partly because Arthur was a notorious spoilsman and partly because the Arthur Administration favored Democrats over Republicans in its Virginia appointments. So, in 1884, he became a Mugwump, one of the gentlemanly reformist Republicans who supported the Democratic candidate Grover Cleveland.

Thereafter Chamberlain considered himself an Independent, but in fact he leaned decidedly toward the Democrats. When Cleveland ran again in 1892—again as a free-trader—Chamberlain condemned the Republican party for its protectionist stand. Alas, the "great party of the war for the Union, of emancipation," had sold itself "unreservedly to tariff beneficiaries and monopolists"! In 1906 Chamberlain wondered despairingly: "When will this d----d nightmare of Theodore Roosevelt be lifted?" The Republican Roosevelt, with more than three years yet to hold office, had long since proved himself too "ignorant and feckless" for the presidency. One of his irresponsible actions had been to invite the black educator and leader Booker T. Washington to the White House and sit down and eat with him.

When Chamberlain denounced Republican aid to "monopolists," he was by no means expressing himself as an economic radical. In the industrial conflicts of the 1880s and 1890s he showed no sympathy with the union leaders and members—with Terence V. Powderly and the Knights of Labor, Samuel Gompers and the American Federation of Labor, or Eugene V. Debs and the American Railway Union. He deplored the tyranny of "the mob, the populace, the proletariat, or the so-called organized forces of labor, the armies led by our Debs, our Gompers, and our Powderly."

As Chamberlain revised his views on race and politics, he lost some of his New England friends of the abolitionist persuasion, who accused him of inconstancy. But he thought of himself as open-minded rather than inconsistent, as simply learning from the observation of events like any conscientious political scientist. "I like to see things with my eyes," he averred, "and not with my prejudices."[21]

While losing a few friends in the North, he regained old ones and made new ones in the South. This necessitated a drastic improvement in his reputation, which among reputable South Carolinians remained very bad for several years after he left the state. The president of the South Carolina Historical Society, in papers he published in 1884 and 1885, had no good word to say for him. In the judgment of this historian, the last of the state's Reconstruction governors had been "the most plausible and the best cultured and the most dangerous." He was "a charlatan and a trickster," the mere "pretence of a Reformer." When at last he "threw off the mask," he revealed himself as a "monster of deceit, of malignity, and of imbecility."

Soon Chamberlain began to renew his friendship with Francis W. Dawson, the English-born editor of the *Charleston News and Courier* who had backed and then abandoned him while he was governor. By 1887 the two men, corresponding regularly, were on the most cordial terms once more. "It's no use! The old love will not *off!*" Chamberlain wrote before long. "I want to keep *au courant* with matters generally in S.C. and I must have the *News & Courier.*" So he subscribed again.

In his cultivation of Southern goodwill, Chamberlain was both helped and hindered by a book that appeared in 1888. This was *Governor Chamberlain's Administration in South Carolina*, a collection of documents that his Yale friend Walter Allen had put together, with connecting narrative, from newspaper clippings, letters, and other records that Chamberlain and his wife, Alice, had saved. The book attested to his exertions on behalf of governmental purity and frugality, and to that extent it tended to improve his image among South Carolina whites, but it also reminded them of what they hated him for—his effort to assure political rights to South Carolina blacks. The volume ended with Allen's assertion that Governor Chamberlain had been a model of "candor" and "sincerity" (by no means a "monster of deceit"). He had devoted himself wholeheartedly to both "the cause of *equal rights* and the cause of *honest government.*"

Chamberlain took no offense when Dawson reviewed Allen's work rather critically in the *News and Courier*. "I am in no way responsible for this book," he hastened to assure Dawson, "except to the extent of placing the material which had been preserved in the hands of Mr. Allen some three years ago, with the single injunction, 'To avoid eulogy, and let the facts and records speak for themselves.'" After Dawson's untimely death the following year, Chamberlain became a trusted friend of Dawson's successor J. C. Hemphill and even enjoyed the privilege of putting unsigned editorials in the paper.[22]

With his increasingly anti-black and anti-Republican pronouncements, Chamberlain gained greater and greater acceptance in South Carolina, until he finally achieved what he had sought and failed to get as governor—a rapprochement with the best people of the state. He had frequent occasion to visit the state after a court appointed him receiver of the South Carolina Railroad in 1889. That same year he was chosen to speak at the annual dinner of the exclusive New England Society of Charleston. Eventually the "good old State of S.C." seemed like home to him. He referred to the "indomitable spirit of our people," meaning the proud, unyielding people of South Carolina, and he came to admire his erstwhile nemesis Wade Hampton as a "true 'natural leader.'"

South Carolinians reciprocated his admiration and affection. His onetime bitter foe, ex-Confederate Colonel Alexander C. Haskell, Hampton's manager in the 1876 campaign, was to eulogize him: "He loved his country, and he was to the end loyal to the State of his adoption, and he came to love the men who had crushed his highest hope in the zenith of his public life." Haskell was to add: "I remember him with love and respect." Alfred B. Williams, a newsman who had reported the campaign with an unabashedly pro-Hampton bias, was to write of

Chamberlain: "He was so fortunate as to live long enough to allow his natural character and clarity of judgment to prevail, to glory in the courage and patriotism that crushed his ambitions and covered him with humiliations, to express his pride in them and claim fellowship with them."[23]

Chamberlain lived long enough for all that, but he lived less than two years beyond his allotted three score and ten, dying of cancer on April 13, 1907. He survived his wife and the last of his four sons, though racked by persistent illnesses himself. As early as 1882-83 he had left his practice temporarily to travel to Europe for the sake of his health, which he believed the strain of his governorship had permanently impaired. In 1897 his physician advised him to quit for good.

At that time he was a sixty-two-year-old widower, living in New York City with an eleven-year-old son he had raised from infancy since Alice's death. He now moved with the boy to the Massachusetts farm where he had spent his own boyhood. After remodeling the farmhouse and filling it with books, he occupied himself with reading and with writing about local antiquities as well as national affairs. But he was to stay there only five years. The boy having succumbed to scarlet fever, Chamberlain could no longer stand the sad and lonely place, and he put it up for sale.

During the five years still left to him he was a wanderer, sojourning in South Carolina, England, Egypt, the Riviera, and ultimately Charlottesville, Virginia, which he was never to leave except to be carried to the Johns Hopkins Hospital in Baltimore and back. While he deteriorated physically, he remained mentally as active and alert as ever. Bedridden, nervous, sleepless, he kept on writing as much as he possibly could. "I was actually so weak," he confessed one day, "that when I had partially raised myself on my pillow and had my pencil in my hand, I could write only a dozen or twenty words, and then give up exhausted and panting." Another day he said his writing cost him almost too much to endure. "My fingers ache and my eyes water with the effort."

On his deathbed he was writing "Some Conclusions of a Free-Thinker," a highly personal essay that was to be published posthumously. It was a confession of his faith—or lack of it. Brought up a New England Puritan, he had associated himself with his wife's church, the Unitarian, after his marriage, he related. Wherever he was, he used to attend some "standard" church of the locality. But in recent years, after much pondering of theological and philosophical tomes, he had come to reject Christianity and all religions as irrational and incredible. His conclusion: "Death ends all."[24]

CHAPTER 20

Lies, Unmitigated Lies (1877-1933)

Albion Winegar Tourgee, unlike Daniel Henry Chamberlain, persisted in advocating Negro rights as long as he lived. Financially, Tourgee proved far less successful, losing his fortune as fast as he had won it. He, too, forced himself to keep on writing despite the handicap of deteriorating health. And he, too, was disillusioned with Christianity, though not to the same degree as Chamberlain. He never gave up his Republican (that is, democratic) ideals, as Chamberlain did his, but he finally abandoned hope for achieving them.

While still at the height of his wealth and fame, he made a slight but significant change in his individuality. During his forty-fourth year he added something tiny to his name, something he had never used before—an accent mark.

Several years earlier, in 1873, when he was not yet nationally famous, a spelling change had been suggested to him by a distant relative who did use the accent. "Isn't it about time that we harmonised upon the orthography of our names?" asked Eben Tourjée, director of the New England Conservatory of Music, Boston. "Should I come to you, or you to me? jée, or gée, which shall it be?" But Albion W. Tourgee considered himself already "too much the property of the public" to take on "an *alias* at this late day." He adopted neither the "j" nor the "é" at that time.

As late as 1881 he was still using plain old "Tourgee," and thus the name appeared on the title page of *A Royal Gentleman*, which came out that year. But there would undoubtedly be advantages in restoring the accent, which some negligent ancestor had dropped in the forgotten past. By Frenchifying the name, the mark would emphasize the Huguenot ancestry of which Albion had always been proud, and it would help to indicate the correct pronunciation, Toor-ZHAY. Too often the pronunciation had been TOR-ghee or Tor-JEE among opponents in North Carolina, Tor-JAY among neighbors in New York State. More important, the accent would add a touch of the distingué, would provide tone befitting an author of such affluence and world renown. In 1882 and after, he was always Albion W. Tourgée.

He needed to do something also about the appellation of his daughter, now approaching puberty. He and Emma had always called her "Lodie," short for Lodolska, Emma's mother's maiden name, which they had fastened on her at birth. As she grew into delicately pretty womanhood, he renamed her Aimée, "beloved." Aimée Tourgée! A mellifluous combination, appropriate for such a lovely girl.[1]

By the time Tourgée took on his new identity, he was already beginning his descent from the status that had seemed to justify it. In collaboration with the noted actor-playwright Steele MacKaye, he prepared and produced a stage version of *A Fool's Errand*, which opened at the Arch Street Theatre in Philadelphia on October 26, 1881. Newspaper critics thought the play too argumentative and not dramatic enough. Audiences, looking for entertainment rather than education, were still less kind. They hissed. In less than two weeks the play closed. Tourgée lost only a little of his reputation, but he lost all the money he had invested in the production.

He was about to make, also in Philadelphia, another investment that was to prove far more disastrous. With the participation of other investors, he undertook to publish, edit, and contribute to a weekly magazine, *Our Continent*. The first issue was ready in February 1882. In the issue for July 12 Tourgée began the serialization of "Hot Plowshares," which the following year appeared as a book, the last in publication but the first in chronology of a six-volume series of historical novels reflecting the sectional controversy from prewar to post-Reconstruction times. But neither his writings nor the contributions of other notable authors, including Oscar Wilde, were enough to save the magazine.

Emma, dubious about the project from the start, became still less enthusiastic as the weeks passed and she stayed in Philadelphia to attend to editorial matters while Tourgée took off for Thorheim, to loaf, fish, or ride out with Aimée. After less than three years, in August 1884, the magazine ceased publication. It had cost Tourgée his entire savings and more: he now faced debts exceeding $70,000. "My poor husband! How his life was embittered, ruined, by his trying to do what he had no capacity to do!" Emma was to exclaim years later, after his death. "His mind was too large to take in business details, and without that ability no one can succeed in such ventures as the *Continent*, which took all his fortune, his ambition, his hopes—everything but his wife."[2]

Tourgée managed to hang on to Thorheim, but he had to mortgage it, and he even had to mortgage the future royalties from his books. He suffered a physical collapse along with the financial one. Stepping off a curb, he wrenched his back in such a way as to reactivate the injury he had incurred during the retreat from Bull Run. Confined to bed for several weeks, he resolutely dictated *An Appeal to Caesar* (1884) to raise money and also to promote his idea of federal aid to education in the South. The book sold well but not well enough to pay off all his debts.

It took him a dozen years to do so. After recovering from his spinal injury, he drove himself to write, write, write—novels, stories, articles, pamphlets, a regular newspaper column. He kept lecturing on the circuit and, as an honorary professor of legal ethics, also at the University of Buffalo law school. He even started another periodical, *The Basis: A Journal of Citizenship*, which lasted only about a year.

At Thorheim, where he did his writing in a spacious study overlooking the lake, it was not all work and no play. He enjoyed his horses and dogs, his sleigh and buggy rides, his strolls in the woods, the parties with his relatives and friends, and the affection of his wife and especially his daughter. Aimée, with something of an artistic bent, illustrated some of his publications. She was a cheerful companion for him but not as active a one as they both would have liked her to be, for her health was rather delicate. She was not to survive her father very long.

Happy though many of his moments were, Tourgée was depressed much of the time. "A rainy, gloomy day with many sad accompaniments," Emma once noted, quite typically, in a diary she had begun to keep. "Albion in despair over his work. Life does not seem worth the struggle anyhow." Tourgée sometimes talked of taking his life if his finances did not improve. Though entitled to a soldier's pension, he long refrained from applying for one; he had too much patriotism and pride. In his desperation he finally did apply, and in 1890 he began to receive monthly payments retroactively from 1863.

After wiping out the last of his big debt, in 1896, he still had to struggle for a livelihood. He gained a little respite when the Republican party hired him to make campaign speeches for William McKinley. After McKinley's inauguration, Tourgée obtained a consular appointment, a kind of federal fellowship that Presidents used to award to literary figures, among them Nathaniel Hawthorne. On July 3, 1897, Tourgée took his last look at his native land as he and Emma sailed for France, where Aimée was to join them.

As consul at Bordeaux, he had an easy enough life, and with a steady if modest income he could write when he felt like writing. But he felt like writing less and less as his health declined. He developed uric acid poisoning, water on the lungs, and diabetes in addition to complications from his war wounds. He thought he was much better after an operation in the summer of 1904. "The doctors made an excavation in my hip and took out a piece of lead which must have been wandering around since Perryville," he recorded on November 23. "I now weigh 175 and feel almost well, except for my hands which are painfully hypersensitive—making writing a burden which has so long been a delight." He lived for five months after penning that and about three weeks after observing his sixty-seventh birthday. He died on May 21, 1905.

In November of that year, members of the Niagara Movement held services throughout the United States to honor the memory of three men who had labored mightily for the liberation of American blacks. The Niagara Movement was a forerunner of the National Association for the Advancement of Colored People, and its leader was William E. Burghardt Du Bois, the Negro champion who (unlike Booker T. Washington) demanded complete and immediate equality of rights. The three "Friends of Freedom" whom Du Bois and his followers honored on this occasion were William Lloyd Garrison, Frederick Douglass, and Albion W. Tourgée.

Tourgée deserved that kind of recognition, whether or not he belonged in the company of such liberators as Douglass and Garrison. For decades he had campaigned unceasingly for equal rights and had encouraged blacks to organize and be militant in demanding them. Again and again he called upon his fellow Republicans to remember their egalitarian principles and not sacrifice them for the interests of big business.

In the case of *Plessy v. Ferguson* he made his greatest single contribution to the egalitarian cause. Homer A. Plessy, an octoroon, had been arrested for sitting in a whites-only coach and thus breaking a Louisiana law that required the segregation of Negroes in separate-but-equal accommodations on railroad trains. When the case reached the Supreme Court, Tourgée served without pay as one of Plessy's counsel and, though not present at the trial, prepared the main brief. In it he argued that segregation is unconstitutional "because it denies equal protection of the law to all classes of citizens; perpetuates inequalities in the enjoyment of their rights; perpetuates race prejudice and deprives citizens of liberty and immunity without due process of law." Unpersuaded, the Supreme Court in its 1896 decision upheld the Louisiana statute. But the Court was to reverse itself in the 1954 school desegregation case, *Brown v. Board of Education*. Tourgée's argument at last prevailed.[3]

So long as he lived, however, Tourgée knew only disappointment in all his idealistic aims. He made no headway with his proposal for reeducating the South. In 1883 a senator from New Hampshire, Henry W. Blair, introduced a bill for federal aid to schools, with the money to be distributed in proportion to the extent of illiteracy and hence mostly to the Southern states. But Tourgée opposed the Blair bill because it would have left the states in control of the funds. Much preferable would be something like the Freedmen's Bureau with its federally supported and independently operated schools, he suggested in 1884. Indeed, the reeducation of the South might already have been well advanced if "the same plan of reconstruction had been put in force immediately upon the close of the war, and the Freedmen's Bureau or some modification of it had been made a permanent national institution."

Northerners instead of Southerners were being reeducated. In an 1884 issue of his ill-fated magazine *The Continent*, Tourgée quoted a Wisconsin veteran who had found his teenaged son and daughter "lamentably ignorant" of the war's causes and the Union's aims. The man discovered why when he looked at the history books the Wisconsin schools were using. "In making text-books for the whole country, publishers have eliminated everything that might offend the Southern people." Agreeing with the Wisconsinite, Tourgée added his own instances of young Northerners, born since the war, feeling guilty about it while young Southerners were being taught to take pride in the Lost Cause and to revere its heroes. "We do not believe in what is termed 'keeping alive the animosities of the war,'" he protested, "but we do believe in keeping in view the underlying principles of right and wrong, of liberty and slavery, of national unity and national dissolution."

History was being "perverted" in leisure reading as well as in schoolbooks. "Not only is the epoch of the war the favorite field of American fiction to-day," Tourgée regretfully noted in 1888, "but the Confederate soldier is the popular hero. Our literature has become not only Southern in type, but distinctly Confederate in sympathy."[4]

The worst was yet to come. In 1902 appeared *The Leopard's Spots: A Romance of the White Man's Burden—1865 1900*, by Thomas Dixon, Jr. Before turning novelist with this book, Dixon, a North Carolinian by birth and upbringing, had been a spellbinding lecturer and preacher, a Baptist with a huge congregation in New York City. Tourgée was acquainted with him; once, as editor of *The Continent*, he had given him some editorial advice. But *The Leopard's Spots* reflected none of Tourgée's views. Instead, it completely reversed his themes, making heroes of his villains and villains of his heroes. It sold more than a million copies, far surpassing *A Fool's Errand* and bringing Dixon fame and fortune that greatly exceeded Tourgée's at its zenith.

Tourgée considered Dixon's novel "entirely worthless as a narrative of events or any analysis of causes," though he conceded that "as a delineation of the southern white man" it was "of inestimable value." He was already disillusioned about the message of his own fiction, and he was confirmed in his disillusionment when he beheld the popular success of Dixon's racist trash. To think that this was the work of an educated person (a graduate of Wake Forest College) and a respected minister of the gospel of Jesus Christ!

In 1901, after President Roosevelt had acted as Booker T. Washington's host, Tourgée wrote to congratulate him for having bravely challenged race prejudice, and to repudiate his own panacea for it—his proposal for reeducation at federal expense. "It was a genuine fool's notion," he confessed to Roosevelt. "I realize now that . . . education does not eradicate prejudice, but intensifies it—Christianity does not condemn or prevent injustice done to the weak by the strong, but encourages and excuses it."

"I have learned something since I wrote 'A Fool's Errand,'" he confided to another correspondent the following year. "I believed in that curious fetich of our modern thought 'Education' as a remedy for wrong." But he could no longer believe in such foolishness. "Now I realize the terrible truth that neither Education, Christianity, nor Civilization mean[s] justice or equality between man and man when one is white and the other colored."[5]

Powell Clayton, too, came to be concerned about the growing distortion of Reconstruction history. The "wildest and most fallacious stories," he once complained, were being told about his own regime as governor of Arkansas. Eventually, he determined to do something to straighten out the record.

After completing his term as United States Senator, in 1877, Clayton had returned to Arkansas, to live in Little Rock and attend to his political and economic interests in the state. In 1882 he moved to Eureka Springs, a resort town in the Ozark Mountains, in a region presumably as healthful as it was scenic, and certainly very different from the hot and humid lowlands around Pine Bluff, where his cotton plantation was located.

Soon he was the leading citizen and the biggest booster and promoter of Eureka Springs. He built and managed the local street railway and served as a director of the Missouri and Northern Arkansas Railroad, president of the Eureka Improvement Company, and president of the Crescent Hotel Company, which owned and operated the hotel where he resided with his family. He also took charge of an educational institution in the resort—a Chautauqua-like summer school for teachers and other interested adults—thus reaffirming the interest in education he had shown when, as governor, he helped to found the University of Arkansas.[6]

While busy with local affairs, Clayton continued to be active in politics. He remained a member of the Republican national committee for forty years, beginning in 1872, and for much of that time he also remained the boss of the state's Republican party. In state politics he had the help of his three brothers—Thomas, William, and John. The Claytons enjoyed the support of blacks who, in the 1880s, could still vote and hold office in southern and eastern counties where the black population was heaviest. In Jefferson County, where the Clayton plantation was located, and where the Claytons shared the spoils with the Democrats, the black Claytonite leader Ferd Havis won election as county clerk and became county boss when John M. Clayton left the office of sheriff in 1886.

Politics could still be rough for Republicans in Arkansas. In 1888 John M. Clayton made bold to challenge the incumbent Democrat, Clifton R. Breckinridge, for his seat in Congress. According to the official count, Breckinridge won reelection by a narrow margin. Clayton decided to contest the returns, and while going about to look for evidence of fraud, early in 1889, he was shot and killed. Breckinridge dismissed the killing as a case of mistaken identity. He said the assassin had really been gun-ning for Powell Clayton, whom he hated as a tyrant who had grossly misgoverned the state.

But Powell Clayton, along with his brothers William and Thomas, suspected that Breckinridge himself was back of the murder. The Claytons hired detectives to investigate, with no result, and so they had to content themselves with arranging for the care of their dead brother's motherless children. Powell Clayton put the two older ones in a boarding school and took the other four to live with his family in the Eureka Springs hotel.[7]

In 1897 he went to Mexico with an appointment, from President McKinley, as minister to that country and, upon the upgrading of the legation to an embassy, as the first ambassador. As a diplomat, his main concern was to settle a claim of the Roman Catholic Church in California against the Mexican government for the confiscation of church-owned land in Mexico. His greatest achievement was to persuade the contestants to refer the dispute to arbitration at the newly established Permanent Court of International Justice at the Hague.

During his ambassadorship he once visited Little Rock to attend a banquet that the Board of Trade was giving for President Roosevelt. Clayton, by virtue of his office, was seated at the presidential table. Governor Jefferson Davis, a Democrat running for reelection, refused an invitation to join the group. Apologizing to Roosevelt, he said he could not sit down to eat with a man who had murdered his aunt. Soon afterward Clayton called at the White House, and Roosevelt joked: "Governor Davis says you murdered his aunt; why didn't you murder his uncle?" What Davis meant, Clayton explained, was that his aunt had died during the 1869 "militia war" and that her death had been hastened by the presence of Clayton's state troops. In fact, Clayton now said, her death was due to puerperal fever, and the troops had nothing to do with it.

In 1905, though still going strong at seventy-two, Clayton retired from the ambassadorship, renounced most of his political and business activities, and took up his residence in Washington, D.C. Now he would have an opportunity to do what he had wanted to do for many years—to write an accurate account of Reconstruction in Arkansas and, particularly, of his own role in it. The wild stories being told by his opponents in Arkansas had long needed correction. And nowadays a biased view, like that of the Arkansas Democrats, was pervading the work of even the most respected and influential historians, North as well as South.

Professor Woodrow Wilson of Princeton University, who held a Ph.D. from the Johns Hopkins University, wrote authoritatively of "unscrupulous men, 'carpetbaggers,'—men not come to be citizens, but come upon an expedition of profit, come to make the name of Republican forever hateful in the South—[men who] came out of the North to use the negroes as tools for their own selfish ends." Wilson was a Virginian and a Democrat, but James Ford Rhodes, an Ohioan and a Republican, agreed with him, describing Reconstruction as "an attack upon civilization" and carpetbaggers as "the vulturous adventurers who flocked from the North."[8]

Clayton became a historian to counteract such historians as Wilson and Rhodes. Day after day he visited the Library of Congress to pore over the files of the *Arkansas Gazette*, the Little Rock organ of the Democrats and disguised voice of the Ku Klux Klan. He also corresponded with state officials in Little Rock. With the data he thus acquired, he supplemented and corrected his own records and memories. Wilson was President of the United States by the time Clayton, in his eighty-second year, wrote the last words of his book, *The Aftermath of the Civil War in Arkansas*. That was just a few days before he died, on August 25, 1914.

He left his wife, his son Powell, and his daughters Lucy, Charlotte, and Kathleen. Powell, Jr., was an army captain, and Lucy the wife of an army major. Both Charlotte and Kathleen had married diplomats, one a Belgian, the other an Englishman. Clayton was eulogized as having had a "high standard of honor and integrity," "sound judgment and unfailing common sense," and "a ready wit and keen sense of humor," and as having been "always loyal" to his friends and always "courteous and gentle" to all. He was buried in Arlington National Cemetery.

His book was published the following year. In it he made a vigorous defense of his governorship, giving an especially detailed account of his victorious war against the Ku Klux Klan. He was also at pains to dispose of the charge that the carpetbaggers had arrived not as bona fide settlers but as adventurers who schemed to grab power and pelf by taking advantage of the Negro vote. The overwhelming majority of Northerners holding office in Arkansas when he did, he now showed, had entered the state before 1867, that is, before the passage of the Reconstruction Act, which gave the ballot to blacks. The small minority who came as late as 1867 "did so when the Democrats were in full power, and before the officers to be elected or appointed, with their salaries and emoluments, had been fixed by the [Reconstructed] State Constitution."

> With a very few exceptions, the Northern men who settled in Arkansas came there with the Federal Army, and . . . were so much impressed with its genial climate and great natural resources as to cause them . . . to make it their future home. A number, like myself and my brother William, had contracted matrimonial ties [with Arkansas women]. Many of them had been away from home so long as practically to have lost their identity in the States [from which they had come]. . . . These were the reasons that influenced their settlement in Arkansas rather than the existence of any political expectations.

That was, to be sure, ex parte testimony, from one of the carpetbaggers himself. Still, he backed his conclusions with abundant and incontrovertible evidence.[9]

Albert Talmon Morgan, more than three decades earlier, had published a book about his experiences as a planter and politician in Mississippi. At the time he wrote it, he was living in Washington, D.C., and supporting himself and his family on a $1600-a-year government salary and a $13-a-month soldier pension.

His federal job, as a second-class clerk in the Pension Office, he owed to Blanche K. Bruce, the black senator from his recent home state of Mississippi, and to Angus Cameron, a Republican senator from his earlier home state of Wisconsin. The clerkship was about as much of an assignment as Morgan was physically able to handle. His war wounds and his malaria, contracted in the service, had left him in such a condition that he could hardly even continue the practice of law. As he stated in 1879, when he first applied for his invalid pension, "his elocution has been impaired, and every effort at continued, clear & loud speech . . . has resulted in great exhaustion"; he "has suffered great loss of his wonted vigor of body, of energy and of will"; and he "is totally disabled from performing continuous manual labor or successfully prosecuting his profession."[10]

Nevertheless, he mustered enough energy and will to finish the long manuscript on his Mississippi career. He could not conclude it without a personal and familial note. "Would you have me marry my daughter to a negro?" people often ask. "What a silly question!" Morgan replies.

> I have never denied nor been ashamed of the fact that my wife and my children have in their veins negro blood; "nigro taint" is the enemy's phrase. The only thing about it which grieves me is the fact that so many of our good boys and girls can see no difference between miscegenation, as practiced in the South, and amalgamation through honorable marriage, or, seeing the true distinction, nevertheless prefer and honor the miscegenationist above the amalgamationist.
>
> Wife and I have been married fourteen years; we have six children. During all the dreary years that have passed since the enemy, by force and murder, took possession of my new field, stole our grand old flag from us, and occupied our temples, this woman and these children have been my refuge.

Morgan hoped the Republican national committee would publish his book, pay him for it, and distribute it as a campaign document in 1884. Instead, he had to pay to have it privately printed. The book appeared, that same year, under the title *Yazoo; or, On the Picket Line of Freedom in the South.*

Morgan could ill afford the expense, and he could afford it even less after Grover Cleveland won the election. Once inaugurated, Cleveland named the Mississippian L. Q. C. Lamar to head the Department of the

Interior, the department within which lay the Pension Office. Lamar—that leader of the revolutionaries who "by force and murder" had driven Morgan and his family from their Mississippi home—was now at the top of the very bureaucracy that sheltered him! Morgan promptly lost his job.

So, in 1885, he had to look for some new means of support. He remembered having gone to Kansas in search of opportunity before ever going to Mississippi, and to Kansas he now took his family, all of them stepping off the train at Lawrence. Here, though they scrimped and his monthly pension rose from $13 to $18, they barely managed to survive. He was "unfortunate in all his business undertakings," as one of the children afterward explained.

After five years in Kansas, Morgan left his family there and, by himself, moved on west to Colorado. Surely a good living could be found there, if anywhere. If not a land of milk and honey, Colorado was at least a land of gold and silver. In Creede, Cripple Creek, Silverton, and other localities he prospected without any luck. Then he settled down in Denver, living at a boardinghouse that belonged to one of his relatives.[11]

If he could not gain a livelihood by digging for gold or silver, perhaps he could do so by talking and writing about them. Attracted by William Jennings Bryan and the "free silver" cause, he abandoned the Republican party and campaigned for the Democratic candidate in 1896 and 1900. He persisted in agitating for a gold-and-silver monetary standard long after bimetallism had become a dead issue. With a partner, H. M. Ware, he conducted a "School of Money" and published *Real Money Magazine.* He also wrote and published books: *The Passing of Gold; or, What Is Lawful Money?* (1908), *On Our Way to the Orient; or, Mr. Bryan, Don't You Know?* (1909), and *The Bank of the Beast* (1910).

To illustrate his point that "money is not wealth," he recalled the time he and other wounded soldiers had lain in the dining room of the Gettysburg Female Seminary while the students looked after them without thought of money.

> And it was neither a "gold," a "silver," nor a "paper" *dollar* that saved me from bleeding to death, but a species of wealth called a gun strap judiciously applied as a substitute for a tourniquet. . . . Opposite where I lay there was a soldier whose eyeballs had been forced from their place by a bullet passing behind them, and they hung out over his lower eyelids. Next to him another with one leg gone. On my right lay another whose tongue had been cut off at the root so that it protruded from his mouth. On my left another whose bowels had been opened. The gable of the building was torn by a shell, the windows of our room pierced by bullets—but none of these things deterred the angels of mercy from ministering: by keeping off the flies, by bandages made from their own night gowns, by food and water, and a look and a touch of tenderest sympathy until Lee had retreated and the battle was won.

Such recollections of the war became less and less relevant as time passed and Morgan aged. In 1912, when he was in his seventieth year, he declared he had few physical reminders of the events of 1861-65 except for his scars and "a perceptible halt in [his] left limb." He claimed to be as happy as any other living veteran: "Aye, the happiest man on top o' Earth—not excepting J. Pirp--- [or] J. D. -----." When he said he was every bit as happy as J. Pierpont Morgan or John D. Rockefeller, he may have merely been facetious, or he may have reflected the genuine cheerfulness of his Christian Science beliefs. In either case, it was fortunate for him that he could disparage money, for he had not yet managed to accumulate any of it.[12]

This did not help his wife and children, however. Ever since leaving them in Kansas, in 1890, he had contributed little or nothing to their support. Instead, to invest in his various enterprises, he had borrowed from his children, especially the oldest, the only surviving son, Albert, Jr. At the age of nineteen, young Bert had left home to make his way in the world. Eventually he held a respectable position as a railway clerk in Indianapolis. He heard from his father occasionally but saw him very seldom.

By 1920, when Bert was nearing fifty, he had begun to wonder whether his parents, separated for more than thirty years, were really married. "Bert," Morgan wrote him, "How can there be any doubt that your mother . . . is my legal wife?" If Bert did have any doubt, he could write to the county clerk in Jackson, Mississippi, for a certified copy of the marriage record, dated August 3, 1870. And Morgan assured his son he had never even thought of marrying any other woman. "On the contrary, where ever I have lived long enough to become acquainted with women I have invariably announced that I have a wife and children living whom I love, and for whom I am making every sacrifice."

After Morgan's 1890 departure for Colorado, Mrs. Morgan and the four girls had stayed on in Kansas for about six years, supporting themselves as best they could. The girls grew into beautiful and talented young women, whom their mother trained as musicians and singers. When they were in their twenties, they began to perform as a professional quartet, appearing in Chicago, New York, Boston, and other cities. Mrs. Morgan went along in the capacity of manager and "chaperone" rather than mother so that, light-complexioned as the girls were, they could pass for white. They kept up the performances for several years. Then one of the sisters died, the others got married, and they ceased to form a musical troupe.

Thereafter, as before, Mrs. Morgan usually stayed with one or another of her daughters, most of the time in New York City. "Mother became a mental healer, Christian Science practitioner and dramatic reader," afterward related the oldest of the girls, Carolyn Victoria, named for her mother. "Those are her professions but she is wonderfully equipped in all phases of literature, art, and religion, and she long ago decided that more children were not to be desired and that people, even married couples, should refrain from the closest intimacy." (Did this decision of hers have anything to do with Morgan's departure in 1890, after twenty years of marriage?)[13]

Before she was fifty, Carolyn found herself "in bad condition mentally," as she later phrased it, and her sister Lucia fell into an even worse condition. No doubt the emotional strain had been enormous for both of these women, marginal persons that they were, maintaining an ambiguous existence in the borderland between the races. Both were sent to what their mother called a "sanitarium for mental cases" in Brattleboro, Vermont. By 1923 Carolyn could refer to herself as "not insane now," and she could recall many things about her parents, including her father's going "into the wilds of Colorado" when she was about fourteen or fifteen. But she remained a patient in the institution along with Lucia, who "could not make a coherent statement" about the past.

Mrs. Morgan now lived with her other daughter, Nina Lillian, a divorcée who wrote poetry, or at least verse, under the pen name of Angela Morgan. Nina, or Angela, had recently moved to England, where she could hope to escape the torment of racial ambiguity so familiar in the United States. Her mother had gone with her, and the two were residing in London when word came from Bert that his father had died in Denver on April 15, 1922. Bert arranged for burial in Indianapolis.

Mrs. Morgan applied for a widow's pension, and she finally got one for the rest of her life, which ended in 1926. But she got it only after much head-shaking on the part of pension officials. "This is an unusual case," one of them remarked. There must have been some reason—a divorce or a legal separation, perhaps—why the pensioner had lived apart from the claimant for so long. "It would look so," Bert conceded, "but my father never made a success and he became so disheartened that he was really ashamed to come home."[14]

Adelbert Ames, after leaving Mississippi politics, in which he had been Morgan's ally, enjoyed a worldly success far beyond what Morgan could even have dreamed of. Ames still had fifty-seven years of life remaining; he was not to die until April 13, 1933. For a time he joined his father in the flour-milling business in Northfield, Minnesota. Then, moving to Tewksbury, Massachusetts (near Lowell, his father-in-law's home), he acquired an interest in textile mills and began to deal in real estate. With the mind of a Yankee inventor, he also thought up a number of improvements in mechanical devices, "ranging from flour mill machinery to a pencil sharpener, from the propulsion of canal barges to extension ladders for fire engines." From his various enterprises he eventually made a fortune, and in his old age he hobnobbed with other venerable millionaires, including John D. Rockefeller himself.

Meanwhile, during the Spanish-American War, he took part as a brigadier-general in the siege of Santiago de Cuba and the battle of San Juan Hill. In Cuba he met and made friends with General Joseph Wheeler, the onetime Confederate cavalry commander. After the war, Ames went to South Carolina on an official mission, to look over some possible sites for army camps.

His experiences now, in 1898, were quite different from those during his previous stay in South Carolina, in 1865 and 1866. "I am surprised at the great change in public sentiment here as compared to what I have known," he wrote to his wife, Blanche. "In this town [Summerfield] are two or three union flags on residences. One or two natives are at home on furlough wearing our uniform. I am treated with great courtesy." The local people, he explained, were pleased at the prospect of getting an army base, with all its pecuniary benefits. "Again, I say this war with Spain in many and devious ways is obliterating Civil War animosities."

Still, the Spanish-American War—and, for that matter, the First and Second World Wars—did not quite obliterate all the old animosities against Ames himself. Mississippi defenders of the Solid South had begun to stigmatize him as a reckless spendthrift when Reconstruction governor. This allegation was being accepted, in both the North and the South, as historical fact.

The historian president of Brown University, in an 1895 *Scribner's* article, stated that during Reconstruction the Mississippi debt had risen from practically nothing to $20,000,000. Ames knew perfectly well that it had totaled no more than about $500,000. He wrote to the author to caution him about the "authorities" he had used. "They have led you into making a $19,500,000 mistake in a $20,000,000 statement." The author corrected his statement in a subsequent book on Reconstruction.

But the Brown president, himself a Union veteran, persisted in giving Mississippi carpetbaggers a bad name. Again Ames sent him a protest. "The Northern men in Mississippi, as a class, were the brave youths who marched at your side for four years of bloody war," he wrote. "They went to Mississippi under the same commendable impulse as had those who have populated this land from one ocean to another. They went to establish new homes." At first, they had nothing to do with politics, and then Congress passed the Reconstruction Act. "It was left for the Union soldiers to practically solve the problem of reconstruction put upon them by a Union Congress." In doing so, they cooperated politically with blacks, and this was the real offense in the eyes of the Southern white. "The southern man has a motive in slandering the reconstructionists. He committed crimes upon crimes to prevent the political equality of the negro."[15]

In 1900, Ames had occasion to correspond with another historian, James W. Garner, a Mississippi native who was then teaching at Bradley Polytechnic Institute in Peoria, Illinois, while writing a dissertation for Professor William A. Dunning at Columbia University. Garner had sent a list of questions for Ames to answer. Why, for example, had Ames left the army in 1870 to go into politics? "My explanation may seem ludicrous now," Ames replied, "but then, it seemed to me that I had a Mission with a large M." What did Ames consider as "some of the merits" of his administration in Mississippi? "My dear Professor, when you appear before St. Peter at the gates of Heaven, what can you say in reply to his query as to 'the merits' of your earthly career?" Ames asked by way of answering. "To say that I acted conscientiously to the best of my ability does not seem to be sufficient."

In this interchange, the old general comes off somewhat better than the callow and bumptious scholar. Ames, feeling that he had nothing to hide, generously offered his personal papers to Garner. "My hope is," Ames said, "that as a young man, as I understand you to be, you will be free from the prejudices and animosities of those days."

Garner's book *Reconstruction in Mississippi,* which he wrote with the aid of the Ames manuscripts, gave grudging praise to the Ames of Reconstruction times for his "personal integrity," "courteous demeanor," and "education and refinement." Garner took him to task, however, for his "prejudice" against Southern whites and his "overconfidence in the mental and moral ability of the black race." His "failure," Garner said, "was due to the circumstances surrounding his advent into Mississippi."

Nevertheless, Garner emphasized, Ames had been guiltless of corruption and was approximately correct in his estimate of the public debt as $500,000. "No well-informed Democratic politician," Garner pointed out, "ever accused him of peculation or plunder." There were "no railroad swindles" and no serious financial scandals during Republican rule in Mississippi. "The only large case of embezzlement among the state officers during the post-bellum period was that of the Democratic state treasurer in 1866"—before the advent of the Republicans.

As the years went by, and idealism gave way to racism throughout the North, Ames felt more and more doubtful about the "Mission with a large M" he once had pursued. In 1926, half a century after the end of his carpetbag career, a *Boston Globe* reporter asked him if he thought it wise to have given ex-slaves the ballot. "That is still a mooted question," he cautiously replied. "Aside from the right or wrong of the policy, I was there to execute the laws of Congress, which took upon itself the task of reconstruction." Three years after that interview, at the age of ninety-three, he responded to another inquiring Mississippi historian, Dunbar Rowland. "The days are many before Christ's Sermon on the Mount will be our practical religion," Ames told him. "Mississippi like other states has a weary task before it."[16]

But Ames had many other things to occupy his mind. Besides his business affairs, he had his family duties, his travels, and his hobbies. Like his fellow carpetbagger Morgan, he fathered six children—two sons and four daughters—but there the similarity ended. All the Ames children were brought up in luxury, and all made a success of life. Both of the sons served in the Spanish-American War and also in World War I. The younger, Adelbert, Jr., earned B.A., LL.B., and Ph.D. degrees from Harvard and became a professor at Dartmouth.

After the death of Blanche's father, Benjamin F. Butler, in 1893, the Ameses shared the Butler mansion in Lowell with her brother Paul. They often summered at the Butler estate on Cape Ann, where they provided a separate cottage for each child. They had the pleasure of cruising in Paul's and Blanche's yacht—in which the family sailed to Montauk Point, Long Island, to pick up General Ames on his return from the Spanish-American War. The Ameses wintered in warmer climes, in California, Florida, the French Riviera, or Italy, where the family owned a villa on Lake Como.

An indefatigable golfer, Ames kept at the game until the day when, in his nineties, he fell down on the links. In the 1920s his favorite golfing partners in Florida were John D. Rockefeller, Sr., and Rockefeller's business associate Henry M. Flagler, the promoter of the railroad down Florida's east coast and all the way to Key West. A newspaper once ran a photograph of Ames and Rockefeller with this bit of doggerel beneath it:

> General Ames and John D!
> John D and General Ames!
> Greatest old cronies you ever will see!
> Calling each other all kinds of names,
> Knowing again their youthful joys,
> Two wise men who are proving that fame's
> Merely a bubble and joy is free.
> John D and General Ames!
> General Ames and John D!

Fame may have been a bubble, but the golfing joy of these two wealthy old men was hardly gratuitous.

While the Ames children leaned toward Unitarianism, the parents remained loyal to the Episcopal Church but supported the children in their liberal causes, such as woman suffrage and birth control. This stand on the children's part did not prevent the arrival of eighteen grandchildren, to whom Ames liked to reminisce about his Maine boyhood, especially about the time his seafaring father took him on a voyage to New York City when he was ten. Almost every year he reminisced about the Civil War in a speech to a veterans' reunion. As his birthdays kept on coming, the newspapers took notice of the "Last General of the Civil War," still "hale and hearty, straight as an arrow."

After he finally died, at ninety-seven and a half, Blanche began to sort and arrange the letters to and from him that she had carefully saved. She was eighty-six and did not expect to live much longer; she wanted to leave, before she died, a record of which her descendants might "justly feel proud." By the end of 1935 she had the letters ready for publication, but was unable to get it done before her death. Not until 1957 did her youngest daughter, Jessie, then seventy-three, see the two volumes of correspondence through the press. On the flyleaf she proclaimed: "TRUTH IS BETTER THAN FICTION."

But truth did not prevail. When the prize-winning book *Profiles in Courage* (1956) came to their attention, Ames's daughters were understandably upset. This book, bearing on the title page the name of John F. Kennedy, then a United States senator from Massachusetts, lauded the Mississippi white-supremacist L. Q. C. Lamar as one of its exemplars of statesmanly courage. In doing so, it slurred Adelbert Ames. "No state suffered more from carpetbag rule than Mississippi," the book asserted, and it exhumed the stale canard about "the extravagances of the reconstruction government" with its "heavy" state debt. By implication, Governor Ames was to blame. Ames's daughters protested repeatedly to Senator (and later President) Kennedy and to his special counsel, Theodore C. Sorensen. They got only evasive replies. No correction was ever made in any of the successive reissues of the Sorensen-Kennedy book.[17]

Henry Clay Warmoth, whom Ames had thought contemptible, came to be equally sensitive about his own reputation as a carpetbagger. He, too, enjoyed a long life as a successful and well-to-do entrepreneur. Unlike Ames, though, he lived out that life in the Southern state of which he had been governor—Louisiana.

When, in April 1877, President Hayes abandoned the carpetbaggers of Louisiana, along with those of Florida and South Carolina, Warmoth did not complain. He had nothing to lose; he was contending for no office at the time, nor did he object to Hayes's Southern policy. Besides, he was preoccupied with something other than politics. He was about to be married.

Always the ladies' man, he had not remained a bachelor for thirty-five years because of a lack of women willing to be wed. One of his many admirers, a Louisiana lady of conservative proclivities, wrote him an anonymous letter in which she referred to his "genius" and his "grand physical beauty." Another, the teenager Elisa Mouton, fell for him when, in 1872, he visited her father in the Cajun country to talk politics with him, a former senator, governor, and secession convention president. After returning to New Orleans, Warmoth received a letter from Elisa that began with the startling words: "I love you." Three years later, though he had done nothing to encourage her, she wrote again, asking for proof that he reciprocated her love. Yet again, in 1876: "Humbly prostrate at your feet (blessed feet!) I supplicate you *come* to see me!"

The bride-to-be, Sally Durand, was a teenager but not a Louisianan. Sally, nineteen, was the daughter of a well-known and wealthy jewelry manufacturer of Newark, New Jersey. Newspapers described her as "a bright, fresh brunette, of soft complexion and brilliant dark eyes," and a "neat figure." They described the groom as "a fine, tall, handsome, dark-haired, dark-eyed cavalier." The wedding, in Newark's Trinity Episcopal Church on the evening of May 30, 1877, was the "culmination of a sensation in the fashionable *monde*." After the ceremony the couple made a brief tour and then sailed for Europe, to spend several months abroad.[18]

On their return the Warmoths settled in Louisiana as master and mistress of Magnolia plantation, forty miles downriver from New Orleans. His partner Effingham Lawrence having died, Warmoth purchased the Lawrence interest in the plantation and in the Magnolia Sugar Refining Company. Here, at Magnolia, the Warmoths raised their family. Their first-born, named for Sally's brother Henry Durand, died at the age of one year, while they were summering with him in Saratoga, New York. Two other sons and a daughter grew to maturity.

Warmoth was an enterprising sugar producer. To get his product more expeditiously to market, he built the New Orleans, Fort Jackson & Grande Isle Railroad and became president of the company. To study the beet-sugar industry (with which he had to compete), he went to Europe with a letter of introduction from President Arthur, which made him a semi-official representative of the United States. To improve the production of cane sugar, he induced the federal government to establish an agricultural experiment station at Magnolia. But he could not persuade the government to maintain a high enough tariff on imported sugar, and, his business becoming less and less profitable, he eventually sold the plantation and the mill.

So long as he and Sally lived there, they enjoyed a reputation as an exemplary host and hostess. Typical of their hospitality was the warm reception they gave a group of congressmen and their wives one cold January day in 1897 (when he was fifty-six and she was forty). The men were members of the House committee on rivers and harbors—who could conceivably do something for Magnolia by providing money to improve the levees that protected its fields from the Mississippi.

"When the train steamed into the plantation yard the master of Magnolia was the first to greet the visitors as they stepped from the platform and entered for the first time the quaint precincts of a sugar plantation," noted a reporter accompanying the group. "Ex-Gov. Warmoth was clad in a great ulster that reached to his feet, and also in the usual smile which lightened up his visage and made it more hospitable than ever." He led them to the mill, which he had started up for their benefit, and showed them its mysteries—"vacuum pans, centrifugals, mixers, carriers, hot room, packeries and everything."

The visitors were even more eager to see how the Negroes lived on a modern sugar plantation, one more than a generation removed from slavery days. They headed for the "whitewashed quarters," some distance from the mill, to be met by an elderly black named Uncle Tom, who deferentially acted as their guide. "Old women and old men, who had grown gray in the service of Magnolia, smiled as they witnessed the advent of the newcomers, and long rows of pickaninnies looked in open-mouthed wonderment as they also gazed at the curious Northerners." Obviously the ex-slaves on the place had not come nearly so far since 1865 as had its master, the Illinois saddler's son.

From the quarters, the guests followed Warmoth to the manor house. Inside, they admired the "elegant parlors" and engaged in pleasant conversation for a while. Then they went in "a little procession down the stairway and into the long dining room where an equally long table was set, filled with an unlimited quantity of good things, and an inspiring array of long-necked and short-necked bottles." Presiding as hostess, Mrs. Warmoth was assisted by Warmoth's sister Bessie and by "the younger members of the master's household." At the end of the repast, when one of the congressmen made an effusive speech of thanks, Warmoth responded with all the grace of an antebellum planter. "In Louisiana we grow sugar cane, we grow corn, we raise rice and pecans," he said, "but most of all do we endeavor to produce a plentiful crop of good fellowship."[19]

While producing his Louisiana crops, Warmoth retained an interest in Louisiana politics, but could not recover leadership of the state's Republican party so long as his old friend and old enemy William Pitt Kellogg held on to it. Kellogg, that other carpetbagger from Illinois, was politically much the more successful of the two. After having been senator and governor, he served a second term in the Senate, from 1877 to 1883, and then a term in the House of Representatives, from 1883 to 1885. He attended seven Republican national conventions, chairing the Louisiana delegation at five of them. Warmoth meanwhile held few and unimportant offices. After withdrawing in favor of Kellogg's gubernatorial candidate, Stephen B. Packard, in 1876, he was elected that year to the state legislature and, in 1879, to a state constitutional convention.

Kellogg having relinquished the party leadership, Warmoth obtained the Republican nomination for governor in 1888, but lost the election by a wide margin. In 1890 he received from President Benjamin Harrison an appointment as collector of the port of New Orleans—the very job that once had formed the power base of the pro-Kellogg and anti-Warmoth "Custom House Ring." Warmoth lost the job in 1893, with Cleveland's return to the presidency, but remained a Louisiana Republican leader, going as a delegate to the national conventions of 1896, 1900, and 1908.[20]

The Republican party in Louisiana, as in other states of the South, had wasted away as the Democrats by various devices discouraged blacks from voting. The party was reduced to little more than a skeleton when the Democrats disfranchised them by statutes and constitutional amendments. As amended in 1898, the Louisiana constitution imposed a property requirement and a literacy test, which blacks had to pass to the satisfaction of a white examiner but which illiterate whites could evade by virtue of a grandfather clause.

Most of the time Warmoth had resisted efforts to deprive Louisiana blacks of voting and other rights. In 1874 he opposed the return of segregated "star cars" to the New Orleans street railway. In 1876 he called for "a fair show for everybody black & white." In 1888, when running for governor, he appealed to Democrats to allow blacks some rights as citizens—if only to keep them from fleeing Louisiana and settling in Kansas or other less oppressive places.

When the Democrats secured the property requirement and the literacy test in Louisiana, the Republicans were divided on the question of Negro suffrage. One faction was for encouraging the blacks to exercise what legal rights they still had. The other, the "Sugar Planters' Faction" or "Lily Whites," was ready to forget about the blacks—until Warmoth rebuked his fellow planters in 1900. "We are to-day the unrecognized wing of the Republican party of the state, because we are not in line with the Republican party of the United States," he declared. "I say there are 15,000 negroes in this State as much entitled to vote as any white man." Warmoth got his way, reunited the party, and established himself as "the boss with an iron hand."

There was no longer much for a Republican to do in Louisiana, however, except to attend party conventions and seek or hold a federal job. By the time of the First World War, Warmoth was a retired politician as well as a retired planter, living with his wife in a fine house in New Orleans. He grew into a dignified and statesmanly-appearing old gentleman, still tall, slender, and straight but with hair and mustache now snowy white.[21]

But he could not live down his reputation as a carpetbagger. He was annoyed when, in 1917, he received a questionnaire from Ella Lonn, who had written a dissertation on Reconstruction in Louisiana but was willing to revise it before publishing it. She asked him such impertinent questions as this: "Will you kindly state why the laws, making you virtually an autocrat, were passed in 1870?" He could have explained that these laws were intended to enable him to protect Republicans from the murderous assaults of Democrats—and that they fell far short of making him "virtually an autocrat," since he lost power long before the end of his single term as governor. "My Dear Miss Lonn," he wrote, instead, "It would be manifestly unsatisfactory for me to attempt to give the history of an important epoch like reconstruction of a state, by answering half a dozen interrogations propounded by an individual who has already put into book form opinions ready for the press, formed from reading only one side of a controversy."

When Ella Lonn's monograph came out, it proved to be not quite so hard on Warmoth as he had had reason to expect. The author pictured him as a kind of dictator who had been responsible for much misgovernment, but she confessed she lacked convincing evidence that he had ever accepted a bribe. Despite her negative finding, a popular history of Louisiana appearing in 1925 alluded to Warmoth—in a chapter on "The

Curse of Carpetbaggery"—as a man now "lolling in luxurious retirement" who had procured his fortune through graft.

From the kind of history taught in the state's schools, at least one Louisianan discovered much to emulate in Warmoth's career as governor. That one was Huey Long, who, after an unsuccessful bid in 1924, was himself elected governor in 1928. He aimed to be all-powerful in the way that Warmoth supposedly had been. Once in office, Long used some of the methods that Warmoth actually had used, entering the legislative halls (like Warmoth) to tell lawmakers how to vote and obtaining laws intended to give him control over local governments and over election officials. To his friends, Long often expressed his admiration for Warmoth as a politician.

Warmoth apparently did not know of Long's admiration for him and certainly did not reciprocate it. Nor did he see any real similarity between Long's career and his own, even when the legislature threatened to impeach Long as it had impeached him. "Gov. Long is making speeches over the state attacking the Legislature for proceeding against him with a view to impeachment," Warmoth noted in his diary on April 21, 1929. "They [the speeches] are disgusting." As a patrician, a former planter from lush Plaquemines parish, Warmoth looked down on the farmer's son from the red-clay hills and piney woods of Winn parish.

By this time, Warmoth was well along in the writing of the memoirs he had begun in the early 1920s. In his memoirs he undertook to refute the "lies, unmitigated lies, notorious and malicious lies" that were still being told about him. He wanted to be remembered as a Southerner and a conservative—as a man who, indeed, had striven during Reconstruction to save Louisiana from the horrors of "Africanization." Either because of a faulty memory or because of deliberate intent, he played down the real Radicalism of his early career (1865-68) in Louisiana politics.

In preparing the memoirs, he went over the diary he had kept during part of that time. He had a typescript made from the small leather-bound notebooks in which he had made jottings with pencil or pen. In the process of transcription he edited some of the passages to tone down their Radicalism. For example, a sentence in the entry for September 24, 1866, referring to a campaign speech he had made in Napoleon, Ohio, originally ran: "They all said I made a great many votes & consolidated opinion on negro suffrage." In the typed version the second clause of the sentence was changed to read: "& consolidated opinion in favor of the party."

As he concluded his autobiographical manuscript, in 1929, Warmoth wrote: ". . . and having not a drop of any other than Southern blood in my veins, I think I may say, at eighty-seven years of age, that I was never a 'Louisiana Carpet-bagger,' though I might, in common parlance, be termed a 'scallawag.'" He was making a final bid for acceptance as a Southerner. But he seemed to forget that, from the white-supremacist point of view, a scalawag was every bit as contemptible as a carpetbagger.

And, though he could claim Southern ancestors, he was himself Northern-born and a Union veteran, hence a carpetbagger, not a scalawag.

His book, *War, Politics and Reconstruction: Stormy Days in Louisiana,* came off the press in 1930. He did not get much of a chance to see what effect, if any, the book would have on his reputation. He died the following year, September 30, 1931, at the age of eighty-nine.[22]

Afterword

More than a century after the end of Reconstruction, writing an essay for his college newspaper, a student in North Carolina referred to carpetbaggers as "ignorant and illiterate." This student, in all innocence, was simply giving expression to what was common knowledge among his Southern peers—what, at home and at school, they were still being brought up to believe. His college, as it happened, was located in the city of Greensboro, once the residence of the carpetbagger Tourgee, who was so ignorant as to have been a university graduate and an academy principal, and so illiterate as to have written a couple of dozen books, among them one of the bestsellers of his time.

In fact, seven of our ten carpetbaggers had a college education or the equivalent, and one of them (Chamberlain) held degrees from both Yale and Harvard, along with a Phi Beta Kappa key. The three who lacked a college degree were by no means uneducated. One of the three (Reed) edited newspapers, and the other two (Warmoth, Morgan) studied and practiced law. Altogether, four of the ten (Tourgee, Morgan, Clayton, Warmoth) authored books, another (Ames) wrote letters that eventually appeared in book form, and still another (Chamberlain) published a number of scholarly articles.

Taken as a group, the ten were much better educated and much more literate than the average for their time—or for our time. It does not necessarily follow, of course, that the rest of the hundreds of carpetbaggers were equally learned or literary, but neither does it follow that the rest were ignorant and illiterate. Probably they were less ignorant and more literate than the rank and file of the Democrats, or Conservatives, who opposed them in politics. This, to be sure, would be difficult to demonstrate, but it would not be hard to show that, in comparison with the outstanding carpetbaggers, the top Southerners opposing them were somewhat lacking in educational and literary attainments.

From the Southern point of view, however, all carpetbaggers were "ignorant" because they did not know any better than to associate politically with blacks. The Republicans from the North were helping to lead a revolution that, for the time being, deprived ex-Confederates of power. The Republicans held offices that the Democrats desired. Early in the political warfare the Democrats hit upon a handy propaganda term for the Northern Republicans in the South. But *carpetbagger* was only a smear word that stuck and continues to stick. The epithet, with its evil connotations, does not really fit any of the men who were presumed to be its most prominent examples.

None of the ten in this book evaded military service, waited until the grant of suffrage to Southern blacks, and then went south to seek election to political office. One of the ten (Reed) had no military record, having been too old to fight, but he arrived in the South, as a federal officeholder, well before 1867; that is, well before Congress passed the Reconstruction Act and thereby gave the vote to Southern blacks. Another (Spencer) did return to the South after the passage of the act, in search of political opportunities under its provisions, but he was a veteran of the Union army.

All the rest were Union veterans and had other than political reasons for remaining in or returning to the South after their military service. Of these eight, all except one (Chamberlain) saw a great deal of action in the war, making honorable and even heroic records. Two (Scott, Ames) were assigned to the postwar South on military duty. Two others (Warmoth, Tourgee) were there as business or professional men. The remaining four (Warner, Morgan, Chamberlain, Clayton) looked for a livelihood as cotton planters.

None of the ten could be correctly described as a roving adventurer who meddled in a place where he had no right to be. True, two of them (Ames, Spencer) were barely residents of the states whose voters elected them to office; both men, though, were constitutionally entitled to run. All the rest intended from the start to make permanent homes in the South. Four (Warmoth, Reed, Warner, Clayton) succeeded in doing so. The other four (Morgan, Scott, Tourgee, Chamberlain) stayed as long as they comfortably could—each of them for ten years or more.

Nor were any of the men penniless when they arrived in the South, though some became more or less impoverished after their arrival. Almost all of them invested in Southern property, some of them (Warner, Morgan, Scott, Tourgee) bringing considerable amounts of money from the North.

In Southern politics the carpetbaggers exerted an influence disproportionate to their numbers, but their influence has been exaggerated. They could wield it only so long as they held the support of a majority of Southerners, black or white. They had no constitutional or legal advantage after 1872, when Congress lifted the Fourteenth Amendment ban on office-holding by ex-Confederate leaders. By 1872, four of our carpetbaggers (Warmoth, Reed, Warner, Scott) were already leaving office, never to be reelected. By 1874, all the others had won their last significant election. The era of so-called "carpetbag-scalawag-Negro rule" persisted as long as a decade (1868-77) only in the states of South Carolina, Florida, and Louisiana.

The question of carpetbaggery and corruption raises the broader question of what, in a particular political context, corruption means. In viewing the late nineteenth century, as in viewing the late twentieth, it is hard to draw a sharp line between legitimate and illegitimate spending in politics. When is a payment a bribe, and when is it a campaign contribution? In the nineteenth century the concept of "conflict of interest" was even less well developed than in the twentieth. So long as a man violated no statute, how far could he properly go in using public office for private gain? During the 1860s and 1870s these ambiguities left a lot of leeway for many politicians, Southerners as well as Northerners, Democrats as well as Republicans.

No doubt there was bribery in the South during Reconstruction—as there was in the North at the same time—but it was not endemic. It varied from state to state, being rife in South Carolina and comparatively infrequent in Mississippi. Nor was it confined to Republicans. If most of the bribe-takers were poor, Republican, and black, many of the bribe-givers (as Warmoth pointed out in Louisiana) were wealthy, Democratic, and white.

In judging the honesty of individual carpetbaggers, we must discount heavily if not disregard entirely what the Democrats said about them. The Democrats accused them of being bent on plunder even before they had been in office long enough to do anything, honest or dishonest. The Democrats kept on slinging the charge of corruption indiscriminately—against men of unquestionable probity as well as against the justifiably suspect. This was part of the Democrats' propaganda technique of the Big Lie.

Of our ten carpetbaggers, all except three (Spencer, Warmoth, Scott) deserve to have the charge of corruption summarily dismissed. One of the three exceptions (Spencer) undoubtedly gave Alabama legislators financial aid, free meals and drinks, and promises of federal jobs in persuading them to reelect him senator. According to his opponents, these favors amounted to bribes, though that kind of politicking was fairly common throughout the country. The other two exceptions (Warmoth, Scott) probably used their positions as insiders to deal profitably with the states they governed, but they would seem to have been guilty of violating no law then in effect.

Like the corruption, the extravagance of the carpetbag governments has been grossly exaggerated. Under those governments, expenditures did increase and there was considerable waste, but most of the money went for new or enlarged state services such as the development of schools and transportation systems. All ten of our carpetbaggers advocated public improvements of that kind; all aspired to reconstruct their respective states economically as well as politically. In promoting railroads through state aid, the carpetbaggers were doing on a larger scale what Southerners themselves had undertaken to do before the war and immediately after it. Almost all the men on our list eventually became advocates of retrenchment.

All ten were responsible, in varying degrees, for causing a disturbance in the relations between the races in the South. As most Southern whites saw it, ideal relations required a continuance of the passivity and deference that had been expected of blacks in slavery days. Southern whites resisted, while carpetbaggers encouraged, the freedmen's exercise of their newly granted political rights. This was the basic reason for the anti-carpetbagger animus.

There remains the charge that the carpetbaggers were interested in the black voter not for his sake but for their own. Among our ten men, the attitude toward blacks varied considerably. Two of the men (Morgan, Tourgee) were seemingly as unprejudiced and as pro-black as any white person of their time, though even they would probably fail to meet the exacting standards of late-twentieth-century militants. Two others (Reed, Warner) were reluctant Reconstructionists who accepted black suffrage and black support without enthusiasm. Two more (Warmoth, Chamberlain) started out as egalitarian Radicals and ended up as disillusioned conservatives, one of the two (Chamberlain) as a fanatical Negrophobe. Another (Ames) thought of himself as a crusader for black rights; he and the remaining three (Spencer, Clayton, Scott) seem to have enjoyed very good rapport with blacks.

We have no way of knowing just how sincere was the interest any of these carpetbaggers took in the cause of equal rights. Regardless, a person's motives for supporting a good cause are historically less important than the fact of his supporting it. None of the carpetbaggers here portrayed comes close to candidacy for sainthood, and perhaps none can even be considered a genuine hero. Each had his frailties, no doubt. But in all fairness we should refrain from comparing a realistic representation of these men with an idealized picture of their Southern white opponents—who, whatever the fine qualities that may have graced them, were defenders and practitioners of racism in some of its ugliest forms. What was once fittingly said about one of the ten carpetbaggers may be fittingly repeated in regard to each of the others: "He may be guilty but my God look at the leprous hands upraised against him."

Acknowledgments

Thanks are due to a number of people who contributed to the realization of this book.

Many writers on Reconstruction and on carpetbaggers have provided information and ideas that saved me a great deal of labor. These authors, too numerous to be listed here, are credited in the back notes of the book.

Several scholars generously made available their notes or other research materials, including copies of many manuscripts. I am beholden to the following: Joseph Logsdon, for information regarding Chamberlain, Morgan, and carpetbaggers in general; Lawrence N. Powell, regarding Spencer; Loren Schweninger, regarding Spencer and Warner; Allen W. Trelease, regarding Clayton; Sarah Woolfolk Wiggins, regarding Warner; and the late T. Harry Williams, regarding Warmoth.

The staffs of various repositories were extremely helpful: the Library of Congress, the National Archives, the Duke University Library, the Yale University Library, the University of North Carolina Library at Chapel Hill, the Ohio Historical Society, and the State Historical Society of Wisconsin. I am especially indebted to Charles M. Adams, James H. Thompson, and other librarians at the University of North Carolina at Greensboro, the library of which sheltered and nourished me for almost a quarter of a century.

Finally, I owe a debt to my late wife, Rose Bonar Current, who served cheerfully as amanuensis, typist, and general assistant during the many years (too many) that the intermittent research dragged on.

Notes

Chapter 1. The Omen of Peace & Reunion

1. Warmoth diary, Aug. 29, Sept. 3, 9, 1863, Mar. 4, 1865, Henry Clay Warmoth Papers, Southern Historical Collection, University of North Carolina Library, Chapel Hill; Henry Clay Warmoth, *War, Politics and Reconstruction: Stormy Days in Louisiana* (New York, 1930), 18-22; Noah Brooks, *Washington in Lincoln's Time,* ed. Herbert Mitgang (New York, 1958), 210-14; Roy P. Basler, ed., *The Collected Works of Abraham Lincoln* (8 vols., New Brunswick, N.J., 1953), VIII, 332-33.

2. Warmoth diary, Dec. 26, 1863, Apr. 3, 4, 5, 6, 7, 1865; Brooks, *Washington in Lincoln's Time,* 222.

3. Warmoth diary, Apr. 14, 16, 17, 18, 19, 20, 1865; Warmoth, *War, Politics and Reconstruction,* 25-27; Brooks, *Washington in Lincoln's Time,* 225-27, 231; *Collected Works of Abraham Lincoln,* VIII, 399-405.

4. Warmoth diary, Apr. 27, 29, 1865; Warmoth, *War, Politics and Reconstruction,* 1-12; John T. Trowbridge, *The South . . . A Journey Through the Desolated States* (Hartford, Conn., 1866), 356, 395; Mark Twain, *Life on the Mississippi* (Boston, 1883), 419-23.

5. Warmoth diary, Jan. 3, Feb. 4, 1864; Trowbridge, *The South,* 397-98.

6. Warmoth diary, May 9, 24, 30, June 2, 1864, May 6, 1865; Warmoth, *War, Politics and Reconstruction,* 23-25; Francis B. Harris, "Henry Clay Warmoth, Reconstruction Governor of Louisiana," *Louisiana Historical Quarterly* XXX (Apr. 1917), 11-16.

7. Warmoth diary, May 14, 1865; Harris, "Warmoth," 17-19; Francis W. Binning, "Henry Clay Warmoth and Louisiana Reconstruction" (Ph.D. dissertation, University of North Carolina, Chapel Hill, 1969 [facsimile, Ann Arbor, Mich., 1980]), 68-71; La Wanda Cox, *Lincoln and Black Freedom: A Study in Presidential Leadership* (Columbia, S.C., 1981), 136-37.

8. Warmoth diary, May 28, 1865; Whitelaw Reid, *After the War: A Southern Tour, May 1, 1865, to May 1, 1866* (New York, 1866), 240-41; Harris, "Warmoth," 19; Binning, "Warmoth," 104-7, quoting *New Orleans Tribune,* June 12, 1865.

9. Warmoth diary, Sept. 19, 1865; J. T. Campbell to Warmoth, June 6, 1865; E. J. Morse to Warmoth, Sept. 19, 1865, Warmoth Papers.

10. Warmoth diary, Sept. 25, 28, 1865; *Chicago Tribune,* Nov. 25, 1865; Harris, "Warmoth," 21; Binning, "Warmoth," 86-87; Peyton McCrary, *Abraham Lincoln and Reconstruction: The Louisiana Experiment* (Princeton, N.J., 1978), 125, 333-34.

11. Warmoth diary, Oct. 3, Nov. 6, 1865; unidentified newspaper clipping, Nov. 13, 1865, Warmoth Papers; Harris, "Warmoth," 19-22, quoting *New Orleans Crescent,* Nov. 4, 1865; Binning, "Warmoth," 87-88.

12. Warmoth to John Sherman, Nov. 15, 1865, John Sherman Papers, Library of Congress; Warmoth diary, Nov. 18, 19, 1865. In *War, Politics and Reconstruction,* ix-x, Warmoth denied that Negroes had been levied upon to pay his expenses as territorial delegate. Yet he conceded quite a bit when he added: "I paid my own expenses with the exception of $1,000 furnished me by the State Committee."

13. Warmoth diary, Mar. 14, Apr. 2, Nov. 30, Dec. 1, 2, 4, 5, 14, 16, 17, 24, 1865.

14. *New Orleans Times,* Dec. 21, 1865; C. W. Stauffer to Michael Hahn, Dec. 19, 1865, Warmoth Papers; L. A. Sheldon to James A. Garfield, Dec. 26, 1865, James A. Garfield Papers, Library of Congress; E. T. Merrick to John Sherman, Feb. 21, 1866, Sherman Papers.

15. Warmoth diary, Jan. 29, Feb. 1, 2, 3, 28, 1866, Thomas J. Durant to Warmoth, Jan. 13, Feb. 14, Mar. 2, 1866, Warmoth Papers; Warmoth, *War, Politics and Reconstruction,* 45.

16. Alfred Shaw to Warmoth, Mar. 22, 1866; J. P. Newsham to Warmoth, Apr. 5, 1866, Warmoth Papers; Sheridan to Henry Wilson, June 29, 1866, Henry Wilson Papers, Library of Congress; Trowbridge, *The South,* 401-3; John R. Dennett, *The South as It Is, 1865-1866* (New York, 1965), 306-10.

17. Warmoth diary, July 29, 1866; Harris, "Warmoth," 24-25; Binning, "Warmoth," 96-97.

18. Warmoth diary, July 30, 1866; Warmoth testimony, Dec. 22, 1866, *Report of the Select Committee on the New Orleans Riots* (39 Cong., 2 sess., House Report No. 16, Washington, D.C., 1867), 40-43; Joe Gray Taylor, *Louisiana Reconstructed, 1863-1877* (Baton Rouge, La., 1974), 110.

Chapter 2. Go South, Young Man!

1. Reid, *After the War,* 159-61; William W. Davis, *The Civil War and Reconstruction in Florida* (New York, 1913), 528-29.

2. Reed to John F. Potter, Nov. 14, 1863, John F. Potter Papers, and WPA field notes for a biographical sketch of Reed, State Historical Society of Wisconsin, Madison; David H. Overy, Jr. "The Wisconsin Carpetbagger: A Group Portrait," *Wisconsin Magazine of History* XLIV (Autumn 1960), 21-25.

3. George Winston Smith, "Carpetbag Imperialism in Florida, 1862-1868," *Florida Historical Quarterly* XXVII (Oct. 1948, Jan. 1949), 110-13, 268-75; Jerrell H. Shofner, *Nor Is It Over Yet: Florida in the Era of Reconstruction, 1863-1877* (Gainesville, Fla., 1974), 6-8; Jonathan Daniels, *Prince of Carpetbaggers* (Philadelphia, 1958), 83-84.

4. Reed to John F. Potter, Nov. 14, 1863, Potter Papers; Overy, "Wisconsin Carpetbagger," 25.

5. Reed to Montgomery Blair, June 26, 1865, Andrew Johnson Papers, Library of Congress; "Southern Emigrants," *Harper's Weekly* XI (Aug. 3, 1867), 492; Smith, "Carpetbag Imperialism," 292-94; Davis, *Reconstruction in Florida,* 350-51, 375.

6. Reed to John Sherman, May 12, 1866, Sherman Papers; Reid, *After the War,* 162-63, 166-67, 171-73; John Wallace, *Carpetbag Rule in Florida* (Jacksonville, Fla., 1888), 5-16; Davis, *Reconstruction in Florida,* 358-59, Shofner, *Nor Is It Over Yet,* 39-40.

7. Spencer to Grenville M. Dodge, May 1, 25, 1865, Grenville M. Dodge Papers, Iowa State Library, Des Moines; Trowbridge, *The South,* 290-91, 380, 448, 450-51; Reid, *After the War,* 207-8, 365, 371-75; Walter L. Fleming, *Civil War and Reconstruction in Alabama* (New York, 1905), 321-22.

8. Spencer to Grenville M. Dodge, Aug. 1, 1865, Dodge Papers; *The National Cyclopaedia of American Biography* (57 vols., New York, 1898-1977, current volumes continuing), XIII, 72.

9. Spencer to Grenville M. Dodge, Oct. 14, 1865, Dodge Papers; *National Cyclopaedia of American Biography,* XIII, 72.

10. Trowbridge, *The South,* 422-27, 433-35, 440-42; Reid, *After the War,* 374-75, 402-3, 405-6.

11. Warner to Willard Warner III, Dec. 2, 1865, Willard Warner Papers, Tennessee State Department of Archives, Nashville (microfilm in the Univ. of Alabama Library).

12. Warner to Lyman Warner, Feb. 23, 1851, and to Eliza Woods, Nov. 10, 1852, June 18, 1853; Eliza Woods to Warner, Sept. 2, 1855; undated "Biographical Note," Warner Papers.

13. Salmon P. Chase to Warner, May 15, 1860; John D. McCarty to W. B. Woods, Feb. 19, 1864; Warner to Willard Warner III, Apr. 27, 1865; "Biographical Note," Warner Papers; Warner to William T. Sherman, Apr. 22, 1866, John Sherman Papers.

14. W. B. Woods to John Sherman, Jan. 28, 1866, Sherman Papers; A. L. Chetlain to the Editor, Feb. 17, 1866, *Chicago Tribune,* Feb. 23, 1866.

15. William T. Sherman to Warner, Jan. 16, 1866; Warner to John Sherman, Apr. 4, June 21, 1866, and to William T. Sherman, Apr. 22, 1866, Sherman Papers; Reid, *After the War,* 454-55; John R. Dennett, *The South as It Is, 1865-1866* (New York, 1965), 302.

16. Albert T. Morgan file, Civil War Service Records, National Archives; Morgan, declaration for invalid pension, Jan. 23, 1879, and affidavit, Apr. 11, 1879; Eleanor Morgan (his mother), affidavit, June 14, 1879, Pension Records, National Archives; Reid, *After the War,* 289-90.

17. O. B. Foster to T. G. Free, Aug. 9, 1865, and William Davis and J. J. B. White depositions, Freedmen's Bureau Records, Mississippi, National Archives.

18. Report of General Wager Swayne, Washington, Mar. 6, 1866, *Chicago Tribune,* Mar. 7, 1866; Albert T. Morgan, *Yazoo; or, On the Picket Line of Freedom in the South* (Washington, D.C., 1884), 17-19, 25-27, 29-33, 38-39, 47-48, 82-84, 99-101.

19. Trowbridge, *The South,* 567-68; Sidney Andrews, *The South since the War as Shown by Fourteen Weeks of Travel and Observation in Georgia and the Carolinas* (Boston, 1866), 1-5.

20. Scott testimony and biographical sketch in J. M. Haag, ed., *The State of Ohio Versus Robert K. Scott* (Toledo, Ohio, 1882), 9-14, 149-50; Scott to J. M.

Thayer, May 6, 1862, Robert K. Scott Papers, Ohio Historical Society, Columbus.

21. Willie Lee Rose, *Rehearsal for Reconstruction: The Port Royal Experiment* (Indianapolis, Ind., 1964), 327-30, 337-39, 356-57; Martin Abbott, *The Freedmen's Bureau in South Carolina, 1865-1872* (Chapel Hill, N.C., 1967), 18-19.

22. Scott to O. O. Howard, Oct. 12, 1866, and to Henry Brakin, Oct. 16, 1866; Scott, Annual Report, Nov. 1, 1866, Scott Papers; Abbott, *Freedmen's Bureau,* 57, 62, 72-74.

23. Scott to O. O. Howard, Apr. 12, June 11, 30, Aug. 9, 1866, and to "Dear Doctor," Aug. 16, 1866; *Chicago Tribune,* Feb. 15, 1866; Abbott, *Freedmen's Bureau,* 25-26, 127, quoting the *Charleston News* as reprinted in the *Columbia Phoenix,* June 5, 1866.

Chapter 3. We Poor Southern Devils

1. W. W. Holden to Tourgee, June 16, 1865, Albion W. Tourgee Papers, Chautauqua County Historical Society, Westfield, New York (microfilm in the library of the University of North Carolina at Greensboro).

2. Roy F. Dibble, *Albion W. Tourgée* (New York, 1921), 11-40, 130-31; Otto H. Olsen, *Carpetbagger's Crusade: The Life of Albion W. Tourgée* (Baltimore, Md., 1965), 1-26.

3. Tourgee to Mrs. Tourgee, July 22, 1865, Tourgée Papers; Olsen, *Carpetbagger's Crusade,* 27.

4. Reid, *After the War,* 28-31; Dennett, *South as It Is,* 155; Edward King, *The Great South* (2 vols., Hartford, Conn., 1875), II, 468-69; Claude G. Bowers, *The Tragic Era: The Revolution after Lincoln* (Cambridge, Mass., 1929), 312-14; Daniels, *Prince of Carpetbaggers,* 150-51, 157-58.

5. H. M. Watterson to Andrew Johnson, June 29, 1865, Johnson Papers; Holden to Tourgee, June 16, 1865; Tourgee to Mrs. Tourgee, July 25, 1865; Mrs. Tourgee to Tourgee, July 27, 1865; J. Clingman, power of attorney to Tourgee, Aug. 9, 1865, Tourgée Papers; Reid, *After the War,* 54.

6. Andrews, *South since the War,* 108-10; Trowbridge, *The South,* 580; Dennett, *South as It Is,* 107-13.

7. Indenture of lease between Cyrus P. Mendenhall and A. W. Tourgee and Seneca Kuhn, Nov. 2, 1965, Tourgée Papers; Trowbridge, *The South,* 581-82; Olsen, *Carpetbagger's Crusade,* 27-30, 32-33.

8. G. W. Welker to Stevens, Dec. 2, 1865, and Marion Roberts to Stevens, May 15, 1866, Thaddeus Stevens Papers, Library of Congress; C. H. Foster to Justin S. Morrill, Feb. 28, 1866, Justin S. Morrill Papers, Library of Congress; Olsen, *Carpetbagger's Crusade,* 41-42, 49-51.

9. Tourgee to Mrs. Tourgee, Aug. 31, 1866, Tourgée Papers; *New York Times,* Sept. 3, 4, 5, 1866.

10. Tourgee to Mrs. Tourgee, Sept. 5, 6, 1866; Tourgee, notes of a speech in 1866, Tourgée Papers; Warmoth diary, Sept. 3, 4, 5, 6, 7, 1866, Warmoth Papers; *New York Times,* Nov. 6, 7, 8, 1866.

11. Tourgee to Mrs. Tourgee, Sept. 6, 16, 19, 28, Oct. 3, 8, 1866; James W. Sampson to Mrs. Tourgee, Oct. 2, 1866; Tourgee, notes of a speech in Pennsylvania, fall of 1866, Tourgée Papers.

12. Warmoth diary, Sept. 11, 12, 13, 15, 16, 18, 20, 21, 22, 23, 24, 1866, and

Feb. 27, 1867, and unidentified newspaper clipping, Sept. 12, 1866, Warmoth Papers.

13. Mrs. Tourgee to Tourgee, Oct. 13, 1866, Tourgée Papers.

14. Jonathan Worth to the editor of the *Greensboro Patriot,* Sept. 10, to Nereus Mendenhall, Sept. 10, Oct. 2, and to R. Y. McAden, Sept. 23, 1866, in J. G. de Roulhac Hamilton, ed., *The Correspondence of Jonathan Worth* (2 vols., Raleigh, N. C., 1909), II, 772-77, 783, 808-9; Worth to ———, Sept. 11, 1865, Jonathan Worth Papers, Southern Historical Collection, University of North Carolina Library, Chapel Hill; Olsen, *Carpetbagger's Crusade,* 56.

15. Mrs. Tourgee to Tourgee, Sept. 3, 1866; unsigned letters to Tourgee, Sept. 3, and Sept. —, 1866, and to Mrs. Tourgee, Oct. 16, 1866, Tourgée Papers.

16. Printed form letter, Nov. 6, 1866, announcing the *Union Register* to begin publication on Dec. 1, 1866; Tourgee agreements with Seneca Kuhn, Dec. 6, 1866, George S. Anthony, Dec. 13, 1866, and Hiram C. Worth, Jan. 1, 1867, Tourgée Papers; Olsen, *Carpetbagger's Crusade,* 60-67.

Chapter 4. To Reconstruct This Godforsaken Country

1. Warner to Sherman, Jan. 26, Mar. 5, 14, Sherman Papers.

2. Warner to Willard Warner III, June 24, 1867, Warner Papers; Sarah Woolfolk Wiggins, *The Scalawag in Alabama Politics, 1865-1881* (University, Ala., 1977), 21-22.

3. Spencer to Dodge, July 1, 1867, Dodge Papers: William M. Cash, "Alabama Republicans during Reconstruction: Personal Characteristics, Motivations, and Political Activity of Party Activists, 1867-1880" (Ph.D. dissertation, University of Alabama, 1973 [facsimile, Ann Arbor, Mich., 1980]), 276-77; Fleming, *Civil War and Reconstruction in Alabama,* 524-30.

4. Spencer to Dodge, Oct. 22, 1867, Dodge Papers.

5. Warner to Sherman, Dec. 9, 19, 27, 1867, and Swayne to Sherman, Dec. 28, 1867, Sherman Papers; Cash, "Alabama Republicans," 89.

6. Spencer to Dodge, Oct. 22, 1867, Dodge papers; W. M. Dunn to Sherman, Nov. 18, 1867, Sherman Papers; F. W. Kellogg to Elihu B. Washburne, Dec. 16, 1867, Elihu B. Washburne Papers, Library of Congress.

7. Buckley to Washburne, Jan. 9, 1868, Washburne Papers; Fleming, *Civil War and Reconstruction in Alabama,* 737.

8. W. M. Dunn to Sherman, Nov. 18, 1867, Sherman Papers; George Ely to Elihu B. Washburne, Feb. 9, 1868, Washburne Papers; Fleming, *Civil War and Reconstruction in Alabama,* 536 ff.; Wiggins, *Scalawag in Alabama Politics,* 37, 40; Richard L. Hume, "The 'Black and Tan' Constitutional Conventions of 1867-1869 in Ten Former Confederate States: A Study of Their Membership" (Ph.D. dissertation, University of Washington, Seattle, 1969 [facsimile, Ann Arbor, Mich., 1980]), 38-40.

9. Cox to Sherman, Mar. 3, 1868, Warner Papers.

10. Warmoth diary, Feb. 27, Mar. 4, 1867, Warmoth Papers.

11. John Lynch to John Sherman, Apr. 20, 1867, Warmoth Papers.

12. W. G. Eliot to John Sherman, Feb. 25, 1867, Sherman Papers; letters to Warmoth from J. D. Rich, Apr. 12, William George, May 6, and Thomas W.

Conway, July 23, 1867, Warmoth Papers; Taylor, *Louisiana Reconstructed,* 144, 147.

13. Warmoth, *War, Politics and Reconstruction,* 51-54, quoting New Orleans Tribune, no date, and *New Orleans Times,* Jan. 25, 1868; Binning, "Warmoth," 110-11.

14. *New Orleans Weekly Republican,* Feb. 29, 1868; Thomas W. Conway to Warmoth, Mar. 15, 1868, Warmoth Papers; W. C. Carroll to Elihu B. Washburne, Mar. 6, 1868, Washburne Papers; Eric L. McKitrick, *Andrew Johnson and Reconstruction* (Chicago, Ill., 1960), 499-500; Binning, "Warmoth," 113-14; Taylor, *Louisiana Reconstructed,* 142, 156-61.

15. Morgan, *Yazoo,* 103, 113; Morgan, Ross & Company to Edward O. C. Ord, Sept. 18, 1867, Army Records of the Fourth Military District, National Archives.

16. Morgan, *Yazoo,* 103, 112-13; Morgan affidavit, Feb. 29, 1867, Army Records of the Fourth Military District; C. T. Comings to J. P. Bardwell, Mar. 1, 1867; D. W. White to A. W. Preston, Apr. 23, 24, 1867; and Allen P. Huggins to A. W. Preston, May 31, 1867, Freedmen's Bureau Records.

17. Allen P. Huggins to A. W. Preston, May 31, June 30, July 15, 31, 1867, and to H. W. Smith, Aug. 31, Sept. 1, 1867, Freedmen's Bureau Records.

18. Morgan, *Yazoo,* 122-28; S. G. Chambers to the Sheriff or Any Constable of Yazoo County, Aug. 21, 1867; affidavit of D. G. Bedwell, Sept. 30, 1867; order of O. D. Green by command of General Ord, Oct. 28, 1867, Army Records of the Fourth Military District; A. P. Huggins to H. W. Smith, Aug. 30, 1867, and to Sheriff of Yazoo County, Sept. 8, 1867, Freedmen's Bureau Records.

19. Morgan, *Yazoo,* 107-8, 132; Daniel Hitchcock to D. Jones, Sept. 21, 1867; A. P. Huggins and others to E. O. C. Ord, Sept. 25, 1867, Army Records of the Fourth Military District; A. P. Huggins to J. W. Sutherland, Sept. 23, 1867, Freedmen's Bureau Records.

20. Morgan, *Yazoo,* 131, 134-38, 142, 149, 156-58; William C. Harris, *The Day of the Carpetbagger: Republican Reconstruction in Mississippi* (Baton Rouge, La., 1979), 115.

21. Morgan, *Yazoo,* 179; Harris, *Day of the Carpetbagger,* 131-32, 140-48; Hume, "'Black and Tan' Constitutional Conventions," 336-39, 342; D. W. White to J. W. Sutherland, Oct. 31, 1867, and to Merritt Barber, Nov. 15, 30, Dec. 12, 31, 1867, Freedmen's Bureau Records.

22. Shofner, *Nor Is It Over Yet,* 165-67; Davis, *Civil War and Reconstruction in Florida,* 469-76, 483; Hume, "'Black and Tan' Constitutional Conventions," 571, 574-77, 585, 588; Wallace, *Carpetbag Rule,* 42-46.

23. Daniel Richards to E. B. Washburne, Nov. 11, 1867, Washburne Papers.

24. Shofner, *Nor Is It Over Yet,* 174-78; Davis, *Civil War and Reconstruction in Florida,* 493-94; Reid, *After the War,* 160; Solon Robinson letter, Feb. 5, 1868, *New York Tribune,* Feb. 12, 1868.

25. Daniel Richards to G. W. Atwood, Jan. 13, 1868, and to E. B. Washburne, Feb. 2, 1868, Washburne Papers; Solon Robinson letters, Jan. 30, Feb. 2, 1868, *New York Tribune,* Feb. 8, 10, 1868; Davis, *Civil War and Reconstruction in Florida,* 494-96.

26. Solon Robinson letters, Jan. 29, 30, 1868, *New York Tribune,* Feb. 8, 1868; Davis, *Civil War and Reconstruction in Florida,* 505-8.

27. Daniel Richards to E. B. Washburne, Feb. 11, 1868, Washburne Papers;

Shofner, *Nor Is It Over Yet,* 180-86; Davis, *Civil War and Reconstruction in Florida,* 509-13; Wallace, *Carpetbag Rule,* 67-74.

28. Daniel Richards to E. B. Washburne, Apr. 14, 20, 21, 29, May 6, 1868, and Lyman D. Stickney to Washburne, May 21, 1868, Washburne Papers; Davis, *Civil War and Reconstruction in Florida,* 520-24; Wallace, *Carpetbag Rule,* 63-64.

Chapter 5. I Believe in the People

1. *The Nation* (New York) VI (Feb. 13, 1868), 123.

2. Hume, "'Black and Tan' Constitutional Conventions," 390, 656. Of the total of 1,027 delegates, Hume identifies 149 as "outside whites" and 257 as blacks but leaves 143 unclassified. If constituting the same proportion of these unknowns as the knowns, the outside whites would total somewhat more than 200, but not all of them were Northerners; some were foreigners.

3. Walter Allen, *Governor Chamberlain's Administration in South Carolina* (New York, 1888), 524-26; James Green, *Personal Recollections of Daniel Henry Chamberlain* (Worcester, Mass., 1908), 3-14; Chamberlain to Eli W. Blake, Jan. 27, 1866, Blake Family Collection, Yale University Library.

4. *New York Times,* Jan. 20, 1868; Peggy Lamson, *The Glorious Failure: Black Congressman Robert Brown Elliott and the Reconstruction in South Carolina* (New York, 1973), 48, 51, quoting the *Charleston Courier,* Feb. 6, 1868.

5. J. Woodruff, reporter, *Proceedings of the Constitutional Convention of South Carolina, Held at Charleston, S. C., Beginning January 14th and Ending March 17th, 1868* (2 vols., Charleston, S. C., 1868), I: 181-83, 278-79, 341-45, 414-17; II, 548-50, 620-21, 681-82, 915-18, and *passim;* Hume, "'Black and Tan' Constitutional Conventions," 431.

6. Green, *Personal Recollections,* 8, says that after becoming a South Carolina planter, Chamberlain "was also employed as a lawyer to prosecute claims in New Orleans by someone who had been stripped of his property in cotton by Government seizure." But Allen, *Governor Chamberlain's Administration,* 526, states that when Chamberlain became attorney general he "had never had a day's practice in the courts." Allen is the more reliable source, since he wrote with Chamberlain's approval and published comparatively close in time (1888) to the event. Green wrote after Chamberlain's death and published twenty years later (1908) than Allen.

7. Scott to "Sir," ———, 1866, and letters to Scott from J. M. Ashley, Jan. 30, 1867, L. C. Clifford, June 29, 1867, and A. T. Porter, July 23, 1867, Scott Papers; Abbott, *Freedmen's Bureau,* 32, 39-47.

8. D. F. Tonely to Scott, Sept. 19, 1867, Scott Papers; Abbott, *Freedmen's Bureau,* 33-34.

9. J. G. Haly to Scott, Oct. 12, 1867; G. E. Weller to Scott, Dec. 6, 1867; Adjutant General's Office, Special Order No. 521, Dec. 19, 1867; Citizens to President Johnson, no date, Scott Papers; Abbott, *Freedmen's Bureau,* 127-28, quoting the *Columbia Phoenix,* Dec. 25, 1867.

10. Letter to Scott from F. L. Cardoza, R. C. De Large, W. J. Whipper, A. J. Ransier, C. P. Leslie, W. E. Hayne, F. J. Morse, Jr., and J. H. Rainey, Mar. 6, 1868, Scott Papers.

11. E. W. Clark, Jr. to Scott, Mar. 16, 1868, Scott Papers.

12. Abbott, *Freedmen's Bureau,* 34; John S. Reynolds, *Reconstruction in South Carolina, 1865-1877* (Columbia, S.C., 1905), 93.

13. Tourgee to Mrs. Tourgee, Mar. 30, 1867, and "Schedule of debts," May 1867, Tourgée Papers; Olsen, *Carpetbagger's Crusade,* 73-75.

14. Tourgee to E. S. Worth, May 24, 1867; E. S. Worth to Tourgee, May 24, 1867; voucher for expenses as registrar, Oct. 14, 1867, Tourgée Papers; Olsen, *Carpetbagger's Crusade,* 70-73, 81-86, 90-91.

15. Jonathan Worth to Thomas Settle, Oct. 22, 1867, to R. P. Dick, Dec. 13, 1867, to C. P. Mendenhall and others, Dec. 14, 1867, to J. A. Gilmer, Dec. 15, 1867, to D. F. Caldwell and others, Jan. 6, 1868, to Henry Joyner, Jan. 7, 1868, to E. A. Jones, Jan. 7, 1868, and to E. R. S. Canby, Jan. 9, 1868, in Hamilton, *Correspondence of Jonathan Worth,* II, 1056, 1084-88, 1113-18, 1120, 1124-27.

16. Tourgee to C. W. Keough, Apr. 16, 1868, Tourgée Papers.

17. Dennett, *South as It Is,* 155; *Greensboro Times,* Feb. 27, 1868; Tourgee to Mrs. Tourgee, Jan. 17, Feb. 8, 10, Mar. 1, 4, 6, 1868, Tourgée Papers.

18. *Constitution of the State of North Carolina, Together with the Ordinances and Resolutions of the Constitutional Convention, Assembled in the City of Raleigh, Jan. 14th, 1868* (Raleigh, N.C., 1868), 113-14; Tourgee to Mrs. Tourgee, Jan. 22, 1868, and to W. M. Coleman, Feb. 4, 1868, Tourgée Papers.

19. *North Carolina Standard* (Raleigh), Jan. 17, 1868; *Raleigh Sentinel,* Jan. 28, 1868; Hume, "'Black and Tan' Constitutional Conventions," 472, 475; J. G. de Roulhac Hamilton, *Reconstruction in North Carolina* (New York, 1914), 256-57, quoting *Raleigh Sentinel,* Jan. 14, 1868, and *North Carolinian* (Raleigh), Feb. 11, 1868.

20. Tourgee to Mrs. Tourgee, Feb. 19, 1868, and draft of his Feb. 21 speech, Tourgée Papers; Olsen, *Carpetbagger's Crusade,* 96-98, 104-5.

21. Tourgee, "A Plan for the Organization of the Judiciary Department," and Tourgee to Nereus Mendenhall, Apr. 28, 1868, Tourgée papers; Hamilton *Reconstruction in North Carolina,* 263, 265; Olsen, *Carpetbagger's Crusade,* 100.

22. Tourgee to Mrs. Tourgee, Mar. 12, 13, 1868; T. A. Byrne notation, Mar. 12, 1868; Tourgee, undated "Sarcastic Resolution," Tourgée Papers; Worth to B. S. Hedrick, May 11, 1868, in Hamilton, *Correspondence of Jonathan Worth,* II, 1200-1201; Olsen, *Carpetbagger's Crusade,* 100.

23. *New York Times,* Mar. 18, 1868; Daniels, *Prince of Carpetbaggers,* 155-57.

24. Tourgee to A. G. Wilcox, Apr. 2, 1868, Tourgée Papers; *North Carolina Standard,* Feb. 4, 1868; Worth to A. M. Tomlinson and Sons, Apr. 11, 1868, in Hamilton, *Correspondence of Jonathan Worth,* II, 1185.

25. *Greensboro Times,* Feb. 20, Mar. 12, Apr. 2, 9, 16, 1868; Tourgee to D. W. Hodgin, Apr. 4, 1868, and to C. W. Keough, Apr. 16, 1868, Tourgée Papers.

26. *Raleigh Sentinel,* Mar. 27, 1868, quoted in Olsen *Carpetbagger's Crusade,* 118; Tourgee to Mrs. Tourgee, Sept. 1, 1866, to General Rutherford, Apr. 4, 1868, and to the *North Carolina Standard,* Apr. 7, 1868, Tourgée Papers.

27. Tourgee to Mrs. Tourgee, May 12, 17, 1868; Holden to Tourgee, May 12, 1868, and Holden and others to Tourgee and Harris, May 16, 1868; admission ticket, May 16, and Tourgee's note, May 16, 1868, Tourgée Papers.

Chapter 6. The Spirit of the Rebellion

1. Blanche Ames Ames, *Adelbert Ames, 1835-1933: General, Senator, Governor* (New York, 1964), 1, 4-5, 23, 61, 264-66, 294-313.

2. John J. Pullen, *The Twentieth Maine: A Volunteer Regiment in the Civil War* (Philadelphia, 1957), 1-3, 36; Ames, *Ames,* flyleaf.

3. Ames to his parents, Feb. 9, Aug. 15, 1865, Feb. 11, 1866, and Ames diary, Nov. 13, 1866, in Ames, *Ames,* 225, 228-29, 236; Ames to his parents, Mar. 24, 1866, in Blanche Butler Ames, comp., *Chronicles from the Nineteenth Century: Family Letters of Blanche Butler and Adelbert Ames* (2 vols., Clinton, Mass., 1957), I, 33.

4. Ames to his parents, Mar. 4, 1866, in Ames, *Chronicles,* I, 31; Ames to his parents, Sept. 25, 1866, in Ames, *Ames,* 234-35.

5. Ames, *Ames,* 239-41, 259-60, 264-66.

6. *Appleton's Annual Cyclopedia, 1868,* 514-15; James W. Garner, *Reconstruction in Mississippi* (New York, 1901), 213-16; Harry K. Benson. "The Public Career of Adelbert Ames, 1861-1876" (Ph.D. dissertation, University of Virginia, 1975 [facsimile, Ann Arbor, Mich., 1980]), 130-33; Harris, *Day of the Carpetbagger,* 52-53, 190-96.

7. Morgan, *Yazoo,* 164-66; John Tyler to D. W. White, Oct. 14, 1868, Freedmen's Bureau Records.

8. Morgan, *Yazoo,* 184, 198; Dick Scott to Alvan C. Gillem, July 10, 1868, Freedmen's Bureau Records.

9. D. W. White to S. C. Green, June 1, 1868; Harry Gilmore and others to A. C. Gillem, June ——, 1868, Freedmen's Bureau Records; Court Martial Orders No. 28, July 28, 1868; Robert Webb and others to Gilem, Aug. ——, 1868, Records of the Fourth Military District.

10. U. Ozanne to Thaddeus Stevens, July 9, 1868, Stevens Papers.

11. W. H. Gibbs to E. B. Washburne, Jan. 18, 29, Feb. 21, Mar. 11, June 30, 1868, Washburne papers. See also C. F. Johnson to Washburne, July 2, 1868: "Knowing that you are in constant communication with the Genl commanding the U. S. army I take the liberty to ask you to lay these facts before him."

12. Lillian A. Pereyra, *James Lusk Alcorn, Persistent Whig* (Baton Rouge, La., 1966), 3-5, 39-55; David Donald, "The Scalawag in Mississippi Reconstruction," *Journal of Southern History* X (Nov. 1944), 447-60.

13. J. L. Alcorn to E. B. Washburne, June 29, 1868, Jan. 1, 1869, Washburne Papers. On Forrest, see the *Cincinnati Commercial* interview with him, Aug. 28, 1868, in *Report of the Joint Committee to Inquire into the Condition of Affairs in the Late Insurrectionary States* (13 vols., Washington, D.C., 1872), XIII, 32-34. On the origin and nature of the Klan, see Allen W. Trelease, *White Terror: The Ku Klux Klan Conspiracy and Southern Reconstruction* (New York, 1971), xv-xlviii, 3-27.

14. "Bloody Knights Ku Klux Klan" to Warmoth, Apr. 27, 1868, Warmoth Papers; Warmoth, *War, Politics and Reconstruction,* 79-81; Taylor, *Louisiana Reconstructed,* 33, 141, 173-74.

15. Harris, "Warmoth," 30-34; Binning, "Warmoth," 122-23; Taylor, *Louisiana Reconstructed,* 174.

16. John E. Gonzales, "William Pitt Kellogg, Reconstruction Governor of Louisiana, 1873-1877," *Louisiana Historical Quarterly* XXIX (Apr. 1946), 2-6.

17. John Hay to Warmoth, July 12, 1868; Kellogg to Warmoth, July 30, 1868, Warmoth Papers.

18. James G. Blaine, *Twenty Years of Congress: From Lincoln to Garfield* (2 vols., Norwich, Conn., 1884-86), II, 400-404.

19. Kellogg to Warmoth, July 30, 1868, Warmoth Papers; Trelease, *White Terror,* 98; Harris, "Warmoth," 34-42.

20. *New York World,* Sept. 30, 1868, quoted in Davis, *Civil War and Reconstruction in Florida,* 482.

21. *Harper's Weekly* XII (Aug. 22, Sept. 12, Oct. 3, 1868), 581, 589, 627.

22. Harris, "Warmoth," 36-37, 42-50; Taylor, *Louisiana Reconstructed,* 173-79; Trelease, *White Terror,* 132-36; James E. Sefton, *The United States Army and Reconstruction, 1865-1877* (Baton Rouge, La., 1967), 213-16.

23. Hahn to Washburne, Oct. 21, 1868, Washburne Papers; L. A. Sheldon to James A. Garfield, Nov. 4, 1868, James A. Garfield Papers, Library of Congress.

24. Kellogg to Warmoth, Dec. 22, 1868, Jan. 4, 17, 1868, Warmoth Papers.

Chapter 7. Turbulent and Lawless Men

1. Orval T. Driggs, "The Issues of the Powell Clayton Regime, 1868-1871," *Arkansas Historical Quarterly* VIII (Spring 1949), 14; John M. Harrell, *The Brooks and Baxter War: A History of the Reconstruction Period in Arkansas* (St. Louis, Mo., 1893), 46-47.

2. *National Cyclopaedia of American Biography,* XII, 262; Harrell, *Brooks and Baxter War,* 50-51.

3. James B. Bradford, report, Jan. 13, 1863; J. S. Marmaduke to G. F. Belton, Oct. 26, 1863; Nathan Kimball to Powell Clayton, Apr. 5, 1864; John Levering to Clayton, Apr. 19, May 16, 1865; Clayton, report, Oct. 27, 1863; Clayton to Levering, Feb. 12, May 22, 1865, in *The War of the Rebellion: A Compilation of the Official Records of the Union and Confederate Armies* (128 vols., Washington, D.C., 1880-1901), series I, vol. XXII, part I, pp. 215, 723-24, 730; vol. XXXIV, part III, p. 49; vol. XLVIII, part I, p. 827; part II, pp. 135, 467, 542.

4. Powell Clayton, *The Aftermath of the Civil War in Arkansas* (New York, 1915), 298-99; Harrell, *Brooks and Baxter War,* 68-69; Trowbridge, *The South,* 391.

5. Clayton, *Aftermath of the Civil War,* 29-31; Reid, *After the War,* 426; Thomas S. Staples, *Reconstruciton in Arkansas, 1862-1874* (New York, 1923), 86-87; J. W. Sprague to John Sherman, Mar. 29, Apr. 4, 1866, Sherman Papers; J. W. Mallet to Thaddeus Stevens, May 28, 1866, Stevens Papers.

6. Clayton, *Aftermath of the Civil War,* 29-31, 299; Driggs, "Powell Clayton Regime," 9-10; Staples, *Reconstruction in Arkansas,* 373.

7. Clayton, *Aftermath of the Civil War,* 13-15, 38-49, 237-41.

8. Driggs, "Powell Clayton Regime," 17-18; Staples, *Reconstruction in Arkansas,* 220-21; Harrell, *Brooks and Baxter War,* 45-47, 61-62; *Chicago Tribune,* Dec. 18, 1867; Clayton, *Aftermath of the Civil War,* 307-8, quoting *Arkansas Gazette,* Aug. 8, 1868.

9. Driggs, "Powell Clayton Regime," 19-20; Clayton, *Aftermath of the Civil War,* 73-74; letters to Clayton from W. Beasley, Aug. 29, 1868; E. H. Mix, Sept. 2, 1868; D. C. Gordon, Sept. 6, 1868; John Havis, Sept. 8, 1868, Governor's Letters Received (Letterbook), Arkansas Historical Commission, Little Rock.

10. Clayton, *Aftermath of the Civil War,* 57-58, 61-63, 73-87; *Testimony Taken by the Joint Select Committee to Inquire into the Condition of Affairs in the Late Insurrectionary States: Arkansas* (Washington, D.C., 1872), 358-98.

11. Clayton, *Aftermath of the Civil War,* 50-51, 96-97, 102-4; Driggs, "Powell Clayton Regime," 21; letters to Clayton from W. P. Anderson, Aug. 31, 1868; W. Hodges, Sept. 22, 1868; D. P. Upham, Oct. 4, 1868; J. Cregan, Oct. 4, 1868; W. E. Spear, Oct. 5, 1868, Governor's Letters Received.

12. Sam Houston to Clayton, Oct. 17, 1868, Governor's Letters Received; Clayton, *Aftermath of the Civil War,* 106-11; John T. Morse, Jr., ed., *Diary of Gideon Welles* (3 vols., Boston, 1911), III, 460-62.

13. Letters to Clayton from J. J. Littleton, Oct. 17, 1868; C. H. Smith, Oct. 30,

Nov. 3, 1868; J. Cregan, Nov. 4, 1868, Governor's Letters Received; *New York Times,* Feb. 1, 1869; Clayton, *Aftermath of the Civil War,* 110-11; Driggs, "Powell Clayton Regime," 22-27.

14. Letters to Clayton from W. Brian, Nov. 6, 1868; J. H. Wilson, Dec. 1, 16, 1868; J. L. Matthews, Dec. 4, 9, 1868; R. F. Catterson, Dec. 7, 1868; D. H. Upham, Dec. 9, 1868; R. L. Archer, Dec. 26, 1868, Governor's Letters Received; telegrams from D. P. Upham, Dec. 19, 1868; K. Danforth, Jan. 20, 1869; E. M. Main, Feb. 15, 1869; G. A. Davis, Feb. 23, 1869; J. M. Brown, Feb. 24, 26, 1869, in a scrapbook labeled "Brooks-Baxter War Telegrams," Arkansas Historical Commission, Little Rock; Clayton, *Aftermath of the Civil War,* 111-28, 137-44.

15. B. F. Rice to Clayton, Nov. 23, 24, 1868, Governor's Letters Received; telegrams to Clayton from B. F. Rice, L. H. Roots, and T. Boles, Jan. 16, 1869, and from J. T. Elliott and L. H. Roots, Jan. 20, 1869, in Brooks-Baxter War scrapbook; *The Nation,* Jan. 7, 1869; Driggs, "Powell Clayton Regime," 28-30; Staples, *Reconstruction in Arkansas,* 374.

16. *The Nation* VI (May 14, 1868), 382. In addition to four of the six states admitted in 1868, the state of Georgia (admitted and then expelled) had a Northern-born man as its newly elected governor. But New York native Rufus B. Bullock had been living in the South before the war and had served in the Confederate army. He therefore should be considered a scalawag rather than a carpetbagger. C. Mildred Thompson, *Reconstruction in Georgia: Economic, Social, Political, 1865-1872* (New York, 1915), 217.

17. W. A. Wright to Scott, July 2, 1868; R. A. Thompson to Scott, July 15, 1868, Scott Papers; *New York Times,* Apr. 25, 1871; Trowbridge, *The South,* 563-64; King, *The Great South,* II, 458-59; Francis B. Simkins and Robert H. Woody, *South Carolina During Reconstruction* (Chapel Hill, N.C., 1932), 113-14; Lamson, *Glorious Failure,* 68-69, 71-72.

18. R. W. Shand to Scott, July 22, 1868; E. F. Whittlesey to Scott, July 24, 1868, Scott Papers; Abbott, *Freedmen's Bureau,* 21, 47-48.

19. Letters to Scott from E. L. Dawes, Aug. 6, 1868; F. J. Moses, Jr., Aug. 13, 1868; D. H. Silcox, Aug. 31, 1868; W. Levinson, Sept. 21, 1868; Scott to Mr. French, Sept. 12, 1868, Scott Papers; R. H. Woody, "Franklin J. Moses, Jr., Scalawag Governor of South Carolina, 1872-74," *North Carolina Historical Review* X (Apr. 1933), 112-15. In 1869 Scott reported real property worth $100,000 and personal property worth $200,000, according to the manuscript federal census for 1870.

20. R. Jones and others to Scott, July 4, 1868; T. L. Tullock to Scott, Oct. 20, 1868; Scott, drafts of proclamations, Aug. 2, 4; Scott to "Dear Genl," Sept 16, 1868, Scott Papers.

21. J. M. Morris to Scott, Oct. 19, 1868; T. L. Tullock to Scott, Oct. 22, 1868, Scott Papers; *Memoirs of William T. Sherman* (2 vols., 1874; Bloomington, Ind., 1957), II, 286-87; Blaine, *Twenty Years of Congress,* II, 397, 400-401; Manly Wade Wellman, *Giant in Gray: A Biography of Wade Hampton of South Carolina* (New York, 1949), 227, 236, 253, 260; Mark M. Boatner III, *The Civil War Dictionary* (New York, 1959), 157.

22. T. J. Mackey to Scott, Oct. 20, 1868; J. V. Meigs to Scott, Oct. 20, 1868; Scott to ——, Oct. 20, 1870; Scott to Messrs. Ransier, Cardozo, and Nash, Oct. 20, 1870, Scott Papers; *Columbia Phoenix,* Oct. 18, 23, 1868, quoted in *Testimony Taken by the Joint Select Committee to Inquire into the Condition of Affairs in the Late Insurrectionary States: South Carolina* (Washington, D. C., 1872), 1248-50; *Report of*

the Joint Investigating Committee on Public Frauds . . . to the General Assembly of South Carolina (Columbia, S.C., 1878), 713; Lamson, *Glorious Failure,* 83-84.

23. Letters to E. B. Washburne from Liberty Billings, June 7, 1868; G. W. Atwood, June 8, 1868; Samuel Walker, June 12, 20, 1868, Washburne Papers; Davis, *Civil War and Reconstruction in Florida,* 531-32.

24. D. Richards to Washburne, May 18, July 19, 1868, Washburne Papers; Davis, *Civil War and Reconstruction in Florida,* 533-36, 542-44, 651; Wallace, *Carpetbag Rule,* 81, 85-87.

25. Davis, *Civil War and Reconstruction in Florida,* 540-41, 544-46, 577-64; Wallace, *Carpetbag Rule,* 86n; Shofner, *Nor Is It Over Yet,* 194-96, 198-99, 203, 225.

26. Davis, *Civil War and Reconstruction in Florida,* 543n, 546-56, 567; Wallace, *Carpetbag Rule,* 87-94; Shofner, *Nor Is It Over Yet,* 204-5.

Chapter 8. Some Good and Some Bad

1. Warner to Willard Warner III, July 3, Dec. 16, 1868; W. T. Sherman to Warner, Aug. 9, 1868, Warner Papers.

2. *Montgomery Advertiser,* July 28, 1868, quoted in John B. Ryan, Jr., "Willard Warner: Soldier, Senator, and Southern Entrepreneur" (Master's thesis, Auburn University, 1971), 55-56; Warner testimony, June 3, 1871, in *Testimony Taken by the Joint Select Committee to Inquire into the Condition of Affairs in the Late Insurrectionary States: Alabama* (Washington, D.C., 1872), 2, 29-30, hereafter cited as *Ku Klux Report: Alabama.*

3. *Congressional Globe,* 40 Cong., 3 sess., pp. 85-86, 553, 861-62; *Montgomery Advertiser,* Feb. 16, 1869, quoted in Ryan, "Warner," 63.

4. Cash, "Alabama Republicans," 211-12; Ryan, "Warner," 64-67, quoting *Montgomery Advertiser,* May 11, 1869. In the Senate Warner said on March 3, 1871: "Senator Spencer's written recommendation of Judge Woods is now on file in the office of the Attorney General." *Congressional Globe,* 41 Cong., 3 sess., appendix, p. 274. When Warner, before his election as senator, was seeking a job as secretary of the Senate, Spencer's close friend Congressman Grenville M. Dodge joined a group of his colleagues in recommending Warner. Robert Schenck and others to John Sherman June 3, 1868, Warner Papers.

5. W. T. Sherman to W. B. Woods, June 23, 1868; Sherman to Warner, May 28, 1870, Warner papers.

6. *Congressional Globe,* 40 Cong., 3 sess., pp. 1089-90; 41 Cong., 2 sess., pp. 788-89, 4643, 4719-22, 5278, 5281; Ryan, "Warner," 63-64.

7. *Congressional Globe,* 41 Cong., 2 sess., pp. 1358-60, 2018-20, 2810-13.

8. Warner to John Sherman, Aug. 23, 1870, Sherman Papers; Cash, "Alabama Republicans," 361-62; Wiggins, *Scalawag in Alabama Politics,* 66.

9. Loren Schweninger, *James T. Rapier and Reconstruction* (Chicago, Ill., 1978), xiii, 75-76; Cash, "Alabama Republicans," 280-82; Wiggins, *Scalawag in Alabama Politics,* 57, 63-64, 66.

10. Sefton, *United States Army and Reconstruction,* 232-33.

11. Schweninger, *Rapier,* 79; Wiggins, *Scalawag in Alabama Politics,* 65.

12. Testimony of William Miller, Charles Hays, Willard Warner, and Arthur A. Smith, *Ku Klux Report: Alabama,* I, 2-5, 14-15, 25-29, 38, 45; Warner, remarks in the Senate, *Congressional Globe,* 41 Cong., 3 sess., pp. 570-76.

13. U. S. Grant to C. W. Buckley, Nov. 21, 1870, Warner Papers; Sch-

weninger, *Rapier*, 79-82; Wiggins, *Scalawag in Alabama Politics*, 66-68; Ryan, "Warner," 83-87.

14. *Congressional Globe*, 41 Cong., 3 sess., pp. 570-76, 2002; appendix, pp. 268-77; Ryan, "Warner," 88-89.

15. *Ku Klux Report: Alabama*, I, 30-31, 34-35.

16. Warner to Willard Warner III, May 5, 1871, Warner Papers.

17. Spencer and others to Grant, Mar. 7, 1871; C. H. Wilson to Boutwell, June 24, 1871; J. P. Sibley to Boutwell, June 25, 1871, General Records of the Treasury Department, National Archives; John Sherman to Warner, May 20, 1871; J. D. Cox to Warner, May 30, June 9, 1871, Warner Papers; Wiggins, *Scalawag in Alabama Politics*, 77-78; Ryan, "Warner," 91-92.

18. Rapier to Boutwell, June 25, 1871; Spencer to Grant, July 6, 1871, General Records of the Treasury Department.

19. Warner to Mrs. Lyman Warner, Nov. 18, 1871, Warner Papers; Rapier to Spencer, Dec. 9, 1871, General Records of the Treasury Department; *Ku Klux Report: Alabama*, II, 887-88; Cash, "Alabama Republicans," 212-14. A Union veteran in Huntsville, arguing for Warner, blamed Spencer for "the *sending* of a *Democrat* to the U. S. Senate and the defeating of Mr. Warner and the cause of the *split* in the *Republican party* and its defeat." D. J. Burke to James A. Garfield, Dec. 18, 1871, Garfield Papers.

20. O. C. Rugg to Spencer, Jan. 4, 1872, General Records of the Treasury Department; Sherman to Warner, Jan. 24, 1872, Warner Papers; Wiggins, *Scalawag in Alabama Politics*, 78; Ryan, "Warner," 92-97.

Chapter 9. The War Still Exists

1. Garner, *Reconstruction in Mississippi*, 228-36; Harris, *Day of the Carpetbagger*, 52-57; Benson, "Ames," 135-41.

2. Harris, *Day of the Carpetbagger*, 58-62; O. H. Clapp to James A. Garfield, July 10, 1869, Garfield Papers.

3. Garner, *Reconstruction in Mississippi*, 233, 237-40; Harris, *Day of the Carpetbagger* 232-36; O. H. Clapp to Garfield, Aug. 9, 1859, Garfield Papers.

4. Ames to John Sherman, Aug. 17, 1869, John Sherman Papers; Ames to William T. Sherman, Aug. 17, 1869, William T. Sherman Papers, Library of Congress.

5. Garner, *Reconstruction in Mississippi*, 243-44; Benson, "Ames," 145-50, quoting Ames to the Adjutant General, Nov. 14, 1869.

6. O. H. Clapp to Garfield, Dec. 8, 1869, Garfield Papers; Pereyra, *Alcorn*, 102-3; Garner, *Reconstruction in Mississippi*, 245-47; Harris, *Day of the Carpetbagger*, 253-57.

7. Affidavits of S. G. Bedwell, Sept. 7, 1880, and I. N. Osborn, July 6, 1881, Pension Records.

8. F. E. Franklin to William Attwood, Apr. 15, 1869, Army Records of the Fourth Military District; Morgan, *Yazoo*, 258-60.

9. James J. B. White to Ames, July 12, 1869, Army Records of the Fourth Military District; Morgan, *Yazoo*, 402-4, 410-12.

10. D. W. Vance to William Attwood, Dec. 4, 1869, Army Records of the Fourth Military District; Morgan, *Yazoo*, 363-65.

11. Garner, *Reconstruction in Mississippi,* 269-71, 281-86; Harris, *Day of the Carpetbagger,* 264, 312-15, 438-40.

12. Morgan, *Yazoo,* 343-56; Morgan, declaration, Mar. 17, 1898, May 23, 1922, Pension Records; *Mississippi in 1875: Report of the Select Committee to Inquire into the Mississippi Election of 1875* (44 Cong., 1 sess., Senate Report no. 527, 2 vols., Washington, D.C., 1876), II, 1695.

13. Harris, *Day of the Carpetbagger,* 324-25, 425-26, 475.

14. Ames, *Ames,* 294-313; Garner, *Reconstruction in Mississippi,* 271, 274-75.

15. *Congressional Globe,* 41 Cong., 2 sess., pp. 2122-23, 2125-35, 2156-69, 2303-16, 2340-49; Ames, testimony, Apr. 27, 1876, *Mississippi in 1875,* I, 17.

16. Ames, *Ames,* 314-30; Ames, *Chronicles,* I, 148, 158, 202, 216, 219-20, 281.

17. Ames, *Ames,* 331-34; Robert Somers, *The Southern States since the War, 1870-71* (1871; University, Ala., 1965), 153-54; Garner, *Reconstruction in Mississippi,* 340-51; Harris, *Day of the Carpetbagger,* 396-99.

18. Ames, *Ames,* 335-42, 346; Pereyra, *Alcorn,* 136-40; *Congressional Globe,* 42 Cong., 1 sess., pp. 406, 569-71; appendix, pp. 117-34.

19. Ames, *Ames,* 347-49; Ames, *Chronicles,* I, 298-91, 308, 313, 341-42; Pereyra, *Alcorn,* 130-33, 141-42; Harris, *Day of the Carpetbagger,* 307-10, 399-405.

20. Ames, *Chronicles,* I, 332, 342-45, 350-51; Pereyra, *Alcorn,* 144-45, 149-50; Garner, *Reconstruction in Mississippi,* 280-81, 291-92; Harris, *Day of the Carpetbagger,* 413-29.

21. *Congressional Globe,* 42 Cong., 2 sess., appendix, pp. 393-96, 402-11; Ames, *Ames,* 367, 369, Pereyra, *Alcorn,* 144-45, 151-53; Garner, *Reconstruction in Mississippi,* 344.

Chapter 10. Juries Are All Ku Klux

1. J. H. Marsh to Mrs. Tourgee, Dec. 21, 1868; Tourgee to J. A. Gray, May 8, 1869; Tourgee to Mrs. Tourgee, May 19, Nov. 21, 1869; H. H. McKethan & Sons to Tourgee, May 26, 1869; M. W. Churchill to Tourgee, May 26, 1869; indentures for the purchase of real estate, Apr. 16, Aug. 21, Dec. 18, 21, 1869, Tourgée Papers.

2. Letters to Tourgee from J. C. Blake, Sept. 25, 1868; G. W. Swepson, Sept. 26, 1868, Jan. 8, 1870, Nov. 20, 1871; C. Dewey, Sept. 29, 1868; J. Rosenthal, Sept. 30, 1868; M. S. Littlefield, May 31, 1869; G. O. Spooner, June 2, 1869; J. J. Bruner, Sept. 16, 1869; Tourgee to Swepson, Jan. 25, 1869; Tourgee to Mrs. Tourgee, May 10, 1869; notice of protest of draft, May 25, 1869; printed notice of "Memorial Ceremonies of the 20th of May," 1869, Tourgée Papers.

3. Tourgee to Mrs. Tourgee, Nov. 18, 19, Dec. 1, 3, 1868, Apr. 13, 28, May 16, 1869, Tourgée Papers.

4. Olsen, *Carpetbagger's Crusade,* 130-32, 137-39, 141.

5. Tourgee to Mrs. Tourgee, Mar. 18, May 13, 14, 1869; S. Pool to Tourgee, Aug. 21, Sept. 16 1869, Tourgée papers; *Raleigh Sentinel,* Apr. 20, 1869, quoted in Olsen, *Carpetbagger's Crusade,* 146.

6. Tourgee, *A Royal Gentleman* (New York, 1881), iii-vii, 310-11, and *passim;* Editor of the Drawer, *Harper's Magazine,* to Tourgee, Mar. 27, 1869; R. M. Tuttle to Tourgee, Nov. 26, 1869, Tourgée Papers. *A Royal Gentleman* was a revised version of *Toinette,* which was published in 1874.

7. "The Slave's Wages," an address to "Freedman Celebration Greensboro, N. C.," Jan. 1, 1870, Tourgée Papers.

8. A. Rankin to Tourgee, July 23, 1868; Thomas Settle to Tourgee, Aug. 8, 1868, Tourgée Papers; Trelease, *White Terror,* 193.

9. *Greensboro Patriot,* Sept. 10, 1868, quoted in Olsen, *Carpetbagger's Crusade,* 145; Tourgee to Mrs. Tourgee, Dec. 3, 1868, May 16, 1869; James McCleery to Tourgee, May 24, 1869; V. C. Barringer to Tourgee, Oct. 4, 1869, Tourgée Papers.

10. Daniels, *Prince of Carpetbaggers,* 190-91; Beth G. Crabtree and James W. Patton, eds., *"Journal of a Secesh Lady": The Diary of Catherine Ann Devereux Edmondston, 1860-1866* (Raleigh, N.C., 1979), xxxiv, 160, 272, 735; Trelease, *White Terror,* 206-7.

11. *Raleigh Sentinel,* May 4, 1869, cited in Olsen *Carpetbagger's Crusade,* 146; undated note (1869) by Tourgee; Tourgee to Mrs. Tourgee, Apr. 28, 1869; Tourgee to editor of *Greensboro Register,* Sept. 6, 1869, and to editor of *North Carolina Standard,* Jan 28, 1870; undated clipping from *Greensboro Patriot,* Tourgée Papers.

12. Olsen, *Carpetbagger's Crusade,* 150-53; Trelease, *White Terror,* 194; Tourgee to Mrs. Tourgee, June 9, 1869, Tourgée Papers.

13. Letters to Tourgee from Thomas Settle, May 12, 1869; W. W. Holden, May 20, 1869; A. L. Murdock, Aug. 7, 1869; Tourgee, "Ku Klux War in North Carolina," Aug. 1870 (written for the *National Standard* of New York but rejected as too long), Tourgée Papers; Tourgee to Thomas Settle, June 24, 1869, Thomas Settle Papers, Southern Historical Collection, University of North Carolina Library, Chapel Hill; Trelease, *White Terror,* 194-95, 205, 209-10.

14. J. W. Stephens to Tourgee, Apr. 20, 1870; John Pool to Tourgee, May 31, 1870; Tourgee, "Ku Klux War in North Carolina," Aug. 1870; Tourgee to editor of *New York Tribune,* Aug. 5, 1870; statement of Patsie Burton to J. G. Hester, Dec. 12, 1872; affidavit of J. G. Hester, Dec. 14, 1872, Tourgée Papers; Olsen, *Carpetbagger's Crusade,* 160-66; Trelease, *White Terror,* 213-15; Hamilton, *Reconstruction in North Carolina,* 499-500, 516, 521-22, 525-26.

15. Tourgee to editor of *New York Tribune,* Aug. 5, 1870; to Joseph C. Abbott, Aug. 5, 15, 1870; to W. W. Holden, Aug. 5, 12, 1870; to U. S. Grant, Aug. 13, 1870; to "My Dear Joe," Sept. 5, 1870; Holden to Tourgee, Aug. 13, 1870; Abbott to Tourgee, Aug. 13, 1870, Tourgée Papers; Olsen, *Carpetbagger's Crusade,* 158.

16. Ralph Gorrell, C. P. Mendenhall, and L. M. Scott to Tourgee, Aug. 15, 1870; Allen Rutherford to Tourgee, Aug. 27, Oct. 15, 1870; Thomas Settle to Tourgee, Sept. 7, 1870; Tourgee to Gorrell, Mendenhall, and Scott, Aug. 16, 1870; to "My Dear Joe," Sept. 5, 1870; to "My Dear Friend," Sept. 7, 1870, Tourgée Papers.

17. Martha F. Stephens to Tourgee, July 20, Sept. 29, 1870; W. W. Holden to Tourgee, Nov. 14, 1870; W. W. Holden to Tourgee, Nov. 14, 1870; Tourgee to Martha F. Stephens, Aug. 12, 1870; to Mrs. Tourgee, Oct. 3, 5, Nov. 1, 1870, to R. Gorell [Nov. 1870]; to V. C. Barringer, Jan. 26, 1871, Tourgée Papers; Olsen, *Carpetbagger's Crusade,* 139; Hamilton, *Reconstruction in North Carolina,* 541-58.

18. Mrs. Tourgee to Tourgee, July 20, Nov. 4, 12, 14, 1870; Tourgee to Mrs. Tourgee, Sept. 24, Nov. 13, 15, Dec. 20, 1870; Angie Tourgee to Tourgee, Oct. 31 1870, Tourgée Papers.

19. G. W. Swepson to Tourgee, Dec. 31, 1870, Jan. 5, 1871; Tourgee to Swepson, Jan. 2, 7, 1871; to G. W. Welker, Jan. 7, 1871; to chairman, Caswell County commissioners, Jan. 7, 1871; to S. S. Ashley, Jan. 26, Feb. 7, 22, 26, 1871; to J. C.

Abbott, Jan. 26, 27, Feb. 6, 10, 15, 1871; to William Mebane, Jan. 28, 1871, Tourgée Papers.

20. Tourgee to J. C. Abbott, Jan. 27, Feb. 8, 1871; to Mrs. Tourgee, Dec. 18, 1871, Jan. 10, 15, 19, Feb. 20, Mar. 20, 1872; to U. S. Grant, Dec. 28, 1871; to Alexander McIver, Feb. 19, 1872; Mrs. Tourgee to Angie Tourgee, Jan. 29, 1872, Tourgée Papers; Olsen, *Carpetbagger's Crusade,* 184-86.

Chapter 11. The Best-Abused Man

1. *New York Times,* Apr. 25, 1871; *Report on Public Frauds, South Carolina,* 188-89, 789, 865-67; *North American Review* CLXXXVI (Oct. 1907), 181; King, *The Great South,* II, 460.

2. W. Sheffield to Scott, Oct. 11, 1871, Scott Papers; F. W. McMaster to Scott, Jan. 4, 1881, and Scott's testimony in Haag, *Ohio Versus Scott,* 15, 149, 166-67; *Napoleon Democrat Northwest,* Aug. 16, 1900; Lamson, *Glorious Failure,* 108-9.

3. Letters to Scott from H. V. Sweringen, Nov. 20, 1868; J. G. Haley, Nov. 4, 1869, Oct. 26, 31, Dec. 6, 1871; W. Sheppard, Nov. 29, 1869; W. Sheffield, Oct. 11, 1871; E. W. Seibels & Co., Apr. 19, 1872, Scott Papers.

4. Letters to Scott from Pressley, Lord & Inglesby, Jan. 21, 1869; C. T. Chase, Apr. 11, 1869; E. Shiver, June 8, 1869; I. I. Stoney, Oct. 24, 1869; J. Holmes and others, Apr. 5, 1870; T. W. Parmele, May 11, 27, 1872; Scott to F. W. McMaster, Apr. 26, 1878; assignment, W. J. Whipper to Scott, Sept. 19, 1869; agreement, T. W. Parmele and Scott, Aug. 13, 1870; agreement, W. W. Hicks and others, Aug. 15, 1870, Scott Papers; Lamson, *Glorious Failure,* 95.

5. Letters to Scott from M. F. Force, Oct. 3, 1868; Grace G. Cochran, June 9, 1869; Win Hood, Nov. 26, 1869; E. P. Alexander, Oct. 1, 1871; G. J. Patterson, Apr. 13, 1872; Wilberforce University, June 1, 1872, Scott Papers.

6. Durbin Ward to Scott, June 11, 1869; W. N. Marsh to Scott, July 31, Sept. 11, 14, 1869; Scott to Henry Clews & Co., Aug. 5, 1870, Scott Papers; Simkins and Woody, *South Carolina during Reconstruction,* 152-55, 208-22.

7. Letters to H. H. Kimpton from C. Vibbard, Apr. 1, 1868, from S. B. White, May 7, 1978, and from several other references; letters to Scott from O. Ferriss (endorsed by John A. Bingham and Thaddeus Stevens), May 11, 1868; R. C. Fenton, May 2, 1868; J. H. Godman, June 8, 1868, Scott Papers; *New York Times,* July 17, 1869; Simkins and Woody, *South Carolina during Reconstruction,* 175-79; F. A. Porcher, "Last Chapter of Reconstruction in South Carolina," *Southern Historical Society Papers* XII (Apr. 1884), 193-95.

8. Letters to Scott from A. Simonds, July 24, Aug. 3, 1868; C. Dewey, Sept. 21, 1868; F. A. Sawyer, Nov. 14, 1868; H. H. Kimpton, Sept. 14, 1869; Henry Clews, Nov. 23, 1869; promissory note, Scott to W. C. Breese, Dec. 19, 1868, Scott Papers; Simkins and Woody, *South Carolina during Reconstruction,* 164, quoting *Charleston News,* n. d.

9. Letters to Scott from J. W. Harrison, Dec. 28, 1868; J. J. Patterson, Sept. 25, 29, 1869; H. H. Kimpton, Sept. 10, 16, 1870; agreement, Scott *et al.* and Patterson *et al.,* July 10, Aug. 9, 1869, Scott Papers; Simkins and Woody, *South Carolina during Reconstruction, 200-8.*

10. Chamberlain to Kimpton, Jan. 5, 1870, quoted in Reynolds, *Reconstruction in South Carolina,* 465-66; N. G. Parker to Scott, Sept. 12, 1870, Scott papers; *Report on Public Frauds, South Carolina,* 849-51, 857-60.

11. *New York Times,* Nov. 21, 1870; Lerone Bennett, Jr., *Black Power U. S. A.:*

The Human Side of Reconstruction, 1867-1877 (Baltimore, Md., 1969), 157-58; Carol K. R. Bleser, *The Promised Land: A History of the South Carolina Land Commission, 1869-1890* (Columbia, S.C., 1969), 28-42, 45, 57-65.

12. H. H. Kimpton to Scott, Apr. 9, 1870, quoting Scott's telegram to Kimpton, Scott Papers; D. M. Porter to Chamberlain, June 6, 1870, and to Parker, June 6, 1870, Samuel Dibble Papers, Duke University Library; Bleser, *Promised Land,* 51-52, 54-65, 69-70, 74-76.

13. Scott to B. F. Whittemore, Jan. 30, 1869; Scott and F. L. Cardozo, document appointing F. J. Moses, July 13, 1869; Y. J. P. Owens to Scott, June 9, 1870; F. A. Townsend to Scott, Sept. 22, 1870, Scott papers; Moses, agreements, Aug. 7, 1869; H. H. Jackson to J. B. Hubbard; B. G. Yocum to Hubbard, Sept. 2, 1870; Moses and L. T. Levin testimony, *Report on Public Frauds, South Carolina,* 674-75, 677-78, 686, 696-704.

14. Letters to Scott from E. Whittlesey, May 4, 1869; N. T. Spencer, Apr. 3, 1870; R. J. Donaldson, Apr. 22, 1870, Scott Papers; Dawson, Woodruff, and Hubbard testimony, 1877, *Report on Public Frauds, South Carolina,* 215-20, 281, 324, 327, 730-31; *Testimony Taken by the Joint Select Committee to Inquire into the Condition of Affairs in the Late Insurrectionary States: South Carolina* (3 vols., Washington, D.C., 1872), I, 258-59; *New York Times,* Nov. 21, 1870.

15. B. G. Whittemore to Scott, June 17, 1870, Scott Papers; *New York Times,* Nov. 21, 1870; Bleser, *Promised Land,* 35-36; Lamson, *Glorious Failure,* 111-14; Bennett, *Black Power U. S. A.,* 188-89; Robert H. Woody, "The South Carolina Election of 1870," *North Carolina Historical Review* VIII (Apr. 1931), 168-86; Wilton B. Fowler, "A Carpetbagger's Conversion to White Supremacy," *North Carolina Historical Review* XLIII (Summer 1966), 288.

16. Scott to Grant, Mar. 16, 1871, Scott Papers; Somers, *Southern States since the War,* 57-58; Lamson, *Glorious Failure,* 113-14, 125-26; William B. Hesseltine, *U. S. Grant, Politician* (New York, 1935), 245.

17. J. W. Harrison to Scott, Apr. 22, 1870; agreement of Scott and others to sell the state-owned Blue Ridge stock to Harrison and others, Nov. 17, 1870; Scott to J. C. Jacobsohn, Jan. 21, 1871, Scott Papers; Scott testimony, 1877, *Report on Public Frauds, South Carolina,* 857-60; Simkins and Woody, *South Carolina during Reconstruction,* 208-22; E. Culpepper Clark, *Francis Warrington Dawson and the Politics of Restoration: South Carolina, 1874-1889* (University, Ala., 1980), 47n.

18. J. W. Harrison to Scott, Aug. 16, 1870, Scott Papers; B. F. Perry to Scott, Mar. 13, 1871, quoted in *Southern Historical Society Papers,* XII, 175-77; *New York Times,* Apr. 25, 1871; *Cincinnati Gazette,* n. d., quoted in *Congressional Globe,* 42 Cong., 1 sess., appendix, p. 124 (Apr. 3, 1871); *Charleston Republican,* May 8, 1871, quoted in *Ku Klux Report: South Carolina,* II, 1250-53; Simkins and Woody, *South Carolina during Reconstruction,* 155-57.

19. Chamberlain to Kimpton, Apr. 23, 1871, quoted in *New York Sun,* Feb. 11, 1878, clipping in the Francis W. Dawson Papers, Duke University Library; Proceedings of the Tax-Payers' Convention, Columbia, May 9-12, 1871, in *Ku Klux Report: South Carolina,* I, 472-75, 486, 492-95, 503, 511; Joel Williamson, *After Slavery: The Negro in South Carolina during Reconstruction, 1861-1877* (1965; New York, 1975), 384.

20. Chamberlain's testimony, June 10, 1871, *Ku Klux Report: South Carolina,* I, 48-49, 52k-53, 57; Scott's testimony, July 9, 1877, and Scott to H. G. Worthington, Sept. 22, 1871, *Report on Public Frauds, South Garolina,* 656-57, 663; Trelease, *White Terror,* 406-7.

21. Letters to Scott from H. H. Kimpton, Oct. 4, 1871; G. W. Waterman, Oct. 17, 1871; N. G. Parker, Nov. 16, 1871; Scott to Kimpton, Oct. 11, 1871; to J. L. Neagle, Oct. 11, 1871; to President, American Banknote Company, Nov. 24, 1871, Scott Papers; testimony of R. B. Carpenter, July 8, 1871, *Ku Klux Report: South Carolina,* I, 227.

22. G. E. Welles to Scott, Dec. 14, 1871; Scott to F. W. McMaster, Apr. 6, 1878, Scott Papers; testimony of Scott, Parker, and Moses, 1877, *Report on Public Frauds, South Carolina,* 583-96.

23. Kimpton to Scott, Apr. 29, May 1, 2, 1872; *John Mackay vs. the Blue Ridge Railroad Company* (June 1871), Scott papers; *Report on Public Frauds, South Carolina,* 613-16.

Chapter 12. The Leprous Hands Upraised

1. Davis, *Civil War and Reconstruction in Florida,* 613; Daniels, *Prince of Carpetbaggers,* 240-41; Wallace, *Carpetbag Rule,* 101-2.

2. Davis, *Civil War and Reconstruction in Florida,* 649, 655, 684-85; Shofner, *Nor Is It Over Yet,* 199-202, 217-19.

3. Davis, *Civil War and Reconstruction in Florida,* 651-52; Shofner, *Nor Is It Over Yet,* 207, 209-11, 243-48, 256; Paul E. Fenlon, "The Notorious Swepson-Littlefield Fraud: Railroad Financing in Florida, 1868-1871," *Florida Historical Quarterly* XXXII (Apr. 1954), 252-54.

4. *Testimony Taken by the Joint Select Committee to Inquire into the Condition of Affairs in the Late Insurrectionary States: Florida* (Washington, D.C., 1872), 78-84, 144-48, 175, 203-4, 212-23; Wallace, *Carpetbag Rule,* 107-13; Davis, *Civil War and Reconstruction in Florida,* 568-85.

5. D. Richards to E. B. Washburne, Jan. 6, 7, 1869, Washburne Papers; *Congressional Globe,* 41 Cong., 2 sess., p. 2813; Wallace, *Carpetbag Rule,* 93-100, 114-26; Daniels, *Prince of Carpetbaggers,* 269; Davis, *Civil War and Reconstruction in Florida,* 612, 615-17, 629-36; Shofner, *Nor Is It Over Yet,* 205-6, 211-12, 219-22.

6. Somers, *Southern States Since the War,* 226, 228; *Cincinnati Commercial,* n. d., quoted in *New Orleans Republican,* Oct. 4, 1871.

7. Warmoth, *War, Politics and Reconstruction,* 88-89, 158-60.

8. *New York Times,* Feb. 4, 1870; T. W. Conway to Warmoth, Aug. 25, 1870; clippings from *New York World,* Feb. 4, 1870; *New York Sun,* Aug. ——, 1870; *New Orleans Republican,* Aug. ——, 1870, Warmoth Papers.

9. J. R. West to Warmoth, Oct. 15, 25, 1871; H. S. McComb to Warmoth, Oct. 30, Nov. 17, 1871; H. C. Dibble to H. S. McComb, Nov. 3, 1871; H. S. McComb to J. R. West, Nov. 6, 1871, Warmoth Papers; *New Orleans Republican,* Sept. 22, 1871, quoting a *Chicago Tribune* interview with H. S. McComb; Taylor, *Louisiana Reconstructed,* 189-202.

10. Letters to Warmoth from W. P. Kellogg, Mar. 6, 17, 1870; L. A. Sheldon, Mar. 10, 1870; J. S. Harris, Mar. 10, 1870; G. A. Sheridan, Mar. 21, 1870; J. F. Casey to G. A. Sheridan, Mar. 15, 1870, Warmoth Papers; Warmoth, *War, Politics and Reconstruction,* 89-91.

11. O. H. Rice to Warmoth, Oct. 27, 1870, Warmoth Papers; Warmoth, *War, Politics and Reconstruction,* 96-102; Harris, "Warmoth," 79; Binning, "Warmoth," 193-98.

12. *New Orleans Bee,* Dec. 12, 1870, clipping, Warmoth Papers; Warmoth,

War, Politics and Reconstruction, 102-9; Harris, "Warmoth," 88; Binning, "Warmoth," 226-27; Taylor, *Louisiana Reconstructed,* 212-15.

13. James Longstreet to Warmoth, Jan. 19, 1871; memoranda of an "understanding" between Warmoth and Democratic legislators, "being the result of two interviews, the concluding one occurring February 9th, 1871"; J. R. West to Warmoth, Apr. 2, 1871, Warmoth Papers; Harris, "Warmoth," 88-91.

14. J. R. West to Warmoth, Mar. 14, 1871; Longstreet to Grant, July 8, 1871; *New Orleans Republican* clippings, Mar. 9, 10, July 2, 6, 1871, Warmoth Papers; Warmoth, *War, Politics and Reconstruction,* 112; Harris, "Warmoth," 92-94.

15. *New Orleans Republican,* Aug. --, 1871, clipping, Warmoth Papers; Warmoth, *War, Politics and Reconstruction,* 112-17; Harris, "Warmoth," 96-101; Binning, "Warmoth," 242-51, quoting *New Orleans Republican,* Aug. 11, 1871.

16. S. B. Packard to Warmoth, Aug. 12, 1871; J. A. Walsh to Warmoth, Aug. 13, Sept. 11, 12, 1871; Warmoth to Walsh, Sept. 11, 12, 1871; *New Orleans Republican,* Sept. 8, 14, 26, clippings, Warmoth Papers; Harris, "Warmoth," 102.

17. L. B. Jenks statement, Dec. 11, 1781; *New Orleans Republican,* Aug. ——, Oct. 4, 1871, clippings, Warmoth Papers; *New York Times,* Aug. 10, 28, 31, 1871; Warmoth, *War, Politics and Reconstruction,* 117-50; Taylor, *Louisiana Reconstructed,* 216-18, 222-27.

18. *New York Times,* Dec. 26, 1869; Clayton, *Aftermath of the Civil War,* 195-202, quoting *Arkansas Gazette,* May 22, Sept. 24, 1869, Feb. 15, July 12, Dec. 15, 1870, Aug. 15, 1871; Harrell, *Brooks and Baxter War,* 52-53, 60-61; James W. Leslie, "Ferd Havis: Jefferson County's Black Republican Leader," *Arkansas Historical Quarterly* XXXVII (Autumn 1978), 240-41.

19. Clayton, *Aftermath of the Civil War,* 226-50; Harrell, *Brooks and Baxter War,* 60, 67; Driggs, "Powell Clayton Regime," 31-34, 53-58; George H. Thompson, *Arkansas and Reconstruction: The Influence of Geography, Economics and Personality* (Port Washington, N.Y., 1976), 231-33.

20. Clayton, *Aftermath of the Civil War,* 257-71; Driggs, "Powell Clayton Regime," 59-62; Thompson, *Arkansas and Reconstruction,* 65, 68, 70, 79-80; Staples, *Reconstruction in Arkansas,* 375-77.

21. Clayton, *Aftermath of the Civil War,* 312-16; Harrell, *Brooks and Baxter War,* 94-95; Staples, *Reconstruction in Arkansas,* 377-78; Driggs, "Powell Clayton Regime," 62-64.

22. Clayton, *Aftermath of the Civil War,* 312-16; Harrell, *Brooks and Baxter War,* 96-97; Staples, *Reconstruction in Arkansas,* 380-81, 384-86; Driggs, "Powell Clayton Regime," 64-72.

23. Clayton's testimony, *Congressional Globe,* 42 Cong., 1 sess., pp. 311-18 (Jan. 9, 1972); Blaine, *Twenty Years of Congress,* II, 508; Driggs, "Powell Clayton Regime," 72-73; Everette Swinney, "United States vs. Powell Clayton: Use of Federal Enforcement Acts in Arkansas," *Arkansas Historical Quarterly* XXVI (Summer 1967), 143.

Chapter 13. Guttersnipes from the North

1. Quotations from *Chicago Tribune,* June 14, July 18, 24, Aug. 14, 26, 1872.

2. *New York Times,* Nov. 15, 1872; Albert Griffin, "'The Infamous Carpet-Bag Governments,'" *Kansas Magazine,* Sept., 1872, pp. 261-62, 265, 268-69,

3. Joseph Logsdon, *Horace White, Nineteenth Century Liberal* (Westport, Conn., 1971), 387.

4. *Chicago Tribune,* Aug. 16, 20, Oct. 4, 8, 10, 1872.

5. Clayton, *Aftermath of the Civil War,* 343-47; Harrell, *Brooks and Baxter War,* 132-39, 142-45; James H. Atkinson, "The Arkansas Gubernatorial Campaign and Election of 1872," *Arkansas Historical Quarterly* I (Dec. 1942), 315-17; Driggs, "Powell Clayton Regime," 73-74.

6. T. J. Mackey to Scott, Feb. 12, Mar. 21, 1872, Scott Papers; *Chicago Tribune,* Aug. 7, 31, 1872; Lamson, *Glorious Failure,* 153-60.

7. T. J. Mackey to Scott, Oct. 1, 7, 1872; George Bliss, Jr., to Scott, Oct. 7, 1872; J. D. Pope to Scott, Oct. 7, 1872; J. D. Pope to Scott, Oct. 28, 1872, Scott Papers; *Chicago Tribune,* Aug. 22, 1872; *New York Times,* Oct. 10, 1872.

8. Alfred Williams to Scott, Oct. 22, 1872; A. Y. Lee to Scott, Dec. 7, 1872, Scott Papers; *Chicago Tribune,* Nov. 2, 1872; *Report on Public Frauds, South Carolina,* 187-88, 875-76, 919-20; Lamson, *Glorious Failure,* 164-71.

9. Horace Greeley to Warner, Aug. 22, 1871; J. D. Cox to Warner, Jan. 30, 1872, Warner Papers.

10. Warner to John Sherman, Feb. 29, 1872, Sherman Papers.

11. Whitelaw Reid to Warner, May 20, 1872; Henry Watterson to Warner, July 25, 1872, Warner Papers; *Chicago Tribune,* June 4, 1872; Wiggins, *Scalawag in Alabama Politics,* 80; Cash, "Alabama Republicans," 362-63.

12. Wiggins, *Scalawag in Alabama Politics,* 88-90; Sarah W. Wiggins, "George E. Spencer: A Carpetbagger in Alabama," *Alabama Review* XIX (Jan. 1966), 45-51; Cash, "Alabama Republicans," 283-88.

13. U.S. Congress, 44 Cong., 1 sess., *Senate Report No. 331* (Washington, D.C., 1876), 1-2, 32-46, 67-79, 90-93, 142-46, 163-69, 203; *New York Times,* Dec. 4, 1872; Fleming, *Civil War and Reconstruction in Alabama,* 755-60.

14. L. W. Reavis to Warmoth, Aug. 13, 1871; Warmoth to Whitelaw Reid, Mar. 12, 1872, Warmoth Papers; *New York Tribune,* Mar. 14, 1872; Harris, "Warmoth," 66-68, 102, 116; Taylor, *Louisiana Reconstructed,* 202-8.

15. *Chicago Tribune,* Apr. 4, 1872; Warmoth, *War, Politics and Reconstruction,* 161-64; Harris, "Warmoth," 119-20; Taylor, *Louisiana Reconstructed,* 227-37.

16. *Chicago Tribune,* Dec. 9, 1872; Warmoth, *War, Politics and Reconstruction,* 197-99; Taylor, *Louisiana Reconstructed,* 237-46; Binning, "Warmoth," 311-19.

17. *Chicago Tribune,* Dec. 7, 10, 12, 14, 17, 24, 1872; *New York Times,* Dec. 7, 10, 1872; Warmoth, *War, Politics and Reconstruction,* 197-220; U.S. Congress, 42 Cong., 3 sess., *Senate Report No. 457* (Washington, D.C., 1873), lx-lxi, 855.

Chapter 14. The Leopard Don't Change His Spots

1. "Imperfect notes of a speech delivered in Corinthian Hall, Rochester, N. Y., 18th July 1872," Tourgée Papers; Olsen, *Carpetbagger's Crusade,* 186-87.

2. Tourgee to Mrs. Tourgee, Jan. 5, 8, 12, 13, 24, 25, 1873; Mrs. Tourgee to Tourgee, May 28, June 29, 1873, Tourgée Papers.

3. Letters to Tourgee from Mrs. Tourgee, June 30, July 2, 1873; D. L. Benjamin, July 19, 1873; J. B. Neathery, July 22, 1873; C. R. Thomas, Jan. 3, 9, 1874; V. Tourgee to Mrs. Tourgee, July 18, 1873; Tourgee to M. B. Anderson, Dec. ——, 1873, Tourgée Papers.

4. Tourgee to Mrs. Tourgee, Jan. 5, 13, 1873, Apr. 27, 29, 1874; letters to Tourgee from J. B. Ford & Co., Oct. 21, 1874; M. B. Anderson, Nov. 19, 1874; J.

A. Royce, Dec. 1, 1874, Tourgée Papers; *Charlotte Observer*, Sept. 24, 1874, quoted in Olsen, *Carpetbagger's Crusade*, 216.

5. Tourgee to M. B. Anderson, May 11, 1874, Tourgée Papers; Olsen, *Carpetbagger's Crusade*, 188, 191.

6. Tourgee to Thomas Settle, Oct. 14, 1873, Settle Papers; Tourgee to Mrs. Tourgee, Nov. 17, 1874, Feb. 4, 16, Sept. 30, 1875; Tourgee to E. B. Taylor, May 3, 1875; letters to Tourgee from J. R. Howard, Jan. 30, 1875; G. S. Hulbert, Sept. 3, 1875; Mrs. Tourgee, Sept. 24, 25, 1875, Tourgée Papers; *Greensboro Patriot*, quoted in Olsen, *Carpetbagger's Crusade*, 207.

7. Tourgee to Mrs. Tourgee, Sept. 10, 23, 1875; "Speech of Hon. Albion W. Tourgee in the Constitutional Convention . . . Sept. 22d 1875," Tourgée Papers; *Journal of the Constitutional Convention of the State of North Carolina Held in 1875* (Raleigh, N.C., 1875), 263-64; Hamilton, *Reconstruction in North Carolina*, 636-43.

8. Printed circular, *Hon. Albion W. Tourgee Will Lecture during the Coming Season (1875-6);* Tourgee to Mrs. Tourgee, Nov. 24, 1875; Tourgee to chairman, U.S. Senate committee on pensions [1875 or 1876]; B. C. Rogers to Tourgee, Apr. 4, 1876, Tourgée Papers; Tourgee to Thomas Settle, June 27, 1876, Settle Papers; Olsen, *Carpetbagger's Crusade*, 208.

9. *New Orleans Times*, Jan. 18, 19, 1873, quoted in Binning, "Warmoth," 343-48.

10. A. F. Gray to Warmoth, Mar. 2, 1873, Warmoth Papers; *Congressional Globe*, 42 Cong., 3 sess., appendix, p. 200; E. Bruce Thompson, *Matthew Hale Carpenter, Webster of the West* (Madison, Wis., 1954), 180-83, 193; John E. Gonzales, "William Pitt Kellogg, Reconstruction Governor of Louisiana, 1873-1877," *Louisiana Historical Quarterly* XXIX (Apr. 1946), 24-25.

11. Warmoth to L. Lexada, Mar. 11, 1873; letters to Warmoth from H. L. Swords, Mar. 2, 1873; A. H. Leonard, Apr. 19, May 12, June 1, 1873; A. S. Herrin, Apr. 26, 1873, Warmoth Papers; Gonzales, "Kellogg," 25-33.

12. M. H. Carpenter to Warmoth, May 7, 1873, Mar. 16, 1874; G. A. Sheridan to Warmoth (two telegrams), Jan. 30, 1874; G. W. Carter to W. S. McMillan, Jan. 31, 1874, Warmoth Papers: Thompson, *Carpenter*, 189-90; Warmoth, *War, Politics and Reconstruction*, 221-39.

13. Letters to Warmoth from Jack Wharton, Sept. 4, Oct. 2, 8, 12, 1874; J. D. Houston, Oct. 12, 1874; H. L. Swords, Nov. 7, 1874; M. H. Carpenter, Nov. 19, 1874, Warmoth Papers; Gonzales, "Kellogg," 38-44, 47-49.

14. G. A. Sheridan to Warmoth, Dec. 18, 20, 1874; J. A. Walsh to Warmoth, Nov. 7, 1873; Warmoth to Walsh, Nov. ——, 1873; clippings from *New Orleans Bulletin*, Dec. 23, 24, 1874; *New Orleans Picayune*, Dec. 27, 1874; *New Orleans Times*, Dec. 27, 1874, Warmoth Papers.

15. *New York Herald*, Dec. 24, 1874; *New Orleans Republican*, Dec. 27, 1874; *Chicago Tribune*, Dec. 28, 1874; *New Orleans Times*, n.d., clippings, Warmoth Papers; Warmoth, *War, Politics and Reconstruction*, 243; Gonzales, "Kellogg," 47-49.

16. Effingham Lawrence to Warmoth, Dec. 2, 1873; O. D. Bragdon to Warmoth, Dec. 14, 1873; City of New Orleans tax receipt, 1873; Warmoth and Lawrence, memoranda of agreement, Apr. 27, Nov. 3, 1874; *Chicago Inter Ocean*, Jan. 11, 1865, clipping, Warmoth Papers.

17. Staples, *Reconstruction in Arkansas*, 407-8; King, *The Great South*, II, 281-83; Clayton, *Aftermath of the Civil War*, 241-50.

18. U.S. Congress, 42 Cong., 2 sess., *House Report No. 2: Affairs in Arkansas*,

Report by Mr. Poland (Washington, D.C. 1874). 145, 424-32; Thompson, *Arkansas and Reconstruction,* 140-47.

19. McClure to S. W. Dorsey or Powell Clayton (telegram), Apr. 17, 1874, Grant Papers; James H. Atkinson, "The Brooks-Baxter Contest," *Arkansas Historical Quarterly* IV (Summer 1945), 124-49; Leslie, "Ferd Havis," 243-44; Thompson, *Arkansas and Reconstruction,* 148-50, 152-53, 155-57.

20. *Report by Mr. Poland,* 501-4; Clayton, *Aftermath of the Civil War,* 349.

21. *New York Times,* Oct. 19, 1874; Atkinson, "Brooks-Baxter Contest," 291; Staples, *Reconstruction in Arkansas,* 429; Thompson, *Arkansas and Reconstruction,* 164.

22. *New York Times,* Mar. 9, 1875; Clayton, *Aftermath of the Civil War,* 309-10; Atkinson, "Brooks-Baxter Contest," 295-96; Staples, *Reconstruction in Arkansas,* 438-40; Thompson, *Arkansas and Reconstruction,* 166, 169, 280; Driggs, "Powell Clayton Regime," 74-75; Hesseltine, *Grant,* 347.

Chapter 15. Political Death of the Negro

1. Ames to Blanche Ames, Nov. 4, 1872, June 28, Oct. 22, 1873, in Ames, *Chronicles,* I, 410, 486, 610; *Congressional Globe,* 42 Cong., 3 sess., p. 464.

2. Ames to Blanche Ames, Sept. 30, Oct. 3, 15, Nov. 10, 1872, in Ames, *Chronicles,* I, 383-84, 387, 393, 416; John R. Lynch, *The Facts of Reconstruction* (1913; Indianapolis, Ind., 1970), 70-73.

3. Blanche Ames to Mrs. B. F. Butler, May 18, 1873, and to Ames, Oct. 3, 1873; Ames to Blanche Ames, July 27, 30, Aug. 27, in Ames, *Chronicles,* I, 455, 496-97, 503, 540, 588; Lynch, *Facts of Reconstruction,* 73-76; Garner, *Reconstruction in Mississippi,* 159-62; Pereyra, *Alcorn,* 159-62.

4. Ames to Blanche Ames, 1873: Sept. 18, Oct. 5, 10, 18, 19, 22, 25, 26, 28, 31, Nov. 5, in Ames, *Chronicles,* I, 571, 589-91, 594-95, 602-7, 609-11, 613-14, 616-18, 624, 626-27; Harris, *Day of the Carpetbagger,* 478-79.

5. Blanche Ames to Mrs. B. F. Butler, 1874: Jan. 25, 30, Feb. 13, Mar. 4, 26, Apr. 4; Mrs. Butler to Blanche, Feb. 6, 19, in Ames, *Chronicles,* I, 640-47, 650-54, 656-57, 667-70; Harris, *Day of the Carpetbagger,* 476-80.

6. Ames's inaugural and messages of Feb. 7 and Mar. 4, 1874; Blanche Ames to Mrs. B. F. Butler, Apr. 26, May 9, 1874, in Ames, *Chronicles,* I, 635, 647-50, 662-66, 672-73, 677; Harris, *Day of the Carpetbagger,* 551-56, 567, 581-83, 608-14, 616-22; Garner, *Reconstruction in Mississippi,* 294, 296-305; Benson, "Ames," 239, quoting the *Brandon Republican,* June 25, 1874.

7. A. T. Morgan to Ames, Mar. 10, 1869 (petition for the appointment of Hilliard as sheriff), Army Records of the Fourth Military District; *Mississippi in 1875: Report of the Select Committee to Inquire into the Mississippi Election of 1875* (44 Cong., 1 sess., Senate Report No. 527, 2 vols., Washington, D.C., 1876), II, 1732-34; Morgan, *Yazoo,* 369-71.

8. *Mississippi in 1875,* II, 1735-40, 1768-69; Morgan, *Yazoo,* 378-84, 388-91. Robert Bowman, "Reconstruction in Yazoo County," *Publications of the Mississippi Historical Society* VII (1903), 115-29, is the reminiscence of a Yazoo City lawyer and Democratic leader. It contains some useful information on the events of 1874 but also some gross errors of fact. E. H. Anderson, "A Memoir of Reconstruction in Yazoo City," *Journal of Mississippi History* IV (Oct. 1942), 187-94, while claiming to be a "recital of true facts," is so egregiously erroneous as to be absolutely useless.

9. Ames to Blanche Ames, 1874: July 31, Aug. 4, 5, 7, 12, Oct. 15, Nov. 4, 20, in Ames, *Chronicles,* I, 693, 698-99, 702, 707-8, II, 28, 65; Garner, *Reconstruction in Mississippi,* 328-30; Benson, "Ames," 245-57.

10. Ames, message of Dec. 17, in Ames, *Chronicles,* II, 74; Benson, "Ames," 249-56; Harris, *Day of the Carpetbagger,* 645-49. In a dispatch from Jackson, dated Dec. 16, 1874, and published in the *New York Times,* Dec. 25, 1874, a correspondent wrote: "Within the past three days I have asked dozens of people why the negroes came armed to Vicksburg. . . . The governor of the State and the lowest field-hand make the same statement— 'they do not know.' . . . Gov. Ames has been charged with advising and directing Crosby to appeal to the negroes for aid, and to order them to support him with arms."

11. Benson, "Ames," 230-31, 233-35, 265-68, and 269, quoting the *Brandon Republican* as reprinted in the Jackson *Mississippi Pilot,* Feb. 13, 1875; Harris, *Day of the Carpetbagger,* 627-32, 651.

12. B. F. Butler to Ames, Mar. 3, 1875; Ames to Blanche Ames, 1875: July 24, Aug. 3, 19, 24, 28, Sept. 1, 2, 3; Garner, *Reconstruction in Mississippi,* 372-75.

13. J. R. Bell to Morgan, Aug. 5, 1874; Morgan to Bell, Aug. 6, 1874, and *Yazoo City Herald,* Aug. 20, 1874, all quoted in *Mississippi in 1875,* II, 1743-44, 1747-50.

14. Morgan, *Yazoo,* 416-17, 420-21, 454, 463-64; *Mississippi in 1875,* II, 1764-65.

15. H. M. Dixon to Morgan, Jan. 11, 1875, *Yazoo City Democrat,* Aug. 31, 1875, *Yazoo City Herald,* Sept. 3, 1875, and Morgan's testimony in *Mississippi in 1875,* II, 1750-52, 1754-59; Morgan, *Yazoo,* 457, 462.

16. *Mississippi in 1875,* II, 1753-60; Morgan, *Yazoo,* 462-85.

17. Ames to Blanche Ames, Sept. 5, 9, 11, 17, 1875, in Ames, *Chronicles,* II, 163, 165, 169, 175, 183; Garner, *Reconstruction in Mississippi,* 378-81.

18. Ames to Blanche Ames, Sept. 7, 1875, in Ames, *Chronicles,* II, 166; George to Pierrepont, Sept. 25, 1875, in *Vicksburg Herald,* quoted in Morgan, *Yazoo,* 479; *New York Tribune,* Sept. 21, 1875, quoted in Harris, *Day of the Carpetbagger,* 666-67; Garner, *Reconstruction in Mississippi,* 389-91. See also the *New York Times,* Oct. 9, 1875, reporting the Washington mission of ex-Senator Pease and other anti-Ames Republicans under the headline: "The Shameful Misgovernment of Gov. Ames Responsible for the Race Troubles."

19. Ames to Blanche Ames, Oct. 9, 12, 1875, in Ames, *Chronicles,* II, 211-12, 216; *Mississippi in 1875,* II, 1760-61, 1783, quoting the *Yazoo City Democrat,* Oct. 9, 1875; Pereyra, *Alcorn,* 172-74; Garner, *Reconstruction in Mississippi,* 375-79, 382-86.

20. Ames to Blanche Ames, Oct. 14, Nov. 1, 4, 1875; Ames to Pierrepont, Oct. 16, 1875, in Ames, *Chronicles,* II, 217-18, 236-37n, 248-49; Pierrepont to Ames, Oct. 23, 1875, in Ames, *Ames,* 441; *Mississippi in 1875,* II, 1801-4; Morgan, *Yazoo,* 403; Garner, *Reconstruction in Mississippi,* 386-89, 392-95. Frank Johnston, "The Conference of October 15th, 1875, between General George and Governor Ames," *Publications of the Mississippi Historical Society* VI (1902), 65-77, misdates the conference and minimizes the role of Chase.

21. Blanche Ames to Mrs. Butler, Dec. 8, 1875, in Ames, *Chronicles,* II, 259; Ames to Charles Colton, Mar. 7, 1876, quoted in Garner, *Reconstruction in Mississippi,* 402.

22. Butler to Ames, Feb. 2, 25, 1876, and Blanche Ames to Mrs. Butler, Mar. 14, 1876, in Ames, *Chronicles,* II, 281, 304-5, 344-45. On Bruce, see William C.

Harris, "Blanche K. Bruce of Mississippi: Conservative Assimilationist," in Howard N. Rabinowitz, ed., *Southern Black Leaders of the Reconstruction Era* (Urbana, Ill., 1982), 3-38.

23. Blanche Ames to Mrs. Butler, Mar. 21, 26, Apr. 2, 1876, and Ames to Thomas J. Durant and Roger A. Pryor, Mar. 28, 1876, in Ames, *Chronicles,* II, 346-47, 351-53, 355; Ames, *Ames,* 490-91; Garner, *Reconstruction in Mississippi,* 406-7.

24. Ames's and Morgan's testimony in *Mississippi in 1875,* I, 1-46, and II, 1729-85 (quotations from I, 45, and II, 1778); *New York Times,* May 2, 1876.

Chapter 16. This Pathway of Political Reform

1. Lamson, *Glorious Failure,* 195-201; Fowler, "Carpetbagger's Conversion," 288; King, *Great South,* II, 462.

2. Letters to Scott from J. G. Haly, Nov. 11, 1872, Dec. 18, 1873, Nov. 11, 1874; —— Welles, Oct. 10, 1873; Isaac B. Smith, Oct. 27, 1873; Wm. Winthrope, Jan. 14, Mar. 21, 1873; J. E. Britton, Apr. 26, 1874; Frank Arnim, Apr. 28, 1874; W. T. Matthews, Mar. 24, 1874, Scott Papers.

3. Scott to President and Congress, Apr. 30, 1874; C. W. Dudley to Scott, Aug. 10, 1874, Scott Papers; *New York Times,* June 21, 22, July 26, 1874; Reynolds, *Reconstruction in South Carolina,* 263-65.

4. Chamberlain to Messrs. Riordan & Dawson, July 31, 1874, Francis W. Dawson Papers, Duke University Library; *Charleston News and Courier,* Sept. 7, 1874, quoted in Ann Kearns Brooks, "A Republican Governor and a Democratic Editor: Their Relationship during the Reconstruction in South Carolina" (Master's thesis, University of North Carolina at Greensboro, 1972), 40.

5. *Charleston News and Courier,* Sept. 15, 1874, quoted in Lamson, *Glorious Failure,* 204; *Wasington Post,* reprinted in *News and Courier,* Nov. 14, 1874, and quoted in Brooks, "Republican Governor," 42-44; R. H. Woody, ed., "Behind the Scenes in the Reconstruction Legislature of South Carolina: Diary of Josephus Woodruff," *Journal of Southern History* II (Feb. 1936), 92-93; Simkins and Woody, *South Carolina during Reconstruction,* 474; Reynolds, *Reconstruction in South Carolina,* 276-79.

6. Dawson to Sarah Dawson, Aug. 2, Sept. 4, 8, 12, 13, Nov. 22, 1874, Dawson Papers; Brooks, "Republican Governor," 49-50; E. Culpepper Clark, *Francis Warrington Dawson and the Politics of Restoration: South Carolina, 1874-1889* (University, Ala., 1980), 10-27, 36-39.

7. Chamberlain to W. J. Magrath, Dec. 24, 1874, Daniel H. Chamberlain Papers, Duke University Library; Lamson, *Glorious Failure,* 205-6, 208-12; Clark, *Dawson,* 40. On the division within the Negro ranks and its significance for state politics, see Thomas Holt, *Black over White: Negro Political Leadership in South Carolina during Reconstruction* (Urbana, Ill., 1977), 1, 4-5, 96-98, 101, 188-93, and *passim.*

8. Chamberlain to Dawson, Jan. 27, Feb. 7, 15, 18, 1875, Dawson Papers; Clark, *Dawson,* 41; Brooks, "Republican Governor," 49-50; Lamson, *Glorious Failure,* 213-19; Holt, *Black over White,* 179-81.

9. Chamberlain to B. R. Riordan, May 11, 1875, Dawson Papers; Chamberlain to Scott, Mar. 12, Apr. 13, Oct. 23, Dec. 24, 1875, and Mar. 29, 1876, Scott Papers; Simkins and Woody, *South Carolina during Reconstruction,* 168-69; Williamson, *After Slavery,* 402-4.

10. Chamberlain to Samuel Bowles, Mar. 30, 1875, Samuel Bowles Papers, Yale University Library; Chamberlain to Dawson, May 5, June 24, 1875, and to Dawson and Riordan, June 9, 1875; Dawson to Sarah Dawson, Aug. ——, 1875, Dawson Papers; Chamberlain to W. M. Grier, May 15, 1875, J. C. Hemphill Papers, Duke University Library; Brooks, "Republican Governor," 67-68; Clark, *Dawson,* 45-47; Lamson, *Glorious Failure,* 215-16; Allen, *Governor Chamberlain's Administration,* 142-44.

11. Chamberlain to Dawson, Oct. 11, Dec. 8, 1875, Dawson Papers; note appointing Scott as a delegate, Nov. 20, 1875, Scott Papers; Brooks, "Republican Governor," 62-63; Lamson, *Glorious Failure,* 219-20.

12. Chamberlain to Dawson, Apr. 20, 1876, Dawson Papers; Woody, "Diary of Josephus Woodruff," 256; Lamson, *Glorious Failure,* 221-23; Holt, *Black over White,* 188-93.

13. Chamberlain to Dawson, Dec. 27, 1875, Jan. 3, 1876, Dawson Papers; Allen, *Governor Chamberlain's Administration,* 192-98; Lamson, *Glorious Failure,* 223-25; Clark, *Dawson,* 49-50; Alfred B. Williams, *Hampton and His Red Shirts: South Carolina's Deliverance in 1876* (Charleston, S.C., 1935), 27.

14. Allen, *Governor Chamberlain's Administration,* 198; Bleser, *Promised Land,* 103-5; Brooks, "Republican Governor," 75-78; Lamson, *Glorious Failure,* 228; Holt, *Black over White,* 187-88; Henry T. Thompson, *Ousting the Carpetbagger from South Carolina* (Columbia, S.C., 1926), 86-89.

15. Chamberlain to Dawson, Jan. 1, Feb. 2, May 22, 1876, Dawson Papers; Allen, *Governor Chamberlain's Administration,* 67-69, 220-21, 272-75, 307-8; Clark, *Dawson,* 60-61; Lamson, *Glorious Failure,* 233-34; Francis B. Simkins, "The Election of 1876 in South Carolina," *South Atlantic Quarterly* XXI (July 1922), 228-32, 234-35.

16. Chamberlain to Dawson, Jan. 26, 30, Mar. 13, Apr. 7, June 25, 1876, Dawson Papers; Chamberlain to Bowles, Feb. 2, 1876, Bowles Papers; Woody, "Diary of Josephus Woodruff," 251, 256; Allen, *Governor Chamberlain's Administration,* 228-35; Brooks, "Republican Governor," 78.

17. Allen, *Governor Chamberlain's Administration,* 258-71; Lamson, *Glorious Failure,* 31, 229-33; Williamson, *After Slavery,* 404-5; Thompson, *Ousting the Carpetbagger,* 96-98.

18. Allen, *Governor Chamberlain's Administration,* 340-45; Thompson, *Ousting the Carpetbagger,* 1-6; F. A. Porcher, "Last Chapter of Reconstruction in South Carolina," *Southern Historical Society Papers* XII (April 1884), 244-45; Manley Wade Wellman, *Giant in Gray: A Biography of Wade Hampton of South Carolina* (New York, 1949), 240-42.

Chapter 17. The Abandonment of Southern Republicans

1. *New York Times,* July 20, 1876; Allen, *Governor Chamberlain's Administration,* 312-26.

2. Wellman, *Giant in Gray,* 238, 242-43; Williamson, *After Slavery,* 407-8.

3. Gary to Dawson, July 25, 1876, Dawson Papers; Allen, *Governor Chamberlain's Administration,* 279, 304-6, 331-39, 374-77; Wellman, *Giant in Gray,* 238, 245-46; Clark, *Dawson,* 62-68, 83; Williams, *Hampton and His Red Shirts,* 90-91; William A. Sheppard, *Red Shirts Remembered: Southern Brigadiers of the Reconstruction Period* (Atlanta, Ga., 1940), 87, 95-109.

4. L. Cass Carpenter to William E. Chandler, Aug. 26, 1876, Chandler Pa-

pers; Allen, *Governor Chamberlain's Administration,* 351-64, 377-80; Lamson, *Glorious Failure,* 235-45; Williams, *Hampton and His Red Shirts,* 196-97; Simkins, "Election of 1876," 236-37; Brooks, "Republican Governor," 85-86; F. A. Porcher, "Last Chapter of Reconstruction in South Carolina," 311-15.

5. "South Carolina Chivalry," *New York Times,* Jan. 16, 1877; Sheppard, *Red Shirts Remembered,* 45-51, 53-54; Simkins, "Election of 1876," 236, 335, 341; Williams, *Hampton and His Red Shirts,* 302, 333, 365.

6. *New York Times,* Oct. 13, 1876; Allen, *Governor Chamberlain's Administration,* 341-42, 351, 365, 385-87, 406-7, 411-15; Williamson, *After Slavery,* 271-72.

7. Allen, *Governor Chamberlain's Administration,* 387-89, 428-29; Simkins, "Election of 1876," 339-40; Williams, *Hampton and His Red Shirts,* 246; Sefton, *United States Army and Reconstruction,* 247. Thompson, *Ousting the Carpetbagger,* 134, says that "in view of the fact that ordinary methods for her [South Carolina's] redemption would not have availed," it was well to consider "whether there was not some palliation for the resort to methods which would never be warranted except as a last resort in time of revolution."

8. *New York Times,* Apr. 30, 1877; Allen, *Governor Chamberlain's Administration,* 435-39, quoting a *New York Times* dispatch of Nov. 28, 1876; Simkins, "Election of 1876," 343-44; Lamson, *Glorious Failure,* 252-54; Thompson, *Ousting the Carpetbagger,* 135-42.

9. Chamberlain to Cameron, Dec. 1, 1876; Hampton to Hamilton Fish, Dec. 3, 1876, Rutherford P. Hayes Papers, Rutherford P. Hayes Library, Fremont, Ohio; *Inaugural Address of His Excellency Daniel H. Chamberlain . . . December 7, 1876* (pamphlet, n. p., n. d.), Hayes Papers; Allen, *Governor Chamberlain's Administration,* 439-41, 444, 454-55; Simkins, "Election of 1876," 345-46; Thompson, *Ousting the Carpetbagger,* 143-57.

10. Chamberlain to A. E. Lee, telegram, Nov. 18, 1876; L. Cass Carpenter to Hayes, Dec. 14, 1876, Hayes Papers; Allen, *Governor Chamberlain's Administration,* 468-69; Simkins, "Election of 1876," 347-48; Lamson, *Glorious Failure,* 261-62.

11. Hampton to Hayes, Dec. 23, 1876; Murat Halstead to Hayes, Dec. 27, 1876; Chamberlain to Hayes, Jan. 2, 1877, Hayes Papers; Alice Chamberlain to W. L. Garrison II, Dec. 26, 1876, William Lloyd Garrison Papers, Boston Public Library; *New York Times,* Jan 5, 1877; Allen, *Governor Chamberlain's Administration,* 464-65.

12. Charles Nordhoff to Charles Foster, Feb. 15, 1877; Joseph Medill to Richard Smith, Feb. 17, 1877; I. C. Deane to Hayes, Feb. 26, 1877, Hayes Papers; Allen, *Governor Chamberlain's Administration,* 469-71.

13. Hampton to Hayes, Mar. 31, 1877; Chamberlain to Hayes, Mar. 31, Apr. 1, 1877, Hayes Papers; Chamberlain to W. L. Garrison II, Apr. 8, 1877, Garrison Papers; *New York Times,* Mar. 28, 29, Apr. 6, 12, 1877; Allen, *Governor Chamberlain's Administration,* 466, 472-73, 479-80.

14. *New York Times,* Apr. 11, 25, 26, May 19, July 5, 1877; Allen, *Governor Chamberlain's Administration,* 481, 483, 485-86, 507-20; Lamson, *Glorious Failure,* 265-66. Hayes noted in his diary, Apr. 11, 1880: "I am not aware of a single instance in which a conspicuous Republican of the South can be said to have been abandoned. Gov. Chamberlain alone has not received office, and he placed himself in an attitude of antagonism which precluded it." T. Harry Williams, ed., *Hayes: The Diary of a President, 1875-1881* (New York, 1964), 270.

15. *New York Times,* Aug. 25, 1877; James Connor to W. D. Simpson, Aug. 24, 1877, quoted in Williamson, *After Slavery,* 415.

16. John B. Dennis to Robert K. Scott, Apr. 5, 1879, Scott Papers; *New York Times,* Nov. 9, 12, 1878; *Report . . . on Public Frauds . . . South Carolina,* 757-63; Allen, *Governor Chamberlain's Administration,* 502-3; Reynolds, *Reconstruction in South Carolina,* 492-93.

17. Scott to F. W. McMaster, undated draft, Scott Papers; J. C. Winsmith to Hayes, Apr. 21, 1877, Hayes Papers; *Report . . . on Public Frauds . . . South Carolina,* 656-57, 857-60; Hampton M. Jarrell, *Wade Hampton and the Negro: The Road Not Taken* (Columbia, S.C., 1949), 123, quoting *Columbia Register,* Aug. 28, 1877.

18. F. W. McMaster to Scott, June 21, Dec. 15, 1877, Mar. 22, 28, 1878; T. J. Mackey to Scott, Aug. 31, 1877; William Dodmead to Scott, Mar. 28, 1878, Scott to McMaster, Mar. 10, Apr. 6, 10, 1878, Scott Papers.

19. J. L. Neagle to Scott, Jan. 20, 1879, and copy of promissory note; E. W. Seibels to Scott, Jan. 21, Nov. 3, 1879; H. H. Kimpton to Scott, Mar. 5, July 3, 8, Sept. 11, 1879; C. O. Witte to Scott, ———, 1880, Scott Papers.

20. Kimpton to Scott, May 3, 1879, Scott Papers; Clark, *Dawson,* 78-80; Williamson, *After Slavery,* 414-17. Williamson has contributed brilliantly to an understanding of the real significance of the fraud investigation and report. But he seems to assume that the report was correct in assigning guilt to Scott. This is, to say the least, questionable. And Bleser, *Promised Land,* 121-22, contends that the findings of Samuel Dibble and his subcommittee "made clear beyond any doubt" that Scott had been one of the "bribe dispensers, bribe gatherers, and embezzlers" and was "guilty of gross fraud." She cites memoranda and affidavits, dated Nov. 1, 1877, in the Dibble Papers, Duke University Library. I have examined those documents and find in them no proof whatsoever that Scott was guilty of Bleser's charges.

Chapter 18. A Fool's Errand

1. Tourgee, manuscript titled "Good Out of Nazareth" and dated Nov. 16, 1876; Tourgee to Dr. Sunderland, Apr. 15, 1877; Tourgee to James C. Young, Aug. 24, 1903, Tourgée Papers; Tourgée, *A Fool's Errand,* ed. by John Hope Franklin (Cambridge, Mass., 1961), 9-20.

2. Tourgee to Mary, July 16, 1877; Lodie Tourgee to Tourgee, Nov. 19, 1877, Tourgée Papers; *New York Times,* Apr. 7, 1878; Olsen, *Carpetbagger's Crusade,* 210-13.

3. Tourgee to Mrs. Tourgee, Aug. 19, 29, 1878, Tourgée Papers; *New York Times,* June 28, 1878.

4. Tourgee to Mrs. Tourgee, Sept. 4, 13, 1878, Tourgée Papers; Olsen, *Carpettbagger's Crusade,* 219-20.

5. Tourgee to Mrs. Tourgee, Sept. 15, 29, Oct. 1, 28, Nov. 6, 9, 11, 1878, Tourgée Papers; *New York Times,* Oct. 5, 1878.

6. Tourgee to Mrs. Tourgee, Nov. 9, 11, 14, Dec. 11, 22, 1878, Tourgée Papers.

7. Tourgee to Mrs. Tourgee, Nov. 17, 25, 27, Dec. 8, 12, 13, 21, 26, 29, 1878, Feb. 14, 1879, Tourgée Papers.

8. Tourgee to Mrs. Tourgee, Jan. 26, 31, Feb. 1, 10, 12, 13, 1879, Tourgée Papers.

9. Tourgee to Mrs. Tourgee, Nov. 14, 30, 1878, Jan. 24, Mar. 9, 10, Apr. 13, 1879, Tourgée Papers.

10. Tourgee to Mrs. Tourgee, Feb. 24, Mar. 2, 6, Apr. 8, 16, 21, 23, 24, 25, May 4, 1879; James W. Albright to Tourgee, May 23, 1879; printed circular, *Valuable Property in the City of Greensboro, N. C., For Sale,* Tourgée Papers.

11. J. R. Howard to Tourgee, Apr. 28, 1879; Tourgee, *A Fool's Errand, by One of the Fools* (New York, 1879), 340-41.

12. Letters to Tourgee from Robert P. Dick, Aug. 21, 1879; W. W. Holden, Aug. 23, 1879; and twelve others, Aug. 23--Oct. 20, 1879, Tourgée Papers; *Greensboro North State,* Aug. 28, 1879, quoted in *New York Times,* Sept. 3, 1879.

13. Memorandum of a contract between Tourgee and Alfred Williams, July 17, 1878; printed circular advertising the *Digest,* [Dec.] 1879; typewritten prospectus of "A Universal Digest," undated but probably Dec. 1879, Tourgée Papers.

14. C. W. Boothby to Fords, Howard & Hulbert, Dec. 22, 1879; V. Tourgee to "Dear Children," Jan. 4, 1880, Tourgée Papers; Tourgee to R. M. Douglas, July 29, 1880, ms. in possession of the Douglas family, Greensboro, N.C.; *Chicago Tribune,* n.d., quoted in Tourgee, *The Invisible Empire* (New York, 1880), 4; Dibble, *Tourgée,* 72-76.

15. Mrs. Tourgee to Tourgee, Jan. 19, 20, 1880; Tourgee to James A. Garfield, Dec. 23, 1880; J. R. Howard to Mrs. Tourgee, Mar. 20, 1881, Tourgée Papers; Tourgee, *Invisible Empire,* 395; Tourgee, *A Fool's Errand,* 360-61; Olsen, *Carpetbagger's Crusade,* 225.

16. J. R. Howard to Chas. H. Blair, Mar. 26, 1881, Tourgée Papers; Dibble, *Tourgée,* 78-83; Olsen, *Carpetbagger's Crusade,* 245, 252-53.

17. Tourgee to Garfield, Dec. 23, 1880, Tourgée Papers; Tourgee, "Aaron's Rod in Politics," *North American Review* CXXXII (Feb. 1881), 136-62; Dibble, *Tourgée,* 76-78; Olsen, *Carpetbagger's Crusade,* 243-44.

18. William L. Royall, *A Reply to "A Fool's Errand, by One of the Fools,"* 2d ed. (New York, 1881), 22-25, 30-37; *New York Sun,* Dec. 9, 1880, quoted in Royall, *A Reply,* 87-89; *New York Tribune,* Jan. 31, 1881.

19. Tourgee, ms. statement on Garfield's death, Sept. 20, 1881, Tourgée Papers; Tourgee, *An Appeal to Caesar* (New York, 1884), 9-20.

Chapter 19. Only a Carpetbagger

1. *New York Times,* Apr. 8, 1876; Wiggins, *Scalawag in Alabama Politics,* 111-16, 120-25; Cash, "Alabama Republicans during Reconstruction," 223-24, 229-33, 235-39, 290-94.

2. "Spencer, George E.," *Biographical Dictionary of the American Congress, 1774-1949* (Washington, D.C., 1950); "Spencer, George Eliphaz," *National Cyclopaedia of American Biography,* XIII (1906), 72.

3. Warner to John Sherman, Jan. 10, 1877, Sherman Papers; Warner to R. B. Hayes, May 18, 1877, General Records, Treasury Department, National Archives; Warner to J. G. Blaine, Jan. 29, 1881, Warner Papers; Cash, "Alabama Republicans during Reconstruction," 229-33, 235-39, 293-94.

4. Warner to R. M. Reynolds, Dec. 23, 1880, July 15, 1881; to W. H. Smith, Jan. 2, 1881; to W. B. Woods, Feb. 2, 8, 1881; to A. E. Buck, Apr. 14, 1881; to J. A. Garfield, May 7, 15, 1881; to J. D. Hardy, May 10, 1884, Warner Papers.

5. W. T. Sherman to Warner, Feb. 5, 1879, Nov. 18, 1880; Warner to W. T. Sherman, May 28, 31, 1880; Warner to J. W. H. Underwood, July 17, 1882; Warner to W. B. Woods, Feb. 5, 1883, Warner Papers; "Warner, Willard," *Na-*

tional Cyclopaedia of American Biography, X (1909), 396; Jonathan M. Wiener, *Social Origins of the New South: Alabama, 1860-1885* (Baton Rouge, 1978), 172-73.

6. Warner to U. S. Grant, Nov. 6, 1880; to C. C. Sheats, Aug. 11, 1881; to James B. Hill, Sept. 19, Oct. 15, 1882.

7. Warner to W. T. Sherman, Feb. 10, 1881; to H. B. Sprague, June 1, 1881; to P. G. Thompson, Jan. 7, 1882; to J. T. Rodd, Feb. 28, 1887, Warner Papers; *National Cyclopaedia,* X, 396.

8. Warner to May Warner, Mar. 4, May 14, 1880, Apr. 1, 1883; to F. I. Wolfe, Dec. 21, 1881; to the Misses Graham, Jan. 5, 1883; May Warner to Warner, Oct. 31, 1885, Warner Papers.

9. Warner to Sister Anne, Apr. 2, 1881; Warner to Western Biographical Publishing Co., Mar. 12, May 5, 1886; C. H. Kibler to Warner, May 3, 1903; "Inscription for Monument," 1906, Warner Papers; *National Cyclopaedia,* X, 396; "Warner, Willard," *Cyclopaedia of American Biographies,* VII (1903), 499; "Warner, Willard," *Biographical Directory of the American Congress, 1774-1949* (Washington, D.C., 1950).

10. King, *The Great South,* 379, 381-82, 385; Wallace, *Carpetbag Rule in Florida,* 251-52; Overy, "Wisconsin Carpetbagger," 35; Shofner, *Nor Is It Over Yet,* 266.

11. *Dictionary of Wisconsin Biography* (Madison, Wis., 1960), 256-57, 299-300; Robert C. Nesbit, *The History of Wisconsin: Urbanization and Industrialization, 1873-1893* (Madison, Wis., 1985), 152, 538.

12. Reed to John L. Mitchell, Nov. 13, 1888, Apr. 7, May 22, 1889, Mitchell Papers, State Historical Society of Wisconsin, Madison; note from an unidentified newspaper, May 27 [1899], Wisconsin Necrology, 6:183a, State Historical Society of Wisconsin; "Reed, Harrison," *National Cyclopaedia of American Biography,* XI (1902), 380.

13. Jane Scott to Scott, Aug. 2, 28, 30, 1879; Knights Templar, Columbia Commandery No. 2, to Scott, June 23, 1880, Scott Papers; Lamson, *Glorious Failure,* 279.

14. This account is derived from the testimony of Scott and others in Haag, *Ohio Versus Scott,* 146-95 and *passim.* On the "withdrawal syndrome," see Robert Berkow, ed., *Merck Manual of Diagnosis and Therapy,* 13th ed. (Rahway, N.J., 1977), 1508-9.

15. Letters to Scott from C. Willard, Dec. 27, 1880; W. J. Whipper, Jan. 1, 1881; Mrs. Lewis Carr and Miriam Carr, Jan. 2, 1881; F. W. McMaster, Jan. 4, 1881; and R. A. Kernan to Waterman (Scott's brother-in-law), Jan. 10, 1881, Scott Papers; *Toledo Blade,* Dec. 27, 1880.

16. Haag, *Ohio Versus Scott,* 21-23, 384-85; *Toledo Blade,* Nov. 5. 1881.

17. John McQueen to Scott, Nov. 7, 1881; F. W. McMaster to Scott, Nov. 18, 1881; Scott to F. W. McMaster, Dec. 1, 1881; *Napoleon Democrat Northwest,* Aug. 16, 1900.

18. Chamberlain to F. W. Dawson, Feb. 13, 1887, Dawson Papers; Chamberlain, *Not "a College Fetich"* (Boston, 1884), *Doctrine of Stare Decisis: Its Reasons and Its Extent* (New York, 1885), *Education at the South* (New York, 1887), "The Harvard Elective System," *New Englander and Yale Review* LXV (Apr. 1886), 359-72; Oscar M. Voorhees, ed., *Phi Beta Kappa Catalog, 1776-1922* (Somerville, N.J., 1923), 813; "Chamberlain, Daniel Henry," *National Cyclopaedia of American Biography,* XII (1904), 176.

19. Chamberlain to Mr. Price, Dec. 28, 1879, Hayes Papers; Chamberlain, "Reconstruction and the Negro," *North American Review* CXXVIII (Feb. 1879),

160-62, 169-72. The next issue of this magazine (Mar. 1879, pp. 224-83) contained a symposium in which public figures Northern and Southern discussed the questions: "Ought the Negro To Be Disfranchised? Ought He To Have Been Enfranchised?" Wade Hampton, one of the contributors, said that "the policy of conferring the right to vote upon the negro, ignorant and incompetent as he was," had been a "dangerous experiment."

20. Chamberlain, "Present Aspects of Southern Question" and "The Race Problem at the South," *New Englander and Yale Review* XLV (Jan. 1886), 31-32, and XLIX (June 1890), 520-23; Chamberlain, "Reconstruction in South Carolina," reprinted from the *Atlantic Monthly* (1901) in Richard N. Current, ed., *Reconstruction in Retrospect* (Baton Rouge, La., 1969), 80; Chamberlain, *Present Phases of Our So-Called Negro Problem: Open Letter to the Right Honorable James Bryce, M. P., of England* (Charleston, S.C., 1904), 24. For an excellent account of Chamberlain's conversion to racism, see Fowler, "Carpetbagger's Conversion," previously cited.

21. Chamberlain to J. C. Hemphill, Feb. 13, 1906, Hemphill Papers; Fowler, "Carpetbagger's Conversion," 294-95, 298-99; Green, *Personal Recollections,* 11-12; Simkins and Woody, *Reconstruction in South Carolina,* 544-45.

22. Chamberlain to Dawson, Jan. 13, Feb. 13, Dec. 21, 1887, May 11, June 8, 19, 1888, Dawson Papers; Chamberlain to Hemphill, June 27, 1904, Hemphill Papers; F. A. Porcher, *Southern Historical Society Papers* XII (1884), 181; XIII (1885), 87; biographical sketch of Chamberlain, *North American Review* CLXXXVI (Oct. 1907), 176. Chamberlain's "Open Letter" to James Bryce appeared originally in the *News and Courier,* Aug. 1, 1904.

23. Green, *Personal Recollections,* 9-10; Fowler, "Carpetbagger's Conversion," 296; *North American Review* CLXXXVI, 178; Williams, *Hampton and His Red Shirts,* 251.

24. Chamberlain to J. C. Hemphill, Aug. 13, 1904, Feb. 13, 1906, Feb. 1, 1907, Hemphill Papers; Green, *Personal Recollections,* 11, 14-15; Chamberlain, "Some Conclusions of a Free-Thinker," *North American Review* CLXXXVI (Oct. 1907), 176-77, 192.

Chapter 20. Lies, Unmitigated Lies

1. Eben Tourjée to Tourgee, Sept. 13, 29, 1873, Tourgée Papers. *A Royal Gentleman* (1881) has Tourgee's name without the accent on the title page, the flyleaf, and page x at the end of the preface. *John Eax, Including also Mamelon and Zouri's Christmas: Life Sketches* (1882) has the name with the accent.

2. Mrs. Tourgée to Mr. Most, June 17, 1905, Tourgée Papers; *Our Continent* II (July 12, 1882), 21-24; *Hot Plowshares,* preface, unpaged; Dean H. Keller, ed., *A Fool's Errand by Steele MacKaye and Albion W. Tourgee* (Metuchen, N.J., 1969), 169-88; Dibble, *Tourgée,* 78-79, 84-91; Olsen, *Carpetbagger's Crusade,* 253-54, 262-64. The name *Our Continent* was changed to *The Continent* with the first issue of volume III (Jan. 3, 1883).

3. Mrs. Tourgée, diary, June 2, 1887, Tourgée Papers; Dibble, *Tourgée,* 110-23, 128-30; Olsen, *Carpetbagger's Crusade,* 248-51, 265-80, 326-31, 352, 354.

4. Tourgée, *An Appeal to Caesar* (New York, 1884), 64-67; Tourgée, "Migma" [Greek for "Mixture," a section of miscellaneous comment by Tourgée], *The Continent* V (Apr. 2, 1884), 443-44; Tourgée, "The South as a Field for Fiction," *The Forum* VI (Dec. 1888), 405.

5. Tourgée to Theodore Roosevelt, Oct. 21, 1901, quoted in Dibble, *Tourgée,* 126-27; Tourgée to E. H. Johnson, May 15, 1902, Tourgée Papers; Olsen, *Carpetbagger's Crusade,* 270, 346; Raymond C. Cook, *Fire from the Flint: The Amazing Careers of Thomas Dixon* (Winston-Salem, N.C., 1968), 112.

6. D. Y. Thomas, "Clayton, Powell," *Dictionary of American Biography*; "Clayton, Powell," *National Cyclopaedia of American Biography,* XVI, 262; "Clayton, Powell," *Cyclopaedia of American Biographies,* II, 57.

7. Clayton, *Aftermath of the Civil War,* 186-93, 249; Leslie, "Ferd Havis," 245-47.

8. Clayton, *Aftermath of the Civil War,* 366-68; Woodrow Wilson, "The Reconstruction of the Southern States," *Atlantic Monthly* (1901), reprinted in Current, *Reconstruction in Retrospect,* 21; James Ford Rhodes, *History of the United States . . . ,* VII (New York, 1906), 168.

9. *National Cyclopaedia of American Biography,* XVI, 262; Clayton, *Aftermath of the Civil War,* 9-11, 298-306.

10. Morgan, declaration for invalid pension, Jan. 23, 1879, and affidavit for pension, Apr. 11, 1879, Pension Records; Frank E. Smith, *The Yazoo River* (New York, 1954), 166.

11. Morgan, application for pension, May 24, 1912; Carrie V. Morgan, affidavit, July 7, 1923; A. T. Morgan, Jr., affidavits, May 10 and Sept. 28, 1923, Pension Records; Morgan, *Yazoo,* 510-11.

12. Morgan to J. L. Davenport, Dec. 25, 1912, Pension Records. Morgan's three books on the money question were all published in Denver; the quotation is from *On Our Way to the Orient,* 12-13.

13. Morgan to A. T. Morgan, Jr., Mar. 15, 1920; Carolyn V. Shannon, affidavit, Oct. 20, 1923, Pension Records.

14. Carrie V. Morgan, application for widow's pension, Nov. 28, 1922; A. T. Morgan, Jr., affidavit, Sept. 28, 1923; H. L. Williams to Commissioner of Pensions, Sept. 29, 1923; E. L. Howard to Commissioner of Pensions, Oct. 27, 1923; and miscellaneous notes, Pension Records.

15. Ames to E. Benjamin Andrews, May 24, 1895, Feb. 29, 1896, Ames, *Ames,* 503, 507-10; Ames to Blanche Ames, Aug. 1, Nov. 2, 5, 1898, Ames, *Chronicles,* II, 636-37, 659, 662.

16. Ames to Garner, Jan. 17, 1900, Ames, *Ames,* 573-75; Ames to Rowland, Mar. 20, 1929, quoted in Terry L. Seip, *The South Returns to Congress* (Baton Rouge La., 1983), 294n; Garner, *Reconstruction in Mississippi,* 290, 320-24, 408.

17. Ames, *Ames,* 500, 516-25, 528-40, 549; John F. Kennedy, *Profiles in Courage* (Cardinal edition, New York, 1957), 136-37.

18. Elisa Mouton to Warmoth, Sept. 28, 1872, Dec. 23, 1875, Mar. 24, 1876; Anonymous to Warmoth, Apr. 30, 1874; unidentified newspaper clippings, 1877, Warmoth papers.

19. Unidentified newspaper clippings, Aug. 9, 1881, Jan. 30, 1897, Warmoth papers; Harris, "Warmoth," 128 29.

20. E. W. Robertson to Warmoth, June 13, 1876, Warmoth Papers; Warmoth, *War, Politics and Reconstruction,* 257; Gonzales, "Kellogg," 93-95, 99-100; Harris, "Warmoth," 128-29; Binning, "Warmoth," 375-77.

21. *New Orleans States,* Jan. 7, 1900; *New Orleans Daily Item,* Jan. ——, 1900, clippings in the Warmoth papers; Binning, "Warmoth," 1-3, 362-73.

22. Ella Lonn to Warmoth, July 3, 14, 1917; Warmoth to Lonn, July 7, 1917; Warmoth diary, Apr. 21, 1929, Warmoth papers; Warmoth, *War, Politics and Reconstruction,* 270; Binning, "Warmoth," 381-85; Taylor, *Louisiana Reconstructed,* 250; T. Harry Williams, *Huey Long* (New York, 1970), 184.

Index

A Fool's Errand, 367–68, 372, 375, 377–79, 397, 402, 405
Abbeville, S.C., 352
Abbott, Joseph C., 205, 206–7, 208, 212
Adaline, 196–97, 210
Adams, Charles F., Jr., 93
Adams, John D., 265
Adams, T. A., 290
Africa, 37
African M. E. Church, 151, 318, 320
Africanization, 420
Afro-Americans, 39, 86, 91; in La., 12–16, 246, 254, 292, 293, 294–95; in S.C., 42–45, 94–96, 113, 114, 143–44, 146, 225–27, 228, 229, 328, 349, 352–53, 362, 396–97; in N.C., 52–53, 65, 104, 107–8, 199, 201–2, 288–89; in Ark., 133, 134, 135, 136, 137–38, 141–42, 268, 305; in Fla., 149, 239; in Ala., 155, 162–63; in Miss., 172–73, 175, 178, 308, 315–16, 317, 321–23, 326–27. *See also* Negro suffrage
Aftermath of the Civil War, The, 408
Alabama, 238, 385, 386; Spencer in, 29–32; Warner in, 32–37; Republican beginnings, 68–73; Warner as senator, 153–60; 1870 election, 160–66; 1871–72 politics, 166–71, 1872 election, 271–76; and Hayes, 383–85; Warner's last years in, 385–89
Alabama & Chattanooga R.R., 157
Alabama Improvement Co., 388
Alabama River, 32–33
Alabama State Journal, 274
Alamance County, N.C., 202, 203, 205, 206, 212, 213, 282, 371
Albany, N.Y., 61, 150
Alcorn, James L.: fears Democrats, 120–22; elected governor, 175–76; elected senator, 179; remains as governor, 186, 188–90; in Senate, 190–91; defeated for governor, 307–9; and bloodshed, 322
Alcorn University, 189
Alden, George R., 151
Allegheny Valley, 41
Allen, Walter, 399
Allendale Mounted Base Ball Club, 355
American Banknote Co., 219, 234
American Federation of Labor, 398
American Historical Review, 396
American Railway Union, 398
American Trust and Banking Co., 256
Ames, Adelbert: background, 112–15; provisional governor of Miss., 115–17, 119; military commander, 172–73; and 1869 election, 174–76; and Morgan, 176–77; elected to Senate, 179; admitted, 181–84; marriage, 184–85; visits Miss., 185–86; debates Blair, 186–89; debates Alcorn, 189–92; runs for governor, 306–9; as governor, 309–12; and Vicksburg riot, 314–17; and 1875 election, 321–24; impeached, 324–25; leaves Miss., 325–26; post-Reconstruction career, 412–16
Ames, Adelbert, Jr., 415
Ames, Blanche (Butler), 112, 114, 181, 186, 315, 317, 323, 413, 415; courtship and marriage, 182–84; visits Miss., 184–86,

Ames, Blanche (*cont.*)
307, 308; as first lady, 309–11, 324; and Ames's impeachment, 325
Ames, Butler, 189, 311, 315
Ames, Edith, 307, 311
Ames, Jessie, 416
Ames, Sarah, 315
Amherst Academy, 92
Amherst College, 396
Amnesty bill, 192
An Appeal to Caesar, 402–3
Anderson, S.C., 217, 218
Andrew, John A., 93
Anthony House, 132, 136, 137, 258
Antietam, Md., 112
Appomattox, Va., 6, 133, 187, 212, 351, 376
Arch Street Theatre, 402
Arkansas, 36, 205, 317; Clayton's arrival, 132–36; Clayton inaugurated, 136–37; militia war, 137–42; prosperity and politics, 255–60; 1872 election, 264–68; Brooks-Baxter war, 299–305; Clayton's last years in, 406–8
Arkansas Central R.R., 299–300, 301
Arkansas Gazette, 138, 140, 141, 255, 256, 265, 408
Arkansas River, 133, 134, 137, 265, 266, 300
Arkansas, University of, 406
Arlington (Lee home), 6; National Cemetery, 384, 408
Army: of Northern Va., 5, 333; of the Tenn., 30, 299, 389; U.S., 81–82, 306
Arthur, Chester A., 397–98, 417
Ashburne, George W., 109
Asheville, N.C., 221
Ashley, James M., 145
Ashtabula, Ohio, 47
Associated Press, 344, 394
Atlanta, Ga., 35, 41
Atlantic Monthly, 373, 396
Augusta, Ga., 349

Baird, Absalom, 22–23
Baltimore, Md., 400
Bancroft, George, 19
Bangor, Me., 214
Bank of the Beast, The, 410
Banking system, 157
Banks, Nathaniel P., 10–12, 18; Mrs., 10
Baptists, 405
Barnwell County, S.C., 352
Basis, The, 403
Bates, Benjamin F., 223
Baton Rouge, La., 9
Baxter, Elisha, 266, 268; in Brooks-Baxter war, 299–305
Bayou Teche, La., 75
Beaufort, S.C., 350
Beauregard, P. G. T., 293, 295
Beecher, James C., 43
Belgium, 122
Benton, Miss., 118
Berkshire Hills, 47, 195
Billings, Josh, 61
Billings, Liberty, 86–90, 148, 240
Bimetallism, 410
Black Belt, 32
Black Crook, The, 212
Black Warrior River, 31
Blacks, *See* Afro-Americans
Blaine, James, G., 260, 362
Blair, Frank: in 1868 election, 124–25, 145–46, 150; denounces Warner, 167–68; debates Ames, 187–88; opposes Clayton, 260
Blair, Henry W., 404
Blake, James P., 93
Bliss, George, Jr., 270
Blue Ridge Mountains, 218
Blue Ridge R.R., 218–21, 228–29, 233–35, 271, 329, 366
Bonds, railroad-aid: S.C., 217–21, 233–35, 237–38, 329, 366; Ark., 256
Bonnie Blue Flag, The, 77
Booth, Edwin, 19
Booth, John W., 7
Boozer, Lemuel, 226
Bordeaux, France, 403
Boston, Mass., 61, 150, 219, 278, 401, 411
Boston Globe, 414
Boston Southern Relief Association, 98
Boutwell, George S., 17, 169–71, 184
Bowen, Christopher C., 226, 234
Bowles, Samuel, 338, 345
Bradley Polytechnic Institute, 413
Brady, Matthew B., 290
Brandon Republican, 316
Brazil, 37
Breckinridge, Clifton R., 406–7
Bricks Without Straw, 378–79
Brindletails, 259, 266
Brinkley, Ark., 265
Bristol Military College, 132
Bristow, Benjamin H., 345, 347
Brooklyn, N.Y., 95
Brooks, Joseph, 138, 140, 259, 266–68; in Brooks-Baxter War, 299–305
Brooks-Baxter War, 299–305

Brown, John, 322
Brown University, 413
Brown v. Board of Education, 404
Bruce, Blanche K., 324–25, 409
Bryan, William J., 410
Buchanan, Robert C., 77–78
Buckley, Charles W., 72, 166
Buffalo, N.Y., 59
Buffalo, University of, 403
Bull Run, Va., 38, 46, 47, 69, 112, 115, 289, 402
Bureau of Freedmen, Refugees, and Abandoned Lands, *see* Freedmen's Bureau
Burke, E. A., 279
Butler, Benjamin F., 55, 61, 77, 112, 114, 181, 184, 192, 293, 307, 312, 319, 415; Warmoth visits, 18; at impeachment, 110; advises Ames, 317, 324–25
Butler, Blanche, *see* Ames, Blanche
Butler, Matthew C., 226, 231–32, 349–50, 351, 362, 366
Butler, Sarah (Hildreth), 18, 184, 185, 311, 325–26
Byerly, D. C., 295–97

"C" letters, 369
Cain, Richard H., 95–96
Cajun country, 74, 246, 416
Calhoun, John C., 217, 232
California, 32, 34, 41, 69, 407, 415
Cambridge, Mass., 93
Cameron, Angus, 409
Cameron, J. Donald, 350, 356
Canby, Edward R. S., 102
Canton, Miss., 279
Cape Ann, 415
Capital punishment, 105
Cardozo, Francis L., 222–23, 332, 334–35, 336, 347, 361, 365, 366
Cardozo, Thomas W., 316
Carlyle, Thomas, 154
Carolina Hall, 357
Carpenter, Matthew H., 290–91, 292–93, 294
Carpenter, R. B., 225–26, 344, 346, 347
Carpetbagger, use of term, 72, 84, 91, 117, 121, 127–28, 131, 153–54, 156, 167–68, 171, 174, 261–62, 387, 420–21, 423
Casey, James F., 245–46, 248–49, 262
Castle Thunder, 6
Castleton, Vt., 24–25
Caswell County, N.C., 102, 203–4, 205, 206, 211–12, 213
Catterson, Robert F., 258–59
Cavaliers, 341
Centennial Exposition, 339
Central College, 41
Chamberlain, Alice (Ingersoll), 214, 338, 341, 346, 355, 361, 399, 400
Chamberlain, Daniel H., 394; background, 91–94; in constitutional convention, 94–98; rebuked by Scott, 99; attorney general, 214–15, 218, 220–21, 228; on land commission, 222–23; in 1870 election, 226–27; in taxpayers' convention, 230–32; and 1872 election, 268–69, 271; elected governor, 328–33; woos conservatives, 333–42; rapprochement with Democrats, 342–48; repudiated by Democrats, 349–53; in 1876 election, 353–57; and Hayes, 357–63; and Hampton administration, 363–66; post-Reconstruction career, 396–400
Chandler, Minnie, 185
Chandler, William E., 278–79
Chandler, Zachariah, 185, 188
Charity Hospital, 250
Charleston, S.C., 40–42, 93, 94, 112, 143, 145, 146, 217, 218, 231, 340, 352, 354
Charleston Chamber of Commerce, 229–30, 338–39
Charleston Club House, 94, 98
Charleston County, S.C., 231
Charleston Courier, 94–95. *See also Charleston News and Courier*
Charleston Daily News, 45, 144, 219, 225. *See also Charleston News and Courier*
Charleston Mercury, 99
Charleston News and Courier: opposes Chamberlain, 331–34; supports C., 334–38, 343, 351; turns against C., 352, 353; on C.'s departure, 361; reconciles with C., 398–99
Charleston Republican, 225, 231
Charlotte, Columbia & Augusta R.R., 217
Charlotte Observer, 284
Charlottesville, Va., 400
Chase, C. K., 323
Chase, Nettie, 17–18
Chase, Salmon P., 149; receives Warmoth, 17–18; and Fla., 25–28; and 1860 convention, 34; at impeachment, 110–111
Chattanooga, Tenn., 35, 47, 169, 170, 387, 388, 389
Cherokee County, Ala., 385
Chester, Ohio, 380
Chester County, S.C., 224, 347

Chester Methodist church, 217
Chicago, Ill., 34, 59, 62, 124, 379, 411
Chicago Tribune, 35–36, 377; on 1872 election, 262, 263, 264–65, 269, 273; on Warmoth, 297; and Chamberlain, 358–59, 359–60
Chickamauga, Tenn., 47
China, 37
Chipola River, 239
Christ, Jesus, 233, 288, 405
Christian Science, 411
Christianity, 373, 400, 401, 405–6
Christ's Sermon on the Mount, 414
Churr, Jacob, 373
Cicero, Marcus, 340
Cincinnati, Ohio, 169, 217, 218, 258, 272, 277, 347, 389
Cincinnati Commercial, 242, 254, 361
Cincinnati Gazette, 230
City Point, Va., 5
Civil rights legislation, 128, 191, 294; Sumner's, 285–86
Clay, Henry, 3
Clayton, Adeline (McGraw), 134, 255
Clayton, Charlotte, 408
Clayton, John M., 255, 300–301, 406–7
Clayton, Kathleen, 408
Clayton, Lucy, 408
Clayton, Powell, 143, 205, 262; background, 132–34; Ark. planter, 134–36; inaugurated governor, 136–37; opposes KKK, 137–41; fights militia war, 141–42; economic policies, 255–57; to Senate, 258–60; in 1872 election, 264–68; and Brooks-Baxter War, 299–305; post-Reconstruction career, 406–8
Clayton, Powell, Jr., 408
Clayton, Thomas, 406–7
Clayton, William H. H., 132, 300, 406–7
Cleveland, Grover, 391, 398, 409, 418
Cleveland, Ohio, 59, 61, 111
Clinton, Miss., massacre, 321
Coahoma County, Miss., 191, 322
Cochran, John R., 223, 363, 365
Cocke, William A., 151–52
Code of Civil Procedure, 372
Colfax, La., 292
Colfax, Schuyler, 19, 292
Collectorship, *see* Customs, collectorship of
Colorado, 374, 410–11
Columbia, S.C., 228, 229, 271, 355; Scott's arrival in, 142–43; burning of, 146, 214; Scott's interests in, 216–17, 329, 364–66, 391–92, 395
Columbia & Charlotte R.R., 268
Columbia Phoenix, 99, 143, 146–47, 147–48
Columbia Union, 225
Columbia Union Herald, 333, 335, 336, 340, 344, 353
Columbia University, 413
Columbus, Christopher, 288
Columbus, Ohio, 41, 47, 111, 359
Confederate money, 35, 217, 283
Congregationalists, 214
Congress, U.S.: considers Reconstruction, 17–20; Joint Committee, 17, 53, 90; passes Reconstruction Acts, 66–67, 68, 69, 73; impeaches Johnson, 107, 109–11, 112, 117, 120, 181; Warner in, 153–60, 166–69; Spencer in, 155–60, 276; Enforcement Acts of, 160, 168, 187, 189–92, 205, 233, 240; Ku Klux Committee, 168, 171, 187, 232–33, 260; Ames in, 181–84, 186–92; Judiciary Committee, 182, 183; Civil Rights Bill, 285–86; Poland Committee, 303–5
Conkling, Roscoe, 183
Conneaut, Ohio, 157
Conservatives, *see* Democrats
Constitution, U.S., 182, 230, 348. *See also* Fifteenth Amendment; Fourteenth Amendment
Constitution Club, 126
Constitutional conventions: Ark., 304; Fla., 87–90; La. 75–76; Miss., 83–84; N.C., 91, 101–7, 287–89; S.C., 91, 94–98
Continent, The, 402, 404–5
Conway, Thomas W., 75, 244
Copperheads, 35, 124, 148
Corinth, Miss., 30, 33
Cornell, Alonzo B., 270
Cornell University, 396
Corruption, 167, 226, 233, 235, 240–41, 243–45, 253, 263, 270, 277, 292, 295, 424
Cotton: claims, 11; Spencer and, 29–31; Warner and, 33, 35–37; tax on, 36, 71; Morgans and, 37–40, 69, 70–71, 80; Chamberlain and, 94; Clayton and, 134–35
Courtland, Ala., 163
Coushatta Massacre, 293
Cox, Jacob D., 73, 169–70, 272
Crane, Joseph G., 173
Crawford, Samuel W., 161, 163–64, 165
Creede, Colo., 410
Crescent Hotel Co., 406, 407
Cripple Creek, Colo., 410

Crosby, Peter, 315–16
Cuba, 413
Cumulative voting, 231, 232
Custer, George A., 349
Custom House Republicans, 277–78, 295
Customs, collectorship of: in New Orleans, 124, 245–46, 248, 418; in Mobile, 156, 169–71

Daily Crescent, New Orleans, 15
Dana, Charles A., 244
Danbury, N.C., 371
Danville, Va., 50
Dartmouth College, 389, 415
Davis, A. K., 308, 312
Davis, Garrett, 183
Davis, Jefferson, 5, 8, 56, 77, 120–21, 182, 200, 243
Davis, Jefferson (Ark. governor), 407
Davis, Joseph, 120
Dawson, Francis W.: denounces Chamberlain, 333–34; befriends C., 334–38; continues support, 338–42; for bipartisan ticket, 342–44, 351; turns against C., 352–53; reconciles with C., 398–99
De Large, Robert C., 222–23, 226, 227, 234
Death penalty, 105
Debs, Eugene V., 398
Debts, state: Ark., 256, 257; Fla., 236–38; Miss., 311, 316, 414, 416; N.C., 105–6; S.C., 218–21, 231, 335–36, 339; exaggerated, 263
Decatur, Ala., 29, 69–70, 163
Decatur, Aberdeen & Vicksburg R.R., 157
Declaration of Independence, 349
Deep River Meeting House, 54, 63
Defiance, Ohio, 393, 394
Delaware, 56, 132
Democrats, or Conservatives, 124–25, 132, 167, 262; in Ala., 155, 156, 160–66, 168, 273, 275; in Ark., 134–35, 138–41, 256, 257, 266, 268, 300, 303, 304–5; in Fla., 86, 90, 149–50, 239–40; in La., 76–77, 122–23, 125–31, 244, 247–49, 254, 277–78, 294–96, 418–19; in Miss., 116, 118–20, 174, 175, 308, 316, 318, 319, 325, 326; in N.C., 102, 104, 107–9, 111, 199, 206, 282, 287–88; in S.C., 91, 101, 145–48, 218, 221, 224–26, 234, 340, 342–43, 345, 348, 350, 352, 355–57, 363–66
Demopolis, Ala., 163
Dent, Louis, 174, 175
Denver, Colo., 374, 377, 378, 397, 410, 412
Denver Times, 377
Detroit, Mich., 185
Devall's Bluff, Ark., 302
Dick, Robert P., 289, 375
Dickinson, J. Q., 239
Digest of Cited Cases, A, 377
District of Columbia, 56
"Dixie," 247, 268
Dixon, Henry M., 319–21, 323
Dixon, Thomas, Jr., 405
Dodge, Grenville M., 30–31, 69, 70, 71, 384
Dorsey, Stephen W., 299–300, 301–2
Doty, James D., 25
Douglas, Robert M., 372, 377
Douglas, Stephen A., 59
Douglas, Stephen A., Jr., 372, 373
Douglass, Frederick: at White House, 5; at Loyalist convention, 55, 58; and Tourgee, 404
Dr. Fitch's Supporter, 38
Dred Scott case, 228
Drennan, Judge, 314
Drury, Warren G., 393–95
DuBois, William E. B., 404
Dumas, Francis E., 76
Dunn, Oscar J., 76, 123, 129, 130, 131, 242, 245, 246, 248, 249, 250–51, 254, 276
Dunn, Thomas C., 344
Durand, Henry, 417
Durand, Sally, *see* Warmoth, Sally
Durant, Thomas J., 14
Durell, E. H., 279–81
Durham's Station, N.C., 196

E. Remington & Sons, 224
Edgefield, S.C., 351–52, 362
Edgefield Advertiser, 343
Edgefield County, S.C., 225, 343–44, 355–57
Edisto Island, 93
Edmunds, George F., 188
Education: and racism, 378, 380–82, 404, 405–6; and classics, 396. *See also* Schools
Egypt, 384, 400
El Cid, 47
Elections: Ala., *1868*, 71–72; *1870*, 160–66; *1872*, 271–76; Ark., *1868*, 141; *1872*, 265–68; congressional, *1866*, 53; *1874*, 294, 315; Fla., *1867*, 86–87; *1868*, 90, 150; La., *1867*, 75; *1868*, 76–78, 131; *1870*, 246–47; *1872*, 276–81; *1874*, 294; Miss., *1868*, 116; *1869*, 118–20; *1871*, 189–90; *1873*, 306–9,

Elections (*cont.*)
312–13; *1874*, 315; *1875*, 317–24; N.C., *1866*, 66; *1867*, 101–2; *1868*, 109, 199; *1870*, 199, 206; Northern, *1867*, 71; presidential, *1872*, 261–64; *1876*, 357–62; S.C., *1868*, 99–101, 145–48; *1870*, 223–27; *1872*, 268–70; *1874*, 333; *1876*, 355–57
Ellenton, S.C., massacre, 354
Elliott, Grace, 346
Elliott, Robert B., 217, 223, 226–27, 269, 271, 328, 332, 346, 392; breaks with Chamberlain, 334–36; backs Whipper, 339, 340, 341; and 1876 election, 352–53, 361
Ellsworth, Hales, 275
Emancipation Proclamation, 198, 298
Emory, William H., 281, 322
Enforcement Acts, 160, 168, 187, 189–92, 205, 233, 240
England, 333, 400
Episcopal church, 183, 184, 297, 389, 391, 415, 417
Erie, Pa., 46–48, 50, 210, 213, 370, 372, 377
Erie Academy, 47
Erskine College, 217, 338
Eureka Improvement Co., 406
Eureka Springs, Ark., 406, 407
Eutaw, Ala., 154; riot in, 163–65, 166

Faneuil Hall, 61
Fernandina, Fla., 24, 26–29
Field, David D., 19, 105
Fifteenth Amendment, 155, 160, 168, 174, 179, 187, 230, 348
Fifth Avenue Hotel, 276, 278
Fifth Massachusetts Cavalry, 93
Figs and Thistles, 373, 375, 377, 379
Finegan, Joseph, 26
First Baptist Church Sewing Circle, 355
Flagler, Henry M., 415
Florence, Ala., 163
Florida, 305, 357, 360, 362, 385, 415; Reed's arrival in, 24–29; Republican party, 84–82; constitution-making, 87–90; Reed takes office, 148–52; Reed as governor, 236–42; Reed's last years in, 389–91
Florida Fruit Growers' Association, 390
Florida Railroad, 26
Fool's Errand, A, 367–68, 372, 375, 377–79, 397, 402, 405
Fords, Howard & Hulbert, 375. *See also* J. B. Ford & Co.
Ford's Theater, 7
Forrest, Nathan B., 121, 311
Fort Smith Herald, 136
Forts: Donelson, 35; Fisher, 35, 112, 181; Sumter, 37, 49, 161, 325, 363; Moultrie, 347, 350
Fourteenth Amendment, 53, 54, 56–57, 62, 66–67, 68, 84, 123, 158, 160, 167, 168, 174, 179, 187, 191, 231, 264, 306, 348
Fowle, Daniel G., 369
Fox Lake, Wis., 37–38
France, 47, 403
Fredericksburg, Va., 112
Free silver, 410
Freedmen's Aid Societies, 27, 66
Freedmen's Bank, 211
Freedmen's Bureau, 19, 21, 27, 32, 36, 39, 51, 52, 66, 71, 72, 74, 75, 79, 82, 83, 85, 90, 95, 106, 113, 118, 148, 173, 240; Scott as officer of, 41–45, 98–100, 143, 144, 225, 230, 269, 329–30, 334; Tourgee on, 404
French Revolution, 12, 55
Friar's Point, Miss., 120, 322
Friends, *see* Quakers
Friends of Universal Suffrage, 13–14
Furman University, 217, 339
Fusionists, 290, 292. *See also* Liberal Republicans

Galesburg, Ill., 62
Gambier, Ohio, 392
Garfield, James A., 173, 385; and Tourgee, 379–82
Garland, Augustus H., 304
Garner, James W., 413–14
Garrison, William L., 92, 361, 404
Gary, Martin W., 228, 231–32, 350–51, 353–55, 366
Gatling gun convention, 251–52
General Butler in New Orleans, 184
George, James Z., 322–24
Georgetown, D.C., 183, 217
Georgia, 157, 158, 160, 322, 386
German Fusiliers, 338
Gettysburg, Pa., 16, 38, 112
Gettysburg Female Seminary, 410
Gibbs, Jonathan C., 88, 90, 151, 239, 241–42
Gibbs, William H., 119–20
Gillem, Alvan C., 116, 118–19, 120, 121

Gleason, William H., 151–52
Godkin, Edwin L., 91
Gold Coast, 285
Goldsboro, N.C., 207
Gompers, Samuel, 398
Goodloe, Daniel, 58
Gordon, John B., 322
Gorrell, Ralph, 209
Governor Chamberlain's Administration, 399
Graham, John A., 106
Graham, John W., 201
Graham, N.C., 203
Graham, William A., 287
Grand Army of the Republic, 73, 194
Grant, Buck, 247
Grant, Jesse, 247
Grant, Julia (Dent), 181, 185, 245, 247, 248
Grant, Nellie, 247
Grant, Ulysses S., 77, 117, 122, 124, 125, 141, 145, 148, 150, 153, 154, 156, 174, 181, 269, 290, 292, 298, 357, 384; removes Warmoth, 3; at Appomattox, 6; and Washburne, 119–20; Alcorn on, 121–22; loses La., 131–32; endorses Warner, 165–66; and Mobile collectorship, 169–71, 385, 387; appoints Ames, 172; repudiates Dent, 175; Tourgee visits, 212; acts against KKK, 228, 233; and La. patronage, 245–49, 250, 252, 254; and 1872 election, 261, 265–66, 271–73, 276, 278, 280–81, 282; and Vicksburg riot, 314–15, 317; and 1875 election, 321–23; and Chamberlain, 333, 345, 350, 356
Grant Parish, La., 292
Greeley, Horace, 19, 38; in 1872 election, 260–61, 269–70, 271–72, 273, 276, 277, 279
Greenback party, 370–71
Greensboro, N.C., 102, 206, 210, 213, 282, 283, 289, 397; Tourgee settles in, 50–51; hostility of, 62–64, 65; 1868 election in, 107–9; Tourgee home in, 193; judicial circuit, 195; and Oberlin, 197; freed people, 198; woodworking business, 210–12; Tourgee attached to, 286–87, 369, 374; T. departs from, 375–76
Greensboro North State, 376
Greensboro Patriot, 62, 63, 64, 199, 201, 208, 286
Greensboro Register, 65, 101, 201
Greensboro Spoke and Handle Factory, 211. *See also* North Carolina Handle Co.
Greensboro Times, 108
Greenville, Miss., 309
Greenville, N.C., 282
Greenville, S.C., 339, 340
Greenville & Columbia R.R., 219–21, 228
Greenville News, 342
Griffin, Albert, 263–64
Guilford Bar Association, 286
Guilford County, N.C., 50–51, 54, 64, 66, 102, 103, 207, 369–71; bar, 208, 286

Hague, the, Holland, 407
Hahn, Michael, 16, 23, 130–31
"Hail Columbia," 107
Haiti, 76
Hamburg, S.C., massacre, 349–50, 351, 352, 354, 362
Hamlet, 19
Hampton, Wade: and burning of Columbia, 146; and 1868 campaign, 146–48; and 1876 campaign, 347–48, 350, 352, 353, 356, 357; and Hayes, 357–60; administration, 363–66; Chamberlain on, 399
Hancock, Winfield S., 77, 78
"Hang Jeff Davis," 107
Harlan, Mary, 19–20, 308
Harper & Brothers, 373
Harper's Magazine, 197
Harper's Weekly, 127
Harris, J. S., 245–46
Harris, James H., 109
Harrison, Benjamin, 391, 418
Harrison, James W., 220, 223, 228–29
Hart, Ossian B., 85, 86, 90
Hartford, Conn., 61
Harvard University, 91, 93, 214, 299, 351, 396, 415
Haskell, Alexander C., 354, 360, 399
Havis, Ferd, 302, 406
Haw River, N.C., 211
Hawkins, Jacob, 280
Hawthorne, Nathaniel, 403
Hay, John, 5, 29, 124
Hayes, Rutherford B., 347, 416; Chamberlain and, 357–62; Scott and, 364; Tourgee and, 367, 369; Spencer and, 383; Warner and, 384–85
Hays, Charles, 163–65, 170
Hebert, P. O., 243
Helena, Ark., 133
Hell-Hole Swamp, 222–23, 364
Hemphill, J. C., 399
Henry Ames, 8, 9

Henry Clews & Co., 220
Henry County, Ohio, 41, 45, 395
Heroes and Hero-Worship, 154
Hesper, 140, 142
Hibernian Hall, 348
Highgate, Carrie (Carolyn) V., *see* Morgan, Carrie V.
Hildreth, Sarah, *see* Butler, Sarah
Hillsboro, N.C., 195, 201, 202, 209
Hinds, James, 138, 140, 154, 266
Hinds, Jerome S., 274, 275
Historical and Biographical Cyclopedia, 389
Hitchcock, Daniel, 82
Holden, William W., 52, 101, 102, 108, 109, 196, 200, 202, 203, 204, 205, 207, 209, 289, 375; welcomes Tourgee, 46–47, 49–50; impeachment of, 210, 287
Holford and Co., 256
Holly Springs, Miss., 309, 319, 322
Holmes, Oliver W., 362
Holt, Joseph, 3
Hornellsville, N.Y., *Valley Times*, 197–98
"Hot Plowshares," 402
Houston, Tex, 13, 74, 244
Howard, Oliver O., 42, 98
Huguenots, 47, 341, 401
Humphreys, Benjamin G., 83; Ames replaces, 115–17, 172
Hunter, Geoffrey, 197
Huntsville, Ala., 163

Idaho, 14
Ilion, N.Y., 224
Illinois, 8, 107, 119, 124, 143, 245
Illinois Central R.R., 279
Impeachments: Ames, 324–25; Cardozo, 336; Chamberlain, 341; Clayton, 259; Holden, 210, 287; Johnson, 107, 109–11, 112, 117, 120, 181; Reed, 148–52, 240–42, 390; Scott, 233–35; Warmoth, 280–81, 420
India, 37
Indiana, 59, 62, 181, 394
Indianapolis, Ind., 59, 62, 411, 412
Ingersoll, Alice, *see* Chamberlain, Alice
Innocents, 128
Interior Department, 409–10
Internal Improvement Fund, 238
Invisible Empire, The, 378, 379
Iowa, 32, 266
Iron industry, 385–88
Italy, 415

J. B. Ford & Co., 284. *See also* Fords, Howard, & Hulbert
Jackson, Miss., 83, 115, 119, 173, 180, 309, 411
Jackson Clarion, 84, 175
Jackson County, Fla., 238–39
Jacksonville, Fla., 28–29, 84, 87, 150, 241, 389, 390, 391
Jacksonville Florida Times, 28
Jacksonville, Pensacola & Mobile, R.R., 238
Jacksonville Republican Club, 85
Jainey Hall, 143
James River, 5
Jay Cooke & Co., 283
Jefferson, Joseph, 74
Jefferson County, Ark., 133, 257, 302, 305, 406
Jefferson Parish, La., 128, 129
Jenkinsville, S.C., 331
Jersey City, N.J., 278
Jesus Christ, 233, 288, 405
Jewell, E. L., 295–97
"John Brown's Body," 180
Johns Hopkins Hospital, 400
Johns Hopkins University, 407
Johnson, A. M., 139
Johnson, Andrew, 49, 55–56, 58, 62–63, 99, 114, 125, 126, 134–35, 163; to Richmond, 5; Warmoth visits, 7–8; restoration plan of, 8, 11–12, 16, 17, 19, 21, 36, 42, 53, 101, 229; Reed and, 28, 85, 89; and Ala., 30–31; "swing around," 59; removes Pope and Swayne, 71–72; removes Sheridan, 75; impeachment, 107, 109–11, 112, 117, 120, 181; backs Humphreys, 115; removes McDowell, 116
Johnson, James M., 136, 142, 257–58, 259
Johnston, Joseph E., 35, 48, 196
Jones, J. M., 203
Judas Iscariot, 288
Judges, election of, 97, 105
Juneau, Solomon, 25

Kansas, 38, 111, 132–33, 143, 263, 267, 410, 411
Kansas Magazine, 263
Kellogg, William P., 130, 131, 278, 279, 297; to Senate, 124; and 1868 election, 125–26; and Casey, 245–46, 250; and 1872 election, 289–93; and 1874 election, 293–98; later career, 418
Kennedy, John F., 416
Kentucky, 56, 183, 225, 279
Kenyon College, 392
Kershaw, J. B., 348

Key, David M., 385
Key West, Fla., 415
Kilbourne, Angie, 369
Kilbourne, Emma, *see* Tourgee, Emma
Kimpton, Hiram H., 218–21, 223, 231, 233–35, 337, 365, 366
King, Edward, 299
Kingsville, Ohio, 377
Kirk, George W., 205
Kirk-Holden War, 205–6, 209
Knights of Labor, 398
Knights of the White Camellia, 125, 126, 128
Ku Klux Acts, *see* Enforcement Acts
Ku Klux Committee, 168, 171, 187, 232–33, 260
Ku Klux Klan: origin of, 121; in Ala., 154, 161–65, 168; in Ark., 138–42, 408; in Fla., 150, 151, 238–40; in La., 122, 125, 128; in Miss., 117, 175, 186–87; in N.C., 199–206, 207, 208, 212–13, 282, 373; in S.C., 221, 227–28, 230, 232–33
Kuhn, Seneca and Hattie, 50, 51, 64–65

Lady Gay, 16
Lafayette Square, 11, 289
Lakes: Chautaugua, 379; Como, 415; Erie, 46
Lamar, L. Q. C., 316–17, 322, 325, 326, 409–10, 416
Land, redistribution of, 42–43, 95–96, 102, 222–23, 364
Lane, Eleanor, 8
Laurens County, S.C., 355–57
Lawhon Iron Co., 388
Lawrence, Effingham, 298–99, 417
Lawrence, Kan., 132, 410
Leavenworth, Kan., 132–33
Lebanon, Mo., 8
Lee, Robert E., 5, 6, 164, 247, 384, 410
Leopard's Spots, The, 405
Leslie, Charles P., 222
Lewisburg, Ark., 138, 266–67
Libby Prison, 6
Liberal Republicans: in Ark. in 1869, 258; in 1872 election, 261, 262, 272–73, 277–78, 282, 290, 292; after 1872, 345
Liberia, 76
Licking Valley, 34
Lily Whites, 419
Lincoln, Abraham, 34, 55, 56, 59, 62, 124; and Warmoth, 3–4; second inauguration, 4–5; on Reconstruction, 6–7; assassination, 7–8
Lincoln Brotherhood, 85
Lincoln, Mary (Todd), 5, 7
Lincoln, Robert T., 19
Lincolnton, N.C., 193
Lindsay, Robert B., 165
Linwood, Ark., 300
Little Rock, Ark., 132, 133, 134, 137–40, 255, 257, 265, 299, 303, 406
Little Rock, Mississippi & Texas R.R., 300
Little Rock, Pine Bluff & New Orleans R.R., 256, 300
Little Rock Republican, 301, 305
Little Sodus, N.Y., 157
Littlefield, Milton S., 211, 381; at N.C. convention, 106–7, 109; lends to Tourgee, 194; in Fla., 236–38, 240–41
Livingston, Ala., 163
London, England, 333
Long, Huey, 420
Long Branch, N.J., 254, 333
Longstreet, James, 128, 156, 247, 249, 250, 278, 279, 280–81, 293
Lonn, Ella, 419
Lookout Mountain, 169
Lost Cause, 362, 390, 405
Louisiana, 305, 357, 360, 362; reorganized, 7; Republican beginnings in, 11–16; territorial delegate, 16–20; massacre, 21–23; reconstructed, 73–78; governor inaugurated, 122–24; 1868 election in, 124–31; Warmoth as governor, 242–49; 1872 election in, 276–81, 289–93; 1874 election in, 293–94; Warmoth's later career in, 416–21
Louisiana Levee Co., 244–45
Louisville Courier-Journal, 273
Lowell, Charles W., 246, 247–49, 250, 251, 252
Lowell, Mass., 184, 189, 307, 308, 324, 412, 415
Lowry, Rebecca Jane, *see* Scott, Rebecca Jane
Loyal Leagues, 118
Loyalists, 51, 54, 63, 372. *See also* Southern Loyalist Convention

McClure, John, 301
McComb, Henry S., 244–45
McDowell, Irwin, 115, 116
McEnery, John, 277, 279, 281, 289–92, 295, 297
McGraw, Adeline, *see* Clayton, Adeline
Mackey, T. J., 144, 270, 271, 351, 359, 364–65

McKinley, William, 403, 407
McLeansboro, Ill., 8
McMaster, Fitz W., 365, 395
McMillan, William L., 291
Macomb, Ill., 62
Macon, Ga., 41
McPherson, Edward, 16–17, 77
McPherson Square, 181
Madison, Wis., 25
Madison House, 274, 275
Madison University, 85
Magnolia plantation, 298–99, 417–18
Magnolia Sugar Refining Co., 417
Maine, 86, 113, 185, 186, 214, 246, 312, 415
Marianna, Fla., 238–39
Marietta College, 34, 389
Marion County, S.C., 342
Marmaduke, John S., 133
Marvin, William, 28
Maryland, 56, 183
Mason and Dixon's line, 387
Massachusetts, 24, 47, 92, 150, 157, 195, 214, 293, 307, 308, 314, 338, 347, 394, 400, 416
Mayflower, 127
Maynard, Horace, 17
Mayville, N.Y., 382
Meade, George G., 87, 89–90
Mechanics' Institute, 21–23, 75, 77, 122, 125, 242, 251, 254, 280–81, 289, 298
Medill, Joseph, 359–60
Melton, Samuel W., 332–33, 334, 336, 344
Memphis, Tenn., 36, 134, 140, 265, 299
Mendenhall, Cyrus P., 51, 54, 207
Mendenhall, Nereus, 54, 63, 105
Mercier, W. Newton, 243
Meridian, Miss., riot, 186–87
Merrick, Chloe, *see* Reed, Chloe
Merrick, Susbanus, 26
Merrimon, Augustus S., 289
Methodist church, 181, 217, 266, 267, 396
Metropolitan Club, 17
Metropolitans, 129, 281, 291
Mexico, 407
Michigan, 98, 148, 157, 392
Michigan Military Academy, 392
Militia: Ala., 154; Ark., 139–42, 300, 302–3; Fla., 150; La., 125–26, 247, 281, 291, 293; Miss., 322–23; N.C., 203, 205–6; S.C., 146, 224–27, 228, 229, 344, 349, 352
Miller, William, 169
Milwaukee, Wis., 25, 390
Minnesota, 113, 185, 189, 325
Minstrels, 259
Miscegenation, 409
Mississippi, 158, 160, 305, 353, 409; Morgans as planters in, 37–40, 78–81; 1867 election, 81–83; constitutional convention, 83–84; Ames in, 114–17; 1868 politics, 117–22; Ames as commander, 172–73; 1869 election, 174–76; readmitted, 181; Ames to Senate from, 181–92; 1873 election, 306–9, 312–13; 1874 election, 315; 1875 election, 317–24; Democrats control, 324–27
Mississippi, Ouachita & Red River R.R., 300
Mississippi plan, 350
Mississippi River, 8–10, 16, 32, 38, 73, 120, 122, 244, 305, 417
Mississippi, University of, 314
Missouri, 8, 56, 124, 167
Missouri & Northern Arkansas R.R., 406
Mitchell, Alexander, 25, 390–91
Mitchell, Mrs. Alexander, 390–91
Mitchell, John L., 391
Mobile, Ala., 32–33, 157, 237; collectorship of, 156, 169–71
Mobile Register, 166
Money, Confederate, 35, 217, 283
Montana, 14
Montauk Point, N.Y., 415
Montgomery, Ala., 32–33, 165, 274
Montgomery Advertiser, 154, 155, 156
Montgomery Mail, 72, 165
Monticello, Fla., 89, 90
Montreal, Quebec, 32
Moore, J. Aaron, 180, 186
Moore, John H., 221
Morehead, James, Jr., 108
Morgan, Albert T., 186, 414; background, 37–40; early hostility to, 78–82; in constitutional convention, 82–84; and 1868 election, 117–19; supervisor and senator, 176–81; sheriff, 312–13; and Hilliard, 313–14; overthrow of, 317–21, 322–23, 324; testifies, 326–27; last years, 409–12
Morgan, Albert T., Jr., 180, 313, 411, 412
Morgan, Angela, *see* Morgan, Nina
Morgan, Carolyn V., 181, 313, 411–12
Morgan, Carrie V. (Highgate), 180–81, 186, 411–12
Morgan, Charles, 37–40, 78, 81, 117–19, 176
Morgan, J. Pierpont, 411
Morgan, Lucia, 411–12

Morgan, Mollie, 79
Morgan, Nina, 313, 411–12
Morgan, William, 313, 314, 317, 319
Morgan, Ross & Co., 78, 81
Mormon women, 13–14
Morrill, Lot M., 183–84, 186
Morton, Oliver P., 290, 291, 294, 345
Moses, Franklin J., Jr., 145, 217, 224, 234, 268–69, 271, 328–29, 331, 332, 340, 344, 345, 351, 359, 363–64
Moses, Franklin J., Sr., 356
Mother's Little Helpers, 355
Moulton, Ala., 163
Mouton, Elisa, 416
Mugwumps, 398
Mule Team, 86–90, 148, 149
Murfreesboro, Tenn., 47
Murphy, Isaac, 136–37
Murrell, John A., 265
Muskingum County, Ohio, 388

Napoleon, Ohio, 62, 98, 337; Scott's interests in, 216, 329, 364–66, 392; murder case in, 393–95
Nasby, Petroleum V., 62
Natchez, Miss., 185, 190, 243, 307, 309
Nation, The, 91, 142, 143, 262
National Association for the Advancement of Colored People, 404
National banking system, 157
National Standard, 205
National Union convention, 53
Neagle, John L., 222, 268, 365
Neenah, Wis., 25, 84
Negro suffrage, 14, 17, 31, 54, 101, 114, 397, 408, 420; Loyalist convention and, 57–59; in North, 68–69; and Reconstruction Act, 74–75, 85; in N.C., 104; in Ala., 155; Scott on, 230; in La., 418–19. *See also* Fifteenth Amendment
Negroes, *see* Afro-Americans
Netty Jones, 140, 142
Nevada, 384
New Bern, N.C., 48
New England, 127, 278, 290, 312, 362–63, 398, 400
New England Conservatory, 401
New England Society, 341, 399
New Hampshire, 37, 86, 404
New Haven, Conn., 93
New Jersey, 44, 85, 148
New Mexico, governorship of, 169–70
New Orleans, La., 4, 73, 184, 237, 281, 292, 300, 361, 377; Warmoth's arrival, 8–11; Republican party, 11–16; news from, 18–19; massacre, 20–23; in 1868, 122, 131; police, 123; lobbyists, 243; "best citizens," 290; 1874 election in, 294–98; Warmoth's last years in, 416, 419. *See also* Customs, collectorship of
New Orleans Bulletin, 295–96
New Orleans *Daily Crescent*, 15
New Orleans, Fort Jackson & Grand Isle R.R., 417
New Orleans & Jackson R.R., 243–44
New Orleans, Mobile & Chattanooga R.R., 244–45
New Orleans, Mobile & Texas R.R., 276
New Orleans Republican, 77, 125, 130, 242, 244, 253, 254, 278
New Orleans Times, 18, 76, 126
New Orleans Tribune, 13, 76, 77
New South, 388
New Testament, 18
New York, 32, 37, 47, 150, 183, 184, 245, 266, 329, 379, 401; constitution of, 75–76, 105, Republican committee of, 270
New York City, 8, 19, 47, 59, 61, 62, 91, 124, 150, 212, 218–19, 223, 233, 236, 256, 276, 284, 293, 300, 362, 411, 415; Tourgee in, 376–79
New York Herald, 62, 63, 277, 303, 344; on Warmoth, 296–97
New York State Bar Association, 396
New York Sun, 243, 337, 380
New York Times, 55, 188, 216, 219, 222, 226, 356, 363, 374; on Scott and Chamberlain, 214–15, 230, 330; on Warmoth, 254, 280; on Clayton, 255, 303–4, 305; on carpetbaggers, 263; Scott in, 269–70; Ames in, 326; on Moses, 330
New York Tribune, 88–89, 205–6, 254, 261, 262, 273; Tourgee in, 206–8; 376–77, 381; on Scott, 269–70; on Warmoth, 276; on Ames, 322
New York World, 127, 221
Newark, N.J., 416–17
Newark, Ohio, 389
Newark Machine Works, 34
Newberry, S.C., 225, 331, 352
Niagara Movement, 404
Nicholson pavement bill, 253
Nickerson's Hotel, 143
North American Review, 380, 396
North Carolina, 385, 401; Tourgee arrives in, 46–50; and Loyalist convention, 54, 56–59; constitutional convention, 91, 101–7; Tourgee's attachment to, 193, 195, 373–74; civil code, 195–96; KKK

North Carolina (*cont.*)
in, 199–206; jails, 211; Littlefield and, 241; 1878 election, 370–72
North Carolina Friends Commission, 380
North Carolina Handle Co., 283, 376. *See also* Greensboro Spoke and Handle Factory
North Carolina R.R., 48, 50
North Carolina Standard, 49, 201
North Carolina, University of, 196, 200, 213
North Carolinian, 104
North Star, 55
Northfield, Minn., 185, 189, 324, 412
Northwestern University, 396
Nunez, William Loring, *see* Spencer, William

Oakly Park, 351
Oberlin, Ohio, 37, 197, 299, 322
Oberlin College, 37, 299, 324
Ocmulgee River, 41
Odd Fellows Hall, 290, 291
Oglesby, Mrs. Richard J., 62
Ohio, 34–36, 37, 47, 95, 98, 111, 143, 145, 153, 157, 183, 235, 359, 379, 384, 385, 388, 389; and Negro suffrage, 68–69; and rebellion, 168; Scott's interests in, 216, 218–19, 234, 391
Ohio, Historical and Philosophical Society of, 217
"Old John Brown," 107
On Our Way to the Orient, 410
Open Door policy, 124
Opium, 41, 143, 215, 392, 393
Orange County, N.C., 202
Orange groves, 29, 75, 241, 298, 389–90
Orchard Lake, 392
Oregon, 357, 360
Orleans Parish, La., 128, 129
Orr, James L., 44, 218, 227, 228, 269
Osborn, Thomas W., 85–86, 88–89, 148–49, 151, 240–42
Our Continent, 402, 404–5
Outlaw, Wyatt, 203, 212, 213, 282
Ozanne, Urbain, 119
Ozark Mountains, 136, 257, 406

Packard, Stephen B., 246, 251, 253, 418
Painesville, Ohio, 47
Palmetto Rifle Club, 348
Panic of 1873, 283, 284, 300, 388
Panola County, Miss., 119
Parker, Albert, 303
Parker, Niles J., 218, 220–21, 222–23, 228, 233–35, 270, 336–37, 365, 366
Parsons, Louis E., 163–64, 170
Parton, James, 184
Pass Christian, Miss., 250–51
Passing of Gold, The, 410
Patterson, John J., 220, 228, 230, 233–35, 271, 337, 344, 346, 347, 352, 365
Pearce, Charles H., 151, 239
Pease, Henry R., 306, 317
Penn, William, 132
Pennsylvania, 30, 41, 46–48, 50, 53, 105, 111, 132, 210, 220, 255, 295; 1866 election in, 60
Pennsylvania R.R., 279
Pennsylvania, University of, 161
Pension Office, 409–10
Peoria, Ill., 413
Permanent Court of International Justice, 407
Perry, Benjamin F., 95, 229
Perryville, Ky., 47, 403
Peru, 209
Petersburg, Va., 38, 112
Petit Jean Mountain, 267
Pettengill, Mr. and Mrs. R. T., 50, 51, 64–65
Phi Beta Kappa, 396
Philadelphia, Pa., 30, 41, 60, 61, 248, 266, 271, 273, 283, 339; Loyalist convention in, 53–59, 109; Tourgee's ventures in, 402
Phillips, Wendell, 92
Phillips Academy, 92
Piedmont R.R., 50
Pierrepont, Edwards, 321–23
Pilgrims, 288, 341
Pilot Mountain, 370
Pinchback, P. B. S., 248, 251, 254, 255, 293; acts as governor, 276–81
Pine Bluff, Ark., 133, 134, 135, 255, 406
Pine Bluff Dispatch, 136
Pittsboro, N.C., 196
Pittsburgh, Pa., 41, 59, 60, 111
Plaquemines Parish, La., 420
Plessy, Homer A., 404
Plessy v. Ferguson, 404
Plymouth Rock, 341
Poland, Luke, committee, 303–5
Pontiac, Mich., 392
Pool, John, 205
Pool, Solomon, 196
Pope, John, 69–70, 87
Post Office Department, 27, 85, 149
Potter, John F., 27

Poughkeepsie, N.Y., 61
Powderly, Terence V., 398
Powers, Ridgley C., 189, 190, 307, 308, 309, 313
Princeton University, 407
Profiles in Courage, 416
Proportional representation, 231, 232
Pryor, Roger A., 323
Pulaski County, Ark., 300
Pure Radicals, 76
Puritans, 113, 290, 341, 400
Purman, W. J., 89, 238–39, 242
Puryear, William, 203

Quakers, 51, 54, 63–64, 105, 181, 207
Quincy, Ill., 62

Railroads, 29, 48–50; Ala., 157; Ark., 134, 137, 255–56, 299–300, 406; Fla., 237–38, 241; Miss., 311; N.C., 106; S.C., 217–21, 228, 231
Rainey, Joseph H., 226
Raleigh, N.C., 35, 103, 200, 262, 289; Tourgee in, 48–50, 367–68, 373; memorial ceremonies in, 194
Raleigh Sentinel, 104, 197, 207; Turner and, 200–201, 203, 204
Raleigh Star, 49
"Rally 'Round the Flag," 106
Randall, Alexander W., 27, 85, 87, 149
Randolph, Mr., 58, 59
Randolph County, N.C., 66
Ransier, A. J., 226–27
Ransom, Edward, 287–88
Rapier, James T., 162, 163, 165, 169–71
Real Money Magazine, 410
Reconstruction: Lincoln on, 6–7; Joint Committee on, 17, 53, 90; Act of March 2, 1867, 66–67, 68, 74, 78, 85, 86, 101, 102, 110, 114, 124–25, 135, 145, 166, 408, 413; Act of March 23, 1867, 60; Act of March 11, 1868, 73; histories of, 406, 407–8, 413–14, 419–21
Reconstruction in Mississippi, 414
Red Shirts, 354–57, 358
Reed, Anna Louise, 25
Reed, Chloe (Merrick), 26–27, 29, 85, 90, 236, 241, 390, 391
Reed, Curtis, 390
Reed, George, 390
Reed, Georgiana, 25
Reed, Harrison, 143; arrival in Fla., 24–29; commands Republicans, 84–87; and constitution, 87–90; elected governor, 90; is impeached, 148–52, 240–42; and railroads, 236–38; and KKK, 238–40; last years of, 389–91
Reed, J. P., 334, 339, 340
Regulators, 44, 150
Reid, Whitelaw, 17–18, 32, 273, 276
Reply to "A Fool's Errand," 380–82
Republicans, 17, 34, 36, 114, 294; Ala., 69–70, 156, 160–66, 169–71, 274, 383–84, 384–85; Ark., 135–36, 140, 141–42, 259, 266, 268, 304–5, 406; Fla., 85–90, 148–52; La., 11–16, 21, 76, 122–23, 125, 128–31, 245–49, 294, 418–19; Miss., 81–82, 116, 120, 174–75, 189–90, 191–92, 318, 320; N.C., 102, 107–9, 111, 287–89; S.C., 99, 145, 148, 224–27, 233, 270, 332–33, 344–45, 348, 350, 363, 366
Returning board, 128, 278–81, 294, 296
Revels, Hiram R., 179, 181–82, 186, 188, 189, 190, 317
Revolutionary War, 347
Rhode Island, 47
Rhodes, James F., 407–8
Rice, Benjamin F., 266, 303
Richard III, 7
Richards, Daniel, 86–90, 240
Richmond, Va., 5–6, 93
Rifle clubs, 354–55, 356
Rio Grande, 93
Riordan, B. R., 337
Rip Van Winkle, 74, 106
Rivers and harbors bills, 157
Riviera, the, 400, 415
Robert E. Lee, 243
Robertson, Thomas J., 344, 350
Robespierre, Maximilien, 12
Rochester, N.Y., 55
Rochester, University of, 47, 197, 283, 284, 379
Rockefeller, John D., 411, 412, 415
Rockingham County, N.C., 195, 202, 213
Rockland, Me., 112
Roman Catholics, 183, 333, 407
Rome, Ga., 387
Rome Courier, 387–88
Roosevelt, Theodore, 398, 405, 407
Ross, Edmund G., 111
Roudanez, Charles, 13, 130
Roudanez, Jean B., 13, 76, 130
Rousseau, L. H., 129–30
Rowland, Dunbar, 414
Royal Gentleman, A, 401

Royall, William A., 380–82
Ruger, Thomas H., 355, 356

St. Ann's Episcopal Church, 184
St. Bernard Parish, La., 128, 129
St. Charles Hotel, 22–23, 77, 250
St. James Parish, La., 21
St. John's River, 29, 389, 390
St. Landry Progress, 77
St. Louis, Mo., 8, 10, 31, 62, 73, 299, 339
St. Pierre's Creek, 93
Salt Lake City, Utah, 13
Sammis, John S., 26
Sandusky, Ohio, 61, 299
Santa Fe, N.M., 170
Santiago de Cuba, 413
Santo Domingo, 249
Saugatuck, Mich., 157
Saunders, William U., 86–90
Savannah River, 349
Sawyer, Frederick A., 144, 226, 269
Saxton, Rufus, 42
Scalawag, use of term, 72, 121, 127, 420–21
Scales, Alfred M., 369–71
Schofield, John M., 20, 126, 128, 140–41, 146
Schools, Southern, 79, 128, 137, 143–44, 174, 177, 179, 180, 181, 237, 247, 256–57, 289, 294–95, 319, 336; in Sumner's bill, 285–86; Tourgee's plan for, 379–80, 382, 404, 405–6. *See also* Education
Schurz, Carl, 263, 273
Scott, Rebecca Jane (Lowry), 144, 216, 365, 366, 392, 394, 396
Scott, Robert K., 262, 347, 359; Freedmen's Bureau head, 40–45, 98–100, 329–30; candidate, 100–101; inaugurated, 142–45; in 1868 election, 145–48; interview, 214–15; interests, 215–17; and railroads, 217–21, 227–28; and land commission, 222–23; and 1870 election, 223–27; and KKK, 227–28, 230, 232–33; and taxpayers, 229, 231–32; impeachment, 233–35; in 1872 campaign, 268–71; and 1874 election, 328–31; Chamberlain on, 337, 339; departs S.C., 364–66; last years, 391–96
Scott, Robert K., Jr., 144, 216, 392–96
Scott, Sir Walter, 341
Scribner's Magazine, 299, 413
Sea Islands, 42–43, 93–94, 350
Searcy, Ark., 139
Second N.C. Union Volunteers, 52–53
Second Wisconsin Regiment, 38
Selma, Ala., 32, 161, 163
Selma, Rome & Dalton R.R., 157
Semi-Tropical, The, 390
Servosse, Comfort, 368, 377
Settle, Thomas, 195, 209, 289; and KKK, 199, 202, 208
Seymour, Horatio, 124, 150
Sharkey, William, 187, 188
Shaw, Alfred, 16, 22–23
Sheboygan, Wis., 157
Shenandoah Valley, 298
Sheridan, George A., 246–47
Sheridan, Philip H., 21, 75, 298
Sherman, John, 16; Warner and, 35–37, 68, 70–71, 73, 153, 156, 161, 170–71, 272, 384–85; Ames and, 174–75, 182, 183
Sherman, William T., 35, 42, 48, 146, 174, 196; Warner and, 36–37, 153, 156, 385–86, 388
Shiloh, Tenn., 42
"Shoo Fly," 268
Sickles, Daniel E., 44, 127–28
Silverton, Colo., 410
Sir Galahad, 113
Slavery, Tourgee on, 197–98
Smalls, Robert, 351, 366
Smith, James Q., 274–75
Smith, Kirby, 133
Smith, William H., 30, 70, 72, 73, 161–64, 274
Smithsonian Institution, 4
Snow, W. H., 211
Society of Friends, *see* Quakers
Socrates, 339–40
Solomon, Hardy, 344
Somers, Robert, 186, 227–28, 242
Sorensen, Theodore C., 416
South Carolina, 305, 391, 394, 395; Freedmen's Bureau, 40–45, 98–100; constitutional convention, 91, 94–98; Scott nominated in, 100–101; Ames in, 113, 114, 413; Scott inaugurated, 142–45; 1868 election, 145–48; 1871 politics, 214–15, 338–42; railroads, 217–21, 228, 231, 235; land commission, 222–23; 1870 election, 223–27; opposition to Scott, 227–33; financial condition, 233–35; 1872 election, 268–71; 1874 election, 328–33; 1876 election, 349–61; Hayes and, 357–63; Hampton administration, 363–66
South Carolina Historical Society, 398

South Carolina Land Commission, 102, 222–23, 364
South Carolina R.R., 221, 399
South Carolina, University of, 143, 146, 328
Southern Loyalist Convention, 53–59, 109
Southwestern Pacific R.R. convention, 339
Spanish-American War, 412–13, 414, 415
Spartanburg, S.C., 344
Spartanburg Herald, 349
Spartanburg & Union R.R., 221
Special Field Order No. 15, 42
Spencer, Bella (Zilfa), 30–31, 69, 70, 384
Spencer, George E., 262, 385, 387; arrives in Ala., 30–32; register in bankruptcy, 69–70, 73; in Senate, 155–60; in 1870 campaign, 161–62, 166, 168; defeats Warner, 169–71, in 1872 election, 272; Senate reelection, 274–76; post-Reconstruction career, 383–84
Spencer, George E., Jr., 384
Spencer William (Nunez), 384
Spotswood House, 6
Sprague, Kate (Chase), 17–18, 20, 114
Sprague, William, IV, 18
Springfield, Ill., 8, 59, 62
Springfield Republican, 338
Stanton, Edwin M., 110
"Star" cars, 122, 294–95
Star-route frauds, 384
"Star Spangled Banner, The," 107, 251
Stars and Stripes, 133
Stearns, M. L., 240
Stephens, John W., 203–4, 206, 213
Stephens, Mrs. John W., 209
Sterling loan, 233
Sterling Medical College, 41
Stevens, Thaddeus, 36, 53, 90, 95, 119, 218; organizes House, 16–17; on Reconstruction, 20; Warner on, 68; at impeachment, 110, 111
Stickney, Lyman D., 26–29, 90
Stokes County, N.C., 370–71
Stoneman's raid, 50
Stowe, Harriet B., 43, 377, 378, 379
Sugar plantations, 9–10, 75, 298–99, 417–18
Sugar Planters' Faction, 419
Summerfield, S.C., 413
Sumner, Charles, 36, 92, 183, 249, 264, 326; and Warmoth, 17; Warner on, 68; Tourgee on, 285
Sumter Watchman, 226
Supreme Court, U.S., 244, 280, 377, 385, 404
Swayne, Wager, 71, 72
Swepson, George W., 200, 211, 371, 372, 380–81; Tourgee's creditor, 194, 289; in Fla., 236–38, 240–41
Switzerland, 360
Sykes, Francis W., 276
Syracuse, N.Y., 26–27, 180

Taft, Alphonso, 350
Taliaferro, James G., 76
Talladega, Ala., 163
Tallahassee, Fla., 85, 87, 88–89, 148, 236, 237, 239, 241
Tallahassee Floridian, 237
Tammany Hall, 345
Taney, Roger B., 228
Taxpayers' convention, 229, 231–32, 329–30
Taylor, Richard, 243
Taylor, Zachary, 243
Tecumseh Iron Co., 385–88
Tennessee, 5, 17, 53, 56, 119, 157, 385, 386, 388, 389
Tennessee Coal and Iron Co., 388
Tennessee River, 29
Tennessee Valley, 29–30
Tenure of Office Act, 110
Terrorism: Ala., 161–65; Ark., 138–42, 408; Fla., 149–50, 238–40; La., 125–26, 128–31; Miss., 117–22, 189, 314–24; N.C., 199–206; S.C., 145–48, 225–27, 349–51, 353–56. *See also* Ku Klux Klan
Tewksbury, Mass., 412
Texas, 133, 299
Texas & Pacific R.R., 157
Thibodeaux, La., 74
Third N.C. U.S. Volunteers, 205
Thirteenth Amendment, 348
Thorheim, 379, 382, 402, 403
Thurman, Allen G., 183
Tilden, Samuel J., 345, 357, 359
Tilton, Theodore, 55, 263
Toinette, 197–98, 284–85, 286, 287, 289, 375, 379
Tokeba plantation, 38–40, 78–81, 178
Toledo, Ohio, 61, 329
Toledo Blade, 62, 394
Topeka, Kan., 263
Tourgee, Aimée, *see* Tourgee, Lodolska
Tourgee, Albion W.: background and N.C. arrival, 46–50; and A. W. Tourgee & Co., 51–52; and Unionists, 52–54; at Loyalist convention, 54–59; in 1866

Tourgee, Albion W. (*cont.*)
campaign, 59–61; and Worth, 62–64, 66; troubles of, 65–66; and Reconstruction Act, 66–67; in constitutional convention, 91, 101–7; elected judge, 107–9; at impeachment, 110–11; as code commissioner and judge, 193–99; and KKK, 199–210; in 1871–72, 210–13; in 1872–74, 282–86; in 1875 convention, 287–89; writes *A Fool's Errand*, 367–68, 372, 375, 397; congressional candidate, 369–72; to N.Y., 375–79; and Garfield, 379–82; later career, 401–6
Tourgee, Emma (Kilbourne), 101, 102, 109, 284, 286, 375; and N.C. prospects, 46, 48, 50; and Greensboro, 62, 64–65, 369, 370; pregnant, 101, 206, 210; home cares of, 193, 196, 197, 283, 287; in Pa., 370, 372; in Denver, 377–79; last years of, 402–6
Tourgee, Lodolska ("Lodie"), 210, 213, 283, 284, 369, 370, 372, 374, 402, 403
Tourjée, Eben, 401
Townsend, Charles H., 84
Townsend, George A., 264–65, 271, 273
Treasury Department, 25, 27–28, 86, 113, 148, 374
Tremont Temple, 61
Trenholm, W. L., 231
Troy, N.Y., 25, 61
Trumbull, Lyman, 277, 290, 291
Turner, Josiah, Jr., 200–201, 203, 204, 209, 288
Turner, Sophia (Mrs. Josiah), 200
Turners Hall, 251, 254
Tuscaloosa, Ala., 31, 70, 163
Tuscumbia, Ala., 163
Tweed, William M., 345
Tweed Ring, 167, 345, 379
Twentieth Me. Regiment, 113

Uncle Tom's Cabin, 43, 377, 378
Union Leagues, 54, 201, 203, 262
Union Pacific R.R., 384
Union Reform party, 225–27
Union Register, see *Greensboro Register*
Unionists, Southern, 51–54, 102, 119, 135, 158–59. *See also* Loyalists
Unitarians, 214, 400, 415
U.S. Association of Charcoal Iron Workers, 387
Utah, 14

Van Buren, Ark., 268
Vance, Zebulon, 369
Venezuela, 169
Vermilion Parish, La., 74
Vermont, 16, 24–25, 124, 188, 225, 290, 299, 303, 412
Vermont, University of, 396
Vickers, George, 183
Vicksburg, Miss., 3, 33, 115, 189, 309, 322, 389; Warmoth at, 9; Morgans arrive in, 38; Ameses in, 185; riot, 314–17
Vicksburg & Nashville R.R., 311
Vicksburg Times, 118, 181
Vienna, Austria, 124
Virginia, 95, 158, 160, 398

Wadmalaw Island, 94
Wake Forest College, 405
Walhalla, S.C., 218
Walker, David S., 86, 89
Wall Street, 396
Walsh, John A., 252–54, 296
Walton, Thomas, 314
War Department, 156
War, Politics and Reconstruction, 421
Ward, Metta, 368
Ward, William I., 204
Ware, H. M., 410
Warmoth, Bessie, 418
Warmoth, Henry C., 143; and Lincoln, 3–8; to New Orleans, 8–11; and Republican party, 11–14; territorial delegate, 14–20; and New Orleans massacre, 20–23; at Loyalist convention, 54, 56–57; in 1866 campaign, 59–62; and Reconstruction, 73–75; elected governor, 75–78; inaugurated, 122–24; and 1868 election, 124–31; as governor, 242–45; and Grant's patronage, 245–49; loses control, 249–54; as Liberal, 264; and 1872 election, 276–80, 289–93; impeached, 280–81; and 1874 election, 293–94; Ames and, 306, 308; post-Reconstruction career, 416–21
Warmoth, Sally (Durand), 416–17, 418
Warner, Eliza (Woods), 33–34, 70
Warner, May, 33, 153, 170, 388–89
Warner, Willard: background, 32–37; in Ohio senate, 68–69; seeks office, 71–73; in U.S. Senate, 153–60, 166–69; in 1870 election, 160–66; and collectorship, 169–71; and 1872 election, 271–76; and post-Reconstruction pol-

itics, 384–85; iron manufacturer, 385–89
Warner, Willard, Jr., 33, 153, 170, 389
Warnersville, N.C., 102
Warren County, Miss., 315–16, 318
Washburne, Elihu B., 72, 130–31, 148; Miss. correspondents of, 119–22
Washington, Booker T., 398, 404
Washington, D.C., 47, 124; Warmoth in, 3–8, 16–20, 247, 290, 291; Reed in, 25, 150; Ames in, 112, 181–84, 326; Tourgee in, 109–11, 212, 382, Morgan in, 326, 409–10; Chamberlain in, 360–61; Spencer in, 384; Clayton in, 407–8
Washington, George, 137
Washington Post, 333
Washington Star, 337
Wasson, Ohio, 61
Waterman, George W., 220
Watterson, Henry M., 49, 273
Weed, Thurlow, 270
Weitzel, Godfrey, 5–6
Welker, George W., 53, 54, 103, 105, 212
Welles, Gideon, 141
Wells, J. Madison, 11, 12, 14, 15, 19, 21
Wentworth, N.C., 195, 199, 202, 213
West, Joseph R., 248–49, 250
West Green Nursery, 51, 52, 62, 65, 101
West Point, N.Y., 112, 113, 184–85
West Virginia, 56
Western Reserve, 47
"When Johnny Comes Marching Home," 271
Whigs, 359
Whipper, William J., 217, 223, 234, 334, 345; and judgeship, 339–42, 352; consoles Scott, 394–95
Whipple, William G., 259
Whistler, James McNeill, 390
White, Horace, 264
White, James J. B., Mr. and Mrs., 38–40, 78–81, 177
White County, Ark., 139
White House, 181, 398; Warmoth at, 3, 5, 6, 247; Ames at, 317; Tourgee at, 382; Clayton at, 407
White Leagues, 293, 294, 297–98
White Liners, 314
Whittemore, B. F., 224
Whytock, John, 300, 301
Wide Awakes, 56
Wilberforce University, 95, 217
Wilde, Oscar, 402
Wiley, Frank A., 204
Willard Hotel, 7
William the Conqueror, 127
Williams, Alfred B., 399–400
Williams, George H., 276, 281, 292, 302–3, 305
Williams, Willoughby, 134
Wilmington, Del., 132, 244
Wilmington, N.C., 236
Wilmington, Charlotte & Rutherfordton R.R., 106
Wilson, Henry, 278
Wilson, James H., 32
Wilson, Woodrow, 407–8
Wilson's Hall, 320, 323
Winn Parish, La., 420
Winona, Miss., 309
Wisconsin, 149, 157, 177, 290, 292; Reed in, 25, 143, 148, 389, 391; Morgan in, 37–38, 176, 404–5, 409
Wofford College, 344
Woman suffrage, 155, 415
Woods, Eliza, *see* Warner, Eliza
Woods, William B., 35–36, 156, 385, 386
Woodstock, Conn., 362
Worcester High School, 92
World War I, 413, 414, 419
World War II, 413
Worth, Jonathan, 52, 62–64, 66, 102, 106, 107
Worthington, H. C., 271
Wright, Jonathan J., 363–64

Xenia, Ohio, 217

Yale Review, 396
Yale University, 91, 92, 214, 338, 396
Yanceyville, N.C., 204
"Yankee Doodle," 107
Yazoo, 409
Yazoo Banner, 117
Yazoo City, Miss., 38–40, 79, 81–84, 117, 118, 177, 180, 314; riot, 317–21
Yazoo City Democrat, 314, 319, 323
Yazoo City Herald, 318
Yazoo County, Miss., 39, 79, 83, 118; supervisors, 176–78; sheriff, 176, 312–14; Democratic coup, 318–21
Yazoo River, 38–39, 78, 79
Yerger, Edward M., 173–74
Young Richmond, 204
Yulee, David L., 85, 90

Zilfa, Bella, *see* Spencer, Bella